PAGE 44

O ROAD

NATION GUIDE
led listings
and insider tips

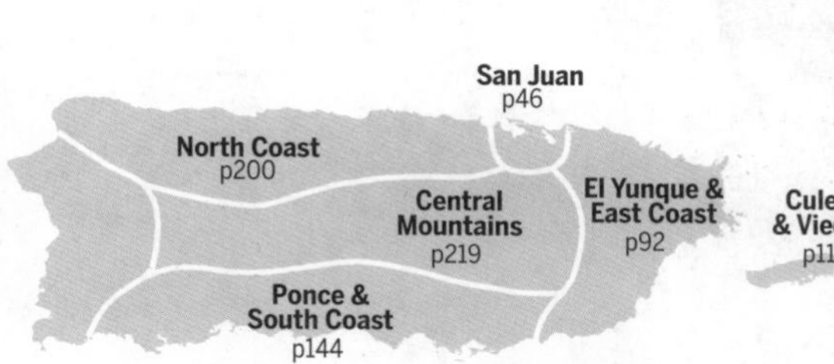

PAGE 277

SURVIVAL GUIDE

VITAL PRACTICAL INFORMATION TO HELP YOU HAVE A SMOOTH TRIP

THIS EDITION WRITTEN ... BY

Nate Cava...

Beth Ko...

welcome to Puerto Rico

Tropical Playground

Puerto Rico is the fodder of many a Caribbean daydream for good reason: this natural jewel box can satisfy the lethargic beach bum, the sunrise rainforest explorer and the budding big-wave surfer – all in a long weekend. Its coral reefs host a riot of tropical fish, its limestone caves in the misty central mountains resound with the chirp of coquí frogs, and its unique collection of forests – some of the wettest and driest in the Caribbean – harbor some of the rarest birds in the world. It's hardly undiscovered – you'll have plenty of company navigating the dripping trails of El Yunque, the perfect waves in Rincón and sunning yourself on some of the best beaches in the world – but with creativity and plucky DIY spirit, you'll find a little piece of this tropical heaven all for yourself.

Cultural Vibrancy

Those curious enough to look beyond the borders of San Juan's condo developments and congested highways reap big rewards from the vibrant culture of this island. You'll get a whiff of it in the tempting smoke from a roasting pig that rises from a roadside *lechonera* (eatery specializing in suckling pig). You'll hear it in the distorted thump of a rowdy, beer-soaked weekend in Boquerón or the polyrhythmic patter of a salsa beat. You'll see it down the quiet hallways of museums celebrating everything

Welcome to Puerto Rico: endless sand, swashbuckling history lessons and wildly diverse tropical terrain. The sun-washed backyard of the USA is a place locals fittingly call the 'Island of enchantment'

(left) Big Tree Trail (p96), El Yunque
(below) Snorkelers, Isla Culebrita (p118)

from failed revolution to classical European painting. Don't be put off by the fast-food chains or unsightly trappings of modern mainland America – Puerto Rican traditions have been shaped by generations of cultural synthesis, celebration and setback, and it emerges today as distinct, spirited and indomitable...if you're willing to look for it.

History

Puerto Rico's history lessons – told through cannon fire and colonization, repression and revolt – offer a palpable sense of the island's dynamic past. There's a bit of legend in every direction: from the fortress walls pocked by cannon fire to the crumbling towers of the sugar refineries that once fired the island's economy. Free-trading colonialists built sparkling European plazas along streets of the harbor cities, while political revolutionaries plotted revolt in misty villages along the twisting spine of the central mountains. Those with a passion for history can wander precolonial Taíno ball courts or steamy coffee plantations, but even if your interest is scant, it's hard not to get caught up in Puerto Rico's fascinating story. While hasty development and cycles of boom and bust leave this island a checkerboard of preservation, the most amazing thing about this island's past is the beguiling weave it creates with the present.

Puerto Rico

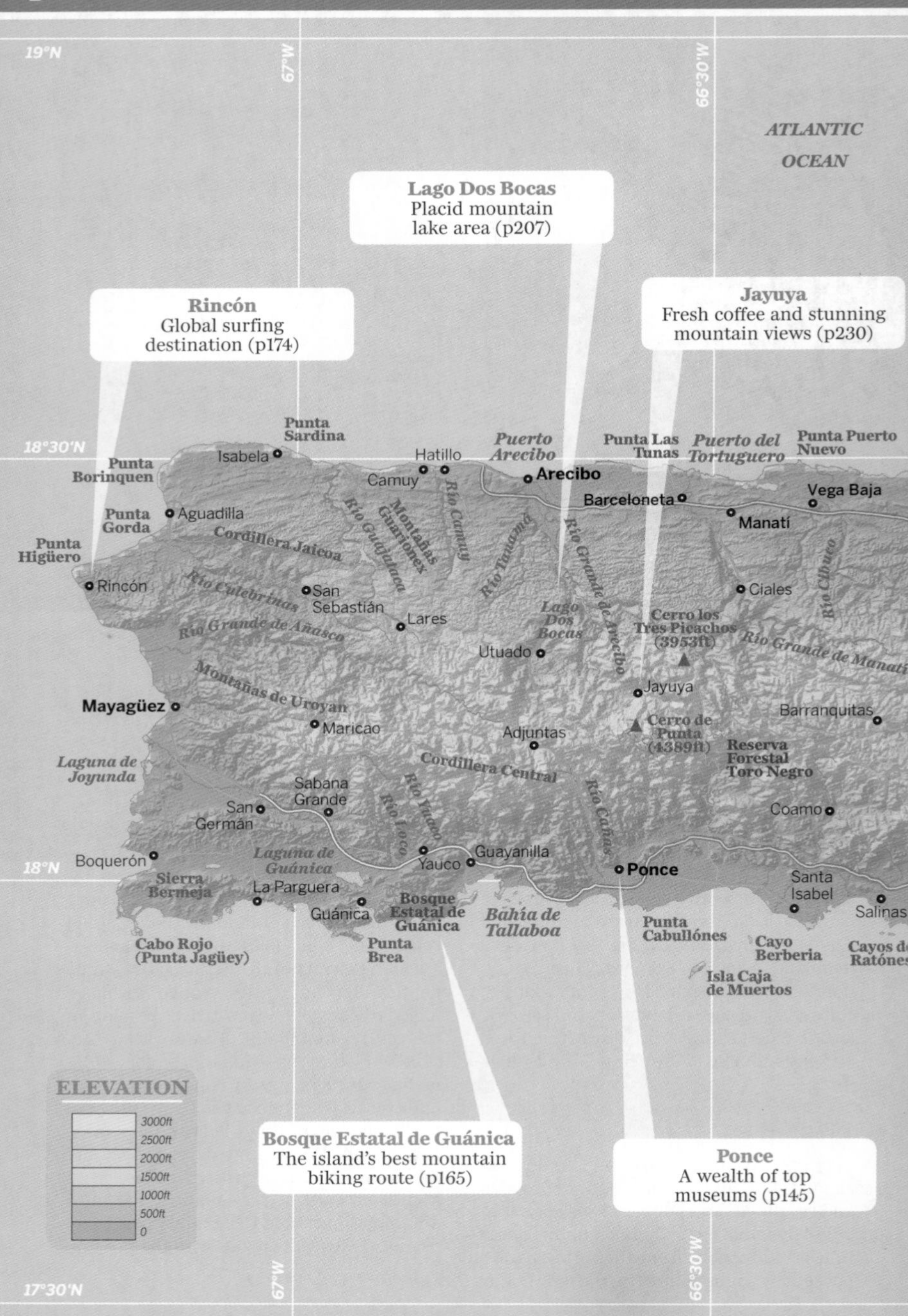

19°N
67°W
66°30'W
ATLANTIC
OCEAN
Lago Dos Bocas
Placid mountain lake area (p207)
Rincón
Global surfing destination (p174)
Jayuya
Fresh coffee and stunning mountain views (p230)
Punta Sardina
18°30'N
Punta Borinquen
Isabela
Hatillo
Camuy
Puerto Arecibo
Arecibo
Punta Las Tunas
Puerto del Tortuguero
Punta Puerto Nuevo
Barceloneta
Vega Baja
Manatí
Punta Gorda
Aguadilla
Cordillera Jaicoa
Montañas Guarionex
Río Guajataca
Río Camuy
Río Tanamá
Río Grande de Arecibo
Río Cibuco
Punta Higüero
Rincón
Río Culebrinas
San Sebastián
Lares
Lago Dos Bocas
Ciales
Cerro los Tres Picachos (3953ft)
Río Grande de Añasco
Utuado
Río Grande de Manatí
Montañas de Uroyan
Jayuya
Mayagüez
Maricao
Adjuntas
Cerro de Punta (4389ft)
Barranquitas
Reserva Forestal Toro Negro
Laguna de Joyunda
Cordillera Central
Sabana Grande
San Germán
Río Yauco
Río Loco
Río Cañas
Coamo
Boquerón
18°N
Laguna de Guánica
Yauco
Guayanilla
Ponce
Sierra Bermeja
La Parguera
Guánica
Bosque Estatal de Guánica
Bahía de Tallaboa
Santa Isabel
Salinas
Punta Cabullónes
Cabo Rojo (Punta Jagüey)
Punta Brea
Cayo Berberia
Isla Caja de Muertos
ELEVATION
3000ft
2500ft
2000ft
1500ft
1000ft
500ft
0
Bosque Estatal de Guánica
The island's best mountain biking route (p165)
Ponce
A wealth of top museums (p145)
17°30'N

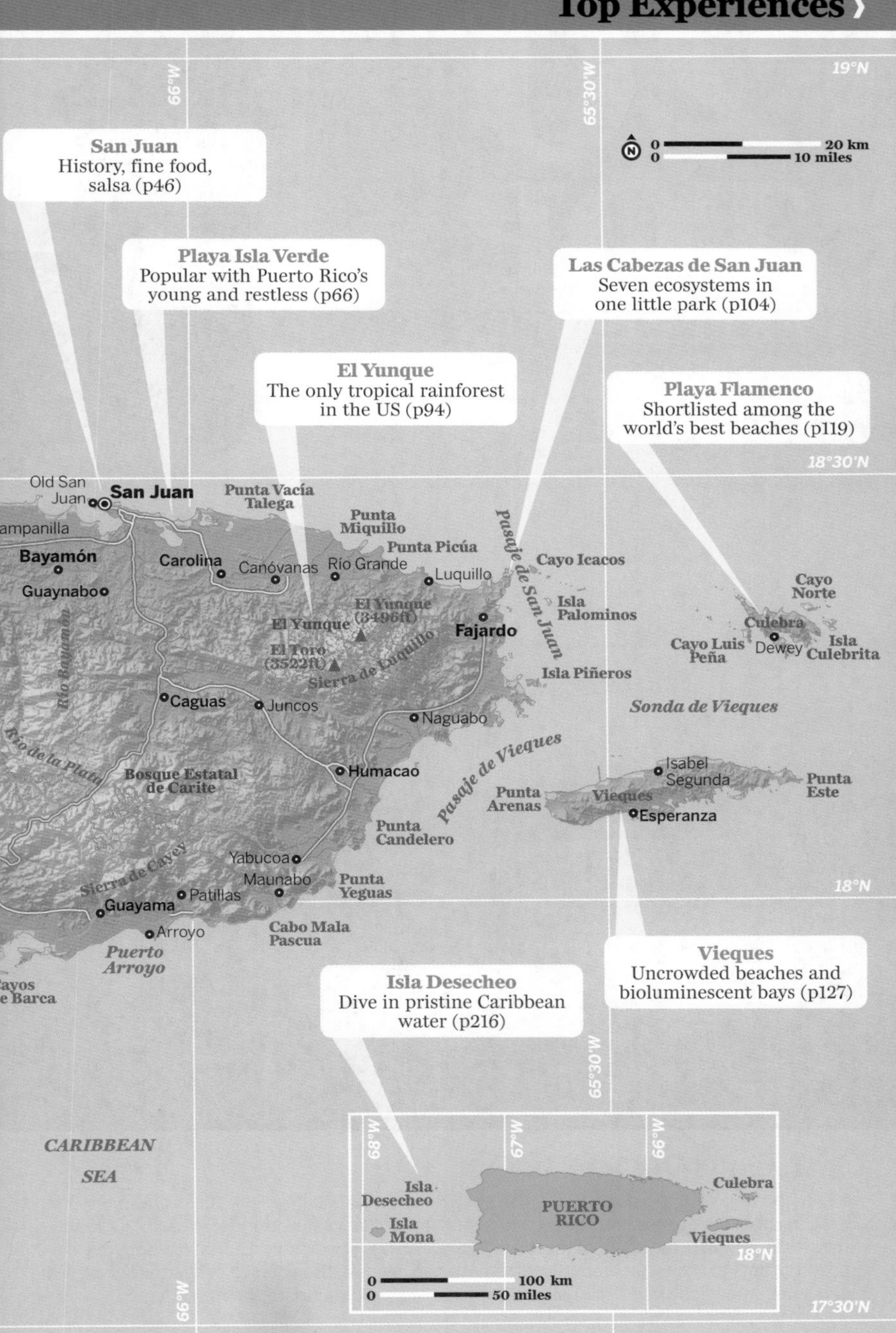
San Juan
History, fine food, salsa (p46)
Playa Isla Verde
Popular with Puerto Rico's young and restless (p66)
Las Cabezas de San Juan
Seven ecosystems in one little park (p104)
El Yunque
The only tropical rainforest in the US (p94)
Playa Flamenco
Shortlisted among the world's best beaches (p119)
Vieques
Uncrowded beaches and bioluminescent bays (p127)
Isla Desecheo
Dive in pristine Caribbean water (p216)
19°N
18°30'N
18°N
17°30'N
66°W
65°30'W
0 20 km
0 10 miles
Old San Juan
San Juan
Bayamón
Guaynabo
Carolina
Canóvanas
Río Grande
Luquillo
Fajardo
Punta Vacía Talega
Punta Miquillo
Punta Picúa
Pasaje de San Juan
Cayo Icacos
Isla Palominos
Isla Piñeros
El Yunque
El Yunque (3496ft)
El Toro (3522ft)
Sierra de Luquillo
Río Bayamón
Caguas
Juncos
Naguabo
Río de la Plata
Bosque Estatal de Carite
Humacao
Pasaje de Vieques
Sonda de Vieques
Culebra
Dewey
Cayo Norte
Isla Culebrita
Cayo Luis Peña
Isabel Segunda
Vieques
Esperanza
Punta Arenas
Punta Este
Punta Candelero
Yabucoa
Maunabo
Punta Yeguas
Sierra de Cayey
Patillas
Guayama
Arroyo
Cabo Mala Pascua
Puerto Arroyo
Cayos de Barca
CARIBBEAN SEA
68°W
67°W
66°W
Isla Desecheo
Isla Mona
PUERTO RICO
Culebra
Vieques
18°N
0 100 km
0 50 miles

20 TOP EXPERIENCES

Mysterious Old San Juan

1 Even those limited to a quick visit find it easy to fall under the beguiling spells of Old San Juan's (p50) cobblestone streets, pastel-painted colonial buildings and grand fortresses. From the ramparts of El Morro, the allure of this place is evident in every direction – from the labyrinth of crooked streets to the endless sparkle of the Atlantic. By day, lose yourself in historical stories of blood and bombast; by night, float along in crowds of giggling tourists and rowdy locals.

Beaches

2 The rub of sand between your toes, the brilliant sparkle of turquoise water and the rhythmic shush of cresting waves – Puerto Rico's beaches have the qualities of a daydream. Take your pick from the golden, crescent-shaped heaven of Playa Flamenco (p119; considered among the world's best beaches); the coconut oil–scented crowds of Playa Isla Verde (p66), Puerto Rico's little slice of Brazil; the secluded, mangrove-shaded hideaways in the south or the roaring surf of the west.

Catch Some Béisbol

3 The bleachers at island *béisbol* (baseball; p272) stadiums reveal a lot more than nine innings of play – it's a vantage on the fickle Caribbean love affair with this sport. Puerto Ricans may never fill the oversized stadiums that dot the island, but the low-key games and dirt-cheap tickets get fans right up in the action. Expect to witness a face-off between upstart farm leaguers looking for their big shot and fading stars of the Major League Baseball looking to go out in a blaze of glory.

Rum Cocktails at Sunset

4 If there's an elixir to help those sunsets imprint your memory forever, it likely comes in a tall, cold glass. From the piña coladas with toy umbrellas to the everyman's Cuba *libre* (rum and Coke with a wedge of lime) you'd be remiss to leave 'King Sugar' without savoring a rum cocktail during a spectacular sunset. Find a comfortable perch in the west – such as Rincón's ultrachill surfer hangout, Tamboo Tavern (p182), or the breezy, upscale comforts at Eclipse (p214) – and sip a taste of paradise.

Bioluminescent Bays

5 Few experiences can inspire the awe of floating in inky waves under a canopy of stars and witnessing one of nature's most tactile magic tricks: the otherworldly sparkle of bioluminescent waters. Swimming or kayaking into Puerto Rico's bioluminescent bays and seeing the jeweled flicker of water drip from your hands or illuminate a paddle stroke promises an experience of profound wonder. The bioluminescent waters in the bays of Vieques (p131; pictured) reveal the phenomenon at its most fantastic.

Las Cabezas de San Juan Reserva Natural 'El Faro'

6 The diverse ecosystem of Las Cabezas de San Juan Reserva Natural 'El Faro' (p104) makes a quick day trip from the high rises of San Juan's urban core and highlights the island's ecological assortment at every turn. After a quick, informative trip through the visitors center, travelers begin the compact tour of the flora and fauna. The sea grass waves along mangrove forest and coral-protected lagoons, while giant iguanas scuttle from underfoot and crabs scurry along the rocky shores.

JERRY ALEXANDER / LONELY PLANET IMAGES ©

Cuisine in San Juan's SoFo District

7 When cruise ships shimmer like floating cities at the docks just offshore, the world-class restaurants of SoFo (short for 'South of Fortaleza,' naturally) rise to the occasion, impressing their international audiences with the most inventive fine dining in the Caribbean. Recent years have seen a revolving door of hot restaurants in this corner of Old San Juan – only the most creative survive. Expect the traditional, elemental essence of Puerto Rican flavors fused with preparations from across the globe.

Ponce's Museums

8 Ponce, the so-called 'Pearl of the South,' boasts a wealth of museums with enough diversity to satisfy the most intellectually rapacious museum hunter. Those interested in the distinctive rhythms of the island should start with Museo de la Música Puertorriqueña (p150), before touring the lovingly restored plantation at Hacienda Buena Vista (p157; pictured) or the best art museum in the Caribbean, the Museo de Arte de Ponce (p150).

Mountain Biking

9 Spending half a day rumbling down the rocky, cactus-lined paths of Bosque Estatal de Guánica (p163; pictured) will traverse some of the most interesting mountain-biking terrain in the Caribbean. They're not well groomed or technical, but trails in this Unesco-protected site, or those in less-traveled karst country forests like Bosque Estatal de Susúa (p197), bring the DIY thrills of the sport to Puerto Rico's unique subtropical wilds.

El Yunque Tropical Rainforest

10 Lush forests, verdant hills and crashing waterfalls attract visitors to El Yunque (p94), the only true rainforests in the US. It's a place to embark on a short hike through the oxygen-rich mist and gawk at Jurassic-sized ferns. You will get wet, so take a raincoat, but bring binoculars, too; of the 26 species found here and nowhere else in the world, you'll want to keep a sharp eye out for the Puerto Rican parrot, one of the 10 most endangered birds on earth.

Architectural Gems

11 If you tried to savor every single example of colonial grandeur – all the fountains and historic squares, every dignified plantation house and buttressed 19th-century town hall – Puerto Rico's architectural gems would demand a month-long stay. But, if just one location outside of Old San Juan earns time on your agenda, take a stroll around the Plaza Las Delicias in Ponce, home to the eclectic Parque de Bombas (p149; pictured). The square is littered with statues, lined by colonial edifices and crowned by the regal Fuente de los Leones (p149; a rescued relic from the 1939 New York World's Fair).

DAN GAIR / LONELY PLANET IMAGES ©

Volunteering with Turtles

12 Seeing the graceful underwater flight of a leatherback sea turtle is one of the most memorable sights for snorkelers and divers in Puerto Rican waters. But environmental conditions, hastened by beachfront tourist infrastructure, have drastically reduced the population of these magnificent creatures over the years. Visitors to Puerto Rico can take part in conservation efforts by volunteering with organizations locally; see p121 for further information.

Kayaking on Lago Dos Bocas

13 Hidden away in the lush vegetation of the central mountains, the calm waters of Lago Dos Bocas allow an experience for kayakers that's entirely more serene than bobbing along on the waves of the open sea. You'll first spy the lake along Rte 143 near the mountain town of Utuado, where travelers can rent boats from little lakeside restaurants. It's an ideal situation – after you work up an appetite with a few hours of paddling, enjoy a feast of inexpensive dishes of freshly caught fish from the lake.

NATIONAL GEOGRAPHIC / GETTY IMAGES

© GEORDIE TORR / ALAMY

Island Wildlife

14 Maybe the syncopated polyrhythmic grooves of salsa rule the island's nightlife, but the chirp of the coquí frogs – whose sound is just like their name – rules the night. These little creatures are the unofficial mascot of the island. The menagerie also includes exceedingly rare birds in the Bosque Estatal de Guánica and lazy reptiles on the remote Isla Mona, often called the Galápagos of the Caribbean. In the waters offshore, the sea life adds to a naturalist's agenda, with waters teeming with tropical fish, coral and sometimes even manatee.

Swimming & Snorkeling

15 Many of the island's most marvelous places for snorkeling and swimming lie out of the heavily traveled tourist corridors, on satellite islands off the main island's east or south coast, and at coral reefs in the southwest. In the morning, waters in these areas are crystal clear and usually calm enough to paddle around for hours enjoying visibility up to 75ft. And what a view – expect a riot of brightly colored fish, coral formations and, if you're lucky, a lazy ray. The consistently clear waters of Isla Desecheo (p216), off the island's west coast, also top any divers' wish list.

Big Wave Surfing at Rincón

16 In winter, the cold weather brings righteous swells to the island's west coast surfing capital of Rincón (p174), where some of the most consistent, varied and exciting surf locations in the Caribbean can be found. And while the double overheads and excellent tubes attract an international set of would-be pros, beginners can paddle out to tamer breaks nearby. At sunset, crowds of locals and visitors replenish themselves with inexpensive eats and ice-cold beer while they mingle in laid-back beach bars and around bonfires on the sand.

Salsa!

17 Let the scholars debate whether the interwoven origins of salsa are rooted in the clubs of New York or the islands of the Caribbean and just feel it. There's no doubt that it lives on as the essential heart beat of Puerto Rico. You'll hear the basic rhythm of the *clavé* (percussion instrument; literally 'keystone') driving Puerto Rican pop music and traditional songs. The secret to grooving to its rhythms on the dancefloor is handed down from one generation to the next.

Sample Lechón with the Locals

18 If you were to draw the Puerto Rican food pyramid, it might only have four elements – rice, beans, plantains and pork. Of these, swine rules the roost; you'll find it fried, grilled, stewed and skewered. But it's the mighty *lechón* (savory, smoky, suckling pig, spit-roasted for up to eight hours) that remains the island's favorite lunch. The roadsides near Guavate (p224) are a virtual parking lot for *lechoneras* (eateries specializing in suckling pig) on the weekends, bringing a festive, down-home atmosphere and a chance for visitors to picnic with the locals.

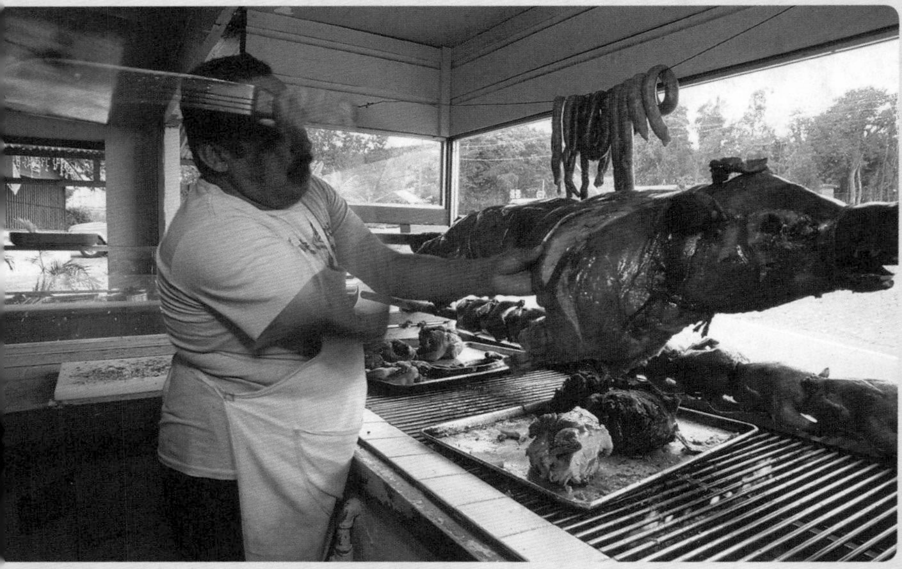

JERRY ALEXANDER / LONELY PLANET IMAGES ©

© EVERYNIGHT IMAGES / ALAMY

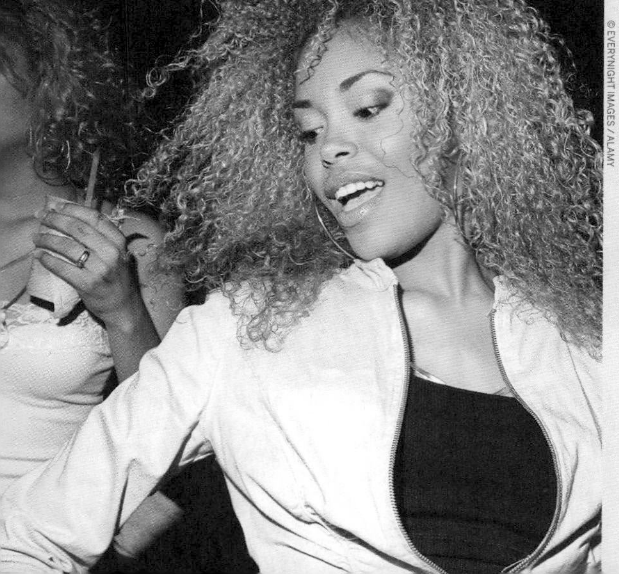

Dance the Night Away

19 Cosmopolitan, stylish and distinctively spiced with the flavors of Latin America, San Juan's nightclubs get started late and party until daybreak. Dress to impress and drink plenty of fluids; it's going to be a long night. The soundtrack here has changed with the times, swapping the salsa of past generations for an au courant mix of trance, techno, house and plenty of reggaetón (the high-energy fusion of reggae and Latino hip-hop). People tend to drink like fish, dance like the devil and throw all caution to the wind.

Fresh Coffee in the Central Mountains

20 The locally sourced food trend in the US has nothing on Puerto Rico's legendary coffee plantations, which offer caffeine junkies a rare opportunity. Here, you can sip a steaming cup of rich, fresh coffee while looking over the rolling hills and quiet valleys where the beans are grown, roasted and brewed. The winding Ruta Panorámica (p221), a white-knuckled scenic route through the mountains, takes travelers past one picturesque plantation after the next, through the village of Jayuya (p230), in the heart of coffee country.

need to know

Currency
» US dollars ($)

Language
» Spanish and English

When to Go

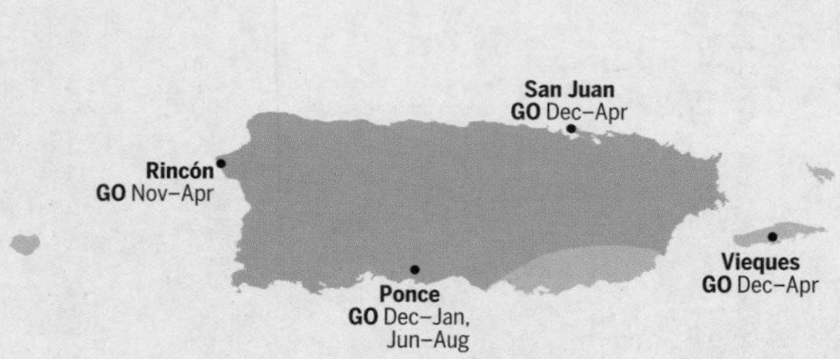

Tropical climate, rain year-round
Warm to hot summers, cold winters

High Season
(mid-Dec–mid-Apr & Jul)

» Crowds escaping the frosty US mainland in winter see hotels rates go up and seasonal attractions come to life.

» In July, local families create a second high season, filling beach towns.

Shoulder
(Sep–Nov & mid-Apr–May)

» Puerto Rico's tourist infrastructure takes a breather to regroup during shoulder season, though there isn't a significant fluctuation in prices or services.

Low Season
(Jun–Nov)

» Apart from July, things get pretty lethargic during hurricane season. Some resorts offer discounted packages but prices at small hotels don't drop precipitously.

Your Daily Budget

Budget less than
$100

» Public transportation: $15

» Budget parador: $60–80

» Eat at cafeterias and stick to museums with free admission

Midrange
$100–200

» Rental car: $25–45

» Double room in midrange hotel: $90–150

» Limit your nightlife budget, self-cater and opt for DIY tours

Top end over
$200

» Double room in boutique hotel: from $180

» Dinner and drinks for two at Mesón Gastronómico: $75

» Guided snorkeling or horseback riding: from $65 for a half day

Money

» ATMs and major American banks are all over the island. Credit and debit cards widely accepted.

Visas

» US visitors won't need a passport; visitors from other countries must have a valid passport. Some nationalities will need a visa.

Cell Phones

» Most US cell phone plans include coverage in Puerto Rico. Travelers from other countries can get prepaid cell phones at one of the ubiquitous malls.

Driving

» Drive on the right; steering wheel is on the left side of the car. Road signs are in Spanish.

Websites

» **See Puerto Rico** (www.seepuertorico.com) Official tourist site.

» **Eye Tour Puerto Rico** (www.eyetour.com) Excellent short videos.

» **To Puerto Rico** (www.topuertorico.com) Food and culture resource.

» **Scurvy Dog's Puerto Rican Blog** (www.robertospuertorico.com) An expat's adventures.

» **Lonely Planet** (www.lonelyplanet.com/puerto-rico) Destination information, hotel bookings, traveler forum and more.

Exchange Rates

Australia	A$1	$1.09
Canada	C$1	$1.05
Europe	€1	$1.48
Japan	¥100	$1.23
New Zealand	NZ$1	$0.80
UK	UK£1	$1.66

For current exchange rates see www.xe.com.

Important Numbers

Country code	☎787
International access code	☎011
Directory assistance	☎411
Puerto Rico Tourism Company	☎787-721-2400
Emergency	☎911

Arriving in Puerto Rico

» **Luis Muñoz Marín International Airport (LMM)**

The LMM airport (see p86) in San Juan provides the same conveniences as any major airport in the US – car rental desks, fast-food restaurants, direct phones for hotel bookings and a well-ordered taxi stand. Taxis set non-negotiable flat rates to all major areas of San Juan.

» **Old San Juan Piers**

If you arrive by cruise ship (see p86), the best dining and shopping of Old San Juan is within a short walk.

Can I Drink the Water?

First-time travelers to Puerto Rico are often a bit trepidatious about the tap water, but there's no cause for concern. Unlike many destinations in the Caribbean, the quality of water here is held to the same standards as any other place in the US, making it 100% safe for drinking. Visitors will see plenty of bottled water for sale, but it's worth considering the environmental impact of all that plastic before purchasing water.

Food safety issues common in other parts of Latin America are also no issue here: milk is pasteurized and dairy products are safe for consumption. Local meat, poultry, seafood, fruit and vegetables are also safe to eat. Although hygiene standards at some roadside *lechoneras* (eateries specializing in suckling pig) might be questionable, you'll rarely go wrong by trusting your instincts and following the crowd.

if you like...

Perfect Beaches

If you've come to laze on the beach and do a whole lot of nothing, there's only one decision to make: where to spread your towel. Generally, the beaches of the north and east are best for swimming.

Puerta de Tierra Tucked away from the towering condos, this is San Juan's best beach (p66)

Playa Flamenco Often shortlisted among the world's best beaches, this pristine strip on Culebra is largely undeveloped (p119)

Playa Santa This south-coast cove stands in the shadow of a majestic 19th-century lighthouse and is perfect for swimming with manatees (p188)

Balneario Boquerón This Blue Flag–certified beach is excellent for strolling and soaking in palm-lined Caribbean scenery (p190)

Ocean Park A magnet for the young and lovely, this is Puerto Rico's version of Rio de Janeiro, with a vibrant weekend scene (p73)

Live Music

Building an itinerary around live music is a surprisingly difficult task in Puerto Rico, where many of the clubs prefer raging reggaetón to live salsa. Here are some of the best bets.

Nuyorican Café This is, bar none, the best place for live music; the musicians carry the torch of Puerto Rican's musical legacy, while the dancefloor steams (p82)

Latin Roots Live bands take the stage nightly at this Old San Juan salsa nightclub (p83)

Picante Lounge Many of the big resorts have a house band of salty codgers, but live merengue and salsa at the Isla Verde Beach Resort is the best of the bunch (p68)

Museo de la Música Puertorriqueña With hands-on displays of instruments and occasional live performances, this Ponce museum looks into Puerto Rico's groove history (p150)

Romantic Getaways

With swaying palms and brilliant-red sunsets, Puerto Rico suffers no lack of romance. San Juan abounds with plush resorts, while options for remote seclusion are scattered around the rest of the island.

Horned Dorset Primavera For very special occasions, this secluded west-coast boutique resort is as romantic as they get (p180)

Gran Hotel El Convento This stately Old San Juan hotel is rich with romantic historic appointments (p71)

Mary Lee's by the Sea These exceedingly fashionable independently owned cliffside apartments are made for couples who want no interruptions (p164)

Malecón House Vieques' newest inn has 10 rooms (some with seaside balconies), mahogany beds and an excellent location (p137)

Inn on the Blue Horizon A handful of bungalows on a bluff define the ideals of the lovers' island retreat (p138)

» Colonial architecture, Old San Juan (p50)

Colonial Architecture

The grand edifices of Puerto Rico's past still sing the hymns of bygone colonial dignity. They're littered around the island, but shouldn't be missed.

Old San Juan There's a picture to be taken down every narrow alley of this historic port town, which has a wealth of lovingly restored buildings (p50)

Plaza Las Delicias Ponce's historical core surrounds this, the grandest public plaza on the island (p147)

Fuente de los Leones Rescued from the 1939 New York World's Fair, this magnificent fountain is the sparkling jewel of Ponce (p147)

San Germán Tucked into the island's southwestern hills lies one of the oldest established cities, where beautifully restored historic homes stand beside the crumbling remains of the neglected ones (p195)

Coamo Before soaking in the thermal baths, visit the city's remarkable San Blás Catholic Church at the edge of the historic central square (p162)

Wildlife-Watching

Under sea and overhead, Puerto Rico's colorful menagerie is ever present.

El Yunque The only rainforest in the US is crawling with lizards and exotic birds; look for the exceptionally rare Puerto Rican parrot (p96)

Bosque Estatal de Guánica This amazingly arid patch of dry forest is teeming with birds, which nest in the cacti and scrub-covered hills (p165)

Isla Mona The so-called Galápagos of the Caribbean is a scarcely traveled nature preserve where visitors can snorkel clear waters with octopus, colorful fish, eels and sharks, and hike past giant iguanas (p198)

Bahía de Jobos Kayakers and hikers navigate the elaborate mangrove channels and coves to spot pelicans, herons and manatee (p160)

Bosque Estatal de Guajataca Keep your eyes in the canopy of this karst country forest and you might spot the rare Puerto Rican boa (p210)

Diving & Snorkeling

Due to big swells on the north coast, most of the best diving and snorkeling lies away from San Juan.

La Parguera Just offshore this southwestern town is 'The Wall,' which drops to over 1500ft and offers the chance to see rare black coral (p170)

Fajardo Enormous coral heads and a great assortment of reef fish – including band-tailed puffers and parrot fish – make this a great destination in the east (p106)

Humacao Excellent for advanced divers, this region has caves and jagged walls, and a mile-long reef frequented by dolphins (p101)

Culebra & Vieques These two islands have many charter trips to tiny, off-lying cays and snorkeling beaches within walking distance of each other (p114)

Isla Desecheo Off Rincón, this island hosts great dives when the sea is calm, with reliable visibility over 100ft (p175)

» Traditional *mofongo* (mashed plantains) served with seafood (p23)

Relaxing at a Resort

From the plush and showy to the remote and cozy, Puerto Rico's spread of resorts is perfect for anyone who wants to feel pampered.

Ritz-Carlton Glitzy and deluxe, the Ritz-Carlton is reigning king of the north coast resorts, featuring a full-service European spa (p74)

Villa Montaña On a moody stretch of coast, this low-profile resort has a remote feel, ecologically sensitive ethos, the best sunsets on the island and turtle adoption programs (p212)

Parador Bahía Salinas Beach Resort & Spa With a lazy eye on the crashing surf, guests laze around the immaculate grounds of this out-of-the-way retreat (p189)

La Concha After a super spiffy upgrade, La Concha is our favorite plush resort in Condado, with lots of attitude and unparalleled views (p72)

Pirates & History

Puerto Rico's strategic importance in the Atlantic channel made it a destination with the peg-leg and plundering set.

Faro y Parque Histórico de Arecibo Kids go crazy for the pirate-themed rides at Aguadilla's family-oriented amusement park (p208)

El Morro This fortress defended the gold of the Spanish crown from one group of pirates after the next; scanning the horizon for ships from its ramparts still captures the imagination (p50)

Cabo Rojo Birthplace of Puerto Rico's most famous pirate, this remote corner of the island has diverse terrain for hiking and hunting for treasure (p188)

Isla Culebrita This little, undeveloped island may not be the actual location of *Pirates of the Caribbean: On Stranger Tides* (the site of the shooting was undisclosed), but the vine-covered, abandoned lighthouse would be an ideal pirate's hideout (p118)

Unique Shopping

From colorful *vejigante* (Puerto Rican masks) to hand-carved saints, Puerto Rico's artisans make one-of-a-kind souvenirs.

Calle del Cristo Some of the best shopping on the island is situated in the shadows of El Morro in Old San Juan. Alongside the cheapie T-shirt and key-chain emporiums, this neighborhood has lots of cool high-end souvenirs (p84)

Artisans Fair Lots of vendors make it easy for cruise-ship crowds to float away with something unique from the island (p84)

Roadside fruit stands When driving through karst country, keep a keen eye out for local farmers hocking locally grown fruits, home-brewed spicy sauces and regionally harvested honey (p200)

Uncharted Studio Every bit as funky as Rincón itself, this local art gallery is filled with affordable one-of-a-kind pieces (p182)

If you like... ancient ruins
The Centro Ceremonial Indígena de Tibes (p156) has ancient ball courts and a glimpse into pre-Columbian island life

Nightclubs

Things may get off to a late start, but when the soundtrack blends a heady mix of hip-hop, reggaetón and salsa, these nightspots see lots of action.

Krash Puerto Rico's best gay club is a blast thanks to an international roster of guest DJs and sweaty dancing (p83)

Red Baron Pub Party hard with college kids who have a seemingly insatiable taste for cheap swill and ear-splitting reggaetón (p187)

Club Lázer A fun and frisky stalwart of San Juan nightlife spinning the most interesting mix of music (p83)

Club Brava With DJs imported from New York and the best sound system in the Caribbean, this is place thumps all night (p83)

Boquerón The narrow streets of this southern beach town are a great place to chase a party, especially on freewheeling summer weekends (p190)

Local Food

Sorry, you'll have to put healthy eating on hold; Puerto Rico's best dishes are meaty as hell and decadently delicious.

Chuletas can-can The house dish at the peerless Restaurante La Guardarraya – a deep-fried pork chop – is worth going *way* out of your way for (p163)

Platano Loco Aguadilla's 'University of Plantains' employs Puerto Rico's favorite starch with devilish creativity (p217)

Guavate lechón Smoky, spit-roasted suckling pig sold at roadside trucks is a taste of heaven (p224)

La mallorca Don't leave Old San Juan before hitting La Bombonera, where this sweet-and-savory ham-and-egg breakfast sandwich was invented (p77)

Mofongo Mashed plantains encases seafood or steak in this signature dish of the island; served everywhere

La Casa de Los Pasteliollos Sway on a hammock while savoring a deep-fried, octopus-stuffed pastry (p159)

Hiking

Don't expect much by way of well-marked trails, but Puerto Rico's hikes offer excellent DIY adventures.

El Yunque Short, easy hikes through this soaking rainforest should top every outdoors agenda (p94)

Bosque Estatal de Guánica With amazing views and a bizarre landscape of cacti and scrub, this blazing hot hike is the weirdest on Puerto Rico (p165)

Corozo Salt Flats, Punta Jagüey & Playa Santa Hike out to rugged cliffs, serene beaches or brackish salt flats in Puerto Rico's untamed southwest (p188)

Bosque Estatal de Guajataca Navigate deep limestone sinkholes, karst country terrain and sudden cliffs in this untouched state forest (p210)

Cerro de Punta You could get here by car, but what fun would that be? Take a rugged DIY hike through the Reserva Forestal Toro Negro to reach the island's highest point (p228)

Isla Mona If you can get here, you'll most certainly hike alone on Puerto Rico's remote wildlife refuge (p198)

month by month

Top Events

1 **Día de los Reyes,** January

2 **Carnaval,** February

3 **Feria Dulce Sueño,** March

4 **SoFo Culinary Fest,** June

5 **Fiesta de San Juan Bautista,** June

January

Travelers looking to escape the cold find balmy solace in Puerto Rico, where temperatures hover between the high 70s and 80s and there's little rainfall.

Fiesta de la Calle San Sebastián

Sponsored by the Instituto de Cultura Puertorriqueña, the Fiesta de la Calle San Sebastián is a four-day shindig of parades, food, dancing and music in Old San Juan. One of the island's hippest street carnivals, it draws in crowds from around the Caribbean and beyond.

Día de los Reyes

The islandwide Día de los Reyes celebration on 6 January toasts the three kings (the Magi) and rivals the popularity of Christmas. Many small towns have festivals in their plazas, with food vendors and live music, and families exchange gifts to celebrate Epiphany.

Whale-Watching

From late January to late March, migrating humpback whales can be seen off west-coast shores. Snorkeling and dive boats double as whale-watching operators, but you may also be able to spot the mammals from the lighthouses at Cabo Rojo and Rincón.

February

Though the mountains are coolest during this time of year, temperatures stay fairly consistent along the coast. It is also one of the driest times of year, with rare, brief afternoon showers.

Maricao Coffee Festival

Held mid month, the annual Maricao Coffee Festival has demonstrations of traditional coffee-making and local crafting. The rugged mountain setting is sublime, and the fresh air fills with the scent of roasting beans.

San Blás de Illescas Half Marathon

Puerto Rico's biggest footrace, the San Blás de Illescas Half Marathon (www.maratonsanblas.com), unfolds in the hills near Coamo. The race has lots of casual runners, but enough notoriety to attract elite runners as well.

Carnaval

During the days preceding Lent, Ponce parties *hard* before giving up vices. While this event is not as wild as Rio de Janeiro's Carnival or New Orleans' Mardi Gras, it's a riot to see parading *vejigantes* (traditional horned masks) and beauty pageants.

March

Snowbird tourists return north, but Puerto Rico's weather remains remarkably beautiful, with warm temperatures and little rain. This might be the slowest month of tourism all year, leaving parks virtually empty.

Cinco Días con Nuestra Tierra

Held in the second week of March, the Cinco Días con Nuestro Tierra (http://agricultura.uprm.edu) is an agricultural-industrial fair, featuring local produce and demonstrations from RUM's agricultural department in Mayagüez. It includes workshops, demonstrations and home gardening exhibits.

Turtle Season

The beaches of Culebra see a lot of action from nesting sea turtles at this time of year. Volunteers can help guard nests from egg poachers – both animal and human – or set up eco-sensitive tours to the island to watch turtles.

Feria Dulce Sueño

The streets of Guayama fill with the elegant gait of Paso Fino horses during the two-day Feria Dulce Sueño (Fair of Sweet Dreams). Competitions take place in a dignified rodeo atmosphere and the city goes horse crazy. It's held in early March.

April

Trade winds bring a bit more precipitation to the north coast, though rainfall is mostly in the afternoon. As temperatures continue to increase, small festivals enliven mountain towns.

Puerto Rico International Film Festival

The Puerto Rico International Film Festival (www.priff.org) is the biggest annual event for the island's burgeoning film industry. The festival's recent move to new digs in the W Retreat & Spa on Vieques underscores its high-class ambition.

Saint's Day

Cities across Puerto Rico celebrate the birthday of patriot and revolutionary independence icon José de Diego (born April 16, 1867). It's a national holiday, celebrated with particular enthusiasm in Aguadilla, where he was born.

Ironwood Wine

Near Ponce, people in little Juana Díaz get tipsy with their Taíno heritage, celebrating Mavi Carnival and toasting a fermented drink made from the bark of an ironwood tree. Festivities include lots of costumes, food and fairly intense hangovers.

Semana Santa

The Catholic holiday of Easter gets celebrated for an entire week at Semana Santa festivals throughout the island. The most vivid festivals will have a procession through the streets to reenact the crucifixion – using a real person tied to a cross.

May

Many of the little agricultural towns of the south celebrate the arrival of spring with the fruit of their harvests – including a delicious assortment of coco, mango, shrimp and oysters.

Feria Internacional de Artesanía

Known locally as FERINART, the Feria Internacional de Artesanía (www.ferinart.org) is a chance for artisans from Puerto Rico and throughout Latin American to show off their wares in Old San Juan. Tents with locally carved masks, paintings and crafts fill the streets below the fort.

Semana de la Danza

Ponce's Semana de la Danza, held in mid-May, features a week of music and dance concerts that celebrate the stately music of string quartets and 19th-century ballroom dance. Many of the events are free.

June

Probably the most active month for festivals on the island, when Puerto Rico celebrates food, jazz and crabs. The summer tourist season – when road-tripping locals join foreigners – swings into high gear.

Heineken JazzFest

Hosted at the Tito Puente Ampitheater in San Juan, the Heineken JazzFest (www.prheinekenjazz.com) draws international artists and jazz fans. An impressive crop of top-drawer salsa and Latin jazz artists perform. It's usually held on the first weekend of June.

SoFo Culinary Fest

The rivalry between San Juan's culinary heavies takes to the street at the SoFo Culinary Fest. The streets of Old San Juan are closed to traffic and the entire neighborhood becomes an alfresco bistro as restaurateurs strut their stuff.

Fiesta de San Juan Bautista

On June 24 Old San Juan explodes with the island capital's *fiesta patronal* (patron saint's festival), Fiesta de San Juan Bautista. Party animals eventually walk backwards into the sea (or sometimes fountains) to demonstrate their loyalty to the saint of Christian baptism.

Festival del Juey

Guánica's mid-June Festival de Juey delights crab eaters and brings an open-air fair to the town's seaside boardwalk. The crustaceans are consumed in every preparation imaginable and washed back with a whole lot of cold beer.

Festival de Flores

Acres of roses, carnations, lilies and begonias brighten up the mountain town of Aibonito with the Festival de Flores at the end of June. Vendors have dirt-cheap plant sales; just be sure to read the Department of Agriculture regulations before flying home with any purchases.

July

Blazing-hot temperatures drive Puerto Rican families to the beaches in droves. This is high season on the south coast, so expect plenty of company at the beach.

Festival Casals de Puerto Rico

World-class instrumentalists play the Festival Casals de Puerto Rico (www.festcasalspr.gobierno.pr), honoring native cellist and composer Pablo Casals. For the past half century this month-long event has offered top orchestral and chamber music events in San Juan.

Puerto Rico Salsa Congress

The competition among professional dancers is cut-throat during the Puerto Rico Salsa Congress, usually held in July in San Juan. Spectators have the chance to see the dance at its highest form.

Fiesta de Santiago

Loíza Aldea's Fiesta de Santiago, held at the end of the month, brings Puerto Ricans of African descent to a fiesta worthy of Bahía in Brazil: parades, fabulous drum ensembles, masks and costumes revive saints and incarnations of West African gods.

August

Every weekend hosts parties for Puerto Rico's patron saints and the tropical rains start to fall, as the island braces itself for the heart of the hurricane season.

San Juan International Billfish Tournament

At over half a century old, the San Juan International Billfish Tournament (www.sanjuaninternational.com) is one of the longest-running deep-sea contests of its kind in the world. And what goes perfectly with fishing? That's right, drinking beer.

Bomba y Plena

The music of plantation workers fills the air at Bomba y Plena festivals during late summer. Explosive drumbeats and folk songs are the custom at a number of them, but reliably rowdy ones happen in Ponce, and in nearby mountain villages of Juana Díaz and Aguas Buenas.

September

Tourism in September can be upended by tropical storms, but the heart of the hurricane season really begins at the end of the month. Still, travelers should keep a close eye on the weather.

Fiesta Nuestra Señora de la Monserrate

The Fiesta Nuestra Señora de la Monserrate in Aguas Buenas, high in the mountains above San Juan, is a favorite among the scarce September festivals. Live music and street food make for a lively atmosphere and the mountain setting is lovely.

October

Though this is the slow tourist season, the island's typical assortment of parties for patron saints are scattered throughout the month. Hurricanes can undermine travel.

Surfing Safari

To kick off the big waves of winter, the island's west coast usually sees a pro-surfing competition at the end of the month. The heart of the action is usually at Rincón, but ask at local surf shops for details.

Día del Descubrimiento de América

Though Christopher Columbus is loathed throughout most of Latin America, Puerto Rico celebrates his arrival – the so-called Día del Descubrimiento de América (Discovery of American Day) – with a smattering of parades and street festivals on October 12.

November

American tourists begin descending on the island as the weather turns cold in the north. Puerto Rico also sees many native sons and daughters return to the island for the holidays.

Festival Nacional Indígena

Although all pure-blooded Taíno have been gone for about 400 years, this Jayuya festival, held mid-month, revives the games, costumes, food and music of the original islanders. As with almost all Puerto Rican fiestas, there is a beauty pageant, this time with women in Indian dress.

Play Ball!

The Puerto Rican League baseball season is in full swing and stadiums throughout the island host teams of aspiring major leaguers, young players hoping to get a bit more experience over the winter and former Major League Baseball players in the sunset of their careers.

December

Christmas lights make central plazas sparkle as Puerto Rico gets geared up for Christmas. Near the end of the month, every town celebrates the nativity.

Waves in the West

Cold fronts push huge waves to the island's east coast, making it the high season for surfing Rincón and beaches near Isabela and Aguadilla. With perfect tubes and tons of tourists, you'll need to reserve a board and lessons early.

Las Mañanitas

Mexican mariachis parade around the square in Ponce during Las Mañanitas, an annual celebration of the Virgin of Guadalupe, patron saint of Mexico. It's a brassy event, with lots of trumpets and drinking, priming the pump for the Christmas festivities.

Hatillo Mask Festival

Held on December 28, the Hatillo Mask Festival features masked devils prowling the streets as incarnations of the agents of King Herod, who sent soldiers to find and kill the Christ Child. Kids think it is great fun to run and hide from the maskers.

itineraries

Whether you've got six days or 60, these itineraries provide a starting point for the trip of a lifetime. Want more inspiration? Head online to lonelyplanet.com/thorntree to chat with other travelers.

Seven Days
Essential Puerto Rico

Touch down in **San Juan** and get to the beach, either Isla Verde, Condado or Ocean Park. Spend the next day weaving through Old San Juan and posing by the ramparts of El Morro. Take a quick nap, then hit Calle Fortaleza for dinner, drinks and salsa.

Start early on day three and go west, watching the waves explode over the breakers at **Playa Mar Chiquita** and winding up the mountain road to the **Observatorio de Arecibo**. Bunk nearby at the restored plantation of **Hacienda Gripiñas**.

Next morning, wind your way along the Ruta Panorámica, heading up toward Puerto Rico's tallest peak in the **Reserva Forestal Toro Negro**, before making your way to historic **Ponce** to dine and sleep. The next day, head east to sample smoky pork at one of the famed roadside *lechoneras* (eateries specializing in suckling pig) in **Guavate**, then continue east to sleep at a beach house in **Yabucoa**. The cool, green interior of **El Yunque** starts day six, which ends on the white sand of **Playa Luquillo**.

Return to San Juan via **Loíza Aldea**, where you can buy a *vejigante* (Puerto Rican mask) before passing the evening hitting the tables of Isla Verde and Condado in the capital.

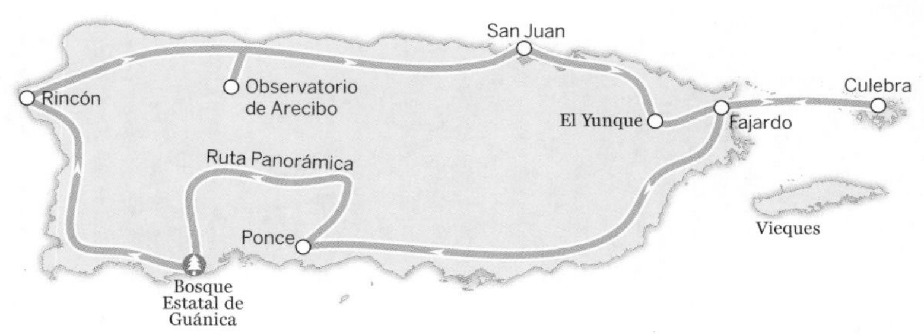

Two Weeks

The Grand Tour

Spend four days in **San Juan** and surrounding areas, getting plenty of beach time and making sure to see Old San Juan. Spend at least one night listing to live salsa and taking in the dancefloor action at Nuyorican Café, the best live music club on the island. Head for **El Yunque** for a day of hiking, then spend the night in **Fajardo** and experience the wonder of the bioluminescent bay.

The next morning head east aboard the ferry for **Culebra** – the quieter, more beautiful and less-developed cousin to Vieques. The next few days will go by too quickly, snorkeling and swimming at some of the best beaches in the world, and taking a charter trip off to the abandoned white-sand paradise of Isla Culebrita.

Now that your batteries are fully recharged, it's time to do some exploring. Make for the mainland and follow the quiet road past the sleepy sugar towns of the south coast toward **Ponce**. Spend a couple days exploring the colonial buildings and excellent food in the so-called 'Pearl of the South.' You can visit La Guancha Paseo Tablado, Centro Ceremonial Indígena de Tibes or make a short detour up the mountain on the **Ruta Panorámica** to do some hiking and sip the island's famous coffee.

Definitely allow one day (preferably with an early morning start so you can be done by mid-afternoon when the sun's at its hottest) for the rugged, bone-dry forest of **Bosque Estatal de Guánica**. After hiking, drive scenic Rte 333 along the south coast and stop to swim at tiny mangrove-enclosed beaches and spend the night in an isolated resort.

You can either spend the day swimming the turquoise water of Playa Santa or head right to the final destination, **Rincón**. The last few days of the trip will be spent surfing (or taking lessons) on perfect waves and soaking up the island's best sunsets with an icy rum drink in hand. Complete the circuit, breaking up the drive with a stop at the **Observatorio de Arecibo**, before arriving back in San Juan for your final evening, dining in style at one of Old San Juan's fine restaurants.

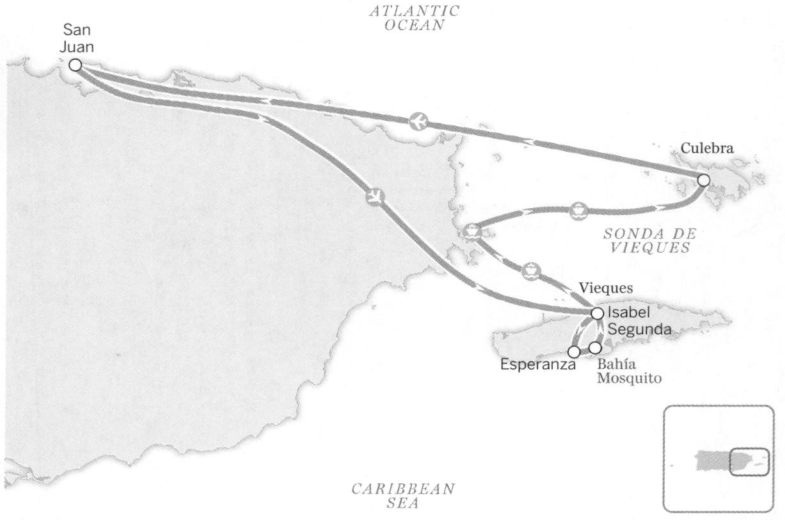

Five to 10 Days
An Escape to Culebra & Vieques

After you land in the capital of **San Juan**, check out the history on offer in the seven square blocks that make up Old San Juan, then hightail it out of town for your island break. A trip to the islands of **Vieques** displays Puerto Rico in its best light: perfect sand, laid-back atmosphere and ramshackle nightlife. Take a scenic flight to leave the capital. It's startlingly cheap and saves you the hassle and expense of renting a car.

Once you touch down in **Isabel Segunda**, pick up your scooter and zip right over to **Esperanza**, the perfect place to get acquainted with the island's beautiful beaches, do a little shopping and slow down to the pace of the tropics. Spend the next few days in Esperanza, spending at least one night in the magically glowing phosphorescent waters at **Bahía Mosquito**. When you tire of lounging around on the beach – and this could be as soon as never – return to Isabel Segunda. Spend a sunny morning out at Fortín Conde de Mirasol, take a quick dip and ditch your flip flops for the nightlife at Al's Mar Azul.

If you haven't quite satisfied your desire for the island life and want to unplug even more, take a ferry back to the mainland and another out to **Culebra** (ferry service between the islands has been suspended). The smaller island just to the north of Vieques is known by Puerto Ricans as a more laid-back alternative to hard-partying Vieques. Culebra doesn't have much by way of fancy resorts and clubs; the focus here is on the world-class beaches, reef snorkeling and wildlife refuges. With few cars on the island and long, deserted stretches of sand, Culebra offers the serenity that can be all too rare on the crowded Puerto Rican mainland. Visitors can soak in the expansive views of the ocean, breathe the fresh island breeze and explore sandy coves. After dark, the little harbor comes alive with affable expats whose love of karaoke crooning is only rivaled by their thirst for cold cans of Medalla. After finding the lolling rhythm of the relaxed place, catch a short flight back to San Juan (its only slightly more expensive than land options) and gape at the aerial views of the rainforest.

Five Days
Exploring the Mountains

Head south from **San Juan** to **Bosque Estatal de Carite** on Hwy 184 for a morning of beautiful hiking and swimming in icy pools (in non-holiday periods Carite is almost empty). On your way, grab lunch from one of the *lechoneras* along the highway near **Guavate**. Head to **Aibonito** next and try to see both coasts of the island from the Mirador La Piedra Degetau.

The next day wind your way west along the island's windiest roads toward the **Reserva Forestal Toro Negro** where you can rouse a park ranger (if you're lucky) and set off on a couple of short hikes, or try your hand at mounting the highest peak in Puerto Rico.

Follow Rte 144 to the mountain town of **Jayuya**, where you can visit the surreal Museo del Cemí and stock up on coffee at the Hacienda San Pedro. Sleep in **Adjuntas** and – if your nerves can handle more blind corners – head north to **Lares** for the island's best ice cream. The final stop on this surreal roller-coaster ride is the **Observatorio de Arecibo**, before heading down the mountain back to the capital.

Seven Days
Puerto Rico's North Coast

San Juan makes a great hub for the first few days of exploring. Old San Juan, the beaches on Isla Verde and the SoFo dining district are vibrant introductions to Puerto Rican culture and history. A great day trip heading east will take in a wild diversity of island ecology at **Las Cabezas de San Juan Reserva Natural 'El Faro'** and allows time to pick up a *vejigante* from **Loíza Aldea**. On the third day, head west after breakfast, taking the vine-covered byways along the shore to **Playa Mar Chiquita** and lunch with the locals at a beachside kiosk. Spend the next day underground – either on your own in the rugged caves of **Bosque Estatal de Guajataca** or as part of a tour of the **Cavernas del Río Camuy**. Choose your adventure for your final few days: either the moody breaks of Puerto Rico's *other* surfing capital, **Aguadilla**, or the chirping coquí frogs and misty mountain fog of a lodge in karst country. Hustle back to San Juan and spend the last night downing mojitos until you get the courage to hit the dancefloor to a soundtrack of live salsa.

Puerto Rico Outdoors

Puerto Rico's Most Memorable Trails

La Mina Trail Navigate through an old mine tunnel in the rainforest, ending at a lovely waterfall.

El Yunque Trail This moderately challenging hike summits the highest point in Puerto Rico's rainforest.

Cueva del Viento Test your navigation skills on the poorly marked trails of the Guajataca forest, and find this spooky cave.

Camino Ballena Hike down a big hill in dry forest and, just when you're getting parched, take a dip in the Caribbean.

Los Morrillos Lighthouse Scramble up to the windswept headlands and old lighthouse overlooking Puerto Rico's remote southwest corner.

This is what you've spent long afternoons at the office daydreaming about: picture-perfect vistas of turquoise water, bushwhacking through the dense canopy of jungle, paddling out in warm waves to catch the sunrise and heavenly surf breaks. The range of outdoor adventures in Puerto Rico is limited only by your ambition, and the island's diverse forests, balmy beaches and crinkled karst formations are calling. This is a place to get out and discover the great outdoors, both sensuously and adventurously, whether by navigating dense forest on foot, perfect waves by surfboard or diving into the depths next to a coral-spiked wall.

Plan Your Surf Trip

Lapped on four sides by warm ocean, Puerto Rico has earned the right to consider itself the 'Hawaii of the Atlantic', with the most consistent surf breaks in the world. Thanks to legendary waves at beaches such as Tres Palmas, Crash Boat and Jobos, Puerto Rico has a deeply ingrained surfing culture based around some of the best waves in the Americas.

When to Go

» **October–April** Winter is the time when cold fronts and low pressure systems from the north bring the biggest waves to Rincón and other surfing destinations on the west and north shores.

When Not to Go

» **December, June–July** Even though you can surf in the west year-round, rates spike in December, when hordes of Americans on Christmas vacation invade, making for crowded waters and competitive accommodations. In June and July there are smaller, if surfable swells, but vacationing Puerto Ricans arrive in droves and many accommodations enforce a three-night minimum stay.

Where to Surf

Although there are opportunities to surf the north and east coasts, the best of Puerto Rico's surfing is off the famous west coast.

» **Rincón** (p175) In 1968 the World Surfing Championships were held at Rincón, and the island hasn't looked back since. Surfers from around the world come here for a long annual season. The huge variety of breaks includes plenty of stuff for beginners and experts. This is Puerto Rico's surfing capital.

» **Aguadilla** (p216) Some locals actually favor the breaks near here, which are generally a bit more challenging than those at Rincón.

» **Isabela** (p212) To avoid the crowds, rent an apartment on the cliff-edge out-of-the way beach towns near Isabela. Playa Jobos, a long beach good for all levels, is here. Gas Chambers is a right-hand break for experienced surfers, while Surfer's Beach is kind to beginners.

Renting Boards & Taking Lessons

» **WOW Surfing School** (p67) Housed in San Juan's Ritz-Carlton hotel, this is a good bet for beginners and new surfers; lessons tackle the relatively easy waves of Playa Isla Verde.

» **Wave Riding Vehicles** (p212) This tiny shop, square in the middle of Playa Jobos, offers rentals and low-key, informal lessons.

» **West Coast Surf Shop** (p175) Centrally located in Rincón, these guys will drop off boards at your hotel room before you arrive.

» **Surf 787** (p175) Groups can rent out the surf villa and get lessons on the beaches in Rincón that are most appropriate for their ability. There's also a kids' camp in summer.

» **Desecheo Surf Shop** (p175) Cheap rentals and a location in the heart of Rincón's stalwart surfer scene make this a good spot to get your bearings.

» **La Selva Surf Shop** (p101) A good place to rent boards if you want to surf the tamer waves off the east coast.

Plan Your Underwater Adventure

Most Caribbean islands boast a formidable diving scene and Puerto Rico can compete with the best of them with an exciting selection of walls, drop-offs, reefs and underwater caves.

Where to Dive

» **Parguera Wall** (p170) The first of Puerto Rico's truly world-class dive areas is near La Parguera in the south. The underwater wall falls from 60ft to over 1500ft due to a huge drop in the continental shelf below the sea bed. With more than 25 named dive sites, the area is awash with trenches, valleys, coral gardens and colorful fish.

» **Isla Desecheo** (p216) Thirteen miles northwest of Aguadilla, Desecheo has a number of spectacular dive sites and visibility that is often at least 100ft.

» **Isla Mona** (p199) This is where real adventurers head for diving. It's expensive to charter a trip, but

SURF ESCAPES FROM SAN JUAN

If the west coast's waves are too big, or if its dudes are too cool or the drive is too far, there are a number of lesser-known options for surfers who want to make a quick day trip from San Juan. Along the north coast there are a few decent breaks for expert surfers around Manatí (p204) and those with less experience can enjoy the shallow-water thrills of boogie boarding. There are even reasonable surfing lessons to be had in the capital, San Juan (p67). Die hards will take what they can get at Balneario Escambrón in Puerta de Tierra (p59), while the best stuff can be found over in Piñones at Los Aviónes. East of San Juan, the best place to surf barrels is at La Pared in Luquillo (p100) or the recently inaugurated wildlife reserve at La Selva (p101).

Surfing Map

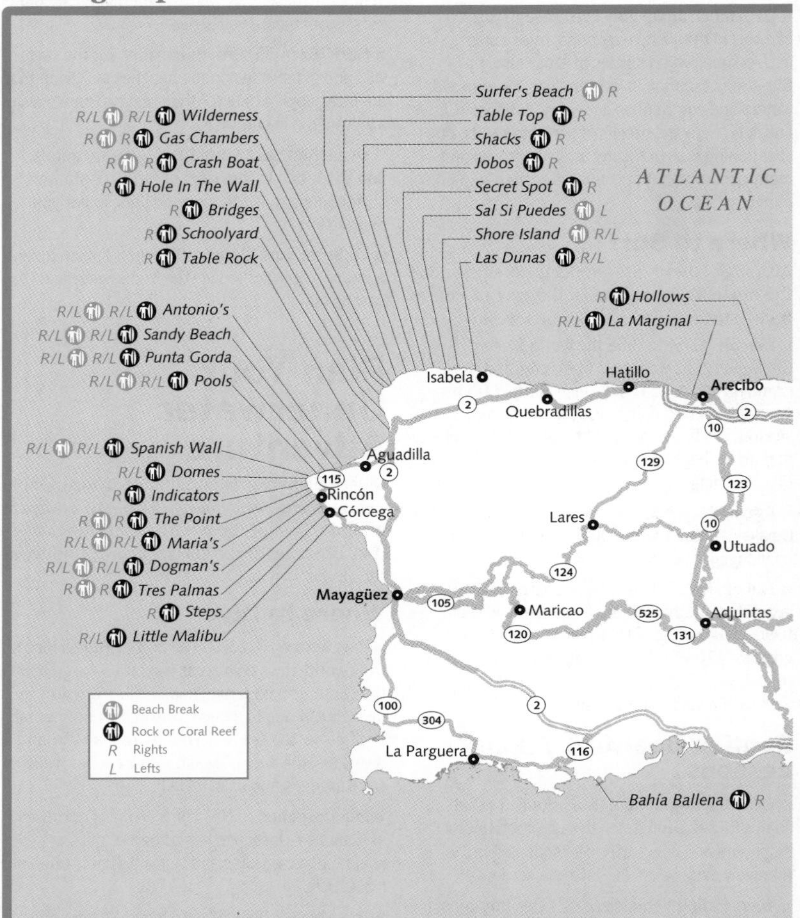

the unblemished waters are frequented by turtles and seals.

Dive Planning Basics

Generally speaking, the waters off the north and west coasts of Puerto Rico are rough and better suited to surfing. You may, however, get some luck on calm days snorkeling the fringe reefs off Condado (p60) and Playa Isla Verde (p66) in San Juan or at either Playa Shacks or Playa Steps in Rincón (p177). Even though west-coast waters are calmer in summer, snorkeling still isn't great there.

Top Dive Operators

Dive operators run day trips out of the major ports and resort hotels around the island (see the On the Road chapters for more details). If you are in the San Juan area, consider a dive trip to the caves and overhangs at Horseshoe Reef, Figure Eight or the Molar. There's decent diving along the chain of islands called 'La Cordillera,' east of Las Cabezas de San Juan (in the Fajardo area), with about 60ft to 70ft visibility. Catch the Drift or the Canyon off Humacao.

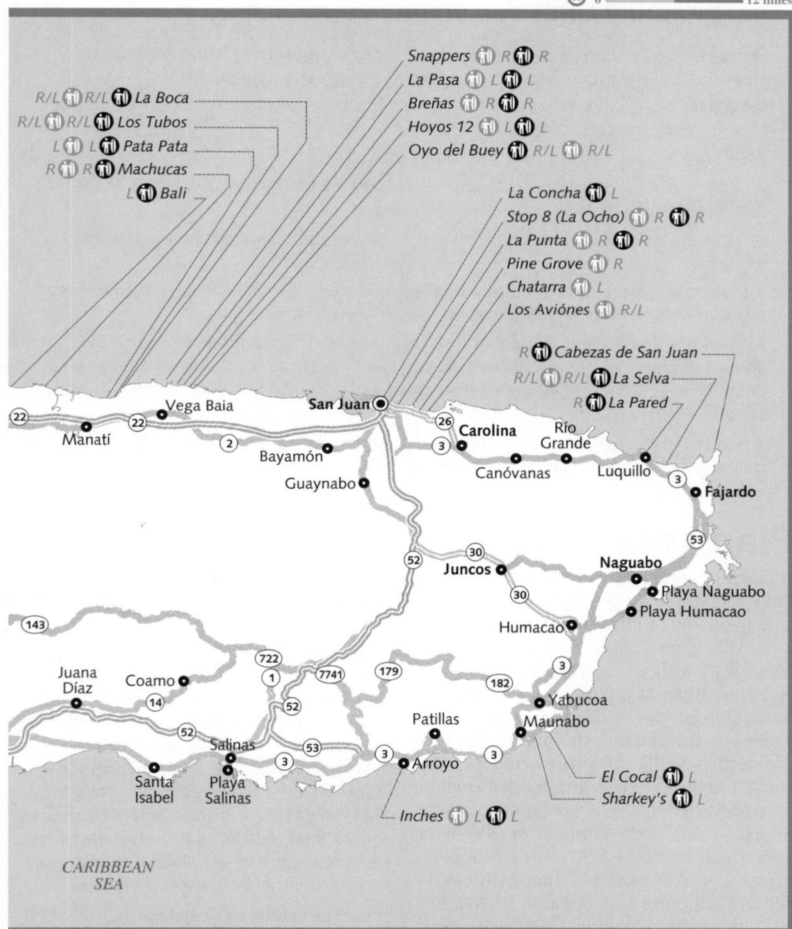

» **Taíno Divers** (p177) In Rincón, this reliable, environmentally sensitive company runs daily trips to Isla Desecheo.

» **West Divers** (p169) The best outfit in La Parguera is in the heart of this fishing village, with regular trips to the famous Wall.

» **Sea Ventures Dive Center** (p107) One of the better operators leaving Fajardo for the northeastern cordillera.

Where to Snorkel

» **Culebra & Vieques** (p120 and p135) The best snorkeling in Puerto Rico can be found off the sheltered islands Culebra and Vieques, where you can snorkel directly from the beach. The former offers Punta Melones and the wonderfully isolated Playa Carlos Rosario, the latter boasts Green Beach and the handily located municipal beach in the main southern settlement of Esperanza.

» **Isla Caja de Muertos** (p151) The south coast faces clear Caribbean waters that suffer low river runoff. Taking the day trip out to this island near Ponce can satisfy hikers as well.

» **La Parguera** (p169) These warm waters have some decent snorkeling, and DIY adventurers can access hidden mangrove beaches via kayak.

SAFETY GUIDELINES FOR DIVING & SNORKELING

Before embarking on a scuba-diving, skin-diving or snorkeling trip, carefully consider the following points to ensure a safe and enjoyable experience:

» Possess a current diving certification card from a recognized scuba-diving instructional agency (if scuba diving).

» Be sure you are healthy and feel comfortable diving.

» Obtain reliable information about physical and environmental conditions at the dive site from a reputable local dive operation.

» Be aware of local laws, regulations and etiquette about marine life and the environment.

» Dive only at sites within your realm of experience; if available, engage the services of a competent, professionally trained dive instructor or dive master.

» Be aware that underwater conditions vary significantly from one region, or even one site, to another. Seasonal changes can significantly alter any site and dive conditions. These differences influence the way divers dress for a dive and what diving techniques they use.

» Ask about the environmental characteristics that can affect your diving and how trained local divers deal with these considerations.

Plan Your Hike

Hiking in Puerto Rico has plenty of potential. But what you actually get out of it depends largely on your individual expectations and how willing you are to strike out on your own (often without a decent map). It would be wrong to paint a picture of the island as some kind of hiker's nirvana. Although the scenery is invariably lush and the coastline wonderfully idyllic, a lack of well-kept paths and a dearth of accurate printed information have thwarted many a spontaneous hiker. Added to this is the commonwealth's compact size; the whole island is only marginally bigger than Yellowstone National Park in the US and supports a population of nearly 4 million people, meaning true backcountry adventures are understandably limited.

Where to Hike

» **El Yunque National Forest** (p96) The most popular hikes by far are in the emblematic El Yunque rainforest, where a 23-mile network of largely paved trails has opened up the area to mass tourism. Hikes here are usually short and easily accessible, and there are plenty of ecominded tour operators happy to guide you through the main sights. The forest also contains Puerto Rico's only true backcountry adventure, the seven-hour trek to the top of El Toro (3522ft) and back.

» **Bosque Estatal de Guánica** (p166) The foil for El Yunque in every way, this forest is on the opposite corner of the island, the climate is bone-dry and instead of palms the trails are lined with cactus. This remote place doesn't have fantastic trails, but it's good for bird-watching and gorgeous views of the Caribbean.

» **Reserva Forestal Toro Negro** (p229) For more dramatic and isolated hikes, head toward the center of the island, on Puerto Rico's misty rooftop. Be prepared to get your shoes dirty here as clouds often shroud the peaks and the trails are invariably damp and muddy. Typical of the numerous forest reserves scattered along the Ruta Panorámica – others include Maricao, Carite and Guilarte – Toro Negro is rarely staffed in low season and you'll be lucky to spot more than a handful of fellow hikers enjoying the views.

» **Bosque Estatal de Guajataca** (p210) The 27-mile network of rough trails is good for a DIY hiker who doesn't mind a bit of bushwhacking, including a side trip to the spooky Cueva del Viento.

What to Expect

With its lush mountains, numerous protected parks and highly developed infrastructure, Puerto Rico ought to be a country perfectly suited to hiking. Yet in reality, decent well-signposted trails are few and far between, and many of the commonwealth's carefully protected forest reserves are rarely utilized.

This paucity of backcountry information can be something of a shock to aspiring wilderness hikers fresh from bushwhacking their way through the Sierra Nevada or dragging their crampons across the European Alps. But, contrary to what the gushing tourist brochures would have you believe, Puerto Rico is no Yosemite. Nor are the Puerto Ricans – with some obvious exceptions – a nation of hikers. Instead, most islanders would much rather drive their cars to the top of the nearest mountain than get their shoes dirty hiking up on a trail. Indeed, Cerro de Punta, the commonwealth's highest peak (4389ft), has a paved road to within a mile of its summit while the poorly maintained hiking path that originates in Jayuya is barely used – except by the odd adventurous visitor.

The key, for confused hikers, is to manage your expectations and do some homework before setting out. In Puerto Rico finding the trailhead can often be more difficult than completing the trail itself.

Outside of El Yunque National Forest (p94), the island's two dozen or so forest reserves are invariably poorly staffed and lacking in any accurate trail maps. But plan ahead and a little-used Eden is yours for the exploring. Persistence is important. Try the Departamento de Recursos Naturales y Ambientales (DRNA; Department of Natural Resources; ☎787-999-2200; www.drna.gobierno.pr in Spanish) in San Juan, ask around at the various adventure tour agencies and – best of all – question the more outdoor-minded locals. You'll be surprised by what you can find.

HIKING ACROSS THE ISLAND

Fondo de Mejoramiento (☎787-759-8366; www.fondodemejoramiento.org, in Spanish) runs day hikes covering the entire length of the island from east to west along the Cordillera Central (Central Mountains). The idea is to cover the whole Ruta Panorámica in different weekend segments over a period of three months (February to April). The 'Ruta' was actually designed by Luis Muñoz Marín in the 1950s primarily as a hiking route.

During specialized Fondo walks – all of which are confined to the paved road – a police escort is provided to ward off the famously zippy Puerto Rican traffic.

Tour Companies & Guides

Several companies in San Juan can organize group trips to Toro Negro that incorporate hiking with various other activities. Acampa Nature Adventure Tours (p229) does a day trip that mixes hiking with zip-lining and climbing with a harness up a waterfall.

To make an organized trek in the company of serious Puerto Rican hikers, take a weekend hike through the Cañón de San Cristóbal (p224) near Barranquitas, where steep cliffs and spectacular waterfalls contribute to some of the island's most serendipitous scenery.

Private guide Robin Phillips (p98) leads all kinds of custom tours of El Yunque's less-traveled south side, including trips to petroglyphs.

Plan Your Cycling Trip

On an island infested with cars, cycling is still in its infancy. But as the traffic gridlock proliferates, it can only be a matter of time before both locals and visitors rediscover the time-saving and health-extolling benefits of two-wheeled transportation.

Where to Cycle

» **Vieques** (p136) The jewel in Puerto Rico's cycling crown has to be pristine Vieques, undoubtedly the best place to organize a creative cycling tour.

» **Cabo Rojo** (p189) The secondary roads on the southwest coast of the island pass gently rolling hills around Guánica, Cabo Rojo and Sabana Grande. There are enough roads here for a two- or three-day trip, including roughshod trails around the Cabo Rojo lighthouse. Reliable bike rentals can be procured at the Wheel Shop (p189).

» **Isabela coast** (p212) This recently developed coastal bike path is great for a casual afternoon ride. You'll pass the crashing surf and plenty of coastal beaches to take a dip. You can rent bikes right along the roadside.

» **Piñones** (p90) The specially designed bike trails in Piñones make for an easy, enjoyable ride on this small island.

» **Central Mountains** (p226) The Toro Verde Nature Adventure Park has a professionally

ALTERNATIVE OUTDOOR ADVENTURES

» Hit the Reserva Forestal Toro Negro with San Juan–based adventure company, Acampa Nature Adventure Tours (p229), and you could find yourself **rappelling** off 60ft cliffs and zip-lining above the tree line.

» **Kitesurfing** has taken off on Playa Isla Verde in San Juan. Get kited out at the locally based Kitesurfpr (p67).

» Rincón is the best place to go for **whale-watching**; humpbacks appear in the Pasaje de la Mona around December. You can organize a boat trip (p177) or sometimes catch a glimpse from outside the Punta Higüero lighthouse.

» Of the various **yoga** retreats on the island, the most transcendental in both mood and setting has to be the early-morning classes at the Casa Grande Mountain Retreat (p208).

» Test your mettle in one of Puerto Rico's famous **running road races**. Events include the World's Best 10K Race (WB10K), the Rincón Triathlon (p178) and the San Blás de Illescas Marathon in Coamo (p161).

groomed single-track trail that offers the island's best mountain biking.

Before You Go

If you want to do serious cycling in Puerto Rico, you'll find that it's more cost-effective to fly with your bike. The options for long-term rentals on the island are scarce and expensive. Also, remember to bring plenty of extra tubes, a spare tire, basic tools and a couple of replacement spokes so the island's combination of rough roads and scarce bike shops doesn't leave you out of commission.

For more general information, contact the **Puerto Rican Cycling Federation** (☎787-721-7185; www.fecipur.com, in Spanish); they know the touring and trail-riding scenes on the island and can point you to an expanding network of safe bike routes.

Travel with Children

Best Regions For Kids

San Juan

Young travelers will be thrilled by San Juan's vibrant culture, wide beaches and kid-friendly museums. San Juan's historic sights have a lot of diversions for kids, and the tunnels and turrets of El Morro and Fuerte San Cristóbal capture young imaginations with stories of pirates and seafaring adventure.

Culebra & Vieques

Snorkeling and swimming in the clear, calm waters is excellent for kids, and the islands host vacation rentals and short-term apartment rentals, which can be an affordable option for families.

El Yunque & East Coast

Rainforests and frogs, drippy palms and mountain lookouts – the easy hikes of the El Yunque rainforest are thrilling for young explorers. The bioluminescent waters of Fajardo are also magical.

West Coast

The west coast has excellent surfing and boogie boarding, with waves big enough or small enough to match your ability. It also gives parents a chance to get off the beaten path.

With so many of the comforts of home and lots of all-ages outdoor adventures, Puerto Rico is an excellent destination for travelers with children. The options for family activities on the island are extensive and happen mostly outdoors; kids and adults find equal pleasure in exploring the waters with a snorkel and fins, the caves with a flashlight or the rainforest with a pair of binoculars.

Puerto Rico for Kids

Puerto Rico is a safe and fun destination for kids, with perhaps the best services for families in the Caribbean. Facilities are comfortable, and you'll receive fewer icy stares from curmudgeonly yachters than you might do elsewhere. Families will find it easy to fill their agendas.

Children's Highlights

Even though many of the island's museums have programs for kids and there's a small kids' museum in San Juan, families will get much more out of their visit if they stick to Puerto Rico's beloved outdoor charms: playing on sandy beaches, swimming in warm water and exploring the island's wildlife.

In general, the beaches of the northeast and east coast are the best for swimming, with the calmest and most beautiful options on Culebra and Vieques. The closest to San Juan are the beaches along Hwy 3 in Luquillo, where there's wide sand, food kiosks and lifeguards. The best of these might be Playa

MIND-BLOWING SIGHTS FOR CHILDREN

Canons at El Morro A deep, mysterious fissure in the earth.
Observatorio de Arecibo This mountain-top radio telescope is like a giant ear listening to the heavens.
Bioluminescent waters at Laguna Grande Sparkling waters make for a surreal night swim.
Marine life in Culebra Coral, tropical fish and clear waters make for excellent snorkeling.
Rainforest flora of El Yunque The soggy trails of North America's only rainforest lead past fascinating flora and fauna.
Watching whales and surfers at Rincón Gaze out to migrating whales and surfers from the cliffs above the waters.

Luquillo, which has well-kept changing rooms and small waves. In the northwest and west the tides are generally rougher and there can be rip tides, so exercise more caution, especially in winter.

If you turn up on the northwest corner of the island, Parador Villas del Mar Hau is an excellent accommodation option, with a beach that's perfect for boogie boarding and large cabañas to easily fit a family. If the waves are still too big, try the Courtyard by Marriot Aguadilla, where kids can run around a bright and colorful on-site splash park.

The best hikes for the whole family are in the rainforest of El Yunque. Unlike virtually every other forest on the island, these trails are well marked, easy to follow and easy enough for shorter legs. A favorite is the popular Big Tree Trail, which ends at a waterfall where kids who are brave enough can take an icy dip. The rainforest also has informative ranger-led walks. Remember that the trails in El Yunque can get pretty crowded after 11am, so it's good to start early. Also, it's essential to bring water on this hike, as there are no facilities on the trails. The Las Cabezas de San Juan Reserva Natural is another great natural area for families, with mini tours through a diverse coastal environment, a tram and lots of skeletons of marine animals.

Families will also find a number of more adventurous activities in parts of the island further afield, though the winding hairpin turns of the central mountains are not recommended. Following the coast, there's lots to keep a family busy: you can ride a horse along the beach in Isabella with Tropical Trail Rides, explore the mysterious subterranean caves at the Río Camuy or hit the pirate-themed historical amusement park in Faro y Parque Histórico de Arecibo.

Planning

Although the fast-food chains and US influence can be a bit off-putting for more adventuresome adults, the familiar sights make Puerto Rico more comfortable for kids. That said, there are several things parents can do to ensure an even smoother visit.

First, call ahead. Puerto Rican attractions can be notoriously unpredictable with their hours of operation – particularly in state-operated parks – so try to confirm opening hours before you go.

Second, know your accommodations. Look carefully at your hotel options to see what offerings they have for kids. Even though many of the hotels have swimming pools, some are comically tiny and not particularly kid-friendly. Others have spacious swimming areas that resemble mini water parks, with slides and splashy playground equipment. Before you book a resort, call to see if it hosts evening programs designed to occupy younger travelers, which can give mum and dad time for a moonlit stroll down the beach. Two of Puerto Rico's megaresorts offer full-day, camp-style programs for children aged three to 15: El Conquistador Resort & Golden Door Spa (near Fajardo on the east coast) and the Palmas del Mar (near Humacao on the east coast).

The Puerto Rico Day Trips (www.puertoricodaytrips.com) website has an exhaustive list of ideas for families, including a list of kid-friendly day trips within one hour of San Juan.

Unless you know someone reliable on the island or you are staying at a big hotel, you'll have difficulty finding a babysitter. There are no reliable agencies that provide this service, but many hotels have day-care programs, activities for older kids, and trusted staff happy to make some extra money babysitting at night.

Finally, families on a budget will want to investigate vacation rentals, which can be more affordable and have cooking facilities. Our favorite website remains Vacation Rentals by Owner (www.vrbo.com).

regions at a glance

San Juan

Nightlife ✓✓✓
History ✓✓✓
Beaches ✓✓

Nightlife

Start with cocktails at a four-star Caribbean fusion restaurant in the SoFo district and join the motley crowd of locals and freewheeling tourists dancing to the libidinous late-night rhythms of a salsa band. Still not done? The casinos are open all night, if you want to press your luck.

History

In Old San Juan history of the Americas comes alive in full color. From the ramparts of grand forts, visitors take in pastel-painted facades and tight cobblestone streets in one direction and the endless sparkle of the Atlantic in the other.

Beaches

This is the little Rio of the Caribbean, where the young, the old and the oily arrive to play under ever-present sunshine.

p46

El Yunque & East Coast

Rainforest ✓✓✓
Bio bays ✓✓
Beaches ✓

Rainforest

The trails leading into El Yunque's humid hills are loaded with surprises: misty waterfalls, the colorful shock of a tropical bird or flower and unexpected views of the canopy-covered hills. And El Yunque is only the beginning of fabulous natural attractions here.

Bio bays

Though Puerto Rico is blessed with several bodies of glowing bioluminescent waters, these are its best. Those who haven't experienced the phenomenon will paddle along in awe.

Beaches

If you don't leave the main island for Culebra or Vieques, Playa Luquillo is Puerto Rico's best beach, perfect for swimming, snorkeling and surfing.

p92

Culebra & Vieques

Beaches ✓✓✓
Snorkeling ✓✓✓
Cycling ✓✓

Beaches

Bar none, these are Puerto Rico's best and most diverse beaches – some of which are commonly listed among the best in the world. Visitors splash around and soak up the essence of the Caribbean daydream.

Snorkeling

The clear water, variety of fish and coral structures are mesmerizing. Unlike snorkel destinations which require a boat, these are within a short swim of the sandy beach.

Cycling

When (or maybe if) you tire of the water, there's plenty of wind-swept coastal rides past fields of wild horses to fill an ambitious afternoon on a bicycle. The network of cycling roads on Vieques isn't difficult and can be extremely rewarding.

p114

Ponce & South Coast

Architecture ✓✓
Museums ✓✓
Archaeology ✓

Architecture
A mix of elegantly restored colonial mansions and tattered historic structures on the verge of collapse, Ponce has some of the most interesting architecture on the island.

Museums
Ponce hosts museums on political revolution, musical heritage and history, but the one that might be worth the trip from San Juan in its own right is the recently renovated Museo de Arte de Ponce.

Archaeology
Just outside the southern capital is the largest Taíno site in the Caribbean, where quiet ceremonial ball courts pay homage to the island's distant past.

p144

West Coast

Surfing ✓✓✓
Diving ✓✓
Adventure ✓✓

Surfing
The Beach Boys didn't sing about Rincón for nothing. The immaculate breaks near the point make for some of the best surfing on the planet. It's a great place to learn too.

Diving
You can leave any number of west coast towns for excellent deep-water expeditions, including a trip to the pristine waters near Isla Desecheo and the illusive Isla Mona.

Adventure
The lonely Cabo Rojo point is a great place for a short cycling tour, but even if you arrive by car a scramble up the lighthouse-crowned point overlooking the Caribbean is heart-racing.

p172

North Coast

Golf ✓✓✓
Surfing ✓✓
Caving ✓

Golf
Dorado's long fairways, challenging courses and jaw-dropping views attract golfers from around the globe. You'll find some of the best courses in the Caribbean within chipping distance of one another.

Surfing
Some claim that while Rincón gets all the glory, the serious surfing happens just to the north, near ramshackle seaside towns like Augadilla and Isabela.

Caving
The karst country's limestone soft hills have made a kind of geological Swiss cheese. This part of the island has enormous networks of caves that are perfect for exploring alone or on underground tours.

p200

Central Mountains

Scenic Drives ✓✓✓
Hiking ✓✓
Rural culture ✓

Scenic drives
Travel along the Ruta Panorámica and you'll discover a part of Puerto Rico that few tourists see. The jagged spine of the central mountains holds the secret to growing rich coffee beans and harboring revolution.

Hiking
Wild scenery and isolation make the untrammeled forests here appealing to gutsy outdoor adventurers. Sure, none of the trails are marked or maintained, but that's part of the fun, right?

Rural culture
The little towns seem lonely until you stumble on the right *lechonera* (eatery specializing in suckling pig), where a plate of smoky pork and a spontaneous dance party appear out of nowhere.

p219

Look out for these icons:

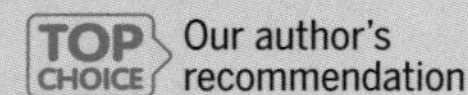

Our author's recommendation

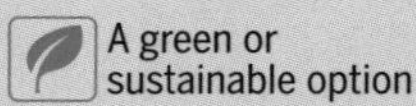

A green or sustainable option

FREE No payment required

See the Index for a full list of destinations covered in this book.

On the Road

San Juan

POP 395,000

Includes »

Best Places to Eat

» Perla (p78)

» Marmalade (p76)

» Niche (p79)

» St Germain Bistro & Café (p76)

Best Places to Stay

» Gran Hotel El Convento (p71)

» La Concha (p72)

» Gallery Inn (p71)

» Casablanca Hotel (p71)

Why Go?

Established in 1521, San Juan is the second-oldest European-founded settlement in the Americas and the oldest under US jurisdiction. Shoehorned onto a tiny islet that guards the entrance to San Juan harbor, the atmospheric old town juxtaposes historical authenticity with pulsating modern energy in a seven-square-block grid of streets that was inaugurated almost a century before the *Mayflower* laid anchor in present-day Massachusetts.

Beyond its timeworn 15ft-thick walls, San Juan is far more than a dizzying collection of well-polished colonial artifacts – it's also a mosaic of ever-evolving neighborhoods. There's seen-it-all Condado, where Cuba's 24-hour gambling party got washed up in the early 1960s; tranquil Ocean Park with its gated villas and strategically located B&Bs; gritty Santurce, relaunched with art galleries after a two-decades-long depression; and swanky Isla Verde, awash with luxurious resort hotels and kitsch casinos.

When to Go

There's no shortage of attractive festivals in San Juan, from the revelrous street party of Festival San Sebastián in mid-January to the citywide celebration of its namesake saint on the week preceding June 24. The SoFo Culinary Festival doesn't have fixed dates, but takes place in late fall and mid-summer. In late July, the nearby town of Loíza Aldea hosts its Fiesta de Santiago, a religious and Afro-Caribbean cultural festival renowned for its colorful masks and exceptional music.

From December through to May, the weather is at its best – highs in the mid-80s, lows in the high 70s and little humidity.

History

It's hard to believe that San Juan was once a deserted spit of land dominated only by dramatic headlands and strong trade winds, but such was the picture when the Spaniards first arrived with their colonization plans in the early 1500s.

Unable to stave off constant Indian attacks or mosquito-borne malaria in the lower lands, they retreated to the rocky outcrop in 1521 and christened it Puerto Rico (Rich Port). (A Spanish cartographer accidentally transposed San Juan Bautista – what Spaniards called the island – with 'Puerto Rico' on some maps a few years later, and the name change stuck permanently.)

The gigantic fortress of El Morro, with its 140ft-high ramparts, quickly rose above the ocean cliffs.

The Catholic Church arrived en masse to build a church, a convent and a cathedral. For the next three centuries, San Juan was the primary military and legislative outpost of the Spanish empire in the Caribbean and Central America. But economically it stagnated, unable to prosper from the smuggling that was pervasive elsewhere on the island.

That all changed after the Spanish-American War of 1898. The US annexed the island as a territory and designated San Juan as the primary port. Agricultural goods such as sugar, tobacco and coffee flowed into the city. *Jíbaros* (country people) flocked to the shipping terminals for work and old villages like Río Piedras were swallowed up.

WWII brought more capital and development as the US beefed up its military defense of the island and the Caribbean. After the war, the monumental economic initiative called Operation Bootstrap began changing Puerto Rico from an agricultural to a manufacturing-based economy, and hundreds of US factories relocated to San Juan to take advantage of tax breaks after the island gained commonwealth status in 1951. Foreign and US banks arrived en masse, the first high-rise buildings went up and the tourist zones took shape along the beachfront of the burgeoning city.

The unchecked growth surge was a nightmare for city planners, who struggled to provide services, roads and housing. By the 1980s, franchises of US fast-food restaurants were everywhere, but there were few places to get a gourmet meal featuring the island's *comida criolla* (traditional Puerto Rican cuisine). Housing developments blighted much of the area.

Unemployment was rampant, and crime was high. Ironically, Old San Juan was considered the epicenter of all that was wrong with the city. Tourists kept to the overdeveloped beaches of Condado, Isla Verde and Miramar.

In 1992, the world marked the 500-year anniversary of Columbus' 'discovery' of the Americas. That celebration gave city leaders the impetus needed to focus on the historic restoration of Old San Juan. The energy and finesse that characterized that effort waned slightly as the decade ended. However, the

SAN JUAN IN...

Two Days

Find a midrange hotel or apartment in Old San Juan. Explore the historical sights of the colonial quarter and dine along **Calle Fortaleza** before heading to **Latin Roots** or **Nuyorican Café** after dark for mojitos and salsa music. Wander over to **Condado** on day two for some sunbathing or beachside water sports.

Four Days

Add a museum crawl around **Old San Juan** and throw in a visit by ferry to the Bayamón **Bacardí Rum Factory**. Find an ecotour company to run you out to **El Yunque** for a day. Finally, scour the nightclubs of the big hotels in **Condado** and **Isla Verde**, and dine at **Perla** and one of the beautiful restaurants at **Gran Hotel El Convento**.

One Week

Head into the burbs for Santurce's two **art museums** or head further south to the **Jardín Botánico** in Río Piedras. Rent a bike and cycle around **Piñones**. Tour the threatened urban waterways and communities of **Caño Martín Peña**. Round it up by hiring some beach toys on **Playa Isla Verde** or trying your luck at **surfing** or **kitesurfing**.

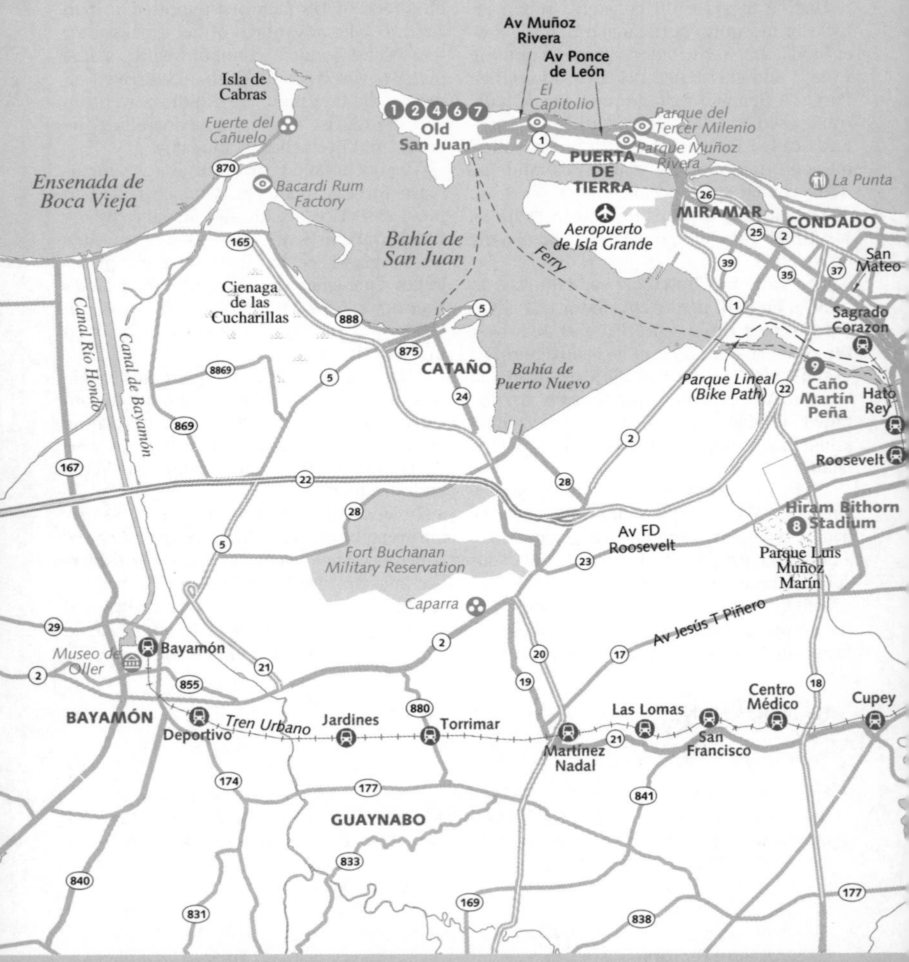

San Juan Highlights

1 Savor a night of colonial luxury in the exquisite **Gran Hotel El Convento** (p71)

2 Feel the rhythm of Puerto Rico at a late-night **Nuyorican Café** (p82) performance

3 Fly and land as you **kitesurf** (p67) and live to tell the tale

4 Play sentry in the colonial tunnels of **Fuerte San Cristóbal** (p55)

5 Explore bike paths, beaches, ramshackle restaurants and precarious coastal ecology in down-to-earth **Piñones** (p89)

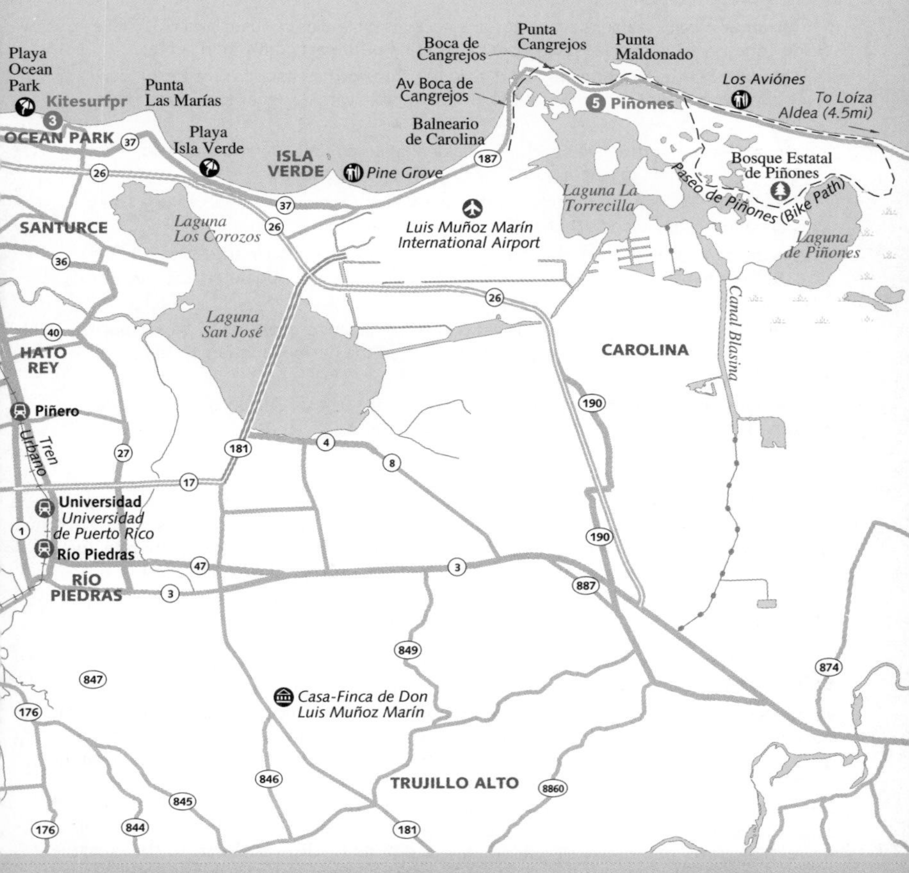

6 Sample the creative fusion cuisine at one of the many **SoFo restaurants** (p76)

7 Dance till you drop at **Latin Roots** (p83), the salsa epicenter of Old San Juan

8 Cheer on the home baseball team as the San Juan Senadores knock it out of the park at **Hiram Bithorn Stadium** (p84)

9 Tour the hidden urban waterways of the **Caño Martín Peña** (p69)

SAN JUAN NEIGHBORHOODS

Metro San Juan, in common with many great cities, is an amalgamation of its neighborhoods, with each area exhibiting its own vicissitudes, atmosphere and charms. Here's a quick rundown of what to expect.

» **Old San Juan** The soul of the city and a gastronome's delight, Old San Juan's seven-square-block Unesco World Heritage site is packed with priceless historical relics and equally pricey restaurants.

» **Puerta de Tierra** This thin slither of land that links Old San Juan with the rest of the city is a strange amalgam of tatty housing projects, salubrious parks and one of the best municipal beaches on the island.

» **Miramar** A leafy residential quarter of eclectic middle-class houses and plush lakeside condos that showcases San Juan's new state-of-the-art convention center.

» **Condado** San Juan's original resort strip has transformed itself from a tacky tourist zone into a revitalized urban neighborhood replete with designer shops and pretty parks.

» **Ocean Park** An attractive beachside residential community punctuated with classy B&Bs, high-rise condos and a quiet, gay-friendly stretch of beach.

» **Isla Verde** The city's premier hotel strip plays host to a mishmash of craning condo towers and swanky resorts that are big on luxury but short on authenticity.

» **Santurce** The once vital city center suffered from dilapidation in the '80s and '90s, but a fine arts center, myriad nightclubs, and a couple of well-appointed galleries have placed it back in the urban reckoning.

» **Hato Rey** San Juan's mini Wall Street is a dense cluster of glass tower blocks and is home to the island's most prestigious ball park and the Caribbean's largest shopping mall.

» **Río Piedras** The low-rise academic quarter is, not surprisingly, replete with cheap shops, a thriving market and an exotic botanical garden.

new century has brought several successful urban regeneration projects such as the super-efficient Tren Urbano (metro) that opened in 2005, a space-age convention center situated in the neighborhood of Miramar, and a clutch of redeveloped hotels in revitalized Condado.

Sights

Most of San Juan's major attractions, including museums and art galleries, are in Old San Juan.

There are a few sights worth visiting in Condado, Santurce and Río Piedras, but schedule serious time for the old town. Be aware that most museums are closed on Mondays.

OLD SAN JUAN

Old San Juan is a colorful kaleidoscope of life, music, legend and history and would stand out like a flashing beacon in any country, let alone one as small as Puerto Rico.

Somnolent secrets and beautiful surprises await everywhere. From the blue-toned cobblestoned streets of San Sebastián, to the cutting-edge gastronomic artistry of SoFo, you could spend weeks, even months, here and still only get the smallest taste.

Add to this the quarter's sensuous yet subtle mood swings: tranquil at dawn, languid during the midday heat, romantic at dusk and positively ebullient after dark.

Mixing ancient with modern, San Juan has embraced the 21st century in the same way it embraced every era that went before – with confidence, innovation and a dynamic joie de vivre.

Far from being just another drop-off point on a busy cruise ship itinerary, this is a city that still lives: listen to the creaking rocking chairs on Calle de Sol, the clatter of dominos in La Bombonera cafe or the spontaneous African drumming ritual echoing around Plaza de Armas. Pure magic.

El Morro FORT

(Fuerte San Felipe del Morro; San Felipe Fort; Map p52; ☎787-729-7423; www.nps.gov/saju; adult/child $3/free; ⏲9am-6pm, free talks on the hour 10am-

5pm) A six-level fort with a gray, castellated lighthouse, El Morro juts aggressively over Old San Juan's bold headlands, glowering across the Atlantic at would-be conquerors. The 140ft walls (some up to 15ft thick) date back to 1539, and El Morro is said to be the oldest Spanish fort in the New World. It was declared a Unesco World Heritage site in 1983.

The National Park Service (NPS) maintains this fort and the small military museum on the premises. Displays and videos in Spanish and English document the construction of the fort, which took almost 200 years, as well as El Morro's role in rebuffing the various attacks on the island by the British and the Dutch, and later the US military.

The lighthouse on the 6th floor has been in operation since 1846 (although the tower itself dates from 1906), making it the island's oldest light station still in use today. After suffering severe damage during a US navy bombardment during the 1898 Spanish-American War, the original lighthouse was rebuilt with unique Spanish-Moorish features, a style that blends in surprisingly well with the rest of the fort. Join a free **lighthouse talk** (English 2:30pm Sat, Spanish 2:30pm) to learn more about the lighthouse and get the chance to enter it (weather permitting). Arrive at least 30 minutes beforehand to get a spot.

If you do not join one of the free guided tours, at least try to make the climb up the ramparts to the sentries' walks along the Sta Barbara Bastion and Austria Half-Bastion for the views of the sea, the bay, Old San Juan, modern San Juan, El Yunque and the island's mountainous spine.

On weekends, the fields leading up to the fort are alive with picnickers, lovers and kite flyers. The scene becomes a kind of impromptu festival with food vendors' carts on the perimeter.

Entry to both El Morro and Fuerte San Cristóbal costs $5.

Fuerte San Cristóbal FORT

(San Cristóbal Fort; Map p52; 787-729-6777; www.nps.gov/saju; adult/child $3/free; 9am-6pm) San Juan's second major fort is Fuerte San Cristóbal, one of the largest military installations the Spanish built in the Americas. In its prime, San Cristóbal covered 27 acres with a maze of six interconnected forts protecting a central core with 150ft walls, moats, booby-trapped bridges and tunnels.

The fort was constructed to defend Old San Juan against land attacks from the east via Puerta de Tierra. The imaginative design came from the famous Irish mercenary Alejandro O'Reilly and his compatriot Thomas O'Daly (hired by Spain). Construction began in 1634 in response to an attack by the Dutch a decade previously, though the main period of enlargement occurred between 1765 and 1783. Seven acres were lopped off the fort in 1897 to ease congestion in the old town, and the following year the Spanish marked Puerto Rico's entry into the Spanish-American War by firing at the battleship USS *Yale* from its cannon battery. The fort became a National Historic site in 1949 and a Unesco World Heritage site in 1983. Facilities include a fascinating museum, a store, military archives, a reproduction of a soldier's barracks, and prime city views.

Entry to both Fuerte San Cristóbal and El Morro costs $5.

La Fortaleza MONUMENT

(Fortress; Map p52; 787-721-7000, ext 2211, 2358 or 2323; www.fortaleza.gobierno.pr; suggested donation $3; tours 9am-3:30pm Mon-Fri) A steep climb along Recinto Oeste takes you to the top of the city wall and the guarded iron gates of La Fortaleza. Also known as El Palacio de Santa Catalina, this imposing building dating from 1533 is the oldest executive mansion in continuous use in the western hemisphere. Once the original fortress for the young colony, La Fortaleza eventually yielded its military preeminence to the city's newer and larger forts, and was remodeled and expanded to domicile island governors for more than three centuries. You can join a guided tour that includes the mansion's Moorish gardens, the dungeon and the chapel. Guided tours run on weekdays except holidays, but the schedule changes daily; you must call on the day you wish to visit in order to reserve, and be prepared for a security gauntlet.

Casa Blanca HOUSE MUSEUM

(White House; Map p52; museum 787-725-1454, tours 787-924-0700; www.icp.gobierno.pr/myp/museos/m13.htm; adult/child $2/1; 9am-noon & 1-4:30pm Tue-Sat) First constructed in 1521 as a residence for Puerto Rico's pioneering governor, Juan Ponce de León (who died before he could move in), the Casa Blanca is the oldest continuously occupied house in the western hemisphere. For the first 250 years after its construction it served as the

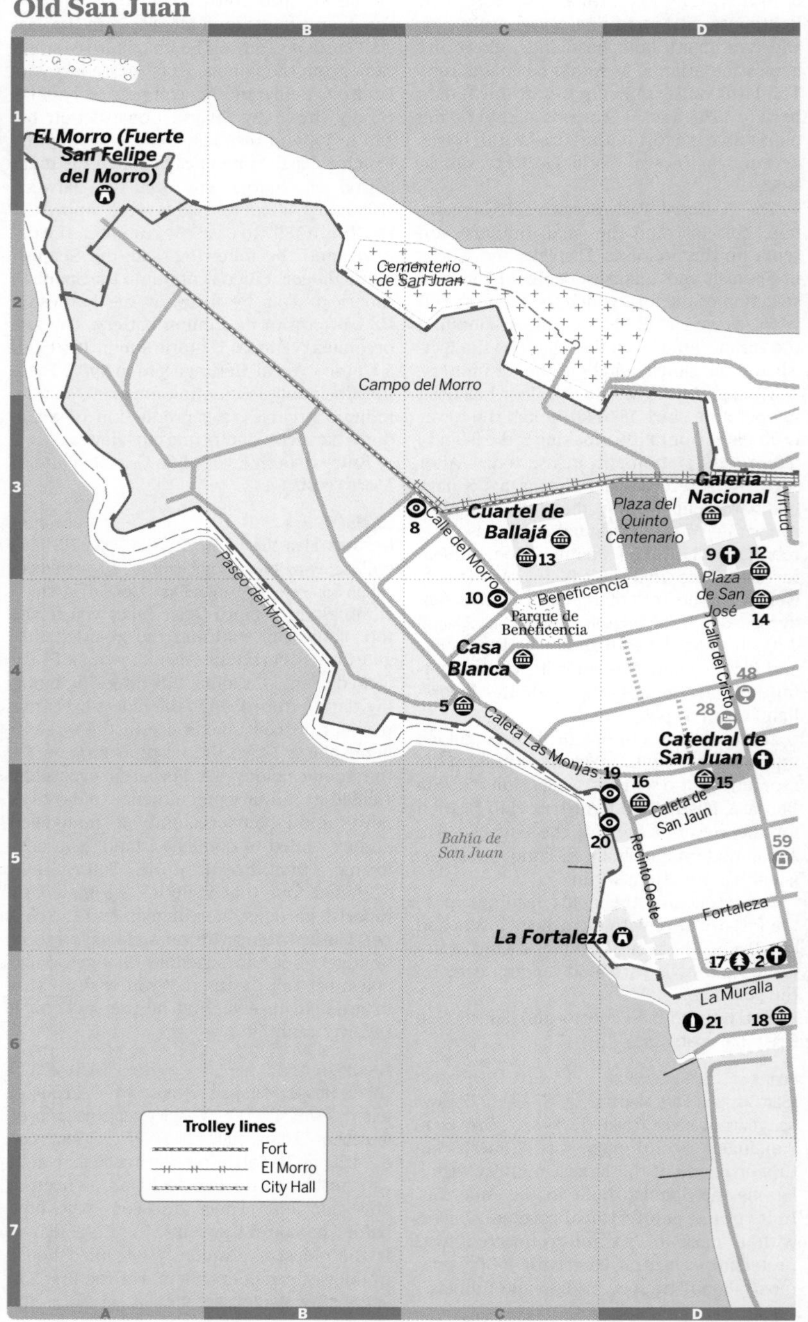
A
B
C
D
1
2
3
4
5
6
7
El Morro (Fuerte San Felipe del Morro)
Cementerio de San Juan
Campo del Morro
Galería Nacional
Virtud
Plaza del Quinto Centenario
Cuartel de Ballajá
8
13
Calle del Morro
9
12
Plaza de San José
14
10
Beneficencia
Parque de Beneficencia
Calle del Cristo
Paseo del Morro
Casa Blanca
48
28
5
Caleta Las Monjas
Catedral de San Juan
19
16
15
Caleta de San Jaun
20
Bahía de San Juan
59
Recinto Oeste
Fortaleza
La Fortaleza
17
2
La Muralla
21
18
Trolley lines
Fort
El Morro
City Hall

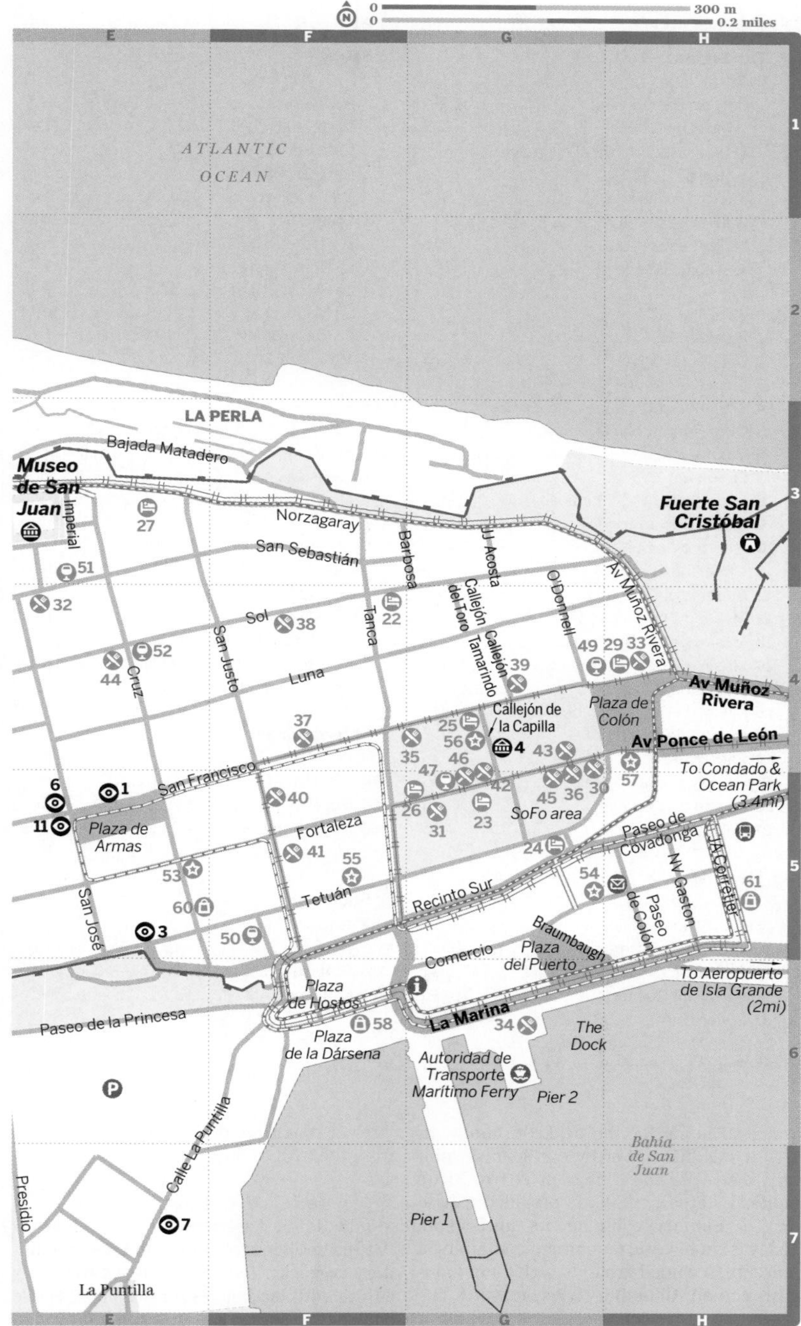

0 300 m
0 0.2 miles
ATLANTIC OCEAN
LA PERLA
Bajada Matadero
Museo de San Juan
Imperial
Norzagaray
San Sebastián
Barbosa
JJ Acosta
O'Donnell
Av Muñoz Rivera
Fuerte San Cristóbal
Sol
Tanca
Callejón del Toro
Callejón Tamarindo
San Justo
Cruz
Luna
Callejón de la Capilla
Plaza de Colón
Av Muñoz Rivera
Av Ponce de León
To Condado & Ocean Park (3.4mi)
San Francisco
Plaza de Armas
Fortaleza
SoFo area
Paseo de Covadonga
JA Corretjer
NV Gaston
Paseo de Colón
Tetuán
Recinto Sur
San José
Braumbaugh
Comercio
Plaza del Puerto
To Aeropuerto de Isla Grande (2mi)
Plaza de Hostos
La Marina
Paseo de la Princesa
Plaza de la Dársena
The Dock
Autoridad de Transporte Marítimo Ferry
Pier 2
Calle La Puntilla
Bahía de San Juan
Presidio
Pier 1
La Puntilla

Old San Juan

Top Sights
Casa Blanca ... C4
Catedral de San Juan ... D4
Cuartel de Ballajá ... C3
El Morro (Fuerte San Felipe del Morro) ... A1
Fuerte San Cristóbal ... H3
Galería Nacional ... D3
La Fortaleza ... D5
Museo de San Juan ... E3

Sights
1 Alcaldía ... E5
2 Capilla del Cristo ... D6
3 Casa de Ramón Power y Giralt ... E5
4 Casa del Libro ... G4
5 Casa Rosa ... C4
6 Diputación ... E5
7 El Arsenal ... E7
8 Escuela de Artes Plásticas ... C3
9 Iglesia de San José ... D3
10 Instituto de Cultura Puertorriqueña ... C4
11 Intendencia ... E5
12 Museo de Casals ... D3
13 Museo de las Américas ... C3
14 Museo de Raíz Africana ... D4
15 Museo del Niño ... D5
16 Museo Felisa Rincón de Gautier ... D5
17 Parque de las Palomas ... D6
18 Paseo de la Princesa ... D6
19 Plazuela de la Rogativa ... D5
20 Puerta de San Juan ... D5
21 Raíces Fountain ... D6

Sleeping
22 AlaSol Apartments ... F4
23 Casablanca Hotel ... G5
24 Chateau Cervantes ... G5
25 Da House ... G4
26 Fortaleza Guest House ... G5
27 Gallery Inn ... E3
28 Gran Hotel El Convento ... D4
29 Posada San Francisco ... H4

Eating
30 Aguaviva ... G4
31 Ayurvedics ... G5
32 Barú ... E4
33 Café Berlin ... H4
34 Café Cala'o ... G6
35 Café Mallorca ... G4
36 Dragonfly ... G5
El Picoteo ... (see 28)
37 La Bombonera ... F4
38 La Fonda El Jibarito ... F4
39 La Madre ... G4
40 La Mallorquina ... F5
41 Manolín ... F5
42 Marmalade ... G5
43 Parrot Club ... G4
Patio del Nispero ... (see 28)
44 St Germain Bistro & Café ... E4
45 Tantra ... G5
46 Trois Cent Onze ... G5

Drinking
47 Blend ... G5
48 El Batey ... D4
49 Los Cuernos ... G4
50 Old Harbor Brewery ... F5
51 Rivera Hermanos Cash & Carry ... E3
52 Taberna Lúpulo ... E4

Entertainment
53 Club Lázer ... E5
54 Latin Roots ... G5
55 Nuestro Son ... F5
56 Nuyorican Café ... G4
57 Teatro Tapia ... H4

Shopping
58 Artisans Fair ... F6
59 Bóveda ... D5
60 Butterfly People ... E5
61 Cigarros Antillas ... H5

ancestral home for the de León family. In 1779 it was taken over by the Spanish military, then with the change of Puerto Rico's political status in 1898, it provided a base for US military commanders until 1966. Today it is a historic monument containing a museum, secluded grounds, a chain of fountains and an Alhambra-style courtyard. The interior rooms are decked out with artifacts from the 16th to the 20th century.

FREE **Cuartel de Ballajá & Museo de las Américas** MUSEUM
(Map p52; off Norzagaray) Built in 1854 as a military barracks, the *cuartel* is a three-story edifice with large gates on two ends, ample balconies, a series of arches and a protected

central courtyard that served as a plaza and covers a reservoir. It was the last and largest building constructed by the Spaniards in the New World. Facilities included officers' quarters, warehouses, kitchens, dining rooms, prison cells and stables. Now its 2nd floor holds the **Museo de las Américas** (Museum of the Americas; ☎787-724-5052; www.museolasamericas.org; adult/child $3/2; ⊙10am-4pm Tue-Sat, guided tours by reservation), which gives an overview of cultural development in the New World. It features changing exhibitions and Caribbean and European American art, most notably an impressive *santos* (small carved figurines representing saints) collection. Hours for both the barracks and the museum are the same.

Galería Nacional MUSEUM
(Map p52; ☎787-725-2670; adult/child $3/2; ⊙9:30am-noon & 1-5pm Tue-Sat) Next to the Iglesia de San José is the former Convento de los Dominicos, a Dominican convent that dates from the 16th century. After centuries of use as a convent, the building became a barracks for Spanish troops and was later used as a headquarters for US occupational forces after the Spanish-American War of 1898. It has been restored to its colonial grandeur and houses galleries of Puerto Rican paintings from the 18th century up through the 1970s, including work by José Campeche and Francisco Oller.

FREE **Catedral de San Juan** CHURCH
(Map p52; 153 Calle del Cristo; ⊙8am-5pm) Although noticeably smaller and more austere than other Spanish churches, the Catedral de San Juan nonetheless retains a simple earthy elegance. Founded originally in the 1520s, the first church on this site was destroyed in a hurricane in 1529. A replacement was constructed in 1540 and, over a period of centuries, it slowly evolved into the Gothic/neoclassical-inspired monument seen today.

Most people come to see the marble tomb of Ponce de León and the body of religious martyr St Pio displayed under glass. However, you can get quite a show here on Saturday afternoons when the limos roll up and bridal parties requisition the front steps. The main entrance to the cathedral faces a beautiful shaded park replete with antique benches and gnarly trees.

Museo de San Juan MUSEUM
(Map p52; ☎787-723-4317; 150 Norzagaray; donations accepted; ⊙9am-4pm Tue-Fri, 10am-4pm Sat

TUNNEL TOURS

Go deeper. And darker. Hour-long **free guided tours** roam the tunnels at **Fuerte San Cristóbal** every Saturday (Spanish) and Sunday (English) at 10:30am. Come at least half an hour beforehand (or earlier) to put your name on the sign-up list. Guides walk you through three of the fort's tunnels, including one that's otherwise closed to the public.

& Sun) Located in a Spanish colonial building at the corner of Calle MacArthur, the Museo de San Juan is the definitive take on the city's 500-year history. The well-laid-out exhibition showcases pictorial and photographic testimonies from the Caparra ruins to the modern-day shopping malls. There's also a half-hour TV documentary (in both Spanish and English) about the history of San Juan.

Iglesia de San José CHURCH
(Map p52; www.iglesiasanjosepr.org; adult/child $1/free; ⊙noon-6pm 2nd & 4th Sat of month, mass 12:30pm 4th Sat) What it lacks in grandiosity it makes up for in age; the Iglesia de San José in the Plaza de San José is the second-oldest church in the Americas, after the cathedral in Santo Domingo in the Dominican Republic. Established in 1523 by Dominicans, this church with its vaulted Gothic ceilings still bears the coat of arms of Juan Ponce de León (whose family worshipped here), a striking carving of the Crucifixion and ornate processional floats. For 350 years, the remains of Ponce de León rested in a crypt here before being moved to the city's cathedral, down the hill. Another relic missing from the chapel is a Flemish carving of the Virgin of Bethlehem, which came to the island during the first few years of the colony and disappeared in the early 1970s. It's also the final resting place of José Campeche (p275), one of Puerto Rico's most revered artists, and the site of Puerto Rico's oldest fresco painting.

Though long-term renovation has transformed the church into a construction site, it's worth visiting during its limited public hours. The exposed structural details of the church are fascinating, and an extensive bilingual exhibit highlights some of the archaeological discoveries made during the restoration process.

Puerta de San Juan GATE

(San Juan Gate; Map p52) Spanish ships once anchored in the cove just off these ramparts to unload colonists and supplies, all of which entered the city through a tall red portal known as Puerta de San Juan. This tunnel through the wall dates from the 1630s. It marks the end of the Paseo de la Princesa, and stands as one of three remaining gates into the old city (the others lead into the cemetery and the enclave of La Perla). Once there were a total of five gates, and the massive wooden doors were closed each night to thwart intruders. Turn right after passing through the gate and you can follow the Paseo del Morro northwest, paralleling the city walls for approximately three-quarters of a mile.

Plaza de Armas SQUARE

(Army Plaza; Map p52) Follow San Francisco into the heart of the old city and it opens on to the Plaza de Armas. This is the city's nominal 'central' square, laid out in the 16th century with the classic look of plazas from Madrid and Mexico.

In its time, the plaza has served as a military parade ground (hence its name), a vegetable market and a social center. Shade trees, banks of seats, and a couple of old-fashioned coffee booths still make the plaza the destination of choice for couples taking their evening stroll. The beat of a *bomba* drum has also been known to light up an otherwise humdrum evening.

One of the highlights of the plaza is the **Alcaldía** (City Hall; Map p52; ☎787-724-7171; www.sanjuan.pr; ⏰9am-4pm Mon-Fri), which dates from 1789 and has twin turrets resembling those of its counterpart in Madrid. This building houses the office of the mayor of San Juan and is also the site of periodic exhibitions.

At the western end of the plaza, the **Intendencia** (Administration Bldg; Map p52) and the **Diputación** (Provincial Delegation Bldg; Map p52) are two other functioning government buildings adding to the charms of the plaza. Both represent 19th-century neoclassical architecture, and come complete with cloisters.

Cementerio de San Juan CEMETERY

(Map p52) Sitting just outside the northern fortifications of the old city, the neoclassical chapel in the cemetery provides a focal point among the graves. The colony's earliest citizens are buried here, as well as the famous Puerto Rican freedom fighter Pedro Albizu-Campos. This Harvard-educated chemical engineer, lawyer and politician led the agricultural workers' strikes in 1934 and was at the forefront of the movement for Puerto Rican independence until his arrest and imprisonment in 1936. A number of muggings have occurred here, so be careful.

FREE **Casa del Libro** MUSEUM

(House of Books; Map p52; www.lacasadellibro.org; 199 Callejón de la Capilla; ⏰11am-4:30pm Tue-Sat or by appointment, closed holidays) Yet another of the old city's tiny museums, the Casa del Libro has temporarily relocated to the SoFo district. Bibliophiles will be in awe of its collection of more than 5000 manuscripts and texts that date back 2000 years. The collection includes one of the most respected assemblages of incunabula (texts produced prior to 1501) in the Americas, including documents signed by King Ferdinand II and his wife Isabela.

Museo de Casals MUSEUM

(Map p52; ☎787-723-9185; adult/child $1/0.50; ⏰9:30am-4:30pm Tue-Sat) On Plaza de San José is the Museo de Casals. A native of Spain's proud but repressed province of Catalonia, world-famous cellist Pablo Casals moved to his mother's homeland of Puerto Rico in 1956 to protest the dictatorial regime of Francisco Franco in Spain. He quickly established the respected Festival Casals for classical music, which became a principal force in the subsequent flowering of the arts on the island (p254).

FREE **Casa de Ramón Power y Giralt** NOTABLE BUILDING

(Map p52; ☎787-722-5834; www.fideicomiso.org; 155 Tetuán; ⏰9am-5pm Tue-Sat) Once the residence of a political reformer and Puerto Rico's first representative to the Spanish court, this restored 18th-century house is now the headquarters of the Conservation Trust of Puerto Rico. A good rainy-day activity, the house contains limited exhibits of Taíno artifacts along with a small gift shop, and highlights the precarious nature of much of the island's ecology. Three environmental films can be shown upon request, in either English or Spanish, and one is an animated short for children. Information is available about tours in San Juan and at the trust's other island properties.

Museo del Niño MUSEUM

(Children's Museum; Map p52; www.museodelninopr.org; 150 Calle del Cristo; adult/child $7/5; ⏲9am-3:30pm Tue-Thu, 9am-5pm Fri, 12:30-5pm Sat & Sun; 👪) An orange-and-green building that sits on the edge of a small shady park houses this museum. Kids love the three floors of hands-on exhibits on health, natural history and science. Favorites include a walk-through cave explaining bats and echolocation, a magnetic food pyramid, a climbing wall (for ages five years and up) and a dress-up station. One area is designed for children from infants up to age three.

FREE **Museo de Raíz Africana** MUSEUM

(Museum of African Ancestry; Map p52; ⏲8am-noon & 1-4:30pm Wed-Sun) Housed in the 18th-century Casa de los Contrafuertes (House of Buttresses) on Plaza de San José, this compact museum displays masks, sculptures, musical instruments, documents and prints that highlight Puerto Rico's connections to West Africa. One exhibit recreates living conditions in a slave ship.

FREE **Museo Felisa Rincón de Gautier** HOUSE MUSEUM

(Map p52; ☎787-723-1897; 51 Caleta de San Juan; ⏲9am-4pm Mon-Fri) This museum is an attractive neoclassical town house that was once the longtime home of San Juan's beloved mayor, Doña Felisa. She presided over the growth of her city with personal style and political acumen for more than 20 years during the Operation Bootstrap days of the 1940s, '50s and '60s. This historic home is a monument to the life of an accomplished public servant.

Capilla del Cristo CHURCH

(Christ's Chapel; Map p52; ⏲Tue afternoon & religious holidays) Over the centuries, tens of thousands of penitents have come to pray for miracles at the Capilla del Cristo, the tiny outdoor sanctuary adjacent to **Parque de las Palomas** (Piegon Park). One legend claims that the chapel was built to prevent people from falling over the city wall and into the sea. Another claims that citizens constructed the chapel to commemorate a miracle.

As the story goes, a rider participating in a race during the city's San Juan Bautista festivities miraculously survived after his galloping horse carried him down Calle del Cristo, off the top of the wall and into the sea. Over the years, believers of the fable have left hundreds of little silver ornaments representing parts of the body – called *milagros* (miracles) – on the altar before the statues of the saints as tokens of thanks for being cured of some infirmity.

You can see the chapel any time, but the iron fence across the front is only open during the listed hours.

Parque de las Palomas PARK

(Pigeon Park; Map p52) On the lower end of Calle del Cristo, Parque de las Palomas is a cobblestoned courtyard shaded with trees at the top of the city wall. *Paloma* means 'dove' or 'pigeon' in Spanish and it's the latter variety you'll encounter here, in their hundreds. Some brave souls come here for the view it affords of Bahía de San Juan. Others just turn up to feed the pigeons. (You can buy birdseed from a vendor by the gate.) Devout Christians have long believed that if you feed the birds and one 'anoints' you with its pearly droppings, you have been blessed by God. Agnostics prefer to look upon it as just plain old bad luck.

Plazuela de la Rogativa PARK

(Small Plaza of the Religious Procession; Map p52) This tiny gem of a park has lovely vistas overlooking the bay and is home to a whimsical bronze sculpture of the bishop of San Juan and three women bearing torches. According to legend, the candles held by the women who walked through this plaza one night in 1797 tricked British lieutenant Abercromby – who was getting ready to lay siege to San Juan with his 8000 troops and flotilla of more than 50 vessels – into believing that reinforcements were flooding the city from the rest of the island. Fearful of being outnumbered, Abercromby and his fleet withdrew.

Escuela de Artes Plásticas NOTABLE BUILDING

(Academy of Fine Arts; Map p52; Norzagaray) The monumental gray-and-white building with a red-roofed rotunda across from El Morro is the Escuela de Artes Plásticas. Built as an insane asylum during the 19th century, this grand building with its symmetrical wings, columns, Romanesque arches, porticos, courtyards and fountains looks more like a seat of government. Today it is the source of more than a few jokes by contemporary art students about the mad dreams that continue to take shape within its walls. See for yourself when students' work go on display at the end of each academic term, or take a look at the sculpture court on the right-hand

TOP HISTORICAL HITS

- **Fuerte San Cristóbal** (p51)
- **Casa Blanca** (p51)
- **Catedral de San Juan** (p55)
- **Caparra** (p89)
- **Casa-Finca de Don Luis Muñoz Marín** (p63)

side of the building, where students can be seen chipping new images from granite.

Paseo de la Princesa STREET
(Walkway of the Princess; Map p52) Emanating a distinctly European flavor, the Paseo de la Princesa is a 19th-century esplanade situated just outside the city walls. Lined with antique streetlamps, shade trees, statues, benches, fruit vendors' carts and street entertainers, this romantic walkway culminates at the magnificent **Raíces Fountain**, a stunning statue/water feature that depicts the island's eclectic Taíno, African and Spanish heritage.

La Princesa NOTABLE BUILDING
(Map p52) Poised against the outside wall of the city, the long, gray and white stone structure that was once a harsh jail now houses the main offices of the Puerto Rico Tourism Company (PRTC; see p86). The bronze statue in front depicts Doña Felisa Gautier, San Juan's revered mayor from 1946 to 1968; see p57 for more information about Doña Felisa.

Plaza de San José SQUARE
Adjacent to the uppermost terrace of the Plaza del Quinto Centenario, where it meets San Sebastián, is the Plaza de San José. This relatively small cobblestoned plaza is dominated by a statue of Juan Ponce de León, cast from an English cannon captured in the raid of 1797. The plaza is probably the highest point in this city and serves as a threshold to four cultural sites on its perimeter.

FREE **Instituto de Cultura Puertorriqueña** NOTABLE BUILDING
(Institute of Puerto Rican Culture; Map p52; ☎787-724-0700; www.icp.gobierno.pr; Calle del Morro; ⏲8:30am-4:30pm Mon-Fri) Once a home for the poor, this buff building with green trim houses the executive offices of this institute. Its sheltered plazas are pleasantly tranquil.

FREE **El Arsenal** MONUMENT
(Map p52; ⏲8:30am-4:30pm Mon-Fri) On the point of land called La Puntilla is a low, gray fortress with a Romanesque proscenium entrance. This is El Arsenal, a former Spanish naval station that was the last place to house Spanish military forces after the US victory in the Spanish-American War. Today the arsenal is home to the fine- and decorative-arts divisions of the Instituto de Cultura Puertorriqueña, and hosts periodic exhibitions in three galleries.

Plaza de Colón SQUARE
(Columbus Plaza; Map p52) Tracing its roots back more than a century to the 400-year anniversary of the first Columbus expedition, the Plaza de Colón lies across the street from the lower part of Fuerte San Cristóbal. The city wall at this end of Old San Juan was torn down in 1897, and the plaza, with its statue of the 'Discoverer' atop a pillar, stands on the site of one of the city's original gated entries, Puerta Santiago. Today the plaza acts as a gateway to much of the traffic entering the city from Av Muñoz Rivera. Buses and taxis congregate on the plaza's south side.

Casa Rosa NOTABLE BUILDING
(Pink House; Map p52) Built as a barracks for the Spanish militia in the early 19th century, this tropical villa in the field leading up to El Morro long served as officers' quarters. The structure has since been restored and now serves as a plush day-care facility for the children of government employees.

Plaza del Quinto Centenario SQUARE
(Map p52) It's surprising to find such a modern square shoehorned in among all the architectural antiques, but this small plaza was built in 1992 to honor the 500-year anniversary of Christopher Columbus' first voyage to the Americas. Constructed for a rumored cost of $10 million and decorated with a craning totem pole – El Tótem Telúrico – of ambiguous significance, the plaza offers great views over El Morro and the ocean and, from a distance, blends in subtly with the surrounding buildings.

LA PERLA

Wedged tightly between the roaring Atlantic surf and San Juan's thick perimeter walls, the compact neighborhood of La Perla marks a rather odd juxtaposition. In truth, this ramshackle hodgepodge of pastel-colored houses and steep, narrow access roads is one of Puerto Rico's most notorious slums –

though, as slums go, it's remarkably picturesque (at least, from a distance).

The standard advice given out by San Juan tour companies is for tourists to steer well clear of La Perla, a potentially dangerous barrio whose international infamy was cemented in a 1966 nonfiction book called *La Vida* by American anthropologist Oscar Lewis. Lewis detailed the tragic cycle of poverty and prostitution lived out by people growing up in La Perla and won a National Book Award for his efforts, though his views weren't particularly welcomed by the quarter's long-suffering residents.

Generally speaking, the cautionary advice on La Perla is pertinent. This is a gritty, high-crime neighborhood with a seemingly incurable drug problem and it would be unwise for a foreigner to wander around.

But hidden among the decrepitude lies a community center, a senior citizens' home, some abstract murals and a handful of talented local artists. Then there's the shabby magnificence of the houses themselves – the turbulent blues, the glinting greens and the foamy browns – that seem pulled right from the ocean.

During the mid-2000s, the Puerto Rican government made regular (unsuccessful) bids to buy out La Perla's residents and redevelop the area.

PUERTA DE TIERRA

Less than 2 miles in length and only one-quarter of a mile broad, this district occupies the lowland, filling the rest of the area that was colonial San Juan. Puerta de Tierra takes its name from its position as the 'gateway of land' leading up to the walls of Old San Juan, which was the favored route of land attack by waves of English and Dutch invaders. For centuries, Puerta de Tierra was a slum much like La Perla, although far less picturesque. It was a place where free blacks and multiracial people lived, excluded from the protection of the walled city where the Spaniards and *criollos* (islanders of European descent) postured like European gentry and maneuvered for political favor.

Today the district is a major driveway for cars entering Old San Juan. There's a housing project here on the south side, but the north coast is the most dramatic oceanside vista in the metropolitan area. Overlooking the wild spectacle of Balneario Escambrón you'll find the Romanesque Capitolio, the Fuerte San Gerónimo and the sun-dappled Parque Muñoz Rivera. The road is a popular jogging route in the day time but is best negotiated by taxi at night.

Fuerte San Gerónimo FORT

(Map p60) This half-forgotten fort is situated at the east end of Puerta de Tierra and was completed in 1788 to guard the entrance to Laguna del Condado (Condado Lagoon). It was barely up and running in 1797 when the British came marching through on their way to San Juan and a short-lived occupation. Restored in 1983, San Gerónimo today is hemmed in by tall modern hotels, but is still worth a closer look. Entered via the walkway behind the Caribe Hilton, the interior of the fort is rarely open, though the exterior walls and ramparts are usually accessible and offer rather fetching views of Condado across the inlet.

FREE **El Capitolio** NOTABLE BUILDING

(Capitol; Map p48; ☎787-724-2030, ext 4616; www.senadopr.us; ⌚8:30am-5pm Mon-Fri, 8:30am-6pm Sat & Sun, tours by appointment) Sandwiched between Av Muñoz Rivera and Av Ponce de León, just east of Fuerte San Cristóbal, is El Capitolio of the commonwealth. Resembling a smaller, Romanesque version of the US Capitol, the building commands an authoritative position in Puerta de Tierra overlooking the wave-lashed coast. The much-revered constitution of the commonwealth, which moved the island a step closer to its citizens' dreams of freedom from colonialism in 1951, is on display inside the 80ft rotunda. Regular sessions of the legislature meet inside, while rallies for and against statehood occur outside every time the government calls for an islandwide plebiscite on the issue.

Parques Muñoz Rivera & Sixto Escobar PARK

(Map p48) Spanning half the width of Puerta de Tierra between the Atlantic and Av Ponce de León, the green space known as **Parque Muñoz Rivera** dates back over 50 years and injects some much-needed breathing space into the surrounding urbanity. It has shade trees, trails, a kids' playground, and a 'Peace Pavilion,' which sometimes hosts community events.

Parque Sixto Escobar (Map p48) – named for the famed Puerto Rican boxer – was the site of the eighth Pan American Games, held in 1979, and is now home to an Olympic athletics track and the gusty Balneario Escambrón.

CONDADO

Beachfront Condado swings to the sound of jangling money – and equally clangorous slot machines. In the 1960s, this is where Puerto Rico's explosive tourist boom was first ignited, spearheaded by exiled Cuban businessmen and rum-drunk Americans in search of the next big thing. But, as fashions ebbed and flowed, Condado's moment as the next Miami Beach never quite arrived. Instead, the more refined action edged gradually east to Isla Verde and abandoned Condado became a lonely hearts club for an unsavory crowd of prostitutes, pimps, drug dealers and high rollers crying into their piña coladas.

It was in the 1990s that things first started to turn around and by the mid-2000s they had almost come full circle. As mainstream tourism headed east, Condado plugged the gaps, attracting assorted celebrities, gay socialites and those in search of the odd hotel bargain. Today, dotted in among the high-rises and condo towers, you'll still find a few old eclectic 1920s villas, along with a handful of pretty parks that serve as spacious windows to the sea. With its traffic-calmed streets and clustered hotels, Condado also retains the kind of relaxed and easily walkable nighttime street scene that Isla Verde lacks.

Besides having a wonderful water view, the **Parque Laguna del Condado Jaime Benítez** (Map p72; www.estuario.org), a new park on the southeastern shore of the lagoon, educates visitors about ongoing mangrove habitat restoration. There are also kayaks available to rent. Its free Cine Verde del Estuario program screens movies alfresco on the second and fourth Saturday of every month. Bring something to sit on.

OCEAN PARK

At the eastern end of Condado lies Ocean Park, with its associated neighborhood of Punta Las Marías, a largely residential collection of private homes and beach retreats that includes a handful of plush seaside guesthouses. The more tranquil beach here is an open secret among the 'in' crowd and is great for windsurfing.

MIRAMAR

Tucked behind Laguna del Condado is the upscale neighborhood of Miramar, named for its lovely sea views, all but blotted out these days by the trim new condo towers of Condado. Distinguished by its mature tree-lined streets and handful of unusual Prairie School architectural creations (think Frank Lloyd Wright meets Arts and Crafts), the area isn't as homogenous as it once was,

Miramar & Ocean Park

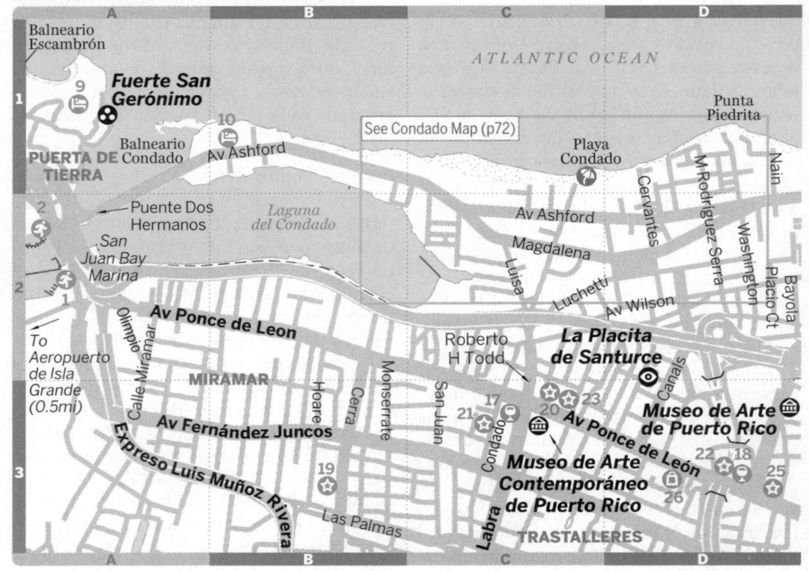

though the yachts berthed at the Club Náutico still gleam like polished diamonds and the new Convention Center drops a few jaws with its outlandish modernist design. Unless you're accommodated here in a hotel, the most you'll probably see of Miramar is from one of its notorious traffic bottlenecks.

SANTURCE

Santurce is one of San Juan's most important barrios, actually incorporating Condado and Miramar, but is usually used to describe the area south of Expressway 26 and north of Hato Rey. Buried in the heart of the modern city, its fortunes have fluctuated markedly since its founding by a Basque Country Count in the 1870s.

The '40s and '50s were a boom time, when color and life seeped from Santurce's energetic streets, spurred on by the buoyancy of Operation Bootstrap. Back then, Santurce was a financial center and a residential quarter of some repute. The nosedive began in the 1970s when the business district headed south to Hato Rey and Santurce suffered a similar fate to many US cities as the upwardly mobile middle classes left to colonize the new suburbs. Left to fester, abandoned with high crime rates and unsightly graffiti, Santurce has worked hard to turn the corner. Its recent 21st-century renaissance has been spearheaded by new art galleries, a performing arts center and a host of trendy clubs.

Museo de Arte de Puerto Rico MUSEUM

(MAPR; Map p60; ☎787-977-6277, for tours ext 2230 or 3230; www.mapr.org; 299 Av José de Diego; adult/student & senior $6/3, admission free 2-8pm Wed; ⏲10am-5pm Tue-Sat, 10am-8pm Wed, 11am-6pm Sun) While the old town's historic attractions are universally famous, fewer people are aware that San Juan boasts one of the largest and most celebrated art museums in the Caribbean. Housed in a splendid neoclassical building that was once the city's Municipal Hospital, MAPR boasts 18 exhibition halls spread over an area of 130,000 sq ft.

But there's far more to this cultural tour de force than just a collection of paintings. Adding distinction to diversity, the facility also boasts a 2.5-acre sculpture garden, a conservation laboratory, a computer-learning center, a 400-seat theater and a museum shop.

The artistic collection traces paintings, sculptures, posters and carvings from the 17th to the 21st century, chronicling such renowned Puerto Rican artists as José Campeche, Francisco Oller, Nick Quijano and Rafael Ferrer.

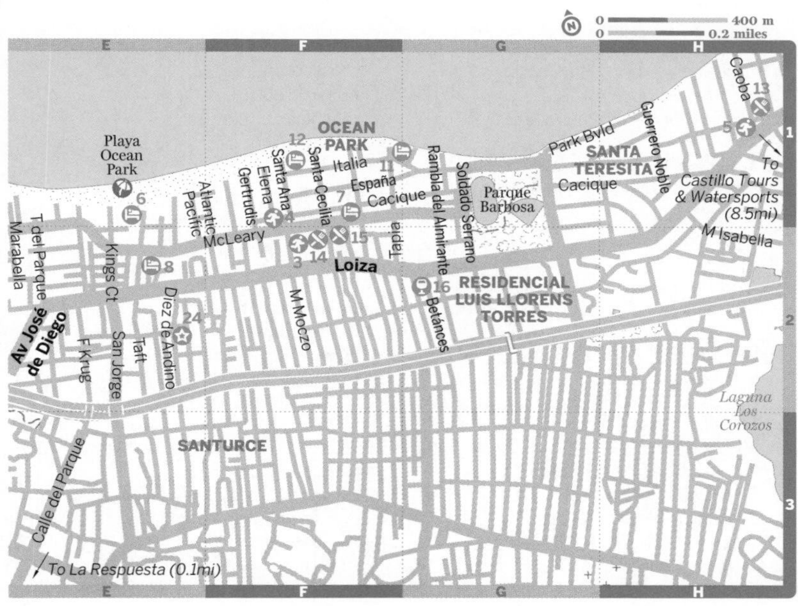

Do not miss the opportunity to take a walk through the gardens, where winding paths invite visitors to stroll past 16 sculptures and more than 100,000 plants in a scene reminiscent of Monet's water lilies.

FREE Museo de Arte Contemporáneo de Puerto Rico MUSEUM
(MAC; Map p60; www.museocontemporaneopr.org; cnr Av Ponce de León & Roberto H Todd; ⏲10am-4pm Tue-Sat, noon-4pm Sun) The Museo de Arte Contemporáneo de Puerto Rico sits just down the road from the Museo de Arte de Puerto Rico in a similarly eye-catching classical Georgian building – the former Rafael M Labra school – dating from 1918. The museum displays art from the mid-20th century onwards and showcases artists from Puerto Rico, the Caribbean and Latin America.

ISLA VERDE

Technically speaking, Isla Verde is in Carolina, a sprawling suburb of San Juan. It's the preferred destination for vacationers who seek what the tourism brochures promise: mega resorts, glitzy casinos and huge swaths of lovely sand beach.

HATO REY

As you head south from Santurce, the urban inquietude of the former business district is replaced by the sleekness of its modern successor. The first signs of the brave new world can be seen at Sagrado Corazon station, a space-age temple to the metro train that is the first stop on San Juan's Tren Urbano. Welcome to Hato Rey, the Caribbean's wannabe Wall Street, a gleaming cluster of glass-sheeted office towers and international banks that reflect not only the crimson afternoon sun but also the lucid dreams of Puerto Rico's economic miracle. Aside from the ubiquitous financial institutions, Hato Rey's primary attractions revolve around shoppers and sports. Just west of the 'Miracle Mile' business district lies the massive Plaza Las Américas (see p84), the largest mall in the Caribbean, along with two major sports arenas – the Hiram Bithorn Stadium and the Roberto Clemente Coliseum.

RÍO PIEDRAS

Keep pushing south and the flatness of Hato Rey soon gives way to the leafy uplands of Río Piedras. Founded in 1714 and existing as a separate town until 1951, Río Piedras is the home of the renowned University of Puerto

Miramar & Ocean Park

Top Sights
Fuerte San Gerónimo ... A1
La Placita de Santurce ... D2
Museo de Arte Contemporáneo de Puerto Rico ... C3
Museo de Arte de Puerto Rico ... D3

Activities, Courses & Tours
1 Benitez Fishing Charters ... A2
2 Club Náutico ... A2
3 It's Yoga ... F2
Kitesurfpr ... (see 11)
4 Tres Palmas ... F1
5 Velauno ... H1

Sleeping
6 Acacia Seaside Inn ... E1
7 Andalucía Guest House ... F1
8 At Wind Chimes Inn ... E2
9 Caribe Hilton ... A1
10 Conrad San Juan Condado Plaza ... B1
11 Hostería del Mar ... F1
Niche ... (see 6)
12 Numero Uno ... F1

Eating
Café Mam ... (see 14)
13 Che's ... H1
14 Kasalta's ... F2
15 La B de Burro ... F2
Pamela's ... (see 12)
Pikayo ... (see 10)

Drinking
16 Pa'l Cielo ... G2
17 San Juan Eagle ... C3
18 Tia Maria's ... D3

Entertainment
19 C787 Studios ... B3
20 Cine Metro ... C3
21 Circo Bar ... C3
22 El Centro de Bellas Artes Luis A Ferré ... D3
23 Krash ... C3
24 RoKA Espacio ... E2
25 Starz ... D3

Shopping
26 Executive Manolo ... D3

ALTERNATIVE ART SPACES IN SANTURCE

Santurce's art scene is blazing hot, with small galleries and cultural spaces organizing cutting-edge art shows and outside-the-mainstream events. A few recommended venues to check out:

» **La Respuesta** (off Map p60; www.larespuestapr.com; Av Fernández Juncos & Calle del Parque) Live music, poetry and art exhibitions.

» **RoKA Espacio** (Map p60; www.rokaespacio.com; Calle Ciales & Diez de Andino) Gallery space featuring visual art and independent cinema.

» **C787 Studios** (Map p60; www.c787studios.com; 734 Cerra) Exhibitions in its gallery, as well as experimental music.

» **Executive Manolo** (Map p60; www.executivemanolo.com; 1416 Av Ponce de León) A quirky shop for clothing and paintings; art and music shows too.

Rico and harbors a thriving academic community. You'll find cheap cafes and amply stocked bookshops here, as well as a cut-price shopping street (José de Diego), and the island's largest farmers market. The university building itself is set in lush, palm-filled grounds and is distinguished by its signature minaret-like clock tower. This is a great place to hang out, shoot the breeze and start taking up those good Puerto Rican vibrations.

Mercado de Río Piedras MARKET

(Paseo de Diego; 9am-6pm Mon-Sat) If you like the smell of fish and oranges, the bustle of people, and trading jests in Spanish as you bargain for a bunch of bananas, this market is for you. As much a scene as a place to shop, the market continues the colonial tradition of an indoor market that spills into the streets.

Next to the Río Piedras stop of the Tren Urbano, the four long blocks of shops and inexpensive restaurants lining Paseo de Diego and facing the market have been closed to auto traffic, turning the whole area into an outdoor mall. You can shop or just watch as the local citizens negotiate for everything from *chuletas* (pork chops) and *camisas* (shirts) to reggaetón CDs. Shoppers will find the market and stores along Paseo de Diego open from early morning to late evening, Monday to Saturday.

FREE **Jardín Botánico** GARDEN

(Experimental Agricultural Station of Puerto Rico; 787-758-9957; www.upr.edu, under 'Servicios a la Comunidad'; 6am-6pm, closed holidays, tours available) This 75-acre tract of greenery is the site of the Estación Experimental Agrícola de Puerto Rico, but is open to the public. Hiking trails lead to a lotus lagoon, an orchid garden with more than 30,000 flowers, and a plantation of more than 120 species of palm. The air smells of heliconia blossoms, as well as of nutmeg and cinnamon trees.

Its small **Museum of Entomology and Tropical Biodiversity** (787-767-9705, ext 2025; http://museo.eea.uprm.edu; Agronomy bldg, 2nd fl; tour by appt) contains three rooms of pinned butterflies, pickled pupae and other creepy-crawlies native to the region.

One of the reasons the garden is so serene is that it's difficult to find. The entrance is nearly hidden on the south side of the intersection of Hwy 1 and Hwy 847, a walk of about a mile from the center of the UPR campus. Call ahead to book a tour; it can be difficult to get the phone answered.

FREE **Museo de Antropología, Historia y Arte** MUSEUM

(787-764-0000, ext 2452; www.uprrp.edu; 9am-4:30pm Mon, Tue, Thu & Fri, 9am-8:30pm Wed, 11:30am-4:30pm Sat) This small but quite engaging museum of anthropology, history and art is worth a stop to see examples of the trove of Taíno artifacts unearthed by university scholars in recent digs. In addition, this museum features revolving art shows and offers scholarly perspectives on island history. Finally, visiting the museum gives travelers a legitimate reason to be snooping around the university campus and opens opportunities for connecting with the students and faculty. The opening hours vary, so call ahead. It lies just inside the entrance to the UPR campus, next to the Biblioteca Lazaro.

Casa-Finca de Don Luis Muñoz Marín HOUSE MUSEUM

(787-755-7979; www.flmm.org/casa.htm; Hwy 181 Km 1.3; adult/child & senior $6/3; 8am-2pm Mon-Fri, 10am-3pm Sat & Sun, tours 10am & 2pm)

START CAFÉ CALA'O
FINISH PASEO DEL MORRO
DISTANCE 3 MILES
DURATION THREE TO FOUR HOURS

Walking Tour
San Juan

Start with an early-morning pick-me-up at **1 Café Cala'o** next to the cruise ships parked by Pier 2, before heading west to visit the friendly folks at the **2 Puerto Rico Tourism Company**. After picking up some informative literature on the sights and sounds that lie ahead, stroll west along **3 Paseo de la Princesa**, a shaded 19th-century esplanade that tracks alongside the formidable old city walls to the brink of the Bahía de San Juan. Pass a former jail that now houses offices and admire the statue of Doña Felisa Gautier, one of the city's most esteemed former mayors. As you feel the refreshing Atlantic breeze hit you face-on, you'll spy the city's legendary perimeter wall as well as an imposing bronze sculpture and fountain called **4 Raíces** that depicts Taíno, European and African figurines rising amid a shower of cascading water.

Behind the fountain, follow the Paseo de la Princesa as it cuts northwest along the waterfront with excellent views over Bahía de San Juan toward the Bacardí Rum Factory. You'll see turreted guard towers called *garitas* carved into the thick city walls here, distinctive conical structures that have become symbolic of Puerto Rico and its rich colonial history. In the 17th and 18th centuries, Spanish ships once anchored in the cove just off these ramparts to unload colonists and supplies, all of which entered the city through a tall red portal known as **5 Puerta de San Juan**, dating from the 1630s.

Pass through the gate and turn right onto Recinto Oeste. This short cobblestoned street leads to the guarded iron gates of **6 La Fortaleza**, a one-time fort that today is more redolent of a well-preserved classical palace. After stopping for a guided tour of this executive mansion, head back northwest, taking a moment to gaze out over the water from the diminutive **7 Plazuela de la Rogativa** and admire its bronze sculpture of a religious procession.

Follow the leafy Caleta de San Juan up the slope to the beautiful Plazuela Las Monjas (Nun's Square), where stray cats stretch and sunbathe and romantic couples linger. Families will want to stop in at the excellent children's museum located here. On the north side of the plaza is 8 **Gran Hotel El Convento**, Puerto Rico's grandest hotel, well worth a casual inspection or a longer stop to dine and drink at one of its evocative courtyard restaurants. To the east lies the 9 **Catedral de San Juan**, a relatively austere religious building whose importance is enhanced by its age (dating from 1540) and the fact that the remains of Juan Ponce de León rest inside.

Cut along Luna for a block before heading right down San José. Take a left onto San Francisco, which will bring you to the 10 **Plaza de Armas**, a small but important square and the hub of the old city. If the effects of your first coffee have worn off you can procure excellent top-ups here from one of the traditional booths that decorate the plaza. Drop south one block and continue east along Fortaleza and you'll soon fall upon the urban inquietude of 11 **SoFo**, Old San Juan's funky restaurant and nightlife quarter that has injected vitality and hipness into the aged colonial core. Break here for your midday meal or window shop the profusion of creative menus and make a plan for dinner. Fortaleza ends in the 12 **Plaza de Colón**, named for the great Genoese explorer and site of the former land entrance to the walled city from Puerta de Tierra. Cut north up Av Muñoz Rivera here and you'll come to 13 **Fuerte San Cristóbal**, the old city's other major fortification, which harbors an interesting museum and theatrical military reenactments, plus fascinating tunnel tours during the weekend.

Walking west along Norzagaray, you can look down at the faded pastel houses of La Perla, San Juan's poorest and most notorious neighborhood, which affront the fierce and tempestuous Atlantic. Hidden in a former market building to your left is the 14 **Museo de San Juan**, which will fill the historical gaps in the story of one of America's oldest colonial settlements. Saturday visitors can revel in the organic bounty of the Old San Juan farmers market, held weekly in the lovely courtyard and returning the building to its original use. A block or two west the 15 **Plaza del Quinto Centenario**, built in 1992 to commemorate the 500th anniversary of Christopher Columbus' 'discovery' of the New World, blends in seamlessly with the older neighboring Cuartel de Ballajá. The latter building houses the 16 **Museo de las Américas**, a museum of changing exhibits on Caribbean and European art. Across the grass expanses of Campo del Morro, kites soar in the sky, picnicking families spread out to feast, and the stately fort of 17 **El Morro** beckons like a brooding sentinel. Stroll the former sentries' walks for iconic panoramic views of San Juan and the sea. If you bought a joint ticket from Fuerte San Cristóbal, you'll get in here at a reduced rate.

On your return, bypass down Calle del Morro to the 18 **Casa Blanca**, the ancestral home for 250 years of the descendants of Juan Ponce de León, and the oldest permanent residence in the Americas.

A stone's throw to the east lies the 19 **Plaza de San José**, with its statue of Juan Ponce de León, cast from an English cannon captured in the raid of 1797. The east side of the plaza contains two small museums that are worth a wander. More antiquity overlooks the plaza from the north in the shape of the 20 **Iglesia de San José**, the second-oldest church in the Americas. The subject of an extensive restoration, its interior contains fascinating murals and a series of displays documenting recent archeological discoveries made during reconstruction work.

You can cut back to the Puerta de San Juan via a network of steep narrow backstreets punctuated with stone staircases. Exiting the city via the old gate, turn right and follow the mile-long 21 **Paseo del Morro**, which hugs the city walls to the far tip of El Morro fort. This stroll is most evocative at the end of the day as the sun sets over the bay and the dark gray shapes of Cataño are transformed into twinkling lights.

This house and farm were once home to the godfather of the Partido Popular Democrático (PPD) and the man who shepherded Puerto Rico into commonwealth status – as well as a 20th-century industrialized market economy in the 1950s and '60s. Today it is a museum honoring the memory of this legendary Puerto Rican figure, and it also serves as a venue for concerts and experimental theater. Call for events, and visit if you want to find out more about the pretty astounding political career of Luis Muñoz Marín. Also take a minute to check out the great vegetation and expansive grounds. Look for the house on the east side of Río Piedras.

Beaches

San Juan has some of the best municipal beaches this side of Rio de Janeiro. Starting half a mile or so east of the old town, you can go from rustic to swanky and back to rustic all in the space of 7.5 miles.

Puerta de Tierra FAMILY BEACH

Imagine it – a sheltered arc of raked sand, decent surf breaks, plenty of local action and the sight of a 17th-century Spanish fort shimmering in the distance.

But, hang on a minute. Are you really still only a stone's throw from Old San Juan and the busy tourist strip of Condado? **Balneario Escambrón** is almost too good to be true, which is probably why a lot of people miss it. Perched on the north end of the slither of land that *is* Puerta de Tierra and abutting majestic **Parque del Tercer Milenio**, this palm-fringed yet rugged beach just might be one of the best municipal options offered anywhere. Adding convenience to enchantment, there are lifeguards, rest rooms and snack bars on hand, along with a large parking lot.

Condado RESORT BEACH

Hemmed in by hotel towers and punctuated by rocky outcrops, Condado's narrow beaches are busier than Ocean Park's but less exclusive than Isla Verde's. Expect splashes of graffiti, boisterous games of volleyball and plenty of crashing Atlantic surf.

The area's official public beach is **Balneario Condado** (Map p60), a small arc of sand, adjacent to the Dos Hermanos bridge, that faces west toward Fuerte San Gerónimo across the inlet. A line of rocks breaks the water here, meaning that the sea is calm and bathing relatively safe. Lifeguards police the area on weekdays, and snack bars are open daily, but bathrooms are few and far between. You can rent beach chairs.

Condado's Atlantic-facing beaches are very popular, especially among families, who congregate around the big hotels, and with gay men, who often populate the sand near the Atlantic Beach Hotel. **Parque de la Ventana al Mar** (Window to the Sea Park; Map p72) has lovely waterfront views and free jazz concerts on the last Sunday of the month.

Ocean Park ACTIVITIES BEACH

Ocean Park's lesser fame is its hidden blessing. Fronted by leafy residential streets and embellished by the odd luxury B&B, its wide sweep of fine, diamond-dust sand that is **Playa Ocean Park** (Map p60) is protected by offshore reefs and caressed by cooling seasonal trade winds. Although it's largely the preserve of trendy lovers of tranquility, anyone can enjoy the very different ambience here. Just pick a road through the neighborhood's low-rise gated community and follow it toward the water.

Playa Isla Verde RESORT BEACH

(Map p74) Resort pluggers will tell you that Playa Isla Verde is the Copacabana of Puerto Rico, with its legions of tanned bodies and dexterous beach bums flexing their triceps around the volleyball net. Other more savvy travelers prefer to dodge the extended families and colonizing spring-break hedonists that stake space here and head west to Ocean Park. Whatever your subjective view, this broad mile-long wedge of sand that lies between Punta Las Marías and Piñones is an undeniable beauty. The downside – if there is one – is access. Cutting in front of the towering condos and plush hotels of Av Isla Verde, the beach is completely obscured from the road and, as a result, lacks the inclusive atmosphere of more-open municipal beaches.

Balneario de Carolina FAMILY BEACH

(Map p48; Rte 187; parking $3; ⏲8am-5pm Tue-Sun) Wedged in between the high-rise-hotel strip of Isla Verde and rustic delights of Piñones, Balneario de Carolina is a fine, clean beach that lacks natural shelter and is positioned a little incongruously right in front of Luis Muñoz Marín International Airport (LMM airport). Equipped with plenty of lifeguards, bathrooms, showers, barbecue pits and rather weird red sculptures, the beach can be pleasantly peaceful in the week if you can ignore the noise from 747s taking off.

Activities

One of the best places in town to buy or rent outdoor gear – including camping equipment – is **Acampa** (☎787-706-0695; www.acampapr.com; 1221 Av Jesús T Piñero, Caparra; ⏰10am-6pm Mon-Fri, 10:30am-5:30pm Sat). It also does a number of good tours all over the island.

Caving & Canyoning

Aventuras Tierra Adentro CAVING, CANYONING
(☎787-766-0470; www.aventuraspr.com; 268a Av Jesús T Piñero, Río Piedras; day trip $150-170; ⏰10am-6pm Tue-Fri, 10am-4pm Sat, tours available on demand) Located a mile west of UPR, Aventuras Tierra Adentro is a favorite store for climbers and hikers in Puerto Rico. It's also a tour operator specializing in rock-climbing and rappelling trips to the Río Camuy caves and canyoning trips in El Yunque. Guides also lead ziplining over the mouth of Camuy's Angeles sinkhole.

Diving & Snorkeling

While Puerto Rico is well known for its first-class diving, San Juan is not the best place for it: strong winds often churn up the water. Condado has an easy dive that takes you through a pass between the inner and outer reefs into coral caverns, overhangs, grottoes and tunnels.

Eco Action Tours DIVING
(☎787-791-7509; www.ecoactiontours.com) In addition to diving, Eco Action Tours can do just about any tour imaginable, from rappelling to nature walks. It operates out of a van and comes to you. It offers San Juan area shore dives ($75, one tank and all equipment) and dives on the east coast.

Caribe Aquatic Adventures DIVING, SNORKELING
(☎787-281-8858; www.caribeaquaticadventure.com; snorkel/1-tank dive incl equipment $50/90) This outfit does dives near San Juan, but also further afield around the islands off the coast of Fajardo (Icacos for snorkeling and Palominos and Palominitos for diving). Lunch and transportation from San Juan are included in trips to Fajardo. The company's shore dives from the beach behind the Normandie Hotel are regarded as some of the best in the Caribbean.

Ocean Sports DIVING
(Map p74; ☎787-268-2329; www.osdivers.com; 77 Av Isla Verde) Has a dive store in Isla Verde and organizes a wide range of dives. It has a full service facility that provides Nitrox, Trimix and rebreathers.

Fishing

Castillo Tours & Watersports FISHING
(Map p60; ☎787-791-6195; www.castillotours.com; 101 Doncella, Punta Las Marías) The Castillo family offers deep-sea fishing for blue marlin, wahoo, tuna and mahimahi, as well as snorkeling and sailing excursions.

Benitez Fishing Charters FISHING
(Map p60; ☎787-724-6265; www.mikebenitezsportfishing.com; San Juan Bay Marina, Miramar) If you want to trade White House gossip while doing some serious deep-sea fishing for dolphin fish, tuna, wahoo and white and blue marlin, book a space on a deluxe 45ft boat captained by the celebrated Mike Benitez, who has carried the likes of former US President Jimmy Carter. Prices start at $210 per person for a four-hour excursion.

Surfing, Boat Trips & Water Sports

San Juan is hardly Rincón in the surfing stakes, but no matter. You'll find the best waves and biggest *surferos* scene east of Isla Verde out toward Piñones and beyond, when the morning and evening breezes glass off a 4ft swell. Popular breaks include Pine Grove and Los Aviónes along Hwy 187.

WOW Surfing School SURFING
(☎787-955-6059; www.gosurfpr.com) This outfit runs full surfing lessons from the Ritz-Carlton on Playa Isla Verde. Lessons include boards, stretching, safety drills, dry-land practice and the real thing. Board rentals (from $25 per day) are also available. Lessons for children.

Tres Palmas SURFING
(Map p60; ☎787-728-3377; 1911 McLeary; short boards/boogie boards per day $36/25) In Ocean Park, Tres Palmas also has 24-hour surfboard and boogie board rentals and lessons. Lessons for children.

Velauno PADDLEBOARDING, WINDSURFING
(Map p60; ☎787-982-0543; www.velauno.com; 2430 Loíza, Punta Las Marías; longboard rental per day $25, windsurfing equipment per hr $20) Velauno is a great place to take windsurfing or paddleboarding classes. On Saturday from 9am to 11am, it offers free paddleboarding lessons at the Laguna del Condado near the Conrad San Juan Condado Plaza.

Kitesurfpr KITESURFING
(Map p60; ☎787-525-1438; www.kitesurfpr.com; Hostería del Mar, 1 Tapia) You can learn how to kitesurf at Kitesurfpr. It also offers islandwide charters and boat support.

SAN JUAN FOR CHILDREN

Puerto Ricans love children – it doesn't matter who they belong to – and they love family, so traveling with youngsters is rarely a hassle, because the Puerto Ricans are doing it too. There are some hotels that won't take children under a certain age, but they are few. Several museums and hotels offer discounts for children – don't be afraid to ask. If renting a car, make sure that the rental agency has a child seat for you, and if taking a taxi any long distance, bring one with you. Children should carry some form of ID in case there's an emergency. You'll rarely encounter any icy or disdainful looks when dining out with your child, but some of the trendier places in Old San Juan, Condado and Isla Verde would be the exception to that rule.

In and around San Juan there are several attractions that children really enjoy. The **Museo del Niño** is always a big hit – as are the many stray cats who nap outside it – and the insect museum at the **Jardín Botánico** will have its ardent fans. **Isla Verde** is the most child-friendly beach, with safe swimming and plenty of beach toys, or you can always head further east to **Luquillo**. For some outdoor exercise hit the **bike trails of Piñones**, or go **kayaking** on the nearby lagoon.

Alternatively you can hop on one of Old San Juan's two handy **trolleys**. For an educational but entertaining delve into Puerto Rican history check out the two splendid forts, **El Morro** and **San Cristóbal**. On a rainy day, the **Casa de Ramón Power y Giralt**, run by the Conservation Trust of Puerto Rico, has interesting exhibits and films.

All the larger hotels have vetted babysitters on speed dial – usually staff who are happy to make some extra money on the side.

15 Knots KITESURFING
(☎787-215-5667; www.15knots.com) In Isla Verde, 15 Knots has kitesurfing lessons for all levels.

Also in Isla Verde, side by side on the beach near the El San Juan Hotel, **Archie's Jet Ski Rental** (Map p74; ☎787-643-4510) and **Watersports 4U** (Map p74; ☎939-969-4510; www.parasailpuertorico.com) can rent you pretty much anything that floats: banana boats, wave runners, kayaks ($20 to $30 per hour), small catamarans (with captain; $60 to $70 per hour), jet skis, water skis and kneeboards. Or get airborne with some parasailing ($60 per person).

Cycling

Forget the notorious traffic jams; cycling in San Juan can actually be good fun, as long as you know where to go. In fact, it is perfectly feasible to work your way along the safe coastline from Old San Juan out as far as Carolina and the bike paths of Piñones.

Rent the Bicycle CYCLING
(☎787-602-9696; www.rentthebicycle.net) Has tours and rents sturdy banana-yellow cruiser bikes for $27 per day, including lock and helmet. Children's bike seats are available for $5. They'll bring a bike to you anywhere in San Juan, or you can stop by the shop at Pier 6.

Vias Car Rental CYCLING
(Map p74; ☎787-791-4120; 4 Rosa) At the Hotel Villa del Sol in Isla Verde, Vias has a handful of mountain bikes and a tandem for rent.

Courses

If you're feeling limber and loose – or would like to be – there are a number of venues offering dance instruction, and yoga classes aren't difficult to find.

Dance

To learn a basic break step or show off your oh-so-effortless moves, the best venue in town is **Latin Roots** (p83). With free nightly salsa classes and awesome music, you can't go wrong. Well…until you mash your partner's toe.

The **San Juan Marriott Resort** (p73) in Condado and the **Courtyard by Marriott Isla Verde Beach Resort** (off Map p74; ☎787-791-0404; Hwy 187; www.sjcourtyard.com/entertainment) offer free salsa classes some nights; call to check current schedule.

Yoga

Well situated in Ocean Park, **It's Yoga** (Map p60; ☎787-677-7585; www.itsyogapuertorico.com; 1950 McLeary; classes $17) offers Pilates and modified Ashtanga classes.

A few accommodations, including the **Casablanca Hotel** (p71, $12) and **Hostería del Mar** (p73, $15 to $30), have classes that are open to the public, and many of the resort hotels offer classes for their guests.

Tours

Rent the Bicycle BIKE TOURS

(☎787-602-9696; www.rentthebicycle.net) Forsake the car and rent a bike! San Juan's biggest and most reliable bike outfit (see p68), it does excellent two-wheeled tours of Old San Juan ($29 to $49), the Condado beaches ($37) and Piñones ($52).

Legends of Puerto Rico CULTURAL TOURS

(☎787-605-9060; www.legendsofpr.com) Debbie Molina-Ramos is a well-respected guide for Legends of Puerto Rico, whose wildly popular 'Night Tales in Old San Juan' tour books up pretty fast. She also does 'Legends of San Juan' ($35 per person) and many others, including an eating and drinking tour (with rum tasting), and tours to El Yunque. Bus trips are available, as are special discounts for families with children (and child-friendly tours, too). Tours are in either English or Spanish.

Conservation Trust of Puerto Rico WILDLIFE TOURS

(☎787-722-5834, ext 242; www.fideicomiso.org) Wildlife lovers should seek out the frequent and well-priced outings of the Conservation Trust of Puerto Rico. Its Old San Juan tours focus on birding ($20) and the city's natural habitats ($5).

Flavors of San Juan FOOD TOURS

(☎787-964-2447; www.flavorsofsanjuan.com; tours $80-95) If eating your way around the old town is more your style, Flavors of San Juan conducts walking tours that give you a crash course in the local cuisine.

Festivals & Events

Aside from Festival San Sebastián, which becomes more adult-oriented during the evening, all of the following festivals retain a congenial atmosphere that is favorable to families. Unless otherwise noted, information on the following events can be obtained by contacting the PRTC.

Festival de la Calle San Sebastián CULTURAL FESTIVAL

For a full week in mid-January, the old city's famous party street, San Sebastián, hums with semi-religious processions, music, food stalls and larger-than-ever crowds. During the day, it's folk art and crafts; at night, it's drunken revelry.

Fiesta de San Juan Bautista CULTURAL FESTIVAL

Celebration of the patron saint of San Juan and a summer solstice party, Latin style. Staged during the week preceding June

DON'T MISS

URBAN WATERWAYS OF SAN JUAN

If you're interested in digging deeper into the cultural and natural history of San Juan, **Excursiones Eco** (☎787-565-0089; www.excursioneseco.com; walking tours $10, boat tours $35-55) lets you get a rare glimpse beyond the city's developed sand beaches, myriad highways and soaring high-rises. With a minimum of four people, Melba Ayala, a young community leader, guides visitors through the Caño de Martín Peña, a 3.5-mile tidal channel that connects the Bahía de San Juan with the Laguna San José. Passengers explore its mangrove forest and bird habitat while learning about its history and current struggles of the low-income neighborhoods surrounding it. Melba also offers walking tours that visit these underserved former squatter communities, which now house close to 27,000 people.

The area is at the center of a burgeoning environmental justice fight. The canal is slated for dredging to improve water quality and access, and some families will need to be relocated because their homes – some without sewage systems – are regularly inundated during seasonal floods. Though these communities were permitted in 2004 to form a land trust – the first in Puerto Rico – that gave them the right to collectively own and manage this land, the government abruptly rescinded it in 2009, taking away much of their bargaining power. They are now fighting large-scale displacement and presumed redevelopment.

A number of tours are available, including boat trips that continue past the airport and end up at Laguna la Torrecilla in Piñones. Reserve two weeks in advance if possible.

GAY & LESBIAN SAN JUAN

Considered to be the most gay-friendly destination in the Caribbean, San Juan has long buried its stereotypical macho image and replaced it with a culture that is remarkable for its tolerance and openness. Santurce is the nexus of the club and cruising scene, but with so many of the capital's hotels and restaurants now run by gay professionals, the finer details of one's sexual preference are usually irrelevant.

Condado and Ocean Park have a number of popular guesthouses, and then there's the delectable **Gran Hotel El Convento** in the heart of the old city.

Most gay clubs have migrated to gritty Santurce, but one of the city's only lesbian clubs, Cups, closed in early 2011. Check for a new standard-bearer. **Krash** can be slightly more mixed than other all-male venues.

Most dining spots can be considered gay-friendly, but perennially popular with the community are **Parrot Club** in SoFo, **Pamela's** inside the Numero Uno guesthouse and **El Picoteo** in the Gran Hotel El Convento.

The free *Conexión G* (www.saliendodelcloset.org) newspaper and website has queer club listings and resources in its *Foro Comunitario* section.

An annual **Puerto Rico Queer Filmfest** (www.puertoricoqueerfilmfest.com) began in 2009, and takes place for a week in mid-November; Pride events are held in early June.

24, the heart of the action – including religious processions, wandering minstrels, fireworks, food stalls, drunken sailors and beauty queens (straight and otherwise) – is in Old San Juan, but the rest of the city gets into the act as well and parties down on the last day of the fiesta at Playa Isla Verde. During this decidedly odd festival, devotees walk backwards into the ocean in the middle of the night – apparently for good luck.

TOP CHOICE Fo Culinary Fest FOOD

Fo's alfresco culinary festival is a semi-annual movable feast that happens in late fall and again in mid-summer. For three nights, a two-block wedge of Fortaleza is closed to traffic and commandeered by local restaurateurs who set up their tables in the street and rustle up their best dishes. Live bands drop by, belly dancers entertain diners and the food is sizzlingly good.

JazzFest JAZZ

Puerto Rico's largest jazz fest, courtesy of Heineken and held from late May to early June, attracts the best Latin jazz artists from all over the Caribbean. The late, great Tito Puente sometimes played here, and Eddie Palmieri still does.

Festival Casals CLASSICAL MUSIC

(www.festcasalspr.gobierno.pr) For over 50 years, renowned soloists and orchestras have come from all over the world to join the Puerto Rico Symphony Orchestra in giving night after night of virtuoso concerts, primarily at El Centro de Bellas Artes Luis A Ferré. Tickets run at around $40, but there are big discounts for students, children and seniors. Dates vary. Check out the website for details.

Festival de Cine Internacional de San Juan FILM

(San Juan International Film Festival; www.festivalcinesanjuan.com) Screens new films over one week in October, with an emphasis on Caribbean cinema. Given the number of Puerto Ricans/Nuyoricans making good on the big screen – J Lo, Benicio del Toro, Jimmy Smits (and Raul Julia, who was given a state funeral when he died of cancer in 1994) – this event has been pulling in bigger luminaries each year.

Sleeping

You'll find ample accommodations in San Juan, though few in the budget category. On the upside, rates for places to stay in San Juan vary significantly (sometimes more than 30%) from season to season. See p278 for details.

Aside from that, San Juan is wide open. Upscale, midscale, boutique or B&B: take your pick. Condado and Ocean Park have the highest concentration of guesthouses and big resort hotels. Isla Verde has a few ritzy boutique options flanked by mega resorts, and Old San Juan's got a handful of historical havens, including the exquisite El Convento, surely the most evocative hotel on the island.

Note that the large hotels tack on a 14% resort fee and charge $15 to $20 per night for parking.

OLD SAN JUAN

Gran Hotel El Convento PARADOR $$$
(Map p52; ☎787-723-9020; www.elconvento.com; 100 Calle del Cristo; r $260-325, ste $535-800; P❄@🛜🏊) Historic monument, tapas restaurant, meeting place, coffee bar and evocative colonial building...without a doubt El Convento is Puerto Rico's most complete atmospheric and multifaceted hotel. Built in 1651 as the New World's first Carmelite convent, this sturdy baroque beacon oozes with priceless old-world relics and subtle 'Siglo de Oro' (Golden Age) charm. Check out the Goya-esque tapestries in the hallway or the late-afternoon tranquility of the enclosed inner courtyard, or wander up onto the roof deck for a plunge in the tiny pool and Jacuzzi that frame sweeping city views over the cathedral and Old San Juan. El Convento's 67 rooms and five suites (2nd-floor rooms have the highest ceilings) are gorgeously decorated with Andalusian tiles, mahogany and thick rugs, plus the service from the bar to the front desk is impeccable. The nightly wine and food reception may preclude outside dinner plans.

Gallery Inn INN $$$
(Map p52; ☎787-722-1808; www.thegalleryinn.com; 204-206 Norzagaray; r incl breakfast $235-355; P❄@🏊) Get ready to do a double take here. This quirky artist-owned hotel will make you feel as if you've wandered inadvertently onto the set of a Harry Potter movie. Showcasing masks, caged birds, trickling water, antiques, paintings and well-thumbed books, the Gallery Inn's cavernous 18th-century compound is the property of local artists Jan D'Sopo and Manuco Gandía (who'll meet guests for a daily 5:30pm cheese and wine reception). Perched romantically above the Atlantic waves and boasting 25 eclectic rooms and a stunning plunge pool, it will be like nowhere else you have ever visited. Three hundred years of art, antiques and history stuffed into one building – staggering. The reception area showcases photos of the Obamas when they overnighted here a few years back.

Chateau Cervantes HOTEL $$$
(Map p52; ☎787-724-7722; www.cervantespr.com; 329 Recinto Sur; r/ste $225/975; ❄🛜) Twelve rooms on six floors, intimate decor and a stunning level of all-round opulence, the Cervantes is about as luxurious as Puerto Rico gets. Designed as a boutique hotel of the highest class by local guru Nono Maldonado, the hotel barely advertises itself from the street – probably because it doesn't need to. Once inside, 'chateau' is definitely the right word in this Parisian-influenced city beauty with its eye-catching art (original, of course) and electronic gadgets deftly splashed around angular rooms that retain a tangible old-town feel. Its restaurant, Panza, serves all meals in high season.

TOP CHOICE **Casablanca Hotel** HOTEL $$
(Map p52; ☎787-725-3436; www.hotelcasablancapr.com; 316 Fortaleza; r incl breakfast $95-195; ❄🛜) Cut from the same cloth as its sister property, longtime favorite Da House, this stylish new SoFo hotel blends a luxurious mix of colonial and contemporary styles. Five floors of rooms (but no elevator) are swathed in vibrant fabrics, and cozy bathrooms sparkle with gorgeous mother-of-pearl sinks from India. Greet the morning with a yoga class on the roof deck with inspirational views of El Morro and El Yunque, or swan around in one of the shaded soaking tubs. Its restaurant fills out a Moorish-style lobby of eye-candy lounges and bold tile work, commanded by a sunburst chandelier.

Da House HOTEL $$
(Map p52; ☎787-977-1180; www.dahousehotelpr.com; 312 San Francisco; r incl breakfast $80-150; ❄@🛜) One of Old San Juan's funkier hotels is also one of its best bargains, with boutique-style rooms kitted out with chic furnishings and decorated with eye-catching contemporary art. Each room is dedicated to a different local artist whose work is displayed within, complete with tantalizing price tags to ponder over. For the musically inclined, one of San Juan's best salsa bars, the Nuyorican, is situated downstairs; for the less enamored (or sleep-deprived), the reception staff will ruefully give out ear plugs.

AlaSol Apartments APARTMENTS $$
(Map p52; ☎787-724-4456; 318 Sol; apt per night/week $116/550; P❄🛜) These handy one-bedroom apartments (three-night minimum stay) have to be one of the best bargains in Old San Juan. Located on neighborly Sol with all of the restaurant and museum action a hop, skip and jump away, the traditional but comfortable rooms have a double bed, futon, kitchenette, bathroom, living room, TV and – almost unheard of in Old San Juan – a parking space out front. Priceless!

Posada San Francisco GUESTHOUSE $
(Map p52; 787-721-7112; 405 San Francisco; r with shared bathroom $45;) The paint was barely dry when we visited this excellent new family-run budget option, and all eight rooms were already snapped up. Spacious and super-clean (one-use shower mats in the six shared bathrooms), the full- and twin-bedded rooms have high ceilings, fridges and classic tile floors. Exquisite 5th-floor-patio views and a guest kitchen seal the deal. Bookable through www.hostelworld.com.

Fortaleza Guest House GUESTHOUSE $
(Map p52; 787-721-7112; 303 Fortaleza; r with shared bathroom with fan/air-con $40/50;) Well located in Old San Juan – though not for the fussy – these basic budget rooms are a good place to meet other travelers. The tiny rooms have either air-con and no natural light or a fan with a somewhat loud streetside balcony. Perks include a small guest kitchen and the excellent Indian and natural foods store across the street. Bookable on www.hostelworld.com.

CONDADO

La Concha RESORT $$$
(Map p72; 787-721-7500; www.laconcharesort.com; 1077 Av Ashford; r $269-319;) Recently reopened after a decade, La Concha will wow you. Spacious and serene white rooms pop with flashes of color, and blue-lit showers exude an otherworldly underwater glow. Add in its three pools (one adults-only), gorgeous indoor and outdoor seating areas, hallways in crayon colors, a 24-hour casino, a sushi bar and the drop-dead gorgeous **Perla** restaurant, and you won't feel the need to venture far. In addition, the hotel lobby is the current place to see and be seen in San Juan, with a sophisticated party scene on weekends. So bring a dazzling outfit or request a room tucked away from the action.

Conrad San Juan Condado Plaza RESORT $$$
(Map p60; 727-721-1000; www.condadoplaza.com; 999 Av Ashford; r $140-539;) Guarding the entrance to Condado like a sparkling concrete sentinel, the Conrad straddles the thin wedge of land that separates the area's eponymous lagoon from the Atlantic Ocean. Housed in two concrete towers connected by an overhead walkway above Av Ashford, the hotel – now a Hilton property – offers the best of both worlds, with stunning views extending in both directions. A swanky lobby redolent of a designer movie set oozes luxury, and guests in the newly renovated oceanfront rooms generally aren't disappointed. Other highlights include a fitness center, a 24-hour casino with live entertainment, a celebrated gourmet restaurant (**Piyako**) and a lovely arc of raked sand that faces the formidable walls of Fuerte San Gerónimo across the inlet.

Coral Princess Inn HOTEL $$
(Map p72; 787-977-7700; www.coralpr.com; 1159 Magdalena; r incl continental breakfast $137-161;) Now we're talking: an independent inn that can compete in the quality stakes with the bigger and plusher opposition. The Coral Princess is a small 25-room boutique hotel that punches way above its weight. Sitting in Condado's midrange bracket, it offers all the luxuries of the fancy resorts – flat-screen TVs, marble floors and original art – but with enough intimacy and Latin

Condado

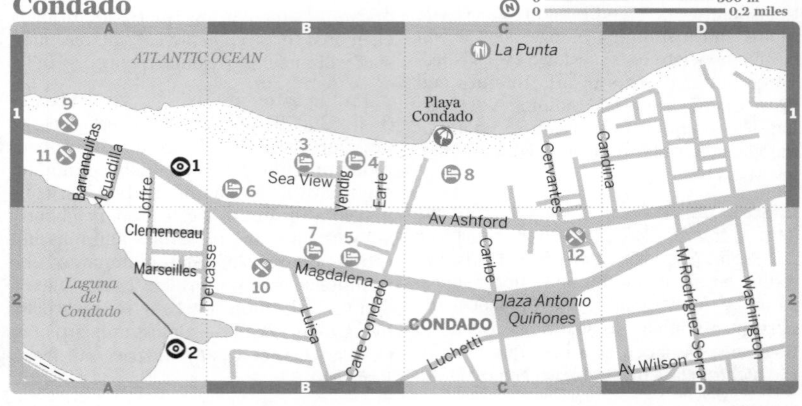

flavor to remind you that you're still in Puerto Rico.

Caribe Hilton RESORT $$$
(Map p60; ☎787-721-0303; www.hiltoncaribbean.com/sanjuan; Rosales; r $279-479; P❄@📶🏊👨‍👩‍👧) The Caribe was constructed in 1949 and played host to numerous celebrities throughout the 1950s and '60s. Its recently renovated rooms are loaded with amenities, and the sprawling pool and beach area includes a lawn chessboard, scores of hammocks and an interesting mini-peninsula with lounge beds. Though it's a bit of an island unto itself, there's good beach access and Old San Juan is a not unpleasant 30-minute walk away.

San Juan Marriott Resort & Stellaris Casino RESORT $$$
(Map p72; ☎787-722-7000; www.marriott.com; 1309 Av Ashford; r $265-325; P❄@📶🏊) The infamous Hotel Dupont Plaza once stood on this site before an arson attack burnt it to the ground, claiming 97 lives, in 1986. Rising in its place a decade later, Marriott has turned a den of notoriety into a pretty beachfront property, with two pools (one with a water slide!) and 525 units. A lot more personable than other resorts in its class, the Marriott boasts enviably modern rooms, a gym, a lavish breakfast buffet and salsa lessons in the lobby lounge.

Condado

Sights

1 Parque de la Ventana al Mar A1
2 Parque Laguna del Condado Jaime Benítez A2

Sleeping

3 Alelí by the Sea B1
4 Atlantic Beach Hotel B1
5 Coral Princess Inn B2
6 La Concha B1
7 Le Consulat Hotel B2
8 San Juan Marriott Resort & Stellaris Casino C1

Eating

9 Hacienda Don José A1
10 José José B2
Perla .... (see 6)
11 Picachos Café A1
12 Via Appia C2

Drinking

La Concha .... (see 6)

Atlantic Beach Hotel HOTEL $$
(Map p72; ☎787-721-6900; www.atlanticbeachhotel.net; 1 Vendig; r $79-119; P❄📶) Formerly the gay nexus of San Juan, this oceanfront hotel now has a more mixed budget-oriented clientele (a strict no-visitors policy has iced out vacation cruising), even if the beach scene remains boys aplenty. After years of the hotel's decline, new management is rounding out an extensive remodel, and rooms now exude a crisp black-and-white minimalism. Overall, the great oceanside location trumps tired common areas and slapdash staff enthusiasm.

Le Consulat Hotel HOTEL $$
(Map p72; ☎787-289-9191; www.leconsulathotel.com; 1149 Magdelena; r $115-135; P❄📶🏊) A mere two blocks from the beach, this new offering has comfortable smallish rooms and a dynamite location within walking distance of Condado's restaurants and nightlife. Incredibly, a flat $5 parking fee covers your entire stay.

Alelí by the Sea GUESTHOUSE $$
(Map p72; ☎787-725-5313; alelibythesea@hotmail.com; 1125 Sea View; r $80-119; P❄📶) A gift to budget-conscious travelers, this modest nine-room guesthouse is the final bastion of inexpensive seaside accommodations in Condado. There's a handy full kitchen, and a spacious view deck fronts the beach.

OCEAN PARK

Hostería del Mar GUESTHOUSE $$
(Map p60; ☎787-727-3302; www.hosteriadelmarpr.com; 1 Tapia; r $104-239; ❄📶) With a desirable beachside location, and greeting guests with an artsy water feature and eye-catching antiques, this whitewashed Ocean Park guesthouse is quiet, intimate and definitively Caribbean. There's no pool, but there is an excellent restaurant in an enclosed gazebo overlooking the beach. Rooms are furnished with a simple rattan-inspired elegance.

Andalucía Guest House GUESTHOUSE $$
(Map p60; ☎787-309-3373; www.andaluciapr.com; 2011 McLeary; r $85-129; P❄@📶) Within striking distance of Ocean Park's excellent restaurants and beaches, this comfortable guesthouse makes you feel like you're part of the neighborhood. Its 11 rooms sport pretty tiling and striking boutique-style color schemes, and some have a kitchen or kitchenette. The super-helpful owners lend out boogie boards

and beach chairs, and there's a cozy terrace deck and courtyard Jacuzzi.

Acacia Seaside Inn HOTEL **$$**
(Map p60; ☎787-727-0668; www.acaciaseasideinn.com; 8 Taft; r $105-210;) A grandiose Spanish colonial–style mansion with a profusion of elaborate staircases, this mini-hotel is a chic smorgasbord of sophistication and style. We're talking funky wall art, an award-winning restaurant, and a pool-sized Jacuzzi complete with granite surround and a Buddha statue imported from China. *Tranquilo,* man.

Numero Uno GUESTHOUSE **$$**
(Map p60; ☎787-726-5010; www.numero1guesthouse.com; 1 Santa Ana; r $149-299;) Pinch yourself – you're still in the middle of San Juan: Ocean Park, to be more precise, the discerning traveler's antidote to Condado and Isla Verde. Hidden behind the walls of a whitewashed 1940s beachfront house, and surrounded by palms and topped by a luminous kidney-shaped swimming pool, the 12 rooms and four apartments are run by a former New Yorker whose soaring vision has inspired an inn of spiffy rooms, intimate service and an exquisite on-site seafood restaurant.

At Wind Chimes Inn INN **$$**
(Map p60; ☎787-727-4153; www.atwindchimesinn.com; 53 Taft; r $80-155;) Linked to the nearby Acacia Seaside Inn, At Wind Chimes is modeled along the same lines: a Spanish-style villa that mixes intimacy with low-key luxuries. It's a pleasant antidote to the resort feel of Condado's other luxury piles. Prices drop in low season, making this even more of a bargain.

ISLA VERDE

Ritz-Carlton RESORT **$$$**
(Map p74; ☎787-253-1700; www.ritzcarlton.com; 6961 Av Los Gobernadores; r $272-1809;) Ritz equals posh, so you'd better pack the trendy slacks and bring along a platinum credit card before booking a night here. Decked out in expensive marble and embellished with Alhambra-esque lions that line the path to the swimming pool, this is San Juan at its swankiest and a favorite hangout of visiting celebrities. Rooms are plush, service heavy on the 'yes sirs and madams' and the communal areas shimmer like winning entries in an international design competition. Parceled inside this carefully manicured tropical 'paradise' are a resident spa, tennis courts, numerous eating facilities and yes, that obligatory casino.

El San Juan Hotel & Casino RESORT **$$$**
(Map p74; ☎787-791-1000; www.elsanjuanhotel.com; 6063 Av Isla Verde; r $259-669;) Decked out in Gothic dark wood, starburst chandeliers and animal-print sofas, the lobby of El San Juan is a theatrical backdrop for the veritable fashion parade of folks prancing in for the legendary nightly entertainment. It's renowned for its flashy casino and rollicking nightlife; if you want stylish rooms, unlimited water features, classy restaurants, Starbucks coffee and a heaving nightlife all in one big happy package, this is the place for you. All rooms have a full or partial ocean view.

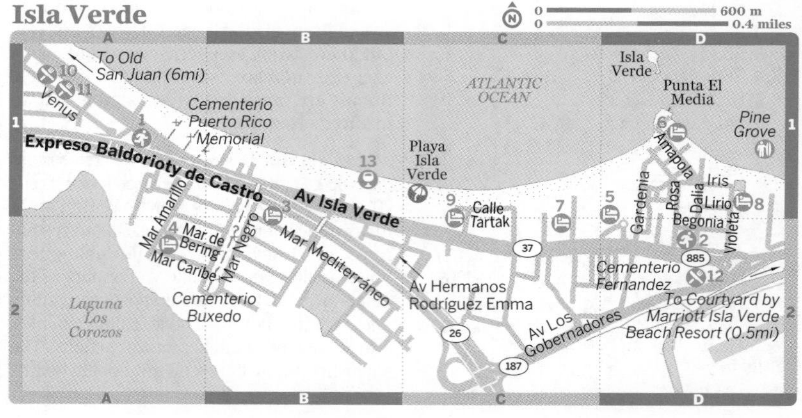

Water & Beach Club HOTEL **$$$**
(Map p74; 787-728-3666; www.waterbeachclubhotel.com; 2 Calle Tartak; r $195-295, ste $325-500; P) Breaking the resort ubiquity of Isla Verde, the Water & Beach Club is – along with the Horned Dorset (p180) in Rincón – Puerto Rico's most celebrated 'boutique' hotel. With a reception area straight out of *Architectural Digest* and elevators that sport glassed-in waterfalls, this is probably the closest San Juan comes to emulating South Beach, Florida. The minimalist rooms are artfully designed and benefit from spectacular beach views, and you have close proximity to its two trendy nightspots. It was undergoing renovations when we visited, including a rooftop lounge remodel.

Hotel La Playa GUESTHOUSE **$$**
(Map p74; 787-791-1115; www.hotellaplaya.com; 6 Amapola; r $109-120, apt $120-195;) Yes, you can stay oceanfront in Isla Verde without breaking the bank. New owners have tinkered under the hood of this 15-room Isla Verde stalwart, quietly constructing a lean, green machine. The new incarnation sports solar hot water heaters, low-power air-con units and a 2000-gallon water catchment system, and its sustainably sourced restaurant recycles its cooking oil for biodiesel. Pretty rooms have new furniture and tasteful Caribbean decor.

InterContinental San Juan Resort & Casino RESORT **$$$**
(Map p74; 787-791-6100; www.icsanjuanresort.com; 5961 Av Isla Verde; r $238-850; P) Probably the least interesting of Isla Verde's craning tourist piles, the InterContinental is, nonetheless, opulent with all of the usual gadgets and marketing ploys you'd expect in a well-appointed four-star place. Though the rooms and facilities are spiffy enough, the El San Juan next door still wins first prize for character and panache.

El Patio Guesthouse GUESTHOUSE **$**
(Map p74; 787-726-6298; 23 Mar de Bering; r $69-90;) Your average Isla Verde visitor probably wouldn't poke a stick at this place, but in the cheaper price bracket it's not a bad bet. A little villa walking distance to the beach and other amenities, it is run by a little old lady who'll bend over backwards to make sure that your rooms are spick-and-span. There's a guest kitchen, and rooms have TVs and fridges.

Coqui Inn MOTEL **$**
(Map p74; 787-726-4330; www.coqui-inn.net; 36 Mar Mediterráneo; r $80-91; P) Bisected by a major expressway, Isla Verde has its ugly side and you'll get a face full of it here. Expect clean, modern but simple rooms with cable TV and free morning coffee. Visitors with ear plugs can take comfort in the price and the proximity to the beach – a short walk across a concrete bridge.

Eating

Few would dispute the fact that San Juan offers the best eating in the Caribbean. Indeed, there are probably enough cutting-edge restaurants here to justify a trip in its own right. When in doubt, head to Calle Fortaleza in Old San Juan, the eclectic heart of San Juan's 21st-century fusion cuisine revolution. Most restaurants have at least one vegetarian dish, though vegans may have a more difficult time.

The recession's hit hard here, with many restaurants altering their menus to include small-plate offerings with more palatable

Isla Verde

Activities, Courses & Tours
- 15 Knots (see 13)
- Archie's Jet Ski Rental (see 5)
- 1 Ocean Sports A1
- 2 Vias Car Rental D2
- Watersports 4U (see 5)

Sleeping
- 3 Coqui Inn B1
- 4 El Patio Guesthouse A2
- 5 El San Juan Hotel & Casino D1
- 6 Hotel La Playa D1
- 7 InterContinental San Juan Resort & Casino C2
- 8 Ritz-Carlton D1
- 9 Water & Beach Club C2

Eating
- 10 Casa Dante A1
- Don José Café (see 2)
- 11 Il Nonno A1
- 12 Metropol D2

Drinking
- 13 Café La Plage B1
- Water & Beach Club (see 9)

Entertainment
- Club Brava (see 5)
- El San Juan Hotel Lobby (see 5)

price tags. It's rare to find dress codes required for dinner.

OLD SAN JUAN

St Germain Bistro & Café INTERNATIONAL $
(Map p52; 156 Sol; dishes $8-14; ⌚11:30am-3:30pm & 6-10pm Tue-Sat, 10am-3pm & 6-10pm Sun; ✎) Kudos to the chef for transforming the main-course salads – so often the dullest dish on the menu – into something fresh, tasty and filling. Then there's the aromatic Puerto Rican coffee, the delicious sandwiches and the homemade cakes, which can only be described as melt-in-your-mouth heavenly. Nestled on the corner of Sol and Cruz, the St Germain is a bright neighborhood place with down-to-earth service, interesting clientele and a distinct European feel. Perfect for lunch, a light dinner or Sunday brunch. Crepes and wine feature for Sunday dinner.

Marmalade FUSION $$
(Map p52; ☎787-724-3969; 317 Fortaleza; dishes $16-29; ⌚6pm-11pm Sun-Thu, 6pm-midnight Fri & Sat; ✎) Promoted as SoFo's best culinary innovator in a street full of them, this starkly minimalist eating establishment is decked out like the Korova Milk Bar in Stanley Kubrick's *A Clockwork Orange*. Step inside the trendy interior to sample house specialties such as paella bites or grilled pears with Parma ham.

Trois Cent Onze FRENCH $$
(Map p52; ☎787-725-7959; 311 Fortaleza; dishes $24-35; ⌚dinner daily, lunch Fri & Sun) With its well-established French connection, 311 has the words 'elegant,' 'refined' and 'sophisticated' written all over it, conjuring up classy European cuisine without too many of those Latino-fusion makeovers (alas, no *mofongo* with a camembert twist here). Glide into one of the island's most romantic interiors, awash with billowing white curtains, flickering candles and delightful Moorish-Andalusian tiles, and order from a menu replete with scallops, duck and foie gras. Not surprisingly, there's a wine list to rival anything in France.

Aguaviva SEAFOOD $$
(Map p52; ☎787-722-0665; 364 Fortaleza; dishes $17-34; ⌚lunch Fri-Sun in season, dinner daily) Seviche's the word at Aguaviva, a trendy SoFo restaurant owned by the same company as Dragonfly and the Parrot Club. It's designed with an arty water/sea-life theme – all turquoise blues and brilliant whites. The house specialty is seafood, in particular the seviche, with plenty of patrons rolling in just to savor an appetizer with a pre-dinner cocktail. Everything from the open-view kitchen to the catwalk clientele is slavishly stylish. But the real test is the food: fresh oysters, lobster yucca gnocchi and swordfish steak *frites* with wild mushrooms.

El Picoteo SPANISH $$
(Map p52; Gran Hotel El Convento, 100 Calle del Cristo; tapas $10-20; ⌚lunch & dinner) One of El Convento's culinary highlights is this terrace tapas bar – suspended above the hotel's central courtyard – that could rival anything in Andalusia. Perennial favorites include tortilla, meatballs, garlic prawns, garbanzos and various cheeses. If you're after something more substantial there's also pizza and paella washed down with sangria. The ambience at Picoteo is terrific and, during the afternoon, the canned music is punctuated with the familiar clack of dominos.

Patio del Nispero INTERNATIONAL $$
(Map p52; Gran Hotel El Convento, 100 Calle del Cristo; sandwiches $12-17, platters $13-24; ⌚breakfast & lunch) Every great Spanish colonial hotel has its shady courtyard and the one at El Convento is the home of the deliciously cool Patio de Nispero, so named for the 350-year-old Nispero tree that resides in its midst. You can enjoy breakfast and lunch here or, even better, escape the hot sun-bleached streets to savor a coffee or an icy mojito during the lazy siesta hour.

Café Berlin INTERNATIONAL $$
(Map p52; 407 San Francisco; dishes $13-22; ⌚10am-10pm Sun-Thu, 10am-11pm Fri & Sat; ☎✎) You've probably heard about the Taíno, the Spanish, the French and the Americans, but the German influence in Puerto Rico is less well documented, unless you wind up sampling sweet pastries on the pleasant terrace here. In a setting that's more Viennese than Caribbean, the Café Berlin serves fresh European-style food with a strong vegetarian/vegan bias. Check out the veggie pizza, the tofu done any which way you want and don't leave without ordering a manjito (a mango-flavored mojito). The sweet Teutonic desserts are positively sinful and the fresh breads melt in your mouth.

La Fonda El Jibarito PUERTO RICAN $
(Map p52; 280 Sol; dishes $9-23; ⌚11am-9pm) Welcome to the neighborhood, *hermano* (brother). El Jibarito is the kind of salt-of-the-earth, unpretentious place that you should reserve to sample your first *mofongo* (mashed plantains) or *arroz con habichue-*

LATIN FUSION IN OLD SAN JUAN

While Old San Juan is well known for its historic Spanish forts and atmospheric cobbled plazas, few outsiders arrive expecting to find a clutch of cutting-edge gourmet restaurants shoehorned in among the quaint 16th-century facades. But hidden inside one of America's oldest urban quarters, streets that once played host to cutlass-brandishing pirates are now the preserve of knife-wielding chefs. San Juan's culinary nexus is situated in the compact neighborhood of **SoFo** (an acronym for 'South Fortaleza St'), a trendy but constantly changing strip of funky wine bars and dimly lit restaurants that has sent many a holidaying food critic home happy. Small, cozy and architecturally interesting, these engaging eating establishments are famous for their Latin-fusion cuisine, an eclectic mix of traditional Latin American ingredients such as rice, beans, pork and plantains, blended with more exotic flavors from Asia, Europe and beyond.

las (rice and beans). A favorite of local families, in-the-know tourists and passing *New York Times* journalists, the meals are simple but hearty, with good pork and prawns, or plantains smashed, mashed and fried just about any way you want. Pull up a seat and chow with the locals.

Barú FUSION **$$**
(Map p52; 150 San Sebastián; dishes $14-28; ⏲6pm-midnight) Very popular with foodies and martini drinkers, trendy Barú mixes it up with the artful use of ingredients such as passion fruit, mango and yams. Dishes include 'yuccafongo' (yucca made like a *mofongo*) with shrimp, pork ribs with ginger tamarind sauce and risotto with shitakes and goat cheese.

La Madre MEXICAN **$$**
(Map p52; 351 San Francisco; mains $15-26; ⏲dinner) Duck quesadilla with wild mushrooms and guacamole? Tuna steak with refried beans? *¿Por qué no?* A sophisticated take on 'modern Mexican,' this hip new restaurant and lounge serves Mexican ingredients with a gourmet twist, as well as delectable margaritas in a rainbow of flavors, including *parcha* (passion fruit), acerola (cherry) and tamarind. The sensory overload continues with tactile frescos, Friday- and Saturday-night DJs, and the occasional wall-projected movie.

Tantra INDIAN **$$**
(Map p52; 356 Fortaleza; dishes $16-23; ⏲noon-1am; 🍸) For purists, eating Masala Dosa in Puerto Rico is probably about as incongruous as chomping on *mofongo* in Madras, but for those willing to drop the cultural blinkers, Tantra's adventurous 'Indo-Latin fusion' cuisine is actually rather authentic. It helps that the chef's from South India. It also helps that the restaurant's Asian-inspired decor, which places exotic lampshades among carved Buddhas, sets your taste buds traveling inexorably east. The pièce de résistance is the belly dancing that kicks off at nine-ish on weekends.

Dragonfly FUSION **$$**
(Map p52; Fortaleza; dishes $14-25; ⏲6-11pm Sun-Wed, 6pm-midnight Thu-Sat) Duck nachos – say no more! One of SoFo's most stylish culinary innovators, this hotspot of Latin-Asian fusion brims nightly with a plethora of self-assured, well-dressed and, frankly, beautiful people. After surviving the shock of your initial entrance (the place resembles a dark, red bordello – all dim lampshades and decorative mirrors), follow up with a hard-hitting Dragon Punch cocktail before you dive into a menu awash with the wonderful and the plain weird (yes, those duck nachos).

La Bombonera PUERTO RICAN **$**
(Map p52; 259 San Francisco; mains $8-16; ⏲7:30am-6pm) The old-fashioned coffee machine hisses like a steam engine, career waiters in black trousers appear like royal footmen at your table, and a long line of seen-it-all *sanjuaneros* (people from San Juan) populate the lengthy row of barstools, catching up on the local breakfast gossip. It shouldn't take you long to work out that La Bombonera is a city institution: it's been around since 1902 and still sells some of the best *pan de mallorca* (sweet bread) in town. Come here for breakfast, lunch or an early-evening snack attack and soak up the unique Latin ambience over a copy of the *Puerto Rico Daily Sun*.

Parrot Club CARIBBEAN **$$**
(Map p52; 363 Fortaleza; dishes $17-28; ⏲lunch & dinner) The menu's in Spanglish, the decor's a lurid mix of orange, blue and yellow, and

DON'T MISS

PERLA

Dine inside a literal architectural oyster at **Perla** (Map p72; ☎787-977-3285; La Concha, 1077 Av Ashford; dishes $22-38; ⏲dinner), where hand-blown glass lamps cast a flattering glow and pearlescent walls undulate and echo into the nighttime sea. The most romantic restaurant in San Juan and the utmost in tropical modernism, this distinctive floating white seashell is a retro stunner. Not surprisingly, aquatic options feature on the menu, though steaks and veggie dishes take a turn. A voluminous wine list (with 30 by the glass) highlights French and Californian selections. Reservations recommended, especially for the coveted window seats.

the waitress could quite conceivably be sporting a pink wig. Welcome to the Parrot Club, where Puerto Rican politicians wind down and enamored gringos live it up. Until the Parrot's opening in 1996, the concept of 'SoFo' didn't even exist. But, with its caustic blend of live jazz and tasty 'nuevo Latino' cuisine, this restaurant quickly set new standards and spawned the ultimate in neighborhood chic – an acronym. Now well into its second decade, the menu continues to win kudos with its eclectic crab cakes *caribeños,* pan-seared shrimp and plantain-crusted dorado.

Café Mallorca PUERTO RICAN **$**

(Map p52; 300 San Francisco; dishes $6-19; ⏲7am-6:30pm) If you spent the previous night in Marmalade or some other haute couture restaurant/club/fashion parade, then bring yourself back down to earth with a lifesaving coffee and breakfast in this cozy nook on San Francisco. Cheap and simple, the Mallorca is where all-night ravers share pick-me-ups and American journalists sift through their travel notes. Zero pretension, but plenty of warm familiarity.

La Mallorquina PUERTO RICAN **$$**

(Map p52; ☎787-722-3261; 207 San Justo; dishes $15-30; ⏲noon-10:30pm Mon-Sat) A must for historically minded food buffs, or food-minded history buffs, La Mallorquina is the grande dame of Old San Juan eateries: it's been around for 150 years, quite a feat in the musical chairs of Fortaleza and its surrounds. It's worth a gander, if only to have a drink at the immense slab of mahogany that is the bar. Should the smells from the kitchen tempt you to stay, try the house specialty, *asopao* (a rice broth stewed with all type of herbs, seafood or meat).

Manolín LUNCH DINER **$**

(Map p52; 253 San Justo; dishes $3-10; ⏲6am-4:30pm Mon-Sat) Elbow in with the local office workers at this snaking counter grill, and fill up on excellent *mofongo* and *churrasco a la parrilla* (skirt steak). Killer air-conditioning hits the spot.

Café Cala'o CAFE **$**

(Map p52; Pier 2; muffins $2.50) It looks just like any other small coffee bar you might roll into in Chicago or Seattle, but in reality Café Cala'o is very different. There are two main reasons for this: the Puerto Rican coffee – which is handpicked from various small farms in the central mountains – is smooth, earthy and not at all bitter, and the people who confect it are trained experts who know as much about coffee as an oenologist knows about wine.

Old San Juan Farmers Market MARKET **$**

(www.mercadoagricolanatural.com; ⏲8am-1pm Sat) Stop by the courtyard of the Museo de San Juan to pick up some organic local produce or coffee, nibble on homemade chocolate, bread or cheese, peruse the handcrafted gifts or tuck into an inexpensive brunch.

Ayurvedics VEGETARIAN **$**

(☎787-721-4369; 304 Fortaleza) Vegetarian self-caterers should made a beeline here – it's one of the best health-food stores on the island.

CONDADO

Pikayo FUSION **$$$**

(Map p60; ☎787-721-6194; Conrad San Juan Condado Plaza, 999 Av Ashford; dishes $30-42; ⏲dinner) Wilo Benet is the island's very own Gordon Ramsay (without the expletives), a celebrity chef par excellence who has uncovered the soul of Caribbean cooking by infusing colonial-era Puerto Rican cuisine with various African and Indian elements. Benet's showcase restaurant, recently relocated to the sleek Conrad hotel, continues to be a splurge-worthy delight.

José José SPANISH **$$$**

(Map p72; ☎787-725-8496; 1110 Magdalena; dishes $22-37; ⏲lunch Tue-Sun, dinner Tue-Fri & Sun)

From the Basque Country's San Sebastián, Chef José Abreu crafts somewhat complicated dishes (think liquid nitrogen, sous-vide vacuum cooking and some serious thought to textures) that you're unlikely to attempt at home. Use the menu as a crutch, or tell the kitchen what ingredients you crave and the chef will improvise a creative custom-made tasting menu. Recent dishes include crabmeat and lobster ravioli with vanilla oil, and pork loin with eggplant caviar and Thai essence.

Via Appia ITALIAN **$**
(Map p72; 1350 Av Ashford; pizzas $8-18; ⏲11am-11pm) The good thing about Condado is that it still retains a smattering of family-run jewels among all the Starbucks and 7-Elevens. Via Appia is one such gem, a no-nonsense Italian restaurant where the pizza is classic and the gentlemanly waiters could quite conceivably have walked off the set of *The Godfather*. Munch on garlic bread or feast on meatballs alfresco, as the multilingual mélange of Av Ashford goes strolling by.

Picachos Café VEGETARIAN **$**
(Map p72; 1020 Av Ashford; dishes $7-11; ⏲8am-7pm Mon-Sat;) Vegetarians, give yourself a pinch. Though not exclusively meat-free, this new out-of-the-way organic cafe serves delicious options such as homemade pastas, natural yogurts and tempting desserts in addition to its signature hot and cold coffee drinks.

Hacienda Don José MEXICAN, PUERTO RICAN **$**
(Map p72; 1025 Av Ashford; dishes $5-22; ⏲8am-10pm Mon-Thu, 8am-11pm Fri & Sat) Condado on the cheap – it can still be done. Indeed, the Don José is more redolent of a Mexican beach bar than a plush tourist trap. Waves lash against the rocks within spitting distance of your pancakes and huevos rancheros, and busy waitresses shimmy around the tiled tables and colorful murals. If your swanky hotel's all-you-can-eat breakfast buffet has worn you out, drop by here for a little bit of local hospitality.

OCEAN PARK

Kasalta's CAFE **$**
(Map p60; 1966 McLeary; sandwiches $5-10, dishes $9-24; ⏲6am-10pm) Wake up with a jolt at Kasalta's, a popular early-morning breakfast haunt tucked into Ocean Park's residential enclave. It's the sort of authentic Puerto Rican bakery and diner that you'll find yourself crossing town to visit daily; the coffee here is as legendary as the sweets that fill a long glass display case and encapsulate everything from Danish pastries to iced buns. Plentiful seating, myriad newspapers and a buzzing local ambience add even more icing to the cake.

Niche INTERNATIONAL **$$$**
(Map p60; ☎787-268-2803; Acacia Seaside Inn, 8 Taft; dinner $24-38; ⏲breakfast Mon-Sat, dinner Wed-Mon) A neighborhood favorite, this super-intimate space inside the Acacia Seaside Inn oozes atmosphere. Little windows in the floor peek through to show water from the underground cistern, and with the wave-shaped banquette seating it feels like you're in a speakeasy under the sea. The emphasis is on fresh local seafood, with dishes such as mahimahi seviche and an award-winning lobster risotto. Serves Sunday brunch too.

Pamela's SEAFOOD **$$**
(Map p60; ☎787-726-5010; Numero Uno, 1 Santa Ana; dishes $16-34; ⏲lunch & dinner) Right on the beach and right on the money, Pamela's is encased inside the elegant Numero Uno guesthouse. Diners sup wine and munch on scallops beside a teardrop-shaped swimming pool while the ocean crashes just feet away. The menu specializes in fresh ingredients plucked from the nearby sea – think jalapeño-ginger shrimp and seafood chowder – though there are surprise twists with everything from Asian to Puerto Rican influences. The place is tucked away, but that hasn't prevented it from becoming an open secret. Reserve ahead.

Che's STEAK HOUSE **$$**
(Map p60; dishes $16-29; ⏲lunch & dinner) Che T-shirts aren't too common in Puerto Rico, where the man who promised to 'create two, three...many Vietnams' in the Americas is regarded with a certain degree of suspicion. That said, you might see the odd red-starred beret in here tucking into *churrasco* and *parrillada* (grilled, marinated steak), or veal chops with a kind of revolutionary zeal. Generally considered to be the best Argentinean food around, Che's is popular with *sanjuaneros* and expats of all political persuasions, who allow themselves to be united momentarily by a bloody good steak.

La B de Burro MEXICAN **$**
(Map p60; 2000 McLeary; dishes $4-10; ⏲11am-10pm, to 9pm Sun) You don't need a mask, tights and cape to sample the best burritos in the Caribbean, but you'd fit right in. A

popular hangout pumping out hearty chimichangas, a cool soundtrack and Old Harbor brew on tap, this funky *lucha libre* (free wrestling)–themed *taqueria* (taco shop) sports a purple wrestling-ring patio, Mexican altars and a ceiling full of *papel picado* streamers. Local kids plant and tend seedlings outside.

TOP CHOICE **Café Mam** VEGETARIAN **$**
(Map p60; 1958 McLeary, Suite 103; dishes $4-7; ⌚10am-7pm Mon-Sat;) Inside the post office parking lot beside Kasalta's, the welcoming community center and cafe of Mujeres Ayudando Madres (Women Helping Mothers) offers tasty and affordable options to support healthy families and pregnant women. Let the little ones run and play while you recharge with freshly made juices, coconut milk shakes, and hearty vegetarian (and vegan) dishes such as a 'fruity burger' – a lentil burger topped with mango sauce, avocado and papaya – or a tofu and hummus wrap.

ISLA VERDE

Metropol SPANISH **$$**
(Map p74; Av Isla Verde; dishes $11-27; ⌚dinner) You can't miss this place – it's right next to the cockfighting arena. It's a neighborhood favorite well known for the plentiful portions and simple (but not plain) Spanish fare. Wandering tourists are sometimes lured out of their upscale resorts and into its inviting fold.

Casa Dante PUERTO RICAN **$$**
(Map p74; 39 Av Isla Verde; dishes $10-26; ⌚lunch & dinner) Casa Dante is a family-run restaurant that serves more variations of *mofongo* than one would think humanly feasible. All are delicious, and you can stick to fajitas, pasta or a basic steak if that's what you prefer.

Il Nonno ITALIAN **$$**
(Map p74; 41 Av Isla Verde; dishes $15-36; ⌚lunch & dinner) A white-tablecloth choice that strikes the right balance between excellent food and reasonable prices, 'the Grandfather' has solicitous service and a pleasant dining room with an old-world feel. A respectable wine list pairs well with dishes such as tortellini with prosciutto and porcini mushrooms or veal shank with saffron risotto.

Don José Café PUERTO RICAN **$**
(Map p74; 6475 Av Isla Verde Km 6.3; dishes $4-18; ⌚24hr) No frills, no formalities, but good food – and it's open 24 hours, though you'd think it wasn't operating at all looking at the heavily tinted windows. Come here for breakfast after one of those exuberant all-night parties and nip your hangover in the bud with two fried eggs, bacon and ham washed down with a strong cup of coffee.

Drinking

Near the UPR campus in Río Piedras, Av Universidad is worth a wander for its many student-oriented bars.

OLD SAN JUAN

Old Harbor Brewery BREWERY
(Map p52; 202 Tizol; ⌚11:30am-1am) Yes beer fans, life does exist beyond Medalla. The only microbrewery on the island, Old Harbor concocts a handful of excellent varieties, including a Coquí lager, the Kofresí stout, a rotating seasonal variety and a 9% double bock brewed for Christmas. Dine on upscale pub fare amid the gleaming copper kettles, or round up a few friends to drain a 64-ounce beer tower. In the 1920s, the building housed the New York Federal Bank. Spent grains become animal feed at local farms or get processed into biofuel.

TOP CHOICE **Rivera Hermanos Cash & Carry** BAR
(Map p52; 157 San Sebastián; ⌚11am-midnight Mon-Sat) A 35-year-old institution run by two Rivera sisters (who didn't bother to change the sign), this cavernous liquor warehouse is a vibrant community hangout for local artists, intellectuals and students, where live salsa and *boleros* (ballads) fill the evenings, and local poets recite to longtime patrons over cheapo Medallas and inexpensive bottles of wine. You can even borrow an instrument for one of the frequent pick-up jam sessions.

Los Cuernos BAR
(Map p52; San Sebastián; ⌚10:30am-midnight, to 3am Fri & Sat) Wedge your way into this long packed bar, where students and young hipsters socialize under a wall of Puerto Rican masks and scribbled-on international banknotes. The draw here is the flavored *chichaítos,* an inexpensive Puerto Rican favorite of rum and anise liquor, available at $1 per shot or $6 for a *caneca de sabores* (premixed flask-sized bottle). It's tasty, sweet and decidedly strong, and you have a choice of 25 flavors, including passion fruit, coconut and ginger.

Taberna Lúpulo BAR
(Map p52; 200 Sol; ⌚noon-late;) The passionate owners of this new craft beer bar,

which serves more than 20 artisan brews on tap (and over 100 in the bottle), rhapsodize about Trappist ales while dishing out beer-infused Puerto Rican comfort food such as a drunken bean soup or bacon-stuffed burger braised with brown ale. Local art students take turns gussying up the interior.

Blend BAR
(Map p52; 309 Fortaleza; ⌚6pm-late) Think dressy, uberchic – and on weekend evenings, uberbusy. Cocooned in an old colonial building on Fortaleza, this fashionable dining and nightlife spot belts out electronic music from Friday to Sunday in its cavernous and moodily lit interior.

El Batey BAR
(Map p52; 101 Calle del Cristo; ⌚11am-7am) If Hunter S Thompson were still alive and living in Puerto Rico, this is where you'd probably find him. Cool, crusty and unashamedly bohemian, the walls of this cavernous drinking joint are covered in graffiti, while the low-key lighting will have you groping in your pockets for spare change to light up the suitably retro jukebox. Across the road from the exquisite El Convento Hotel, El Batey is a place to down shots, shoot pool and ramble soulfully about when Elvis was king and the Bacardí bottles still came from Cuba. There's no phone, but a helpful soul drew one on the wall.

CONDADO, OCEAN PARK & ISLA VERDE

La Concha BAR
(Map p72; 1077 Av Ashford, Condado) Take your rightful place with the beautiful people at the undisputed hot spot of San Juan. On weekend nights, the lobby bar explodes with activity and chic cocktail-bearing waitresses in space-age outfits and wedge heels do their best to swivel through. Things get progressively wilder as the night turns to morning, with dancing to DJs and live music.

Pa'l Cielo BAR
(Map p60; 2056 Loiza, Ocean Park; ⌚5pm-2am Wed-Sun) Caribbean kitsch rules at this bohemian bar modeled after a rural roadside food shack. Dolled up in colored lights, with artsy little *altares* and tropical murals, its funky mismatched tables get pushed aside after midnight for DJs or live salsa, reggae and hip-hop.

Café La Plage BAR
(Map p74; 4851 Av Isla Verde, Isla Verde; ⌚noon-midnight Sun-Wed, noon-late Thu-Sat) Cozy up in a bed on the beach, comb the sand with your toes and make bedroom eyes from behind a flavored mojito. Secreted behind the Beach House Hotel, this palm-shaded lounge has a stylish yet relaxed vibe, with live jazz Thursday nights and lounge sounds Friday and Saturday.

Water & Beach Club BAR
(Map p74; 2 Calle Tartak) The soon-to-be-renamed lounges situated in Isla Verde's Water & Beach Club are popularly considered to be two of San Juan's most esteemed watering holes, where San Juan's well-heeled and the well-endowed come to swap email addresses. One dominates the swank roof space – due to reopen soon after an extensive remodel – and the other is located off the chic white-on-white ground-floor lobby. They're interconnected by a space-age elevator decorated rather surreally with its own water feature.

SANTURCE

Tia Maria's GAY BAR
(Map p60; 326 Av José de Diego; ⌚11am-3am) She admits to being almost 30, though the boys who pack Tia Maria's are aged across the spectrum and turn up from all over the island for the cheap drinks, good company and perhaps a game of pool. Tuesday-night karaoke.

San Juan Eagle GAY BAR
(Map p60; www.eaglepuertorico.com; 1204 Av Ponce de León; P) Bust out (or out of) those chaps! The men of Puerto Rico have anxiously awaited this brand-new addition to the popular Eagle leather bar franchise.

☆ Entertainment

Old San Juan is the center of the city's nightlife, hosting what is popularly considered to be the hottest and hippest entertainment scene in the Caribbean. Walk the aesthetic streets of the historical quarter after dark and you'll encounter scores of people striding the cobblestoned streets (and sometimes hugging the curbs). For a condensed late-night scene, hit the bars of San Sebastián or the trendy restaurant and cocktail lounges of SoFo's Fortaleza.

Beyond the old town, there's usually action at the major resort hotels, particularly Condado's La Concha and Isla Verde's El San Juan. The gay nightlife scene has mostly migrated to grittier Santurce, where there's a cluster of activity along the Av Ponce de León corridor between Condado

FEAR & LOATHING IN SAN JUAN

Long before *Fear and Loathing in Las Vegas* and the sharp, stylized prose that gave birth to 'Gonzo' journalism, US writer Hunter S Thompson earned a meager living as a scribe for a fledgling Puerto Rican English-language weekly called *El Sportivo*, based in San Juan.

Thompson first arrived in the Puerto Rican capital in 1960 on the cusp of an unprecedented tourist boom. With the Americans recently ushered out of Cuba by a belligerent Fidel Castro, the rum party had moved defiantly east as corrupt businessmen and nascent tour companies attempted to re-create the tawdry nightlife and glitzy casinos that had once run rampant in Havana.

Attracted raucously into the melee, Thompson lapped up the louche bars with hungry relish. To finance his Caribbean sojourn he vied for a job with the (now defunct) *San Juan Star*, a newspaper then edited by subsequent Pulitzer Prize winner William Kennedy (author of the novel *Ironweed*) but, after being passed over in favor of more reliable fodder, he set his sights dangerously lower. For the literary world, it was a fortuitous demotion. Money was tight but rum mysteriously abundant in 1960s San Juan and, while many of Thompson's experiences quickly evaporated in back-to-back drinking binges, the essence of the era was later to emerge rather dramatically in his seminal book, *The Rum Diary*. Published in 1998 (nearly 40 years after it was written), the novel is a thinly veiled account of Thompson's alcohol-fuelled journalistic exploits as seen through the eyes of Paul Kemp, a struggling freelance writer caught in a Caribbean boomtown that was battling against an incoming tide of rich American tourists. Kemp, rather like Thompson, was a young chancer, eager to make his mark in a city that was getting its first insight into the decadence and depravity of the American Dream. Transfixed and reviled in equal measure, he regularly plied the streets of Old San Juan drinking rum for breakfast and gate-crashing free press parties for lunch.

However, built on precarious foundations, Thompson's Puerto Rican honeymoon didn't last. The writer left San Juan nine months after he arrived and made tracks for America's west coast. His characteristically manic *Rum Diary* scribblings, released 40 years later, offer a rare glimpse of an island at an important turning point in its history and a snapshot of a journalistic genius in the making. Hailed today as a modern classic, the book has been made into a Hollywood movie starring Johnny Depp, due for release in 2011.

and Av José de León. Consider a taxi if you're going solo.

Live Music

A number of the resort hotels have live music in their lobbies, usually on weekends. Try the El San Juan or the San Juan Marriott Resort in Condado for salsa and merengue bands, and dancing from 8pm until late.

Nuyorican Café LIVE MUSIC
(Map p52; www.nuyoricancafepr.com; 312 San Francisco, Old San Juan; ⌚8pm-late) If you came to Puerto Rico in search of authentic salsa music, the legend still lives on at the Nuyorican Café. San Juan's hottest nightspot – stuffed into an alley off Fortaleza, opposite a nameless drinking hole – is a congenial hub of live Latino sounds and hip-gyrating locals that easily emulates its famous New York namesake. You get everything from poetry readings to six-piece salsa bands that squish onto the stage here. And you'll meet people too – the Nuyorican is refreshingly devoid of pretensions or dance snobbery. Things usually get interesting around 11pm.

Nuestro Son LIVE MUSIC
(Map p52; 259 Tetuán, Old San Juan; ⌚6pm-late) You'll hear it before you see it, so follow your ears to this loud and proud dive bar and live-music-venue club concealed on a darkened backstreet. The crowd's local, the cover's always cheap, and the fervent sounds of rock, bossa nova, *bomba* and *trova* – '*anything* but reggaetón' – propel you through the door.

Coliseo de Puerto Rico LIVE MUSIC
(www.coliseodepuertorico.com; 500 Arterial B, Hato Rey) Across the street from the Hato Rey Tren Urbano station, this

18,000-capacity arena books musical superstars from Iron Maiden to Marc Anthony.

Dance Clubs

Latin Roots DANCE HALL

(Map p52; www.thelatinroots.com; Comercio, Old San Juan; admission $5-10 Thu-Sat; ⏲6pm-2am Thu-Sat, 6pm-midnight Mon-Wed, 2pm-midnight Sun) Salseros, need a fix? The Latin Roots is the closest you'll get to 24/7 salsa, with free lessons from 6pm to 10pm daily and live bands every night from 8pm (2pm and 6pm on Sundays). It's also a popular Puerto Rican restaurant; you'll find a lively mix of locals and tourists swiveling on the dancefloor.

Club Brava NIGHTCLUB

(Map p74; www.bravapr.com; El San Juan Hotel & Casino, 6063 Av Isla Verde, Isla Verde; admission $10-20; ⏲10pm-late Thu-Sat) A swinging club inside the El San Juan Hotel, Brava frequently get breathless reviews from celeb spotters and all-night dance fanatics. The two-level interior is small, and the music a mix of dance, reggaetón and salsa. The atmosphere's electric and the people-watching possibilities in the lobby beforehand strangely voyeuristic. Dress up, bring your credit card and get ready to jive to what is touted as the best sound system in the Caribbean. Thursday and Friday are 21+; Saturday 23 and over.

El San Juan Hotel Lobby HOTEL

(El San Juan Hotel & Casino, 6063 Av Isla Verde, Isla Verde; ⏲8pm-2am Thu-Sat) If you want to dance but discos aren't your style, try the salsa and merengue bands here. Professional dancers move among the crowd getting everyone in motion. Live music adds to the fun.

Krash GAY NIGHTCLUB

(Map p60; 1257 Av Ponce de León, Santurce; admission $6-10; ⏲10pm-late Wed-Sat) Hot dancing is de rigueur and theme nights are the staple here. DJs shake the house with the latest club sounds from LA, New York and beyond.

Circo Bar GAY NIGHTCLUB

(Map p60; 650 Condado, Santurce; admission free; ⏲9pm-late; P) Primarily a video bar from Sunday through Wednesday – with a karaoke detour on Thursdays – this place gets sweaty and snug on weekends, when high-energy dancing gets everyone up close and personal. Amid the flashing TV screens you'll find a youngish male crowd wriggling to hip-hop or chilling out on the walk-through smoking patio.

Starz GAY NIGHTCLUB

(Map p60; 365 Av José de Diego, Santurce; admission $5; ⏲10pm-late Sat) Meet some new friends across the street at popular **Tia Maria's** and then boogie the night away at this exuberant mostly male discotheque. DJs spin disco, trance, techno and house sounds, pausing for a 3am drag show.

Club Lázer NIGHTCLUB

(Map p52; 251 Cruz, Old San Juan; ⏲10pm-late) It's been around for a while and it's still a big draw, with three levels to wander and laser lights slicing across the dancefloor. The music tends toward reggaetón and hip-hop, with things heating up by midnight. Strippers (male and female) set the tone on Saturday nights.

Classical Music, Opera & Ballet

El Centro de Bellas Artes Luis A Ferré THEATER

(Bellas Artes; Map p60; ☎787-620-4444; www.cba.gobierno.pr; Av Ponce de León, Parada 22½, Santurce) Built in 1981 in Santurce, this center has more than 1800 seats in the festival hall, about 700 in the drama hall and 200 in the experimental theater. The three concert halls fill when the Puerto Rican Symphony Orchestra holds one of its weekly winter performances. International stars also perform here, and it's the major host to the annual Festival Casals. In 2009, the complex completed the new 1300-seat Pablo Casals Symphony Hall.

Theater

Teatro Tapia THEATER

(Map p52; ☎787-480-5000; Plaza de Colón, Old San Juan; tickets $10-30) Something of a city emblem, the Teatro Tapia on the south side of Plaza Colón is an intimate neoclassical theater designed in the Italian style with three-tiered boxes and an elegantly decorated lobby. Dating from 1832 and named after the so-called Father of Puerto Rican literature, Alejandro Tapia y Rivera, the building has long acted as a nexus for the island's rich cultural life and has hosted big names in opera, stage and ballet from around the world. The theater was restored extensively in 1949 and then again in 1976, 1997 and 2007. Experts today rate it as the oldest freestanding drama stage in the US and its territories.

The Tapia's contemporary performances are usually in Spanish and frequently feature new works from Spain or Latin America. The acting is professional and performances attract Puerto Rico's literati and social elite.

Cinemas

Movie theaters can be found in most of San Juan's major shopping centers. Check www.caribbeancinemas.com for most theaters and showtimes islandwide. Be sure to ask someone you trust whether the movie house is in a safe area before you go wandering around its locale after dark. The average cost of a cinema ticket is adult/child/senior $6.75/4/4.

Fine Arts Café CINEMA
(☎787-765-2339; Popular Center, Torre Norte, Hato Rey) With Miramar's Fine Arts Cinema closed for remodeling, this is the island's only true art-house cinema, showing a good selection of independent films from around the world. It's across from the Hato Rey Tren Urbano station.

Plaza Las Américas Cinema CINEMA
(☎787-767-4775; Plaza Las Américas, Hato Rey) In the Hato Rey district, this 13-screen multiplex is very popular.

Cine Metro CINEMA
(Map p60; ☎787-722-0465; Parada 18, 1255 Av Ponce de León, Santurce) This classic, restored cinema is in Santurce, edging towards Miramar.

Movie buffs should refer to p70 for information on the city's annual cinema festival.

Casinos

Although it may not be Vegas, San Juan has certainly developed a reputation for being Las Vegas-on-sea, a mantle it stole from Havana when Castro threw the mob and their gambling syndicates out of Cuba in 1959. As a result a lot of travelers and islanders come down here purely for the action. All of San Juan's large resort hotels have casinos, and the gaming houses have now expanded to offer Caribbean Stud Poker, Let It Ride, Pai Gow Poker and the Big Six Wheel, as well as the standard blackjack, roulette, craps, baccarat and minibaccarat. Most of the city's casinos are open between noon and 4pm, and 8pm and 4am, though a few are 24-hour.

Sports

Home of the Montreal Expos in 2003 and 2004, **Hiram Bithorn Stadium** (Map p48; Plaza Las Américas, Av Roosevelt) is a small ball park and home to the San Juan Senadores (www.senadoresbaseball.com). It's named after the first Puerto Rican to play in the majors.

The **Roberto Clemente Coliseum** (Map p48; ☎787-754-7422; Roosevelt Ave) is another big sports arena. Come here to see the resident Gigantes de Carolina baseball and soccer teams.

Shopping

Popular Puerto Rican souvenirs include *santos* crafts, domino sets, cigars, rum and coffee. The best arts and crafts shopping is in Old San Juan, though most of the schlocky T-shirt shops are there too. San Francisco and Fortaleza are the two main arteries in and out of the old city, and both are packed cheek-by-jowl with shops. Running perpendicular at the west end of the town, Calle del Cristo is home to many of the old city's chicest establishments.

Worth looking out for are the jewelry shop and gallery of **Bóveda** (Map p52; 200 Calle del Cristo; ⌚10am-6pm) and **Butterfly People** (Map p52; 257 Cruz; ⌚11am-6pm Sat-Thu), where you'll find unusual art incorporating insects. Cigar fans interested in the craft should stop by the open storefront of **Cigarros Antillas** (Map p52; ⌚9am-5pm) to see workers roll by hand.

Artisans Fair MARKET
(Map p52; Plaza de La Dársena) Head here for more traditional arts and crafts offerings. It's generally open whenever there's a cruise ship in port.

Mercado de Río Piedras MARKET
(Paseo de Diego, Río Piedras) Of course, there's also the market for produce, meats and bargain clothing; see p63.

Plaza Las Américas MALL
(⌚9am-9pm Mon-Sat, 11am-7pm Sun) The Caribbean's largest shopping mall has 300 stores and is situated in Hato Rey.

Plaza Carolina MALL
(off Hwy 26; ⌚9am-9pm Mon-Sat, 11am-6pm Sun) Offers US standards such as JC Penney and Sears among its 240 shops; it's east of the city off Hwy 26 (Expreso Baldorioty de Castro) in Carolina.

Borders BOOKS
(☎787-777-0916; Plaza Las Américas, 525 Av FD Roosevelt, Hato Rey) A large selection of mostly English-language books, plus a cafe.

LA PLACITA DE SANTURCE

Revitalized after an injection of municipal funds, the once dilapidated **Santurce marketplace** (Map p60) rocks just like old times. The show starts not long after dawn when bleary-eyed market traders stock up their permanent stalls with homegrown treats from around the island. There's chayote from Barranquitas, pumpkin from Coamo, pineapple from Lajas, and mango from Mayagüez – all glowing colorful, tasty and fresh in the morning sun.

Materializing mid-morning, inquisitive shoppers arrive en masse to finger and bag the best produce, before sitting down for a hearty lunch in one of the square's many family-run cafes.

At 5pm, with the market winding down for the evening, the square undergoes a heady transformation, particularly on Fridays. Still dressed in their smart work attire, groups of exhausted office clerks roll in to drink, chat, de-stress and unwind. As the myriad bars fill up, ties are loosened, a salsa band lets rip from a makeshift stage, and a bright and infectious energy infiltrates the humid yet congenial surroundings. It doesn't take long for the dancing to start. A shimmy here, a holler there, and suddenly the whole square is alive with inebriated marketing reps kicking off their high heels and slick-haired business analysts salsa-ing like repressed Ricky Martins into the morning light. Come 6am and there's little left, save for a handful of all-night revelers nursing premature hangovers and the familiar clatter of early-morning traders setting out their wares for another day of business.

Information

Dangers & Annoyances

Safety-wise, San Juan is comparable with any other big city in the mainland US. Though you'll hear stories of robberies, drugs and carjackings, the worst most visitors will face is tripping up over an uneven paving stone on the way back from the local bar. Take all the usual precautions and you'll minimize any risk of trouble.

Don't leave your belongings unguarded on the beach, don't leave your car unlocked and don't wander around after dark in deserted inner-city areas or on unpoliced beaches. Areas to avoid at night include La Perla, Puerta de Tierra, parts of Santurce (especially around Calle Loíza) and the Plaza del Mercado in Río Piedras.

Old San Juan is relatively safe and well policed. However, visitors are not encouraged to enter the picturesque yet poverty-stricken enclave of La Perla just outside the north wall at any time of day or night without a local escort.

Emergency

You may find that the telephone directory and tourist publications list nonfunctioning local numbers for emergency services. In *any* kind of emergency, call ☎911.

Hurricane warnings (☎787-253-4586; www.nhc.noaa.gov)

Medical emergencies (☎787-754-2550)

Rape crisis hotline (☎800-981-5721, 787-765-2285)

Tourist zone police (☎911, 787-726-7020; ⌚24hr) English spoken.

Internet Access

Internet cafes are hard to come by, but most lodgings have wi-fi. A number of plazas in Old San Juan have free hot spots.

Cybernet Café Condado (1128 Av Ashford; ⌚9am-10pm Mon-Sat, 10:30am-10pm Sun; per hr $9); Isla Verde (5980 Av Isla Verde; ⌚10am-10pm Mon-Sat, 6-10pm Sun; per hr $9)

Diner's Internet (311 Tetuán, Old San Juan; per hr $5)

Seafarers' House (161 O'Donnel; ⌚10am-7pm Mon-Wed, Thu & Fri 10-6pm, 10am-9pm Sun; $5.50 per hr) Longer hours when cruise ships in port.

Laundry

Condado Cleaners (63 Condado) Promises a fast turnaround, and delivers too.

Medical Services

Ashford Presbyterian Community Hospital (☎787-721-2160; 1451 Av Ashford) This is probably the best-equipped and most convenient hospital for travelers to visit.

Walgreens Old San Juan (cnr Cruz & San Francisco); Condado (1130 Av Ashford; ⌚24hr) US drugstore chains including Walgreens are all over the city.

Money

Banco Popular Old San Juan (cnr Tetuán & San Justo) Near the cruise ship piers and Paseo de la Princesa; Condado (1060 Av Ashford); Isla Verde (Av Isla Verde) Charges no commission to cash up to $300 in traveler's checks.

Post

Old San Juan Post Office (Map p52; 100 Paseo de Colón; ⌚8am-4pm Mon-Fri, 8am-noon Sat) The one likely to be most convenient for travelers.

Tourist Information

The Puerto Rico Tourism Company distributes information in English and Spanish at two venues in San Juan, the LMM airport (Terminal C) and near the cruise ship terminal in Old San Juan.

Puerto Rico Tourism Company (PRTC; ☎800-223-6530, 787-721-2400; www.seepuertorico.com); LMM airport (☎787-791-1014; ⌚9am-8pm); Old San Juan (Map p52; ☎787-722-1709; Edificio Ochoa, 500 Tanca; ⌚8:30am-8pm Mon-Wed & Sat, 8:30am-5:30pm Thu, 8:30am-6:30pm Fri, 9am-8pm Sun)

Getting There & Away

Air

International flights arrive at and depart from Luis Muñoz Marín International Airport (LMM airport), which is about 8 miles east of the old city center. See p289 for information on airport services and international carriers that fly to San Juan.

Several airlines provide services between San Juan and other parts of the commonwealth. Private aircraft, charter services and many of the commuter flights serving the islands of Culebra and Vieques arrive at and depart from San Juan's original Aeropuerto de Isla Grande, on the Bahía de San Juan in the city's Miramar district. See p291 for details.

Cruise Ship

More than a dozen cruise lines include San Juan on their Caribbean itineraries, and as the second-largest port for cruise ships in the western hemisphere, the city is visited by more than a million cruise-ship passengers a year. All ships dock at the piers along Calle La Marina near the Customs House, just a short walk from the cobblestoned streets of Old San Juan. See p290 for details.

Público

There is no islandwide bus system; públicos form the backbone of public transportation in Puerto Rico and can provide an inexpensive link between San Juan and other points on the island, including Ponce and Mayagüez. For more details see p295.

In San Juan the major público centers include LMM airport, two large público stations in Río Piedras (Centro de Públicos Oeste and Centro de Públicos Este) and – to a lesser extent – Plaza de Colón in Old San Juan. These are the places you should go first if you want to attempt to understand the intricacies of the fun – but sometimes difficult to fathom – público system.

Getting Around

To/From the Airport

The bus is the cheapest option. Look for the 'Parada' sign outside the arrivals concourse at LMM airport. The B40 bus will get you from the airport to Isla Verde or Río Piedras. From Isla Verde you can take bus T5 to Old San Juan and Condado. From Río Piedras you can take bus T9 to Santurce and Old San Juan.

There are also taxi vans at the arrivals concourse. It's a fixed flat fee per carload (printed on the window) of $10 to Isla Verde, $15 to Condado and Ocean Park, and $19 to Old San Juan. Add another dollar for each piece of luggage, and another buck if it's after 10pm.The taxi reps discourage sharing, but you'll save money by finding someone going your way.

Getting to LMM airport from hotels in the San Juan area is easy. Staff at virtually all of the midrange and top-end hotels will arrange for a taxi or airport shuttle van to pick you up in front of your lodging at your request.

Bicycle

San Juan is in the dark ages when it comes to provisions for cyclists. The big operator in the central tourist areas is Rent the Bicycle (p68), but it only has chunky cruiser-style bikes. Rather surprisingly, cyclists can navigate a pleasant and safe cross-city route by following the shoreline from Old San Juan through Condado and Isla Verde as far as Piñones (the last part is on a designated bike lane). There is an additional bike path in Parque Lineal in Hato Rey. Elsewhere, getting in and out of the city by bike is difficult and – given the audacity of drivers – not always advisable.

Bus

The **Autoridad Metropolitana de Autobuses** (AMA; Metropolitan Bus Authority & Metrobus; ☎787-294-0500, ext 514 or 524) has a main bus terminal (Map p52) in Old San Juan near the cruise ship piers. Buses cost 75¢ and run until 10pm. Since the bus companies aren't big on disseminating information, it's almost impossible to track down a current map, and the routes change somewhat frequently, it's a good idea to confirm bus lines with your lodging or a local. These are the routes taken most often by travelers (bus numbers are followed by associated route descriptions):

T5 Old San Juan, Stop 18, Isla Verde (via Loiza)

T9 Old San Juan, Sagrado Corazon (train station), Río Piedras

C10 Sagrado Corazon (train station), Ocean Park (via Loiza), Condado, Stop 18, Isla Grande airport/Convention Center

B21 Old San Juan, Isla Grande airport/Convention Center, Condado, Sagrado Corazon (train station)

B40 Isla Verde, LMM airport, Río Piedras

C53 Old San Juan, Condado, Ocean Park (via McLeary), Isla Verde

In Old San Juan there is a handy free trolley bus that plies routes around the old quarter, with three routes. The trolley starts and finishes a block away from the main bus terminal, toward the piers, but you can get on and off at any one of two dozen designated stops.

Car

If you can avoid driving in the city, by all means, do so. Traffic, parking and the maze of thoroughfares make having, let alone driving, a rental car in the city a challenge.

In Old San Juan, there are two handy parking facilities on Recinto Sur just as you enter town: Covadonga, above the bus station, and Dona Fela, about three blocks further west. Both charge about $1 for the first hour, and 50¢ to 65¢ for additional hours. The town's cheapest lot, **La Puntilla** (787-723-7422), charges about $5 per day.

For access to El Morro or the nightlife of San Sebastián, check out the underground lot (beneath Plaza del Quinto Centenario off Calle Norzagaray) at the upper end of town.

For car rental, both **Avis** (800-331-1212; www.avis.com) and **Hertz** (800-654-3131; www.hertz.com) have offices at LMM airport.

Ferry

The commuter ferries of **Autoridad de Transporte Marítimo** (787-788-1155; per trip $0.50) connect the east and west sides of Bahía de San Juan, Old San Juan and Cataño. In Old San Juan, the ferry dock is at Pier 2, near the tourism office. The ferry runs every 30 minutes from 6am to 9pm.

Metro

The Tren Urbano connects Bayamón with downtown San Juan as far as Sagrado Corazón on the south side of Santurce. Efficient trains run every 10 to 15 minutes in either direction between 5:30am and 11:30pm. Bicycles are permitted with a special free permit. The 16 super-modern stations are safe, spacious and decked out with acres of eye-catching art and polished chrome. The line, which is a mix of sky-train and underground, charges 75¢ for any journey, regardless of length. For more information contact **Tren Urbano** (866-900-1284; www.dtop.gov.pr).

Taxi

A government taxi scheme sets trip prices in the main tourism zones. From Old San Juan, trips to Condado or Ocean Park cost $12, and $19 to Isla Verde. Journeys within Old San Juan cost $7.

Outside of the major tourist areas, cab drivers are supposed to turn on the meter for trips around town, but that rarely happens. Insist on it, or establish a price from the start. Meters – when or if they do go on – charge $1.75 initially and $1.90 per mile or part thereof. You'll also pay 50¢ for up to three pieces of luggage. There's a $1 reservation charge; add a $1 surcharge after 10pm.

Taxis line up at the south end of Fortaleza in Old San Juan; in other places they can be scarce. Don't make yourself a mugging target by standing on a deserted street waiting for one to pass by – call from the nearest hotel. Try **Metro Taxi Cab** (787-725-2870) or **Rochdale Radio Taxi** (787-721-1900); they usually come when you call.

AROUND SAN JUAN

Cataño & Bayamón

Together, Bayamón and Cataño have a denser concentration of strip malls than any other area in Puerto Rico, which may be one reason why tourists don't seem to be flocking across the bay. Other reasons could be the heavy industrialization, traffic that could make you pull your hair out and air that's often fouled with noxious chemicals. Nonetheless, there are a few things worth seeing in Bayamón and Cataño, although nothing warrants staying overnight.

To get here, you can take the ferry from Old San Juan and enjoy a quick harbor tour along the way. The Tren Urbano links Santurce, Hato Rey and Río Piedras to Bayamón; from Old San Juan/Condado you can catch bus B21 to Sagrado Corazon station and the start of the train route.

If you head about a mile north of town to where Hwy 165 meets Hwy 870, you can follow the latter to a secluded picnic site amid the dramatic setting of Isla de Cabras.

Sights

FREE **Bacardí Rum Factory** LANDMARK
(Map p48; 787-788-8400; www.casabacardi.org; Hwy 888 Km 2.6; tours 9am-4:30pm Mon-Sat, 10am-3:30pm Sun) Called the 'Cathedral of Rum' because of its six-story distillation tower, the Bacardí Rum Factory covers 127 acres and stands out like a petroleum refinery across from Old San Juan, near the

THE BACARDÍ STORY

Although today the Bacardí brand retains its headquarters in the Bahamas and runs the largest rum factory in the world in Puerto Rico, its roots were sown several hundred miles to the west, in Cuba, a country with whom the company's powerful bosses have allegedly been at loggerheads for the last 50 years.

Founded in 1862 in the city of Santiago de Cuba, the world's largest rum dynasty was the brainchild of Don Facundo Bacardí, an immigrant from Catalonia, Spain, who had arrived on the island in 1830 at the age of 16. Recognizing the unusual quality of the sugarcane in Cuba's eastern valleys, Facundo began experimenting with rum distillation using molasses until he was able to produce a refined, clear spirit that was filtered through charcoal and aged in oak barrels.

The new drink quickly caught on and, in time, Facundo passed his burgeoning rum business down to his sons Emilio and José. Emilio went on to become a well-known Cuban patriot during the Second Independence War against the Spanish and, in the 1890s, was exiled briefly for his revolutionary activities. He returned to Cuba a hero in 1898 and was promptly named as Santiago's first mayor. It was during this tempestuous period that Bacardí concocted its two famous rum cocktails, the Daiquiri (named after a Cuban beach) and the Cuba *libre*, both mixed with its signature clear rum.

After the repeal of the US prohibition laws in 1932, Bacardí began expanding its operation outside Cuba, opening up a bottling plant in Mexico and establishing the Cataño distillery in Puerto Rico, a move that enabled it to combine cheap labor costs with direct entry into the American market. When the new Cuban leader Fidel Castro began nationalizing businesses islandwide in 1960, the company was promptly relocated overseas, lock, stock and rum-filled barrel, abandoning a 100-year tradition.

In the years since, a colorful web of intrigue has grown around the company, and political plots and conspiracy theories abound. Yet, despite controversy, Bacardí has remained the world's most popular rum, selling more than 240 million bottles annually in 170 countries. In Puerto Rico, the Cataño factory reigns as the so-called cathedral of rum, churning out over 70% of the company's annual global production.

entrance to the bay. The world's largest and most famous rum-producing family started their business in Cuba more than a century ago, but they began moving their operation to this site in 1936. Today the distiller produces some 100,000 gallons of rum per day and ships 21 million cases per year worldwide.

In exchange for two free drinks, you'll be escorted on a tram tour that lasts about 45 minutes. To get to the Bacardí factory, take a público (about $3 per person) or walk 15 minutes from the ferry terminal in Cataño along the waterfront on Calle Palo Seco (Hwy 888). At Km 2.6 north of town, look for the Cathedral of Rum and other Bacardí factory buildings to your left, rising above the landscape. Free tours visit a reproduction of the original factory every 30 minutes on the half-hour.

Isla de Cabras & Fuerte del Cañuelo SCENIC OUTLOOK

Located at the end of Hwy 870, north of the Bacardí Rum Factory and the settlement of Palo Seco, **Isla de Cabras** (Goat Island; Map p48; ☎787-788-0440; www.parquesnacionalespr.com; parking $3) is perhaps the greatest seaside refuge in metro San Juan for travelers craving privacy and nature. There isn't much here except some shade trees, some gazebos for picnicking, a rocky seashore, waves and litter. You can fish, but the offshore currents are too dangerous for swimming. The ruins at the north end of the island mark a late-19th-century leper colony.

On the island's south end stand the remains of **Fuerte del Cañuelo** (Cañuelo Fort). The fort, which is nothing but ruins today, dates from 1610 and once shared the responsibility of protecting Bahía de San Juan with El Morro, which is across the channel marking the entrance to the bay.

FREE **Museo de Oller** MUSEUM

(Map p48; ☎787-785-6010; ⊙8am-noon & 1-4pm Mon-Fri) Located in the former city hall on the plaza of Bayamón's historic district, this art and history museum pays tribute to native son Francisco Oller (1833–1917), considered the first Latin American impressionist. Most of Oller's great works are displayed elsewhere, but the restored neoclassical museum building is worth a peek if you are in the area. The collection includes some Oller portraits, Taíno artifacts, and sculptures.

Caparra MUSEUM

This is the site of Juan Ponce de León's first settlement on the island, established in 1508. The site was rediscovered in 1936, and only the foundations of a few buildings remain. There is a small **museum** (Map p48; ☎787-781-4795; Hwy 2 Km 6.4; admission free; ⏲8am-4:30pm Mon-Fri) featuring Taíno artifacts that is open irregularly. Located on a highly commercial section of Hwy 2 east of Bayamón in Guaynabo, the site is only worth a visit to ponder why the great conquistador ever imagined this spot on the fringe of a mammoth swamp could possibly be suitable as a location for a colony.

Piñones

Of the many arresting cultural contrasts visible in Puerto Rico, none is as striking as the abrupt transition from modern San Juan to pleasantly ramshackle Piñones, gateway to the east coast. The two worlds are linked by Punta Cangrejos, a small bridge on Rte 187 that spans Boca de Cangrejos (Crabmouth Point); once you cross it, 'resort-land' quickly becomes a distant memory.

Do as the visiting *sanjuaneros* do on weekends and saunter along the sandy curves that are backed by spiky pine groves, nosh on seafood snacks and *coco frío* (ice-cold coconut milk) sold at roadside stands, and soak up the strong Afro-Caribbean culture that permeates Loíza Aldea and Carolina, two neighboring towns that maintain strong indigenous identities in the face of urbanization.

Both a state forest – Bosque Estatal de Piñones – and a neighborhood of its parent municipality, Loíza Aldea, further to the east, Piñones presents an alternative to the high-rise condos and casino hotels of Isla Verde to the west, and the massive pharmaceutical plants of Carolina to the south. During vacations and on weekends, this entire stretch is filled with *sanjuaneros* and locals enjoying lots of African-influenced music, food and drinks.

Whatever is happening in laid-back and rural Piñones is happening on Rte 187, which parallels the ocean. Entering from the west side, coming from Isla Verde, there's a high bridge to cross and then immediately a sign on the left saying *'Bienvenidos a Boca de Cangrejos'* (Welcome to Crabmouth Point). The sign leads up a small incline and onto a cliff overlooking the water. It's a popular drinking place and offers fabulous views, especially at sunset. There are also several popular restaurants and *friquitines* here. *Friquitines,* also known as *buréns* in Piñones, are food kiosks of all shapes and sizes (and states of hygiene) that line the coastal road. Proprietors roast plantains, whole fish, codfish fritters and skewered pieces of seasoned pork over wood fires (it's a good idea to avoid oysters, seviche and other raw or lightly cooked dishes).

The road circles and brings you back down onto Rte 187. Parking is available on the cliff top. About a mile down the road is another concentration of popular beach shacks, set just a little off the road overlooking the ocean.

Reefs just offshore create good surfing conditions and protect bathers from the full force of ocean swells, and on the days the ocean's just too rough, there's the recently completed Paseo de Piñones, a first-rate nature trail and bike path along the beach and through the forest reserve.

There are few accommodations and no real sense of the town beyond what is immediately visible along Rte 187; eventually Rte 187 hits Rte 951, which returns to Hwy 3.

History

In the 16th century most of this fertile low-lying coastal region was farmed and inhabited by local people. Once the Spanish arrived and took over in 1719, huge tracts of land were turned into massive sugarcane plantations and captured natives were forced to provide the necessary labor, although they resisted mightily. Unable to keep many of their farmhands from melting into the nearby mountains, plantation owners began shipping in African workers, and sometimes stole them from other Caribbean islands. Most of the 30,000 residents living in the municipality today are freed descendants of these Yoruba slaves. The region is justifiably proud of its Afro-Caribbean heritage: Loíza Aldea is named after Luisa, a powerful *cacique* (Taíno chief) who ruled the area before the Spanish conquest.

GETTING AWAY FROM IT ALL

You don't have to run to the hills to get away from it all. In fact, some of San Juan's greatest escapes can be found only a mile or two from the city center.

The **Corporación Piñones Se Integra** (COPI; ☎787-253-9707; www.copipr.com) is a community-based nonprofit organization that is involved in improving the facilities in Puerto Rico's poorer barrios, particularly Loíza. Concurrently, it is working hard to keep the island's traditional Afro-Caribbean culture alive. Headquartered in the **Centro Cultural Ecoturístico de Piñones** (Rte 187, Boca de Cangrejos, Loíza), situated to the right of Rte 187 immediately after you cross the bridge at Boca de Cangrejos, the organization promotes some of Puerto Rico's best *bomba y plena* (Afro–Caribbean drum music) performances one Friday a month. Call for schedule.

Sitting on land that was recently saved from the developer's bulldozers via direct community action, COPI has also pledged to protect the region's priceless but precarious ecology. To discover it for yourself, you can hire kayaks at the cultural center to explore the adjacent lagoon.

Beaches

Piñones' wild beaches contrast sharply with the well-raked expanses of Isla Verde not two miles to the west – and this is part of their attraction. You can find a choice spot almost any place where Rte 187 parallels the coast. The most picturesque and deserted beaches start at around Km 9. For swimming, avoid the corals at the western end of the strand of beaches. Unfortunately, this is where most of the food stands are, and it's where the bus from San Juan ends its route. Nonetheless the walk east is a pleasant ramble along a dedicated hiking/biking path.

Activities

To see a patch of the rarely viewed coastal wilderness, you can rent a kayak ($10 per person per hour) from COPI and explore the **Laguna la Torrecilla**, which features fish, birds and the occasional manatee.

If the surfing is good at Piñones, you will see rows of cars with board racks parked by a good break. Or you can check ahead with one of the San Juan surf shops before you go.

For bicycling, head across to the 5-mile-long Paseo de Piñones bike trail, running from the east end of Isla Verde along the shores of Playa Piñones and into the Bosque Estatal de Piñones. You can rent bikes from COPI but they're in pretty awful shape. It's best to rent them in Old San Juan.

Eating & Drinking

Although the ocean vistas, open-air seating and shade from the tall pine trees make the food kiosks a terrific place to kick back with a *coco frío* or beer, hygiene is not always a top concern for vendors in Piñones. If your stomach hasn't acclimatized yet, hit one of the more established restaurants listed below.

Piñones has countless bars, restaurants and beach shacks and names come and go. To list them all would be nigh on impossible and detract somewhat from the joy of wandering between them and ending up where your senses carry you.

Waterfront Restaurant SEAFOOD
(☎787-791-5989; Rte 187; mains $10-26; ⏲10am-10pm; 👪) Right off the bike path at Km 5, this airy place has comfortable seating and a dynamite shrimp, octopus and lobster *asopao*. Its *mofongo* can be ordered with either seafood or soy meat.

Soleil Beach Club SEAFOOD
(www.soleilbeachclub.com; Rte 187 Km 4.6; mains $10-25; ⏲11am-11pm Sun-Thu, 11am-1am Fri & Sat) With a breezy oceanfront location, this more upscale place has two floors to drink in the views and a menu of seafood-based Caribbean cuisine that's kept the buzz going for almost 15 years. Try the *mofongo* with crab, shrimp, conch or octopus, and the excellent the *tres leches* cake. It caters a lot of special event banquets.

Reef Bar & Grill SEAFOOD
(☎787-791-1374; mains $7-18; ⏲10:30am-10pm Sun-Thu, 10:30am-3am Fri-Sun) To get started you might want to try its seafood and African-flavored sides.

Puerta del Mar PUERTO RICAN
(mains $8-20; ⏲lunch & dinner, Fri & Sat until late) Serves classic *mofongo,* fritters, deep-fried fish and burgers.

Information

Dangers & Annoyances

Avoid walking along deserted strips of beach after nightfall, and be aware that some drug activity takes place on the beaches toward the west side of town. Don't venture onto the beach in that area at night. Watch your speed while driving; transit cops love to patrol scenic Rte 187.

Getting There & Away

The C45 bus picks passengers up in front of the Cockfight Arena on Isla Verde (connect with T5 for the rest of San Juan) and runs all the way to the settlement at the west end of the beach at Piñones. Walk a mile to the east for some decent swimming beaches. You can also cycle to Piñones from San Juan.

Loíza Aldea

Take Hwy 187 east from San Juan to catch some fresh air and rural scenery (and escape the commerce and traffic jams on Hwy 3). The road eventually breaks out of the Piñones forest. When you cross a bridge spanning the island's largest river, the Río Grande de Loíza, the road brings you to the center of Loíza Aldea, commonly called Loíza. This town is a largely rural municipality in the coastal lowlands east of LMM airport, and it includes Piñones as well as three other districts.

Loíza dates from 1719 and has a rich Taíno heritage. Sadly, there's little infrastructure to support tourism, and none of the settlements here are scenic. Most of the 30,000 residents are poor. There are only two reasons for a traveler to visit: a church and a fiesta. You will find some kiosks set up along the roads in Loíza that sell the usual snacks, but there's nowhere to sleep at night. Stay in nearby Piñones, San Juan or at any number of places around Luquillo, El Yunque or Fajardo.

Sights

At the northern end of the plaza, **La Iglesia del Espíritu Santo y San Patricio** (Church of the Holy Ghost and St Patrick) appears every bit as proud and colonial as the cathedral in Old San Juan, and stands out from the humble collection of surrounding modern buildings.

The church dates from 1646 and took its name from the patron saint of Ireland to honor Puerto Rico's famous Irish mercenaries, who designed many of the fortifications of Old San Juan.

Festivals & Events

Puerto Rico's African soul is unveiled for nine days every July and August in the **Fiesta de Santiago**, a cultural extravaganza of drums, masks and hybrid religious iconology relating to the Catholic Saint James the Moor Slayer.

Shopping

Handmade *vejigantes* (Puerto Rican masks) carved by local artisans are available in many places in Loíza (and are generally of higher quality for less money than what you'll find in San Juan). Wander the streets around the town center and you'll see plenty of colorful creations quite literally staring out at you.

Estudio de Arte Samuel Lind ART GALLERY
(☎787-876-1494; www.samuellind.com; Rte 187 Km 6.6) This is the most famous shop in town. The studio, which is open to visitors when someone is at home, is 2 miles south of town on Rte 187 and sells the artist's paintings, sculptures and serigraph prints. To drive there, head toward Río Grande until you see a sign for the studio. Turn left and stop at the third house on the left. Públicos from San Juan to Rio Grande will stop at the studio on request. About 20 other mask makers work in the area.

Information

The center of the town is called the Plaza de Recreo, known as La Plaza, and is just east of the bridge over the Río Grande de Loíza.

Getting There & Away

You can catch a público to Loíza's plaza from Río Piedras in San Juan for a few dollars, which is not a bad way to go during the Fiesta de Santiago, when traffic into Loíza on Hwy 187 and Hwy 188 can be more frightening than a *vejigante*. Públicos return to Río Piedras from a terminal in Loíza (three blocks away from the plaza), but usually only during daylight hours.

El Yunque & East Coast

Includes »

Best Places to Eat

» La Estación (p108)
» Pasta y Pueblo (p102)
» Pasión por el Fogón (p108)
» *Friquitines* in Luquillo (p102)
» Aquamar Steakhouse & Seafood (p112)

Best Places to Stay

» Casa Cubuy Ecolodge (p99)
» Rainforest Inn (p98)
» Luquillo Sunrise Beach Inn (p101)
» Ceiba Country Inn (p107)
» Casa Flamboyant (p98)

Why Go?

The east coast is Puerto Rico shrink-wrapped; a tantalizing taste of almost everything the island has to offer squeezed into an area not much larger than Manhattan. Sodden rainforest teems with jungle waterfalls and noisy wildlife at El Yunque National Forest, the commonwealth's giant green lungs and biggest outdoor attraction. Down at sea level, beach hedonists bask on the icing-sugar sand of Playa Luquillo.

Golfers and resort-seekers will find a different kind of nirvana: the highest concentration of mega resorts outside San Juan.

Scruffy Fajardo is the island's uncrowned water-sports capital, where adventurers kayak, dive, snorkel and fish, and rich yachters park their sailboats.

Cutting through the region like a thin, green ribbon is the Northeast Ecological Corridor, a slender tract of undeveloped and endangered pristine land featuring Las Cabezas de San Juan Reserva Natural 'El Faro,' a tiny nodule of coastline harboring one of Puerto Rico's stunning bioluminescent bays.

When to Go

Noteworthy annual events in Luquillo include the Fiesta de los Platos Típicos (Traditional Food Festival) in November, and on the third Saturday in April the Sierra Club promotes the preservation of the Northeast Ecological Corridor with a child-friendly turtle festival (Festival del Tinglar). An April kite festival is a fun event in Fajardo.

Note that hurricane season – early June through late November – can bring sodden conditions to El Yunque, with the possibility of trails being closed due to mudslides and flooding some years.

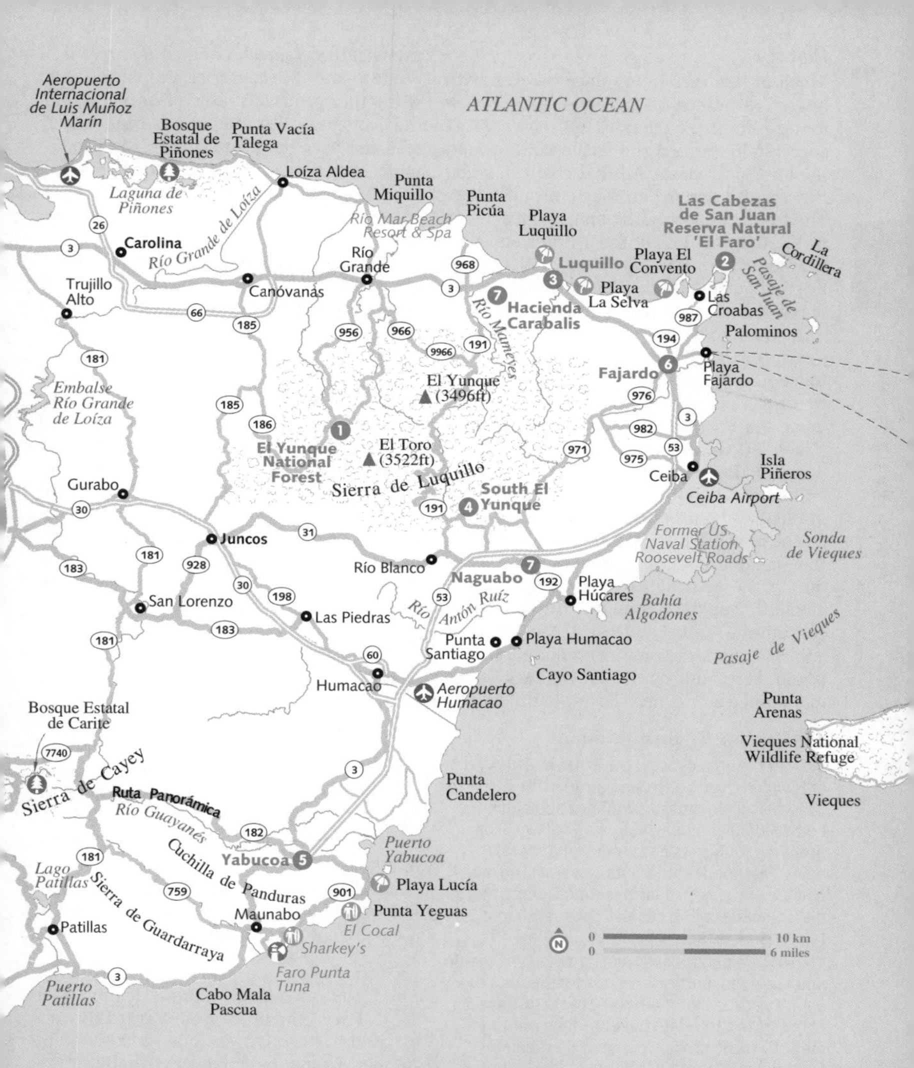

El Yunque & East Coast Highlights

1. Ramble through the moist rainforest flora in **El Yunque National Forest** (p94)
2. Admire the sea views, iguanas and seven different ecosystems in **Las Cabezas de San Juan Reserva Natural 'El Faro'** (p104)
3. Surf the local break and swim at one of the island's best beaches at **Luquillo** (p100)
4. Explore hidden waterfall pools and petroglyphs on **El Yunque's quiet south side** (boxed text, p98)
5. Kick back at one of the pretty oceanfront paradores near low-key **Yabucoa** (p112)
6. Drink in the mesmerizing water with a **kayak tour** (p106) of Fajardo's glowing bioluminescent bay
7. Traipse the forest or beachside landscape with a **horseback riding trip** on the north (p110) or south coast (p101)

History

Much of this region was once covered with lighter variations of the dense foliage now found only in El Yunque, but native Taíno successfully farmed the fertile land around the low-lying coasts. All that changed when the Spanish arrived en masse around 1700. The tremendous wealth of natural resources in El Yunque – lots of fresh water and timber, for example – attracted settlers, and existing farmlands were quickly turned into massive sugar plantations by colonizers.

A small gold rush added to the need for a strong labor force, and after most of the indigenous population was either wiped out by disease or forced deep into the mountains, the Spanish brought in West African slaves in considerable numbers. Descendants of those Yoruba people make up the bulk of the 30,000 residents who live in the municipalities around El Yunque today.

The next wave of colonization came when the US took control of the island in 1898, during the Spanish-American War, eventually setting up the commonwealth status that continues to this day. Most of the highways and existing infrastructure on this part of the island were built by the US military, which maintained a base near Fajardo until 2003.

Getting There & Around

Most of the east coast is traversable via Hwy 3 or Hwy 53. Once you leave San Juan, be it on Rte 187 (the scenic route via Piñones and behind Loíza Aldea) or on the main drag of Hwy 3, be prepared for bursts of concentrated development (fast-food restaurants, several strip malls and the occasional pharmaceutical plant) and distant views of El Yunque. Públicos (shared taxis) serve most towns.

There are public vans running between Fajardo and San Juan, but to penetrate further into the countryside, a car or bike is necessary. It is easy to organize a tour into the El Yunque rainforest (see p97). The driving trip from San Juan to Fajardo takes about two hours (without traffic). From San Juan to Yabucoa it's about three hours (again, without traffic).

With its high concentration of cars, the northeast is not the most pleasant part of Puerto Rico in which to cycle. But stay off the main arteries of Hwys 3 and 66 and two-wheeled transport is possible.

El Yunque

Covering some 28,000 acres of land in the Sierra de Luquillo, this verdant tropical rainforest is a shadow of what it was before axe-wielding Spanish conquerors arrived in the 16th and 17th centuries. But, in common with other protected reserves on the island, the ecological degradation has been largely reversed over the past 50 years, and today, under the auspices of the US Forest Service, El Yunque National Forest is once again sprouting a healthy abundance of dense tree cover.

Compared with other Puerto Rican forest reserves, El Yunque is well staffed and crisscrossed by an excellent network of signposted trails. But adventurers beware. In contrast to national parks in the mainland US, there's no true wilderness experience to be had here. Unlike North Americans, Puerto Ricans have never truly incorporated wilderness hiking in the national psyche. As a result, most of El Yunque's hikes are short, paved and relatively mild compared with the trails of Yellowstone and Yosemite. Crowds populate El Yunque's popular spots in peak season, but if you stray off the standard tourist routes, there are still plenty of places to slip under the radar.

Sights

Once you've entered El Yunque National Forest, all of the forest's visitors centers, major attractions and trailheads appear as Hwy 191 twists, turns and climbs steeply on its way south toward the summit. (It's also possible to follow Hwy 186 along the west side of El Yunque, but if you want to experience the forest's heart, Hwy 191 is the road to take.)

In addition to short and long hiking trails in El Yunque, there are a few places directly accessible by road within the forest.

La Coca Falls WATERFALL

The first spectacular natural feature you see as Hwy 191 climbs south toward the forest peaks is an 85ft cascade as the stream tumbles from a precipice to the right of the highway onto boulder formations. The gate is open every day from 7:30am to 6pm.

Yokahú Tower SCENIC OUTLOOK

Less than a half mile further up the mountain, past La Coca Falls, this 65ft, Moorish-looking stone tower was built as a lookout in 1962. This is the first good place for vistas of the islands to the east, but there are better vantage points higher up on the mountain. The tower often gets crowded with tour groups. Pass it by unless you have a lot of time and the view to yourself.

El Yunque

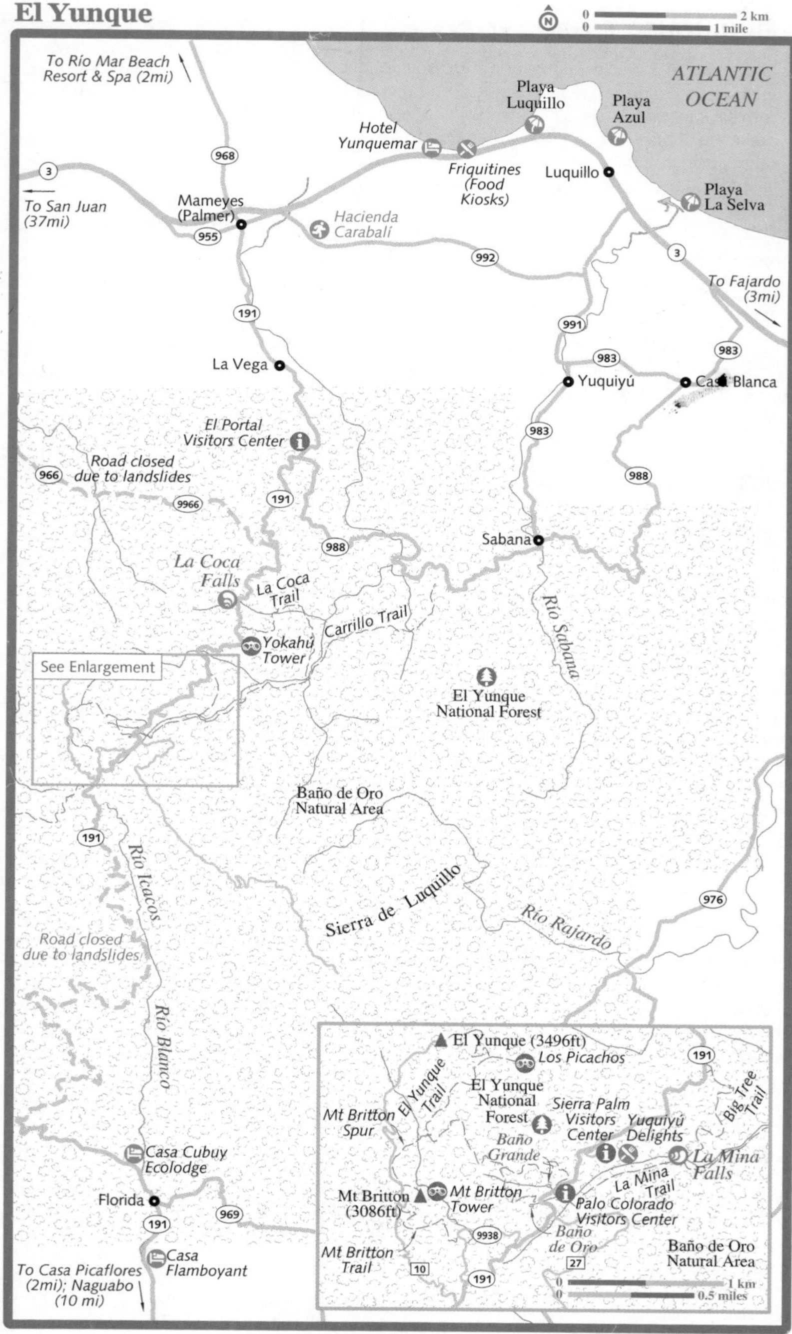

To Río Mar Beach Resort & Spa (2mi)
ATLANTIC OCEAN
Playa Luquillo
Playa Azul
Hotel Yunquemar
Friquitines (Food Kiosks)
Luquillo
Playa La Selva
To San Juan (37mi)
Mameyes (Palmer)
Hacienda Carabalí
To Fajardo (3mi)
La Vega
Yuquiyú
Casa Blanca
El Portal Visitors Center
Road closed due to landslides
Sabana
La Coca Falls
La Coca Trail
Carrillo Trail
Yokahú Tower
See Enlargement
Río Sabana
El Yunque National Forest
Baño de Oro Natural Area
Sierra de Luquillo
Río Rajardo
Río Icacos
Road closed due to landslides
Río Blanco
Casa Cubuy Ecolodge
Florida
Casa Flamboyant
To Casa Picaflores (2mi); Naguabo (10 mi)
El Yunque (3496ft)
Los Picachos
El Yunque Trail
El Yunque National Forest
Sierra Palm Visitors Center
Yuquiyú Delights
Big Tree Trail
Mt Britton Spur
Baño Grande
La Mina Falls
La Mina Trail
Mt Britton (3086ft)
Mt Britton Tower
Palo Colorado Visitors Center
Baño de Oro
Mt Britton Trail
Baño de Oro Natural Area

EL YUNQUE'S FLORA & FAUNA

More than 240 species of tree and 1000 species of plant thrive in this misty, rain-soaked enclave, including 50 kinds of orchid. El Yunque is also the island's major water supply, with six substantial rivers tracing their sources here. The fauna is characterized by the presence of the critically endangered Puerto Rican parrot *(el higuaca)* and more than 60 other species of bird, nine species of rare freshwater shrimp, the coquí frog, anole tree lizards and the 7ft-long Puerto Rican boa.

Four forest zones define El Yunque. The tabonuco forest grows below 2000ft and receives less than 100in of rain. This area is characterized by tall, straight trees such as the tabonuco and ausubo, and palms, epiphytes (including many orchids), flowers and aromatic shrubs of many kinds.

The palo colorado forest grows above 2000ft in the valleys and on gentle slopes. Here annual rainfall averages as much as 180in. This area is lush with ancient colorado trees (some more than 1000 years old). Vines and epiphytes hang from the trees.

Above 2500ft, look for sierra palms along the streams and on the steep valley slopes. The so-called mountain palm tree dominates here in the third zone, the palma sierra forest, with mostly ferns and mosses growing beneath.

The highest forest zone, the cloud forest, grows above the Palma Sierra Forest and sees up to 200in of rain per year. Trees here are generally twisted from strong trade winds and are less than 12ft tall (hence the term 'dwarf forest' commonly applied to this ecosystem). Mosses and lichens hang from trees and cover the forest floor. Red-flowering bromeliads stand out like beacons in the fog.

Baño Grande & Baño de Oro SCENIC OUTLOOK

Baño Grande, a former swimming hole built during the Depression, lies across Hwy 191 from the Palo Colorado Visitors Center. A little further along the road, Baño de Oro is another former swimming hole that is now a popular spot for photo opportunities. The water hole takes its name from the Río Baño de Oro, which feeds the pool. The name means 'bath of gold' in English, and Spaniards gave the river this name because they mined for gold here in the 16th century. The Baño de Oro Natural Area surrounding the pool is the catchment area for the river and pool.

La Mina Falls WATERFALL

If you really want to paddle in some water, take the 30-minute walk from Palo Colorado down the mountain to the swimming hole at the base of La Mina Falls. Here you'll find a water cascade, quite stunning in its natural beauty. Come early if you want tranquility, because it's popular with cavorting families.

Activities

With more than 23 miles of well-maintained trails, and plenty of rugged terrain, El Yunque has a plethora of easy day hikes. Come prepared (think rain poncho and good shoes) and remember there are no water, trash or rest room facilities.

It's a good idea to check in at the visitors center for the latest weather update before heading out for a trek. El Yunque's weather caters to the unique needs of its ecosystem. Sudden surges of light rain can occur anytime during the year in this dense rainforest, but that goes with the territory – throw on some protective gear and get on with your day. During hurricane season El Yunque gets very wet indeed. Some trails might be closed due to mudslides, and streams swell enormously. Winter nights in the Luquillo mountains can be damp and a little chilly.

Big Tree Trail HIKING

Half an hour each way, this trail through tabonuco forest to La Mina Falls contains bilingual interpretive signs that highlight sights such as a 300-year-old ausubo tree. This short 0.86-mile trail is moderately difficult; its name comes from (surprise!) the size of the vegetation along the way. It's probably the most popular trail in the park. The trailhead is at Km 10.4 on Hwy 191.

La Coca Trail HIKING

If getting off the beaten path is your bag, try this deceptively challenging trail. Wilder and less maintained than some of the more popular forest rambles, this 1.8-mile (one way) hike descends through thick tabonuco forest and enormous ferns and crosses several rocky streams. You'll get muddy and have to do some scrambling, but the rewards of private waterfalls and dipping pools more than make up for it. Long pants are recommended and good shoes are a must, and most folks take three to four hours for this out-and-back trek because of the slippery terrain and tempting swimming.

The trailhead is just up the road past the falls of the same name – just before the Yokahú Tower – and there is a small parking lot here.

La Coca made its mark on El Yunque history when a US college professor disappeared here for 12 days in 1997, claiming after his rescue that he got off the trail and was lost. The Forest Service, which had enlisted a search party of 60 volunteers and aircraft, was hardly amused.

Mt Britton Trail HIKING

If you are short on time and want to feel as if you have really 'summited,' take the 0.8-mile, 45-minute climb up through the mid-level types of vegetation into the cloud forest that surrounds this peak, which is named after a famous botanist who worked here. This is a continuous climb on paved surfaces to the evocative stone Mt Britton Tower, built in the 1930s. When not shrouded by clouds, the panoramic views extend over the forest to the Atlantic Ocean and the Caribbean. The trailhead is at the side of Hwy 9938, which veers off Hwy 191 south of the Palo Colorado Visitors Center. The more adventurous and fit can connect to El Yunque Trail via the 0.86-mile Mt Britton Spur.

El Yunque Trail HIKING

On a clear day, never-ending views extending to Vieques and Culebra reward hikers tackling the almost 1500ft of elevation gain on this trail. This is the big enchilada for most visitors, taking you to the top of El Yunque (3496ft, 1049m) in 1½ hours or longer. Starting on Rte 191 Km 12.2 opposite the Palo Colorado Visitors Center, the 2.4-mile trail is mostly paved or maintained gravel as you ascend through cloud forest and then dwarf forest to the observation deck, which is surrounded by microwave communication towers that transmit to the islands of Culebra and Vieques. If you want a rock scramble from here, take Los Picachos Trail (0.17 miles) to another old observation tower and feel as if you have crested a tropical Everest. You can return via a different route by descending down the Mt Britton Spur/Mt Britton Trail and then down Rtes 9938 and 191 to your start point.

Tradewinds-El Toro Trail HIKING

Scheduled for extensive repairs and closures over the next few years, this trail is the closest El Yunque gets to a true backcountry adventure. Although the 7.8-mile round-trip to El Toro (3522ft) and back might not sound particularly daunting, wet conditions, thick mud and poorly maintained paths render it an all-day excursion for most hikers (some parties even camp out overnight). El Toro is El Yunque's highest point and the trail up from Hwy 191 traverses dense jungle broken by intermittent views of both coasts. During the ascent you'll pass through all four forest life systems, ending up in a haunting dwarf forest above 3000ft characterized by its ghostly epiphytes and ubiquitous mist.

The trailhead for the Tradewinds Trail is situated at Km 13.3 on Hwy 191, behind a locked gate where the road ends. The unpaved path climbs 3.9 miles to the summit of El Toro, from where you can either retrace your steps or continue west on the similarly vague El Toro Trail to Km 10.8 on Hwy 186 (2.1 miles from El Toro and 6 miles from Hwy 191). From here you'll need to return the way you came, or arrange for a car to pick you up and take you back to the start.

Aspiring hikers should contact the forest visitors center for current road conditions and trail status.

Tours

San Juan–based tour operators (see p287) are handy in that they can transport you to and from the park, highlight the main sights and provide you with a mine of interesting information.

DON'T MISS

LA MINA TRAIL

The forest's newest trail was opened in 1992 as an extension of the Big Tree Trail, although it can be done in isolation from its starting point at the Palo Colorado Visitors Center. The trail heads downhill through palo colorado forest to La Mina Falls and an old mine tunnel. Mostly paved, it's an easy though often slippery 0.7-mile walk down, but a bit of a hike back up. The payoff here is the photo-worthy falls, which drop 35ft into a perfect natural swimming pool.

WORTH A TRIP

GO FURTHER INTO THE COUNTRYSIDE

If you have an aversion to large crowds, give El Yunque's northern highlights a body-swerve and head instead to the region's alternative entrance road just west of the town of Naguabo. Since mudslides closed the central section of Hwy 191 in the 1970s, this southern portion of the rainforest has remained relatively isolated and unexplored.

Spend the night at one of the wonderful south side lodgings (p98) up the precipitous and winding Hwy 191. From there, you can procure directions to a number of nearby hiking and swimming spots, or hire local expert **Robin Phillips** (787-874-2138; www.rainforestfruitfarm.com; rainforest day tour $125, 2hr petroglyph tour $53) to guide you to some of the area's natural highlights.

Forest Adventure Tours RAINFOREST
(787-888-1880; www.fs.fed.us/r8/caribbean/recreation/recreation_forest_adventure_tours.shtm; adult/child & senior $5/3; tours 11am-1:30pm Wed-Sun) In addition to the standard options, the National Park Service offers guided one-hour hikes from the Palo Colorado Visitors Center. This organization aims to offer visitors a better understanding of conservation and forest management.

Eco-Action Tours RAINFOREST
(787-791-7509; www.ecoactiontours.com) This outfit is another good ecosensitive operator, which offers half-/full-day tours for $58/68, for hikes to Mt Britton and La Mina Falls. Guides are knowledgeable, environmentally conscious and eager to talk about the rainforest ecosystem. They'll pick you up from your San Juan hotel.

AdvenTours RAINFOREST
(787-530-8311; www.adventourspr.com) An ecosensitive guiding company offering bird-watching tours and night hikes (for nocturnal animals and bioluminescent fungi) in El Yunque National Forest.

Sleeping

Several beautiful inns, B&Bs and guesthouses have opened up along the edges of El Yunque – not actually within the national forest, but along its fringe, which still feels very wild. The proximity to the rainforest means lots of loud animal activity: the sound of chirruping coquí will send you to sleep, and you'll wake to wild birds whistling. Some places are accessible along the north section of Hwy 191, coming from Río Grande (Luquillo beaches are only a few minutes away). Other accommodations are on the south side, also on Hwy 191. Due to mudslides, south side accommodations must be accessed from the Naguabo entrance to El Yunque. These are good choices if you want to be in close proximity to day trips in and around Fajardo. Most have minimum stays.

NORTH SIDE

Rainforest Inn INN $$
(787-378-6190; www.rainforestinn.com; off Hwy 186; r incl breakfast $155-165; P) Bordering the national forest, this former coffee estate plantation has two two-bedroom units with beautiful (and lovely smelling) reclaimed cedar beams and luxurious details such as a claw-foot bathtub and antique mahogany and satinwood furniture.

Outside, the property has views of El Yunque Peak and a private path leads to a stunning waterfall pool. The inn attracts a good number of scientists and educators, who sometimes sign up their (adult) kids for the inn's volunteer apprenticeship program in carpentry, masonry and electrical work. No children under 12 years of age.

Villa Sevilla INN $$$
(787-887-5889; www.villasevilla.net; Rte 956 Km 7.8, Río Grande; r $150-250; P) One of the finest El Yunque accommodations, Villa Sevilla is a private estate with five different sets of digs, a gorgeous saltwater swimming pool and foliage-framed Atlantic views. There's the three-bedroom Bella Vista chalet and Hacienda Las Palmas, the two-bedroom La Casita and Villa Escondido, and the one-bedroom Pablo's Place. All apartments have kitchen, satellite TV, washer/dryer and linen. They're ideal for couples and families on longer stays. The service here is top-notch and the rainforest surroundings magnificent.

SOUTH SIDE

Casa Flamboyant INN $$$
(787-874-6074; www.elunque.com/flamboy.html; Hwy 191 Km 22.2; r incl breakfast $200-250;)

Some hotels try to create their own 'faux' paradise, others are located where paradise already exists. Tucked way up high in the mountains and offering panoramic views of El Yunque and three waterfalls, the Casa Flamboyant is of the latter variety. It was once owned by a top New York City art dealer, and its past house guests include Federico Fellini and Robert Mapplethorpe. With its three gorgeous rooms with private bathrooms, and a curious Hawaiian screw pine that could have been lifted from a Dr Seuss book, this is as elegant as Puerto Rico's rainforest gets. Guests love to watch storm clouds march past en route to glowering El Yunque while lounging in the pool. Adults only.

TOP CHOICE Casa Cubuy Ecolodge GUESTHOUSE **$$**
(787-874-6221; www.casacubuy.com; Hwy 191 Km 22; r incl breakfast $110-125; P) If listening to a frog symphony, conversing nightly around the dinner table, and relaxing on a shady balcony within hammock-swinging distance of a mystical tropical rainforest has you dashing for your jungle apparel, then this could be your place. Cocooned atop the winding Hwy 191 on El Yunque's wild and isolated southern slopes, Casa Cubuy Ecolodge offers a welcome antidote to the modern Puerto Rico of crowded beaches and spirit-crushing traffic. Ten cozy rooms rise just inches from the ethereal green forest, and a covered communal patio replete with games and books encourages multilingual guest interaction. To top it all, the lodge even guards its own private trail to a nearby waterfall and natural swimming pool. For something a bit more upscale, ask about its three Sierra Palms rooms (doubles with breakfast $130) just down the road. It also operates a nearby restaurant in season.

Casa Picaflores INN **$$**
(787-874-3802; www.casapicaflores.com; off Hwy 191; studio incl breakfast $149, 3-bedroom villa incl breakfast $345; P) Spend the night in a luxurious three-bedroom house or nestled into a cozy casita (small house), surrounded by abundant fruit trees and majestic mahogany boughs. The lodgings are furnished with organic bedding and linens, and the grounds contain a vegetable garden fertilized by the waste from its tilapia nursery. A river-fed pool is in the works.

Eating

Yuquiyú Delights PUERTO RICAN **$**
(Hwy 191 Km 11.3 & Km 4.0;) The small food concessions situated next to the Sierra Palm picnic area and inside the El Portal Visitors Center are the only real 'restaurants' in the forest. It does decent burgers ($7 to $8), *comida criolla* (traditional Puerto Rican cuisine) and smoothies and should replenish your legs ready for a few more miles of hiking. The Sierra Palm location has the larger menu. A few smaller kiosks sell snacks and soft drinks around Km 7 on Hwy 191.

Information

First port of call for aspiring rainforest explorers should be the **El Portal Visitors Center** (787-888-1880; www.fs.fed.us/r8/caribbean; Hwy 191 Km 4.3; adult/under 15yr/senior $4/free/2; 9am-5pm, closed Christmas Day). Built in 1996, El Portal is an intelligently landscaped visitors center that offers reams of information about both El Yunque and tropical rainforests in general. The facility has interactive exhibits, a 17-minute film in both English and Spanish, a walkway through the forest canopy and a gift shop. You can also pick up free basic maps and information on the forest. If you don't feel like paying the admission tariff or want to avoid crowds on weekends, head to one of the other visitors centers further up the mountain, where you can pick up brochures and basic maps for no charge.

It's worth enduring the switchbacks and steep road to get to the **Palo Colorado Visitors Center** (Hwy 191 Km 11.9). Most of the short and spectacular hiking trails leave from this spot. The picnic area – which includes a series of sheltered concrete platforms hidden in the jungle, overlooking a ravine of rushing water – is hard to match anywhere on the island. The staff here offers first-aid service, and there's also a gift shop with maps and the like.

CAMPING IN EL YUNQUE

At the time of research, there was an indefinite moratorium on camping within El Yunque National Forest. A number of trails had suffered weather-related damage from landslides and fallen trees, and authorities were conducting an assessment of safety procedures for visitors. Check the forest website (www.fs.fed.us/r8/caribbean) or call for updates. In the past, it's been free to camp – within certain boundaries – and a permit was required.

The **Sierra Palm Visitors Center** is a free visitors center on your way up the mountain. It is not always staffed, but it has a picnic area, rest rooms and a food concession, Yuquiyú Delights.

Getting There & Away

There's no public transportation to El Yunque. The only way to get here is by private car, taxi (expensive), or in a pre-arranged tour (p97). You can see the rainforest from San Juan even though it lies 25 miles to the southeast. Driving from San Juan, there will be signs directing you from Hwy 3 to Hwy 191. Turn right and keep your eyes peeled for more signage directing you to Hwy 191 and El Yunque National Forest. Just after the road starts to rise abruptly into the mountains, you enter El Yunque National Forest.

Take note that some highway maps suggest that you can traverse the forest on Hwy 191 (or access El Yunque from the south via this route), but south of the Palo Colorado Visitors Center, Hwy 191 has been closed by landslides for years. Some road maps also suggest that El Yunque can be approached via a network of roads along the western border of the national forest. Don't try it: these roads are rugged, untraveled, unmaintained tracks that dead-end in serious jungle. El Yunque is not immune to thievery, so if you park in a remote area to take a stroll, be sure to lock up and don't leave anything of value in plain sight in the car.

Luquillo & Around

POP 20,000

In many ways Luquillo is a typical Puerto Rican town; a physically beautiful coastal strip of magnificent beaches backed by a dull, uninspiring mishmash of condo towers, strip malls and unsightly urban sprawl. But here, in the island's congested northeastern corner, beauty easily outweighs the beast. Playa Luquillo, the mile-long crescent of surf and sand to the west of the town, is regularly touted as being the commonwealth's finest balneario (public beach) and the proverbial home of Puerto Rican soul food. Meanwhile, winking a velvety shade of purple in the background, the crenellated ridges of El Yunque proffer a ghostly invitation.

Central Luquillo doesn't have much worth exploring and little in the way of history. Surfers flock to the beach at the La Pared break, giving the area a sporty laid-back vibe. But most travelers head a mile west to Puerto Rico's so-called Riviera, the insanely popular Luquillo Beach that is as famous for its ramshackle strip of permanent food kiosks as it is for its icing-sugar sand and sheltered bay.

Luquillo traces its history to an early Spanish settlement in 1797 and its name to a valorous *cacique* (Taíno chief), Loquillo, who made a brave standoff against early colonizers here in 1513. These days the 20,000-strong town is bypassed by the arterial Hwy 3 that carries traffic to Fajardo. Here you'll find little of lasting architectural note save for a couple of craning condo towers that do their best to block out views of El Yunque.

Thanks to Luquillo's popularity with vacationing *sanjuaneros* (people from San Juan), público links with the capital are fairly regular during the week. If you're going to the beach, make sure you disembark next to the kiosks, a mile or so before Luquillo Pueblo. Most of the shops and stores of interest to visitors are alongside Playa Azul, or on Fernandez Garcia.

Beaches

Playa Luquillo BEACH
(Balneario La Monserrate; admission free, parking $4.50; ⌚8am-5pm daily) Luquillo is synonymous with its balneario, the fabulous Playa Luquillo. Set on a calm bay facing northwest and protected from the easterly trade winds, the public part of this beach makes a mile-long arc to a point of sand shaded by evocative coconut palms. The beach itself is a plane of broad, gently sloping yellow powder that continues its gradual slope below the water. Although crowds converge here at weekends and during holidays, Luquillo has always been more about atmosphere than solitude. With its famous strip of about 60 food kiosks congregated at its western end, it's also a great place to sample the local culinary culture, including scrumptious *surullitos* (fried cornmeal and cheese sticks). There is a bathhouse, a refreshment stand, a security patrol and well-kept bathrooms.

You do not have to park in the balneario lot if you want to visit the beach. Playa Luquillo extends at least another mile to the west. If you pull off Hwy 3 by the long row of food kiosks, you can drive around to the ocean side of the stalls and park under the palms, just a few steps from the beach and with more cold beer and *pastelillos* (fried dumplings) than you could consume in a year.

Playa Azul BEACH
If Playa Luquillo feels too busy (and it does get cheek-by-jowl in high season), head for

Playa Azul, east around the headland and in the town itself, directly in front of the condominium development of the same name. While the beach is more exposed to the trade winds, seas and dangerous riptides (people have drowned), Playa Azul is just as broad, white and gently sloping as Luquillo. Snorkeling enthusiasts particularly enjoy these waters, but swim with great caution.

A friendly contingent of surfers hangs out at the east end of this beach – known as 'La Pared' (the Wall) – waiting for an offshore breeze to glass off a 3ft break. Pick up an 'I (heart) La Pared' bumper sticker to look like a local.

Playa Seven Seas BEACH

Scrambling over a stone jetty at the east end of Playa Azul will take you to a strand of beach and bays that stretch over 5 miles to the Playa Seven Seas balneario in Las Croabas (p105). The western section of this undeveloped beach is known as **Playa La Selva**; the eastern end is called **Playa El Convento** and features a beach house that is a retreat for government officials.

Activities

Benefiting from a fabulous beachside location and proximity to the rainforest, Luquillo is well-positioned for both aquatic and land-based adventures. Ask locals for directions to **Las Paylas**, a pair of natural **waterslides** located off Hwy 983.

Surfing

While not exactly hard-core, Luquillo's waves are less crowded and less daunting than the west coast's.

La Selva Surf Shop SURFING

(787-889-6205; 250 Calle Fernández García) Well-stocked and friendly, La Selva Surf Shop rents out surfboards ($40 per day) and bodyboards ($20) and offers the latest on surf conditions at La Pared (literally two blocks away), La Selva (further east) and around the Humacao area to the south.

Bob's East Island Surfing Adventures SURFING

(787-435-1760; www.rainforestrental.com) Offers surfing lessons ($60 per person) as well as rentals.

Kayaking

For a guided kayak tour along the coast, check out a host of different day and night options from mobile operations, including **Las Tortugas Adventures** (787-809-0253; www.kayak-pr.com), whose tours focus on the importance of environmental conservation, and **Enchanted Island Eco Tours** (787-888-2887), whose trips have a similar vent as those of Las Tortugas. Prices start at about $55.

Golf

The **Berwind Country Club** (787-876-3056; www.berwindcountryclub.net; Hwy 187 Km 4.7, Río Grande; greens fee $50) is open to the public Sunday to Friday. The greens fee includes a golf cart.

Río Mar Beach Resort & Spa is frequented for its two excellent courses: the Greg Norman River Course and the Tom and George Fazio Ocean Course. Nonguests pay $165 for morning tee times and $130 after 2pm.

Horseback Riding

Hacienda Carabalí HORSEBACK RIDING

(www.haciendacarabalipuertorico.com; Hwy 992 Km 5.1; adult/child per hr from $30/20) This 600-acre eco-adventure ranch southwest of town does trail rides on Paso Fino horses along the Río Mameyes and into the foothills of the rainforest, and two-hour rides include time for swimming and a picnic. Beach rides and simple jaunts around the ranch are also offered, as well as two-hour mountain-biking tours along rainforest trails. Aluminum bikes, with helmet and gloves, are provided for $50 per person.

Sleeping

For decades Puerto Ricans and adventure travelers have camped with impunity at Playas La Selva and El Convento. During holidays and on high-season weekends, you'll have plenty of company. Think twice, though, if it looks like you'll be out there alone. Groups of young men have been known to roam the area looking for vulnerable targets. Muggings do occur.

TOP CHOICE **Luquillo Sunrise Beach Inn** HOTEL $$

(787-889-1713; www.luquillosunrise.com; A2 Costa Azul; d incl breakfast $125-155; P ❄ @) Filling a gap in the midrange market, the Luquillo Sunrise Beach Inn is caressed by cooling Atlantic sea breezes in each of its spiffy 17 ocean-facing rooms. There's a communal patio and all upper-floor rooms have large balconies overlooking the beach. Other facilities include a conference room, satellite TV and an excellent compilation of local information, restaurant menus and maps. Luquillo plaza is two blocks away and the famous balneario and food kiosks are a 30-minute stroll along the beach.

Hotel Yunquemar HOTEL **$$**
(☎787-889-5555; www.yunquemar.com; No 6 Calle 1, Fortuna Playa, Luquillo; r incl breakfast $95-115; P❄📶≋) The name Yunquemar sums it up. Lying in the shadow of El Yunque and within pebble-pitching distance of the *mar* (sea), you've got the best of both worlds here. A comfortable family-run hotel with its own swimming pool and beach, and a pool table and wide-screen TV tucked down in the enormous basement, it's a quiet respite a few minutes' drive from central Luquillo.

Río Mar Beach Resort & Spa RESORT **$$$**
(☎787-888-6000; www.wyndhamriomar.com; 6000 Río Mar Blvd; r/ste from $200/340; P❄@📶≋👪) The Río Mar inhabits an entire hill just west of Luquillo. Spread over a mammoth 500 acres on former plantation land, there are two golf courses here along with a 600-unit high-rise hotel facility with the obligatory casino. It's better landscaped than some of the island's mega resorts, with dotted palms and imaginative art that pays a nod to indigenous island culture. On-site restaurants offer a choice of sushi, Italian, Puerto Rican or grill fare.

Rainforest & Ocean View Inn INN **$$**
(☎787-889-1807; www.rainforestoceanviewinn.com; Hwy 992 Km 4; d $165, each additional person $15; P❄≋) As well as offering horseback rides and mountain biking, Hacienda Carabalí runs a new 12-room inn. Set on a hill with a lovely pool and the stellar views promised by the name, the large dark-wood rooms have fridge, microwave and coffeemaker, plus a separate loft area that works well for families (guests can include two kids under 12 years of age without extra charge). The only drawback is the satellite location – you need to call the main office if you need anything, and the good restaurant (dishes $9 to $28) down near the stables only opens for lunch and dinner.

Balneario La Monserrate PRIVATE CAMPGROUND **$**
(☎787-889-1807; Hwy 3, Playa Luquillo; powered sites $17; P) There are more than 30 campsites and a bathhouse at this beachside spot. It's insanely popular in summer, but best avoided in the quiet winter months (when it's often closed).

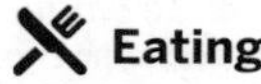

Eating

Luquillo's famous line of 60 or so **friquitines** (also known as *quioscos, kioskos* or just plain food stalls) along the western edge of Hwy 3 serve some of the tastiest treats around, from outstanding *comida criolla* to top-notch steaks. Some are very basic, others are upscale restaurants, so walk the line and follow your senses – or the locals.

TOP CHOICE **Pasta y Pueblo** ITALIAN **$**
(Calle 14 de Julio; dishes $10-15; ⏲dinner Tue-Sun; ✔) On a gravel lot around the corner from the Luquillo Sunrise Beach Inn and a half block from the beach, this unassuming little shack with fold-down windows slings some plate-licking fabulous food. It's run by local surfers, and there's often a crowd waiting to dine on pasta laced with seafood or more traditional sauces. Don't leave without trying the guava cheesecake or strawberry flan.

Boardriders Rum Shack RESTAURANT **$**
(Playa La Pared; dishes $7-20; ⏲lunch & dinner daily, plus brunch 10am-2pm Sat & Sun) A friendly beachside hangout festooned with Christmas lights, you can stash your board in its surf shop next door and refuel on fish tacos, beer-battered chicken fingers and burgers before your next set at La Pared. Or come for weekend brunch and watch someone else's wipeouts while you finish off some banana-stuffed French toast. Stop by around 6pm on Sunday for reggae and rumba bands.

Miramar Café CARIBBEAN **$$**
(152 Fernández García; dishes $14-23; ⏲2-10pm Wed-Sun) Lobster *asopado* (stew), coconut calamari and fried cheesecake are some of the faves of this new white-tablecloth eatery. On a corner of the central plaza, it's another popular dinner spot, with a decent wine selection and fantastical floor-to-ceiling murals.

Erik's Gyros & Deli MEDITERRANEAN **$**
(352 Fernández García; dishes $6-10; ⏲7am-6pm Mon-Sat, 8:30am-2pm Sun; 📶) It doesn't look like much, but locals swear by this place a few blocks south of the main plaza in downtown Luquillo. If you're missing gyro sandwiches or have an incurable penchant for feta cheese and a mochaccino, this is the place. Breakfasts too.

Brass Cactus RESTAURANT **$$**
(Hwy 193 Km 1.3; dishes $8-22; ⏲11am-midnight Sun-Thu, 11am-2am Fri-Sat) Not at all prickly, the Brass Cactus serves big plates of American pub fare with the odd traditional dish thrown in. Children will find lots to eat (burgers, fries, chicken fingers) and the down-home decor (think license plates hanging from the walls) will give them plenty to look at. Around 11pm on weekends the Cactus gets more of a club vibe, with patrons coming in to drink rather than eat.

La Exquisita Bakery BAKERY **$**
(Cnr 4 de Julio & Jesús Piñero; dishes $1-4; ⏲6am-8pm Mon-Sat, 8am-3pm Sun) Well perhaps not 'Champs Élysées' exquisite, but, as far as Luquillo goes, this place could satisfy a few sweet tooths. Slap-bang in the town's sleepy main square, this is where locals gather for cakes, pastry, coffee and sandwiches.

☆ Entertainment

Aside from the makeshift barbecues and myriad people-watching possibilities, you only have a couple of options here (outside of the swankier bars in the Río Mar). Then again, the beach itself is often a full-on party, especially at weekends.

Guava's LIVE MUSIC
(Playa La Pared; ⏲to 2am Fri & Sat) A bohemia trio plays at this restaurant on Sunday, and on Friday and Saturday nights, the tables are cleared and you can take a turn to live salsa, merengue or borchata with a splendid beach view.

El Flamboyán BAR
(Hwy 193 Km 1.2; ⏲8am-midnight Wed-Mon) Rub some chalk onto your pool cue and twist the top off your Medalla beer (preferably by hand); yes, the Flamboyán is one of those rustic open-sided seaside bars with heavy stone tables and perennially popular pool tables that serves simple food and $2 bottles of beer. The local gang shows up on weekend evenings to witness the sporadic African drumming.

ℹ Getting There & Away

Hwy 3 will take you to Rte 193 (aka Calle Fernandez Garcia), which is the main artery of Luquillo. It passes right by the Plaza de Recreo, the town's central plaza.

Públicos run regularly during the week from the Río Piedras terminal in San Juan to and from the Luquillo plaza ($5 to $8).

Fajardo & Around

POP 37,000

For the uninitiated observer, Fajardo is no oil painting. A spread-out municipality of just under 40,000 inhabitants, it sprawls like an untidy suburb between the El Yunque foothills and the sea. Part downbeat ferry port, part luxury boat launch, part swanky resort and part busy commuter town, there's little rhyme or reason to this hard-to-fathom conurbation spread over seven wards, although there are plenty of amenities and ample hotels hidden amid the characteristic low hills and small hidden bays.

But delve beneath the outer turbidity and Fajardo has its raison d'être. A mecca for wealthy yacht owners and tourists heading to the gargantuan Conquistador (a mega resort that once featured in the 1964 James Bond movie *Goldfinger*), Fajardo reigns as one of Puerto Rico's biggest water-activity centers and is the primary disembarkation point for the Spanish Virgin Islands of Vieques and Culebra.

You can do everything from diving in the waters of the coral-rich La Cordillera islands to exploring one of Puerto Rico's three bioluminescent bays here. On dry land there's the affectionate fishing 'village' of Las Croabas with its creaky fishing sloops, and the commonwealth's oldest colonial lighthouse. There's even a rather attractive and ecologically important nature reserve – Las Cabezas de San Juan – juxtaposed, in true Puerto Rican fashion, against the ubiquitous out-of-town shopping infestations.

Founded in 1760, downtown Fajardo, which lies between Rte 194 and Hwy 3, has little to show for 250 years of history. Yachters head a few miles south to Puerto del Rey, the largest marina in the Caribbean, while the most interesting sights for travelers – including the bioluminescent bay, the nature reserve and the well-maintained Playa Seven Seas – punctuate the strung-out neighborhood of Las Croabas to the north.

◉ Sights

Culture-vultures should look elsewhere: Fajardo has few interesting historical artifacts and little indigenous culture. The area's best activities can be enjoyed on the beach, in or under the water, or at the small but il-

Fajardo & Around

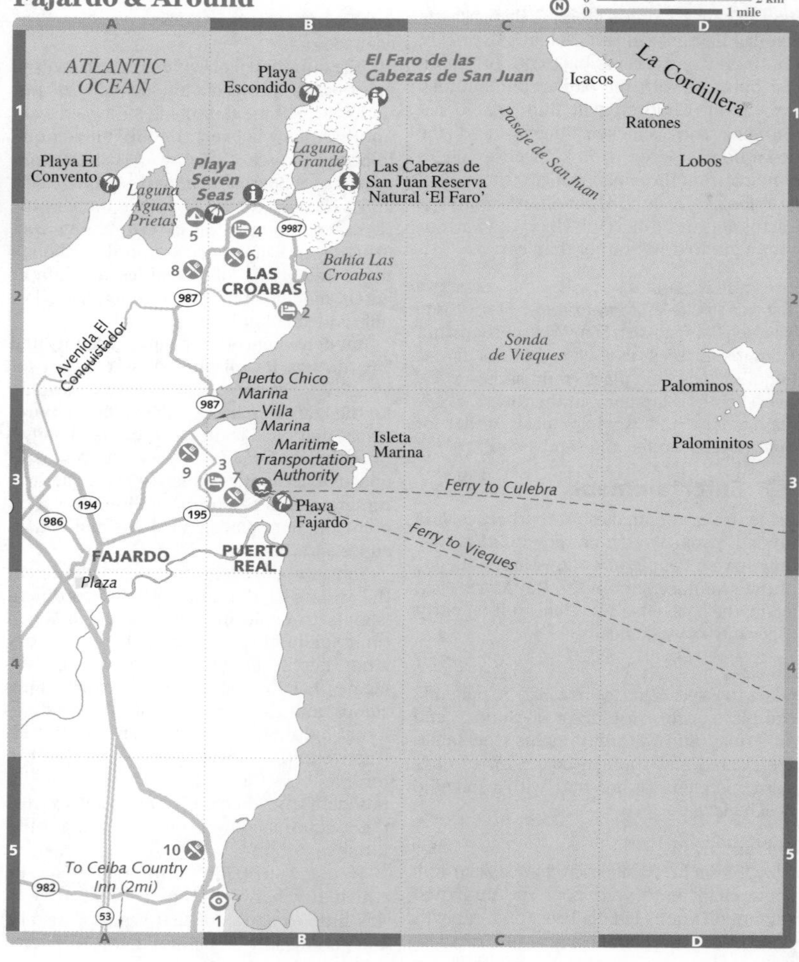

luminating Las Cabezas de San Juan nature reserve.

The city is quite spread out and most navigation will require a vehicle. Hwy 3 divides the city and connects you to other roads leading to popular attractions. Taking Rte 195 from Hwy 3 will bring you to the ferry docks; follow signs that say 'Embarcadero' or 'ferry' until arriving at Rte 987. There the roads split at a toe-tappingly-long traffic light: continuing straight on Rte 195 goes to the docks, while turning left onto Rte 987 passes Villa Marina and eventually brings you to the beach, the nature reserve and Las Croabas.

Buy a good road map if you plan to venture far off Hwy 3, as the rural roads can be confusing.

Las Cabezas de San Juan NATURE RESERVE
(☎787-722-5882/860-2560; www.fideicomiso.org; Hwy 987 at Las Croabas; adult/child $8/5; ⏰9am-4pm Wed-Sun, Spanish tours 9:30am, 10am, 10:30am & 2pm, English tours 2pm) A 316-acre nodule of land on Puerto Rico's extreme northeast tip, the Las Cabezas de San Juan Reserva Natural 'El Faro' protects a bioluminescent bay, rare flora and fauna, lush rainforest, various trails and boardwalks, and an important scientific research center. De-

Fajardo & Around

spite its diminutive size, the reserve shelters seven – yes *seven* – different ecological systems, including beaches, lagoons, dry forest, coral reefs and mangroves. Animal species that forage here include big iguanas, fiddler crabs, myriad insects and all kinds of birds. Such condensed biodiversity is typical of Puerto Rico's compact island status and 'Las Cabezas' is highlighted as an integral part of the commonwealth's vital – but dangerously threatened – Northeast Ecological Corridor (see www.sierraclub.org/corridor for more information).

Adding historical value to a potent natural brew is the splendidly restored 1882 **Faro de Las Cabezas de San Juan**, Puerto Rico's oldest lighthouse. Adorned with rich neoclassical detail and topped by a distinctive Spanish colonial tower, it overlooks the peninsula's steep, craggy cliffs where the stormy Atlantic meets the Sonda de Vieques (Vieques Sound). Situated in the eponymous natural reserve on a craggy headland, it today houses an information center and an observation deck, open the same hours as the reserve, which offers spectacular views of El Yunque.

There are about 2 miles of trails and boardwalks that lead through the park, but you can't follow them on your own: you must take a guided tour. This lasts more than two hours, including the short tram ride through the dry forest section. New **night tours** (2hr tours adult/student & senior $20/10) explore the grounds, lighthouse and bioluminescent lagoon on Thursday, Friday and Saturday at 7pm. Reservations are required for all tours, and can be made on the reserve's website.

You can get a glimpse of some of the reserve by simply walking east down the narrow beach from the Playa Seven Seas. Better yet, take a kayak tour (see p106) at sunset, and head into **Laguna Grande** after dark for the green-glowing, underwater 'fireworks' of bioluminescent micro-organisms. Make sure you go in a kayak or sailboat; engine pollution is slowly killing the very microorganisms that create the bioluminescence. Check that you're not doing anything to harm the environment before making deals with local boat owners.

Playa Seven Seas BEACH

(www.parquesnacionalespr.com; admission free, parking $5.35) On the southwestern shore of the peninsula of Las Cabezas, Playa Seven Seas is a sheltered, coconut-shaded horseshoe-shaped public beach. While it's not quite as pretty as Playa Luquillo, fear not – it is attractive. The beach gets packed on weekends and during summer.

For good snorkeling or to get away from it all, follow the beach about a half mile to the northeast along the Las Cabezas property to an area known as **Playa Escondida** (Hidden Beach). The reefs are just offshore. Taking the trail to the west eventually brings you to the nearly empty **Playa El Convento**, with its beach house for government officials.

Bahía Las Croabas SCENIC OUTLOOK

You find this spot where Hwy 987 ends at a little seaside park rimmed by seafood restaurants and bars looking east across the water to the peaks of Culebra. There is not much of a beach here, but there's a view of the offshore islands and the air blows fresh with the trade winds. The anchorage accommodates the fishermen's co-op and the last half-dozen *nativos,* the 'out-island' sloops

SEEING THE BIOLUMINESCENT LAGOON

Not everyone counts themselves a kayaker, but there are two other options for witnessing the bioluminescence of Fajardo's **Laguna Grande**.

» **Eco-Action Tours** (www.ecoactiontours.com) and **Bio Island** (www.bioislandpr.com) do electric boat trips for $45 to $50 per person.

» The **night tours at Las Cabezas de San Juan** (see p105) visit the grounds by foot and tram and then spend time down at the lagoon.

that everyone around here once used for fishing and gathering conch or lobster. The fishermen here are friendly, and you can probably strike a deal with one of them for a boat ride.

Puerto del Rey MARINA
(www.puertodelrey.com; Hwy 3 Km 51.4) Standing behind a breakwater in a cove 2 miles south of Fajardo, this is the largest marina (1100 slips) in the Caribbean. You will find a complete marina village here with restaurants, stores, laundry facilities, banking and all manner of boat-hauling and maintenance capabilities. Many yachts stop here to take advantage of the marina's courtesy carts and Fajardo's supermarkets when stocking up for a winter in the tropics or the ride back home to the US. Travelers will find that many of the sailing, diving and fishing charters run from here. It's about 5 miles south of Villa Marina.

Activities

Fajardo is decidedly amphibian – life is as exciting in the water as it is on land. This coastal region is blessed with many tiny islands (not to mention Culebra and Vieques) that provide fabulous opportunities for swimming, snorkeling, diving, fishing or just relaxing on a quiet beach.

Boat Trips

Almost all sailing trips advertised for travelers on the island sail out of one of the marinas in Fajardo. The operators listed here have been around for a while and know the area well, but there are many more good choices if these are all booked; *Que Pasa* (the island's tourism magazine) updates listings of new charter operators throughout the year. Many will pick you up in San Juan.

Erin Go Bragh Charters SAILING, SNORKELING
(www.egbc.net; Puerto del Rey Marina) Offers day sailing and snorkeling adventures (with barbecue lunch provided), sunset dinner cruises, as well as overnight charters to Vieques or Culebra and term-charters beyond to the Virgin Islands.

East Island Excursions SAILING
(☎787-860-3434/409-2485; www.eastwindcats.com; Puerto del Rey Marina) This outfit has glass-bottomed catamarans that are in high demand, so book early. All kinds of day trips to the La Cordillera islands are offered, and it even does quick runs over to St Thomas. One of the catamarans has a water slide that launches you right into the ocean. Day trips start at $69 per person.

Traveler SNORKELING
(www.ecoadventurespr.com; Villa Marina; snorkeling tour from $65) Offers similar daily tours as other operators, with all-you-can-eat salad bars and snorkeling equipment provided for reasonable prices.

Kayaking

This is absolutely the most entrancing way to see Fajardo's bioluminescent attractions – and the most environmentally sound as well. Swimming has been banned in the bay since 2007. Many companies don't have excursions on Sunday nights.

Yokahú Kayaks KAYAKING
(www.yokahukayaks.com; bay tour $45) This operator provides equipment, and the guides are very professional. Children under six years of age aren't allowed on the night trips, which generally last two hours.

Kayaking Puerto Rico KAYAKING
(www.kayakingpuertorico.com) Runs numerous tours, including the bioluminescent lagoon, daytime snorkel tours and full day trips including kayaking, snorkeling and an excursion to El Yunque ($109).

Akuadventures KAYAKING
(www.biobaypr.com) Uses clear kayaks on its tours of the bioluminescent bay, enabling paddlers to see the aquatic fireworks from all angles.

Fishing

Capt Osva Alcaide FISHING, SNORKELING
(☎787-547-4851; www.deepseafishingpr.com) Offers half- and full-day deep-sea fishing

charters out of Fajardo, and snorkeling to Icacos and Palominos islands. A full day (six people maximum) with lunch costs $950.

Diving

Caribbean School of Aquatics DIVING
(☎787-728-6606; www.saildiveparty.com; Villa Marina) Operating since 1963, the Caribbean School of Aquatics has National Association of Underwater Instructors (NAUI) and Professional Association of Dive Instructors (PADI) scuba classes, and Captain Greg Korwek will take you on all-day boat trips to the best spots around La Cordillera and elsewhere; two-tank dives start at $119 per person.

La Casa del Mar DIVING
(☎787-860-3483; www.scubapuertorico.net; 1000 Ave Conquistador) Set inside the grounds of El Conquistador resort, this PADI-certified outfit is great for all levels. A 'bubblemaker' appeals to the younger crowd, while more-experienced divers can take the trips to local reefs (one/two tanks $69/99). A two-tank dive in Culebra is $125.

Sea Ventures Dive Center DIVING, SNORKELING
(☎800-739-3483, 787-863-3483; www.divepuertorico.com; Puerto del Rey) With three outlets in Fajardo, Palmas del Mar and Guánica, staffed by very experienced professionals, Sea Ventures offers one-week PADI certification courses. For those who just want the basics or already know how to dive, there are usually trips to Palominos and Icacos daily (one/two tanks $65/119, including gear). Snorkel excursions are available for $45 to $60.

Sleeping

Officials don't hassle people who pitch tents on Playa El Convento, which is reached by the path heading west from Playa Seven Seas. The area is popular, so you'll usually find at least one or two tents up at all times; avoid pitching here if there are no other campers though – muggings do occur.

Ceiba Country Inn INN $$
(☎787-885-0471; www.ceibacountryinn.com; Hwy 997 Km 2.1; d incl breakfast $85-125; P❄📶) A classic mountain retreat with friendly new owners – and even friendlier pets – this place has nine units overlooking the Caribbean and the offshore islands. On a clear day Culebra floats along the horizon. Picture a landscaped hillside villa with decks, barbecue grill and lounge, and the sounds of the forest coming alive at dusk. From San Juan, take Hwy 3 past Fajardo until the road becomes Rte 53. Take exit 5 (Ceiba North) and then make a right onto Rd 975 and go 1 mile. Turn right onto Hwy 977 and follow the signs.

Passion Fruit B&B INN $$
(☎800-670-3196; www.passionfruitbb.com; Hwy 987 at Hwy 9987; r $95-130; P❄📶🏊) A tropically themed guesthouse with a personal touch, the Passion Fruit is quite likely to inspire plenty of summer passion with its poolside breakfast spread and colorful 3rd-floor honeymoon suites. Upstairs rooms are best. Discreet, private and bang for your buck.

Fajardo Inn PARADOR $$
(☎787-860-6000; www.fajardoinn.com; 52 Parcelas Beltrán, Hwy 195; r $110-300; P❄@📶🏊👪) Perched on a hill overlooking the scruffy Fajardo corridor (and distant sea views), the Spanish-hacienda-style Fajardo Inn is hard to miss. With two beautiful swimming pools, crazy golf, kids' playground, tennis court and a gym so huge it would look impressive in New York's Upper East Side, this peach-hued Puerto Rican parador exudes comfort, charm and a refreshing blend of unhurried ambience. Rooms are large and uncluttered, with cable TV, massive beds, wood furnishings and a daily dose of complimentary Puerto Rican coffee. A miniresort without the wristband.

El Conquistador Resort & Golden Door Spa RESORT $$$
(☎787-863-1000; www.elconresort.com; 1000 Ave El Conquistador; r from $280; P❄@📶🏊👪) A 900-unit mega resort that encompasses a steep coastal escarpment a few clicks northeast of Fajardo, this minitown boasts its own cove, cable car, mock Andalusian village, and – just in case you were harboring any James Bond allusions – private fantasy island. If your idea of a good vacation revolves around golf, tennis, spa pampering, water sports, fine dining and gambling – with lots of company – this could be your bag. Mind the resort and parking fees.

Playa Seven Seas Camping PUBLIC CAMPGROUND $
(☎787-863-8180; Hwy 987; campsites per tent $10) One of Puerto Rico's safest beaches, Playa Seven Seas near Las Croabas fills up fast. Make sure you reserve in advance if you plan to come during summer or holidays.

Showers and bathrooms are available and there's a restaurant on the beach.

Eating

Reservations are recommended in high season.

TOP CHOICE La Estación CARIBBEAN **$$**
(787-863-4481; Hwy 987 Km 4; dishes $9-20; dinner Fri-Wed;) Done up like an artist's funky loft, this playfully converted gas station has a jeep dashboard bar on the patio and a candlelit dining room hung with classic bicycles. Just around the corner from the El Conquistador, this indoor/outdoor eatery serves heaving portions of *mofongo* (mashed plantains), skirt steak and even a few good veggie items, on heavy wooden pedestals, with delicious sauces and an eye-fluttering passion fruit vinaigrette salad dressing. The outdoor barbecue gets fired up when the weather's good, and there's a pool table in the separate bar area (open until 2am Friday and Saturday, otherwise until midnight) that's fun for evening entertainment.

Pasión por el Fogón PUERTO RICAN **$$**
(787-863-3502; Rte 987 Km 2.3; dishes $14-38; dinner Wed-Mon) Lobster medallions, filet mignon and chicken stuffed with sweet banana and bacon – sound tasty? The governor of New York, Mariah Carey and Carlos Delgado obviously thought so, as they've all eaten here at one time or another. Listed as one of Puerto Rico's leading Mesónes Gastronómicos, Pasión por el Fogón is situated opposite the Villa Marina and – in keeping with its name – has a real passion for cooking.

Calizo Seafood SEAFOOD **$$**
(787-863-3664; Hwy 987 Km 5.9; dishes $17-35; 5-10pm Mon-Fri, 1-11pm Sat & Sun) On a bend in the road near Playa Seven Seas, Calizo produces seafood, steaks and paella with a gourmet flourish. Dine in the outdoor courtyard with thatched umbrellas and a spreading palm tree or in the air-conditioned dining room with pretty blue- and yellow-tiled tables and work by local artists. Though seafood's the highlight, the Caribbean-infused steaks (tamarind grilled mignon) and desserts (mango cheesecake and malanga brûlée) are excellent too.

Puerto Nativo PUERTO RICAN **$$**
(787-430-8448, Hwy 3 Km 50.5; mains $10-25; lunch & dinner Tue-Sun) A new eatery near the Ceiba airport, Puerto Nativo creates tasty variations on Puerto Rican favorites, with half a dozen varieties of *mofongo* on offer, as well as fried pork, fresh seafood and meat dishes such as the *empanada de res al caballo* (breaded steak topped with fried egg). Relax with a drink (the bar closes at 2am Friday and Saturday and stays open until midnight otherwise) on the large wooden porch and don't miss the live *música bohemia* on Fridays.

Blue Iguana MEXICAN **$**
(dishes $7-17; 11am-11pm) The **Fajardo Inn** has two restaurants, but this one is by far the best, with great Mexican fare, sharp service and unbelievably cheap prices (for sizable portions). In the earlier hours it's a good option for families; later on the pool table and ample bar attract a drinking crowd. On weekends it's very popular after 10pm, especially for Friday-night karaoke.

Golden Sweet Bakery BAKERY **$**
(Hwy 195; dishes $4-6; 6am-5pm;) Along the ferry terminal route just east of the Hwy 987 intersection, this large sit-down bakery cafe creates pastries on-site, serves breakfast all day and claims an 'intermittent' wi-fi signal. Make a quick stop for some freshly squeezed orange juice, or settle in for a sandwich and a serving of bread pudding.

Entertainment

The casino (which opens at 4pm), bars and restaurants at the **El Conquistador Resort & Golden Door Spa** are open to the public; you're perfectly welcome to try your luck at the tables or take in a floor show from the bar no matter where you lay your head later that night. Be prepared to fork over $3 an hour for parking.

Blue Iguana gets busy on weekend nights during high season, and **Puerto Nativo** has live music on Friday nights.

Shopping

The malls are on Hwy 3 just north of town if you need a supermarket or superstore fix.

Information

Fajardo mayor's office (www.fajardopr.org; cnr Muñoz Rivera & Dr López; 8am-noon & 1-4:30pm Mon-Fri) There's no real tourism office in town, but the mayor's office does what it can.

HIMA San Pablo Hospital Fajardo (787-863-0505; www.mlteam.com/HIMA; Rte 194 off Av Conquistador; 24hr) The largest hospital along the east coast and your best option for medical issues.

Wash-n-Post (Santa Isidra shopping center; ⌚8am-7pm Mon-Sat, 11am-5pm Sun) Across the street from the Villa Marina shopping center, this one-stop FedEx and Western Union service also has fluff-and-fold.

Getting There & Away

Air

The small **Ceiba airport** (24-hour parking $9) opened in 2008 on the old Roosevelt Roads Naval Station, replacing Fajardo as the regional airport. It's approximately 6 miles south of Fajardo. Typical one-way fares are approximately $30 to Vieques (15 minutes), $40 to Culebra (15 minutes) and $90 to St Croix (30 minutes). To get there by car from Fajardo, take exit 2 onto Hwy 3 and follow the airport signs. From Naguabo and the south, use exit 6 to approach it via Hwy 978.

Air Flamenco (☎787-801-8256; www.airflamenco.net) Scheduled flights go to Vieques, Culebra and both San Juan airports.

M&N Aviation (www.mnaviation.com) Has on-demand charter service.

Vieques Air Link (☎787-534-4221; www.viequesairlink.com) Offers the most daily flights and the best fares, with service to destinations including Vieques, Culebra, St Croix, St Thomas, Tortola, as well as San Juan's Isla Grande ($50).

Call for availability of charter flights. A público from the airport to the ferry terminal is fixed at $12 for up to four passengers.

Car

There's a spacious outdoor parking lot on the right-hand side of the road as you approach the ferry docks. The lot is surrounded by secure fencing and has 24-hour surveillance. Parking here costs $5 a day. Note that most rental car contracts prohibit taking cars on the ferry to Culebra or Vieques.

World Car Rental (☎787-860-4808; Rte 195 at the docks; per day from $43; ⌚7:30am-8pm Mon-Fri, 7:30am-5:30pm Sat & Sun) Super-close to the public parking lot, this small outfit offers cars at daily and weekly rates.

Avis (☎787-885-0505; www.avis.com) At the Ceiba airport; will transfer you to/from the ferry without charge, and offers one-way rentals at a higher daily rate.

Thrifty (☎787-860-2030; www.thrifty.com; Puerto Del Rey Marina; $60 drop-off fee) and **Enterprise** (☎787-860-6868 central Fajardo, 787-801-3722 El Conquistador; www.enterprise.com; $40 drop-off fee) also permit one-way rentals.

Ferry

The ferries to Vieques and Culebra leave from the **Maritime Transportation Authority** (Autoridad de Transporte Marítimo or ATM; ☎787-863-0705; www.atm.gobierno.pr) for the islands. The terminal is about 1.5 miles east of town in the run-down Playa Fajardo/Puerto Real neighborhood (follow the signs to either). For the ferry schedule for Culebra, see p126; for Vieques, see p143.

Público

The **main público stop** is off the plaza in the old commercial center of town; but you will also find públicos at the ferry terminal (to meet incoming ferries) and near the seafood restaurants in Las Croabas. Some of the públicos at the ferry terminal will take you to Luquillo ($2, 15 minutes), and to and from the Río Piedras section of San Juan ($4 to $6, 1½ hours), but you might need to take one into the center ($1) and transfer first. For other trips, you'll need to negotiate a fare with a taxi. If you are coming from San Juan and going to the ferry dock, make sure to tell the driver to go all the way to the port.

Taxi

You can always find taxis at the ferry terminal to take you to Luis Muñoz Marín International Airport (LMM) in San Juan ($80). Based in Fajardo, **Alvaro Cuellar** (☎787-590-9001) charges $60 to $65.

Naguabo & Around

POP 26,700

There are two parts to modern Naguabo: the so-called downtown – which you'll curse for its nutty traffic and impossible-to-understand one-way system – and the laid-back and local Playa Húcares, where you might want to linger for views, a snooze, and lunch in one of its down-to-earth seafood restaurants. Pretty Playa Húcares bay was one of the set locations for *The Rum Diary* movie (see the boxed text, p82).

Sights

Playa Húcares doesn't actually have a beach – the waterfront is a rock seawall overlooking a bay. It does, however, have a dramatic view of Vieques, 10 miles out to sea, and Cayo Santiago, closer to the coastline. It's worth visiting to get a look at the brightly painted fishing sloops and the two Victorian mansions that stand like sentinels over the sleepy little boardwalk, officially named Malecón Arturo Corsino. One of the mansions, the Castillo Villa del Mar, is on the National Registry of Historic Places (despite the dilapidation and the graffiti) and was once home to a restaurant and art gallery where local painters showed their work. These days it's a run-down old eyesore, but the mansion next to it has been somewhat restored, giving rise to hopes that both structures will eventually be returned to their former state of grace.

On weekends people flock to the line of open-air seafood restaurants just across the street for freshly caught *chillo* (snapper) and *sierra* (kingfish). If you follow Hwy 3 a half mile further south, you'll see about 2 miles of thin, tree-lined, vacant beach. Beyond this, the road carries you into the tiny village of **Playa Humacao**. Dilapidated Playa Humacao has one bright spot: there is a pristine balneario and *centro vacacional* (vacation center) at the neighborhood west of the village. **Punta Santiago** has become a bit of a weekend and holiday hot spot, and its bright *friquitines* offer lots of succulent treats such as *arroz con jueyes* (rice with crab chunks) and shark nuggets. During the busy season it's fun and upbeat and nowhere near as crowded as Luquillo.

Activities

Most outfitters operate out of the mammoth Palmas del Mar resort. Golfers can make reservations at either of the two **golf courses** (☎787-656-9040). The greens fee for the 6800yd Reese Jones course is $135 ($95 after 1pm) for nonguests; the old course (called 'the Palms') has similar prices.

The largest tennis facility in the Caribbean, the resort has 20 **tennis courts** (☎787-656-9043), but you must make a reservation. Court fees are $20 per person an hour during the day, and $30 at night.

Barefoot Travelers Rooms HANG GLIDING, KAYAKING
(☎787-850-0508; www.barefoottravelersrooms.com; Punta Santiago) Active folks should contact Barefoot Travelers Rooms about hang gliding instruction ($149 per tandem flight) in El Yunque and kayak/snorkel excursions ($40 per person) to the periphery of Cayo Santiago.

Captain Frank López FISHING, SNORKELING
(☎787-316-0441) The captain offers fishing or snorkeling trips and sea excursions to Cayo Santiago. Prices are negotiable: start your bidding at about $35. Look for *La Paseadora* boat at Playa Naguabo.

Sea Ventures Dive Center DIVING, SNORKELING
(☎787-863-3483; www.divepalmasdelmar.com; Marina de Palmas) Organizes diving and snorkeling trips to Cayo Santiago and the deeper sites offshore (there are 35 within a 5-mile radius). Prices start at $60/119 for a half-day snorkel/dive including gear. It also does afternoon snorkel trips to Vieques ($75) and Culebra ($120).

Rancho Buena Vista HORSEBACK RIDING
(☎787-479-7479; www.ranchobuenavistapr.com) Boards about 70 horses, including hunters and jumpers. One-hour trail rides cost about $45 (eight years and older), and it's $20 for kids' pony rides.

Sleeping

There are several pretty guesthouses tucked into the south side of El Yunque that can be reached from Naguabo (see p98), and some excellent accommodations along the coast.

Casa Libre Puerto Rico GUESTHOUSE **$$**
(☎787-874-6414; www.casalibrepr.com; 188 Calle 8, Playa Húcares; r incl breakfast $110; P❄📶≋) All three of the rooms at this new guesthouse have attractive furnishings and comfortable beds. The friendly Puerto Rican and Californian hosts make a dynamite full breakfast, and will lend movies from their huge DVD library. Reserve the purple room upstairs for breathtaking El Yunque and water views.

Barefoot Travelers Rooms GUESTHOUSE **$**
(☎787-850-0508; www.barefoottravelersrooms.com; Punta Santiago; r $73-83; ❄📶≋👪) At this homey three-room guesthouse located in a gated community a block from the beach, your detail-oriented hosts really do walk around shoeless – when they're not giving hang gliding instruction. Amenities include a gorgeous guest kitchen, a book library, and an ample living room with television and DVD player, plus complimentary morning coffee.

Palmas del Mar RESORT **$$$**
(☎787-850-6000; www.starwoodhotels.com/fourpoints; 170 Candelero Dr, Humacao; r $155-290; P❄@📶≋) Covering 2700 acres, this massive complex is significantly larger than most of Puerto Rico's state forests and is a world unto itself. At its opulent core lies a huge cluster of privately owned villas (ranging in price from $365,000 to $9 million)

CAYO SANTIAGO

In 1938 a team of scientists from the University of Puerto Rico and Columbia University in New York decided to turn Cayo Santiago into a research area. Five hundred rhesus monkeys were let loose on the peaked, hazy island just offshore from Punta Santiago, and today 900 descendants of these primates run rampant on the 39 tropical acres.

Only researchers and scientific personnel from the Caribbean Primate Research Center (http://cprc.rcm.upr.edu) are permitted on the island, but visitors can eyeball monkeys from their boat (don't forget that monkeys can swim). There's fabulous snorkeling around a sunken ship not far from the shore.

and time-share units built around a marina, 6.5 miles of beach and two golf courses. Of more interest to itinerant travelers are the casino and token hotel: the Four Points by Sheraton, which has 107 amply furnished rooms and access to any of the resort's 20 restaurants.

Centro Vacacional Punta Santiago VACATION CENTER **$**
(☎787-852-1660; www.parquesnacionalespr.com; Hwy 3 Km 72.4, Playa Humacao; RV powered sites $25-40, cabins/villas $70/110; P❄≋) This spot has a balneario, 36 cold-water cabañas and 63 air-conditioned villas in a coconut grove on a pristine beach. Each unit can accommodate up to six people, but you need to bring your own linen.

Eating

The easygoing strip of Playa Húcares is a cheapskate's heaven, and perfect for a bit of do-it-yourself research. Comb the kiosks and holes-in-the-wall at the north end for great *empanadillas* (dough stuffed with meat or fish), *mojito criollo* (rum, mint and lemon) sauce on fresh fish and tasty *surullitos*. Lovers of hot sauce should drop by the La Playa Liquor Store mini-mart to buy one of the fiery *piques* crafted by a local Thai resident.

El Makito SEAFOOD **$$**
(Hwy 3, Playa Húcares; mains $12-25) The tanks say 'fresh Maine lobsters,' even though these pincerless live specimens are the Caribbean variety, but no matter. From its second-story perch on the *malecón* (pier), the 'little shark' has an excellent view of the water from its shaded patio seats. The menu's long, with seafood pastas, the requisite laundry list of *mofongos,* and shrimp, conch and octopus done up in myriad configurations.

Restaurant Vinny PUERTO RICAN **$$**
(mains $14-26; ⏲8am-7pm Mon-Thu, 8am-7pm Fri-Sun) Across from El Makito, Vinny does a bang-up lunch for $5.50 and the best *empanadillas* on the island.

Getting There & Away

Público vans in Playa Naguabo park near the promenade. For a few dollars, they go to Naguabo or Humacao, from where you can move on to the greener pastures of Fajardo, Ponce or San Juan.

The Palmas del Mar resort can arrange for a minivan to haul you to and from LMM airport in San Juan – about a 45-minute trip in normal traffic. During peak season, it charges $90 to $100. For reservations call ☎787-285-4323.

Yabucoa & Around

POP 37,900

Surrounded by hills on three sides and ocean on the other, Yabucoa sits on a tract of well-watered fertile land that once played host to Puerto Rico's all-encompassing sugar industry. Unless you have a penchant for poking around the ruins of old sugar mills, the town holds little for modern-day travelers. Out on the periphery, it's a different story. Yabucoa is the starting point for two dramatic drives: the famed Ruta Panorámica and the less heralded, but no less spectacular, Hwy 901 that tracks the coast between Playa Lucía and the Punta Tuna lighthouse. On this road you'll find accommodations, restaurants and two of the island's most isolated surfing spots.

If you are traveling south to Yabucoa from the Humacao area, take the Hwy 53 toll road to avoid the traffic on Hwy 3. This lightly traveled section of road bisects miles of sugarcane fields and estuary where three mountain rivers meet.

Sights & Activities

The balneario at **Playa Lucía**, near the intersection of Hwy 901 and Hwy 9911 in Yabucoa, has great shade under its coconut trees and several little beach bar-restaurants just off its premises. **El Cocal** is one of the few good surfing spots in the area (ask for directions at the balneario). Further southwest toward Maunabo is Sharkey's, another decent surf break where you're likely to have the waves to yourself.

Off Hwy 901 along the coast, you can ponder the ruins of **Hacienda de Santa Lucía**, an old sugar plantation a mile north of Playa Lucía. Don't expect a haunted mansion; there's only one wall left. **Central Roig** is the still-active, old-time sugar hacienda and mill on the same road.

Lovers and solitary types like the view from the base of the **Faro Punta Tuna** (9am-3:30pm Wed-Sun), the lighthouse just southeast of Maunabo; it's also a wetland reserve and nesting ground for leatherback and hawksbill turtles. From Hwy 901, take Hwy 760 toward the ocean. A path leads down to the extremely secluded **Playa Larga**.

Sleeping

Caribe Playa INN $$
(787-839-6339; www.caribeplaya.com; Hwy 3 Km 112; r $98-135; P) You will spot this place where Hwy 3 runs along the seashore between Maunabo and Patillas. Tucked right on the shore under a slanting plantation of coconuts, this inn has 26 units, many with beachfront balconies; most rooms have a kitchen sink and fridge, but no stove. There's a restaurant on the premises and a natural pool carved into the rocky coast. A licensed therapist can do beachside massages for $55 an hour.

Parador Palmas de Lucía PARADOR $$
(787-893-4423; www.palmasdelucia.com; cnr Hwy 901 & Hwy 9911; d/tr $102/126; P) Just when you thought mall-infested Yabucoa was uninhabitable, you hit the end of the road at Playa Lucía and stumble upon what is surely one of Puerto Rico's best paradores. Backing up onto the beach, but with its own secluded pool and restaurant, the Palmas de Lucía is a light, airy place with huge, clean rooms decked out with rather plush furnishings. To add spice to an already strong brew, there's also a small but well-kept gymnasium, which offers a good alternative to jogging around Yabucoa's traffic-clogged roads. Good service is par for the course at this family-friendly hotel, and it makes an excellent launch pad for a lengthy road trip across the Ruta Panorámica.

Parador Costa del Mar PARADOR $$
(787-266-6276; www.tropicalinnspr.com; Hwy 901 Km 5.6; d/tr $102/126; P) A younger sibling of the Palmas de Lucía (it's owned by the same family), Costa del Mar fits the same price and comfort bracket. Its position on a grassy bluff overlooking the ocean at the start of spectacular Hwy 901 gives it extra kudos, as do the vividly colored flowers, luminous pool and brilliant-yellow paintwork. But there's substance under the superficiality. You can also bank on five-star cleanliness, zippy service and gym, sauna and a 100yd trek to the beach.

MaunaCaribe PARADOR $$
(787-861-3330; www.tropicalinnspr.com; Hwy 901 Km 1.9, Maunabo; d $102; P) Another relation to the area paradores listed above, this oceanside option boasts a dazzling infinity pool, flat screen televisions and rooms with new blonde wood furniture and a muted tropical flair. Recently remodeled, the pastel-painted complex is still saddled with a sterile cookie-cutter suburban layout, but the many amenities, including a spacious restaurant and bar, more than compensate.

Playa de Emajaguas Guest House GUESTHOUSE $
(787-861-6023; Hwy 901 Km 2.5; d/tr $60/80;) The no-frills Emajaguas Guest House nestles in verdant mountain foothills above a stunning deserted beach near El Cocal and Sharkey's surf breaks. It's light on luxuries and close to nature; you come here for the rustic surroundings and the sense of isolation. The once grand house shelters seven scruffy efficiency apartments with private bathrooms and kitchenettes, and cats and roosters roam about the property. Grab a hammock and turn off, tune in and drop out.

Eating

Aquamar Steakhouse & Seafood RESTAURANT $$
(787-861-1363; Hwy 901 Km 1.7, Maunabo; dishes $12-33; 11am-10pm Mon-Wed, 11am-11pm Thu-Sun) Just past the police station and basketball court in Maunabo and a few paces from sandy beach, Aquamar specializes in exotic meats such as ostrich and wild boar. Not so adventurous? Then peruse the lengthy menu for standout conch and octopus or the pas-

tas and risottos. Its classy warehouse-sized dining room is flanked by the restaurant's 300 varieties of wine, or you can sit in the breezy bar area facing the water. Live local groups entertain on Saturday night.

El Nuevo Horizonte PUERTO RICAN **$$**
(Hwy 901 Km 9.8; dishes $17-29; ⌚11am-9pm Thu-Sun) Just a mile or two west of Parador Costa del Mar, the view rarely gets better than it does from this place. This restaurant is perched high on the mountainside overlooking the Caribbean. You can smell the *asopao de langosta* (lobster stew) cooking 200yd before you get here. A cauldron of the stew will set you back about $25 and serves at least two people.

El Mar de la Tranquilidad PUERTO RICAN **$$**
(Hwy 3 Km 118.9; dishes $10-20; ⌚noon-8pm Fri-Sun, noon-5pm Tue-Thu) Once the road returns to sea level (heading west), look for this establishment on the seaward side of Hwy 3. Beer on the outdoor terrace is a rare pleasure, and you can get *salmorejo de jueyes* (land crab in tomato sauce), lobster and some decent cocktails.

ℹ Getting There & Away

Públicos link Yabucoa to Humacao ($2) and taxis can take you to Maunabo ($10). Both have onward connections to Fajardo and San Juan. A new tunnel on Hwy 53 connects Yabucoa and Maunabo, although the oceanside Hwy 901 is a far more scenic route (especially if you're on a bike).

Culebra & Vieques

POP 11,100

Includes »

Best Places to Eat

» Susie's (p124)
» Conuco (p139)
» El Eden (p124)
» Coconuts (p139)
» El Quenepo (p140)

Best Places to Stay

» Hix Island House (p138)
» W Retreat & Spa (p138)
» Palmetto Guesthouse (p121)
» La Finca Caribe (p139)
» Flamenco Campground (p124)

Why Go?

Separated from mainland Puerto Rico by a 7-mile stretch of choppy ocean, the two bejeweled Caribbean havens of Culebra and Vieques have sizable populations of American expats and maverick locals and are noticeably slower and more easygoing than their main-island counterpart.

Disembark for a few days and you'll uncover a wealth of surprises: wild horses in Vieques, endangered turtles in Culebra – and people of rare courage, many of whom were instrumental in the fight to reclaim their prized islands from the US Navy in 1975 (Culebra) and 2003 (Vieques) after more than 50 years of military occupation.

The main drawcard for contemporary visitors is the unsullied beaches – Vieques and Culebra protect some of the best arcs of sand in the Caribbean – and the unblemished countryside, which glimmers invitingly with nary a golf course or casino to break the natural vista.

When to Go

September and October can be pretty slow on the islands, with many restaurants taking a break or cutting back their hours. But it's also a good time to find lodging discounts and have less company on the island ferries.

The best viewing of the bioluminescent bay in Vieques is during the new moon; some operators don't go out when it's full. From April through June, wildlife fans can volunteer for a turtle-egg protection project on Culebra.

The famous Caribbean trade winds gently buffet these two islands, but it is still hot, hot, hot just about every day of the year.

History

Some 500 years ago the islands east of Puerto Rico, including Culebra and Vieques, were disputed territory between the Taíno and the Caribs. Groups from both tribes came and went from the islands according to the season – probably to hunt the turtles nesting here. Vieques had more fertile, flatter land for farming and therefore was the more popular island. The first real settlement came to Culebra during the early 16th century, when Taíno and Carib refugees from Borinquen gathered here and on Vieques to make peace with each other, pool their resources and mount a fierce (but ultimately unsuccessful) campaign to drive the

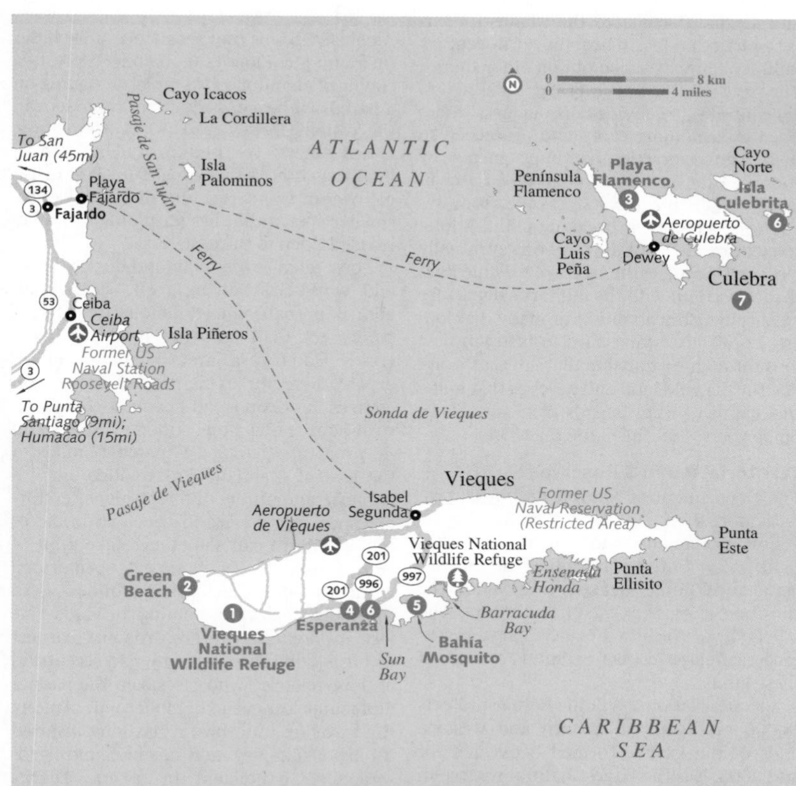

Culebra & Vieques Highlights

1. Trail mongooses and wild horses and explore abandoned navy bunkers on a backcountry exploration of the **Vieques National Wildlife Refuge** (p129)
2. Swap four wheels for two and go for a picturesque spin to **Green Beach** (p135) on bike-friendly Vieques
3. Find dilapidated US tanks and a refreshing lack of tourists on paradisial **Playa Flamenco** (p119)
4. Eat, drink, play or just plain chill on the colorful 'strip' in laid-back **Esperanza** (p131)
5. See aquatic stars on a serene but distinctly surreal evening boat tour of bioluminescent **Bahía Mosquito** (p131)
6. Hike the gentle hills on the offshore islands **Isla Culebrita** (p118) and **Cayo de Tierra** (p132)
7. Plunge in and **dive** (p120) the reefs and sunken treasures of Culebra's clear waters

Spaniards from the big island. When Spain conceded Puerto Rico and her territories to the US following the Spanish-American War in 1898, both Culebra and Vieques became municipalities of the Republic of Puerto Rico. Therefore, residents are recognized as US citizens (half of them are expat Americans, in any case).

For most of the 20th century, the US Navy and Marine Corps used the islands for target practice and for rehearsing 20th-century military actions carried out on other shores. The navy left Culebra several decades ago to concentrate its activities on Vieques, where it set up a military camp and proceeded to hold regular practice bombings in nearby waters. After an errant bomb killed a civilian in 1999, *viequenses* (people from Vieques) reached their breaking point. A long struggle ensued, but the navy was eventually ejected. Of course, the tracts of pristine land that opened up with the military's departure have caught the attention of many developers. Locals are trying hard to bring in new jobs through sustainable tourism that won't destroy the wild land and beaches that make the Spanish Virgin Islands truly special. So far so good – but the battle rages on.

Territorial Parks & Reserves

The Department of Natural Resources protects more than 1500 acres of land along the Península Flamenco and from Monte Resaca (640ft) east to the sea. Named the Culebra National Wildlife Refuge, it includes the coastline as well as 22 offshore cays. The **US Fish & Wildlife Service** (www.fws.gov/caribbean/refuges/culebra) administers all of these lands.

Vieques National Wildlife Refuge protects 18,000 acres on the eastern and western ends of the island. Formed between 2001 and 2003, it is the largest natural reserve in Puerto Rico and offers visitors a chance to mountain bike, hike, snorkel and swim on newly opened beaches and pristine land.

Getting There & Around

There's frequent air service from San Juan to both Vieques (see p142) and Culebra (see p126). Cheaper and more environmentally friendly are the government-run ferries that run from Fajardo to Vieques (see p143) and Culebra (p126) regularly, though the passage can be bumpy. In January, ferry passengers can sometimes spot humpback whales.

Many travel agencies will tell you that cars are a must on Culebra and Vieques. However, with a little extra effort and some lung-expanding leg work, both islands can be negotiated via a mixture of públicos (shared taxis), taxis, bicycles and your own two feet.

Currently, there's no scheduled ferry or direct flights between Vieques and Culebra; air or boat charters (see p126) are the only option.

Culebra

POP 1818

An elusive lizard (not seen since 1974) hides in a unique mountain 'boulder' forest, a couple of abandoned US tanks lie rusting on a paradisial beach, a sign on a shop door in the 'capital' Dewey reads 'Open some days, closed others.' Welcome to Culebra, the island that time forgot; mainland Puerto Rico's weird, wonderful and distinctly wacky smaller cousin that lies glistening like a bejeweled Eden to the east.

Long feted for its diamond-dust beaches and world-class diving reefs, sleepy Culebra is probably more famous for what it *hasn't* got than for what it actually possesses. Home to a large population of US expats, there are no big hotels here, no golf courses, no casinos, no fast-food chains, no rush-hour traffic, no postmodern stress and *no problemas, amigo*. Situated 17 miles to the east of mainland Puerto Rico, but inhabiting an entirely different planet culturally speaking, the island's peculiar brand of offbeat charm can sometimes take a bit of getting used to. Don't expect open-armed cordiality here. Culebran friendliness is of the more backwards-coming-forwards variety. It's home to rat-race dropouts, earnest idealists, solitude seekers, myriad eccentrics, and anyone else who's forsaken the hassles and manic intricacies of modern life. Among the traveling fraternity, it has long inspired a religiouslike devotion in some, and head-scratching bafflement in others. There's but one binding thread – the place is jaw-droppingly beautiful.

History

First hunting grounds for Taíno and Carib tribes, then a pirate stronghold during the days of the Spanish Empire, much of Culebra's 7000 acres has remained essentially the same ever since two-legged creatures took to walking its shores. The US Navy grabbed control of most of the island early in the 20th century and didn't cede its lands back to the locals until 1975. Some modern structures went up on the newly accessible land rather rapidly, but resident expats and

Culebra

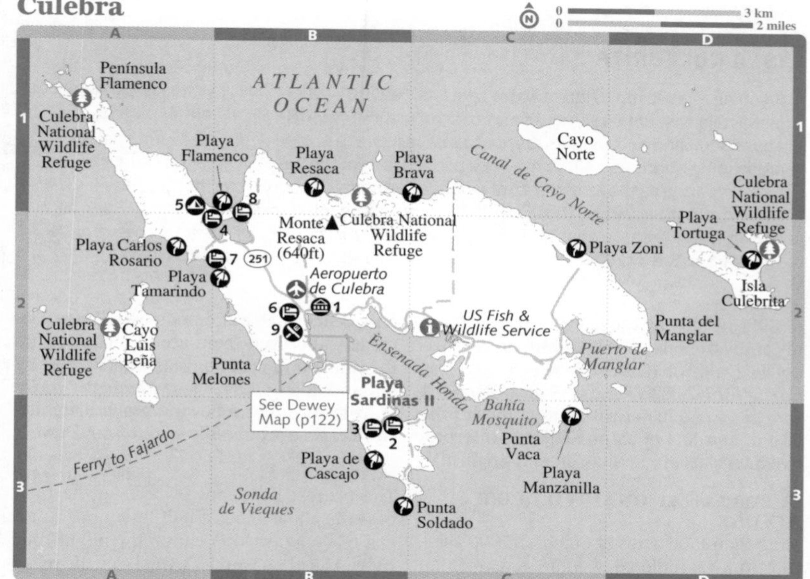

Culebra

Sights

1 Museo Histórico de Culebra B2

Sleeping

2 Bahía Marina B3
3 Club Seabourne B3
4 Culebra Beach Villas B2
5 Flamenco Campground A1
6 Palmetto Guesthouse B2
7 Tamarindo Estates B2
8 Villa Flamenco Beach B1

Eating

9 Barbara Rosa B2
Club Seabourne .... (see 3)

native-born *culebrenses* (people from Culebra) were very quickly able to find a common language and they have continued to work together quite fiercely to hold overdevelopment and commercialization at bay.

Sights

Heading left away from the dock will bring you to Calle Pedro Márquez, usually referred to as the 'main road,' which leads into Dewey, the island's principal settlement.

The main road eventually leads out to the single-landing-strip airport on Rte 251; if you continue past the airport you get to Playa Flamenco. If you take Rte 250 east you'll come to turnoffs for Playas Resaca and Brava, eventually winding up at Playa Zoni. Another road, Calle Fulladoza, heads south to Punta Soldado.

Isla Culebrita and Cayo Norte are two of the more popular cays off Culebra and are easily visited; there are about 18 others surrounding the island.

DEWEY

Nestled on a thin knob of land between two glistening bays, Dewey is Culebra's diminutive main town and the launching pad for Culebra's rustic attractions. A languid settlement that awakes from its slumber for the arrival and departure of the ferry, it's more of a rural backwater than drop-dead gorgeous Caribbean idyll. Named after an illustrious US admiral, it's a place where no one's in a hurry, and residents stop to chat about what hot commodities have turned up at the grocery store.

Belying expectations for a town so small, but reflecting Culebra's strong expat draw, Dewey contains a high ratio of chefs running excellent restaurants, and even an energetic dose of low-key nightlife.

WORTH A TRIP

ISLA CULEBRITA

If you need a reason to hire a water taxi, Isla Culebrita (Map p117) is it. This small island, just a mile east of Playa Zoni, is part of the Culebra National Wildlife Refuge. With its abandoned and decaying 1880s lighthouse, six beaches, tide pools, reefs and nesting areas for seabirds, Isla Culebrita has changed little in the past 500 years. The north beaches, such as the long crescent of Playa Tortuga, are popular nesting grounds for sea turtles, and you may see these animals swimming near the reefs just offshore. Bring a lot of water, sunscreen, a shirt and a hat if you head for Isla Culebrita, because there is little shade here. See p120 for details on renting and hiring boats to reach this island.

Built in 1905 by the navy for use as a munitions warehouse, the little **Museo Histórico de Culebra** (Culebra History Museum; Map p117; ☎787-742-3832; Rte 250; ⏰10am-3pm Sat & Sun) has some historical photographs of the island, and lots of Taíno artifacts. Interpretive materials are in Spanish and English.

CULEBRA NATIONAL WILDLIFE REFUGE

More than 1500 acres of Culebra's 7000 acres constitute a national wildlife refuge (Map p117), which US President Theodore Roosevelt signed into law almost 100 years ago, and which is protected by the Department of Natural Resources. Most of this land lies along the Península Flamenco, and from Monte Resaca east to the sea, and includes all of the coastline as well as more than 20 offshore cays, with the exception of Cayo Norte. The **US Fish & Wildlife Service** (Map p117; ☎787-742-0115; www.fws.gov/caribbean/refuges/culebra; ⏰7am-4pm Mon-Fri) administers these lands. Monte Resaca, Isla Culebrita and Cayo Luis Peña are open to the public from sunrise to sunset daily, and all have some fairly challenging hikes. Stop by the office on the east side of Ensenada Honda for maps, literature and permission to visit other sections of the refuge.

CAYO LUIS PEÑA

Less visited than Isla Culebrita, Luis Peña (Map p117) is the island of peaks, rocks, forests and coves you'll pass just a few minutes before the ferry lands you at Culebra's dock. This island is another part of the wildlife refuge, and it has a collection of small sheltered beaches. Luis Peña is a short kayak or water taxi trip from town; it has good beaches and snorkeling all around the island.

Beaches

Culebra's beaches offer wild natural beauty, but little in the way of tourist facilities. The only beach that has amenities is Playa Flamenco, and even these are limited. Be sure to bring lots of water/snacks when venturing out and don't take risks swimming if you're on your own. The following beaches are listed clockwise around the island from Dewey.

Punta Melones SNORKELING BEACH

The nearest beach to town. Take the road past the clinic about a half mile north until you reach a development on the hill to your right. Ahead on your left, you'll see the rocky Melones point with a navigation light; to the right of the point is a stony beach. If you head down to this beach, you will find great snorkeling at both ends. The point's name comes from the prevalence of a species of melon cactus in this part of the island. It's a good idea to bring shoes you can wear in the water; cacti line the seafloor. There's also not a lot of shade on the beach, so strong sunscreen is imperative.

Playa Tamarindo SNORKELING BEACH

A little bit beyond Melones, this is a very good snorkeling beach. It's accessible by foot by either turning off the Dewey–Flamenco Beach road at the bottom of the hill just before the lagoon, or from an unmarked trail west off the Flamenco parking lot. This is an often-overlooked beach; it's not as flashy and fabulous-looking as others are, but offers a good combination of sun and shade, gentle currents and lots of underwater life for good snorkeling.

Playa Carlos Rosario SNORKELING BEACH

If you follow a path west from the parking lot at Playa Flamenco, about a 15-minute hike over the hill will bring you to Playa Carlos Rosario, an antidote to the crowds at Playa Flamenco and one of the best snorkeling areas in Puerto Rico. But don't get confused: Playa Carlos Rosario is not the first beach you'll reach along this path.

To reach Carlos Rosario, head north from this first beach, cross the narrow peninsula, and head down to the sandy basin and shade trees. A barrier reef almost encloses this beach, and you can snorkel on either side of it by swimming through the boat channel – look for the white plastic bottle marker – at the right side of the beach. But be *very* careful: water taxis and local powerboats cruise this channel and the reef, and in 1998 a longtime Culebra resident and diver was struck and killed by a boat.

For really spectacular snorkeling, work your way along the cliffs on the point south of the beach, or head about a quarter mile north to a place called the **Wall**, which has 40ft drop-offs and rich colors.

Playa Flamenco FAMILY BEACH

Stretching for a mile around a sheltered, horseshoe-shaped bay, Playa Flamenco is not just Culebra's best beach; it is also generally regarded as the finest in Puerto Rico, and quite possibly the whole Caribbean. In fact, certain discerning travel writers have suggested that it is among the top 10 in the world. While individual musings may sound trite, there is no denying that this gentle arc of white sand and crystal surf is something special. Backed by low scrub rather than craning palms, and equipped with basic amenities, Flamenco is the only public beach on the island. It is also the only place where you are allowed to camp. Facilities include two guesthouses, a collection of kiosks (selling both snack food and beach gear), toilets, outdoor showers, lifeguards, picnic tables and a parking lot. There are no full-blown restaurants or stores in the area, so visitors should stock up with provisions in Dewey before they arrive.

In contrast to the main island's gargantuan resorts, Flamenco is refreshingly rustic and crowd-free. In the winter months you'll feel like Robinson Crusoe contemplating the clarity of the water here, while on a busy day in summer with perhaps 200 people spread across nearly a mile of beach, it will still seem half-deserted. The name comes from the nearby lagoon, which attracts flamingos in winter.

Playa Resaca SECLUDED BEACH

A *resaca* is an undertow and a metaphor for a hangover, an allusion to the state of the water perhaps, or the way you will feel after climbing up and down 640ft Monte Resaca to reach it. Not well maintained nor easy to find, the trail is a 40-minute hike that involves scrambling – you'll want to wear sturdy shoes. The **US Fish & Wildlife Service** (☎787-742-0115) manages the trail here; call for directions to the trailhead. Monte Resaca, the island's highest point, is characterized by an ecologically unique boulder-strewn forest on its upper slopes that harbors rare types of flora and fauna (mainly lizards). It's a deceptively tough (and sometimes prickly) climb. Bring lots of water and

FLAMENCO'S MILITARY PAST

Up until the early 1970s, Flamenco was part of a live firing range used by the US Navy for target practice. First requisitioned by the military in 1902 to counter a rising German threat in the Caribbean, Culebra's beaches were used to stage mock amphibious landings and myriad ground maneuvers. In 1936, with WWII in the offing, the Flamenco peninsula yielded to its first live arms fire and the beach was regularly shelled.

Burgeoning decade by decade, the military operations reached their peak during the late 1960s at the height of the Vietnam War, with the navy simulating gun attacks and submarine warfare. When the US government hinted at expanding the Culebra base in the early 1970s, public sentiment quickly turned bellicose. In what would become a dress rehearsal for the Navy–Vieques protests (see p134) 30 years later, a small committed group of Puerto Rican protesters – including Independence party leader Rubén Berríos – initiated a campaign of civil disobedience that culminated in squatters accessing the beach and having to be forcibly removed by police. Despite arrests and imprisonments, the tactics worked. In 1975 the US Navy pulled out of Culebra and the beach was returned to its natural state.

Well almost... More than 30 years later you can still find graphic evidence of the war games that once wreaked havoc on Flamenco. At the beach's western end, contrasting rather sharply with the diamond-dust sand and translucent water, two rusty, seaweed-covered tanks sit like ghostly reminders of past military maneuvers.

sunscreen and don't try swimming from the beach.

Playa Brava SECLUDED BEACH

The beauty of Brava lies in the fact that there is no road here; you *have* to hike – make that bushwhack – about 30 minutes along a little-used trail that is often overgrown with sea grape and low scrub. The rewards are immense when you finally clear the last mangrove and are confronted with an isolated but stunning swath of sand that glimmers with a fierce but utterly enchanting beauty.

To get here, travel around to the eastern side of Ensenada Honda. Pass the Km 4 marker and turn left a little way past the cemetery. Follow this road until the pavement ends and you come up against a chain gate near a few small houses, some of which are fashioned from shipping containers. This is the entrance to a cattle farm, but it is also a public right-of-way, so park your car or bike and head due north on the trail beyond the gate. The second half of the trail leads through a grove of trees that sometimes attracts butterflies.

Playa Zoni SECLUDED BEACH

Head to the extreme eastern end of the island and you'll eventually run out of road at Playa Zoni. It's a straightforward 20-minute drive – but the road can be treacherous after heavy rains: it's paved, but sometimes large chunks wash away, with one steepish section that can rattle the nerves of flatlanders. There's a small parking spot next to the sign alerting you to the fact that endangered turtles cross the beach. Zoni is long and straight, with beautiful Caribbean islands popping up in the distance, but again, it's an isolated place, so don't swim alone.

Some locals think this is a better beach than Flamenco; it doesn't have quite the same soft sand and gentle curves, but it certainly is stunning in its own right and is usually less crowded. Be careful entering waters for a few days after a storm: sometimes the heavier currents will have pulled sand away from the shoreline that usually covers rocks; it will eventually wash back in, but until then there's the distinct possibility that you can bang your shins on some very sharp projections.

Punta Soldado FAMILY BEACH

This site on the extreme southwestern tip of the island has a rocky beach and good snorkeling. To get here, follow the road south across the drawbridge for about 2 miles, passing Club Seabourne and finally scaling a steep hill. Here the pavement stops, and it's a bumpy dirt road down to the beach. You will see the reef about 50yd offshore to the southeast. Locals bring their children to snorkel in the shallow waters here.

Activities

Diving & Snorkeling

Despite reef damage caused during the US Navy testing era, Culebra retains some of Puerto Rico's most amazing dive spots, including sunken ships, coral reefs, drop-offs and caves. Highlights include the *Wit Power* tugboat (which sank in 1984), the Geniqui Caves, the El Mono boulders, and the fish-filled, water-world of Cayo Ratón. Good snorkeling can be accessed from many beaches, in particular Playas Carlos Rosario, Tamarindo and Melones. Don't rely on local maps for accessible entrance spots – ask the locals.

Two-tank dives run from $90 to $100 with the island's two main dive operators, **Culebra Divers** (Map p122; ☎787-742-0803; www.culebradivers.com), located across from the ferry dock, and **Aquatic Adventures** (☎787-742-0605; www.diveculebra.com). The latter also offers snorkel trips ($50, including equipment and lunch) that go to at least two different locations.

Culebra Divers and Culebra Bike Shop rent snorkeling equipment for $10 per day, and most boat captains will also arrange snorkel tours.

Kayaking

Culebra Bike Shop KAYAKING

(Map p122; ☎787-742-0589; www.culebrabikeshop.com; Calle Fulladoza) Rents two-person kayaks for $50 per day.

Kayaking Puerto Rico KAYAKING

(☎787-435-1665; www.kayakingpuertorico.com) This Fajardo-based operator runs regularly scheduled 3½ hour kayak and snorkel trips to Cayo Luis Peña for $65.

Boat Trips

Drop-off at and pickup from Isla Culebrita costs about $45 per person. Trips to Cayo Norte are generally combined with snorkeling and lunch, and start at $50 per person.

Boat captains recommended for charters and water taxi services include **Willy** (☎787-742-3537), **Brad Stephens** (☎787-435-6546) and **Carlos** (☎787-435-3662).

Captain Bill Penfield (☎787-215-3809) runs highly recommended catamaran trips from Bahía Marina.

KEEPING WATCH OVER TURTLES

Two of Culebra's most isolated beaches – Resaca and Brava – are nesting sites for the endangered leatherback sea turtle, the largest living sea turtle in the world. The nesting season runs from April through early June. Though this project was more active in the past, each year a few volunteers are accepted by the Department of Natural Resources to monitor the delicate egg-laying process. Volunteers travel out to the beaches, where they count eggs, measure turtles, and document the event for environmental records. At the same time, participants are able to witness one of nature's most transfixing and timeless events in stunning close-up.

For more information on how to volunteer for this, and other wildlife conservation initiatives in Puerto Rico, see p288.

Fishing

The real fish hawk on the island is **Chris Goldmark** (☎787-742-0412; www.culebraflyfishing.com; per half-day $240). He can take you out to the flats for some superb bonefishing, or offshore for the big stuff.

Cycling

With its hills, dirt trails and back-to-nature ruggedness, Culebra is an excellent place to bike – not just for exercise but also as a handy means of transportation. **Dick & Cathie's Rentals** (☎787-742-0062) rents good-quality mountain bikes ($17 per day) and offers free road service if you get a flat. Call and they'll swiftly deliver a bike to you in their old-fashioned VW van – just like that! Next to Dinghy Dock, **Culebra Bike Shop** (Map p122; ☎787-742-0589; www.culebrabikeshop.com; Calle Fulladoza) offers identical prices and delivery, and has a few child-seats available.

Surfing

The island's not known for great waves, but you can sometimes catch some action at Carlos Rosario, Zoni and Punta Soldado. Culebra Bike Shop rents boogie boards for $7 per day.

Hiking

Rejoice! The island is your oyster. The 2.5-mile hike from Dewey to Playa Flamenco is along a paved road with some inclines, but the destination is idyllic. You can veer off to Playa Tamarindo from a junction just before the lagoon. Playa Carlos Rosario is reached via a trail that starts at the west end of Playa Flamenco. The hike to Playa Brava begins at the end of a back road that cuts north from Rte 250 just past the graveyard. The trail rises to a ridge and then drops to the beach via thick bushes. The toughest hike on the island is the rough trail to Playa Resaca that traverses the eponymous mountain. The trailhead is about 2 miles from Dewey.

Sleeping

In addition to guesthouses, inns and hotels, Culebra has an excellent selection of rental properties of all shapes and sizes dotted around the island. **Culebra Vacation Planners** (Map p122; ☎787-742-3112, 866-285-3272; www.culebravacationplanners.com) can fix you up with some stunners, and travelers with disabilities or special needs can also be catered for. It lists basic rooms for under $100 and mansions with views of the British Virgin Islands for up to $750 per night.

DEWEY

TOP CHOICE **Palmetto Guesthouse** GUESTHOUSE $$
(Map p117; ☎787-742-0257; www.palmettoculebra.com; r $95-115; ❄@🛜) Run by two ex–Peace Corps volunteers from New England, this business is a super-friendly and accommodating escape. Five guest rooms have the run of two kitchens, a deck, a handy book exchange and a sporty magazine pile. Situated not far from the airport, it's a 10-minute stroll to Dewey – the perfect distance for walking off a hearty dinner. Snorkel gear, beach chairs and boogie boards are yours for the taking, and there's free pickup and drop-off from the ferry terminal or the airport.

Villa Fulladoza APARTMENTS $$
(Map p122; ☎787-742-3576; www.culebra-island.com; Calle Fulladoza; apt $75-90; 🛜) Super-cute and colorful, Villa Fulladoza offers seven bright fan-cooled studio apartments with delicious ocean breezes. The shared patio is shaded by a swaying mango tree and, if you are lucky enough to enjoy your own private water transportation, there's a boat dock.

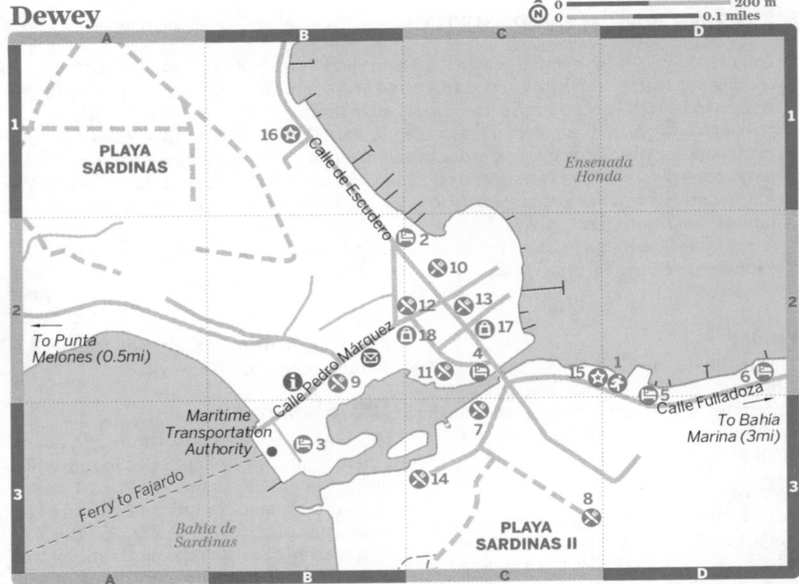

Casa Ensenada GUESTHOUSE $$
(Map p122; ☎787-742-3559; www.casaensenada.com; r $125-175; ❄📶) This pleasant guesthouse just north of town on the waterfront at Ensenada Honda is handily placed for almost everything. The inn has three units (accommodating two, four or up to six people) with kitchen or kitchenette, separate entrance and air-conditioning. There are a lot of unexpected extras here such as free use of a kayak, free boat dock, beach towels, grill, hammocks and a spacious breezy patio.

Villa Boheme GUESTHOUSE $$
(Map p122; ☎787-742-3508; www.villaboheme.com; Calle Fulladoza; r $98-139; ❄📶) A recent remodel has spiffed up this well-situated guesthouse already endowed with a breezy communal patio, lovely bay views, kayak rentals and proximity to town (not to mention the Dinghy Dock restaurant next door). A few of the colorful rooms are equipped with kitchenette for guests who don't care to make use of the shared cooking facilities. Rates dip in low season.

Mamacita's GUESTHOUSE $$
(Map p122; ☎787-742-0090; www.mamacitasguesthouse.com; 64 Calle Castelar; r $89-125; ❄📶) Screaming lurid pink, pastel purple, green, blue and perhaps a little yellow, Mamacita's is the raffish Caribbean crash pit you've been dreaming about. And although the water's invariably cold, and the reception staff will have probably gone home by the time your boat arrives, there's something strangely contagious about this old Culebra stalwart. The 10 rooms are simple but attractive, the vibe in the adjacent bar fun and casual, and the on-site restaurant a living legend.

Posada La Hamaca HOTEL $$
(Map p122; ☎787-742-3516; www.posada.com; r $89-155; ❄📶) Next to Mamacita's, La Hamaca has a tough act to follow and lies somewhat in its neighbor's shadow. It's a shame, because it's not a bad option. Rooms are basic but comfortable and overlook the canal, while location wise you're right in the heart of Dewey with plenty of eating options within walking distance. The front desk is an excellent source of local information.

Hotel Kokomo HOTEL $
(Map p122; ☎787-742-3112; www.culebra-kokomo.com; r $44-138; ❄📶) If you're anxious to dump your bags in the first visible crash pad in order to get out exploring, then Hotel Kokomo, the bright yellow building

Dewey

Activities, Courses & Tours

1 Culebra Bike Shop D2
Culebra Divers .... (see 3)

Sleeping

2 Casa Ensenada C2
Culebra Vacation Planners .... (see 3)
3 Hotel Kokomo B3
Mamacita's .... (see 11)
4 Posada La Hamaca C2
5 Villa Boheme D2
6 Villa Fulladoza D2

Eating

7 Colmado Milka C3
Dinghy Dock .... (see 15)
8 El Eden C3
9 Heather's B2
10 Holística Aimée C2
11 Mamacita's C2
Panadería Tropical .... (see 3)
12 Pandeli C2
Spot .... (see 9)
13 Superette Mayra C2
14 Susie's C3

Entertainment

15 Dinghy Dock C2
16 El Batey B1
Gretchen's Da Bar .... (see 3)
Mamacita's .... (see 11)

Shopping

17 Butiki C2
18 Galería de Regalos C2

right across from the ferry dock, is just the ticket. Rooms, while still basic, are clean and cheery enough. Check your room before committing – some are much better than others, and one is windowless. The two penthouse apartments are much more luxurious, sleeping four or six people.

SOUTH OF DEWEY

Club Seabourne HOTEL $$$
(Map p117; ☎787-742-3169; www.clubseabourne.com; r $199, villa $239-359; P❄📶🏊) A deftly designed and recently upgraded small hotel that blends seamlessly into the southern portion of the island, Club Seabourne is Culebra luxury-style, with an outdoor bar, a secluded swimming pool, kayak and bike rentals and a restaurant decked out with tablecloths and wineglasses. The welcoming lobby has a library and relaxing club chairs, while the individual villas have sea views and are deliciously tranquil.

Bahía Marina RESORT $$$
(Map p117; ☎787-278-5100; www.bahiamarina.net; Punta Soldado Rd Km 2.4; r $219-295; P❄📶🏊) One of the island's newer accommodations is also one of its most luxurious – in fact, it's Buckingham Palace by Culebra standards. Billed as a condo resort, this is not your average high-rise environmentally unsound concrete block. Abutting a 100-acre nature preserve, it has 40 one- and two-bedroom apartments with modern kitchenettes, water pressure (a recent invention in this part of the world), cable TV, swimming pools, three restaurants and live music at weekends.

PLAYA FLAMENCO AREA

Villa Flamenco Beach APARTMENTS $$
(Map p117; ☎787-742-0023; www.culebra-island.com; studios $125-135, apt $150; P❄) Gentle waves lulling you to sleep, a night sky replete with twinkling stars, and one of the best beaches on the planet just outside your window; this six-unit place would be a winner even if it was just a roof and four walls. To make your stay more comfortable, the management has added self-catering kitchen facilities and inviting hammocks. It's open December through September and is right next to the Culebra Beach Villas.

Culebra Beach Villas APARTMENTS $$
(Map p117; ☎front desk 787-742-0517, 787-767-7575; www.culebrabeachrental.com; apt $146-350; P❄📶) The only visible building on the beach is this three-story Caribbean villa with wraparound balconies. It acts as the main building to a small complex that rents out 33 self-catering apartments (leased out by many different brokers) with kitchen and cable TV for between two and eight people. The setting is stunning, though you'll have to stock up on provisions in Dewey, 2.5 miles away.

Tamarindo Estates APARTMENTS $$
(Map p117; ☎787-742-3343; www.tamarindoestates.com; r $156-169; P❄@🏊) The Tamarindo is Culebran to the core; rustic, isolated and set facing one of the Caribbean's most serendipitous views, overlooking Cayo Luis Peña and a national wildlife refuge. Being Culebra, the accommodations – which comprise 12 self-contained cottages spread over 60 acres – are not New York luxury. Then again, you probably didn't come here to watch

Hollywood movies on a flat-screen TV. Nestled near the water's edge there's a pool and restaurant, and remote Playa Tamarindo is a five-minute stroll down the road.

Flamenco Campground PUBLIC CAMPGROUND $
(Map p117; ☎787-742-0700; www.flamencobeachcampground.com; campsites $20; P) The only place you can legally camp in Culebra is just feet from the paradisial Playa Flamenco. Report to the office at the entrance and you will be assigned a spot. Six people maximum per tent. There are outdoor showers with water available between 4pm and 7pm; bathrooms are open 24/7. The campground's pretty safe and reservations aren't usually necessary.

Eating

Perhaps because of the high expat population, Culebra is very vegetarian-friendly – every place has meat-free options or will make some if asked, and the markets even carry soy milk. Be warned that some restaurants close or pare back their hours during the September and October low season.

DEWEY

TOP CHOICE **Homeless Dog Café** INTERNATIONAL $
(☎939-452-9563; dishes $8-12; ⏲4pm-2am Wed-Mon; 🖉) No one's going to confuse tiny Culebra for the amenity-rich island of Manhattan, but this food delivery service (to anywhere on the island!) is a scrumptious luxury. Ask your accommodations for the menu, which boasts mostly steak and chicken dishes and sandwiches such as a shrimp po'boy. There's a second menu of sushi rolls, and it bakes its own bread and desserts.

Susie's CARIBBEAN $$
(Map p122; ☎787-742-0574; dishes $17-23; ⏲6-10pm Tue-Sun; 🖉) Beautifully presented Puerto Rican food with Asian accents, this Culebra favorite curates a rotating collection of crowd-pleasing dishes, always including fresh fish such as grouper and snapper. Diners can choose from tables at the long purple banquettes indoors – where Susie herself might pop out to momentarily escape the kitchen's heat – or the pleasant outdoor dockside seating. Be forewarned: Susie's island mash – a side of yucca, malanga and potatoes – may become your next comfort food. Reservations recommended.

El Eden CARIBBEAN $$
(Map p122; ☎787-742-0509; dinner mains $17-25; ⏲9am-9pm Wed-Sat; 🖉) Come hungry. A liquor store with an excellent and eclectic wine selection, its restaurant is the special-occasion dinner choice for Culebra residents. Set with patio tables frocked in mismatched tablecloths, it's not an elegant place, but feels that way nonetheless, with owners Richard and Luz greeting everyone like long-lost friends. Dishes including lobster risotto and melt-in-your-mouth gnocchi with pesto sauce come in huge portions, and desserts such as caramel pecan fudge cake or rum-laced bread pudding will initiate extended after-dinner strolls. Reserve ahead.

Barbara Rosa RESTAURANT $
(Map p117; dishes $8-14; ⏲dinner Thu-Mon) *You* are the waiter at this diminutive restaurant/bistro. You're also in Barbara's house – her front verandah to be more exact, so tread carefully. When you've decided what you want, take the menu into the front room and holler through the kitchen hatch at the busy Barbara as she scurries around the kitchen. Hey presto, 15 minutes later out comes fish-and-chips, a juicy burger or a plate of homemade crab cakes. It's rather quaint, once you get your head round the system. Bring your own booze.

Mamacita's CARIBBEAN $$
(Map p122; mains $15-21; ⏲lunch & dinner daily, breakfast Fri-Sun; 🖉) Always buzzing with activity, Mamacita's offers some of the best-presented food outside of San Juan, along with zero pretension and laid-back, quirky service. Fish and meat plates are tasty, seasoned and creative, and the menu – which always includes at least one vegetarian option – changes daily, as displayed on a handwritten blackboard. Of all the places on the island, this is where expats, locals and visitors mingle best. Fun is in the air at weekends when the *bomba* drums get warmed up. Don't feed the iguanas – they're enormous already.

Dinghy Dock SEAFOOD $$
(Map p122; Calle Fulladoza; mains $10-29; 🖉) Unusually for Puerto Rico, the DD has an all-you-can-eat salad bar to quell your early hunger pangs, and you can chomp on your lettuce and cucumber while watching the kitchen staff throw morsels of food to the giant tarpon that swim right up to the deck. Fish is the obvious specialty here – fresh catches such as swordfish and snapper done in creole sauces. The busy bar is a frenzy of expats nursing Medalla beers and

acts as the unofficial island grapevine. If you haven't heard it here first, it's not worth hearing.

Heather's PIZZA $

(Map p122; pizza $8-20;) In the center of town, across from the town hall, Heather's is a popular hangout at night and a great pizza parlor. It gets popular in high season, so expect a wait.

Spot INTERNATIONAL $

(Map p122; dishes $8-16; lunch Mon & Wed-Fri, tapas dinner Mon & Fri, to 2am Fri) Coffee connoisseurs rave about the espresso drinks, and locals will usually direct you here for the twice-weekly tapas and the plethora of lunch choices including salads, grilled paninis, pita sandwiches and burgers. The tiny place has style – with an array of red Chinese lanterns, a checkerboard floor and a cobalt blue counter. Island restaurant workers trickle in after work on Friday nights to kick back and play darts.

Pandeli CAFE $

(Map p122; dishes $4-7; 6am-4pm;) This popular early-morning deli/cafe sells pastries, pancakes, salads, sandwiches and coffee. Come 8am it's inundated with schoolkids and stray travelers. A good place to take breakfast and lunch and catch up on the local gossip.

Panadería Tropical BAKERY $

(Map p122; dishes $2-7; 5:30am-1pm Mon-Sat, 6:30-11:30am Sun & holidays) Grab a few *quesitos* (sweet cheese pastries) on the way to the early ferry, or have this small bakery fix you up with a tasty sandwich. Egg and pancake breakfasts served until 10:30am.

Colmado Milka SUPERMARKET

(Map p122; 7am-7pm Mon-Sat, to 1pm Sun) Across the bridge past Mamacita's, Colmado Milka is the island's second-largest supermarket. It even stocks a number of vegan items.

Superette Mayra SUPERMARKET

(Map p122; 8:30am-1:30pm & 3:30pm-6:30pm Mon-Sat) Here you'll find all of the basic food supplies along with other, nonedible essentials such as washing powder, diapers and toilet rolls.

Holística Aimée HEALTH FOOD

(Map p122; 126 Calle de Escudero; 10am-6pm Mon-Fri;) A small selection of health foods.

On Fridays, a fruit-and-vegetable vendor sets up under some shady trees near the airport, across the street from Carlos Jeep Rental.

SOUTH OF DEWEY

Club Seabourne CARIBBEAN $$

(Map p117; 787-742-3169; mains $16-35) As well as being an upscale inn, Club Seabourne has an outstanding eatery. With 36 tables arranged around a mosquito-free screened-in porch, you can sup on wine (the place has its own wine cellar), chomp on seviches and feast on steak filet mignon while enjoying calming views of glistening Ensenada Honda framed by palms. The adjacent poolside bar and gazebo hosts a popular happy hour and can conjure up a formidable mojito.

☆ Entertainment

The island's nightlife revolves around its many funky bars and restaurants.

Gretchen's Da Bar BAR

(Map p122; 3pm-midnight Sun-Thu, to 2am Fri & Sat;) Slink past the 'wanted dead or alive' roster of patrons with delinquent bar tabs and order a whipped-cream-topped bushwacker or a piña colada blushing sherbert pink with grenadine. There's always something happening at this dockside hot spot, whether it's soulful karaoke on weekends, tourists playing Wii bowling while waiting for the ferry, an open mic poetry performance or just a gaggle of locals chowing down with sushi rolls ($8 to $18) from the in-house **Juanita Bananas** restaurant.

El Batey BAR

(Map p122) Not a large place, but seemingly big enough to accommodate the majority of Culebra's population at weekends, when locals swing by to shake a leg to reggaetón with a bit of salsa and merengue mixed in. During the week the place is esteemed for its cheap burgers, cold beers and pool table.

Mamacita's BAR

(Map p122) Mamacita's has a lively happy hour and after-dinner scene. On weekends, locals, expats and yacht crews favor this place, with its open-air deck and Friday-night DJ. Mamacita's really smokes when *bomba y plena* drummers show up to rock the patio every Saturday night with *bomba* rhythms, as well as salsa and merengue. Everybody dances!

Dinghy Dock BAR

(Map p122) The 'dock' has karaoke on Thursdays – aarghhhh!

Shopping

Galería de Regalos SOUVENIRS
(Map p122; cnr Calles Pedro Márquez & Castelar; ⌚10am-5pm) A colorful gift-and-clothes shop that sells República de Culebra stickers and plenty of other unique knickknacks.

Butiki ART
(Map p122; cnr Calles de Escudero & Romero) Run by an American expat, this local art shop sells paintings, jewelry, masks, T-shirts and plenty more. Almost everything is island-made.

Information

Few establishments have meaningful street addresses on Culebra; descriptive addresses are generally used here. Basic island maps are handed out by hotels and car-rental agencies. All of the services listed here are in Dewey.

Dangers & Annoyances

Culebra breeds swarms of mosquitoes, especially during the rainy season (May to November). Some of the daytime species have been known to carry dengue.

Emergency

Police (☎787-742-3501)

Internet Access

Most accommodations have wi-fi, and Gretchen's Da Bar across from the ferry terminal is a handy free hot spot.

Culebra Community Library (⌚10am-2pm Thu-Sat & Mon-Tue; 👪) In a trailer across from El Eden restaurant, this welcoming volunteer-run library has three computers ($5 per hour donation requested) and wi-fi. Visitors can borrow from its excellent selection of books and magazines, in (mostly) English and Spanish. Excellent children's room.

Media

Culebra Calendar (www.theculebracalendaronline.com) is the island newsletter and has complete listings of upcoming events, jobs, tide tables and articles on important Culebra issues.

Medical Services

Despite its small population, Culebra has good health services. Basic toiletries are carried in local shops, but it's wise to bring things such as condoms, saline solution and contact-lens supplies.

Clinic (☎787-742-3511; ⌚7am-4pm Mon-Fri) In town on the road to Punta Melones; has drugs and resident doctors. There's no pharmacy on the island, but the clinic can order prescriptions, which get flown over from the mainland.

Hospital (☎787-742-0001; ⌚24hr) Adjoining the clinic, the hospital has a 24-hour emergency room. The island also keeps a plane on emergency standby at the airport for medical transport to the main island.

Money

Banco Popular (Calle Pedro Márquez; ⌚8am-3:30pm Mon-Fri) There's an ATM here.

Post

Post office (Calle Pedro Márquez; ⌚8am-4:30pm Mon-Fri, to noon Sat) Super-efficient, well-cooled and right in the center of town.

Tourist Information

Try www.islaculebra.com or www.culebra-island.com for good general information.

Tourist office (Map p122; Calle Pedro Márquez; ⌚8am-noon & 1-4:30pm Mon-Fri) Islandwide information can be found at this counter outside the Alcaldía (Town Hall) on the main street 200m from the ferry terminal, though you may need to rouse a worker from the inside office.

Getting There & Away

Air

Culebra gets frequent air service from San Juan ($65 to $95 one way) and Ceiba ($30 to $45 one way).

Air Flamenco (☎787-724-1818; www.airflamenco.net) Has regular scheduled flights to San Juan's Isla Grande and to Ceiba.

Culebra Air (☎787-427-4808; www.culebraairservices.com) and **M&N Aviation** (☎877-622-5566; www.mnaviation.com) offer regional charter service, with flights to San Juan averaging a bit over $100 per person on full three- or eight-seater planes.

Vieques Air Link (☎888-901-9247; www.viequesairlink.com) Flies about four times daily to/from San Juan's Isla Grande.

Boat

A number of companies offer charter services, which can be economical for groups. See Boat Trips (p120) for a list of recommended captains.

Interisland Water Taxi (www.interislandwatertaxi.com) Based in Fajardo, this operator offers Culebra–Vieques charters ($535 for six people), and service to St Thomas.

Ferry

Ferries of the **Maritime Transportation Authority (ATM)** Culebra (Map p122; ☎787-742-3161; www.atm.gobierno.pr; ferry dock, Dewey; ⌚8-11am & 1-3pm Mon-Fri); Fajardo (☎787-863-0705; ⌚8-11am & 1-3pm Mon-Fri) travel between Fajardo and Culebra thrice daily and take about an hour and a half. Round-trip passenger fares are $4.50. Boats leave Fajardo daily at 9am, 3pm and 7pm, and Culebra at 6:30am, 1pm and 5pm. A cargo ferry takes two hours and runs two to three times daily Monday through Friday. However, Puerto Rican rental car contracts prohibit taking cars on the ferry. Schedules change, so confirm times. Good luck trying to reach an ATM employee by phone.

Ticket offices open one hour before departure; arrive at least 30 minutes in advance of sailing. Tickets can sell out during holiday periods and busy summer weekends, and island residents get priority over visitors with tickets. No advance phone or internet reservations are available.

The little ferry dock fronts a strip of shops and the Kokomo Hotel. Cab drivers and public vans also congregate here.

Getting Around

Most of the island's natural attractions are not near the town, and chances are that your guesthouse or other rental isn't either. So you might need to organize a ride, by either rental car or taxi at some point.

Biking, kayaking and water taxis are good options for reaching far-flung attractions around the island. See p120 for details.

To/From the Airport

If you have not arranged an airport pickup/drop-off with your guesthouse proprietor, you'll need one of the island taxis; $5 to $15 will get you just about anywhere on the island.

Car & Scooter

It's not usually necessary to hire a car on Culebra (there are too many cars on the island as it is); the Dewey area is all walkable, and it's easier to walk than drive in town due to one-way streets and some parking congestion. Flamenco Beach is a not unpleasant 30-minute hike, and everywhere else can be easily reached by público, taxi or, if you're energetic, bicycle. See p121 for details of bike hire.

If you really can't be parted from your four wheels, or just need something for the day, **Jerry's Jeeps** (☎787-742-0587), across from the airport, rents well-used vehicles for $45 to $50 per day that you won't stress about keeping pristine. Around the corner, the big local player **Carlos Jeep Rental** (☎787-742-3514; www.carlosjeeprental.com) rents compact cars ($57), jeeps ($66), golf carts ($46) and Yamaha scooters ($45; by law passengers must wear closed shoes and long pants). **Dick & Cathie's Rentals** (see Cycling p121) has a few funky VW Things for $45 a day, and **Thrifty** (☎787-742-0110; www.thrifty.com) has a small franchise at Bahía Marina (p123). Reserve ahead in high season.

Taxi

There is taxi service on the island, but they're basically público vans designed to get large parties of people back and forth between the ferry dock and Playa Flamenco (where they will be partying or camping) for a couple of dollars per person.

Willy (☎787-742-3537) generally meets every ferry and also arrives at your door when booked. Also try **Ray** (☎787-225-5717) or **Carlos** (☎787-975-3513).

Vieques

POP 9300

Measuring 21 miles long by 5 miles wide, Vieques is substantially bigger than Culebra and distinctly different in ambience. Though still a million metaphorical miles from the bright lights of the Puerto Rican mainland, the larger population here has meant more luxurious accommodations, hipper restaurants and – unfortunately – more petty thievery (particularly on the beaches).

Vieques was where Puerto Rico's most prickly political saga was played out in the public eye. For over five decades the US Navy used more than two-thirds of the island for military target practice. The war games ended in 1999 after a misplaced 500lb bomb caused the death of a Puerto Rican civilian and set in motion a protest campaign that led to the navy's long-awaited withdrawal.

Since the official military withdrawal in 2003, Vieques has regularly been touted as the Caribbean's next 'big thing,' with a pristine coastline ripe for the developer's bulldozer. Fortunately, environmental authorities swept in quickly after the handover and promptly declared all of the former military land (70% of the island's total area) a US Fish & Wildlife Refuge. The measure has meant that the bulk of the island remains virgin territory to be explored and enjoyed by all.

Development elsewhere has been slow and low-key. Although many guesthouses and restaurants have expanded their business since 2003, much of this growth has centered on ecoventures and small but luxurious boutique hotels. The island has no golf, gambling or Las Vegas–style glitz, and the only real resort is the newly opened and much-hyped W hotel, built on the site of another former resort complex. The pace or scale of development seems unlikely to change in the short term. Vieques' residents – many of whom are US expats – are fiercely protective of their Caribbean nirvana.

The name 'Vieques' is a 17th-century Spanish colonial corruption of the Taíno name *bieque* (small island). The Spaniards also called Vieques and Culebra *las islas*

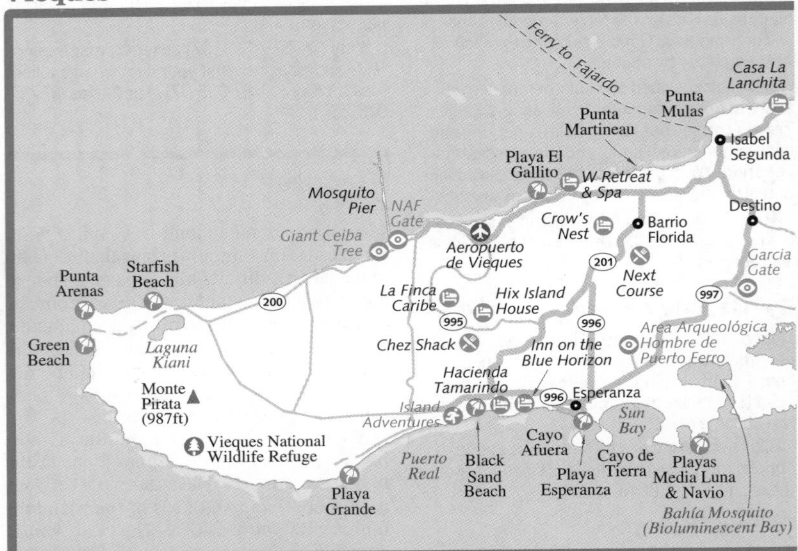

inútiles (the useless islands) because they lacked gold and silver. But over the centuries, residents and visitors who share affection for this place have come to call Vieques 'Isla Nena,' a term of endearment meaning 'Little Girl Island.'

These days Vieques is synonymous with its gorgeous beaches, semiwild horses and unforgettable bioluminescent bay.

History

When Columbus 'discovered' Puerto Rico on his second voyage in 1493, Taíno people were living peacefully (save for the occasional skirmish with Carib neighbors) on Vieques. With the expansion of Puerto Rico under Ponce de León, more Taíno fled to the island; Caribs joined them and the two groups mounted a fierce resistance to Spanish occupation. It failed. Spanish soldiers eventually overran the island, killing or enslaving the natives who remained.

Even so, Spanish control over the island remained tentative at best. In succeeding years, both the British and French tried to claim the island as their own. In reality, Vieques remained something of a free port, thriving as a smuggling center.

Sugarcane plantations covered much of Vieques when the island fell to the Americans in 1898 as spoils from the Spanish-American War, but during the first half of the 20th century the cane plantations failed. Vieques lost more than half its population and settled into near dormancy; the remaining locals survived as they always had, by subsistence farming, fishing and smuggling.

Shortly after WWII broke out, the US Navy showed up on Vieques and grabbed about 70% of the island's 33,000 acres to build military bases (see p134). They held onto it until May 2003 when, after four years of peaceful protests, the land was ceded to the US Fish & Wildlife Refuge. In the years since, Puerto Rican, US and international developers have been salivating at the prospect of building mega hotels and more. But for the time being, ecotourism, construction, cattle raising, fishing, ordnance clearing and some light manufacturing (such as the General Electric assembly plant) bring money and jobs to the island.

Sights

With about 10,000 people, Vieques is considerably more populated than its sleepy sister island, Culebra. Consequently, it has two towns to Culebra's one. The main settlement, Isabel Segunda (Isabella II), is on the north side where the ferry docks. Most people run through Isabel Segunda en route

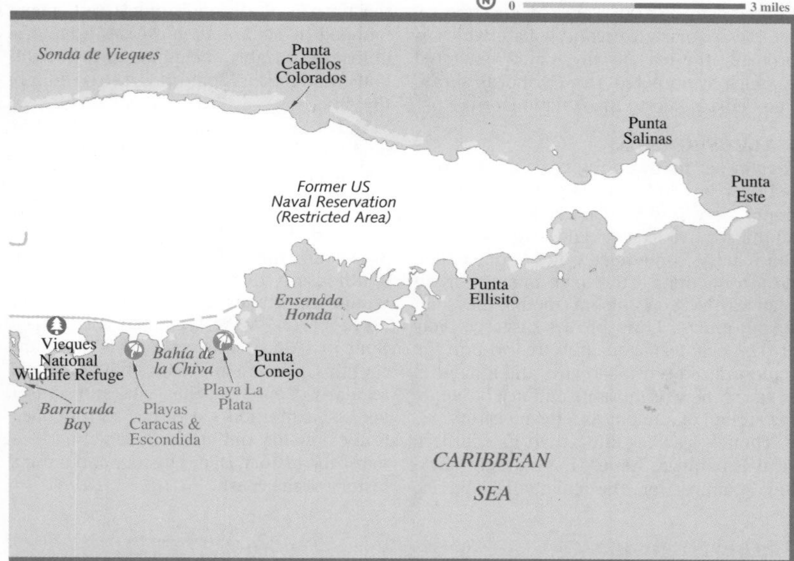

to Esperanza, on the Caribbean side. Esperanza is indisputably prettier, with a public beach, and a *malecón* (waterfront promenade) lined with numerous attractive and entertaining restaurants and guesthouses.

Hwy 200 originates in Isabel Segunda and heads west past the airport as far as Green Beach on the island's western tip. To get to Esperanza, take either of two routes south over the mountains: Hwys 201/996 or Hwy 997. If you take the latter route, you will pass along the navy fence as you descend from the summits. The Garcia Gate is clearly visible on your left. Head through the gate and follow the signs to pristine beaches in the former military zone (now a national wildlife refuge).

VIEQUES NATIONAL WILDLIFE REFUGE

This 18,000-acre **refuge** (Map p128; www.fws.gov/caribbean/refuges/vieques) occupies the land formerly administered by the US military. The 3100-acre western segment – used mainly as a storage area during the military occupation – was instituted in 2001. The 14,700-acre eastern segment, which includes a former live firing range (still off-limits), was inaugurated two years later in 2003.

The refuge protects vast tracts of largely pristine land containing four different ecological habitats: beaches, coastal lagoons, mangrove wetlands and forested uplands. It also includes an important marine environment of sea grasses and coral reefs. Many colorful species survive in these areas, including the endangered brown pelican and the Antillean manatee. Vieques' dwarfish thicket-strewn forest, which includes some indigenous cacti, provides one of the best examples of dry subtropical forest in the Caribbean.

Existing as a military site until May 2003, much of the refuge's land is still officially off-limits to visitors. A potentially dangerous no-go zone is Punta Este in the far east of the island, where live ordnance is still being removed. Other restricted areas in the east include most of the north coast east of Isabel Segunda, along with the south coast east of Playa La Plata (Orchid Beach). The most easily accessible area is the narrow ribbon of land that abuts the road leading from the Garcia Gate to La Plata.

Most of the hilly western part of the refuge is open for business, and includes a lonely swath of colorful wildflowers and scores of (mostly sealed) cavernous military-style bunkers that were used to store ammunition.

Perhaps the finest **Giant Ceiba Tree** (Map p128) in Puerto Rico is situated on the right-hand side of the road as you head toward

Green Beach, adjacent to the Mosquito Pier. Rumored to be 400 years old, the tree resembles a gnarly African baobab, which is probably the reason why it was venerated so much by uprooted Afro-Caribbean slaves. The Ceiba is Puerto Rico's national tree.

ISABEL SEGUNDA

A calm yet hardworking coastal town dotted over low hills on Vieques' north coast, nontouristy Isabel Segunda is the island's administrative center and capital. Sometimes busy, sometimes quiet – depending on ferry activity – the town is more urban than anything on Culebra (though that's not saying much). Lines of cars disgorge daily at the dock, teenagers grab free wi-fi in the underutilized central square, and a handful of snazzy new restaurants pull in a burgeoning stream of affluent American visitors.

Though less beguiling than its southern rival Esperanza, Isabel II is no ugly duckling. Named for the enigmatic Spanish queen who reigned between 1833 and 1868, the town is the island's oldest settlement, founded in 1843, and showcases a handful of historical sights, including an 1896 lighthouse and the last Spanish fort to be built in the Americas.

Isabel Segunda hosts the bulk of the island's services. But with only 5000 residents and more wild horses than wine waiters, it's a long way from sparkling modernity.

El Faro de Punta Mulas SCENIC OUTLOOK

(Map p130) One of Puerto Rico's 16 historic lighthouses, this pastel-shaded historic monument stands on the hilly point just north of the Isabel Segunda ferry dock. Built in 1896, it was restored in 1992 and contains a small museum that's open irregularly. Come for the vista and sunset, not the exhibition – a rather paltry collection of photos and artifacts depicting local maritime history, island history and natural history of the coast.

Isabel Segunda

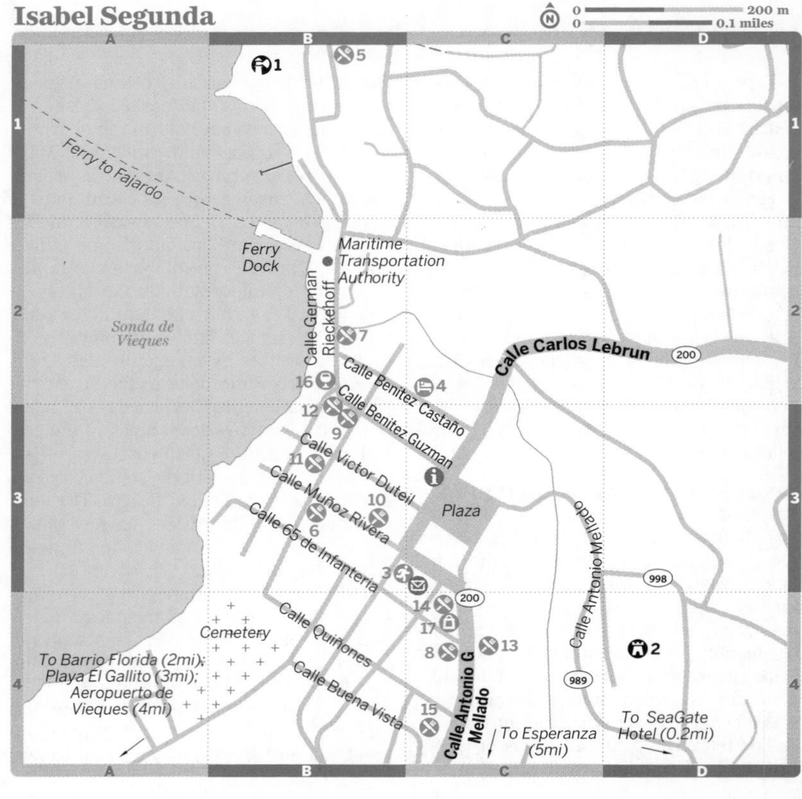

Fortín Conde de Mirasol FORT

(Map p130; 471 Calle Magnolia; donations accepted; ⌚8:30am-4:20pm Wed-Sun) This small fort, on the hill above Isabel Segunda, is the last Spanish fort constructed in the Americas (1840s). Although never completed, the fort has ramparts and a fully restored central building that houses a history and art museum. It currently serves as a museum that showcases the island's 4000-year-old Indian and colonial history.

ESPERANZA

Esperanza is the quintessential Caribbean beach town; a shabby-chic cluster of wooden shacks and colorful open-fronted restaurants that has lifted many a dampened mainland spirit. If you've been fighting your way through the traffic and suburbia of San Juan, this could be your nirvana; an exotic but laid-back mélange of infectious Latin music and friendly streetside salesfolk peddling rum, reggae and bioluminescent kayaking trips.

Set on Vieques' calm southern shores, Esperanza's waters are deep, clear and well sheltered to the north, east and south by two tall, lush islands. The white concrete railings of the modern *malecón* rise quaintly above the town's narrow beach and, if you arrive at sunset, you will see twinkling lights and hear ebullient music pouring from the cafes and restaurants that line the Calle Flamboyán 'Strip' facing the Caribbean.

Some 25 years ago, Esperanza was a desolate former sugar port with a population of about 1500. Its residents survived by fishing, cattle raising and subsistence farming. But then a couple of expatriate Americans in search of the *Key Largo,* Bogart-and-Bacall life discovered the town and started a bar and guesthouse called 'Bananas'. Gradually, word spread among independent travelers, and a cult following took root. Protected (rather ironically) by the presence of the US military on Vieques, Esperanza, despite a recent growth in popularity, has managed to retain much of its rustic pioneering spirit and remains an evocative but fun place to visit.

Isabel Segunda

Sights

1 El Faro de Punta Mulas B1
2 Fortín Conde de Marisol D4

Activities, Courses & Tours

3 Blackbeard Sports B3

Sleeping

4 Casa de Amistad C2

Eating

5 Barefoot Be'stro B1
6 Buen Provecho B3
7 Café Mamasonga B2
8 Cantina La Reina C4
9 Coconuts B3
10 Conuco B3
11 Morales Supermercado B3
12 Panadería & Repostería Lydia B3
13 Panadería La Viequense C4
14 Roy's Coffee Lounge C4
15 Shawnaa's C4

Drinking

16 Al's Mar Azul B2

Shopping

17 Caribbean Walk C4
Siddhia Hutchinson Gallery .... (see 6)

Bahía Mosquito NATURE RESERVE

(Bioluminescent Bay; Map p128) Locals claim that this bay, a designated wildlife preserve about 2 miles east of Esperanza, has the highest concentration of phosphorescent dynoflagellates not only in Puerto Rico, but in the world (see p266). Indeed, it's also known as Bioluminescent Bay – and it's magnificent.

A trip through the lagoon is nothing short of psychedelic, with hundreds of fish whipping up bright-green sparkles below the surface as your kayak or electric boat passes by (no gas-powered boats are permitted – the engine pollution kills the organisms that create phosphorescence). But the best part is when you stop to swim: it's like bathing in the stars.

You can just drive east on the rough Sun Bay road (you'd better have a 4WD, though, because the road's a mess) and jump in for a swim at any point that's glowing. However, an organized trip will give you far more opportunity to really take in the spread of phosphorescence without getting stuck in a huge pothole along the way.

There's another inlet to the east, Barracuda Bay, that's also filled with dynoflagellates, but tour operators don't venture out that far.

Reservations are highly recommended for boat tours and kayak rentals in high season. For more information, see Boat Trips (p135) and Kayaking (p135).

Esperanza

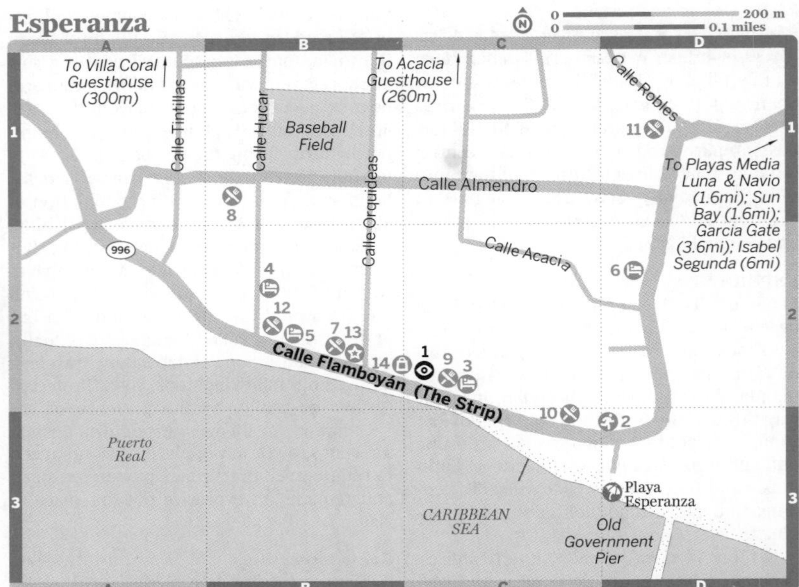

Vieques Conservation & Historical Trust — MUSEUM

(Map p130; www.vcht.com; 138 Calle Flamboyán; donations accepted; 9am-5pm) Founded in 1984 to save the island's bioluminescent bays, the trust operates the tiny Museo de Esperanza, which contains exhibits on the ecological efforts of the trust, the island's natural history and its early Indian inhabitants. Behind the gift shop, the museum runs what is supposedly the smallest aquarium on earth, a series of tanks in which baby sea creatures are displayed for a few weeks before being returned to the ocean. There are also exhibits on the island's archeological and natural history, an internet facility, and tours available (see p136).

Cayo de Tierra — SCENIC OUTLOOK

(Map p128) A teardrop of land between the *malecón* and Sun Bay reached by a slender sandspit (or by wading, if storms have washed it out), Cayo de Tierra has a few irregularly maintained trails that make for an interesting ramble. At the northern tip is a large hyper-saline lagoon teeming with birds, including ospreys and pelicans. The island's high point peaks at 80ft, with wind sculpted trees and impressive Vieques views. The most direct route there is to walk east along the beach from the Esperanza pier.

Area Arqueológica Hombre de Puerto Ferro — LANDMARK

(Map p127) You will find this site marked by a small sign on Hwy 997, east of Esperanza. About a half mile east of the entrance to Sun Bay (Sombé balneario), take the dirt road on your left (it heads inland). Drive for about two minutes on a rutted dirt road until you find the burial site of the Indian known as the 'Hombre de Puerto Ferro'. Big boulders identify a grave where a 4000-year-old skeleton (usually on exhibit at the Fortín) was exhumed. Little is known about the skeleton, but archaeologists speculate that it is most likely the body of one of Los Arcaicos (the Archaics), Puerto Rico's earliest known inhabitants; this racial group made a sustained migration as well as seasonal pilgrimages to the Caribbean from bases in Florida.

Until the discovery of the Hombre de Puerto Ferro, many archaeologists imagined that the Arcaicos had reached Puerto Rico sometime shortly after the birth of Christ; the presence of the remains on Vieques could push that date back nearly two millennia if controversy surrounding the skeleton is resolved. Visitors can stop by the excavation site, but besides the original boulders, there's not much to see.

Esperanza

Sights

1 Vieques Conservation & Historical Trust C2

Activities, Courses & Tours

2 Blue Caribe Kayaks D3

Sleeping

3 Bananas C2
4 Esperanza Inn B2
5 Malecón House B2
6 Rainbow Realty D2

Eating

Bananas .... (see 3)
7 Belly Button's B2
8 Colmado Lydia B1
9 Duffy's C2
10 El Quenepo C3
Farmers Market .... (see 1)
11 La Tienda Verde D1
12 Trade Winds B2

Drinking

Duffy's .... (see 9)

Entertainment

13 Lazy Jack's Pub & Pizza B2

Shopping

Kim's Cabin .... (see 14)
14 Vieques Flowers & Gifts B2

Beaches

Vieques' beaches are as legendary as Culebra's – and there are more of them. Environmentally speaking, the US occupation was a blessing in disguise, in that it has left many of the island's more remote beaches in an underdeveloped and pristine state. Now protected in a national wildlife refuge, areas such as Bahía de la Chiva, Caracas and Green Beaches are clean, untrammeled and paradisial. Others, encased in the former weapons-testing zones, remain closed off and are, effectively, virgin territory. Closed roads leading to contaminated areas are clearly marked as such, but if you have questions about whether an area is safe, check with the **US Fish & Wildlife Service** (787-741-2138; www.fws.gov/caribbean/refuges/vieques).

Unfortunately many of Vieques' beaches are prone to petty theft. No matter how remote your beach, don't leave your valuables unguarded while you swim or snorkel, especially on the beach in downtown Esperanza – they'll be gone in a heartbeat.

Ask locals for directions to Black Sand Beach between Esperanza and Playa Grande.

Playa Esperanza FAMILY BEACH

(Map p132) The advantage of slender Playa Esperanza is that it is within shouting distance of the *malecón* and most of Esperanza's bars, restaurants and guesthouses. The downside is that it is often dirty with litter, seaweed and – even worse – shards of glass. Tread carefully.

Cayo Afuera SNORKELING BEACH

(Map p128) A popular option is to journey from Playa Esperanza across to the nearby islet of Cayo Afuera, an uninhabited pinprick of land that is part of the Mosquito Bay Reserve. It's situated a few hundred meters across the bay; many intrepid locals elect to swim (not advisable unless you are a strong swimmer and are aware of the local weather conditions), while others kayak or take a boat. There is great snorkeling here, both under the ruined pier and on the ocean side of the islet where a sunken sailboat languishes beneath the surface. Antler coral, nurse sharks and manatees have also been spotted in the vicinity.

Sun Bay FAMILY BEACH

(Sombé Balneario; Map p128) This long half-moon-shaped bay, less than a half mile east of Esperanza, is the island's balneario (public beach), with all the facilities you have come to expect in Puerto Rico, including a cafe (open Wednesday through Sunday). Measuring a mile in length, Sun Bay is rarely busy. Indeed, such is its size that even with 100 people congregated in its midst it will still appear almost deserted. The beach is also not always staffed, so you can often drive in without paying the usual $2. If the gate is locked, take the easy walk east along Playa Esperanza, and then walk across the narrow sandspit to Sun Bay.

Playas Media Luna & Navio SECLUDED BEACHES

(Map p128) If it really is isolation you're after, continue east on the dirt road past Sun Bay, and you'll enter a forest. Go left at the fork in the road. In a couple of hundred yards, you'll stumble upon **Playa Media Luna**, a very protected, shady beach that is excellent for kids. Beyond this on the same road is **Playa Navio**, where bigger waves are the domain of bodysurfers. Both of these beaches served

THE NAVY-VIEQUES PROTESTS

In a country where the national status is more often a topic of apathy than anarchy, the 1999–2003 protests against the US Navy presence on the island of Vieques were something of a wake-up call. First requisitioned by the US military in 1941, Vieques was originally intended to act as a safe haven for the British Navy during WWII, should the UK fall to the Nazis. But after 1945 the US decided to keep hold of the territory to use as a base for weapons testing during the ever chillier Cold War. Taking control of more than 70% of the island's total land in the east and west, the military left the local population to live in a small strip down the middle while they shelled beaches and dropped live bombs on offshore atolls. On average the military bombed Vieques 180 days a year and in 1998 alone dropped a total of 23,000 explosive devices on the island.

With the public ire raised, things came to a head on April 19, 1999, after Viequense civilian guard David Sanes Rodríguez was accidentally killed when two 225kg bombs missed their target and exploded near an observation post he was manning. The incident triggered a massive campaign of civil disobedience that reached far beyond the shores of Vieques, recruiting Puerto Ricans and non–Puerto Ricans worldwide. The most common form of protest involved demonstrators entering the military base illegally and setting up makeshift encampments. The campaign gained international notoriety in May 2000 when more than 700 protesters were arrested for trespassing, including notable celebrities such as Robert Kennedy Jnr and Rubén Berríos, leader of the PIP (Puerto Rican Independence Party). Other names who threw their weight behind the cause were Jesse Jackson, Ricky Martin, boxer Felix Trinidad and Archbishop of San Juan Roberto González Nieves.

As in Culebra 25 years earlier, the pressure and publicity finally paid off; in 2001 Puerto Rican Governor Sila María Calderón brokered a deal with US President George W Bush promising that the US military would leave Vieques by May 2003.

Slowly but methodically, the clean-up campaign continues still. Furthermore, after decades of heavy shelling, various health and environmental bodies have reported that Vieques' eastern beaches are heavily contaminated and that its citizens have a cancer rate 27% higher than the Puerto Rican average.

You can track the status of the navy's clean-up of the island at http://public.lantops-ir.org/sites/public/vieques.

as sets in the 1961 film version of the famous William Golding novel *The Lord of the Flies*.

If you climb the rocks at the west end of Playa Navio, you'll find a path along the shore that you can follow to find petrified clams and corals dating from 50 million years ago.

Playas La Plata, Caracas, Garcia, Escondida & Bahía de la Chiva SECLUDED BEACHES

(Map p128) These south-shore beaches, which used to be on navy land, can be reached by entering the Garcia Gate on Hwy 997. New signage makes it easy to find your way around, and the road's paved east as far as Playa Caracas.

Calm and clear **Playa Caracas** (Red Beach) is reached on a paved road and has gazebos with picnic tables to shade bathers from the sun. **Garcia Beach** is lesser known and has less shade, meaning that fewer people decamp here. **Playa Escondida** (Secret Beach) is also in the vicinity. This deliciously deserted stretch of sand has absolutely no facilities – just jaw-dropping beauty.

Bahía de la Chiva (Blue Beach), at the east end of the former Camp Garcia road, is long and open, and occasionally has rough surf. If you happen upon this beach during Semana Santa (the Holy Week preceding Easter), you'll see hordes of faithful Catholics camping on the beach, where they pray and party in honor of the death and resurrection of Jesus Christ. There's good snorkeling here at an island just off the coast. **Playa La Plata** (Orchid Beach), further eastward, is as far as you can go at present. This gorgeously secluded beach has sand like icing sugar and a calm sea that seems to shimmer in a thousand different shades of turquoise, cobalt and blue.

Playa El Gallito (Gringo Beach) RESORT BEACH

(Map p128) The site of the chic new W resort, El Gallito has a great reef for snorkeling just 10yd offshore, but seas can be very rough here from December to March, when trade winds can blow from the northeast.

Starfish Beach FAMILY BEACH
(Map p128) On the north side of Laguna Kiani is the most wonderful beach on Vieques for children, with gentle surf, crystal-clear waters and immense starfish to catch the eye lying all along the shore. It's a really good place for families to relax, and perfect for teaching youngsters the look-don't-touch approach to fragile ecosystems.

Green Beach & Punta Arenas SECLUDED BEACH
(Map p128) Punta Arenas and Green Beach are excellent places for a quiet picnic, some family-friendly snorkeling, and up-close views of the big island and El Yunque across the water. To get here, pass through the former Naval Ammunitions Facility (NAF) Gate and head west for about 20 minutes through pastoral landscapes and herds of wild horses. At the western tip of the island, the road turns to dirt and you can park in the clearings.

The strand here is not very broad and is punctuated with coral outcroppings, but there are plenty of shade trees. Snorkeling reefs extend for miles, and you can expect to have this place pretty much to yourself, except on summer weekends, when a lot of yachts out of Fajardo come here on day trips. Since this beach is generally sheltered from the trade winds, you definitely want bug repellent.

Playa Grande SECLUDED BEACH
(Map p128) Playa Grande has a long, narrow strip of sand and water that drops off very quickly (not good for children or weak swimmers). If you head west on Rte 996 past Esperanza to Rte 201, you'll eventually come to a dead end where you can park and hit the sand.

Activities

Diving & Snorkeling

Blackbeard Sports DIVING, SNORKELING
(Map p130; ☎787-741-1892; www.blackbeardsports.com; 101 Calle Muñoz Rivera, Isabel Segunda) Blackbeard offers two-tank scuba dives from $100 and Professional Association of Dive Instructors (PADI) certified basic open-water courses from $350. You can also rent snorkel/scuba gear for $15/50 a day.

Nan-Sea Charters DIVING, SNORKELING
(☎787-741-2390; www.nanseacharters.com) This outfit does two-tank boat dives from $100, leaving from Esperanza. Shore dives (from $50), night dives and snorkel trips are also available.

Heaven Caribe SNORKELING
(☎787-909-9685) Does two-hour snorkeling excursions to Cayo Afuera via kayak for $30 per person. Children are welcome.

Boat Trips

Vieques Sailing SAILING
(☎787-508-7245) Captain Bill and his boat *Willo* offer a variety of sailing trips. Pick from a half-day sailing and snorkeling trip ($50) to offshore coral reefs, or an all-day sailing excursion to the south tip of the Bermuda Triangle that includes snorkeling, beach time and lunch ($110).

Island Adventures ELECTRIC BOAT
(Map p128; ☎787-741-0720; www.biobay.com; Rte 996 Km 4.5) If you want to see the bioluminescent bay without paddling, Island Adventures offers 90-minute tours ($32) in an electric boat just about every night, except when there's a full moon. Groups are often a little on the large side.

Marauder Sailing Charters SAILING
(☎787-435-4858; www.viequessailing.com; Esperanza) Runs full-day sailing excursions on a classic 34ft sloop, with two snorkel stops, a gourmet lunch prepared onboard and beverages included for $100 per person.

Kayaking

Vieques Adventure Company KAYAKING
(☎787-692-9162; www.viequesadventures.com) This operator has totally clear kayaks that let you see the action as you glide across the water on its unforgettable bio bay tours ($45). Groups

> **ARE YOU A BIO-HAZARD?**
>
> If you're going to take a dip in the bioluminescent bay, make sure not to kill it with curiosity. Sunscreen and insect repellant are harmful to the dynoflagellates that light up the waters, and there's concern that swimming might be banned in the future (as it has been in Fajardo's Laguna Grande) if visitors don't keep it clean. Conscientious outfitters should make this clear when you sign up for a trip, but always make sure you rinse off these substances before going to the bay.

are small, so reserve well ahead. It also does fly-fishing tours via kayak.

Abe's Snorkeling & Bio-bay Tours KAYAKING, SNORKELING
(787-741-2134; www.abessnorkeling.com; Esperanza) Abe's offers guided kayaking and snorkeling trips to Cayo Afuera, a few hundred meters offshore (adult/child $35/17.50). This is a great trip for beginners and families. Its ecofriendly bio-bay tour (adult/child $30/15) is equally child-friendly, with kayaks that can accommodate families of three or even four.

Blue Caribe Kayaks KAYAKING, SNORKELING
(Map p132; 787-741-2522; www.enchanted-isle.com/bluecaribe; Calle Flamboyán, Esperanza) Located right on the Strip, Blue Caribe rents out kayaks ($10/30 for one/four hours), runs bioluminescent bay tours ($30) and does daytime kayak/snorkeling trips ($35) around Cayo Afuera.

Fishing

Fishing is sublime in Vieques. Imagine Florida Keys with about one-tenth of the fisherfolk and enough bonefish, tarpon and permit to stock a mini ocean. Fishing boats can also allow you access to isolated stretches of coastline in the former naval zone.

Two local operators, **Caribbean Fly Fishing Company** (787-741-1337; www.caribbeanflyfishingco.com) and **Amity Fishing Charters** (787-502-3839; www.viequessportfishing.com) charge $350 for a half-day excursion.

Horseback Riding

At the SeaGate Hotel (p137), **Penny Miller** (787-741-4661) runs highly recommended guided trail rides through the mountains or by the ocean, whatever you prefer. Tours cost $65 for two hours.

Cycling

Some of the best bicycling is along Hwys *995*, *996* and 201, which wind through the countryside north and west of Esperanza and are light on traffic. Both of the companies listed here offer excellent bike tours.

Blackbeard Sports CYCLING
(Map p130; 787-741-1892; 101 Calle Muñoz Rivera, Isabel Segunda) Blackbeard rents out North American standard bikes from its store in Isabel Segunda for $25 per day including helmet. It also rents child seats. Its website has a downloadable bike map of western Vieques.

Vieques Adventure Company CYCLING
(787-692-9162; www.viequesadventures.com) Based on the south side of the island, delivers good-quality mountain bikes, helmets and locks to your doorstep for $25 per day.

Tours

The Vieques Conservation and Historical Trust (see p132) offers in-depth naturalist and cultural history tours to places including the Playa Grande sugar mill and Cayo de Tierra. See its website for the schedule.

For bicycle tours of the island, both the Vieques Adventure Company and Blackbeard Sports offer excellent options for easy amblings or round-the-island adventures. Prices range from about $20 to $25 per hour.

Car-free visitors should check out **Kiani Tours** (787-556-6003) for a two- to three-

VIEQUES BY BIKE

A hidden blessing of the erstwhile US occupation is that Vieques remains refreshingly undeveloped and ideal for cycling. Free from the main island's legendary traffic jams and unforgiving drivers, this 135-sq-mile slither of land has subsequently become a little-heralded biker's paradise.

As well as renting out bikes, helmets, locks and child-seats, the island's main bike outlets organize guided rides around the island. If you're up for going it alone, they can furnish you with maps, routes and insider tips. A few suggestions:

» The main road from Isabel Segunda to Esperanza is Hwy 997, but head west on Hwy 200 and then south on Hwy 201 and you'll find a quieter, more pleasant alternative route. Halfway along, you can detour up Hwy 995, another lovely country road.

» The ultimate Vieques loop involves heading west out of Isabel Segunda on Hwy 200 all the way to Green Beach (the last section is unpaved). After some shore snorkeling and an idyllic picnic lunch, swing south through the old military bunkers to Playa Grande before linking up with Hwy 996 to Esperanza.

hour historical tour ($30 to $35 per person) of the island. It can also arrange drop-off and pickup to Playa Caracas/Bahía de la Chiva for $10 person, with a three-/four-person respective minimum.

Sleeping

Vieques is a rural island. You can expect to hear chickens, dogs, cats, cattle and horses making their barnyard noises day and night. Travelers will find guesthouses in both of Vieques' main towns, as well as elsewhere. Many places have a minimum stay during high season.

Just like Culebra, Vieques is an open-minded and tolerant community, and you can safely assume that all tourist accommodations here are gay-friendly. Many guesthouses and restaurants on the island are owned by lesbian or gay expats.

If you're looking for a rental agent, try gay-friendly **Rainbow Realty** (Map p132; 787-741-4312; www.viequesrainbowrealty.com; 278 Calle Flamboyán, Esperanza) in Esperanza. **Vieques Fine Properties** (787-741-3298; www.viequesfineproperties.com) can also help you out. These agents represent a variety of vacation properties ranging from apartments to villas.

If you wish to camp, just east of Esperanza you can pitch your tent at **Sun Bay** (Sombé balneario; 787-741-8198; campsites $10; Wed-Sun). A security guard works here in the evenings. If you don't require facilities or security, you can camp at Playa Media Luna or Playa Navio with a free permit from the Sun Bay office of the **Departamento de Recursos Naturales y Ambientales** (DRNA; Department of Natural Resources & Environment; 787-741-8683; daily but sporadic).

ISABEL SEGUNDA

There are a few accommodations in the heart of town, easily reached on foot from the ferry. Other offerings exist up just above the lighthouse on North Shore Rd, an area called Bravos de Boston. They're not far as the crow flies, but a long uphill trek on foot.

TOP CHOICE **Casa de Amistad** GUESTHOUSE $$

(Map p130; 787-741-3758; www.casadeamistad.com; 27 Calle Benitez Castaño; r $75-105;) A fun and comfortable place to crash slap-bang in the middle of town, friendly Casa de Amistad has seven stylish rooms for rent with air-con and private bathrooms (two of the bathrooms, though private, are separated from bedrooms). Communal areas include an honor bar, sitting room/library, kitchen, landscaped yard and swimming pool, and rooftop deck.

Casa La Lanchita APARTMENTS $$

(787-741-8449; www.casalalanchita.com; 374 North Shore Rd, Bravos de Boston; r $115-185;) La Lanchita turns out 12 spiffy suites with private bathroom and full kitchen on the ocean's edge. The building's a whitewashed three-story colonial beauty that resembles an old plantation house rising up over the Atlantic, albeit with a few salt stains. Bonus features include beach gear, view balconies, a library and a placid pool with kids' section. On clear days you can see St Thomas.

SeaGate Hotel GUESTHOUSE $$

(off Map p130; 787-741-4661; www.seagatehotel.com; r incl breakfast $80-200;) Situated on a hill high above the town, the SeaGate is a bit of a hike from the ferry dock, most of it uphill. But once you get here, it's a different world. Horses roam freely in the surrounding grounds (and can be rented for horseback riding, see p136), lush vegetation fills the garden, and views of the surrounding countryside are panoramic. The crux comes with the animals. This place is dog-friendly, so if sharing a house with myriad canines ain't your cup of tea, you might want to try something a little closer to town.

ESPERANZA

A number of small guesthouses line Calle Flamboyán, the town's main commercial street.

TOP CHOICE **Malecón House** INN $$$

(Map p132; 787-741-0663; www.maleconhouse.com; 105 Calle Flamboyán; r incl breakfast $160-250;) With its travertine floors, beautiful fabrics and light wood furniture, this spacious new upmarket inn kicks Esperanza's accommodations up a few notches. Looking out over the water from a quiet section of the main street, two of the 10 rooms have private seaside balconies, one has a four-poster mahogany bed and all have a clean and uncluttered feel. There's a good book library and helpful owners, plus a free poolside show in the lush garden – watching iguanas graze in the trees overhead.

Acacia Guesthouse APARTMENTS $$

(off Map p132; 787-741-1059; www.acaciaguesthouse.com; 236 Calle Acacia; apt $110-150) Clean and airy are two words that spring to mind when you glimpse inside the four well-laid-out apartments encased in this three-story whitewashed building situated on a rise above Esperanza's beachside strip. From the 2nd- and 3rd-floor decks and rooftop patio you have spectacular views over hills and sea, and virginal St Croix is visible on clear days. The units have full kitchens, comfortable furnishings and friendly owners who live just across the street. There's also a free washing machine, and complimentary air-con courtesy of the breezy trade winds that spread their freshness across the private terrace.

Esperanza Inn GUESTHOUSE **$$**
(Map p132; ☎787-741-2225; www.esperanzainn.com; Calle Hucar; r $95-100, 1-/2-bedroom apt $135/200;) You'd be hard-pressed to lack anything here at this longtime guesthouse with friendly new owners and a coterie of sweet outdoor cats. Comfortable rooms are spacious and impeccably clean, and there's the chance to chat with fellow travelers as you whip up something in the guest kitchen, grab a Medalla from the honor bar, or duck in for a morning caffeine fix. Apartments with balconies and full kitchens sleep six to eight people, and an ample grassy backyard contains a small pool.

Villa Coral Guesthouse GUESTHOUSE **$$**
(off Map p132; ☎787-741-1967; www.villacoralguesthouse.com; 485 Calle Gladiola; r $85, 2-bedroom apt $160-185;) At this six-unit Spanish-style charmer, the tranquil roof deck and pleasant bougainvillea-fringed front veranda dispel any lingering stress. Located in a quiet residential area a few minutes' walk from the action, rooms sport colorful contemporary textiles and bathroom sinks tiled like dreamy waves.

Bananas GUESTHOUSE **$$**
(Map p132; ☎787-741-8700; www.bananasguesthouse.com; 142 Calle Flamboyán; r $70-100;) New management has updated Esperanza's original budget guesthouse-restaurant, and its seven rooms – three with air-con – now sport fresh paint, Indian-print linens and new bedding. The rear rooms back onto jungle, and a few of the rooms open onto private porches. Light sleepers should note that the house bar closes at around 1am on weekends.

ELSEWHERE ON THE ISLAND

TOP CHOICE **Hix Island House** APARTMENTS **$$$**
(Map p128; ☎787-741-2302; www.hixislandhouse.com; Hwy 995; apt incl breakfast groceries $175-310;) Ecohip, new-age-minimalist, environmental-austere; to describe the Hix house in a single sentence is nigh-on impossible, suffice to say that the place inspires robust opinions across the spectrum and is guaranteed to be like nowhere else you have ever visited. Designed by cutting-edge Canadian architect John Hix, this unique guesthouse consists of four industrial concrete blocks that arise out of the surrounding trees like huge granite boulders (or the island's abandoned navy bunkers). Hosting 13 rooms, the ethos here is minimalist, ecological and close to nature – the idea is that the rooms open up to give you the feeling that you are actually living in the forest. Further green credentials are earned through solar panels, recycled water and natural air-conditioning (trade winds), and daily yoga classes are available. It's a brave and surprisingly attractive experiment.

W Retreat & Spa RESORT **$$$**
(Map p128; ☎787-741-4100; www.wvieques.com; Hwy 200 Km 3.2; r from $499;) Breathlessly trendy and uberchic, Vieques' only resort has been the darling of the design set since it unfurled its showy feathers in 2010. Coffee-table books on green living and urban trespass are scattered about the lobby lounge, a glammed-out art explosion with bursts of color and texture from striped rugs and furry pillows. All 156 rooms (oceanside are the quietest) have private balconies or patios and discreetly hidden TVs, and stock Bliss bath products in open bathrooms with both showers and washing-board-styled tubs. Other hotel features include a full spa, a signature **restaurant** (dinner mains $22-39; ⏱breakfast & dinner) by chef Alain Ducasse, a beachside fire pit with wraparound sofa, three pools and two beaches (though the surf can be quite rough). A not unsubstantial nightly resort fee ($60) includes whisking to and from the W's private airport lounge, plus yoga classes, access to the fitness center and tennis courts and use of snorkel gear. Some guests have noted that, like a hot club that hasn't quite hit its stride, staffing and amenities can be strained on busy weekends.

Inn on the Blue Horizon INN **$$$**
(Map p128; ☎787-741-3318; www.innontheblue horizon.com; d $160-370;) Small is beautiful. The Inn on the Blue Horizon was surely invented with such a motto in mind. With only 10 rooms harbored in separate bungalows wedged onto a stunning ocean-

side bluff a few clicks west of Esperanza, the sense of elegance here – both natural and contrived – is truly breathtaking. The luxury continues inside the restaurant and cozy communal lounge, which overlook an Italianate infinity pool fit for a Roman emperor. Children aged under 14 years not permitted in high season.

La Finca Caribe GUESTHOUSE **$$**
(Map p128; ☎787-741-0495; www.lafinca.com; Hwy 995; r $95, cabins $110-165, house $195; P) Finca Caribe is Vieques personified. Sitting high up on a mountain ridge seemingly a million miles from anywhere (but only actually 3 miles from either coast), it's the kind of rustic haven stressed-out city slickers probably dream about. Despite its back-to-nature facilities – outdoor communal showers, shared kitchen and hippyish decor – it has a religious following and has inspired gushing reviews from numerous top newspapers and magazines. The secret lies in the nuances. Picture the swaying hammocks, the unhurried games of croquet, the tangible proximity of nature…

Hacienda Tamarindo GUESTHOUSE **$$$**
(Map p128; ☎787-741-8525; www.haciendatamarindo.com; s incl breakfast $180-240, d incl breakfast $195-345; P@) Lying along Hwy 996 about three-quarters of a mile west of Esperanza, on a hill looking across fields to the Caribbean, this is one of the largest guesthouses (16 rooms) on the south side of the island. Rooms or suites are tricked out in 'Caribbean deluxe' style, which means lots of elegant doors opening to wrought-iron balconies filled with bougainvillea. During high season, children must be aged over 15 years to stay here.

Crow's Nest HOTEL **$$**
(Map p128; ☎787-741-0033; www.crowsnestvieques.com; r incl breakfast $146-283; P) Perched – figuratively speaking – in the Barrio Florida in the hills above Isabel Segunda, the Crow's Nest enjoys a rural airy setting with pink bougainvillea contrasting with its rippling turquoise swimming pool. More functional than luxurious, the rooms here have lounging area and kitchenette. The too-new-to-review **Veritas restaurant** (Caribbean lobster macaroni and cheese, mmm…) also sits on the property.

Eating

Many of the newer, high-end and American-run restaurants require reservations, especially on weekends in high season.

ISABEL SEGUNDA

Conuco PUERTO RICAN **$$**
(Map p130; ☎787-741-2500; 110 Calle Muñoz Rivera; mains $12-20; lunch Wed-Fri, dinner Wed-Sun) A new place with a modern take on Puerto Rican cuisine, Conuco is named for Taíno garden plots. Chef Rebecca Betancourt injects culinary magic into a revamped traditional home complete with entranceway veranda and a corrugated metal roof that echoes in the rain. Standouts include the *bacalaítos* (cod fritters), mahimahi with passion fruit and coconut sauce and the *piónono* (sweet yellow plantains stuffed with ground-beef stew). Romantic and refined, this is the north side's best spot for a dinner date.

Coconuts CARIBBEAN **$$**
(Map p130; ☎787-741-9325; cnr Calles Benitez Guzman & Baldorioty de Castro; mains $11-29; dinner Fri-Tue) Foodies shouldn't miss the non-stop stream of creative offerings generated by top-notch chef Michael Glatz. Under a softly lit patio with palm trees and a salsa soundtrack, dine on the signature sushi pizza (a tempura rice crust adorned with ahi tuna and spicy sauce), or make yourself choose from the long list of daily specials. Don't miss sampling the basil-and-goat cheese or toasted-coconut-rum ice creams. Reservations a must in high season.

Cantina La Reina MEXICAN **$**
(Map p130; 351 Calle Antonio G Mellado; mains $9-17; lunch & dinner Dec-Apr, shorter hr May-Nov) Ensconce yourself inside this dramatic blood-red building for California-style Mexican fare accompanied by a laundry list of tequilas. Guacamole, fajitas and *chilaquiles* (tortilla chips with eggs) feature, though the sugar-dusted churros and ice cream has its rabid fans. The walls are covered in religious objects and revolutionary iconography, and there's a romantic upstairs roof deck and a pool table to boot.

Barefoot Be'stro SEAFOOD **$$**
(Map p130; ☎340-514-0124; Bravos de Boston; mains $9-24; 8-11am & 5-9pm Wed-Sat) The open air dining room is topped by a thatched roof, the patrons dine at mosaic beach tables and benches, and the chef prepares meals in a seascape-festooned food cart. You could call it gourmet casual or upscale island, but either way it works. The seafood is prepared with a tropical flair, with favorites including variations on Caribbean lobster.

Roy's Coffee Lounge CAFE $
(Map p130; 355 Calle Antonio G Mellado; mains $7-10; ⏲8am-2pm daily, dinner Tue & Thu high season; 📶) At this artsy little haven on the main drag, you'll usually find a clutch of folks checking their email while sipping espresso drinks on the back garden patio. In addition to simple breakfasts, there's a full bar and grill food such as burgers and quesadillas, and the big brownies and sticky cinnamon rolls are always a treat.

Panadería La Viequense BAKERY $
(Map p130; Calle Antonio G Mellado; dishes $3-8; ⏲6am-4pm Mon-Sat, to 2pm Sun) If it's breakfast you're after, this is the place to come for your 6am eggs or hangover-curing coffee. If you miss the 11am cutoff you can feast instead on decent baked goods, tortillas and sandwiches. Service is no-nonsense and fast, the decor clean and modern, and the clientele local with a smattering of in-the-know tourists. Don't miss its photo gallery of early-20th-century Vieques.

Shawnaa's PUERTO RICAN $
(Map p130; 327 Calle Antonio G Mellado; dishes $6-8; ⏲10:30am-2pm Mon-Fri) Bring a big appetite to Shawnaa's buffet. It's full of superb *comida criolla* (traditional Puerto Rican cuisine) dishes that you can take out onto the patio or consume in the shaded interior.

Panadería & Repostería Lydia BAKERY $
(Map p130; cnr Calles Benitez Guzman & Plinio Peterson; snacks $1-5; ⏲4am-noon) With a 4am opening call, this veritable hole-in-the-wall bakery-cum-coffee bar is ideal for insomniacs, late-night party animals and ferry workers on the graveyard shift. Stop by for caffeine, pastries, sandwiches and sweet bread, and fight with the locals for one of the two plastic tables that furnish the sidewalk.

Café Mamasonga DINER $
(Map p130; ☎787-741-0103; 566 Calle German Rieckehoff; mains $6-15; ⏲Sun-Fri) At this petite tropical eatery a few paces from the ferry terminal, you can sit outside to gaze at the water and watch cars bump over the grate out front. Start your day with a American-style breakfast or come by later to fill up on seafood stew, fettuccini alfredo or crab cakes with mango habañera sauce.

If you're looking to stock up on provisions, try **Morales Supermercado** (Map p130; 15 Calle Baldorioty de Castro); there is a second store a mile west of Isabel Segunda on the road to the airport (Hwy 200). For a gourmet selection of island-scarce produce, artisan breads, Angus beef steaks and two dozen varieties of cheese, check out **Buen Provecho** (Map p130; cnr Calles Muñoz Rivera & Baldorioty de Castro; ⏲10am-6pm Tue-Sat).

ESPERANZA

El Quenepo INTERNATIONAL $$
(Map p132; ☎787-741-1215; 148 Calle Flamboyán; dishes $20-32; ⏲dinner Tue-Sun mid-Nov–Easter & Wed-Sun Easter-Aug) The destination restaurant of Vieques, Esperanza's upscale El Quenepo has a lovely interior and an equally delectable menu. The food is catch-of-the-day fresh – a family of seven brothers supplies the seafood – and the decor is very chic. A few suggestions to get your mouth watering: whole Caribbean lobsters, *mofongo* (mashed plantains) made with breadfruit grown in its backyard and a lovely *churrasco* (charcoal-broiled Argentinean steak). Reservations highly recommended.

Duffy's RESTAURANT $
(Map p132; Calle Flamboyán; dishes $10-13; ⏲lunch & dinner; 🍸) At this convivial bar opening out onto Esperanza's main strip, the laid-back street atmosphere infiltrates the shady interior where expats and locals mingle over microbrew beer paired with wraps, fish tacos or burgers (including the meat-free variety). For tasty food, upright prices and good company, look no further.

Trade Winds CARIBBEAN $$
(Map p132; Calle Flamboyán; dishes $5-24) Unpretentious dining at its finest. Sit back in a wide chair on the breezy verandah and enjoy scrumptious scrambled eggs or island-spiced fish and meat dishes later in the day.

Belly Button's BREAKFAST $
(Map p132; Calle Flamboyán; dishes $5-10; ⏲breakfast & lunch, sporadic dinner) Consisting of a small collection of alfresco tables located outside a kitchen trailer on the *malecón*, this expat-run breakfast phenomenon conjures up enough food to keep you going until 6pm. Order a mug of gourmet coffee, season your eggs with locally made and sweat-inducing Komodo Dragon hot sauce, and make plans for a day of breathtaking action – or indolence.

Bananas RESTAURANT $
(Map p132; Calle Flamboyán; dishes $9-12; ⏲lunch & dinner) More popular for drinks

DON'T MISS

CHEZ SHACK

What do '60s psychedelic band the Mamas and Papas and Vieques' most bohemian restaurant have in common? They both owe at least a part of their success to expat impresario and restaurateur Hugh Duffy. In the 1960s Duffy owned a restaurant called 'Love Shack' on the nearby island of St Thomas, where he hosted folk-music nights with a quartet of spaced-out hippies called the New Journeymen. It was an important first break. But while the Journeymen changed their name to the Mamas and Papas and headed off to LA for some California Dreamin', Duffy transplanted himself just 13 miles to the west, where he opened up **Chez Shack** (Map p128; ☎787-741-2175; Hwy 995 Km 1.8; dishes $18-30; ⊙dinner Wed-Sun mid-Nov–May), a quirky Caribbean hangout that quickly began to rival the luminous bio-bay as *the* place to go on Vieques. Two decades later both Duffy (now pushing 90) and the shack are still rustling up fine dinners that have become almost as celebrated as his erstwhile protégées. Monday is the big night, with live reggae and an outdoor grill featuring chicken, fish or steak. Make reservations.

than dinner, Bananas weighs in with excellent salads, sandwiches and seafood, as well as inexpensive daily specials. Its upstairs bar has sigh-worthy water views.

For groceries, **La Tienda Verde** (Green Store; Map p132; Calle Robles) and the **Colmado Lydia** (Map p132; Calle Almendro), near the baseball field in the center of town, are your best bets in Esperanza, but that's not saying much. On Saturday, stop by the small **farmers market** (⊙11am-4pm Sat) at the Vieques Conservation and Historical Trust for excellent local produce, baked goods, honey and hot sauce. Some vendors will barter.

ELSEWHERE ON THE ISLAND

Next Course FUSION $$
(Map p128; ☎787-741-1028; Hwy 201; mains $22-38; ⊙dinner Fri-Wed, shorter hr low season; ✎) Another new upscale option, this one's cocooned away on Hwy 201 and serenaded by a throaty chorus of frogs. Offering 'cuisine inspired by travel,' Next Course borrows influences from Thai, Mexican and Persian kitchens, with an emphasis on fresh local food, and some of its fruit harvested onsite. A sampling of choices might include poached lobster with white truffle risotto and prosciutto-wrapped asparagus or tender barbecued ribs that fall off the bone. After dark, orient yourself by its tiki torches and strings of patio lights.

Inn on the Blue Horizon INTERNATIONAL $$
(Map p128; dinner mains $24-29; ⊙breakfast & dinner) A mile west of Esperanza on Hwy 996, this inn offers casual, elegant gazebo dining with a view like the name implies. Reservations are a must.

Drinking

The local police sometimes set up sobriety checkpoints. Don't drink and drive.

Al's Mar Azul BAR
(Map p130; Calle Plinio Peterson) Al's shelters the ghosts of Charles Bukowski and Ernest Hemingway and is the nexus of local gossip. Locals come to play pool, and expats come to drink…and drink. Visitors teeter somewhere in between. Karaoke crooners fill the place Saturday nights.

Duffy's BAR
(Map p132; Calle Flamboyán) Esperanza's best bar carries more than 30 varieties of bottled microbrews, such as Kalamazoo Stout and Two-Hearted Ale, in addition to a yummy tropical cocktail menu. Try a *parcharita* – a concoction of passion fruit and tequila with a sweet and salty rim.

For upscale atmosphere, drop over to the hotel bars at the W (p138) or the Inn on the Blue Horizon (p141).

Entertainment

On Monday, Chez Shack boogies to live reggae.

Lazy Jack's Pub & Pizza BAR
(Map p132; Calle Flamboyán) Another popular *malecón* bar, with music most nights of the week. Depending on the day, you can play at an open jam, embarrass yourself over karaoke, kick back with a thin-crust pizza while

grooving to a reggae band, or shake it at the Saturday-night dance party.

Shopping

Siddhia Hutchinson Gallery ART
(Map p130; cnr Calles Muñoz Rivera & Baldorioty de Castro; 9:30am-4pm) The gallery of artist and designer Siddhia Hutchinson exhibits her first-class paintings of colorful tropical scenes and the pottery, jewelry and sculpture of other local artists.

Vieques Flowers & Gifts CRAFTS
(Map p132; 134 Calle Flamboyán) On the Strip in Esperanza, this shop has everything from local crafts, pottery, clothes and – of course – fresh flowers.

Caribbean Walk ART
(Map p130; 353 Calle Antonio G Mellado; 10am-3pm, closed Wed & Sun) Tiny, but full of local art, this creative shop in Isabel Segunda harbors intricate jewelry and plenty of other dexterously sculpted crafts.

Kim's Cabin JEWELRY
(Map p132; 136 Calle Flamboyán) Carries lovely silver jewelry made with beach glass.

Information

Unless otherwise noted, all of the places listed here are in Isabel Segunda. While some actual street addresses exist on Vieques, citizens and businesses rarely use them.

Emergency

Dial 911 for emergencies.

Fire (787-741-2111)

Police (787-741-2020)

Internet Access

In Isabel Segunda, wi-fi's available at Roy's Coffee Lounge (p140), and there's a free hot spot in the plaza, right in front of city hall.

Blackbeard Sports (Map p130; 101 Calle Muñoz Rivera; per hr $6; 8am-5pm Mon-Sat, 10am-3pm Sun) Has a small business center with PCs and wi-fi.

Vieques Conservation & Historical Trust (Map p132; Calle Flamboyán 138, Esperanza; per 30min $5; 11am-4pm) Half a dozen computer terminals; wi-fi $5 per hour with your own laptop.

Media

Vieques Events (www.viequesevents.net) A bilingual monthly magazine with a local calendar of events and phone directory, plus schedules for yoga classes, AA meetings, and anything else that's happening on the island.

Medical Services

Hospital Susan Centeno (787-741-0392; Rte 997 Km 0.4; clinic 7am-4pm Mon-Fri, emergency 24hr) Just south of Isabel Segunda on Hwy 997.

Farmacia San Antonio (787-741-8397; Calle Benítez Guzman; 8am-6pm Mon-Fri, 9am-noon & 1:30-6pm Sat) For basic supplies and over-the-counter remedies.

Money

It's a good idea to carry cash on the island (but watch out for petty thieves) as the ATMs have been known to run dry. At the time of research, all the island's ATMs were in Isabel Segunda, including a few in markets. Credit cards are widely accepted.

Banco Popular (Calle Muñoz Rivera; 8am-3:30pm Mon-Fri) ATM here.

Cooperativa de Ahorro y Crédito Roosevelt Roads (Calle Muñoz Rivera; 8:15am-4:30pm Mon-Fri, 8:15am-noon Sat) Another ATM just across the street from Banco Popular.

Post

Post office (Map p130; Calle Muñoz Rivera 97; 8:30am-4:30pm Mon-Fri, 8am-noon Sat) Across from the Banco Popular, this is the island's only post office.

Tourist Information

Good websites include www.enchanted-isle.com and www.vieques-island.com for useful directories of island businesses, services and accommodations.

Puerto Rico Tourism Company (PRTC; Map p130; www.gotopuertorico.com; Calle Carlos Lebrun 449; 8am-noon, 1-4:30pm) Friendly, helpful and bilingual staff on hand every day to give out information, brochures and the classic Vieques map, www.theviequesmap.com.

Getting There & Away

Air

Públicos greet most flights and will take you anywhere you want to go on the island.

The island has lots of air services from San Juan – both LMM International and Isla Grande airports – and Ceiba. There are more than 20 flights a day to/from San Juan's Isla Grande and LMM airports. Round-trip prices start at $220 (25 minutes) from LMM, $126 from Isla Grande and about $65 (10 minutes) from Ceiba. Check with any of the following carriers for more up-to-date information.

Air Flamenco (787-724-6464, 787-741-8811; www.airflamenco.net) and **M&N Aviation** (787-791-7008; www.mnaviation.com) fly charters from San Juan and Ceiba for the same price as the scheduled carriers. Call for availability.

Air Sunshine (☎800-327-8900, 787-741-7900; www.airsunshine.com) flies directly to St Thomas, St Croix and Tortola in the British Virgin Islands. It also carries people between San Juan LMM and Vieques, charging the same rates as the other carriers.

Cape Air (☎866-227-3247, 787-741-7734; www.flycapeair.com) flies six times a day from San Juan LMM airport.

Seaborne Airlines (☎866-359-8784; www.seaborneairlines.com) has service to San Juan LMM airport, Isla Grande and St Croix and one weekly nonstop service to St Thomas.

Vieques Air Link (☎888-901-9247, 787-741-8331, San Juan–Vieques flights, ☎787-741-3266, 787-534-4222 Ceiba–Vieques flights; www.viequesairlink.com) is the major carrier, with an office in Isabel Segunda. It currently flies to Culebra (via Ceiba) for $70.

Ferry

The high-speed passenger ferries of the Maritime Transportation Authority (Autoridad de Transporte Marítimo or ATM) run between Fajardo and Vieques four times a day. Boats leave Fajardo at 9:30am, 1pm, 4:30pm and 8pm and Vieques at 6:30am, 11am, 3pm and 6pm. Passage takes one hour 15 minutes, weather permitting. The round trip costs a giveaway $4. A thrice-daily cargo ferry sails from Fajardo to Vieques (weekdays only, two hours), but rental car contracts prohibit bringing cars on the ferry.

Confirm the passenger ferry schedule in advance, as it does change occasionally. Frustratingly, advance reservations are not sold; the ticket offices usually open one hour before departure. Holiday weekends and summertime are peak times when tickets can sell out. In these situations, Vieques residents get priority and visitors can get bumped. In Fajardo call the **Maritime Transportation Authority** (ATM; ☎787-860-2005, 800-981-2005; www.atm.gobierno.pr; ⏲8-11am & 1-3pm Mon-Fri) for vehicle reservations (required), or call the **Vieques office** (Map p130; ☎787-741-5018; ⏲8-11am & 1-3pm Mon-Fri) at the ferry dock in Isabel Segunda. Note that these offices rarely answer their phones though!

Getting Around

Bicycle

Vieques is excellent for cycling, and partaking in a little two-wheeled transport will help ease the proliferation of cars that goes hand in hand with tourist growth. The road across the island from Isabel Segunda to Esperanza is less than 6 miles in length and can be tackled by any moderately fit cyclist. See p136 for bike rental.

Car & Scooter

You may not need wheels for your whole stay, as most of the main facilities are located within close proximity to each other in the center of the island. Most rentals are Suzuki Samurai jeeps (about $50 to $70 a day), and reliable operators include **Island Car Rentals** (☎787-741-1666), **Maritza's Car Rental** (☎787-741-0078; www.maritzascarrental.com) and **Coquí Car Rental** (☎787-741-3696). Reserve ahead in high season.

Fun Brothers (☎787-435-9372) rents two-passenger Yamaha scooters (with helmets) for $50 a day from a kiosk at the east end of Esperanza Strip.

Public Transport

If you have not arranged for a rental car at the airport or an airport pickup/drop-off with your guesthouse proprietor, you'll need one of the island taxis; $10 to $15 will get you just about anywhere on the island. Públicos usually greet both ferries and airplanes, and will take you where you need to go, but you can't be in a hurry to get there. You'll pay between $3 to $5 per person to travel between Isabel Segunda and Esperanza, with públicos running fairly regularly.

Taxi

For a ride, try one of the following cabs:

Alba Melendez (☎787-206-0456)
Carlos & Denisse (☎787-447-8697)
Eric (☎787-741-0448)
Edna Robles (☎787-630-4673)

Ponce & South Coast

POP 527,450

Includes »

Best Places to Eat

» La Casa de Los Pastelillos (p159)

» Archipielago (p153)

» Restaurante La Guardarraya (p163)

» Alexandra (p165)

» Aguazul (p170)

» Café Café (p154)

Best Places to Stay

» Mary Lee's by the Sea (p164)

» Copamarina Beach Resort (p165)

» Ramada Ponce (p153)

Why Go?

The Caribbean-facing south coast offers the chance to unplug, escape the cruise ship crowds and take a DIY journey into Puerto Rico's past.

The proud southern capital of Ponce – the so-called Perla de Sur (Pearl of the South) – stands in elegant disrepair, where haute eateries neighbor slouching colonial facades. Along coastal Hwys 2 and 3, crumbling chimneys of sugar mills stand beside their graying industrial replacements – chemical and pharmaceutical factories. But for all these dichotomies, there's a certain unpolished charm in picturesque southern towns.

The still waters of the south won't compare with the postcard-perfect beaches on the Atlantic, but beyond a typical day at the beach, travelers can kayak the maze of mangroves, hike the arid hills of the dry tropical forest and float in the surreal glow of the Bahía de Fosforescente.

When to Go

With some of the most consistent weather in the world, the dry, sunny climate is always inviting, though the June through August can be blisteringly hot. When school is out during this period, Puerto Rican families fill the sun-washed plazas, wander through colonial buildings and enjoy alfresco dining at the ubiquitous seafood shacks. Even though the arid, breezy atmosphere doesn't change much in winter, the typically languid pace slows to a crawl between September and May, only picking up for local festivals during the extended Christmas holiday.

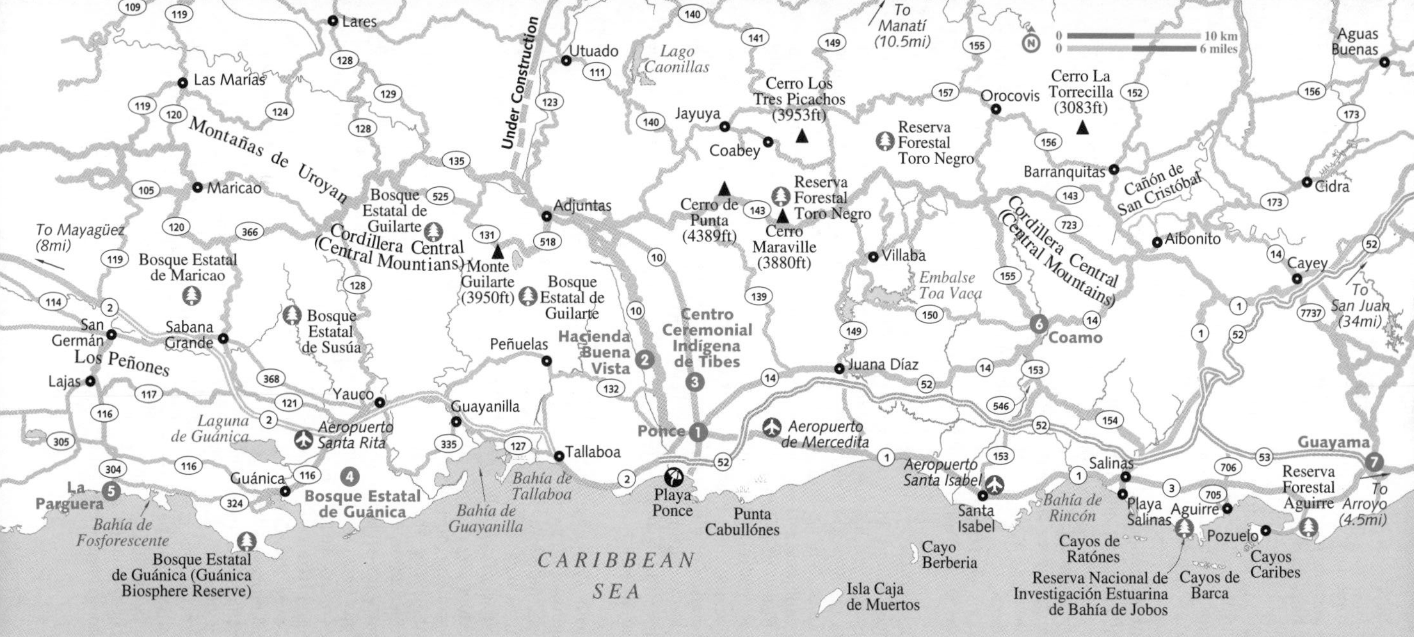

Ponce & South Coast Highlights

1 Fall in love with *Flaming June* at the **Museo de Arte de Ponce** (p150)

2 Stroll the grounds of an immaculately restored coffee plantation at **Hacienda Buena Vista** (p157)

3 Connect with the mysterious Taíno past, on the ball courts of **Centro Ceremonial Indígena de Tibes** (p156), the island's largest archaeological site

4 Hike or mountain bike the dusty, birding trails at **Bosque Estatal de Guánica** (p165)

5 Stagger down the crooked streets of **La Parguera** (p167) after snorkeling its cays

6 Soak at the **Baños de Coamo** (p162), once thought to be the fountain of youth

7 Sway on a hammock while lunching on golden, octopus-stuffed pastries at **La Casa de Los Pasteliollos** (p159) in Guayama

History

The rolling foothills and broad coastal plains of the south coast were home to a number of indigenous tribes and were first colonized by Spaniards, who raised cattle and horses for the colonial expeditions in Mexico and South America in the 16th century. In 1630 they built a hamlet on a port between the mountains and the coast which would eventually become Ponce.

For more than a century, goods and materials flowed through the welcoming harbors. Ostensibly the port of Ponce was only open to Spanish vessels trading directly with Spain, but the watchful eyes of the island governor were a universe away – over the mountains in San Juan – and free trade flourished, bringing goods, currencies, and people from across the New World and Africa.

When slave revolts erupted in the neighboring French-held island of Saint-Domingue in the 1790s and South America between 1810 and 1822, many wealthy refugees fled to the south coast, buying land to grow coffee and sugarcane. Soon they imported former slaves from Caribbean colonies to meet the ever-increasing American appetite for sugar, coffee and rum. Production and profits from agriculture skyrocketed throughout the 19th century, when sugar barons built cities with elegant town squares, neoclassical architecture and imported French fountains.

The Spanish-American War ended the freebooting days, bringing military occupation, uniformly enforced trade laws and an economic freefall. Hurricanes devastated the coffee industry, sugar prices fell, and the US government decided to develop San Juan, not Ponce, as a strategic port. When the Depression hit in the 1930s, the region fell into an economic hibernation.

These days the south limps along littered with contradictions between the past and the future: cranes mark Ponce's continual, if poorly planned, urbanization. The breathtaking sunsets over the Caribbean are marred by huffing factory smokestacks, and the smooth roads that cut through the ramshackle towns are often choked with traffic, only affording occasional glimpses of the land's lush beauty. These paradoxes make Ponce and the surrounding south coast the place where the 18th and 21st centuries have collided, and an area of constant surprise.

PONCE

Ponce native son and author Abelardo Díaz Alfaro famously called Ponce a *baluarte irreductible de puertorriqueñidad* – a bastion of the irreducible essence of Puerto Rico. Strolling around the sparkling fountains in the central square and narrow streets of the city's historic center evokes the stately spirit of Puerto Rico's past. Unfortunately, the neighborhoods that surround the square bear witness to some woeful characteristics of Puerto Rico's present: irreducible snarls of congested traffic, economic stagnation and cookie-cutter urban sprawl. Even though the honking and ceaseless construction are signs of the city's growth, the communities surrounding San Juan have grown much faster, unseating Ponce's status as Puerto Rico's second-most populated metropolis.

The city has a more easygoing spirit than other major cities on the island, with businesses that open late and close early, couples who stroll circles around the city's fountains and spend breezy evenings 2 miles south at the shoreline. There, at a developed facility called La Guancha Paseo Tablado, clusters of restaurants and cafes draw families for open-air dinners on the weekend. After the kids go to bed, the drinks flow and the area jumps with a booming mix of reggaetón and salsa.

History

Unlike many destinations in the north, where history buffs have to do some digging, Ponce's celebrated past is a marquee feature. Present in preserved Spanish colonial buildings, statuary and more than a dozen museums, history is most readily visible at the city's historic Plaza Las Delicias. Those interested in the island's precolonial indigenous roots are only a short drive from Puerto Rico's largest and most educational archaeological site, the Centro Ceremonial Indígena de Tibes.

The earliest western settlement saw a number of clashes between Spanish Conquistador Ponce de León (from whom the town gets both its name and one of its many nicknames, 'City of Lions') and the Taíno tribes, but the region was claimed for the Spanish Crown in 1511. The city was established around 1630, when the Spaniards built the first incarnation of the current cathedral and named it for the patron saint of Mexico, the Virgen de Guadalupe.

As the first port of call in the region – far from Spanish authorities in San Juan – Ponce grew fat off the rewards of smugglers in the late 1600s. By the mid-1700s Ponce's bourgeois society wanted at least a patina of respectability; Spanish merchants and wealthy refugees from nearby Saint-Domingue (where slave revolts radically changed the order of things) poured resources into legitimate enterprises such as tobacco, coffee and rum. Sugar, too, became an important business, and entire plains (the same denuded ones you see today) were shorn of greenery and replaced with silky, lucrative sugarcane. The added wealth and polyglot mixture of Spanish, Taíno, French and West Indian peoples helped establish Ponce as the island's earliest artistic, musical and literary center. The parlors of the bourgeoisie echoed with postured *danza* (an elegant ballroom dance with Caribbean origins), while satirical, boisterous strains of *bomba y plena,* two distinct yet often associated types of folk music, were shared by laborers.

That golden age ended in 1898 when Spain rejected America's demand to peacefully observe Cuban independence, which spurred the start of the Spanish-American War. Compared with modern definitions, it wasn't much of a scuffle, but the five-month skirmish included an American invasion that landed in Guánica. By the time the 1898 Treaty of Paris was signed, the United States held colonial control of not only Puerto Rico and Cuba, but also Spanish colonies in the Pacific.

Under American colonial rule, Puerto Rico's economy was drastically transformed and Ponce's sugar fields were lucrative for industrialized investors. In 1899 however, a pair of hurricanes (one of which, San Ciriaco, was among the longest ever recorded in the Atlantic) devastated the sugar fields and Ponce's industry never fully recovered.

These hurricanes started a period of long decline in the region. First went the sugar, then the region's coffee trade took a nosedive the 1920s. In the harsh economic conditions of following decades, Ponce became a hotbed of civic unrest. It boiled over during the Ponce Massacre of 1937, which politically alienated Ponce from the rest of the island. Ponce was already on its knees by the time the Americans' Operation Bootstrap, an ambitious island-wide industrialization project, dealt a region a near-fatal blow by favoring the development of ports on the north coast.

Through the later half of the 20th century, Ponce limped along producing textiles and cement, though it was only relatively recently that Operation Bootstrap's other impetus – tourism – began to have a positive affect the region. It has gradually reestablished itself as a historic center for tourists (helped dramatically by a highway connecting it to San Juan) and entered the modern age with an economy augmented by producing plastics, rum and pharmaceuticals.

PLAN YOUR TRIP

» Book a tour at the Hacienda Buena Vista (p157).

» Call ahead to nature reserve offices to check on trail conditions and seasonal variations in offerings.

» Look at the www.seepuertorico.com website to plan visiting one of the south's famous festivals.

 Sights

Should you ever get lost in Ponce, just look to the skies for a sign from God: the town's two infallible landmarks are the towering steeples of the Catedral Nuestra Señora de Guadalupe, which sits regally at the center of the lovely Plaza Las Delicias, and an enormous concrete-and-glass cross, El Vigía, which overlooks the town to the north.

As you navigate your way through the outskirts of Ponce, its first impression, characterized by traffic jams and mini malls, is less than inspiring. But the soul of Ponce is its idyllic Spanish colonial plaza and the surrounding grid of streets. These blocks host picturesque historic buildings painted in pastels and outfitted with ornate second-story balconies, shuttered windows and solid wooden doors. Some are elegantly restored, many are slouching in a broken-hearted state of disrepair, but the area makes for a romantic stroll.

Plaza Las Delicias SQUARE

Within this elegant square you'll discover the heart of the city and two of the city's landmark buildings, Parque de Bombas and Catedral Nuestra Señora de Guadalupe. The smell of *panaderías* (bakeries) follows churchgoers across the square each

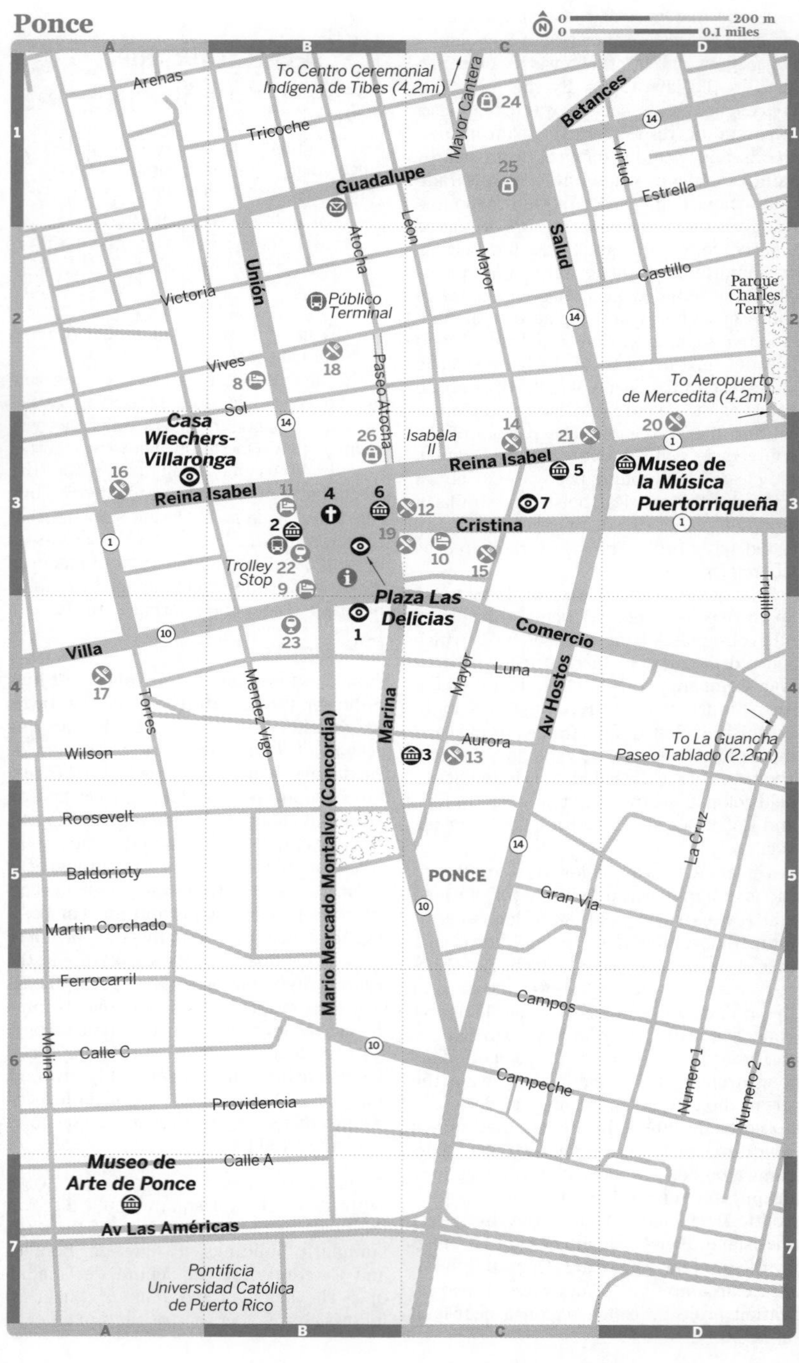

To Centro Ceremonial Indígena de Tibes (4.2mi)
Arenas
Tricoche
Mayor Cantera
Betances
Guadalupe
Virtud
Estrella
Léon
Atocha
Salud
Mayor
Unión
Victoria
Castillo
Parque Charles Terry
Público Terminal
Vives
Paseo Atocha
Sol
To Aeropuerto de Mercedita (4.2mi)
Casa Wiechers-Villaronga
Isabela II
Reina Isabel
Museo de la Música Puertorriqueña
Cristina
Trolley Stop
Plaza Las Delicias
Comercio
Trujillo
Villa
Luna
Torres
Mendez Vigo
Mayor
Marina
Av Hostos
Aurora
Wilson
To La Guancha Paseo Tablado (2.2mi)
Mario Mercado Montalvo (Concordia)
Roosevelt
La Cruz
Baldorioty
PONCE
Gran Via
Martin Corchado
Ferrocarril
Campos
Molina
Calle C
Campeche
Numero 1
Numero 2
Providencia
Museo de Arte de Ponce
Calle A
Av Las Américas
Pontificia Universidad Católica de Puerto Rico
0 200 m
0 0.1 miles

Ponce

Top Sights

Casa Wiechers-Villaronga A3
Museo de Arte de Ponce A7
Museo de la Música Puertorriqueña D3
Plaza Las Delicias B3

Sights

1 Casa Alcaldía B4
2 Casa Armstrong-Poventud B3
3 Casa de la Masacre de Ponce C4
4 Catedral Nuestra Señora de Guadalupe B3
5 Museo de la Historia de Ponce C3
6 Parque de Bombas B3
7 Teatro La Perla C3

Sleeping

8 Casa del Sol Guest House B2
9 Hotel Bélgica B3
10 Hotel Meliá C3
11 Ramada Ponce B3

Eating

12 Archipielago C3
13 Café Café C4
Café Tomas .... (see 14)
14 Café Tompy C3
15 Cesar's Comida Criolla C3
16 Chef's Creations A3
17 Edan Deli & Juice Bar A4
18 King's Cream B2
19 King's Cream C3
20 La Casa de Las Tias D3
21 Rincón Argentino C3

Drinking

Archipielago .... (see 12)
22 Kenepa's at Café Plaza B3
23 La Taberna B4

Shopping

24 Mercade Juan Ponce de León C1
25 Nueva Plaza del Mercado C1
26 Utopia B3

morning, children squeal around the majestic fountain under the heat of midday, and lovers stroll under its lights at night. Even as the commercial banks and the fast-food joints encroach at the edges (a Burger King and a Church's Chicken mar the plaza's west side), reminders of the city's prideful history dominate the plaza's attractions, including marble statues of local *danza* icon Juan Morel Campos and poet/politician Luis Muñoz Marín, Puerto Rico's first governor. The **Fuente de los Leones** (Fountain of Lions), a photogenic fountain rescued from the 1939 World's Fair in New York, is the square's most captivating and vibrant attraction.

FREE Catedral Nuestra Señora de Guadalupe CATHEDRAL
(Our Lady of Guadalupe Cathedral; 6am-1pm Mon-Fri, 6am-noon & 3-8pm Sat & Sun) The twin bell towers of this cathedral cast an impression of piety over the plaza, even as young punks gather to show off skate tricks on its steps. It was built in 1931, in the place where colonists erected their first chapel in the 1660s, which (along with subsequent structures) succumbed to earthquakes and fires. Its stained-glass windows and lovely interior are picturesque, but be mindful of the fact that this is a fully functioning church, with a number of daily services.

FREE Parque de Bombas NOTABLE BUILDING
(9:30am-5pm) *Ponceños* (people from Ponce) claim that the eye-popping Parque de Bombas is Puerto Rico's most frequently photographed building – not too hard to believe as you stroll around the black-and-red-striped Arabian-style edifice and make countless, unwitting cameos in family photo albums. Originally constructed in 1882 as an agricultural exhibition hall, the space later housed the city's volunteer firefighters, who are commemorated in a small, tidy exhibit on the open 2nd floor. Since 1990, the landmark has served the perfect function of a tourist information center – even the most hapless tourist can't miss it – where a pleasant, bilingual staff will sell you tickets for a trolley and point you in the right direction for local attractions and amenities.

FREE Casa Wiechers-Villaronga HISTORICAL HOME
(8:30am-4:30pm Wed-Sun) Perhaps the most grand of Ponce's historic homes, this mansion was designed by Paris-educated *ponceño* architect Alfredo Wiechers. The carefully preserved Victorian details – such as the multidirectional pipeworks of the ancient shower and the hand-carved bedroom furniture – speak to the grand lifestyle of its former residents. Tours begin by request (better in

Spanish, though possible in English). Those who don't get their thrills from Victorian living might find some by climbing the twisting iron staircase to the neoclassical rooftop gazebo for a bird's-eye perspective of the neighborhood.

Casa Armstrong-Poventud HISTORICAL HOME
(admission $3; ⏲8:30am-4:30pm Wed-Sun) After restoration for the better part of a decade, Casa Armstrong-Poventud's caryatid columns emerged from behind a veil of scaffolding. Though infrequently open, it holds a modest display about the family who lived here and historic photos of the square.

FREE **Casa Alcaldía** NOTABLE BUILDING
(Town Hall; ⏲8am-4:30pm Mon-Fri) Facing the south side of Plaza Las Delicias, Ponce's city hall was built in the 1840s. The last public hanging on the island happened in its courtyard, where current galleries were formerly cells. Its balcony has seen speeches by four US presidents – Teddy Roosevelt, Hoover, Franklin Roosevelt and George HW Bush. The waggish head of Carnaval, El Rey Momo, also makes pronouncements from here.

Teatro La Perla NOTABLE BUILDING
(Pearl Theater; cnr Mayor & Cristina; ⏲lobby 8am-4:30pm Mon-Fri) The restored 1000-seat Teatro La Perla recently reopened for theatrical and musical performances. The columned entrance, designed by Calderoni, the father of Puerto Rico's neoclassical style, was completed in the 1860s. It took 20 years to rebuild after an earthquake in 1918, but has since played a crucial role in the city's performing arts world, underscored by the Instituto de Musica Juan Morel Campos, a music conservatory, across the street. The theater is empty most of the year, but becomes an important performance center during festivals.

TOP CHOICE **Museo de Arte de Ponce** ART GALLERY
(MAP; www.museoarteponce.org, in Spanish; 2325 Av Las Américas; adult/senior & student $6/3; ⏲10am-5pm) *Brush Strokes In Flight,* a bold primary-colored totem by American pop artist Roy Lichtenstein, announces the smartly remodeled MAP, where an expertly presented collection ranks among the best in the Caribbean. It is itself worth the trip from San Juan. A $30 million renovation celebrated the museum's 50th anniversary and the smart curation – some 850 paintings, 800 sculptures and 500 prints, presented in provocative historical and thematic juxtapositions – represents five centuries of Western art. The greatest-hits collection of Puerto Rican painters is stirring (look for the wall-sized *Ponce* by Rafael Ríos Rey in the rear of the museum). The building's blanched edifice, winged central stair and hexagonal galleries were designed by architect Edward Durell Stone, who created Washington DC's Kennedy Center and the MOMA in New York. The exceptional pre-Raphaelite and Italian baroque collections, which traveled to the Prado and Tate museums during the 2009–10 renovation, are offset by impressive installations and special exhibits (which occasionally cost a small extra fee).

A complete tour of the museum takes about three hours, but if you only have time for a quick peek, spend some time sitting in awe of Edward Burne-Jones's ghostly, half-finished *The Sleep of Arthur in Avalon* (look for the unfinished, blank eyes of the attending queens) and Lord Leighton's erotic *Flaming June,* the museum's sensual showpiece. Set across from the Universidad Católica, the MAP is about 10 blocks to the south of Plaza Las Delicias.

Museo de la Música Puertorriqueña MUSEUM
(www.icp.gobierno.pr; cnr Reina Isabel & Salud; admission $1; ⏲8:30am-4:30pm Tue-Sun) After the MAP, this spacious pink villa designed by Juan Bertoli Calderoni, father of Puerto Rico's neoclassical style, offers Ponce's best museum experience. A guided tour showcases the development of Puerto Rico's sound, allowing hands-on demonstrations of indigenous instruments. The collection of Taíno, African and Spanish instruments – especially the handcrafted four-string guitar-like *cuatros* and three-string *trios* – and careful explanation of Puerto Rican musical traditions are highlights. The museum also hosts a three-week seminar on drum building in July, and holds concerts in its courtyard.

La Guancha Paseo Tablado BOARDWALK
Commonly known as 'La Guancha,' this rebuilt public boardwalk is 3 miles south of the city center near the relatively lonely Ponce Hilton. Refurbished in the mid-1990s, it's a haven for picnicking families and strolling couples. Its chief points of interest include a concert pavilion, a well-kempt public beach and a humble observation tower. There's a handful of open-air bars and food kiosks,

THE PONCE MASSACRE

In the turbulent 1930s, Puerto Rico's troubled economy created revolutionary fervor across the island, but it was in Ponce, with its reputation for culture and sophistication and large student population, that a march for independence went terribly wrong.

Originally the marchers had a parade permit for the demonstration, which was staged in the plaza on Palm Sunday, March 21, 1937, but at the last minute the governor of Puerto Rico withdrew permission.

Angered, the nationalists defied the prohibition and marched. Slightly fewer than 100 young men and women faced off with 150 armed police near Plaza Las Delicias. When the nationalists started singing 'La Borinqueña' – the national anthem – a shot was fired and the entire plaza erupted in gunfire. Seventeen marchers and two police officers died. Not one civilian carried a gun, and most of the 17 died from shots in the back. While the US government chose not to investigate, the American Civil Liberties Union did, and confirmed that the catastrophe warranted its popular name, 'Masacre de Ponce' (Ponce Massacre). Now a small museum appropriately called the **Casa de la Masacre de Ponce** (cnr Marina & Aurora; admission $1; ⌚9am-4pm Wed-Sun), is housed in the building that held the offices of the Nationalist Party in 1937, keeping the memory alive.

and a couple of fine-dining restaurants too, making it a popular date spot. Weeknights are quiet but the place picks up with a breezy, festive atmosphere on the weekends.

Museo de la Historia de Ponce MUSEUM
(51-53 Reina Isabel; adult/child $3/1 ⌚9am-5pm Wed-Mon) This history museum is extensive for a city of fewer than 200,0000 people – more evidence of Ponce's reverence for history. Located in the 1911 Casa Salazar, on the same block as the Teatro La Perla, the museum has 10 galleries displaying centuries of the city's history in ecology, economy, education, architecture, medicine, politics and daily life. A refreshingly Ponce-centric perspective on the development of Puerto Rican culture, the building itself is an architectural treasure that blends typical *ponceño criollo* detailing with Moorish and neoclassical elements.

El Vigía SCENIC OUTLOOK
(17 El Vigía; admission $4; ⌚9am-5:30pm Tue-Sun) It doesn't really compare with the hilltop cross in Rio de Janeiro, but the 100ft reinforced-concrete Cruceta El Vigía looking over Ponce is one of the city's more reliable points of orientation. The site was first used for a similar purpose in the 19th century, when the Spanish Crown posted lookouts here to watch for smuggling along the coast. Today, the site is on shared grounds with the Museo Castillo Serrallés and a scrubby Japanese garden, but it still offers an expansive view. The $4 elevator ride to the top is optional; the view is probably better in the open air at the base, without the hazy obstruction of worn Plexiglas windows. A combined ticket with Museo Castillo Serrallés costs $9.50.

Museo Castillo Serrallés MUSEUM
(Serrallés Castle Museum; www.castilloserralles.org, in Spanish; 17 El Vigía; adult/child & senior $6/3; ⌚9:30am-5:30pm Tue-Sun) On the same property as the mammoth cross, this is the house of Ponce's rum dynasty, the Serrallés family. Docents lead bilingual walking tours through the lovely Moorish-style castle. When the somewhat exhausting hour-plus tour ends you can order snacks and drinks at the cafe and relax on the terrace under the red-tiled roof, enjoying a view of the city below and the quiet burble of the garden's fountains. A combo ticket with El Vigía costs $9.50.

Activities

Swimming

Aside from the modest beach to the east of La Guancha, Ponce doesn't have much by way of sand. There's almost never a sizable surf and it can't compare with the Atlantic shore, but it's a stone's throw from La Guancha's cafes and restaurants and perfect for a few hours of lounging. It's often jammed on the weekend.

Snorkeling

In not-so-distant memory, a government boat carried swarms of people to the now-quiet beaches on Isla Caja de Muertos, but since the ferry was repurposed to the Fajardo–Vieques–Culebra run, the wilds have

WORTH A TRIP

ISLA CAJA DE MUERTOS

The name of Isla Caja de Muertos – which translates to Coffin Island – seems cribbed from the script of a swashbuckling adventure flick, but the big lizards here run a lazy show, trotting across dusty, cacti-lined trails and over the mangrove marsh. The morbid moniker is thought to have come from an 18th-century French author's observation that the island's silhouette looked like a casket.

There's not much to see, but the opportunity for a daylong escape from the congestion of Ponce can be pleasant. It hosts some of the best snorkeling around and plenty of tranquil, if somewhat rocky, stretches of beach. Day hikers wander past endangered plants and reptiles that thrive in the climate and a regal 19th-century lighthouse, occasionally used as a station for biologists. If you need more action, try a low-impact tour (p151) to scuba at the 40ft Wall, just offshore. The only way to make the 3-mile trip is through **Island Ventures Water Excursions** (☎787-834-8546; www.islandventurepr.com, in Spanish; $17 round-trip; reservations necessary). Leave a message if there's no answer.

reclaimed the place. Today Island Ventures Water Excursions sends boats on reservation and can offer group rides around the bay. It arranges a package including snorkeling gear, beach chair, umbrella and lunch for $35. In high season look for its kiosk on La Guancha. It can also accommodate two-tank dives for $65 to the Wall off the island's shore, which is magnificent with the right conditions.

Festivals & Events

Carnaval CARNIVAL

Ponce's Carnaval is a time of serious partying. Events kick off on the Wednesday before Ash Wednesday with a masked ball, followed by parades, a formal *danza* competition and the coronation of the Carnaval queen and child queen. The party ends with the ceremonial burial of a sardine (the traditional significance of which has been washed away by booze) and the onset of Lent. Each parade and all of the critical activities take place in Plaza Las Delicias in front of Casa Alcaldía. If you're planning to visit Ponce during Carnaval, make your hotel and transportation reservations at least three months in advance.

Semana de la Danza DANCE, MUSIC

Held in mid-May, this 'Week of Dance' has parades and dance events. The (humorously stuffy) Ponce Municipal Band performs in Plaza Las Delicias as well-groomed couples offer postured examples of the form of dance that goes along with what's regarded as 'Puerto Rico's classical music.' It's in the right place; Ponce was home to high society and composers who made *danza* a distinctive art form at the turn of the 19th century.

Fiesta de Bomba y Plena MUSIC, DANCE

Drummers and *pleneros* (*plena* singers) arrive from all over the island to participate in this festival of *bomba y plena,* the singing, dancing and drumming style that evolved in Ponce from citizens of African descent who came en masse to work the cane fields. Held in August, with major events at the Rafael 'Caro' Maldonado baseball park.

Sleeping

If you're planning on spending any quality time in Ponce, it's best to make your bed at one of the hotels surrounding the Plaza Las Delicias, instead of the bland chain resorts outside of the city center. The sterility of the Hilton and Holiday Inn might comfort the most cautious gringo, but the local flavor is nil and prices soar for accommodations that are only questionably more comfortable.

Hotel Meliá HOTEL **$$**

(☎787-842-0260, 800-44-UTELL; www.hotelmeliapr.com; 2 Cristina; r incl continental breakfast $100-140; P ❄ @ ≋) Just east of the plaza, this independent, historic hotel might remind you of favorite three-star hotels in Spain and Portugal. The grand lobby is plusher than the basic rooms, but everything is clean and functional, the building is monumental and the staff is friendly and helpful. Continental breakfast is served on a sunny rooftop deck and the beautifully renovated pool makes an attractive bonus. The 80 rooms are spread over four floors and bit by bit they are being updated. The beds are big and bathrooms fully modernized. The hotel has been in the family for generations – check out the pictures on the wall for a look at Ponce in its prime – and the manager/co-owner will happily tell you its history.

Ramada Ponce HOTEL $$
(☎787-813-5050; www.ramadaponce.com; cnr Reina Esquina & Unión; d incl continental breakfast $135-200; P❄📶🏊) Standing grandly over a corner of the plaza, this historic facade emerged from the scaffolding after years of preservationist dispute under the Ramada banner. Even though it doesn't escape the bland feel of a chain (cardboard waffles), the historic building, location and clutch of amenities makes it the best option in town. Of the two connected buildings, the best rooms face the square, with black-and-white-tiled floors and balconies; those in the back are clean but have little by way of atmosphere. The courtyard pool is tiny, but hip design elements and an open-air bar make it worth a drink.

Hotel Bélgica HOTEL $
(☎787-844-3255; www.hotelbelgica.com; 122 Villa; r $70-90; P📶❄) A traveler favorite for years, the Bélgica, a 20-room hotel bearing a creaking colonial ambience with 15ft ceilings and wrought-iron balconies, is just off the southwest corner of Plaza Las Delicias. The hallways are a bit of a maze and dimly lit, but the place is charming. The basic rooms are strictly functional; ones near the front allow you to stare out over the plaza from a private balcony, but be prepared for noise on weekend nights. The wi-fi is spotty, and works only in the lobby.

Ponce Hilton & Casino RESORT $$$
(☎787-259-7676; www.hilton.com; 1150 Av Caribe; r $210-280; P❄@🏊) This 153-room Hilton stands within a gated area 6km south of town, near La Guancha boardwalk on the Caribbean. It's the most deluxe place in town, with well-manicured grounds, on-site golf, a nightclub, restaurants and a casino. It suffers from a lack of local flavor; sun-pink golfers and wealthy Americans are wont to gripe about their last round and the quality of the buffet. Even so, it can be the only place in town to catch live music and it's the only hotel in Ponce with ocean views.

Casa del Sol Guest House GUESTHOUSE $
(☎787-812-2995; 97 Unión; r incl breakfast $60-90; ❄@🏊) Take your chances with this nine-room guesthouse, where the quality of rooms vary greatly. Within steps of the plaza, its shared balconies look over the street and there's a private terrace out the back with a small hot tub. It can be a great value (especially since prices seem somewhat negotiable), but pay in cash; there are lots of reports of dubious credit card charges.

Also recommended:

Howard Johnson HOTEL $$
(☎787-841-1000; www.hidpr.com; Hwy 1 Km 123.5; d $111; P📶❄🏊) Not much personality, but abundant in chain hotel comforts including wi-fi, exercise room, game room and a terrific pool. A pristinely clean option and very near the airport.

Holiday Inn & Tropical Casino HOTEL, CASINO $$
(☎787-844-1200; www.sixcontinentshotels.com; 3315 Ponce By Pass; r $110-160; P📶❄@) Perched atop a hill west of town, this place has a small casino, modern rooms and bilingual staff. The poolside bar offers views of the Caribbean and surrounding mountains.

Quality Inn El Tuque HOTEL $$
(☎787-290-0000; www.eltuque.com; Rte 2 Km 220, 3330 Ponce By Pass; d $119; P❄@🏊) This tucked-away option with tons of space and a big pool for families adjoins a speedway and (summer) water park. In winter, the only company may be the pet turtles.

Eating

With a little effort, diners will be rewarded by a crop of creative chefs working in Ponce's city center. For something cheap and on-the-go, there are carts around Plaza Las Delicias where a hot dog with the works ($1.50) comes saddled with mustard, ketchup, onions, peppers, processed cheese, meaty chili and crispy shoestring potato chips. Perhaps by way of suggestion, many of them also sell gum and antacids. If you're up for a drive to the port area, *ponceños* will point you to a couple of traditionally popular seafood places with white tablecloths, water goblets, an armory of silverware and waiters in vests. La Guancha is a good bet for open-air cafes and restaurants, which take on a festive atmosphere at sunset.

TOP CHOICE **Archipielago** CARIBBEAN FUSION $$$
(☎787-812-882; www.archipielagopr.com; Cristina 76; mains $15-40; ⏲lunch & dinner Wed-Fri, dinner Sat & Sun) With a bird's-eye view above Parque de Bombas, the sleekly designed rooftop restaurant Archipielago has single-handedly upped the ante on Ponce's fine-dining scene. The blend of Caribbean

flavors – chicken and pork stuffed with sweet plantains, an upscale version of local root vegetable stew and lobster with curry – punch up the menu's more traditional continental plates, such as crusted mahimahi. The service is excellent and there's often live music on weekends. The food and the scene can be a tad inconsistent (our second visit, replete with Velveeta croquettes and bickering lawyers, was a disappointment) but the views of the city never miss. No doubt: Ponce's best.

King's Cream ICE-CREAM PARLOR **$**
(9223 Marina; cones $1-3; ⏲8am-12am) On warm evenings, lines stretch down the sidewalk at this institution, located across from Parque de Bombas. Smooth blended tropical licks have big chunks of pineapple, coconut, almond and passion fruit, and come piled high for just over $1. If the line is too long, find the other location a few blocks north of the plaza on Vives, between Unión and Marina.

La Casa de Las Tias CARIBBEAN, FUSION **$$**
(46 Reina Isabel; mains $15-30; ⏲lunch & dinner) In a cozy historical home, 'the aunts' kitchen is overseen by Wilda Rodriquez, one of Ponce's most creative, least pretentious chefs. The unhurried service and atmosphere may lack a little polish, but whimsical specials (such as the fantastic midweek 'Deli & Burger Queens Night') balance traditional and fusion Puerto Rican dishes, such as the seafood stew and rib eye glazed with a guava reduction.

Café Café CAFE **$$**
(www.cafecafeponce.com; 46 Reina Isabel; mains $15-30; ⏲Mon-Fri 8:30am-10:30pm, Sat 11am-3pm) For the best coffee in Ponce and an excellent breakfast, start at this art-filled, bilingual cafe. The coffee beans couldn't be fresher – they're roasted next door – and the egg scrambles excellent. For lunch, try the *mofongo* (mashed plantains) *'a caballo,'* stuffed with corned beef and topped with a fried egg. When the students are in town, the cobblestoned patio is great for mingling.

Cesar's Comida Criolla CARIBBEAN **$**
(near cnr Mayor & Cristina; dishes $2-14; ⏲lunch) The ultimate hole-in-the-wall for *comida criolla* (traditional Puerto Rican cuisine), this humble joint might be rough around the edges, but the savory piles of pork, chicken and seafood (most served with rice and beans) are the city's best home cooking and best dressed in the homemade hot sauce. Daily offerings are scrawled on the chalkboard.

Café Tompy & Café Tomas CARIBBEAN **$$**
(☎787-840-1965; cnr Reina Isabel & Mayor; mains $4-20; ⏲lunch & dinner) The no-frills cafeteria lunch counter at Tompy is Ponce's most reliable lunch, drawing locals who pile up plates of assorted *comida criolla* – most of which costs around $7 – and park at the plastic tables. The adjoining Tomas has similarly tasty food with sit-down service, table linen and higher prices (mains $11 to $30).

Also recommended:

Chef's Creations FUSION **$**
(☎787-848-8384; 100 Reina Isabel; mains $6-$12; ⏲lunch) A menu changes daily, leaning toward international fusions of local fare, such as the delicious Paella Con Tostones.

Rincón Argentino STEAK HOUSE **$$$**
(☎787-284-1762; cnr Salud & Reina Isabel; mains $10-26; ⏲dinner) This upscale steak house is mannish, though romantic, boasting a lengthy wine list.

Edan Deli & Juice Bar VEGETARIAN, DELI **$**
(cnr Villa & Torres; mains $2-7, ⏲lunch; 🌿) Within an organic grocery store, this deli offers veggie and vegan salads and sandwiches and fresh juices.

Drinking & Entertainment

Ponce nightlife is at the mercy of capricious college crowds who pack little restaurant-cum-bars around the plaza to slam drinks and grind to reggaetón. Hot spots change often and last as long as some celebrity marriages. The scene at La Guancha is also festive, but a bit more reserved and populated with families earlier in the evening. Both the Ponce Hilton and the Holiday Inn have modest casinos, but there's more stylish action at the Hilton, where there's also a club.

TOP CHOICE **Archipielago** COCKTAIL LOUNGE
(www.archipielagopr.com; Cristina 76; ⏲lunch & dinner Wed-Fri, dinner Sat & Sun) Those who don't eat at Ponce's elegant newcomer should at least visit the rooftop lounge for expert cocktails and the stunning view. The passion fruit mojito crowns a bar menu rounded out by frosty bottles of Puerto Rican craft beer and wine by the glass.

Akua LOUNGE BAR
(Blvd Miguel Pou, Plaza Nuevo Mundo; ⏲5pm-late) Sure, it's in a strip mall en route to the Ponce airport, but this ultrahip lounge bar is home

to Ponce's see-and-be-seen crowd, who sip cocktails served on the stem and nod along while DJs spin hip-hop, Brazilian, and light house music. The furnishings are as sleek as the patrons. During high season, Akua opens for lunch.

Kenepa's at Café Plaza BAR
(3 Unión; ⌚5pm-late) After graduating from the Calle Luna party scene, a slightly classier crowd comes here to thin their blood on juice drinks and beer. The tables on the sidewalk fill quickly, especially when it hosts live music or DJs. When it gets late, the crowd migrates into the narrow quarters to dance.

Hollywood Café BAR, POOL HALL
(www.hollywoodcafeponce.com; Rte 1 Km 125.5; ⌚6pm-late) Off the beaten path in the neighborhood near the Howard Johnson hotel, a mid-20s crowd sprawls into the parking lot from Thursday to Sunday, getting rowdy with Latin rock, competitive pool and cheap swill. Wednesdays are famous for the 'Noche Del Pelao' – 'night for the flat broke'.

La Taberna BAR
(119 Villa; ⌚4pm-late Thu-Sat) This delightfully seedy little place is right off the main square. A young crowd knocks back innumerable $1.75 Medallas, watches sports on a vintage TV and blasts music at ear-splitting levels.

Shopping

Paseo Atocha, just north of the plaza, is closed to traffic, serving as a busy pedestrian marketplace with food stands and cheap goods. Here and along the cross streets merchants create a street-bazaar feel with racks of clothing, leather goods and suspiciously affordable designer wear.

Amazingly, Puerto Rico's historic center doesn't have a single bookstore; if you are hard up for something to read in English, you'll have to drive back to San Juan or Mayagüez.

Utopia SOUVENIRS
(78 Reina Isabel; ⌚7:30am-6pm Mon-Sat, from 11am Sun) Selling colorful *vejigantes* (Puerto Rican masks), *santos* (small carved figurines representing saints) souvenirs and Puerto Rican trinkets, Utopia is the nicest souvenir shop on the square. The bonus? The little bar up front will sell six-packs of beer to go, the only such place on the plaza.

Nueva Plaza del Mercado MARKET
(between Mayor & Estrella; ⌚6am-6pm Mon-Sat) Winding through crowds of shoppers on Paseo Atocha will lead you to the city's most exciting indoor market, four blocks north of the plaza. The selection of produce – freshly hacked off the vine – is marvelous, and can be complemented by less healthful options such as cheapie sweets and fried snacks, as well as lottery tickets. Just up the block, the slightly more crowded **Mercade Juan Ponce de León** has stalls hocking pan-religious voodoo charms and salsa tunes on vintage vinyl platters, reconditioned boots and hand-rolled cigars.

Information

Internet Access

Many hotels have internet service for guests and the Plaza Las Delicias has wireless connectivity, a terrific convenience for travelers with a laptop.

Mariana Suarez of Longo Biblioteca (Villa; ⌚9am-9pm Mon-Sun) A short walk from the plaza, this bright facility is part of Archivo Municipal de Ponce and contains an impressive $114-million digital-computing and education center. Puerto Rico Telephone footed the bill and did it right, with 50 new computers, laptop stations and wireless access.

Medical Services

Emergency (☎911)

Hospital Manuel Comunitario Dr Pila (☎787-848-5600; Av Las Américas, east of Av Hostos) 24-hour emergency room. Recommended.

Walgreens (Rte 2 Km 225; ⌚24hr) The only pharmacy that can accommodate a late-night need for aloe.

Money

Banks line the perimeter of Plaza Las Delicias, so finding a cash machine is no problem. Most of the banks are open from 9am to 4pm weekdays, plus Saturday mornings.

Post

Post office (93 Atocha; ⌚8am-4pm Mon-Fri, 7am-noon Sat) Four blocks north of Plaza Las Delicias, this is the most central of the city's four post offices.

Tourist Information

Puerto Rico Tourism Company (PRTC; www.letsgotoponce.com; Parque de Bombas, Plaza Las Delicias; ⌚9am-5:30pm) You can't miss the big red-and-black structure in the middle of the park, where friendly, English-speaking members of the tourist office are ready with brochures, answers and suggestions.

Getting There & Away

Air

Four miles east of the town center off Hwy 1 on Hwy 5506, the Aeropuerto de Mercedita (Mercedita Airport) looks dressed for a party, but still waiting for the guests to arrive. **Cape Air** (www.capeair.net) has four flights a day to San Juan (one way/return $87/152) and **jetBlue** (www.jetblue.com) also services Ponce from a number of American cities.

Car

Cruising to Ponce from San Juan is easy on the smoothly paved A-52 (Hwy 52), a partially toll-controlled highway called the Autopista Luis A Ferré. You'll know you've arrived when you pass through the mountains and drive through the towering letters by the roadside reading 'P-O-N-C-E.' The city center is about 2 miles from the south shore and 2 miles from the foothills of the Central Mountains to the north.

You don't have to drive through the center of town to get through Ponce – two bypass roads circle the city to the south. The inner road is Av Emelio Fagot/Av Las Américas (Hwy 163). The faster route is the outer road, Hwy 2, called the 'Ponce By Pass' which hosts the town's biggest mall and loads of American chain stores. To reach the port, take the freshly paved route just east of the square, Rte 12. It becomes a divided highway south of the Ponce By Pass. Follow the signs to La Guancha.

Público

There's a nice, new público (shared taxi) terminal three blocks north of the plaza, near Plaza del Mercado, with connections to all major towns. There are plenty of long-haul vans headed to Río Piedras in San Juan (about $20) and Mayagüez (about $10).

Getting Around

It may be possible to fly to Ponce directly, but navigating the area in depth largely requires a car as público transport can be time-consuming and maddeningly erratic.

To/From the Airport

Taxis tend to gravitate to the Plaza Las Delicias. Expect to pay $15 for the 4-mile taxi trip to or from the airport.

Car

Rental car agencies are mostly located at the airport, including the following:

Avis (☎787-842-6184)
Dollar (☎787-843-6940)
Hertz (☎787-842-7377)

Taxi

Hailing a cab at the Plaza Las Delicias is much quicker than calling for one. It's $1 to drop the flag and about $1.50 per mile, but meters are used infrequently, so ask about the price before you get an unpleasant surprise. **Coop Taxi del Sur** (☎787-848-8248) and **Ponce Taxi** (☎787-642-3370) are reliable.

Trolley

The city tourist office operates a trolley and a 'chu chu' train for visitors ($2), which are informative and entertaining. Supposedly both follow the same route, but the two-hour trolley ride makes stops, allowing passengers to get out and snap photos, while the train makes no stops, completing its circuit in about an hour. Of the two options, the trolley is recommended. There are supposed to be regular trips between 8am and 7:30pm, but drivers seem to change the schedule and routes on a whim. They all leave and return to the stop in front of the Casa Armstrong-Poventud, on the west side of Plaza Las Delicias. Inquire at the tourist desk in Parque de Bombas before planning your day around a ride.

AROUND PONCE

The city around Ponce's historic center sprawls with the unsightly blandness of an American suburb, but navigate the roads into the rural area a bit further out and there are a number of worthy sights for an afternoon.

Sights

Centro Ceremonial Indígena de Tibes ARCHAEOLOGICAL SITE
(Tibes Indian Ceremonial Center; ☎787-840-2255; Hwy 503 Km 2.2; adult/senior & child $3/2; 9am-4pm Tue-Sun, closed major holidays) Puerto Rico owes the discovery of its most significant archaeology site to tropical storm Eloíse, which hit Ponce in 1975 and caused the Río Portugués to overflow its banks. When the floodwater retreated from local farmland, it exposed the ruins of Tibes, an ancient ceremonial center. The government quickly expropriated more than 30 acres, and archaeologists, historians, engineers and geologists moved in. To date they have excavated slightly more than 5 acres of the property.

While Tibes lacks the dramatic scale of a place like Uxmal in Mexico, the evidence of Igneris and other pre-Taíno cultures found here makes it among the most important archaeological sites in the Caribbean. The

SOUTH COAST ROAD TRIP

Since the south coast offers visitors a chance to soak up the charms of Puerto Rico's Caribbean coast at a leisurely pace, it's crucial to get off the highways and travel on the older system of back roads, Hwy 1 and Hwy 3. Weaving your way through scrappy coastal towns, visitors can break at the roadside kiosks for a smoky plate of pork and join the weathered codgers for a few cold Medallas and a few bets on the mechanical horse races, known as *picas*. Don't expect much by way of beaches – the only place for any kind of quality hidden swim in the area is off Hwy 333, near Guánica – but for a deep dive into the essence of the region, you have to get off the highway.

You'll see plenty of the crumbling brick smokestacks of former sugar refineries east of Ponce. Tiny dots on the map such as Arroyo and Aguirre (a ghost town) are largely abandoned, standing in picturesque disrepair. It may not match the postcard vision of the Caribbean, but there's no chance of suffering the tourist mobs of the north.

site is in the foothills north of town and is a recommended way to spend an afternoon.

Current excavations have uncovered seven *bateyes* (Taíno ball courts), two ceremonial plazas, burial grounds, 200 skeletons, pottery, tools and charms. As you tour the manicured setting – with its *bateyes* and plaza rimmed by bordering stones (some with petroglyphs) – guides explain that the first settlers on this spot were Igneris, who probably migrated from the Orinoco Valley of Venezuela and arrived at Tibes about AD 300. They were farmers and sought out fertile river valleys to grow their staple crop of cassava.

As part of their cassava culture, the Igneris became fine potters, making vessels for serving and storing food. Many of these bell-shaped vessels have been found buried with food, charms and seashells in more than 100 Igneri graves. Individuals were buried in the fetal position in the belief that they were bound back to the 'Earthmother' for rebirth. Many of the Igneri graves have been discovered near or under the *bateyes* and walkways constructed by the pre-Taíno, who probably came to the site around the first millennium.

In a tidy **museum** you can see some of the weapons, *cemíes* (deities) and tools that they used. You will also see some reconstructed pre-Taíno *bohíos* (huts) amid this natural botanical garden with fruit trees, including the popular *guanábana* (soursop). There's a cafeteria open seasonally.

All visits include a **tour**, which takes about an hour and includes a movie and a visit to the museum, holding Indian ceremonial objects, pottery and jewelry. Sometimes the tour gets full, so you should make reservations in advance.

Tibes lies about 2 miles north of Ponce at Km 2.2 on Hwy 503. If you're driving this route, the best way to not get lost is to follow the brown signs leading to Tibes: pick these out on Hwy 14 (Calle Fagot) on the northeast side of Ponce. It's also easy to get there on a público from Ponce (see p156), which costs about $6, but getting back can be tricky as públicos don't frequently pass the site.

Hacienda Buena Vista HISTORICAL PLANTATION
(☎787-284-7020; Rte 123 Km 16.8; adult/child $8/5; ⊙Wed-Sun by reservation) The overgrown coffee fields and lovely, rusting historic buildings of Hacienda Buena Vista make up one of the best-preserved 19th-century coffee plantations in Puerto Rico. Wandering its grounds while listening to the song of the coquí frogs makes a tranquil historical day trip. Now, as in its heyday, the ingenuity of the irrigation and growing techniques are impressive, captured in the network of diverted waterway from the nearby Río Canas that still slowly turns the enormous water wheel and the industrial-era kitchen. Spontaneous travelers may miss out – you absolutely must call in advance to book a reservation. There are several tours daily, including one in English, and a small gift shop where you can purchase locally grown beans. The plantation is marked on many area maps and with some road signs near the center of Ponce, though the winding route through the countryside takes the better part of an hour.

Hacienda Buena Vista is 5km from the city center on Rte 10. There are some signs from the main roads, but getting here requires asking some directions. Conversely, top hotels from Ponce and San Juan can arrange taxi service to the site and tours.

Arroyo

On the southeast corner of the island, Arroyo seems to have dozed off shortly after the reign of 'King Sugar' and never quite awakened. It's the first town on the south coast you'll hit heading clockwise along the island from San Juan and typical of many of the seaside burgs in the area, with economies that hobble along through a trickle of tourism and small commercial fishing ventures. The dusty main drag, Calle Morse, passes 19th-century structures and salt-weathered wooden homes with drooping tin roofs and shuttered windows, eventually ending at the still, blue Caribbean.

Like Ponce, Arroyo was a rough-and-tumble smugglers' port during colonial days, when New England sea captains built many of the slouching wooden houses. Arroyo's five minutes of fame came when Samuel Morse, inventor of the telegraph, installed lines here in 1848. Citizens named the main street after Morse and praise him in the town's anthem.

Entering the village from Hwy 3 to Calle Morse, you'll notice that the upside of Arroyo's isolation is a lack of commercial development – there's not a Burger King in sight. But, despite its relative charms, the sleepy town is of little interest for travelers and only worth the detour for those with time to spare.

Hwy 3, the old southern coastal road, skirts the edge of town but Hwy 753 becomes the main street, which has a smattering of eateries and watering holes.

Sights & Activities

The narrow strand adjoining the Centro Vacacional Punta Guilarte has a **balneario** (public beach) and is the only decent beach around, even though the waters suffer from pollution. It's about 3 miles east of Arroyo on a property with grills and tables. Parking costs $2.

Antigua Casa de Aduana MUSEUM
(Old Customs House; ☎787-839-8096; 67 Morse; ⏲9am-4pm Wed-Sun) The elaborately carved former customs house is filled with Morse memorabilia. Call ahead, as hours vary with the season and the building is often closed for 'renovations.'

Sleeping

Centro Vacacional Punta Guilarte PUBLIC CAMPGROUND, CABINS $
(☎787-839-3565; Hwy 3 Km 126; campsites/cabins/villas $10/65/109; P❄≋) About 2 miles east of Arroyo, this well-maintained government facility has rustic cabins and slightly more refined (read: hot water and air-con) villas, 40 basic campsites and a pool. The cabins sleep six. The place bustles during the summer months, when you should reserve a room well in advance through the San Juan office of the **Compañía de Parques Nacionales** (CPN; National Park Company; ☎787-622-5200). In winter, you might have it mostly to yourself.

Information

Arroyo Tourist Office (87 Morse) During peak season in summer, you might get lucky and find someone here, but don't count on it; the hours are erratic.

Getting There & Away

Most públicos bound for Guayama will take you the few extra miles into Arroyo for a nominal charge, leaving you at the terminal near the town hall on Calle Morse. It might take a while to get a público back to Guayama ($4), but from there you can find a connecting ride to Río Piedras in San Juan or back to Ponce.

Guayama

A few miles up the hill from the coast is Guayama, Arroyo's bigger, less attractive older sister. The two cities have been linked since colonial days when the shadowy brokering of Arroyo's ports fattened the wallets of Guayama's society families. In the century since, these sisters have grown apart, with the sprawling asphalt parking lots of big box stores and commercial development offering evidence of how Guayama has left ragged little Arroyo behind.

Today, Guayama's 45,000 residents pay the rent with jobs at pharmaceutical factories that lie west of town, and the place once called the 'City of Witches' (a result of Santería worship brought here by African laborers) suffers from the contemporary spells of hasty development and heavy traffic. If you can make your way through the labyrinth of one-way streets you'll discover the jewel of the city, a **fountain** in the plaza that was imported from France in 1918.

During the first weekend of March the upscale **Feria Dulce Sueño** (Fair of Sweet Dreams) brings thousands of equestrian zealots to town for a Paso Fino horse race.

Sights

FREE **Centro de Bellas Artes** ART GALLERY
(Rte 3 Km 138; 9am-4:30pm Tue-Fri, from 10am Sat) This fine arts center stands just west of town in the former home of the Puerto Rican High Court. The collection focuses on emerging and established Puerto Rican artists (including a somewhat humorous set of reproductions), but the most stunning objects on display are the intricately carved gourds of folk artist César Ruiz, and the religious statues in the lobby. The adjoining galleries are hung with student works from the school across the street and some dusty dioramas on Taíno culture. A casual tour is available in English.

Museo Casa Cautiño HISTORICAL HOME
(cnr Palmer & Vicente Pales; adult/child $1/0.50; 9am-4pm Tue-Sun) On the north side of the plaza, this museum was built as a *criollo*-style town house in 1887 to house the wealthy Cautiño family, who profited from the trio of cane, cattle and tobacco. Almost 100 years later, the government claimed the property for back taxes (a common event on the island, which has saved many heirlooms). Now the house has been restored to its dignified Victorian state, with Oriental carpets and period furnishings.

Sleeping & Eating

No need to put a varnish on it: Guayama's sleeping choices aren't good. If it's late and you're tired, consider pulling in here, but better sleeping options abound to the east. For eats, inexpensive fare comes from the cafeterias by the central plaza, but the best food is a few miles down the road, in the fishing community of Pozuelo.

Hotel Brandemar HOTEL $
(787-864-5124; www.brandemar.com; end of Rte 748; r $54-75; P ❄ ≋) Following a twisting road through a residential neighborhood just outside of town, you'll come to the Brandemar, a serviceable family-run hotel that is Guanica's best by a nose. It's a small compound of buildings including a hotel with inexpensive, no-frills rooms situated around a pool, buttressed by a building with well-stocked bar and restaurant with fresh seafood. There's a small beach just paces away, but the shore is no good for swimming.

El Molina HOTEL $$
(787-866-1515; Hwy 54 Km 2.1; r from $97; P ❄ ≋) Set on 9 acres of a former sugar plantation, this 20-room inn is dominated by a crumbly old sugar mill, and is a solid bet for travelers looking for a place to rest their heads and little more. Its adjoining sports bar/restaurant turns into a thumping nightclub on the weekends, which can be exciting or unruly, depending on whether you want to party or sleep. The relatively big price tag reflects a sellers' market.

TOP CHOICE **La Casa de Los Pastelillos** SEAFOOD $$
(Rte 7710 Km 4; mains $3-30; 10:30am-6pm Mon-Wed, 10:30am-10pm Thu, 10:30-11pm Fri) After seeing the sorry excuse for what passes for *pastelillos* (fried dumplings) elsewhere – dry as dirt and suffering under heat lamp – you might not recognize the namesake of this seaside patio restaurant. The ambitious variations of the fried staple (shark? octopus? pizza?) are made to order, arriving as greasy, seafood-stuffed slices of heaven. More ample, healthful options are also lovingly made, based around fresh catches. Add in the view of crashing waves and dreamy hammocks tied between palms, and this is the best lunch spot on the south coast.

Also recommended:

El Suarito CARIBBEAN $
(cnr Derkes & Hostos; mains $2-5; breakfast-10pm Mon-Sat) Popular with local wags, this cafeteria dishes eggs and toast, cheap pork chops and beer.

Rex Cream ICE-CREAM PARLOR $
(24 Derkes; cones $1-3; 9:30am-10:30pm) Exquisite ice cream made with seasonal fruit.

Getting There & Away

Públicos gather at the parking structure two blocks southeast of the plaza. Local services to neighboring towns including Patillas and Salinas cost $3 and longer hauls to San Juan or Ponce are about $8. Coming by car, you can't miss town – it's at the junction of Hwy 3 and the Hwy 53 toll road.

Bahía de Jobos

Hwy 3, the slow route, along the south coast, has a worthy highlight in the sprawling Reserva Nacional de Investigación Estuarina de

Bahía de Jobos, which has hiking trails, and a labyrinth of mangrove canals. The marshy reserve borders a nearly abandoned sugar town, Aguirre, which makes a compelling detour.

Sights & Activities

Reserva Nacional de Investigación Estuarina de Bahía de Jobos NATURE RESERVE

Bursting with wildlife and rarely visited, the National Estuarine Research Reserve at Bahía de Jobos is an enormous protected mangrove bay, one of the largest and least visited patches of coastal wilderness in Puerto Rico. The Bahía de Jobos covers almost 3000 acres of brackish water, including associated coastal wetlands and 15 offshore mangrove cays known as Los Cayos Caribes. West of the research reserve, the Reserva Forestal Aguirre adds even more undeveloped coastal land to this wilderness. Though the low-lying mangrove marsh won't impress like the immediate, overwhelming natural beauty of El Yunque or Guánica or with miles of hiking trails, it's an excellent place for bird-watching and those seeking wilderness isolation.

Start at the reserve's **lab & visitors center** (787-864-0105; Hwy 705 Km 2.3; 7:30am-noon & 1-4pm Mon-Fri, 9am-noon & 1-3pm Sat & Sun). This is one of the largest and best educational nature centers on the island, with displays on conservation work and the surrounding reefs and wildlife. In addition to the menagerie of brown pelicans, great blue herons, black-crowned night herons, snowy egrets, ospreys, peregrine falcons and American oyster catchers, this is probably the best place to see manatees (sea cows) in Puerto Rico. Well over 100 feed here (best seen early in the morning) and play free, untroubled by humans. There are also dolphins and hawksbill sea turtles in the area.

You can go on a superb short hike along the **Jagueyes Forest Interpretive Trail**, which twists around mangroves, wetlands and salt flats for about 30 minutes, with bilingual signs posted along the way. The path is mostly on an elevated boardwalk and can be reached from the visitors center by driving west on Rte 3, then turning left at Km 154.6. This is also right near our favorite lunch spot on the coast, La Casa de Los Pastelillos (p159).

The mangrove channels also make an excellent kayaking route, and rangers are working on developing a route with docks and posted signs. However, without nearby kayak rentals, this is only appealing to a handful of locals.

Aguirre GHOST TOWN

Crumbling monuments to the sugar industry are evident everywhere in the southeast, but there's no more heartbreaking reminder of departed 'King Sugar' than sleepy Aguirre, which borders the Bahía de Jobos and is so far off the beaten path that it doesn't appear on many tourist maps. The moldering sugar town was booming in the early 20th century, complete with a mill, company stores, hospital, theater, hotel, bowling alley, social club, golf course, marina, executive homes and narrow-gauge railroad. This was the planned private community of the Central Aguirre sugar company, and at its height (around 1960) it processed 12,500 tons of sugarcane per day. Declining prices for sugar, foreign competition and escalating production costs drove the company under in 1990 and Aguirre became a virtual ghost town. The rusting train tracks remain, as does a weedy **golf course** (787-853-4052; Rte 705 Km 1.6; tee fee $20-25 weekdays, $30-35 weekends; 7am-6pm Tue-Sun).

Getting There & Away

The only way to visit the Reserva Nacional de Investigación Estuarina de Bahía de Jobos and Aguirre is by car. Take Hwy 705 south from Hwy 3. Watch for the barely visible sign pointing to 'Historic Aguirre.'

Playa Salinas

Salinas proper, the town at the center of the south coast's agricultural economy, lies about a mile north of the coast and a mile south of the highway. Even though it's the birthplace of baseball legends Roberto and Sandy Alomar and a pair of Miss Universe queens, the town itself isn't so easy on the eyes; like many other small cities in the region, it has never replaced the sugar-based economy.

The coastal barrio of Playa Salinas fares a bit better. The name is a bit of a misnomer since there's no actual sand, but the geographical features of its harbor make it an important port for the northern Caribbean. With deep water and a dense barrier of coastal mangroves, it's an ideal 'hurricane hole.' Even when the seas are still, the port attracts scores of yachts, and though many of them are captained by retired Americans and Europeans, locals will be wont to gab about frequent celebrity sightings.

Following Rte 701 along the coast you'll pass a cluster of candlelit surf-and-turf joints and arrive at the Marina de Salinas, a complex that includes the Posada El Náutico hotel. Travelers looking for a berth aboard a cruising sailboat headed to the Dominican Republic, the Bahamas, the US, Cuba or Jamaica will do well to check the bar within the Marina de Salinas, especially in late March and early April. If you can't get a ride, it's still a good place to watch the boats roll in and out of the harbor.

Sights & Activities

Even if you don't stay at the Posada El Náutico, most activities in the water are available through the front desk of the **Marina de Salinas** (☎787-824-3185; 8-G Playa Ward), where you can rent kayaks ($20 half day) and water bikes. They'll also help arrange day trips, deep-sea fishing expeditions and jaunts to the local cays.

With a blasting stereo and boisterous families, trips on the **La Paseadora** (☎787-824-2649; dock near El Balcón del Capitan; tours $3, trips to local cays $5) leave weekend mornings in good weather. They offer snorkeling tours and round-trips to a nearby island with a beach.

East of town on Hwy 3 is the office of the **Departamento de Recursos Naturales** (Department of Natural Resources; ☎787-864-0105; Playa Ward), which can provide information and a place to pay fees for the many surrounding natural areas.

Sleeping & Eating

The mess of streets leading to Playa Salinas is a bit confusing to navigate, but Rte 701 leads to the small commercial district of Playa Ward. From here, you can navigate around the bay via largely unmarked roads.

Marina de Salinas & Posada El Náutico HOTEL, MARINA $$
(☎787-824-3185; www.marinadesalinas.com; Playa Ward; r $95-135; P❄≋@📶) This is the best coastal hotel east of Ponce, part of the all-in-one marina complex that has clean rooms decorated with some tropical flair, a pool, playground, cafe and a slightly more upscale restaurant overlooking the harbor. Find it easily by heading south on Rte 701, past the line of seafood restaurants. The snack bar near the pool is where the cruising fraternity, mostly American, comes for cheap breakfasts in the morning and cheap beers through the afternoon. Although rare, it might be possible to hitch a ride to a neighboring island if you hang around here long enough.

Manatee Eco Resort & Loco Pelicano Restaurant HOTEL, RESTAURANT $$
(☎787-824-6688; Calle A Sector Playita No 286; r $84-125; P❄≋) It's not clear what efforts this self-defined 'eco' hotel makes for the environment, but after a recent facelift it is a more economical option across the harbor from the Marina de Salinas. The rooms are a bit dark, but have tiled floors, mini-refrigerators and microwaves. The restaurant turns out excellent mussels and dramatic sunset views. You can also rent kayaks to navigate the bay for $40 a day, and, according to the amiable hosts, there are scores of manatees in the area.

Balcon de Capitan SEAFOOD $$
(Calle 54, Hwy 701; mains $10-30; ⏲lunch & dinner) Although the slow economy has hidden many Playa Salinas restaurants behind shutters, the Capitan soldiers on, earning its Mesón Gastronómico status through fresh plates of red snapper, a good seafood-stuffed *mofongo* and tangy *mojo isleño* (a thin tomato-based sauce). The dining room, often frigid with air-conditioning, is a pleasant enough place for dinner, though in high season the open-air patio gets lively with a boozy mix of locals and yachters.

Getting There & Away

You cannot miss where the públicos gather in the lot near the town plaza. You can get to Guayama for about $3 or Ponce for $6. To get to Playa Salinas and the marina, you have to walk about 1.5 miles or negotiate with your público driver.

From the east, Hwy 3 becomes Hwy 1 as it passes through Salinas. From Ponce, drivers should take Hwy 1 east or the Hwy 52 toll road to Hwy 1 south.

Coamo

Ponce de León's obsessive search for the fountain of youth – which, according to some historians, was sought in hopes of curing sexual impotence – led not only to the discovery of North America, but perhaps also to the founding of this city, still famous for its thermal springs. León's lagging libido might be responsible for making Coamo one of the oldest colonial settlements on the island, a place that also staged a decisive battle of the Spanish-American War.

Coamo today is a major chicken-processing center with more than 30,000 residents. The main draw for travelers continues to be the *baños* (baths) south of town. Over the years they've hosted former US President Franklin Roosevelt and millions of visitors.

Coamo also hosts a famous footrace, the hilly 20km **San Blás de Illescas Marathon** (actually more like a half-marathon), in February.

Sights & Activities

Baños de Coamo THERMAL BATHS

(Coamo's Baths; admission $3; 8am-6pm) After a recent facelift, the Baños de Coamo – once filling a fairly dreary set of cement tubs – have taken on the air of a modern spa. The spa has been a destination for centuries. Today, the facility has handsome changing rooms, piped-in jazz and a small cafe. It's doubtful that you'll have a very tranquil soak because of the close quarters, but for fans of thermal waters it is certainly worth a detour. Note that swimsuits are required – bathing au naturel isn't tolerated by local families.

Though both pools are small and can get crowded, taking a dip early in the morning, during a rain shower or at dinnertime might give you the place to yourself. While the upper pool has thermal water at about 110°F and the lower one is cooler, both are good places to take in the scene as trade winds blow across the fields and down the Río Coamo on their way to the sea.

To get here, take Hwy 153 from Hwy 1 or Hwy 52. Head north for about 3 miles and look for the sign that points off to the left (west) to the Parador Baños Coamo, which is Rte 546. You'll pass a number of recent condo developments and a golf course, before coming to a parking area at the bottom of a hill. The parador is next to the river, which flows near the right side of the fence. You'll see some ruins and two pools built high on the side of the riverbank.

There's very little public transportation to the *baños*. A público from Ponce will drop you at the intersection of Hwys 546 and 153, about 1 mile away ($5). For more money it may go on to the baths, but you'll need to arrange it in advance.

If you're interested in poking around town after a dip, check out **San Blás Catholic Church** on the plaza, which has paintings by the island masters Campeche and Oller, including a painting of one of Oller's girlfriends being tortured in purgatory. As in Guayama, Coamo has also converted an old mansion on the plaza into a **museum**; it opens upon a request through the town hall.

Sleeping & Eating

You'll pass loads of kiosks on the roads around Coamo, many of them roasting pork and seafood and dishing out lunches for about $5. If you want to sit down (and have an aversion to fast-food) it's a bit of a hunt, though there are several cafeterias in the blocks surrounding the town square.

Parador Baños de Coamo HOTEL **$$**

(787-825-22186; www.banosdecoamo.com; end of Hwy 546; r $85-95; P) Situated around an enormous *Samanea saman* (rain tree), this is the most recent incarnation of the hotels that have stood on the site for 150 years. This one has been here since the 1970s, though the ruins of its predecessors give it a historical colonial feel. Lizards scurry around the grounds and guests enjoy an open-air bar and thermal pools. The rooms are modern, if a little worn. Things are quiet in low season. Nonguests can use the hotel's swimming and thermal pools between 10am and 5:30pm for $5/3 per adult/child.

La Ceiba MEXICAN, PUERTO RICAN **$$**

(Rte 153 Km 13; mains $8-16) After a morning at the pools, this breezy, brightly painted, open-air Mexican spot is a great roadside stop. It has daily specials of Puerto Rican pork, rice and beans and passable Mexican standards, such as grilled chicken or steak burritos. Beware the potent margaritas.

WEST OF PONCE

Yauco & Around

Yauco is Puerto Rico's coffee capital, where well-scrubbed public squares, friendly tourist office and a hillside of brightly painted houses stand in gleaming contrast to the ragged little burgs that dot the southwest highway. Hidden up in the hills, the city was founded in 1758 by merchants tired of pillaging pirates. Now famous for bold coffee, yucca plantations and art deco, colonial and creole architecture, the so-called 'City of Coffee' is a perfect stop for supplies before heading into the Guánica forest or a day trip from Ponce.

To get here, exit Hwy 2 at Km 359 and go right on Calle 25 de Julio, which runs alongside **Parque Arturo Lluberas**. You'll be in town when you reach the Yauco Garden, a large, futuristic tree sculpture that might have developed from plans drawn by Dr Seuss. East of the plaza, in the basement of the brightly painted Alejandro Franceschi Art Museum is the **tourist office** (787-267-0350; cnr 25 de Julio & Batences; 8am-3pm Mon-Fri, 9am-2pm Sat & Sun), with information about precolonial ruins and **trolley tours**, which run regularly in summer and by appointment in low season.

Sights

In sharp contrast to the modern Parque Arturo Lluberas is the city's more traditional **Plaza de Recreo**, just a few blocks up the hill upon which the massive **Iglesia Católica Nuestra Señora del Rosario** casts a long shadow over domino players and strolling lovers. The plaza hosts a small wireless cafe where you can sample local coffee, and sits just off a bustling stretch of shops on Calle Comercio, which has a number of jewelers who will make gold pendants with your name on them.

FREE Casa Museo de la Música HISTORICAL HOME

(15 Calle Santiago Vivaldi Pacheco, around the cnr from Casa Franceschi; 1-3pm Mon-Fri, 8am-noon Sat & Sun) Musicians might find a bit of diversion in this former home of local composer Amaury Verey Torregrosa, though the wilting creole house has little inside except some faded sheets of music and old photos.

FCentro de Arte Alejandro Franceschi MUSEUM

(cnr 25 de Julio & Batence; 8am-3pm Mon-Fri, 9am-2pm Sat & Sun) The city's immaculate little art museum is housed in a 1907 building chock-full of Victorian oil paintings and gilded frescoes.

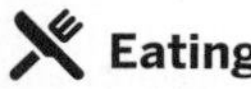

Eating

For something inexpensive to eat, stroll down Calle Comercio, which has good cafeterias and cafes. The same strip also has a franchise of the delightful Ponce institution, **King's Cream** (27 Comercio; 9am-8pm).

> **DON'T MISS**
>
> **CHULETA CAN-CAN**
>
> On an island that seems crazed for pork, the **chuleta can-can** is king. It's the specialty at the Restaurante La Guardarraya (p163).

TOP CHOICE Restaurante La Guardarraya PUERTO RICAN $

(787-856-4222; www.laguardarraya.com; Rte 127 Km 6; mains $7-13) You'll see the signs announcing Chuletas Can-Can all over the island, but this charming 1957 institution is the place that invented the dish. What is it? A slab of pork, with the ribs and fat left on, prepared with a row of delicate cuts so that when the whole thing gets deep-fried, the fat blossoms to resemble the underskirt of a cancan dancer. Intense? You better believe it. Sided with rice, beans, plantains and a pitcher of water it makes for an *amazing* (if decadent) meal. The historical ambience of the restaurant – it's set on stilts in a tropical forest clearing outside of Yaoco, with lazy fans spinning overhead, waiters with well-groomed mustaches and lots of pride – makes for one of the best dining experiences on the island.

Guánica & Around

A plush resort east of town draws international travelers, but Guánica doesn't much notice the happenings of the relatively rich and famous: it exudes the feel of a simple fishing village where folks unwind after a long week of tending the lines at open-air bars along the *malecón* (waterfront promenade). The village sprawls from the edge of a scrubby town square and a row of bars and restaurants facing a large factory across the bay. However, just east of town the Bosque Estatal de Guánica is stunning, perched in hills above the sea; after a long day in the sun there, Guánica is a low-key spot to recharge with a few cold ones and a meal of the freshest seafood – some of it caught only hours earlier by the guy at the end of the bar. Guánica is a few miles south of Hwy 2 on Rte 116.

Activities

Route 333 encounters several decent options for swimming before ending at the best one, **Bahía de la Ballena**. It twists and turns right

Guánica & Around

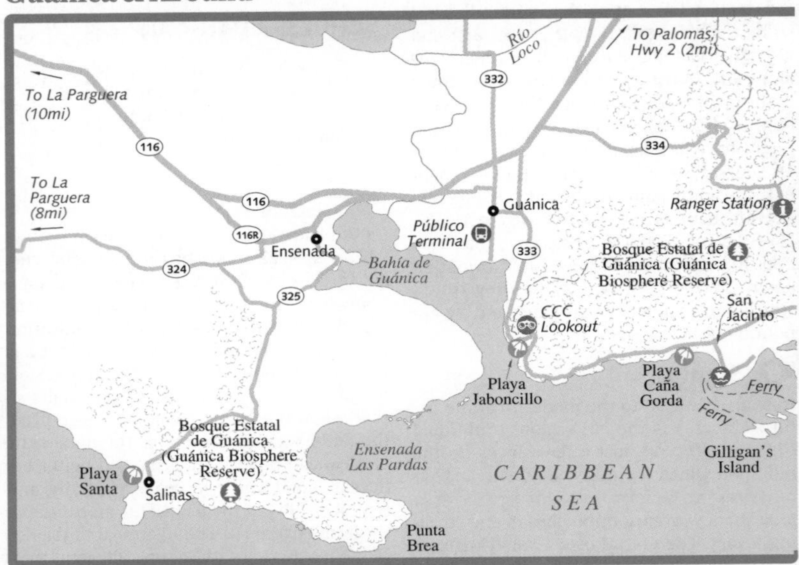

along the coast, but keep your eyes peeled for unmarked dirt paths along the way where you can fight your way through mangroves to find sparsely populated waters.

Playa Caña Gorda (Stout Cane Beach; Hwy 333 Km 6.2; parking $3) is the balneario adjacent to the southern edge of the dry forest on Hwy 333 and where the locals come to grill fresh fish, play volleyball and lie around in the shade. The modern facilities are the most developed in the area, including a small shop with cold soda and sunblock.

Gilligan's Island and **Isla Ballena** (Whale Island) are small mangrove islands off the tip of the Caña Gorda peninsula and technically part of the dry forest reserve. Neither is too sandy, but both offer good sunbathing and passable snorkeling. The ambitious can reach these via kayak (rentals are available at Playa Caña Gorda and the Copamarina Resort) or you can catch a small **ferry** (adult/child $6/3; 9am-5pm Tue-Sun) in front of Restaurante San Jacinto every hour, barring bad weather. If Gilligan's is packed, pony up a couple more dollars to the captain and try the less-visited Ballena.

At the very end of Rte 333 is the most secluded beach, a long crescent of mixed rocky and sandy shore bordering **Bahía de la Ballena**. The road ends at the east end of the bay, and you can park along the road to picnic and sunbathe (you can also pick up the Vereda Meseta trail here).

Sleeping

A community of vacation houses and guesthouses called San Jacinto dominates the highlands of the small Caña Gorda peninsula. If you're looking for a cheap option, drive up there and poke around, as many houses rent rooms.

TOP CHOICE **Mary Lee's by the Sea** APARTMENTS $$
(787-821-3600; www.maryleesbythesea.com; 25 San Jacinto; studios from $120, apt $250) This immensely charming guesthouse run by Mary Lee Alverez is one of the most isolated and charming stays on the island. Set on a steep hillside overlooking the mangrove cays and the Caribbean, guests have little choice but to unplug (no cell service, no televisions) and relax. Each apartment is appointed with ultrahip, brightly colored furnishing and many have decks, hammocks, barbecue and sea views. One even has a bathroom that opens into a private garden shower. Mary Lee herself is a character, a doting host who came here to dive 50 years ago and never left. There are stairs that lead down to a dock where you can relax by the water, or

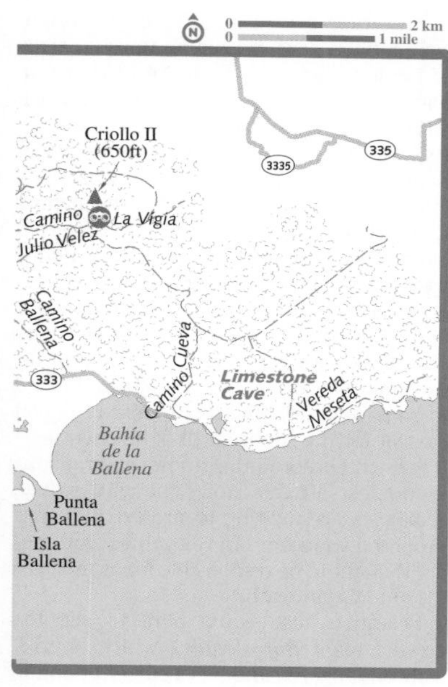

rent boats and kayaks for a reasonable fee. Note that Mary Lee does not accept credit cards.

Copamarina Beach Resort RESORT **$$$**
(☎800-468-4553; www.copamarina.com; Hwy 333 Km 6.5; r $190-400, villas $859; P❄@📶≈) This full-service resort is the most upscale vacation retreat on the southwest coast of Puerto Rico, just east of the balneario on a shallow bay. It's relatively pricey but worth it: the immaculate grounds include a pair of beautiful pools, tennis courts, and two upscale restaurants. There's even an on-site dive shop and a 24-hour service desk. Most of the plush, elegantly outfitted rooms open to ocean breezes and swaying palms, making it idyllic for honeymooners, who drag beach chairs into the shallow waters under the shade of the palm trees. The only drawback is the resort's isolation but, for those who enjoy peace and quiet, it can also be its greatest attribute.

✕ Eating & Drinking

Alexandra FUSION **$$**
(☎800-468-4553; www.copamarina.com; Hwy 333 Km 6.5; dishes $15-35; ⊙lunch & dinner) If one dish could represent the menu at this upscale resort restaurant, it'd be lobster tail in mango and mustard sauce. Savory, inventive and decidedly upscale, the fusion Caribbean and New American dishes here are as elegant as the linen-draped dining room. The food is a match for the dreamy location, and the atmosphere is completed by doting waiters and couples who toast special occasions. Reservations are recommended.

Cafeteria El Aleman CAFETERIA **$**
(106 Ochoa; dishes $1-8; ⊙lunch & dinner) If your dream of the Caribbean includes sipping a high-octane rum drink out of a coconut, this tiny red-roofed roadside cafeteria is the answer to your prayers. Patrons park themselves on stools at the shoulder of the road, choose their coconut (and their poison – the house recommends Cutty Shark) and order thick, homemade sandwiches and sundry *comida criolla*.

ℹ Getting There & Away

Públicos vans stop on the plaza in Guánica, a few blocks west of the shore. Getting between Ponce and Mayagüez costs about $7. During summer and on sunny weekends vans connect to the beach at Caña Gorda or the ferry dock to Gilligan's Island, but don't count on it.

If you're driving to Guánica, follow Hwy 116 south from the expressway.

Bosque Estatal de Guánica

The immense 10,000-acre expanse of the Guánica Biosphere Reserve is one of the island's great natural treasures and a blank slate for the outdoor enthusiast. Trails of various lengths and difficulty make loops from the visitors center, lending themselves to casual hikes, mountain biking, birdwatching and broad views of the Caribbean.

This remote desert forest is among the best examples of subtropical dry forest vegetation in the world – a fact evident in the variety of extraordinary flora and fauna – present at every turn. Scientists estimate that only 1% of the earth's dry forest of this kind remains, and the vast acreage makes this a rare sanctuary, crossed by 30-odd miles of trails that lead from the arid, rocky highlands, which are covered with scrubby brush, to more than 10 miles of remote, wholly untouched coast. Only a two-hour drive from the humid rainforests of El Yunque, this crumbling landscape and parched vegetation makes an unexpected, thrilling contrast.

In 1981 the UN acknowledged the value of this dry forest by designating it a Unesco 'biosphere reserve.' This accolade, Unesco says, makes it one of 529 such preserves in 105 countries around the world, where scientists and local people work with government agencies to create model land management.

To get to the eastern section of the reserve and the **Ranger Station** (787-821-5706; 9am-4pm), which has some photocopied trail maps and brochures, follow Hwy 116 southeast toward Guánica town from Hwy 2. Turn left (east) onto Hwy 334 and follow this road as it winds up a steep hill through an outlying barrio of Guánica. Eventually, the road crests the hills, ending at the ranger station, a picnic area and a scenic overlook of the forest and the Caribbean.

The southern extent of the eastern section of the forest – including Bahía de la Ballena (Whale Bay) and the ferry to Gilligan's Island – is also accessible by Hwy 333, to the south of Guánica. Parking is free.

There are no hotels in the forest but the nearby towns of Guánica, La Parguera and Ponce have many places to stay. Bring food and water for hikes; there are no kiosks or food stands anywhere inside the forest.

Climate

The dry forest owes its unusual microclimate to the presence of the nearby Central Mountains. This mountain range creates, guides and exhausts tropical rainstorms as the easterly trade winds drive warm, moist air over the cool peaks. As a consequence, the cordillera gets totally inundated with rain while Guánica, located to the south, gets very little – usually about 35in a year, which mostly falls from June to September.

Meanwhile, December through April is so sunny, hot and dry that the deciduous trees shed all of their leaves. Temperatures fluctuate between 80° and 100°F, virtually tropical desert conditions. The flora and fauna that survive here are hearty and attuned to these conditions.

Wildlife

Just over half the forest, in the highest elevation, consists of deciduous trees, while near the coast there's more than 1000 acres of semi-evergreen forest and scrub forest; at the waterline are the familiar mangroves. One of the most unusual plants here is the squat melon cactus with its brilliant pink flowers that attract hummingbirds. Another plant, with the unseemly name of the Spanish dildo cactus, grows into huge treelike shapes near the coast and attracts bullfinches and bats.

The forest's uneven rainfall and drainage patterns have created an unusual array of habitats for more than 700 varieties of plants (many in danger of extinction), which attract a large number of birds. Some studies claim that almost all of the bird species found in Puerto Rico turn up in Guánica – fans say the area is better for bird-watching than El Yunque. Guánica is a preferred habitat for nine of the island's 14 endemic species, including the Puerto Rican woodpecker, the Puerto Rican emerald hummingbird and – the ultimate prize for bird-watchers – the exceedingly rare 'prehistoric' Puerto Rican nightjar, of which there are estimated to be as few as 1500. The nightjar is a good mascot for the subtle thrill of its environs – it lives and nests on the ground and remains motionless all day. Long thought extinct, ecologists are fighting to protect it from a proposed wind farm in Guayanilla; turbines are thought to be responsible for as much as 5% of nightjar deaths.

Scientists also come here to see the crested toad *(Bufo lemur),* which is critically endangered and has a current population estimated to be in the hundreds; the *Amelva wetmorei* lizard, with its iridescent tail; and the purple land crab. Green and leatherback turtles still lay their eggs here, but their hatchlings may be in a losing contest against the predation of mongooses, which have overrun the island since their introduction to control the rats in the cane fields.

Geography

The Bahía de Guánica divides the forest into two sections. The highest elevation here is 650ft Criollo II, and many of the forest's hills rise abruptly from the coast to nearly equivalent heights. The terrain is undulating, with steep slopes in the east and moderate, rolling terrain in the west. Limestone underlies most of the forest and is overlaid by several yards of calcium carbonate. Erosion by both water and sun has created sinkholes, caves and a forest floor that often looks like brittle Swiss cheese.

Hiking

Thorn-lined paths, endless dry scrub and unrelenting sun might scare off the crowds, but Guánica's lengthy system of hypnotic trails yields a million surprises – private vistas of the Caribbean, a flutter of exotic birds and the shocking color of cacti flowers.

TOP FIVE CARIBBEAN VIEWS

» **Fuerte Caprón** (p167) A hike through the brushy hills of Puerto Rico's bizarre dry forest brings you to a fort overlooking the turquoise horizon.

» **El Vigía** (p151) This huge concrete cross on a Ponce hilltop takes in the Pearl of the South and the sea.

» **Rte 333** After a white-knuckled drive around Guánica, pull over to chill out on tiny beaches hidden by mangroves.

» **La Guancha Paseo Tablado** (p150) Watch the ships roll in and out of the port at this boardwalk observation deck.

» **La Casa de Los Pastelillos** (p159) Swing on a hammock between palm trees and enjoy endless views at this hidden-away lunch favorite.

The 1-mile **Camino Ballena** trail starts from the dusty parking lot of the ranger station, descending on a partially paved old road through some gnarled and wild scenery and eventually ending at a beautiful stretch of beach. As you leave the forest office, you'll pass a mahogany plantation and deciduous forest, passing chalky limestone scrub and cacti. A small side trail at the 1km marker will send you to the cool ravine where the 700-year-old 'Centenario' Guayacán tree lives, before you continue on an easy downhill hike past agave and twisted gumbo limbo trees and eastward along Rte 333 toward Camino Cueva. After relaxing on the shore, the most challenging part of the hike is the return.

The best for bird-watchers is the 2-mile circular hike on the **Camino Julio Velez**, leaving from the ranger station and following a broad path through several areas inhabited by big birds. With a short detour to La Vígia, a fabulous lookout, it can be completed in a leisurely hour.

Ending at an observation tower built by conservationists, **Fuerte Caprón** doesn't go through the most eye-catching vegetation, but it's an easy, meandering 2.5-mile walk with changes in gradation to get your heart pumping. It takes about 60 minutes to get to the CCC tower lookout, then the trail continues for another 30 minutes before coming to a dead end.

Although none of the foliage is particularly dense and getting lost isn't easy, be safe and bring water, sunscreen and bug repellent; the sun can be brutal and there's little shade. Protective clothing helps with insects, thorns and the poisonous *chicharron* shrub with its reddish spiny leaves. Trails open and close seasonally to protect the wildlife and minimize human impact, so it's hard to plan specifics about your hike until you get there. Like other Puerto Rican forest ranger posts, staffing at the ranger station is erratic. Parking is free.

Getting There & Away

From Hwy. 2, turn south onto Rte 116 and follow signs to take a left on Rte 334. The beaches along the south part of the forest are accessed via Rte 333. No público service visits the forest.

La Parguera

La Parguera is a lazy, lovable seaside town, a somewhat disorderly magnet for vacationing Puerto Ricans and US expats who spend most of the morning in bed, most of the day on the water, and most of the weekend popping open cans of Medalla. During the day, the streets empty as fishermen and divers navigate the maze of mangrove canals to the open water to catch snapper and shark or dive the 40ft Wall.

During the long summer months between Easter and September, La Parguera parties hard despite its diminutive population. The bars, all disheveled and covered in beer banners, blast salsa and reggaetón, and the streets fill with students and travelers. Little mobs of friends traverse the crooked, disorderly sidewalks arm in arm with a wobble in their step.

At the busy waterfront, boats shuttle tourists to the glowing waters of the town's big draw – Bahía de Fosforescente – simultaneously diminishing its glow with the pollution from their motors.

The ramshackle mix of new and old buildings has a chaotic charm, from the houses on stilts over the water to vacation condo developments that have arisen on upland fields.

La Parguera

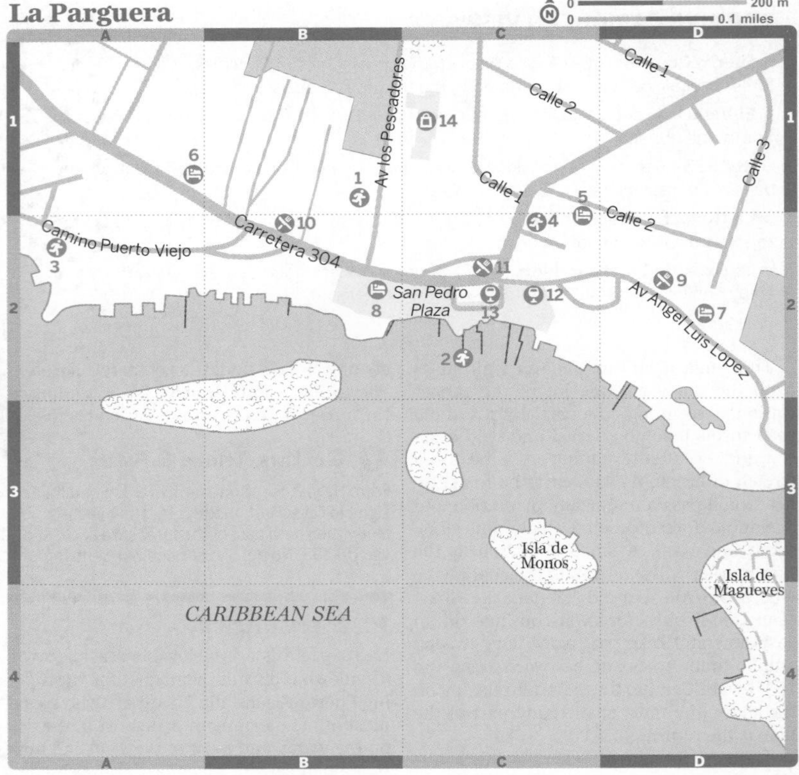

Even though many of the streets don't have signs, it doesn't take long to get oriented; Rte 304 brings you into town and takes a sharp bend at the water to become the main drag. It's lined with shops, trinket galleries, bars and cafeterias.

Sights

Bahía de Fosforescente NATURE RESERVE

The once-glittering waters remain La Parguera's biggest draw, but environmental conditions from boat tours and developments have dimmed the spectacular show. Still, it can be interesting for those who have never seen the phenomenon – boats visit the Bahía Monsio José and Bahía La Parguera east of town. Both are reached via narrow canals through the mangrove forest and, if you come here at night, bioluminescent microorganisms in the water put on a surreal light show (see p266). However, the motorboats and pollution have killed many of the organisms in Parguera's bays, so today the best way to see bioluminescent water is on Vieques; see p131. Nevertheless, the $7 ride on the **Fondo de Cristal** (☎787-899-5891) is the least expensive way to witness this glowing water in Puerto Rico. If you want to be ecologically minded, however, skip this bay for a place where nonpolluting kayaks or electric boats are used – and tell motorized-boat operators why you're saying no.

Isla Mata la Gata & Isla Caracoles BEACH

These two mangrove cays lie less than a half mile offshore and can be worth a visit after the other dusty sights nearby. The sandy strands on the seaside are really the only places in La Parguera to spend a traditional day at the beach, but both are overused and the sand is not spectacular. You can come here in your own rental boat or kayak, but the boat operators at the town docks will also take you for a $7 round-trip.

La Parguera

Activities, Courses & Tours

1 Aleli Kayak Rental ... B1
2 Cancel Boats ... C2
3 Parguera Fishing Charters ... A2
Vento Lera ... (see 14)
4 West Divers ... C2

Sleeping

5 Glady's Guest House ... C2
6 La Parguera Guest House ... A1
7 Nautilus Hotel ... D2
8 Villa Parguera ... B2

Eating

9 Aguazul ... D2
10 La Empanadilla ... B2
11 Yolanda's ... C2

Drinking

12 El Karacol ... C2
13 Mar y Tierra ... C2

Shopping

14 Ocean View Mall ... C1

Isla de Magueyes & Isla de Monos ISLANDS

Magueyes Island lies about 200yd south of the boat docks and is used as a marine science station for the Universidad de Puerto Rico. The island was formerly a zoo, though now it's overrun by some frighteningly large iguanas, many of which were originally brought from Cuba. They occasionally make their way to the mainland. Monkeys held for research on Isla de Monos (Monkey Island), about a mile to the west, have also escaped and are breeding ashore – pests to local farmers, but amusement for children and local wags.

Activities

Diving & Snorkeling

West Divers DIVING, SNORKELING

(☎787-899-3223; www.westdiverspr.com; Rte 304km 3.1) With a pair of offices, West Divers is the best diving operation in the area and our favorite on the south coast. It offers three-hour snorkeling trips ($40) and day-long two-tank trips to the Wall ($100). If you're in a party smaller than three, call ahead to inquire about joining another group.

Boating & Boat Trips

Travelers have a number of vendors to choose from in this town. **Cancel Boats** (☎787-899-5891; boats per hr about $30), at the town docks, has a lot of loyal customers renting its 15ft whaler-type boats with 10HP engines. Competitor **Torres Boat Service** nearby has similar prices, all of which get better with larger groups.

Across the street from the shopping center is **Aleli Kayak Rental** (☎787-899-6086; 1-/2-person kayaks per hr $10/15, half day $30/40, full day $50/60), which is the most ecologically responsible way to see the magical waters. It can also arrange ecotours through the mangrove channels. For any rentals, call ahead, as opening hours are variable.

Kitesurfing & Windsurfing

The sheltered waters of the bay and reliable breeze makes this an excellent destination for windsurfing and kiteboarding. For all related inquiries, ask Eddie Rodríguez, who runs an excellent water sports shop, **Vento Lera** (☎787-808-0396; Ocean View Mall; windsurfing rentals from $45).

Fishing

You can fish the reefs for grouper, snapper and mackerel, or head into deeper water for blue marlin, tuna and dorado. **Parguera Fishing Charters** (☎787-382-4698) runs half- and full-day trips (from $175) on its 31ft Bertram from a well-marked dock at the west end of town.

Festivals & Events

Fiesta de San Pedro PARTY

Named after the abundant pargo fish, La Parguera hosts the Fiesta de San Pedro to honor the patron saint of fisherman in June. The party closes the main street, where there's live music, food kiosks, children's activities and vendors who pour untold gallons of Medalla.

Sleeping

There are plenty of sleeping options within walking distance of La Parguera, so unless it's the peak of summer or during a festival, it won't be hard to find a comfortable place to sleep for under $100. Guesthouses and a pair of larger, slightly more polished hotels are within walking distance of the dock.

TOP CHOICE **La Parguera Guest House** MOTEL $$

(☎787-899-3993; www.pargueraguesthouse.com; Carretera 304 Km 4; r $85; P❄@⌔) This cheerfully painted guesthouse is the best deal in town, right on the strip with 18 clean, small rooms all with a small refrigerator and cable TV. There are also two apartments; one sleeps

DIVING THE WALL

Although landlubbers can have plenty of fun in Parguera, divers know the real draw – the underwater treasure hidden 6 miles offshore.

The Wall (advanced dive, 50ft to 125ft) features a 'swim-through' at the base of an immense reef that has a sheer 60ft drop. Plenty of good diving takes place above that mark, but the real treat is wiggling in and out of the 'swim-through' hole and checking out the impressive reef structure at 80ft and below. Divers have reported seeing manatees, dolphins, manta rays and much, much more.

Some other diving highlights near La Parguera:

» **Motor** (novice, 55ft to 75ft) An unclaimed airplane motor adds mystery to a reef.

» **Barracuda City** (novice, 60ft to 70ft) You'll get the hairy eyeball from big silver predators.

» **Super Bowl** (intermediate, 55ft to 75ft) Swim-throughs and overhangs.

» **Chimney** (intermediate, 55ft to 75ft) A north-facing ledge honeycombed with holes.

» **Black Wall** (intermediate, 60ft to 130ft) A smaller version of the big coral wall.

» **Two for You** (advanced, 55ft to120ft) This reef looks like an underwater flower shop.

» **Fallen Rock** (advanced, 65ft to 120ft) A magnet for abundant coral and bright-blue fish.

six and goes for $120, another sleeps eight and can be had for around $150. Prices go up during peak season.

Villa Parguera HOTEL $$
(787-899-7777; www.villaparguera.net; Carretera 304 Km 3.6; r $107-187;) On the main street across from the church, this two-story hotel with 63 units is a longtime favorite of travelers, and the closest to luxury that you're going to find in town. It's a modern and reliably clean choice. There is a gourmet restaurant and nightclub on-site, which does a campy show on the weekends.

Glady's Guest House GUESTHOUSE $
(787-899-4678; 42 Calle 2; r $60-74;) This great, if nondescript, guesthouse is run by a family who live downstairs. The tidy grounds are a few steps from the center of the action, but just far enough away to allow a good night's sleep.

Nautilus Hotel HOTEL $
(787-899-4004; www.nautiluspr.com; 238 Av Angel Luis Lopez; r Mon-Fri $65, Sat & Sun $70-90;) Just east of the center of town, the Nautilus is a well-appointed modern place with 18 rooms.

Parador Villa del Mar HOTEL $$
(787-899-4265; 3 Av Albizu Campos; r $99-109;) On a hilltop outside of town, this family operation has 25 rooms and a swimming pool – all extremely clean.

Eating & Drinking

It's easy to follow your nose here; there are plenty of bars and food kiosks at the waterfront. Nightlife in La Parguera is an outdoor affair: people drink, eat and stroll from one end of the waterfront road to the other.

TOP CHOICE **Aguazul** CARIBBEAN $$
(mains $10-22; lunch & dinner Tue-Sat, lunch Sun) The focus on fresh local, organic ingredients and a menu of homemade raviolis, *churrasco* (grilled meat) and creole fish dishes with haute presentation leaves Zoe with few peers. Finish with a plate of fresh local cheese and it's the best fine dining in La Parguera. Aguazul is located on Rte 304, near Hotel Nautilus.

La Empanadilla CAFETERIA $
(Carretera 304, near La Parguera Guest House; empanadas $1-2; lunch until late) The best place for cheap empanadas in town – nothing costs over two bucks. In terms of atmosphere, this beat-up cafeteria doesn't have much polish, but it more than makes up for it in character. The empanadas with *pulpo* (octopus) are the best.

Yolanda's CARIBBEAN $
(www.yolandasbarandgrill.com; Carretera 304 Km 3.2; mains $6-13; lunch until late) The high-pitched roof and wood trim offer Yolanda's a South Seas atmosphere. It serves savory lunch specials and stiff drinks and in the

evening the patio makes a great place to party.

Mar y Tierra BAR, POOL HALL

(Carretera 304; ⌚4pm-midnight, later on weekends) This stands out among the cluster of places packed together between the main street and the docks. It is more of a pavilion with indoor and patio seating than a traditional bar, and it pumps out live Latin rock and salsa on the weekends. Right in the center of town, it's impossible to miss.

El Karacol BAR

(Carretera 304, at the docks; ⌚4pm-midnight, later on weekends) This brightly lit bar/diner has the ambience of a fluorescent-lit fast-food chain, making a bizarre partner to the dark and noisy adjoining game room. The 'sangria coño' is its famous drink, which tastes like rum-spiked wine and can pack a wicked hangover.

Information

Ocean View Mall (Ave los Pescadores) One block off Rte 304; has a book exchange, a well-stocked, brightly lit grocery store, and a contract post office.

Getting There & Away

Públicos come and go irregularly from a stop near the small waterfront park and boat piers in the center of the village. Service is basically local and travels to nearby towns such as Lajas ($1), where you can move on to bigger and better van stands in bigger and better municipalities.

The fastest way here is on Hwy 116, off Hwy 2, from Guánica or San Germán. Follow the signs for the last couple of miles on Hwy 304.

West Coast

POP 364,600

Includes »

Best Places to Eat

» A 2 Tiempos (p197)
» Horned Dorset Primavera (p181)
» La Marea (p192)
» La Rosa Inglesa/English Rose Inn (p181)
» E Franco & Co (p186)
» El Bohió (p194)

Best Places to Stay

» Parador Bahía Salinas Beach Resort & Spa (p189)
» Blue Boy Inn (p179)
» Villa Vista Puerto (p189)
» Casa Islena (p179)
» Horned Dorset Primavera (p180)
» Centro Vacacional Boquerón (p191)

Why Go?

Across much of Puerto Rico the most impressive sight is the languid, azure sparkle of ocean, but in the west it's the visceral opposite – a place to get out in the water, paddle like mad and ride one perfect wave after another back toward shore. Its pièce de résistance is Rincón, a surfin' safari outpost (named in a Beach Boys song, for goodness' sake!) where grizzled beach bums, moneyed surf junketeers and stoned locals catch waves in the salty dawn and mingle around beach bonfires at twilight.

As well as taking the drop on flawless surf, Porta del Sol (Gateway to the Sun) is a grandiose land of stormy shorelines, low-key resorts and down-to-earth fishing villages, where deep-fried cod fritters from a Caribbean food shack are considered a gourmet meal and the spirit of slacker independence is as mellow as the stunning sunsets are arresting.

When to Go

Welcome to the endless summer: the west coast is pleasantly hot all year round. It gets heavy rain in late summer and early fall, but otherwise, expect it to be sunny, breezy and around 80°F nearly every day. If you're here to surf, winter is ideal. Cold fronts bring big waves to the western beaches, when average crests of 5ft or 6ft can grow as large as 25ft. In December and February, you may also spot migrating whales offshore. Those who aren't here to ride will find the calmer waters more inviting for swimming and deep-sea fishing in summer.

History

The consensus is that Columbus first arrived in Puerto Rico in November 1493 and docked somewhere off the west coast (though there is some dispute as to actually *where*). Fifteen years later he was followed by Juan Ponce de León, who landed near Cabo Rojo before heading off north to found the settlement of Caparra. San Germán, the island's second-oldest city, was founded near Mayagüez in 1511 and moved to its present site in 1573. More recently, the west has spawned many great liberal thinkers including Dr Ramón Emeterio Betances, the inspiration behind the revolutionary Grito de Lares (p245) in 1868. The details of this abortive rebellion were fine-tuned in a series of safe houses on the outskirts of Mayagüez.

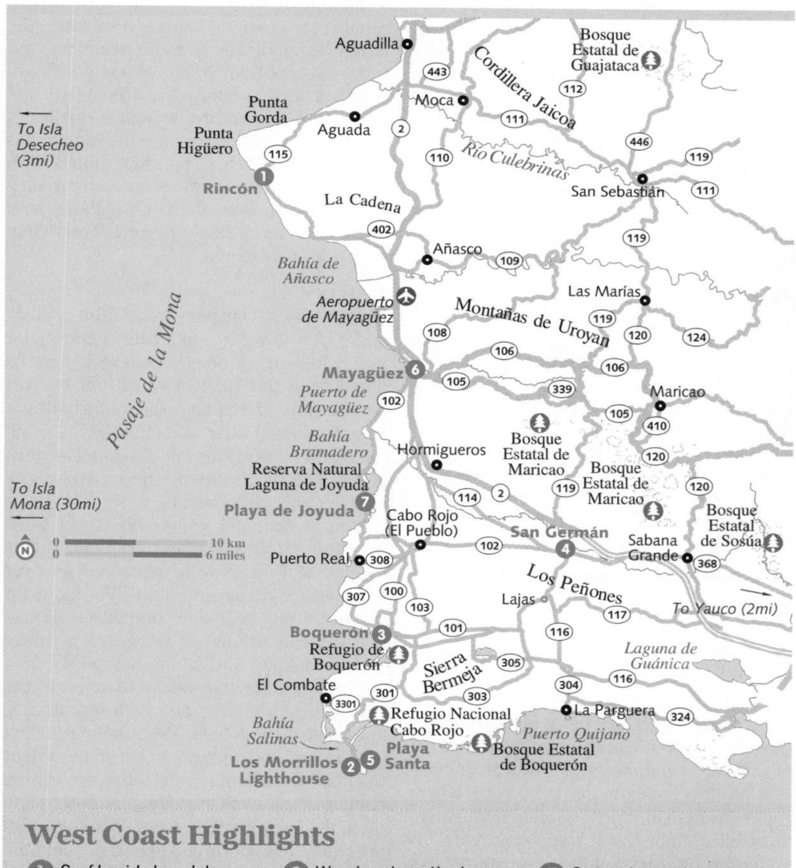

West Coast Highlights

1. Surf beside beach bums and vacationing businessmen on the legendary breaks of **Rincón** (p175)
2. Peer at the endless sea from the top of the **Los Morrillos Lighthouse** (p188), overlooking Playa Santa
3. Wander along the long stretches of sand before bar-hopping down the strip in **Boquerón** (p193)
4. Explore historic streets and some of the west's best food in **San Germán** (p195)
5. Swim alongside curious manatees at **Playa Santa** (p188)
6. Get giddy on **Sangria de Fido** (p186), the local punch of Mayagüez
7. Lunch on fresh seafood in **Playa de Joyuda** (p194), Puerto Rico's 'Gourmet Golden Mile'

Territorial Parks & Reserves

The 4775-acre patchwork of the Bosque Estatal de Boquerón is split into eight different segments spread around the Cabo Rojo area. Of these, the Refugio Nacional Cabo Rojo is a favorite of casual outdoor enthusiasts; it's great for bird-watchers, and the flat, guided trails would be easy for young children. There's a visitors center and guided hikes, and the views of the Caribbean from its outlooks are excellent.

Two others are also secluded. The Refugio de Boquerón has mangrove wetlands and excellent bird-watching opportunities, and the Reserva Natural Laguna de Joyuda plays host to numerous species of waterfowl.

Further east, in the foothills of the Central Mountains, the 3300-acre Bosque Estatal de Susúa exhibits an interesting blend of dry forest and tropical jungle. Still, the best opportunity for hiking and nature lovers is in the nearby Bosque Estatal de Guánica.

Getting There & Around

The west is easily accessed by Hwy 2, the island's nominal ring road – although it's not as fast as the newer toll roads further east. Públicos (shared taxis) serve most of the main towns, with Mayagüez acting as the regional hub. You can fly direct from the US into Aguadilla airport 30 minutes' northeast of Rincón. Mayagüez also has its own airport (flights from San Juan and the US Virgin Islands only). The area around Cabo Rojo southwest of Hwy 2 is ideal for cycling.

Rincón

POP 15,200

You'll know you've arrived in Rincón – 'the corner' – when you pass the group of sun-grizzled gringos cruising west in their rusty 1972 Volkswagen Beetle with surfboards piled on the roof. Shoehorned far out in the island's most remote corner, Rincón is Puerto Rico at its most unguarded, a place where the sunsets shimmer scarlet and you're more likely to be called 'dude' than 'sir.' This is the surfing capital of the island and one of the premiere places to catch a wave in the hemisphere.

For numerous Californian dreamers this is where the short-lived summer of love ended up. Arriving for the Surfing World Championships in 1968, many never went home. Hence Rincón became a haven for draft-dodgers, alternative lifestylers, back-to-the-landers and people more interested in catching the perfect wave than bagging $100,000 a year in a Chicago suburb.

Breaking anywhere from 2ft to 25ft, Rincón's waves are often close to perfect. The names are chillingly evocative: Domes, Indicators, Spanish Wall and Dogman's. The crème de la crème is Tres Palmas, a white-tipped monster that is often dubbed the 'temple' of big-wave surfing in the Caribbean.

Though Rincón is crawling with American expats (many of them residents), the tourist/local divide is more seamless and less exclusive than in the resorts out east. However, with a new, more affluent surfing generation demanding a higher quality of living than their hippie parents, Rincón has developed a clutch of boutique hotels with upmarket services aimed at surfing Gen X yuppies. Indeed, these days those with boards are more likely to be lawyers than high-school dropouts.

History

Rincón traces its history to the 16th century and a few low-key sugarcane plantations. And while many people believe it gets its name from the Spanish word *rincón* (corner) because of its shape, the municipality is actually named after one of the area's original planters, Don Gonzalo Rincón. For most of its history, the town survived on cane farming and cattle-raising.

Things changed when the World Surfing Championships arrived in 1968. Glossy images of Rincón were plastered all over international magazines and TV – the word was out. Every year since then has seen successive generations of wave riders make the pilgrimage. And while they pursued an endless summer, they began to invest in the community, building their own restaurants, guesthouses and bars. Eventually, Rincón's perfect surf and permanent beach bums lent the place the vibe it retains today, something similar to a Hawaiian surfing outpost.

As the baby-boomer generation of surfers got older, they continued to harbor romantic images of Rincón. But when they returned with their own children, they demanded better accommodations, slicker restaurants and a broader variety of activities – and the town responded. Today, you can rent distinctive vacation homes or stay in luxurious hotels. While the old-style bunkhouses are gone, imaginative and moderately priced guesthouses remain a staple in Rincón.

Sights

Rincón is more of a region than a town, encompassing a municipal center surrounded by clusters of commercial areas. The municipal center is only about four square blocks, encircling the Catholic church and the Presbyterian church that face each other across the traffic-crowded Plaza de Recreo. This core has essential services but most of the inns, restaurants and beach attractions lie north or south.

The best swimming beaches are south of the village, as are many of the larger hotels. A number of different snorkeling and surfing sites lie north and west of town, along Hwy 413. Moving further north, Hwy 413 climbs into steep hills.

Punta Higüero Lighthouse LIGHTHOUSE
Nicknamed El Faro, the Punta Higüero lighthouse dates from 1892 and rises almost 100ft. It was restored in 1922 after being severely damaged by a tsunami set off by the devastating 1918 earthquake. The 26,000-candlepower light has been automated since 1933 and still helps ships navigate the Pasaje de la Mona.

There's a small **museum** (admission free; 10am-2pm) inside the lighthouse building, which has artifacts from shipwrecks and relays anecdotes from the area's maritime history. The principal reason to come here, however, is for the view. Five great surf breaks are nearby, and sometimes humpback whales come within 100yd of the coast.

The historic lighthouse crowns **Parque Pasivo El Faro**, a pleasant city park that makes a breezy place for a sunset picnic, or to spy migrating whales during winter.

Bonus Nuclear Power Plant LANDMARK
A curious landmark, this green dome poking out from behind the palm trees behind the Punta Higüero Lighthouse once housed the first nuclear-powered electricity-generating facility in the Caribbean. Back in the days when the Beach Boys led the surfin' safari, the Boiling Nuclear Superheater Plant (known half-sarcastically by the acronym of Bonus) was a prototype of the superheater reactor.

The plant only produced about 16,000kW of energy and never functioned properly. In its short life from 1960 to 1968, it suffered a reactor failure and drew scorn from environmentalists. The US government filled it with cement and tried converting the building into a museum, only to discover – shocker – that a failed nuclear power facility wasn't popular with tourists.

During the next 40 years Bonus became a rusting relic of the nuclear age and a favorite canvas for graffiti artists, who scrawl slogans to vilify nukes or praise marijuana. Locals named a surf break after it: Domes, one of Rincón's most consistent breaks. In the past decade the building has been declared 'clean' and a museum was again considered, but it currently opens only by appointment through the **Puerto Rican Electric Power Authority** (787-521-4060; www.prepa.com).

Activities

Surfing

Surfing is the prime attraction, so if you're arriving in high season, make arrangements for rentals or lessons as early as possible. If you're just looking for a casual arrangement, there are shacks with boards to rent by the major surfing areas.

There are several reliable surf schools that get very high marks from former students.

Rincon Surf School SURFING, YOGA
(787-823-0610; www.rinconsurfschool.com) Rincon Surf School often does lessons at Sandy Beach and is a good bet for beginning adults. Also on offer here are surf-and-yoga combo packages, and lessons specifically for women.

Surf 787 SURFING
(787-448-0032; www.surf787.com) The coolest kid on the block, Surf 787 also has a suite of packages, all-inclusive surf vacations, adult getaways and a kids' surf camp. The instructors here, who are all CPR and water safety certified, also offer lessons for couples and small groups.

West Coast Surf Shop SURFING
(787-823-3935; www.westcoastsurf.com; 2e Muñoz Rivera; 10am-2pm) Right off the Plaza de Recreo, this sleekly designed, modern surf shop sells and rents top professional gear. The owners have great local knowledge and can organize lessons for any standard or age at short notice. They will deliver rental gear to your hotel room so it's ready when you arrive.

Desecheo Surf Shop SURFING, SNORKELING
(787-823-0390; www.desecheosurfshop.com) One of the many well-positioned options on the road to the lighthouse, this place can rent a surfboard to fit conditions for about $35 a day; boogie boards cost about $15. It also sells clothes and rents snorkeling equipment.

Rincón & Around

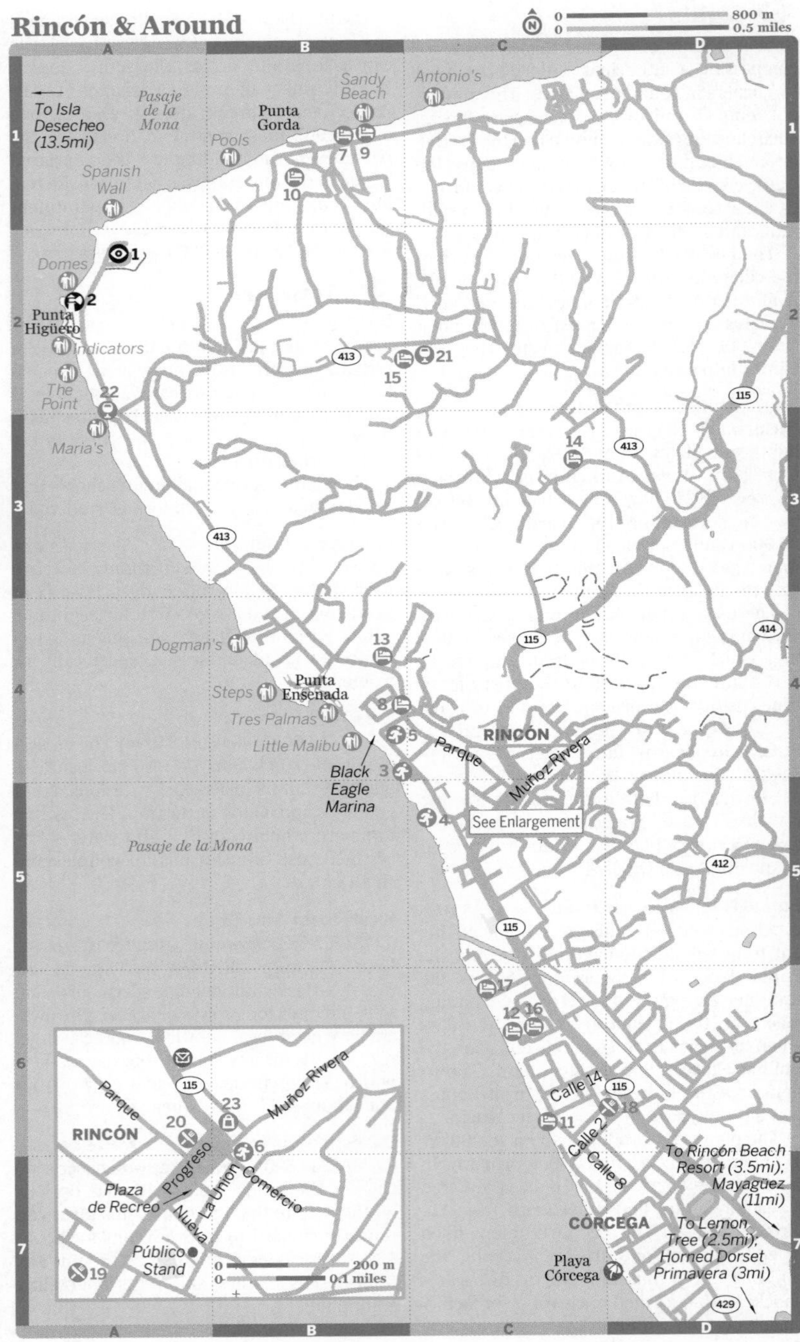

Rincón & Around

Sights

1	Bonus Nuclear Power Plant	A2
	Museum	(see 2)
	Parque Pasivo El Faro	(see 2)
2	Punta Higüero Lighthouse	A2

Activities, Courses & Tours

3	Capital Water Sports	B4
4	Rincón Balneario	C5
5	Taíno Divers	B4
6	West Coast Surf Shop	B6

Sleeping

7	Beside the Pointe	B1
8	Blue Boy Inn	B4
9	Casa Islena	B1
10	Casa Verde Guesthouse	B1
11	Coconut Palms Guesthouse	C6
12	Hotel Villa Cofresí	C6
13	Island West Properties	B4
14	La Rosa Inglesa/The English Rose Inn	C3
15	Lazy Parrot Inn	B2
16	Parador Villa Antonio	C6
17	Rincón of the Seas	C6

Eating

18	Antojos	D6
	La Rosa Inglesa/English Rose Inn	(see 14)
19	Libanesa Bakery	A7
	LPR	(see 15)
20	Rincón Cash & Carry	A6
	Tapas Bar	(see 9)

Drinking

21	Banana Dang	C2
22	Calypso Tropical Café	A2
	Rock Bottom Bar & Grill	(see 10)
	Tamboo Tavern	(see 7)

Shopping

	Lazy Parrot Tropical Gift Shop	(see 15)
23	Uncharted Studio	B6

Diving & Snorkeling

Because of the rough water this is not a great place for snorkeling, but snorkelers will fare much better in summer, when the water is calmer. Head for either **Playa Shacks** or **Playa Steps** near Black Eagle Marina for the best of what the beaches have to offer.

Rincón has two good dive shops thanks to the popularity of diving the pristine reefs around Rincón and Isla Desecheo.

Taíno Divers DIVING, SNORKELING
(☎787-823-6429; www.tainodivers.com; Black Eagle Marina; 2-tank dive $129, snorkeling $95) Located inside the little marina north of town, this is probably the best outfit on the west coast; its guides are responsible, professional and very environmentally aware. It does almost daily runs to Desecheo (8am to 2pm) and shorter trips to nearby reefs (8am to noon). Snorkel trips, one-tank dives, whale-watching and sunset cruises are also available, as well as chartered deep-sea fishing trips.

Desecheo Surf & Dive Shop DIVING, SNORKELING
(☎787-823-0390; www.desecheosurfshop.com; El Faro Road; half-day board rental $20-25) You'll pass this low-key rental shop en route to the lighthouse. They also offer lessons and dive gear, but no dive trips.

Swimming

The surf is often too rough for swimming at many sites along the coast. Fortunately, there's the safe and newly renovated **Rincón balneario** (public beach) about half a mile from the Plaza de Recreo. Here you'll find rest rooms, showers, some temporary food shacks and a new mall, which contains the tourist office, harbor restaurant and lookout tower.

There is also good, safe swimming on the adjacent strand in front of Parador Villa Antonio and Hotel Villa Cofresí.

Kayaking

You can rent kayaks from **Capital Water Sports** (☎787-823-2789; Sunset Village, Rincón Balneario) and at Taíno Divers for approximately $25 an hour for use around the balneario.

Fishing & Whale-Watching

Taíno Divers does responsible **whale-watching tours** (about $55 per person for a two-hour tour). Boats are required to keep a minimum distance from the gentle giants, but less scrupulous operators don't always adhere to that rule. Taíno Divers can also take you on half-day deep-sea fishing excursions for about $600 per chartered boat (eight people maximum). Whale-watching is also possible from the Punta Higüero lighthouse park in December.

SURF BEACHES

As far as surfing folklore goes, Rincón wins the ultimate accolade: it's mentioned in a song by the Beach Boys. Released in 1962, *Surfin' Safari* names Rincón as the place where 'they're walking the nose,' surfer slang for moving forward on the board toward the front. For walking the nose or simply taking in the action from shore, here's a guide to Rincón's hottest surf beaches (running south to north):

» **Little Malibu** Just north of the marina. OK in winter, with easy 4ft breaks. Good for beginners.

» **Tres Palmas** The big kahuna, with breaks of up to 25ft. Requires *bon courage* and a long paddle out. Handle with care.

» **Steps** Also known by its Spanish name, *Escalera,* this is the 'inside' break to Tres Palmas' 'outside' break. Good snorkeling spot when it's calm.

» **Dogman's** A local favorite that is anything but predictable. Expect waves that are high and hollow.

» **Maria's** A good right, but needs a decent swell. Three times a year the waves break big, but otherwise it's average.

» **The Point** In front of the lighthouse, this one is not for amateurs. Waves can break big here while Maria's is lying flat.

» **Indicators** Good powerful rights. Watch out for rocks and a pipe and coral bottom.

» **Domes** Named for the nearby former nuclear facility. Good rights with the occasional left. A strong undercurrent, but probably the most consistent spot in Rincón.

» **Spanish Wall** A beautiful secluded spot only reachable by a rough path, this place gets up in winter and can be particularly fabulous after a cold front.

» **Pools** Offers a few shallow reef-break peaks that can occasionally barrel.

» **Sandy Beach** Good beginner's beach with decent waves when the swell is right.

» **Antonio's** Used heavily during the 1968 World Surfing Championships, this has a right wall with a shorter left. Two take-off points spread the crowd.

Makaira Charters FISHING
(☎787-823-4391/299-7374; www.makairafishingcharters.com; half/full day $575/850) Captain Pepi Alfonso is a licensed US Coast Guard who runs deep-sea fishing charters for up to six people and can sometimes split charters if your party is smaller. Drinks are included, but bring your own food – no bananas though (an old fishing superstition)!

Festivals & Events

Rincón Triathlon RACE
(www.rinconpr.com/triathlon/home.htm) This triathlon has been going since 1982, which is pretty much ancient history in the triathlon world. Held every June, it's a classic ironman contest that's starting to draw some quality international athletes – it makes for a serious fiesta for spectators.

Sleeping

Rincón has some of the best-value accommodations on the island, especially in its small, boutique properties. Still, reservations are recommended, particularly in high season, from November through February, when the town is overrun by surfers.

Rincón is also awash with vacation-rental properties of all shapes and sizes. To make your search easier you can enlist the services of **Island West Properties** (☎787-823-2323; www.rinconrealestateforsale.com), which maintains an office on Hwy 413 about a mile out of town toward the lighthouse. Villa rentals with one to eight bedrooms go for between $120 and $700 per night.

Most of the guesthouses (and a few bar-restaurants) are in the hills north of town, especially on a loop of road that circles down to the north-facing beach and rejoins Hwy 413 a mile further to the northwest.

Many of the accommodations (as well as restaurants and pubs) listed here do not have street addresses per se; in these cases we provide descriptive addresses.

NORTH OF TOWN

Most of the following accommodations, and some other scrappy options not listed, are along Hwy 413, north of town.

TOP CHOICE Casa Islena HOTEL $$

(787-823-1525; www.casa-islena.com; Hwy 413, Beach Rd; r incl breakfast $185-205; P ❄ @ ≋) A high-class option in the heart of Rincón's best surfing, Casa Islena is an elegant Mediterranean-style guesthouse on a magnificent, moody stretch of ocean. It's a magnet for discerning jet-setting surfers; guests work out the sore muscles at morning yoga under palms and navigate the walled-in gardens to nine lovely sea-view rooms. Breakfast is at the bar next to the sparkling pool, afternoon snacks are plates of lime-dressed grilled fish from the Tapas Bar (p181). The nightly dinner show includes a spectacle of roaring surf and setting sun. As with all of Rincón's best places, you'll certainly want to book early.

Blue Boy Inn HOTEL $$

(787-823-2593; www.blueboyinn.com; 556 Black Eagle St; r $175-215; P ❄ ≋) This elegant little inn near the old marina is an excellent midpriced option with very private rooms, a doting staff and the best breakfast around. This isn't a good place for families (it suggests no children under 12 years of age), nor is it ideal for avid surfers (the best breaks are north of town) but the tiled terraces of rooms are hidden among the leafy gardens and exude a romantic, secluded atmosphere. In the evening, guests can cook at the outdoor kitchen near the pool or sit around the crackling fire pit before retiring to their rooms, where high-thread-count sheets cover sleigh beds. It has boogie boards and bikes for its guests to use, free of charge.

Beside the Pointe HOTEL $

(787-823-8550; www.besidethepointe.com; r $75-125; P ❄) The social centerpiece of Sandy Beach, this guesthouse has a happening bar and restaurant, Tamboo Tavern (p182), rooms that are outfitted like small, tiled-floor apartments, and lots of unpretentious character. Few rooms have good views, but many have cooking facilities and kitchenettes, and they're slowly being upgraded with flat-screen televisions. If you choose one of the rooms up front, expect plenty of background noise after hours.

Tropical Treehouse CABANAS $$

(541-499-3885; www.tropical-treehouse.com; off Hwy 115; d $100-125, apt for up to 10 people $350 P ❄) Built on 25 acres of bamboo forest high above the Rincón shore, this cool ecoretreat is your chance to live in a Swiss Family Robinson–style tree house, built with woven bamboo, screened in with mosquito netting and perched high off the ground. There are only three choices – 'Sunset Hooch,' 'Luna Hooch' and the large main house, which sleeps 10 – but all have bamboo furniture, basic kitchen facilities and a fantastically sustainable ethos (they're even solar-powered). It's rustic and quirky, so it's better for those looking for a back-to-nature excursion than a plush retreat. Set on a ridge in the dense jungle forest, this is a true escape from civilization. As such, getting here can be a bit tricky, as it's on unmarked roads off Hwy 115. Calling ahead for detailed directions is essential.

Lazy Parrot Inn HOTEL $$

(787-823-5654; www.lazyparrot.com; Hwy 413 Km 4.1; r $125-165; P ❄ @ ≋) Claiming the middle ground between high quality and high quirky, the Lazy Parrot captures the unique essence of Rincón without scrimping on the home comforts. A venerable inn crammed full with all kinds of parrots – including real ones, carved ones, inflated ones and stuffed ones – it occupies the high country above Rincón, offering glimpses of the sparkling ocean. Rooms are comfortable, but not flashy; the restaurant, LPR (p182), is a culinary corker; and the inviting pool and Jacuzzi – not to mention the leafy Bamboo Bar – are positively sublime (especially at night). The staff is friendly and the clientele well-dressed gringos with surfing aspirations.

Casa Verde Guesthouse GUESTHOUSE $

(787-605-5351; www.enrincon.com; Beach Rd off Hwy 413; apt $70-180; P ❄) Cheap and fun, this sea-green guesthouse is the place to stay if you want to stumble to bed after indulging in Rincón's scrappy party scene. It's a bit rough around the edges, with horses in front and an adjoining party hall (Rock Bottom Bar & Grill, p182), but Casa Verde is a surfer-friendly guesthouse with supermodern accommodations. There are one-, two- and three-bedroom choices available – with the added plus of a late-night bar scene right next door.

LOCAL KNOWLEDGE

JOAQUIM CRUZ: RINCÓN SURFER

Rincoń was the first place in Puerto Rico to sponsor surfing in a big way after the 1968 World Championships. It also embraces surfing culture in its entirety, with friendly people, plenty of places to stay, a decent local mayor, rural tranquility and an excellent array of other sports. Ten years ago I was surfing with my friend, Rasta, up at Crash Boat Beach near Aguadilla. The swell was so awesome that the local dudes with boogie boards were actually fighting with each other for space in the water. I took a gorgeous wave and dropped down, turning as I went, hand on the wall. I think I took the tube three times before I ran out of water and hit the shore. There was this guy behind me watching and whooping. I'm not sure whether he was wishing he was up there with me or he was just sharing in the moment.

Favorite Surf Spot

Dogman's, because the waves there are really hollow. Often the waves elsewhere are just as high, but Dogman's invariably has the best tubes.

Best Time of Year

From the second week in October through April.

After-Surf Party

Go to bars like the Calypso (p182), where you can hear good bands playing Latin, rock, salsa and reggae.

As told to Brendan Sainsbury

SOUTH OF TOWN

Horned Dorset Primavera RESORT **$$$**
(787-823-4030; www.horneddorset.com; Hwy 429 Km 0.3; r from $650; P ❄ @ ≋) Undoubtedly the best small resort in Puerto Rico, and perhaps even the Caribbean (though you may have to remortgage your house to stay here), this place rightly claims to offer the 'epitome of privacy, elegance and service,' and it certainly delivers. There are 30 suites in private villas that are furnished with hand-carved antiques and come equipped with their own private plunge pools (just in case you get bored of the communal infinity pool, which overlooks the setting sun). It is a beautiful, quiet playground for an international set of travelers who are quite comfortable with life's finer things. Dripping with exclusivity, the Horned Dorset doesn't accept children under 12 years of age, shuns TVs in the rooms and encourages people to dress up – especially for dinner (see p181). It's a long way from Rincón's surf scene, but it's blissful.

Lemon Tree SUITES **$$**
(787-823-6452; www.lemontreepr.com; Hwy 429 Km 4.1; r $110-185) You can wrap yourself in a Japanese *yurkata* (robe) and enjoy fresh morning coffee on your private oceanfront deck at this luxury beachside property. Six self-contained suites with fully furnished kitchens are decorated in thematic tropical colors. There's the indulgent Banana suite with its Jacuzzi tub and terrazzo floors, or the three-bedroom Papaya suite with its flat-screen TV and sweeping beach views. An extra bonus is the on-site PADI–certified Lemon Tree Divers.

Coconut Palms Guesthouse GUESTHOUSE **$$**
(787-823-0147; www.coconutpalmsinn.com; 2734 Calle 8, Comunidad Estela; r $75-150) Sandwiched in between Rincón's more upscale southern resorts lies this fun and unpretentious guesthouse in a residential neighborhood just off Hwy 115. The Coconut's best feature is its fern-draped and bird-filled courtyard along with its lovely setting right on a calm, nonsurfing stretch of beach. It has a number of adjoining rooms, many with pull-out futons, making it ideal for small groups traveling on a smaller budget or those who want to relax with a good book and laze around on the sand.

Hotel Villa Cofresí HOTEL **$$**
(787-823-2450; www.villacofresi.com; Hwy 115 Km 12.3; r $115-160; P ❄ ≋) There's nothing too fancy here, but fabulous customer service,

squeaky-clean rooms and king-size beds make this a safe, if slightly bland option. It seems like someone plucked a better-than-average Days Inn out of a highway exit in Ohio and dropped it in the tropics. There's also a large pool and water-sports concession on the property and the restaurant/bar is renowned for its high-octane coconut drinks.

Rincón of the Seas RESORT **$$$**
(☎787-823-6189; www.rinconoftheseas.com; Hwy 115 Km 12.2; r $235-495; P ❄ @ ≋) This is a resort with all the usual upscale touches, yet it somehow retains a more laid-back Rincón feel than the bigger piles further east. Maybe it's the tasteful antiques that adorn the lavish lobby, or the gaggles of nouveau-riche surfers who congregate around the swimming pool. Parked right on a calm stretch of beach, the Rincón is a modern hotel with a swath of beautifully landscaped grounds. Regular rooms go for under $200 in summer, but travelers with a penchant for art deco can fork out more than $400 for the special ocean-view suite. There are tons of on-site amenities and staff more than willing to hook you up with snorkeling and diving adventures.

Rincón Beach Resort RESORT **$$$**
(☎787-589-9000; www.rinconbeach.com; Hwy 115 Km 5.8; r/ste $240/459; P ❄ @ ≋) Not quite as luxurious as the Dorset, this neighboring resort is also outside of Rincón proper. It's a boutique hotel that has some private villas, a gorgeous beach and lots of opulent amenities for guests. If you like all-inclusive places where you rarely have to leave the property unless it's to head into the water, then try this place – tennis, massages, golf and more right at your fingertips. The rates for suites drop in low season.

La Rosa Inglesa/ English Rose Inn B&B **$$**
(☎787-823-4032; www.larosainglesa.com; follow signs from Hwy 413 interior; r $115-200) High in the hills, this B&B meets a high standard of cleanliness and comes with the best breakfast in town.

Parador Villa Antonio PARADOR **$$**
(☎787-823-2645; www.villa-antonio.com; Hwy 115 Km 12.3; r $115-170; P ❄ ≋) Rincón's token parador is atypical of the genre: family-friendly, affordable and good with the basics.

Eating

A lot of Rincón's guesthouses and hotels also serve food, so the list of restaurants in this small municipality is impressive. Vegetarian options can be had at most places.

Horned Dorset Primavera FRENCH FUSION **$$$**
(☎787-823-4030; www.horneddorset.com; Hwy 429 Km 0.3; mains $30-50; ⊙dinner) Elegant, exclusive and extraordinary, this is among Puerto Rico's best fine dining options – where you climb the sweeping staircase to the black-and-white-tiled dining room of billowing lined drapes and an atmosphere right out of a colonial Caribbean culinary dream. Suffice to say, the stunning French-influenced food is dreamy, relying on seasonal, daily menu dishes that marry seasoned duck and tropical fruit reductions, grilled mahimahi, chateaubriand, porterhouse steaks and delicately prepared seafood dishes. Few surf bums turn up here; the clinking wine glasses toast marriage proposals and business deals, and patrons outfit themselves accordingly. Smart casual attire is required.

La Rosa Inglesa/ English Rose Inn BREAKFAST **$**
(☎787-823-4032; www.larosainglesa.com; follow signs from Hwy 413 interior; breakfasts $7-11; ⊙breakfast) The trick to this, Rincón's exceptional breakfast place, is the crusty homemade breads and savory home-stuffed sausage, which turn the egg dishes and omelets into a real event. The upscale surfers shovel down breakfast burritos and poached eggs after surfing the morning away, enjoying a view of the water. It's kind of a pain to get here, situated as it is way up in the hills above town, but the best breakfast in town and great views are ample reward. To find it, look for signs off Hwy 413…or follow the crowd.

Tapas Bar TAPAS **$$**
(☎787-823-1525; www.casa-islena.com; Casa Islena, Hwy 413, Beach Rd; tapas $7-10; ⊙11am-3pm & 5-9pm) Casa Islena's Tapas Bar serves delicious tapas washed down with rum-laced sangria. Imagine grilled swordfish in spicy coconut broth, and skirt steak marinated in ginger, soy and garlic, enjoyed over a scarlet-streaked sunset. The restaurant also follows a good environmental code using filtered water (no plastic), biodegradable takeout containers and sustainably harvested seafood.

LPR CARIBBEAN FUSION **$$**

(☎787-823-5654; www.lazyparrot.com; Hwy 413 Km 4.1; mains $16-21; ⏲noon-9:30pm) Though the food has been serious for years, the place formerly known as Smilin' Joes has taken it up a notch after changing the name to LPR (for Lazy Parrot Restaurant, a part of the Lazy Parrot Inn, p179). The dining room is finished with elegantly rustic trimmings and overlooks the pool, the green hills and the ocean. Try the sesame-ginger *churrasco* steak or the mango-glazed chicken breast and choose something full-bodied from the comprehensive wine list. Then there's the guesthouse itself, which provides a strangely romantic setting (considering all the parrot paraphernalia) with its cleverly lit swimming pool and strategically positioned Rum Shack bar, which lives by its rather Hemingway-esque motto 'Conserve water – drink rum.'

Libanesa Bakery BAKERY **$**

(52 Muñoz Rivera; snacks $3-7) Of all the bakeries in Rincón, this takes first prize for freshness and variety. It's in the heart of downtown.

Antojos CARIBBEAN **$$**

(☎787-823-4377; Hwy 115 Km 11.2; dishes $8-14) Fish is served up with *comida criolla* (traditional Puerto Rican cuisine) side dishes, such as rice, beans and fried plantains. Nothing fancy, reliably hearty.

Rincón Cash & Carry SUPERMARKET

(⏲10am-6pm Mon-Sat, 10am-4pm Sun) For self-caterers. In the town center, across from the Plaza de Recreo.

Drinking

TOP CHOICE **Calypso Tropical Café** CAFE, BAR

(⏲noon-midnight) Wall-to-wall suntans, svelte girls in bikini tops, bare-chested blokes nursing cold beers, and syncopated reggae music drifting out beneath the sun-dappled palm trees; the Calypso is everything you'd expect a beachside surfers' bar to be – and perhaps a little more. All that's missing is a prepsychedelic-era Brian Wilson propping up the jukebox (then again, Brian never *could* surf). On the ocean side of the leafy road to the lighthouse, Calypso hosts the oldest pub scene in Rincón and regularly books live bands to cover rock, reggae and calypso classics. Not surprisingly, it's a microcosm of the region at large and *the* place to go to find out about surf gossip, weather and waves.

Tamboo Tavern BAR

(www.besidethepointe.com; Sandy Beach; ⏲noon-midnight) The patio bar of the Beside the Pointe guesthouse overlooks some of the best sand in Rincón. But the scene on the waves is only a slice of the quality atmosphere, which is completed by great burgers, and a young and vivacious local crowd who drink a little too much and dance a little too close. With a congenial après-surf scene, it has occasional live music, but the sound system is pretty good and the twilight beach panorama is something to behold. It's been shortlisted by *Esquire* among the best bars in America, and it's easy to see why.

Banana Dang CAFE

(www.bananadang.com; Hwy 413 Km 4.1; ⏲7am-7pm Mon & Wed-Sat, 9am-7pm Sun; @ wi-fi) Set up in 2007 by two committed coffee and banana addicts from LA, Banana Dang comes pretty close to delivering the best shots of caffeine on the island. Next door to the Lazy Parrot Inn in the hills above Rincón, it's well worth stopping off here to – in the words of the owners – think, drink and link (yes, there are computer terminals and wi-fi access). The banana smoothies are memorable, too.

Rock Bottom Bar & Grill BAR

(Beach Rd off Hwy 413; ⏲noon-2am) Rock Bottom is a 'tree-house'-style bar situated next to the Casa Verde Guesthouse (p179) in the Sandy Beach neighborhood. It has ladies nights, surf videos, tasty bar snacks (buffalo wings and mozzarella sticks) and a novel, less tacky version of karaoke that it calls the 'Acoustic Jam.' This is the kind of place that looks like a postdrunken disaster area by day, but come after dark and it's a charmer.

Shopping

Uncharted Studio GALLERY, CUSTOM T-SHIRTS

(www.theunchartedstudio.com; Plaza de Recreo; ⏲10am-5pm) This excellent and extremely hip gallery, right on the central square, deals the work of local artists, cool custom T-shirts, screen prints and paintings. If you're going for some local artwork that's a discerning cut above the painfully cheesy airbrushed pictures of dolphins and whales, this is the place to look.

Lazy Parrot Tropical Gift Shop GIFT SHOP

(☎787-823-5654; www.lazyparrot.com; Lazy Parrot Inn, Hwy 413 Km 4.1; ⏲9am-6pm) In the Lazy Parrot Inn, this shop is a must-stop for parrot lovers. You will also see Lisl Voigt's handmade sea-glass jewelry here.

Information

Emergency

Police station (787-823-2020) In the south corner of the village off Nueva.

Internet Access

Banana Dang (www.bananadang.com; Hwy 413 Km 4.1; per 30min $3; 7am-7pm Mon & Wed-Sat, 9am-7pm Sun) Wi-fi and terminals available here.

Surf's Up (Hwy 115 Km 12; per 30min $3; 6am-8:30pm) Internet, wi-fi, coffee and bagels.

Medical Services

Farmacia Nogueras (787-823-1704; 11 Muñoz Rivera) Downtown next to the Plaza de Recreo.

Rincón Centro de Salud (787-823-5171/2795/3120; 28 Muñoz Rivera) In town next to Paco's Grocery, this health center is a block south of Plaza de Recreo.

Money

There are ATMs in the lobby of almost every hotel and in many bars, so finding cash won't be a problem.

Banco Popular (9am-2:30pm Mon-Fri, 9am-noon Sat) Downtown near Plaza de Recreo. Has an ATM.

Western Bank (9am-2:30pm Mon-Fri, 9am-noon Sat) Also downtown near Plaza de Recreo, with an ATM.

Post

Post office (7:30am-4:30pm Mon-Fri, 8:30am-noon Sat) A quarter mile north of the Plaza de Recreo on Hwy 115.

Tourist Information

The Tourism Association of Rincón puts out a great, amusing map, complete with site descriptions, cartoon drawings and essential phone numbers (it's completely not to scale). You can get one from your innkeeper. Sometimes you can get a map for free; sometimes it's $1.

Tourism Association of Rincón (888-237-2073; www.rincon.org) For a complete list of the area's offerings, check out the virtual office here. There are links to accommodation websites.

Tourist Information Center (787-823-5024; Sunset Bldg, Cambija St; 8am-4:30pm Mon-Fri) In the Sunset Building adjacent to Rincón public beach.

Getting There & Away

Rincón doesn't have an airport, but there are two in the area. If you are coming from San Juan, fly into Mayagüez. Aguadilla's Aeropuerto Rafael Hernández generally has a couple of flights a day from the New York area or Miami.

The público stand is just off Plaza de Recreo on Nueva. Expect to pay about $5 if you are headed north to Aguadilla or $3 to go south to Mayagüez (you can access San Juan from either of these cities). Both trips take about 40 minutes.

In spite of what your map might suggest, the easiest way to approach the town is via the valley roads of Hwy 402 and Hwy 115, both of which intersect Hwy 2 south of the Rincón peninsula.

Getting Around

Now for the bummer: Rincón – despite its mantle as an 'alternative' beach haven – has little provision for nonmotorized transport. A spread-out community with minimal public transport, Rincón has few sidewalks and almost no facilities for bicycles (the nearest bike rental is in Aguadilla; see p215). The only reliable way to get around the area is by rented car, taxi, irregular públicos or – if you're energetic and careful – walking. You will pay $18 or more for a taxi from either the Aguadilla or Mayagüez airports. Car rentals can also be found at both of these destinations (see p218 and p188) or you can try **Angelos** (787-823-3438; Hwy 115 Km 12), in the town itself.

Mayagüez

POP 89,080

Like many of Puerto Rico's midsized cities, it takes some digging to discover the charm of Mayagüez. The 'Sultan of the West' is largely a transportation point for visitors to the west or those making the weekend junket to the Dominican Republic. The commonwealth's underrated and slightly disheveled dock town is the island's third biggest – behind San Juan and Ponce – though it has few comparable attractions. Still, savvy travelers will sense some vibrancy here, mostly thanks to a hard-partying student population and some ambitious restoration projects, many of which were completed before hosting the 2010 Central American and Caribbean Games.

Founded in 1760 by émigrés from the Canary Islands, Mayagüez had an inauspicious early history considering its current

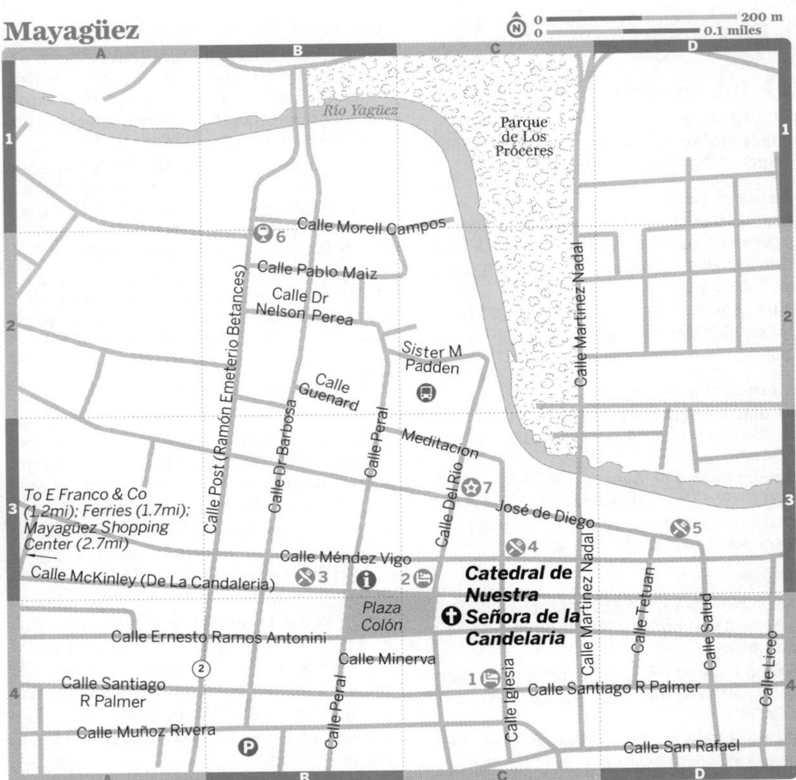

size and importance. The emerging economy was based on fruit production and agriculture, and even today the city remains noted for the sweetness of its mangoes. In the mid-19th century Mayagüez developed a contrarian nature and sheltered numerous revolutionary thinkers including Ramón Emeterio Betances, architect of the abortive Grito de Lares (p245). Disaster struck in 1918 when an earthquake measuring 7.6 on the Richter scale all but destroyed the central business district, but the city rose from the rubble.

Mayagüez today boasts a large university (specializing in sciences), numerous historic buildings, a couple of parks and a lovely central plaza. It's also a center of Puerto Rican gastronomy and drinking, with a pair of 19th-century bakeries celebrated for a locally famous delicacy known as *brazo gitano* (gypsy's arm; a jam sponge cake presented in the style of a Swiss roll). For drinkers, there's a raucous college bar scene and an out-of-the-way place brewing an insanely sweet rum-and-wine cocktail known as Sangria de Fido.

Little visited by tourists who veer northwest to Rincón or south toward Cabo Rojo, Mayagüez has enough distractions to fill a long afternoon (including Puerto Rico's only zoo and planetarium), the delightful Yagüez theater and a lively student nightlife. Then there's the congenial *mayagüezians* (people from Mayagüez), always up for a spontaneous fiesta, such as **Cinco Días con Nuestro Tierra**, an agricultural-industrial fair (see p24).

Sights

Catedral de Nuestra Señora de la Candelaria — CHURCH

Consecrated in 1760, Mayagüez' original Catholic church was replaced by the current model in 1836. The cathedral suffered many blows over the subsequent 100 years,

Mayagüez

Top Sights

Catedral de Nuestra Señora de la Candelaria C4

Sleeping

1 Hotel Colonial C4
2 Howard Johnson Downtown Mayagüez C3

Eating

3 Rex Cream B3
4 Ricomini Bakery C3
Stoa's .... (see 2)
5 Vegetariano La Familia D3

Drinking

6 El Garabato B2

Entertainment

7 Bleu Bar & Tapas C3
Red Baron Pub .... (see 6)

culminating in the 1918 earthquake, which destroyed its ceiling, and a lightning bolt that toppled one of its bell towers. Ambitious renovation plans were drawn up by architect Luis Perocier in 1922, but due to lack of funds they were never truly realized.

The full refurbishment wasn't actually completed until 2004. The cathedral now sparkles afresh and survives as one of Puerto Rico's most evocative ecclesial monuments with gilded scenes from the life of Christ behind the altar.

Zoológico de Puerto Rico ZOO
(Bario Miradero, Hwy 108 interior; adult/child $10/5, parking $3; 8:30am-4pm Wed-Sun) After a multimillion-dollar top-to-bottom renovation, the only real zoo on the island has joined the modern standard of facilities with natural-looking environments, wheelchair-accessible paths and a conservationist bent. Of the 600-odd species of reptiles, birds, amphibians and mammals the highlight is the brightly polished arthropod and butterfly house, where kids squeal at glass enclosures of giant tropical cockroaches and brightly painted butterflies that flutter about. The aviary, where visitors walk on an elevated boardwalk through a large net-enclosed area, has a number of bright tropical species as well. Off Hwy 108, the zoo is just to the northeast of the university in the same neighborhood as the agricultural research station and city park.

Recinto Universitario Mayagüez UNIVERSITY
(RUM; www.uprm.edu, in Spanish; 259 Post) More than 13,000 students are enrolled in a host of disciplines at this university. Over the years, RUM has become the premier math and science campus of the University of Puerto Rico system and boasts internationally respected programs in agriculture and engineering, as well as in the physical and biological sciences. The campus lies just out of town off Calle Post (Hwy 2). Though visiting campus can offer a glimpse into Puerto Rican higher education, it may be easier to commune with students over beers on the bustling strip of Calle Post. The university also boasts two excellent sports mascots; men's teams are the Tarzáns, while the women's teams are the Janes!

FREE **Estación Experimental Agrícola Federal** AGRICULTURAL CENTER
(http://eea.uprm.edu; Av Paris; 7am-4pm Mon-Fri) Wandering through the Estación Experimental Agrícola Federal, the tropical agricultural research station of the US Department of Agriculture, is a bit like wandering through a geeky botanical garden, what with the neatly labeled plantations of yams, plantains, bananas and imported tropical 'cash crops' such as cinnamon trees from Sri Lanka. Today, the station also throws many of its federal grants behind biofuels and tropical medicine. The adjacent city park known as **Parque de los Próceres** (Patriots' Park; dawn-dusk), on the south side of Hwy 65, also has verdant walkways and together these make an interesting stroll. These grounds lie just southeast of the RUM campus.

Sleeping

Howard Johnson Downtown Mayagüez HOTEL $$
(787-832-9191; www.hojo.com; 70 Calle Méndez Vigo; d $111-133; P) The stained-glass windows in this freshly remodeled central hotel are left over from the building's history as a monastery, a fact also evident in the smallish rooms and somber heavy wooden doors. Some rooms, with a bit more space and brightly colored bedspreads, are geared toward families, though most of them are oriented toward business travelers, with desks, mini-refrigerators and flat-screen televisions. It has a bit of a corporate feel, but there are perks in the small courtyard pool and absolutely enormous collection of

bottles at the on-site tapas bar, Stoa's. For discounts, book online.

Mayagüez Resort & Casino HOTEL, CASINO $$
(787-831-7575; www.mayaguezresort.com; Rte 104 Km 0.3; r $189-335;) This hotel-and-casino combo is the plushest option in town and locals pack into the casino to drink and play slots. Located off Hwy 2 north of town, this 140-unit property – with tennis courts, pool and casino – will seem strangely familiar to travelers who have frequented the hotels of Isla Verde or the megaresorts that populate Fajardo and the east coast. Surprisingly, it is not on the water, but on 20 acres of tropical gardens – actually an adjunct to the nearby agricultural research station – and it boasts a lovely river pool (the coolest in this part of the island), which winds between tropical plants and large rock formations.

Hotel Colonial HOTEL $
(787-833-2150; www.hotelcolonial.com; 14 Calle Iglesia; s/d incl breakfast $49/99;) With a bit of negotiation, these 29 rooms can be an affordable option in the center of town, but the rooms are a bit bleak, with plastic-covered mattresses and dim lighting. Still, there's local charm in the long staircases and Moorish tiling of these historic digs, especially considering the building was once a home for nuns.

Eating & Drinking

TOP CHOICE **E Franco & Co** BAKERY, CAFE $
(www.brazogitano.net, in Spanish; 3 Manuel Pirallo; dishes $7-16) Most of Puerto Rico's culinary legends are less than 20 years old, but this salt-of-the-earth grocery-store-cum-cafe has been here for more than 150 years and is still drawing in punters from as far away as San Juan for a monthly stock up. Cocooned in the waterfront warehouse district, Franco's is an upmarket place with tables scattered around a glass-topped deli counter in the style of an old English tearoom. Order your lunch from a set menu and you'll receive a complimentary *brazo gitano* that goes down well with a cup of fine Puerto Rican coffee. Stocked with assorted condiments, fresh-baked goods and opulent hampers, the store affords plenty of people-watching opportunities as shoppers from around the island arrive to pick up their favorite treats.

Stoa's TAPAS, BAR $
(70 Calle Méndez Vigo; dishes $2-8; breakfast, lunch & dinner;) Don't be fooled by the simple first impression of this lunch counter, located in the lobby of Howard Johnson; Stoa's has the best selection of wine in western Puerto Rico. There's a diverse offering by the glass, and by the bottle the sky's the limit, with imports from Italy, Spain, France and California. The food is elegantly presented but nothing exceptional – a menu of grilled sandwiches and hot and cold tapas – but it's all carefully made and hits the spot after a few glasses.

Rex Cream ICE-CREAM PARLOR $
(Calle Méndez Vigo; cones $1-3) Rex is a small Puerto Rican ice-cream chain that was founded in Mayagüez in the 1960s by Chinese immigrants who came to the island via Costa Rica. This signature store near the central plaza is still something of a local tradition and gets full, particularly on public holidays. Among the numerous weird and wonderful flavors you can sample are corn sherbet and tamarind.

Ricomini Bakery BAKERY, CAFE $
(101 Calle Méndez Vigo; dishes $2-8; 5am-1am) The Ricomini bakery and deli has been on this corner for well over a century and is still packing them in. A place with a lunch counter, some tables and basic groceries, this is a de facto social hub of downtown Mayagüez: deals are made here, relationships forged (and broken), and gossip boisterously exchanged. The deals are good too; you can roll up for steaming coffee, scrambled eggs, a slice of the famous *brazo gitano* or a delicious toasted Cubano sandwich, stacked with ham, roasted pork, cheese and pickles.

Vegetariano La Familia VEGETARIAN $
(787-833-7571; 151 José de Diego; mains $5-12;) Bankers, teachers, students, office workers and itinerant travelers – they all line up here at another Mayagüez classic where the portions are huge, the tastes are rustic and the price is…well…peanuts. The lunch buffet on its own is a sight to behold – tofu dishes and salads stretching across a big table. Then there are the rice dishes, the pasta, the beans and the strangely tasty vegan lasagna. Even incurable carnivores have been known to lick their lips.

TOP CHOICE **Sangria de Fido** BAR, CAFE
(75 Calle Dulievre, off Hwy 106; 6pm-late Wed-Sat) Wilfrido 'Fido' Aponte became something

of a local legend for his potent sangria – a blend of Bacardi 151 and extraordinarily sweet tropical fruit juice. The drink grew such a cultish following that, according to boozy locals, Bacardi offered a king's ransom for the recipe, which Fido refused. His heirs still produce a few varieties of the 'wine cocktail' and sell them out of a garage in a residential neighborhood of Mayagüez. It's delicious stuff, but the high sugar content ensures a memorable hangover. A small on-site cafe also serves food. To find this place, head east out of town on Hwy 106 and turn left into a residential neighborhood on Arturo Gigante. Make a left on Dulievre.

El Garabato BAR
(102 Calle Post; ⏲1pm-2am) In the same banner-covered building as Red Baron but on the 1st floor, El Garabato is more of a typical pub than a dance hall. Here students swing by for a quick one between classes or stop to play dominoes with the regulars. Happy-hour prices are laughably low – $2 for a mixed drink and $1 for a beer.

☆ Entertainment

The tight knot of here-today-gone-tomorrow student bars at the end of Calle Post has a gregarious nighttime buzz, especially on weekends. It might be a little hard to get a read on, since places fall in and out of favor so quickly, but just follow the crowds. In summer, when the students are out of session, it can be dead as a doornail and you'll have to find one of the many dive bars, where workers from the local Medalla factory seem to volunteer for endless quality-control testing. For entertainment and upscale atmosphere, head to the Mayagüez Resort & Casino.

Red Baron Pub NIGHTCLUB
(102 Calle Post; cover with live band $6; ⏲9pm-2am) This place has been a juggernaut on the Mayagüez party scene since the mid-'80s, and has adapted well with its reliable charms: supercheap drink specials, ear-splitting music and events aimed at college kids looking to blow off some steam. The dance club above El Garabato, Red Baron often has a DJ spinning reggaetón, rap, hip-hop and Spanish rock. Lots of students get tanked-up downstairs and then come up to work the dancefloor and enjoy a bird's-eye view of the city until the small hours. Cash only.

Bleu Bar & Tapas NIGHTCLUB
(63 Calle de Diego; ⏲6pm-late Wed-Sat) Many a blurry weekend evening ends up in the thumping, stainless steel–dressed confines of this large dance club. There's a small cover when notable DJs are on the turntables, and a menu of fried snacks to help you soak up the booze.

Information

General Hospital Dr Ramón Emeterio Betances (☎787-735-8001; Rte 2 Km 157)

Tourist Information Office (cnr Calles McKinley & Peral; ⏲8am-4pm) In the main square; well stocked with local maps and has helpful staff.

Getting There & Away

Air

The Aeropuerto de Mayagüez is about 3 miles north of town, just off Hwy 2. **Cape Air** (☎800-352-0714; www.flycapeair.com) currently has several flights daily to and from San Juan ($81 one-way). **Continental Airlines** (www.continental.com) also flies directly to Mayagüez from several cities in the US.

Car & Motorcycle

Hwy 2, part of the island's nominal ring road, brings you to town from the north or south. While this is a four-lane road, it is plagued by traffic lights. Hwy 105 is the west end of the Ruta

RARE BOOKS

Puerto Rico's lack of bookstores can leave a bookworm starving. Few hotels have book exchanges and there are almost no major booksellers outside of San Juan. The lone exception is a godsend: **Borders Mayagüez** (☎787-833-4333; 975 Hostos; ⏲10am-10pm Mon-Sat, 11am-7pm Sun). This large, bilingual bookstore is situated in the Mayagüez Mall off Hwy 2, just west of town. It carries a complete selection of travel guides, historical nonfiction about the island, and maps. If you're embarking on the long, winding, often beguiling Ruta Panorámica through central Puerto Rico, this is an excellent place to pick up a detailed road map and reading material for the quiet nights in the mountains.

Panorámica, which leads from Mayagüez into the mountains and to Maricao.

Ferry

For years, Mayagüez was Puerto Rico's gateway to the Dominican Republic, at least by sea, but recently the operator, **Ferries del Caribe** (787-832-4800) ended its thrice-weekly runs across the Pasaje de la Mona due to a dispute with the Mayagüez Port Authority about docking fees. Its massive M/S *Caribbean Express* has made a few alternate runs between San Juan and the Dominican Republic (a 16-hour trip), but the suspension of regular service makes it difficult to plan in advance.

At the time of research, one-way tickets from Mayagüez started at $115 for a sleeping chair and $165 for a single cabin, though no scheduled service was planned.

Público

The público terminal is in Barrio Paris, about four blocks north of Plaza Colón. Públicos make the trip to west-coast beach towns such as Aguadilla and Rincón (each about an hour away), and the long trek to San Juan ($20 to $28, plan on four hours at least).

Getting Around

A few taxis usually show up at the airport when the flights arrive from San Juan; if none are there, or if you need to get to the airport, call **White Taxi** (787-832-1115). The one-way fare to town is about $8.

To rent a car you will find vendors at the airport or in Mayagüez Shopping Center, 2.7 miles south of town on Hwy 2, including **Enterprise** (787-805-3722).

Cabo Rojo

Cabo Rojo (Red Cape) is the name of both a small administrative town (10 miles south of Mayagüez and 8 miles west of San Germán) and the wider municipality that surrounds it. To add to the confusion, it is also the name used to describe the rugged coastline that constitutes Puerto Rico's extreme and rarely traveled southwestern tip. Got it?

Characterized by rust-red limestone cliffs that fall precipitously away into the ocean, the region is dominated by the Faro de Cabo Rojo (Red Cape Lighthouse), which sits atop a wild and windswept promontory surrounded by coastal mangroves, dry cacti and crystalline salt pans.

Busy Hwy 2 cuts inland between Mayagüez and Yauco, leaving this rather isolated corner of the island refreshingly untrammeled. There's an extensive patchwork of wildlife refuges here along with a quiet network of country roads that make for excellent cycling. Closer to the lighthouse you'll find trails, extensive salt pans and the bejeweled Playuela Beach. In-the-know locals will tell you in surreptitious whispers that this is one of the island's best stretches of sand.

The comparatively underwhelming Cabo Rojo municipality incorporates the settlements of Boquerón, El Combate, Playa de Joyuda and Cabo Rojo (El Pueblo), which lies 10 miles north of the eponymous cape. There's little to see in the town today aside from a small museum dedicated to local heroes such as Ramón Emeterio Betances, the father of Puerto Rico's independence movement, and Roberto Confresí, a once notorious local pirate. The best selection of accommodations lie in Boquerón and the best restaurants in Joyuda.

Sights & Activities

Corozo Salt Flats, Punta Jagüey & Playa Santa NATURE RESERVE, LIGHTHOUSE

Vast salt flats surround the rocky, dramatic narrow peninsula in the southwestern tip of the island. You'll pass pools of evaporating brine and mounds of salt waiting to be shipped to market alongside the dirt road as you head south toward the headland of Punta Jagüey. This can be a bizarre, picturesque and adventurous place to explore, a place where scrub forest gives way to an elevated headland surrounded by steep limestone cliffs and amazing views of the ocean.

Go south over the bone-rattling PR 301 until it stops, and choose your adventure: either park on the left and follow the trails out to an immaculate crescent beach known as **Playa Santa**, where a protected bay makes excellent swimming for both humans and manatees, or follow trails continuing south to climb the windswept headlands crowned by **Los Morrillos Lighthouse** (10am-6pm Wed-Sun, with seasonal variations). We like starting with Los Morrillos, which has been smartly remodeled with an observation deck looking over the surreal turquoise of Playa Santa's water and across the expanse of Caribbean.

If a volunteer is on hand at the lighthouse, they might offer a casual history of the area, where humans have been gathering salt since AD 700. When the first Spaniards arrived, they quickly took over the evaporation pools used by the Taíno to collect salt and expanded the business, making it a sustaining force in the local economy until efficient sugarcane farming arrived in the 18th century.

For a lonely drive through undeveloped coastal plains or a cycling adventure, approach Cabo Rojo from La Parguera via Hwy 304, Hwy 305 and Hwy 303. Then follow Hwy 301 south until it turns to dirt, where you'll traverse a spit of sand between Bahía Salinas (Salt Bay) and the aptly named Bahía Sucia (Dirty Bay).

FREE Refugio Nacional Cabo Rojo NATURE RESERVE
(Hwy 301 Km 5.1; ⏲8am-4pm Mon-Fri) This refuge is about a mile north of the Hwy 301 turnoff to El Combate. Its visitors center contains displays on local wildlife and wildlife management techniques. Outdoors you will find bird-watching trails among the ruins of an old farmstead in the Valle de Lajas (Lajas Valley). This area around the plains and shores of Cabo Rojo is a major winter ground for migratory ducks, herons and songbirds, and more than 130 bird species have been sighted here. You can arrange guided hikes through the refuge at the Centro Interpretativos Las Salinas de Cabo Rojo.

FREE Centro Interpretativos Las Salinas de Cabo Rojo NATURE CENTER
(Hwy 301 Km 11; ⏲8:30am-4:30pm Wed-Sat, 9:30am-5:30pm Sun) A small center further south along Hwy 301 toward the lighthouse explains the geology and ecology of the salt pans. It is staffed by knowledgeable eco-sensitive guides who give thorough explanations of local flora and fauna. Across the road is a three-story wooden lookout tower that offers a bird's-eye view of the salt pans, a major bird migratory corridor. There is also a small network of hiking and mountain-biking trails here (though no place to rent a bike), which lead to a stretch of very long beach on the island's west side. This is not perfect sand – much of it is dotted with mangrove forest – but it is excellent for private swimming.

Cycling

There are numerous cycling trails around the Cabo Rojo lighthouse and wildlife refuge. The condition of the trails is a bit sketchy – expect to catch a branch or two in the face – but they access some solitary stretches of beach that are blissfully refreshing. Ask at the Centro Interpretativos Las Salinas de Cabo Rojo for details. The nearest bike rental is at the **Wheel Shop** (☎787-255-0095; www.wheelshoppr.com, in Spanish; Hwy 100 Km 5.9) in Cabo Rojo (El Pueblo). Expect to pay from $20 per day.

Sleeping & Eating

TOP CHOICE Parador Bahía Salinas Beach Resort & Spa RESORT $$
(☎787-254-1212; www.bahiasalinas.com; Hwy 301 Km 11.5; r incl breakfast $192; P❄@🏊📶) As if the location wasn't enough – rust-red cliffs, salt flats and an adjacent wildlife refuge – the rooms in this gorgeous, palm-shaded boutique parador have balconies, sleigh beds and tropical flowers. The grounds are immaculate too – drape-covered sun loungers and canopy beds look over an undisturbed stretch of ocean and the infinity pool that frames some of the island's most spectacular sunsets. Added to this is the award-winning Aqua al Cuello Restaurant and an environment around a little harbor where guests enjoy perfect serenity. In contrast to bigger resorts, this low-rise, low-key place threads its luxury quite seamlessly into the surrounding landscape. During high season there can be a three-day minimum stay, though better deals can be had at other times of year.

Villa Vista Puerto ECOLODGE $$
(☎787-255-4144; www.caborojopr.com/vistapuerto.html; off Hwy 307; r from $100 P) This hand-built ecolodge is a unique choice for travelers looking to get off the beaten path and book an environmentally sensitive stay. Set high on a hillside overlooking Puerto Royal and the surrounding jungle, there's a guesthouse for two and a rustic-chic canvas-topped cabana, both of which have hand-built driftwood furniture, a spacious indoor area, a great outdoor cooking area and use of a jungle shower. The place is perfect for couples who want to *really* get away, and though it's isolated from dining and entertainment options, it's in the heart of some stunning nature.

Aqua al Cuello Restaurant CARIBBEAN FUSION $$
(☎787-254-1212; www.bahiasalinas.com; Parador Bahía Salinas Beach Hotel, Hwy 301 Km 11.5; meals $8-28; ⏲lunch & dinner) On a beautiful deck

over the water, this breezy dining destination cooks up equally beautiful food that has bagged Puerto Rico's best Mesón Gastronómico award in recent years. The mahi-mahi in creole sauce is plated with style and backed up by some surprising specials. Ever tried kangaroo?

Information

The Porta del Sol branch of the **Puerto Rico Tourism Company** (PRTC; ☎787-255-1560; www.gotopuertorico.com; La Campana Bldg, Muñoz Rivera; ⏲8am-4pm) is located in Cabo Rojo (El Pueblo).

Getting There & Away

There is no regular público service available to the Punta Jagüey area, which is the most remote corner of the island. Some days there is a morning público that runs between the town of Cabo Rojo (El Pueblo) and the point, but you can't count on it. A more reliable option is to come by rental car or bike (following the route from La Parguera via Hwy 304, Hwy 305 and Hwy 303).

Boquerón

POP 8000

Boquerón is something of the wild child of west coast fishing towns, a place that pulses with the colorful beats of the Caribbean, and colorful characters who wander among wooden-shack restaurants and open-air food stalls. Rightly famous for its sheltered balneario and up-and-coming marina, Boquerón is surrounded by a verdant patchwork of refuges, nature reserves and state forests – a nuance that lends the settlement a refreshing small-town, semirural feel. Down here in the island's extreme southwestern corner, a tangible sense of isolation contrasts with the maelstrom elsewhere and many stressed-out *sanjuaneros* happily tackle the three-hour drive from the capital to bliss out on the region's palm-shaded beaches.

Historically, Boquerón's legacy is possibly even older than Caparra's. Certain scholars have claimed that this is where Columbus first set anchor when he 'discovered' the island of Puerto Rico in 1493. However, no town existed here until the 1700s and the new colony's administrative focus was ultimately centered further to the east.

Boquerón attracts travelers of all types, from wealthy yachters to brightly dressed Rastafarians, and has lately become a favorite destination for islanders. But with few restaurants outside the standard mom-and-pop luncheonettes, the atmosphere remains informal and relaxed. There's a lot of fun to be had at the waterfront, particularly at night when the two main roads are shut down to traffic and people can indulge in the favorite Caribbean pastime of *limin'* – hanging out, chilling, and moving from one bar to another with a drink in hand.

Sights

Refugio de Boquerón WILDLIFE REFUGE

The western part of the Bosque Estatal de Boquerón is protected as the Refugio de Boquerón, a 400-acre patch of mangrove wetlands, about 2 miles south of town between the coast and Hwy 301. This is an excellent area for bird-watching; more than 60 species are commonly sighted. A number of duck species migrate here in the winter, as well as osprey and mangrove canary. An excellent way to see this sanctuary is to rent a kayak (p191) and paddle south across Bahía de Boquerón (Boquerón Bay). The **main office** (☎787-851-7260; Rte 101 Km 1.1, Boquerón; ⏲7:30am-3:30pm) can provide more information and has a 700ft walkway leading into the mangroves. Or stop at Km 1.1 just off Rte 101 and start walking along the trail you see there. Insect repellent is a must-carry in dry season, as is water, and always watch where you put your feet: tiny crabs scuttle about.

Beaches

Just east of town, the **Balneario Boquerón** (parking $5) ranks among the very finest public beach facilities in Puerto Rico; it's a terrific place to swim or spend the day lounging. The mile-long arc of sand gets insanely busy on high-season weekends, but it's still big enough to carve out a relatively quiet space, and the beach area is backed by coconut palms and ample grassy lawns and showers, changing rooms, toilets and picnic tables. Designated as one of only five Blue Flag beaches on the island for its environmental management, water quality and ecology programs, it's popular with Frisbee-throwing families who come here at weekends. To get there, turn left (heading towards town) off Hwy 101 at the Boquerón Beach Hotel and proceed along a small spur road for a quarter-mile. You can also reach the beach on foot from downtown Boquerón; a small footbridge connects at the end of Calle José de Diego.

Playa Buyé is a smaller palm-fringed beach that's about 2½ miles north of town off Hwy 307.

Activities

Diving & Snorkeling

Nearby La Parguera has good diving and snorkeling opportunities as well; see p169.

Mona Aquatics DIVING, SNORKELING
(787-851-2185; www.monaaquatics.com; Calle José de Diego) Next to the *club náutico* (marina), west of the center of town, Mona Aquatics has a 40ft dive boat – *Orca Too* – that takes you on local dives ($105) or longer excursions to Isla Desecheo ($150). Prices include snack, weights, instruction and two dives and get cheaper if you have a group. It also rents out snorkeling gear and occasionally operates boats across the rough passage to Isla Mona.

Kayaking

Along Calle José de Diego, there are a number of vendors renting kayaks and other gear to get in the water. This is a great option if you want to explore the mangroves east of town.

Boquerón Kayak Rental KAYAKING
(787-255-1849; Calle José de Diego) Has pedal boats and surf bikes, as well as kayaks (all from $15 per hour). Boat rides are also available. Cash only.

Sleeping

Unless it's high season, there is likely to be plenty of space in Boquerón. In addition to the accommodations listed below, there are a number of private homes with rooms or apartments to rent. Look for signs nailed to telephone poles along Calle José de Diego.

Centro Vacacional Boquerón CABANAS $
(787-851-1900, reservations 787-622-5200; apt s/d $68/109) Though primarily marketed toward Puerto Rican families, this excellent, enormous government-operated complex is the best of its kind in Puerto Rico, a sprawling village of basic apartments that hold six people and have a bathroom, kitchen, bunk beds and ceiling fans. They come in two classes – cabanas, a basic option with no air-con, and villas, which are more modern and have air-con. An excellent budget option, the spare rooms are no-frills and a bit like summer camp – you even have to provide your own linen. But activity rooms, a convenience store and a first-aid station are on the premises and the beach outside your door is one of the best on the island. The place gets booked a year in advance for summer and holidays, but stands half-empty in low season.

Shamar Bar-Restaurant & Hotel GUESTHOUSE $
(787-851-0542; Calle José de Diego; r $100) Clean, bright and comfy – though not particularly quiet – the upstairs rooms are good crash pads if you want to be in the thick of Boquerón's small but vibrant commercial strip. For history buffs, the Shamar is the oldest commercial building in Boquerón and has been a working bar for more than 50 years. The upstairs rooms facing the water have small balconies.

Adamari's Apartments APARTMENTS $
(787-851-6860; Calle José de Diego; r $70-90; P ❄) Adamari's is the tall building right next to Parador Boquemar, with a launderette out the front. The nine clean efficiency apartments (each with a kitchenette and many with ocean views) are serviceable and good value for the price. They all have cable TV, which is nice, and mattresses covered in some kind of protective plastic, which is not.

A NIGHT AT THE BEACH

Camping at Puerto Rico's beaches is illegal, but some of the large, developed facilities at public beaches around the island, including **Balneario Boquerón**, have government-operated cabanas to rent. These facilities vary in quality – some are little more than cinder-block apartments with a kitchenette and a grill, others are a bit more plush, with balconies and barbecue grills. Still, they make an affordable way to stay on the beach. Here's the catch: since they are mostly for Puerto Rican families, they are poorly marketed to tourists, and guests have to bring their own linen. Contact the Centro Vacacional Boquerón.

Plus, if you like to sleep, this puts you a bit out of earshot from Boquerón's party people.

Parador Boquemar HOTEL $
(787-851-2158; Calle José de Diego; r $85-110;) There's a bit of a rabbit-hutch feel to the 60 generic rooms here, which are piled on top of each other over three crowded stories in a building that has seen better days. That said, because this is Boquerón and because you're essentially 'downtown,' the Boquemar is rather popular. The rooms are clean, but probably about what you might expect from a slightly worn American motel. In common with standard Puerto Rican paradores, there's a pool, an above-average on-site restaurant and friendly, down-to-earth service.

Cofresí Beach Hotel HOTEL $
(787-254-3000; www.cofresibeach.com; 57 Calle Muñoz Rivera; apt $89-219;) For families, this is a nearly uniform recommendation – each unit is fully equipped with a microwave and TV and its location in a residential neighborhood is a bit out of the downtown craziness. There's a limited maid service available by prearrangement, and a view of the bay from the pool.

Wildflowers INN $
(787-851-1793; 13 Calle Muñoz Rivera; r $109-125;) A Victorian-era house in the heart of Boquerón, Wildflowers feels like a misplaced New England B&B. Doubling up as a gallery, the cozy rooms and sleek communal areas display the work of local artists. There's no maid service or breakfast, but economically priced rooms can sleep up to four and there's shared use of a microwave and coffee machine along with private refrigerators. Dark-wood floors and furnishings add a dash of 19th-century romance.

Buýe Beach Resort CABANAS $
(787-255-0358; Hwy 30 Km 4.8; cabins $75;) Located on a popular beach north of town, this clean and simple operation has 16 cinder-block-and-tile cabins on the beach. Each one accommodates three to four people and includes a private bathroom and kitchen. There is a coin laundry here, too.

Boquerón Beach Hotel HOTEL $
(787-851-7110; www.boqueronbeachhotel.com; r $88-149;) At the turnoff for the balneario, this is a clean and efficiently run modern hotel, but beware of the beach tag – it's actually on a busy road.

Eating

The cheapest eats are from the kiosks along Calle José de Diego, where vendors stand proudly beside piles of oysters and clams, which are shucked open, juiced with fresh lemon or hot sauce and slurped down on the spot. There are also numerous vendors serving *pinchos* – chunks of grilled chicken, pork or seafood, sometimes doused with barbecue sauce and sided with bread – between $2 and $4.

La Marea SEAFOOD, CARIBBEAN $
(5 Calle José de Diego; mains $8-15; lunch-10pm) The motley and amiable crew of locals, sunwashed yachters and young Puerto Rican honeymooners nod along to reggae at this house of strong drinks, seafood and Borquerón's finest casual dining. The interior is a classy notch above most of the alfresco dining on the strip, and sidewalk tables are a place to order and watch the action stumble by. The dishes – shrimp-stuffed plantains and cuts of fresh fish – are a good match for the unpretentious elegance. The bar serves labor-intensive mojitos and spot-on piña coladas, while offering the most impressive wine list in town.

Galloway's Bar & Restaurant SEAFOOD $$
(Calle José de Diego; dinner mains $12-24) 'Snowbirds Welcome' reads the sign out the front, but those four-seasoned spring-breakers from Minneapolis you've just spied on the waterfront deck aren't the only birds pecking at the food. Small black-feathered creatures will make a beeline for any spare tasty morsel, so hold on to your seafood crab salad and freshly prepared octopus. Something of a local legend, Galloway's combines great seafood with a picturesque waterfront setting on Boquerón's rustic downtown strip. With lots of space to run around and an unflappable staff, it's terrific for children too.

Pika-Pika MEXICAN $$
(224 Calle Estación; mains $12-24) Although discerning fans of Mexican cuisine might be a bit underwhelmed by the cheese-covered Puerto Rican/Tex Mex fusions, this high-class cantina located on the road in and out of Boquerón's is a place to escape the thumping. It's dimly lit and cool, and patronized by families and groups of friends. Deep-dish burritos and tacos are savory and can be prepared vegetarian-style. The margaritas are lethal!

Entertainment

The minute you hit the ground running in Boquerón you can tell from the shabby-chic bars and relaxed Caribbean ambience that this is a party town.

Shamar Bar-Restaurant & Hotel BAR
(Calle José de Diego) Shirtless dudes knock back beers at the bar, overdriven reggaetón blasts out of the speakers on the sidewalk, and the pool table becomes a psychological battleground; the Shamar is that kind of place – laid-back, cool and friendly on its own terms. The bar gets jammed at happy hour, but the street's a good refuge, as the space out front offers up a nightly show – if the awe-inspiring sunsets don't get you, the wobbly people-watching will. Dress down, polish up on Puerto Rican slang, and try not to look too square when you start moving along to the music. If you need something to soak up the drinks, there's a menu of deep-fried delights. Try the empanadas or the tasty *surullitos* (fried cornmeal and cheese sticks).

Galloways Bar & Restaurant BAR
(Calle José de Diego) All pretense of being a restaurant is dropped by 9pm on weekends, when a fun-loving yuppie crowd shows up for live 1980s and '90s rock. There's also occasional Spanish guitar music.

Getting There & Away

The easiest way to get to Boquerón by público is via the town of Cabo Rojo (El Pueblo). From April to August, it's easy to find one for about $3. From El Pueblo, you can also catch a van to Mayagüez ($5, 40 minutes), Ponce ($9, two hours) or San Germán ($5, 20 minutes).

If you're driving from El Pueblo or Mayagüez, follow Hwy 100 south to Hwy 101 and turn right (west). Driving from San Germán, it's a straight shot west on Hwy 101 south of Lajas.

Playa de Joyuda

Just north of Boquerón and south of Mayagüez, little Joyuda is a dining destination – famous for its string of seafood restaurants and known islandwide as the Milla de Oro del Buen Comer (Gourmet Golden Mile). It might be a bit generous to call these places 'gourmet,' but the seafood can be very fresh, and more than a dozen family-owned establishments line a 3-mile oceanfront stretch of Hwy 102, specializing in oysters, crab and shrimp. Often, you can get a seat right over the water and look down at startlingly large carp who loll up to lazily beg for table scraps.

While Joyuda isn't a beach haven, there are plenty of accommodation options in this ramshackle west coast outpost, and with a couple of decent sailing and dive operators and a nearby nature reserve, there's enough outdoor adventures to work up an appetite for an evening of shellfish. Just offshore, the tiny Isla de Ratones has a white sandy beach and is great for snorkeling.

Sights & Activities

The heart of the 300-acre **Reserva Natural Laguna de Joyuda** is a saltwater lagoon a mile long and a half mile wide, with a depth that rarely exceeds 4ft. The sanctuary is of great importance to waterfowl and other migratory birds that come here to prey on more than 40 species of fish. Humans come here for the same reason.

The reserve is also home to another of Puerto Rico's famous bioluminescent bodies of water, like those in La Parguera and Vieque, but free of commercial tourism. After dark, microorganisms give the dark water a green glow. Travelers with access to a kayak can launch a nighttime exploration of the lagoon; watch for the access road off Hwy 102 near Parador Perichi's.

For trips or tours around the area on a 33ft lobster boat, try **Tourmarine Adventures** (787-375-2625; www.tourmarinepr.com; Rte 102 Km 14.1). If you've got a big enough group (10 or more people), the owner might arrange trips to Isla Mona...if you can get a permit. There are also snorkeling trips offered around the nearby cliffs ($40 without equipment), deep-sea fishing in the Pasaje de la Mona ($400 per half-day charter) and diving off Isla Desecheo ($75 per person). The owner also has a handful of apartments for rent.

Sleeping

There's no luxury here and few good deals, so better sleeping options are on other parts of the west coast. Still, if you find yourself in Joyuda for the evening before a charter, try one of the following.

Parador Joyuda Beach HOTEL $$
(787-851-5650; Hwy 102 Km 11.7; r $70-125; P) Up the road from Parador Perichi's and the Joyuda Plaza, this hotel is actually *on* a narrow strand of beach. It's not exactly

Boquerón, but the snorkeling right offshore is OK, as long as the wind stays southerly. The hotel has a restaurant, a swimming pool and 41 standard rooms with those ubiquitous flowery bedspreads and terra-cotta tiled floors. Arrive expecting a tropical-flavored motel and you shouldn't be disappointed.

Hotel Costa de Oro Inn HOTEL **$**
(787-851-5010; Rte 102 Km 14.7; r $50-85;) A tiny pool and spotless rooms make this little guesthouse the best value within miles. There are no big luxuries on the property, but you'll be very comfortable. There's also a small cafeteria on site where mains come for a $4 bargain.

Joyuda Plaza HOTEL **$**
(787-851-8800; Hwy 102 Km 14.7; r $65-125; P) This 55-room hotel is within walking distance of Joyuda's best food and drink. Despite dark rooms, it boasts serviceable facilities, a pair of pools and a friendly staff.

Parador Perichi's HOTEL **$$**
(787-435-7197; Rte 102 Km 14.3; r $75-139; P) Close to Joyuda Plaza, Perichi's is Joyuda's fanciest place, which isn't saying much. Although it's definitely seen better days, the 41 rooms have air-con and there's a large pool.

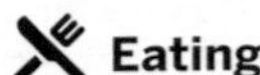

Eating

Joyuda is a great place for a bit of culinary exploration, and it would take weeks of tasting to settle on a favorite. Park your car or bike, stroll up and down the strip a few times and see where your nose leads you. For informal dining, locals swear by El Bohió, Raito and Vista Bahía. Others champion El Gato Negro. You might end up in all or none of these, sampling lobster, *mofongo* (mashed plantains), oysters or crab. Joyuda's restaurants aren't always fancy in terms of decor, but the food is legendary – and for good reason. If you're really short on time try one of these proven favorites.

El Bohió SEAFOOD **$**
(www.restauranteelbohiojoyuda.com, in Spanish; Hwy 102 Km 13.9; dishes $9-21; lunch & dinner Thu-Tue) The best seafood in town is the subject of fierce debate among locals, but this place is a certain contender, with a long list of shellfish and fresh fillets done in a variety of styles and waitstaff offering recommended fresh catches. What really puts El Bohió over the edge is the atmosphere – it's perched on stilts right above the crystal water, enjoying an uninterrupted view of the sea.

Tino's SEAFOOD **$$**
(Hwy 102 Km 13.6; dishes $10-28; lunch & dinner Wed-Sun) If you want a really nice meal – with real silverware and without paper plates that bend under their load – then Tino's is your best bet in Joyuda. It's not got the pretty views, but it does have the tourist office's stamp of approval as a Méson Gastronómico. The special of the house is worth pulling over for – a seafood-piled *mofongo* that comes in two sizes, though the small is still big enough to feed a couple.

Island View SEAFOOD **$**
(Hwy 102 Km 13.7; dishes $7-21; lunch & dinner Thu-Tue) Great views of the few small cays that dot the water off the coast and big steaming dishes of seafood specialties, such as rice and crab, have made Island View very popular.

Getting There & Away

Joyuda isn't on a regular público route, but you can drive here easily enough from either Mayagüez or Cabo Rojo on Rte 102. Alternatively, take a taxi or hire a bike from the Wheel Shop in Cabo Rojo (p189).

El Combate

This gritty seaside settlement wedged incongruously between Boquerón beach and the Cabo Rojo lighthouse is at the end of Hwy 3301, a short spur branching west from Hwy 301. Those with limited time can skip it – it's an untidy sprawl of tawdry guesthouses, backyard trailer-camping sites, beach houses and restaurants, all covered in Bacardi banners. But while the down-at-heel bar scene might be a little on the rough side, the thin 3-mile-long strip of sand that affronts the Pasaje de la Mona is a perennially popular vacation spot for Puerto Rican families and college kids looking for some fun on the weekends.

Named after a 1759 colonial turf war to control the lucrative salt flats to the south, El Combate (The Battle) retains its wayward and embattled image, sprawling at the junction of a couple potholed roads and the sea. Ask around enough and you might run into a couple locals who still pride themselves on being known as Los Mata con Hacha (Those Who Kill with Axes) for their historical penchant to wield sharp weaponry against rivals from the nearby town of Lajas.

Sleeping & Eating

This is a seasonal place, and as such has a handful of basic guesthouses and apartments for rent that open only in summer. You won't find luxury, but visitors here spend little time indoors.

Combate Beach Hotel & Restaurant HOTEL $
(787-254-7053; Hwy 3301 Km 2.7; d/q $90/110; P) A favorite oasis in El Combate, this hotel is right on the beach about a quarter of a mile from all the development in town. The motel-style rooms are simple but clean with private bathrooms. They're also the best rooms you're going to get in town. There's a casual restaurant serving seafood and *comida criolla* and the whole place runs smoothly under the watchful eyes of the proprietors.

Annie's Place BAR $
(Hwy 3301 Km 2.9; mains $5-15) Breeze from the ocean drifts in the open floor plan of Annie's, a bar and restaurant with great *empanadillas* (dough stuffed with meat or fish), lobster soup, fish salad and homemade burgers. Overlooking the long public beach, this has the best atmosphere of El Combate bars, and it gets very popular in the early evening, when young kids on double dates drop by to play billiards and watch the sun set.

Getting There & Away

Públicos run frequently to and from the town of Cabo Rojo (El Pueblo) from April to the end of August ($2). In Cabo Rojo, you can connect to Mayagüez ($4, 30 minutes) or Ponce ($8, two hours).

If you're arriving by car, El Combate is at the bitter end of Hwy 3301. Go west at the turnoff from Hwy 301.

San Germán

POP 35,527

Puerto Rico's second-oldest city (after San Juan), San Germán is also one of its best preserved. Founded in 1511 near present-day Mayagüez on the orders of Juan Ponce de León, the original coastal settlement was moved twice in its early life to escape the unwelcome attention of plundering French corsairs. The current town, which lies about 10 miles inland from the Cabo Rojo coast, was established in 1573 and once administered a municipality that encompassed the whole western half of the island. Downsizing itself over the ensuing four centuries, contemporary San Germán (named for Germaine de Foix, the second wife of Spain's King Ferdinand) is far more unassuming than the colonial capital of yore, although the historical buildings – some of which date from the 17th century – retain a quiet dignity. For those interested in colonial creole architecture, this little town can only be bested by Ponce and Old San Juan.

Despite its rich architectural heritage and lofty listing on the National Register of Historic Places, San Germán is largely ignored by its modern inhabitants and by tourists. As a result, the classic four-square-block colonial center – laid out in an unusual irregular pattern – is a veritable ghost town after dark. The city's one downtown hotel sports cobwebs and few of the numerous historic buildings are open for public viewing, even if the trio of excellent restaurants all might be worth a small detour.

Fortuitously, San Germán's semi-abandonment lends it an air of authenticity. It is also one of the few settlements in Puerto Rico where the central city core hasn't been demeaned by thoughtless development.

Sights

Iglesia de Porta Coeli CHURCH
This small, squat building might not look like much, but it is actually one of the oldest surviving ecclesial buildings in the Americas. Originally constructed between 1606 and 1607 on the orders of Queen Isabella of Spain, it once served as the chapel for a Dominican monastery that stood on this site until the 1860s. Atop a long, steep flight of steps overlooking Plaza Santo Domingo, the current structure dates from 1692. The Porta Coeli ('Heaven's Gate' in Latin) has an interior with ausubo pillars and roof beams, and a ceiling made from palm wood, which is typical of construction in Puerto Rico during the 17th and 18th centuries. Inside, a small **museum** (Plaza Santo Domingo; admission $1; 8:30am-4:30pm Wed-Sun) displays statues of the black Virgin of Montserrat, folksy carvings of Christ imported from the early days of San Juan, choral books dating back 300 years and other curios.

San Germán

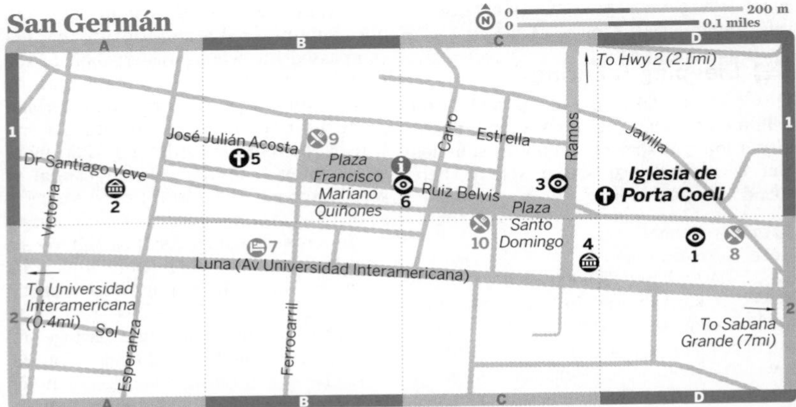

Catedral de San Germán de Auxerre

CHURCH

(⏲8-11:30am & 1-3pm Mon-Fri, 8-11am Sat, mass 7am & 7:30pm Mon-Sat, 7am, 8:30am, 10am & 7:30pm Sun) San Germán's cathedral is named for the town's patron saint and is noticeably grander than the diminutive Porta Coeli. Facing Plaza Francisco Mariano Quiñones, it dates back to 1739, but major restorations and expansions over the years (especially in the 19th century) have created a mélange of architectural styles, including colonial, neoclassical and baroque elements. This is an active parish; if you visit for a Saturday or Sunday service, take note of the crystal chandelier that helps to light the main nave and the trompe l'oeil fresco.

Viejo Alcaldía

HISTORIC BUILDING

The old city hall, which acts as a dividing line between the city's two central squares, is a classic example of a 19th-century colonial municipal building with its stately facade and cool inner courtyard. The building currently serves as a police station and the headquarters for San Germán's rather low-key tourist office (p198).

Universidad Interamericana

UNIVERSITY

(Luna) Founded in 1912, this university is now the largest private facility of its kind in the western hemisphere. The 267-acre campus just west of San Germán is probably the most attractive college setting in Puerto Rico and it draws about 6000 students from all corners of the globe. There are branch campuses in San Juan, Arecibo, Barranquitas, Bayamón, Fajardo, Guayama and Ponce, and tens of thousands of students work toward degrees in both its Spanish and English programs.

San Germán

Top Sights
Iglesia de Porta Coeli ... D1

Sights
1 Casa Acosta y Flores ... D2
2 Casa de Lola Rodríguez de Tío ... A1
3 Casa Morales ... C1
4 Casa Perichi ... C2
5 Catedral de San Germán de Auxerre ... B1
6 Viejo Alcaldía ... C1

Sleeping
7 Parador Oasis ... B2

Eating
8 A 2 Tiempos ... D2
9 Chateaux De Auxerre ... B1
10 Tapas Café ... C2

Casa de Lola Rodríguez de Tió

MUSEUM

(☎787-892-3500; 13 Dr Santiago Veve) Built in 1843 in a neoclassical creole style and said to be an excellent example of local 17th-century domestic architecture, this house is reputedly the most continually occupied residence in the town. Its most famous resident was a 19th-century poet and patriot named Lola Rodríguez de Tió, who was exiled in the 1860s for her revolutionary activities. Lola's mother was a descendant of Ponce de León. The house is supposed to act as a museum, but is often closed. Phone ahead.

The following historic homes are not open to the public, but are beautifully preserved examples of valuable architectural heritage.

Casa Perichi HISTORIC RESIDENCE
(94 Luna) Situated on the main drag, this house is a 1920s estate that's been on the National Register of Historic Places since 1986. Its eclectic architectural style featuring wraparound balconies and decorative wood trim has been called 'Puerto Rican ornamental artisan.'

Casa Morales HISTORIC RESIDENCE
(38 Ramos) This Victorian-era house was built soon after the American occupation in 1898. With its gables, porches and roof turrets, it is redolent of a Queen Anne–style structure from the plush neighborhood of a US mainland city.

Casa Acosta y Flores HISTORIC RESIDENCE
(70 Dr Santiago Veve) Built in a crisscross of styles, this house, dating from 1917, exhibits elements of creole, Victorian and art nouveau architecture and looks like a wedding cake.

Sleeping

Villa del Rey HOTEL $$
(787-642-2627; www.villadelrey.net; Rte 361 Km 0.8; r $85-110; P) Your only alternative to the antiquated Oasis is this family-run country inn just north of town. A sturdy midrange option, it has big rooms, suites with kitchenettes, and an unhurried west-coast ambience (you may have to holler to raise the receptionist). Certainly fit for the kids – though perhaps not for a *rey* (king).

Parador Oasis HOTEL $
(787-892-1175, 800-942-8086; 72 Luna; r $75; P@) If you wanted luxury, you've come to the right place – the catch is you're 20 years too late. Hidden under the cobwebs of the lackluster modern-day Oasis is a once grand dame of Puerto Rican paradores. Today, the place is down on its luck and seemingly bereft of guests, with the air of Miss Havisham's house in Charles Dickens' *Great Expectations*, bearing carpet that is coming up at the seams, and artwork that is downright bizarre. Still, the Italianate pool still glistens invitingly and the staff tries hard to plug the gaps. Framed testimonies on the wall highlight favorable reviews from years past; the most recent dates from 1984.

Eating

TOP CHOICE **A 2 Tiempos** CARIBBEAN FUSION $$
(787-892-9600; www.a2tiempos.com, in Spanish; Dr Santiago Veve 70; mains $10-20; dinner Wed-Sat, lunch & dinner Sun) This intimate destination restaurant, in a warmly finished 1912 creole home, is regarded among Puerto Rican foodies with awed reverence. The atmosphere has the feel of a 19th-century Caribbean parlor, and the artfully presented plates include creative offerings such as the Filete José – a filet mignon encased in

WORTH A TRIP

BOSQUE ESTATAL DE SUSÚA

Juxtaposed between the dry coastal flats and the humid mountain foothills of the Cordillera Central, this foggy forest's diminutive 3300 acres is no Yellowstone, but what it lacks in acres it makes up for in peaceful solitude. Well off the main tourist trails and notoriously difficult to find, Susúa is invariably deserted year-round – save for the odd binocular-wielding ornithologist (the forest boasts 44 species of bird) and tapped-in mountain biker.

To get here, drive east out of Sabana Grande on Rte 368 to Km 2.1. Turn left and keep going until you arrive at the shack for the **Departamento de Recursos Naturales y Ambientales** (DRNA; Department of Natural Resources & Environment; 787-721-5495; 7am-3:30pm Mon-Fri, 9am-5pm Sat & Sun). There's not much in the way of amenities at the entrance – just a few picnic tables, a toilet, a scattering of fire pits and some campsites (though you'd be wise to check on availability/hours before arrival; camping per tent costs $6).

The hiking trails leaving from the entrance are typical of most on the island: poorly marked and somewhat hard to find. Rangers might help with a hand-drawn, worryingly simplistic map. For mountain bikers, there's a very challenging 6.3-mile trail that incorporates river crossings and a technical ravine reverently called La Pared (Wall). The nearest bike rental is in the town of Cabo Rojo (see p189).

a flaky, lobster-filled pastry. Unpretentious and memorable, it's among the very best small dining rooms on the island, especially when there's a live jazz combo in the corner.

Chateaux De Auxerre FRENCH CARIBBEAN **$$$**
(16 Estrella; ⌚dinner Wed-Fri, lunch & dinner Sat & Sun) Late brunch in the courtyard of this centrally located, recently remodeled 19th-century town house rewards a morning of exploring the west coast. The morning dishes are exceptional – strong coffee and eggs with fresh, seasonal vegetables – and in the evening the menu assumes a French classicism. Watchful servers and linen table dressings also elevate this to among the most upmarket dining experiences in the region.

Tapas Café TAPAS **$**
(48 Dr Santiago Veve; tapas $4-11; ⌚dinner Wed-Fri, lunch & dinner Sat & Sun) The food and atmosphere are both great at this cafe, which seems like it'd fit in among the Triana district of Seville. Flamenco drifts under the high ceilings, and bullfighting paraphernalia adorn the walls, while the kitchen turns out delicious fare such as *albondigas* (meatballs), *queso manchego* (Manchego cheese), *tortilla española* (Spanish omelette) and *jamon serrano* (cured Spanish ham).

Information

The government recently changed the name of Calle Luna to Av Universidad Interamericana; nobody uses it, however, so addresses in this book still refer to Calle Luna.

San Germán Tourism Office (Viejo Alcaldía, Plaza Francisco Mariano Quiñones; ⌚8am-4pm) This office also runs the San Germán trolley bus around the town's main sights, but schedules are erratic.

Getting There & Away

San Germán enjoys frequent público services to and from Ponce ($7, 90 minutes) or Mayagüez ($5, 45 minutes). It lies just south of the Hwy 2 expressway, so if you are driving here from the west coast, follow Hwy 102 from the town of Cabo Rojo (El Pueblo).

Isla Mona

Few wilderness adventures in the Caribbean can compare with a trip to Isla Mona, a wild, deserted speck in the ocean some 50 miles to the west of the main island. And although few people ever visit Mona, the 14,000-acre island looms large in the imagination. It's a place where the beauty of limestone caves and turquoise water coexists with the dangers of a rugged environment. Then there's the island's long, romantic history, told in Taíno petroglyphs and swashbuckling stories about sunken galleons, treasures of gold and skeletons of 18th-century pirates.

A nature reserve since 1919 and uninhabited for more than 50 years, Mona is very difficult to visit. Concerns about safety caused the DRNA to close the island to visitors for months, so if you are even considering a trip here, start your inquiries as soon as possible – it can take about four months of planning to secure permits and transportation.

While the DRNA provides toilets and saltwater showers at Playa Sardinera, Mona is a backcountry camping experience. You're required to pack everything in and out – including bringing your own water and hauling out your garbage. The rangers and police detachment (in an occasionally manned station at Playa Sardinera) can provide basic first aid and have radio contact with the main island, but beyond that, you are on your own in a beautiful – if hostile – environment.

History

Mona was first settled about 1000 years ago as pre-Columbian peoples migrated north through the Caribbean archipelago. Petroglyphs in some caves and the subtle ruins of *bateyes* (Taíno ball courts) are the chief remnants of the Indian presence. Columbus stopped here on September 24, 1494 (at the end of his second New World voyage) and remained several days to gather water and provisions for the long trip back to Spain. When the Spaniards returned in 1508, with an expedition led by Juan Ponce de León, Mona had become a sanctuary for Taíno people escaping slavery.

The Spanish eventually claimed the island to guard the ship traffic to and from the gold coast of the Americas, but abandoned it after two decades when they couldn't afford it. Uninhabited and defenseless, Mona was a haven for pirates by the late 1500s, when French corsairs used it as staging ground for their attacks on the Spanish colony at San Germán.

During the next 300 years, Mona became the refuge of a host of privateers, including Sirs Walter Raleigh and Francis Drake, John Hawkins, William Kidd and the Puerto Rican buccaneer Roberto Cofresí.

In the early 20th century it was mined for bat guano (exceptional agricultural fertilizer!) and made headlines when a German submarine fired on the island, thinking it was a post for the Allies, in the early 1940s.

Following Civilian Conservation Corps (CCC) activities on the island, the comings and goings of treasure hunters, WWII and a scam to turn Mona into an airbase, the government of Puerto Rico slowly began to take seriously its duty to protect the island as a nature preserve, and eventually prohibited development. Finally, after almost 500 years of human interference, Mona returned to her wild state.

Wildlife

Although the dry, semitropical climate might suggest an area with little variety in vegetation, Mona claims about 600 species of plants and 50 species of trees. Four of the plant species are endemic, unknown to the rest of the world. If you are exploring here, wear protective clothing. Mona has four types of venomous trees and bushes: indio, papayo, manzanillo and carrasco. Almost 3000 acres of the island consist of cactus thickets, while 11,000 acres are in scrub forest.

The biggest stars of the island's wildlife menagerie are the giant rock iguanas, *Cyclura stejnegeri* (similar to the iguanas at Anagada in the British Virgin Islands and Allan's Cays in the Bahamas), ferocious little buggers with sharp teeth and claws, and which charge when threatened.

Between May and October, Isla Mona's beaches are important nesting grounds for a number of species of marine turtle, including the chronically endangered Carey turtle.

Sights & Activities

Isla Mona is almost a perfect oval, measuring about 7 miles from east to west and 4 miles from north to south. Most of the island's coastline is made up of rough, rocky cliffs, especially along the north side. The south side, meanwhile, has a number of narrow beaches that fringe the highlands. The most approachable of these beaches is **Playa Sardinera**, where you will find toilets, showers and the concrete living quarters of the rangers and police detachment. The airfield, lying about a mile further east, has been closed since 1999.

The island's terrain consists of a broad rim of coastal plain that rises gently to a central mesa. Because the land is flat and overgrown, it is difficult to find landmarks on the horizon. More than a few people have gotten lost here – including the pirate William Kidd and a boy scout who died from dehydration and exhaustion in 2001. The basic photocopied map you get from the DRNA in San Juan is useless; the US Geological Survey (USGS), an agency of the US Department of the Interior, publishes a better map ($8).

You will find spectacular 150ft visibility (or better) for **diving** in the waters around the island. There are excellent barrier and fringe-reef dives filled with lagoons and ruts on the south side of the island. Divers particularly enjoy the sharp drop-off along one reef that creates an overhanging wall; some fascinating creatures come to drift in its cool shadow.

Aside from diving, the only thing to do here is geek out on the nature.

Tours

Acampa Nature Adventure ORGANIZED TOUR
(787-706-0695; www.acampapr.com) Organizes four-day trips of the island with guided hikes; billed as 'roughing it with all the comforts.'

Adventures Tourmarine BOAT CHARTER
(787-375-2625; www.tourmarinepr.com; Rte 102 Km 14.1, Playa de Joyuda) The esteemed Captain Hernández is based in Joyuda in Cabo Rojo and is an old Mona hand; call for prices and availability.

Mona Aquatics GUIDED DIVE TRIPS
(787-851-2185; Calle José de Diego; www.monaaquatics.com) Can arrange custom trips to the island…for the right price.

Getting There & Away

The only way to get to Isla Mona is by boat, and it's difficult unless you are a part of an organized trip. It is also extremely expensive; about $800 each for groups of 10 people. If you are prone to seasickness, beware: the Pasaje de la Mona makes for a rough crossing.

North Coast

POP 1 MILLION

Includes »

Best Places to Eat

» Platano Loco (p217)

» One Ten Thai (p217)

» Heladería de Lares (p211)

» Villa Dorada d'Alberto Seafood Restaurant (p203)

» Eclipse (p214)

Best Places to Stay

» Casa Grande Mountain Retreat (p208)

» Punta Maracayo Hotel (p208)

» TJ Ranch (p208)

» Villa Montaña (p212)

» Courtyard by Marriot Aguadilla (p216)

Why Go?

Wedged between the vine-tangled crags of karst country and the spectacular fury of the Atlantic Coast, this region's charms await those who explore winding, tree-lined byways. It's a nearby escape from the island's overdevelopment, a place to hike through caves, patronize roadside food trucks and comb the beach to see what the tides have brought in. The sights here have neither the untouched exotic natural spectacle of El Yunque nor the rustic allure of the central mountains, but this quick escape has more than enough DIY adventures for travelers with no fixed timetable.

Learn to surf in less-crowded waters, gape at the world's largest radio telescope or ride some of Puerto Rico's most bicycle-friendly roads: the north coast has loads of opportunity to see another side of Puerto Rico – and still make your dinner reservation in San Juan.

When to Go

Outside of the island's rainy months (late summer to early fall), the north coast is generally sunny, although big Atlantic storms can come barreling out of nowhere to whip the waves into a white-capped frenzy. Inland, the humidity increases, but on the shore the 80°F temperatures aren't at all oppressive. Since there's only a difference of a few degrees between the coldest month, January, and the warmest, August, the region offers consistently sunny, breezy days year-round. Crowds are generally biggest during winter (December through March) on the US mainland.

North Coast Highlights

1 Surf the storied waves at **Playa Jobos** (p212)

2 Put a mountain-sized ear to the heavens at **Observatorio de Arecibo** (p206)

3 Trot along in the sand and snorkel with **Tropical Trail Rides** (p212)

4 Cruise on a bicycle past the surfers carving the waves at **Isabela** (p211)

5 Picnic near the most spectacularly rough north coast beach, **Playa Mar Chiquita** (p204)

6 Embark on a DIY cave hike at the lonely **Bosque Estatal de Guajataca** (p210)

7 Sink into a decadent fried plantain and pork sandwich at **Platano Loco** in Aguadilla (p217)

History

The north coast contains one of the island's largest and oldest Native American ceremonial sites near Utuado, an archaeological find that provides dramatic proof that a well-organized Taíno culture thrived on the island before the arrival of the Spanish. Though Arecibo is the third-oldest city on the island, there is little of historical note remaining on the north coast outside of a couple of picturesque Spanish-colonial lighthouses. The 20th century saw a burgeoning of San Juan's suburbs westward into satellite towns such as Vega Alta and Manatí. At the same time a concerted effort has been made to protect karst country through tree-planting projects and the formation of half a dozen forest reserves in the 1940s.

Territorial Parks & Reserves

The north coast is dotted with small karst-country parks and reserves, although they're not nearly as well equipped (or as well trodden) as El Yunque. From east to west, there's the diminutive 1000-acre Bosque Estatal de Vega and the equally tiny Bosque Estatal de Cambalache. Around Arecibo the heavily populated San Juan suburbs give way to larger reserves such as the 5000-acre Bosque Estatal de Río Abajo, which has better-maintained trails and a wider range of facilities, although even this pales in comparison to the Parque de las Cavernas de Río Camuy, one of Puerto Rico's most oft-visited tourist attractions. Nestled in the northwest, the Bosque Estatal de Guajataca has caves, *mogotes* (hillocks) and plenty of signposted trails.

ℹ Getting There & Around

Aguadilla has an international airport that is widely used by vacationers heading for the west coast beaches and scientists keen to study the stars at the Observatorio de Arecibo. Públicos run between the smaller coastal towns and from San Juan out to the main population centers along Hwy 2. Renting a car is probably the most popular option for getting around. The Isabela region is good for cycling.

Dorado

POP 35,000

For those who love golf, Dorado is pure gold, legendary for its exceptional courses. With over 35,000 inhabitants, it boasts five championship-standard golf courses that are an international draw. If you're not interested in an amble down the fairways, several stunning local beaches offer a welcome break from the clubhouse banter. If you're only interested in beaches, bypass Dorado for locales further west.

Founded in 1842, Dorado first became a resort town in the early 1900s when the Rockefeller family started building a Caribbean Shangri-la. The venture went public in 1958 when Laurence Rockefeller, the well-known philanthropist and conservationist, opened up the region's first hotel, the Dorado Beach, a pioneering ecoresort where no building was taller than the surrounding palm trees. And though there have been some formidable resorts here over the years, today many golfers opt for time-shares and condo rentals, robbing the hotel scene of its once-ritzy image.

Away from the resorts, Dorado has a timeless public beach in town and an even prettier free option a few miles to the west at Cerro Gordo. Back in town, the original 19th-century settlement, with its teardrop-shaped lights rimming the main plaza, is a pleasant spot to while away a lazy afternoon.

El Dorado's urban core is spread out, and the route between PR 22 and the coast is almost entirely developed. Rte 165 turns into Calle Méndez Vigo, the town's central road.

Sights

Museums

Dorado has a trio of small museums, none of which is too remarkable, but a decent

NORTH COAST GRAND SLAM

Despite the precipitous terrain, the north coast showcases some of Puerto Rico's biggest outdoor attractions, many of which can be tackled in an ambitious day trip from San Juan. A 'grand tour' for weekend warriors includes the Río Camuy caves, the Observatorio de Arecibo (the largest radio telescope in the world) and the Parque Ceremonial Indígena Caguana – all must-sees on any itinerary and all consequently crawling with day-trippers. For an alternative escape, forge south into the mountain foothills around Río Abajo, where placid lakes and out-of-the-way retreats make a tranquil respite from the island's congestion.

breather between golf rounds. The **Museo y Centro Cultural Casa del Rey** (Calle Méndez Vigo) is an old Spanish garrison that displays antique furniture; the **Museo del Plata** (Industria; ⌚8am-4pm Mon-Sat) showcases local art, sculpture and paintings; and the **Museo de Arte e Historia de Dorado** (cnr Calles Méndez Vigo & Juan Francisco; ⌚8am-3:30pm Mon-Sat) gives you the rundown on local history and archaeology. Admissions are free.

Activities

Golf

Look no further. With expertly groomed holes, impeccably maintained greens and gentle Atlantic breezes, Dorado has the best golf courses in the Caribbean, period. There are five 18-hole courses here and all remain open despite the changes to the hotel which used to administrate them. Four of the most famous courses are now under the umbrella of the **Dorado Beach Club** (☎626-1001; www.doradobeachclubs.com), an upscale vacation facility housed partially in a former Hyatt. The famed **East Course** is the green jewel – Jack Nicklaus ranked its 540yd 4th hole, a double dogleg with a pair of ponds and amazing views, among the world's best. It's also listed among the planet's finest golf courses by *Golf Digest*. Next door lies the 6975yd **West Course**, while across the road you'll find the **Pineapple** and **Sugarcane** courses at the Plantation Club. Booking tee time at any of these can be done through the **Plantation Club Pro Shop** (☎626-1010; www.doradobeachclubs.com) or through its website. Dorado's fifth and newest course is the Chi Chi Rodríguez–designed **Dorado El Mar** (☎796-3070) at the Embassy Suites. Greens fees at these courses range from $100 to $150 for guests and $130 to $190 for nonguests depending on tee times.

Beaches

Although nobody is advertising it, there is, in fact, a public beach in Dorado where you can swim. **Balneario Manuel Morales** (parking $3) is at the end of Rte 697. But it's a rather boring bit of sand surrounded by rocky outcrops and marred by litter. For a far better experience try Playa de Cerro Gordo, several miles to the west.

You can also get to nearby Toa Alta's beach, **Punta Salinas**, about 20 minutes east of Dorado on Rte 165. It's got food kiosks, lifeguards, restrooms and basketball courts.

Sleeping & Eating

Dorado's guests mostly stay in time-shares and eat at the American fast-food restaurants lining the main roads. If you're here to golf and have a taste for something more adventurous, try the area by the public beach, where open-air snack bars sell lots of deep-fried delights and cold beer.

Embassy Suites Dorado del Mar Beach & Golf RESORT **$$**
(☎796-6125; www.embassysuitesdorado.com; 201 Dorado del Mar Blvd; r $150-300; P ❄ @ ≈ ☒) Dorado's newest resort has taken center stage since the gargantuan golf hotels have transformed into time-shares. Close to town amid a phalanx of gated communities, it has a Chi Chi Rodríguez–designed course, a business center, a gym, tennis courts and specialty restaurants. The open-plan lobby is a fountain-filled state-of-the-art extravaganza where smooth-talking salespeople in Hawaiian shirts leap out from behind pillars and try to sell you time-shares. If you can survive this relatively innocuous form of initiation, you could be in for a ball.

Villa Dorada d'Alberto Seafood Restaurant SEAFOOD **$$**
(99 Calle E; dishes $12-25; ⌚lunch & dinner) With gentlemanly waiters in black tie and linen napkins, this is Dorado's classiest joint, serving seafood platters to a soundtrack of schmaltzy elevator music. On the weekends it's a scene as tables of locals buzz with date night, and remains one of the only places around that draws vacationers out of their all-inclusive slumber. Afterwards you can wander next door to Katrina or out to the public beach, where romantic guitars play Puerto Rican and Cuban classics.

El Ladrillo SEAFOOD **$$**
(☎796-2120; www.elladrillorestaurant.com; 334 Calle Méndez Vigo; dishes $15-35) El Ladrillo has been a culinary anchor of downtown Dorado for decades; it exudes old-world charm, with dark wood, exposed brick and thick steaks. Naturally, it serves seafood as well; everything from octopus salad to lobster *asopao* (an island specialty, a delicious thick stew). It also functions as a mini art gallery; the walls are crowded with colorful paintings from locals.

La Terraza SEAFOOD **$$**
(cnr PR 693 & 697; dishes $10-40; ⌚dinner) The atmosphere at this terraced roadside restaurant is a bit less buttoned-up than Dorado's

DON'T MISS

PLAYA MAR CHIQUITA

With foaming, furious waves, bizarre rock formations and a protected wading pool, Playa Mar Chiquita is the most spectacular beach on this coast.

other options, and the surf-and-turf menu is the best of the cluster of restaurants at the junction. It serves a mean paella, and the 2nd-floor rooftop terrace offers distant views of the sea. Expect occasional live salsa music – although it's usually pop rock from Hollywood soundtracks.

Getting There & Away

It is easy to get a público to and from Río Piedras in San Juan (40 minutes) or the ferry terminal in Cataño (about $4; 20 minutes).

Manatí & Around

POP 16,000

Modern Manatí, which was named for the endangered manatee (sea cow) that once prospered in these waters, is an industrial hub for workers in local pharmaceutical factories and a nearby pineapple-canning plant. But skirt the industrial eyesores and you'll uncover some little-heralded beaches along with two inland forest reserves among the sinkholes and limestone *mogotes* of karst country.

Manatí sprawls between the two east-west island thoroughfares of Hwy 2 and Expressway 22 (a toll road). The beaches and Laguna Tortuguero lie on a thin coastal strip to the north, while the Bosque Estatal de Vega lies just south of the main highways, approximately 6 miles to the east. The Bosque Estatal de Cambalache is situated 5 miles west of Manatí, a mile or so north of Expressway 22.

Sights & Activities

Laguna Tortuguero LAGOON

(☎844-2587; ⌚8am-4pm Wed-Fri, 6am-6pm Sat & Sun) This lagoon is the only natural lake in Puerto Rico, making its protection extra precious. It is also one of the most ecologically diverse spots on the island, listing 717 species of plant and 23 different types of fish. Hiking around this pretty spot yields ocean views, and you can also fish and kayak in the lake – though you'll have to bring your own equipment. Ask the rangers on duty about the trails, though they're pretty obvious. Some locals use them for jogging. One of the lake's more surprising problems is a caiman infestation. In the 1990s there was a craze to buy striped South American caimans. Locals soon discovered they don't make good pets. Hundreds were ditched in the lagoon, with unfortunate results for the ecosystem. Rangers have an extermination program to get the population under control. In theory, caimans only hunt at night, but be alert for them. To get to Tortuguero from Hwy 22, take Exit 41, take a right on Hwy 2, then left on Rte 687 until you see a big sign for the lagoon on your left.

Bosque Estatal de Cambalache NATURE RESERVE

Cambalache covers an area of just 1000 acres, making it smaller than a lot of Puerto Rican resort hotels. The entrance to this compact, out-of-the-way forest reserve lies west of Barceloneta, in front of – wait for it – a Job Corps facility. Despite this rather inauspicious introduction, the forest is ecologically varied and characterized by distinctive karstic formations; countless *mogotes* pop straight up from the landscape to heights of 160ft. Its many caves provide homes for fruit bats, which often swarm like bees into the evening sky.

The forest has a picnic area, 8 miles of hiking trails, two designated trails for mountain bikes (though they're often washed out), one that is wheelchair-accessible, and two camping areas. Note that a permit is required for cycling, but on our last visit there was no one checking for them and no way to obtain them in advance, except for calling the Departamento de Recursos Naturales y Ambientales (p278) in San Juan in advance. Basic on-the-ground information can be obtained at the **ranger station** (☎878-7279; Hwy 682 Km 6.6; ⌚7:30am-4pm) to the right of the entrance gate. Since the forest only enjoys a couple of thousand visitors in any given year, the ranger should be very pleased to see you, if he's there at all.

Beaches

An anomaly among Puerto Rican beaches, **Playa Mar Chiquita** isn't alongside a main thoroughfare, has no long strand and isn't good for swimming and surfing. Still, the pure drama of this place makes it a favorite beach on the island. Here, two goliath coral formations protect a small, shallow cove and tidal pools from the raging crash of the Atlantic, which sprays foam in unpredictable bursts. In the aftermath, the texture of the coral rushes with a network of tiny waterfalls into the protected tidal pools. The protected cove can be calm enough to wade or snorkel at times, but this is the kind of beach best for just standing in awe of nature, chilling in the small sandy area with a book or picnicking alongside Puerto Rican families.

There's a hardly visible sign to the beach off Hwy 685, about 2 miles north of Manatí and just beyond the entrance to the town of Boquillas. If you miss the sign, go north on Hwy 648 (about a mile east of Boquillas). This road takes you over a steep hill to the beach, which lies at the bottom of an escarpment where the plateau of the coastal plain has been hollowed out into caves.

As you continue east on the seaside road (which has now become Hwy 686), you'll pass through a coastal forest. When the road creeps back to the edge of the coast, the long strand of **Playa Tortuguero** will be on the left. A couple of miles further east is a normal balneario (public beach), **Playa Puerto Nuevo** – a narrow crescent of sand sheltered by a broad headland to the east and surrounded by clusters of beach homes.

If this place seems too tame for you, head east from here on Hwy 692, a road that comes to a halt in a mile or so at the spot where the Río Cibuco joins the sea. The beach along this road is exposed and punctuated with reefs and rocks. To the south lie cow pastures and savannas. This beach is known variously as **Playa de Vega Baja** and **La Costa Roja**. Strong riptides make it dangerous for swimming, but the surfing can be excellent and the peace you find sitting here under a coconut palm may be as good as it gets in Puerto Rico.

After a long detour inland (to clear the swampy mouth of the Río Cibuco), the network of coastal roads takes you to one more surprising beach as you head east. **Playa de Cerro Gordo** (parking $3) lies at the end of Hwy 690. This was once the north coast's best-kept secret, but word is definitely out; the government just pumped several million dollars into creating restrooms, showers, fire pits and other beach necessities to put Cerro Gordo on the tourist map – and the additions have improved what was already a first-rate area. Camping is possible here.

DON'T FORGET THE QUARTERS

If you're making the day trip across the north coast, don't forget to bring enough change for the tolls…in cash! The total one-way trip across PR 22 is $3.75, with a toll increase due in the near future. If you get caught without cash, you'll have to pull over, complete a pile of paperwork and find another toll booth to pay later – a doubly unpleasant detour. Those with exact change get the fast lane, marked 'Autos Cambio Exacto Con Monedas.'

Sleeping & Eating

Camping in this area, like much of the rest of the island, is not an easy option, due to unmanned ranger stations, conflicting information and erratic office hours. With persistence, the following are options.

Bosque Estatal de Cambalache PUBLIC CAMPGROUND $
(campsites per person $6) To camp in karst country at this forest, you need to make reservations. There are two campsites: La Boba holds four tents and La Rosa holds eight. A free permit is required; contact the DRNA in San Juan.

Playa de Cerro Gordo PUBLIC CAMPGROUND $
(☎883-2730; campsites $13; ⏱beach 8am-6pm) There's camping available on this popular beach west of Dorado. Lifeguards are present daily, and the food kiosks sell the usual fried finger foods that you can eat at pine picnic tables. If you're camping in the summer call ahead for a reservation and don't expect privacy. Parking costs $3.

Getting There & Away

While you can get to and from Manatí by público (about 45 minutes from San Juan), you'll need wheels to avoid being stuck in the undesirable town with no way of getting around the sights. By car, Manatí can be reached from the east or west via Hwy 2, or by taking Hwy 149 south from Hwy 22.

Arecibo & Around

POP 101,000

As you approach Arecibo in the crawl of traffic, it's hard to imagine that this sprawling modern municipality of nearly 101,000

SKIP THE CLIMB?

It's quite a hike up the trail to the Observatorio de Areciba, but worth it. Those having trouble making the steep ascent by foot can ask rangers for a ride in a shuttle.

people is Puerto Rico's third-oldest city, after San Juan and San Germán. Founded in 1556, the original town was named after an esteemed *cacique* (Taíno chief) and gained notoriety in 1702 when Spanish captain Antonio Correa thwarted a full-scale British invasion off the coast. Little of historical note remains in the present-day city, save a restored cathedral and Spanish-colonial lighthouse in a campy amusement park. Veer further inland and the view gets a lot more interesting.

Arecibo's greatest claim to fame is the world's largest and most sensitive radio telescope, the Observatorio de Arecibo, several miles up the hills to the south, in the heart of karst country. Harboring a fascinating museum and a view worthy of a futuristic James Bond film set, the observatory is open for public viewing and reigns as one of the island's most rewarding must-sees. Back on the coast you can pass a short afternoon at the lighthouse and its surrounding historical park or saunter off in search of ancient Taíno petroglyphs in one of the north coast's many karstic caves.

The popular Hatillo Mask Festival, held on December 28, is one of Puerto Rico's most symbolic ceremonies whose innovative masks and costumes adorn the front of numerous books, postcards and tourist literature.

Sights & Activities

TOP CHOICE Observatorio de Arecibo RADIO TELESCOPE

(☎878-2612; www.naic.edu; adult/child/senior $6/4/4; ⏰9am-4pm Dec 15-Jan 15 & Jun 1-Jul 31, 9am-4pm Wed-Sun off season) The Puerto Ricans reverently refer to it as 'El Radar.' To everyone else it is simply the largest radio telescope in the world. Resembling an extraterrestrial spaceship grounded in the middle of karst country, the Arecibo Observatory looks like something out of a James Bond movie – probably because it is (007 aficionados will recognize the saucer-shaped dish and craning antennae from the 1995 film *Goldeneye*).

The 20-acre dish, operated in conjunction with Cornell University, is set in a sinkhole among clusters of haystack-shaped *mogotes,* like earth's ear into outer space. Supported by 50-story cables weighing more than 600 tons, the telescope is involved in the SETI (Search for Extraterrestrial Intelligence) program and used by on-site scientists to prove the existence of pulsars and quasars, the so-called 'music of the stars.' Past work has included the observation of the planet Mercury, the first asteroid image and the discovery of the first extra-solar planets.

Top scientists from around the world perform ongoing research at Arecibo, but an informative visitor center with interpretative displays and an explanatory film provide the public with a fascinating glimpse of how the facility works. There's also a well-positioned viewing platform offering you the archetypal 007 vista.

To get to the observatory follow Hwys 635 and 625 off Hwy 129. It's only 9 miles south of the town of Arecibo as the crow flies, but the rollercoaster ride through karst country will make it seem more like 90.

Parque de las Cavernas del Río Camuy CAVES

(☎898-3100; Hwy 129 Km 18.9; adult/child $12/6, parking $2; ⏰8am-5pm Wed-Sun & holidays) The beguiling networks of stalagmite ornamented caves at Río Camuy is the third-largest network of its kind in the world, formed by the soft karstic limestone that shapes the hills on this remarkable part of the island. This park is *big* – spread over 10 miles with multiple entrances. A visit here can be an unearthly, slightly creepy diversion from the typically sunny shore, if you have the time and patience to put up with the crowds.

Over the years, the caves have been shelters for indigenous people, home to millions of bats that help keep the island's insect population under control, and a source of fertilizer. But no modern explorers went to the trouble of making a thorough investigation of the caves until 1958. Shortly after, the government purchased 300 acres of land around the caves to establish a nature preserve and the Speleological Society of Puerto Rico mapped them. In 1986 the attraction opened as a tourist facility.

Call the park for local conditions (too much rain causes closures), and arrive before 10:30am to avoid crowds or a long wait. Don't expect much contact with the spectacular underground formations either. Your visit begins with a film at the visitor center and a trolleybus through the jungle into a 200ft-deep sinkhole to **Cueva Clara de Empalme** (Clear Cave Junction), where you take a 45-minute guided walk. Here you walk past enormous stalagmites and stalactites, and into rooms littered with boulders. At one point the ceiling of the cavern reaches a height of 170ft; at another you can see the Río Camuy rushing through a tunnel.

After leaving the cave from a side passage, you take another tram to the **Tres Pueblos sinkhole**, which measures 650ft across and drops 400ft. Forty-two petroglyphs that you can now inspect have been found in **Cueva Catedral** (Cathedral Cave).

The last tour leaves at 2pm if you want to see all three areas, or at 3:45pm if you want to see just one sinkhole. All told, the fun of the visit here depends on the size of the crowds, your patience and the tour guide (some of them seem bored stiff).

You can get off the beaten path underground by joining **Expediciones Palenque** (☎823-4354, 306-4382; www.expedicionespalenque.com; full-day $90), which offers daylong caving trips, and a host of other cool trips hiking, rappelling and body rafting the Río Camuy.

Parque Ceremonial Indígena Caguana — PARK

(☎894-7325; adult/child $2/1; ⏲9am-4pm) Like the archaeological site at Tibes near Ponce, this Taíno ceremonial site, off Hwy 111, has no monumental ruins; the power of the place comes from the natural botanical garden of ceiba, ausubo and tabonuco trees that shade the midslopes of the central mountains. There are 10 ceremonial *bateyes* (Taíno ball courts), dating back about 800 years to original Taíno inhabitants. Stone monoliths line many of the courts; some weigh up to a ton, but most are small. Quite a few have petroglyphs, such as the famous Mujer de Caguana, who squats in the pose of the traditional 'earth mother' fertility symbol.

Caguana is a place to walk and reflect, not to be thrilled by exhibits or enormous ancient monuments. Nevertheless, there is a small **museum** with artifacts and skeletons on the property, and a gift shop that sells inexpensive but attractive reproductions of Taíno charms, including the statues called *cemíes*.

Lagos Dos Bocas & Caonillas — LAKES

These two lakes – each more than 2 miles long – fill a deeply cleft valley at a point where karst country gives way to the jagged spine of the central mountains, east of Hwy 10 and north of Utuado. The lakes are the principal reservoirs for the north-central part of the island, and they can provide a tranquil escape if the beaches are too congested.

In calm weather, you can ride Dos Bocas' free launch, which serves as a taxi service to the residents in the area. The boat landing is on Hwy 123, on the west side of the lake. Boats leave almost every hour. You can disembark at restaurants around the lake or just sit back and enjoy the two-hour ride. You can similarly pick up the boat launch on the other side of the lake at the end of Hwy 612, about 3 miles beyond the Casa Grande Mountain Retreat. Along the shore there are several *comida criolla* (traditional Puerto Rican cuisine) restaurants, some of which hire kayaks.

Bosque Estatal de Río Abajo — STATE FOREST

This 5000-acre forest has a **visitors center** (☎880-6557; ⏲8am-4pm) just off Hwy 621, halfway between Utuado and Arecibo, and some of the most rugged terrain on the island. Situated in the heart of karst country, the forest's altitude jumps between 700ft and 1400ft above sea level. The steep sides of the *mogotes* are overrun with vines, and the forest is a jungle of tropical hardwoods, including Honduran mahogany and Asian teaks, and huge clumps of bamboo.

The remains of the lumber roads cut by the loggers and the Civilian Conservation Corps (CCC) workers have now become trails. The two best are the **Visitors Center Trail** (a 500m-long stroll with three gazebos set up along the way) and **Las Perdices** (about 2km long). Others are often poorly maintained or affected by recent weather conditions. Enquire at the visitor center and you should be able to piece together a more substantial hike through karst country. The Visitors Center Trail has water, interpretive displays and occasional wildlife lectures.

To reach Bosque Estatal de Río Abajo from San Juan, take Hwy 22 west toward Arecibo. Turn south on Rte 10 toward Utuado. Turn west on Hwy 621 and continue to Km 4.4 and the park entrance.

The ranger station is near the entrance, where Hwy 621 snakes into the forest. At the end of this road, there is a picnic and recreation area and an aviary, where the DRNA is working to reintroduce the Puerto Rican parrot and other endangered species.

Faro y Parque Histórico de Arecibo AMUSEMENT PARK
(☎817-1936; Rte 655; adult/child $10/8; ⊙9am-6pm Mon-Fri, 10am-7pm Sat & Sun) This theme park off Hwy 2 is a bit gimmicky and overpriced, though it does offer a glimpse of the historic Arecibo lighthouse and is a good place to break up the long drives across the North Coast if you're traveling with the kids, who will likely get into the pirate-themed stuff. Judging by the squeals of delight, Blackbeard's Pirate Ship was a hit. Perched on a headland on the hill at Punta Morrillos, east of Arecibo, the **Faro de los Morrillos**, dating from 1897, is an excellent example of Spanish neoclassical architecture with its whitewashed facade and gracefully refined cylindrical shape. Inside, a tiny **museum** displays artifacts salvaged from shipwrecks. There are fantastic views of the Atlantic Ocean and karst country from the roof.

Elsewhere the park boasts a reconstructed Taíno village, two pirate ships, a pirate's cave, a mini-zoo and a substantial children's playground.

Beaches

There are two passable beaches in the area of the Faro de los Morrillos, though much better beaches are along the coast to the east. On the cove side, south of the point and the commercial pier, just off Hwy 681, you will see the manicured facilities of a **town beach** with broad sand and totally protected water. This is a great place for families.

If you follow the road past the lighthouse (less than a quarter of a mile), you come to the **Balneario Morrillos** (parking $3). There is a big parking lot and all the usual facilities. The beach is about a half-mile of low dunes and white sand, and it usually gets plenty of surf.

Sleeping & Eating

TOP CHOICE **Casa Grande Mountain Retreat** GUESTHOUSE $$
(☎888-343-2272; www.hotelcasagrande.com; Hwy 612 Km 0.3; r $95-115;) Materializing in the heart of Puerto Rico's gorgeous karst country, the Casa Grande is the perfect place to escape the daily grind. Nestled in its own steep valley and run efficiently by an ex-New York lawyer, the ecologically congruous hotel stops you in your tracks and forces you to slow down. While there are no TVs or phones in any of the 20 rooms, there are daily yoga classes, a scrumptious on-site restaurant (which only serves breakfast) and each of the rooms has a porch where you can swing along on the hammock and watch the mist roll across the hills. This is a place to completely unplug. Note that its website also has an option for work-exchange stays.

Punta Maracayo Hotel HOTEL $$
(☎544-2000; www.hotelpuntamaracayopr.com; Hwy 2 Km 84.6; r $89-119; P) With excellent service, modern rooms and lots of colorful common spaces, there's no contest that Punta Maracayo is the best option along the dreary north coast highways. Although the facility itself is a bit similar to a quality highway hotel in the US, it does well to dress things up with fresh tropical flowers in the lobby, wicker furniture and bold modern art. The pool area in back is a great option for people traveling with children, as it is spacious.

Parador El Buen Café HOTEL $$
(☎898-1000; Hwy 2 No 381 Km 84; r $95-160; P) Little more than a journey-breaker on Hwy 2 between San Juan and the west coast, El Buen Café is a clean and efficiently run parador with bright bedspreads and relatively cheerful ambience. The friendly staff, pool and adjacent cafeteria-style restaurant are the perfect antidote to any suppressed road rage, though Punta Maracayo, just half a mile up the road, is much nicer. It's 5 miles west of Arecibo.

TJ Ranch CABINS $$
(☎880-1217; www.tjranch.com; Rte 146; cabins $100; P) A charming stop on any karst country driving/cycling tour, TJ Ranch is a little-known Eden that harbors three beautiful cabins surrounded by lush foliage next to Lago Dos Bocas. It's actually a working coffee plantation and the congenial hosts are known to be formidable cooks who will concoct all sorts of mini-feasts from the ultimate Puerto Rican cookbook.

El Buen Café CAFETERIA $
(☎898-1000; Hwy 2 No 381 Km 84; dishes $6-15; ⊙5:30am-10pm) This no-nonsense cafeteria-style roadhouse – frequented by day trippers, truckers and retirees – is open all

START ARECIBO
FINISH FARO Y PARQUE HISTÓRICO DE ARECIBO
DURATION THREE TO FOUR HOURS WITHOUT BREAKS (TWO DAYS BY BIKE)

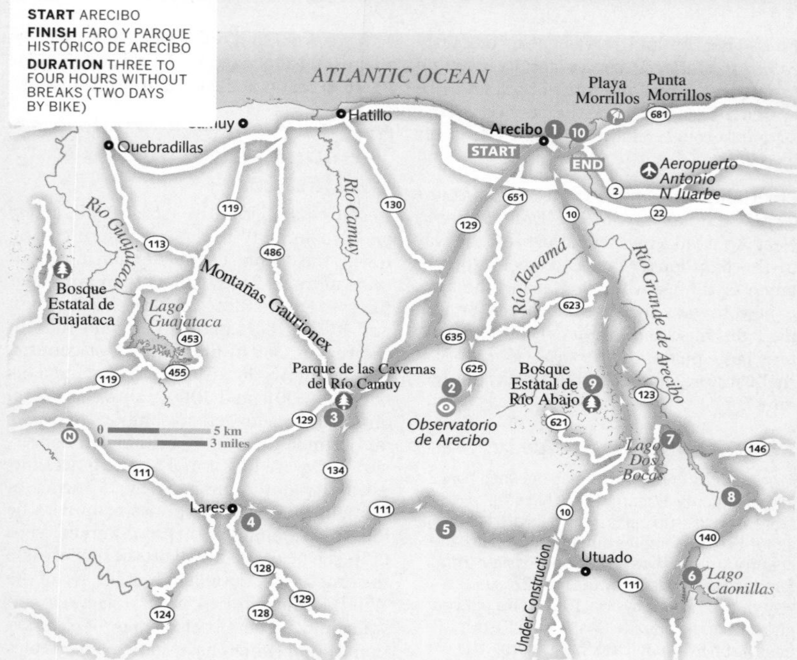

DISTANCE 60 MILES
SEASON ANYTIME IT'S NOT RAINING

Driving/Cycling Tour
Karst Country

Start in ❶ **Arecibo**, a town perfectly situated to fuel up for the trip, and head south toward Lares, birthplace of the *independenista* movement. Take a scenic detour along the way to the ❷ **Observatorio de Arecibo**, the world's largest radio telescope and a surreal sci-fi vision in the jungle. Afterwards stop at the ❸ **Parque de las Cavernas del Río Camuy**, where you'll find a network of dripping caves which can be a great place to cool off. Honing in on Lares, you'll want to stop in the main plaza for ice cream from the renowned ❹ **Heladería de Lares**. Next, head east on Hwy 111 (up and down lots of ridges) to the ❺ **Parque Ceremonial Indígena Caguana**, a quiet park which was once used for worship and ballgames of indigenous Taíno people. After a quiet walk, follow signs toward Utuado, but turn off for a short detour to either of the visually stunning mountain lakes in the area, ❻ **Lago Caonillas** or ❼ **Lago Dos Bocas**. You'll find serene accommodations and early-morning yoga nearby at the ❽ **Casa Grande Mountain Retreat**. Regular boats ply the lake and ramshackle restaurants sell all the regular Puerto Rican favorites. You can walk off the deep-fried cod fritters by pausing at ❾ **Bosque Estatal de Río Abajo** up Rte 621, where former lumber roads have been converted to trails. Stay on Hwy 10 as it approaches the edge of Arecibo city and hook up with Hwy 681. That will bring you down to the ❿ **Faro y Parque Histórico de Arecibo**, where a picturesque lighthouse stands guard over the Caribbean.

hours (nearly) and serves cheap but tasty *comida criolla*. It serves a salty *bacalao* (a salty cod stew) and lots of pork and rice options. Like the food, the service is consistent throughout the day and the locals love it.

Lighthouse Bay Restaurant PUERTO RICAN $ (☎878-5658; dishes $6-19; ⏲lunch & dinner) Near Arecibo's commercial pier on the way to the lighthouse, this is a good stop for lunch or dinner when you are in the area, or if you want to go to the beach or visit the lighthouse and Cueva del Indio. It's $18 for a large platter of *mariscos* (four types of shellfish) or you can go light with a burger for $7.

Getting There & Away

Arecibo's city center is trapped between Hwy 2 and the Atlantic Ocean – it's a thin strip of restaurants and strip malls. The main attractions lie about 15 to 20 minutes outside of town in karst country, just off Hwy 129. It is accessible from San Juan or Aguadilla by the Hwy 22 expressway, or from Ponce by Hwy 10. Catch a público just east of the plaza to San Juan ($10, two hours) and to Aguadilla ($8, 1½ hours).

Lago Guajataca

Beautiful and serene, Lago Guajataca has some of Puerto Rico's best fishing - on the north side of the lake are two clubs for anglers hoping to catch the tucunare fish that are stocked in this lake. Right in the middle of karst country, the easiest approach to the lake is along Hwy 2 to Rte 119, and then into the forest to the **DRNA** (☎896-7640; Rte 119 Km 22.1; ⏲6am-6pm Tue-Sun). You'll need to get a permit here if you want to fish and you can pick up a loaner bamboo fishing pole (no bait) from the office. You are also free to use the bathrooms (with showers) and picnic tables. Kayaking is allowed in the lake, but it's best to bring your own kayak. Swimming in the lake is prohibited.

If you want to stay the night shoreside, try the rustic Hotel Lago Vista. It's also good for a bite to eat, as is the Cafetín Vista al Lado.

QUICK GREEN ESCAPES

- » Bosque Estatal de Guajataca (p210)
- » Laguna Tortuguero (p204)
- » Parque de las Cavernas del Río Camuy (p206)
- » Bosque Estatal de Río Abajo (p207)
- » Lagos Dos Bocas & Caonillas (p207)

Bosque Estatal de Guajataca

Despite its diminutive size (2300 acres) and proximity to the northwestern coastal towns, the Bosque Estatal de Guajataca contains more trails (27 miles) than any other forest in Puerto Rico – including El Yunque – and it's the best place for a wild hike in the region. Set in dramatic karst country, the distinctive local terrain rises and falls between 500ft and 1000ft above sea level and is characterized by bulbous *mogotes* and rounded *sumideros* (funneled depressions). Covered by a moist subtropical forest and watered annually by 75 inches of rainfall, there are 45 species of bird to be found here along with 186 different types of tree. One of the highlights of the forest is the limestone Cueva del Viento (Cave of the Wind), which is rich with stalactites and stalagmites. There is also a pair of observation towers, which have some picnic tables where locals gather around grills, and plantations of blue mahoe trees. The area is a favorite habitat of the endangered Puerto Rican boa.

Compared to other Puerto Rican forests and parks, the trails in Guajataca are relatively well marked, though it's wise to procure a map beforehand to see how the various paths link up. True to form, the **ranger station** (☎872-1045; Rte 446; ⏲8am-5pm) near the trailheads, 5 miles into the forest, is not always open, and when rangers do emerge they don't always have much in the way of printed information. The moral: come prepared. The best bet is to call the Aguadilla office of the DRNA (p218) before you arrive at the forest, find things closed and feel a little lost. Be warned that 'official' maps of the area are usually hand-drawn, photocopied and not to scale.

There are no eating facilities in Guajataca forest.

Sights & Activities

Most of the main hikes depart from, or near, the ranger station on Rte 446. The most popular is the 1.5-mile **Interpretative Trail** that passes the **observation tower** and several other points of interest (be sure to hike to the observation tower to get the best

WORTH A TRIP

HELADERÍA DE LARES

For unbiased visitors, sleepy Lares is famous for two reasons. First, it was the site of the short-lived Grito de Lares (p245) independence call in 1868, and second, it sells some of the best ice cream on the island, if not in the Caribbean.

To the chagrin of modern-day *independistas*, the bulk of the people who visit the town these days come to consume large quantities of ice cream rather than plot surreptitious rebellion; and what better place to do it? Their fixation is the understated **Heladería de Lares** (☎897-3290; Plaza de Recreo, Lecaroz; ⏰10am-5pm Mon-Fri, 9am-6pm Sat & Sun), an ice-cream store that occupies the ground floor of a three-story building in the town's pleasant main plaza. Though it may not have sparked any history-shaping insurrections since its inception four decades ago, the store's crafty concoction of over 1000 exotic ice-cream flavors, including avocado, *arroz con pollo* (chicken with rice) and – urghhhh – garlic, could certainly be seen as revolutionary.

Wacky, wonderful or just plain weird, Heladería de Lares today is celebrated across the island and is well worth a mile or two's diversion from a karst-country driving tour for a fleeting sample. If you prefer your garlic in a curry rather than a cone, don't worry. There are plenty of delicious traditional flavors to choose from such as chocolate, almond and vanilla.

views of the surrounding countryside). It's a moderate walk that takes about two hours. **Trail Number One** breaks off from the Interpretative Trail and heads toward **Cueva del Viento**. There, wooden stairs will take you down into the depths of the dark cave (bring a flashlight). Let rangers know if you are going into the caves.

Sleeping

Nino's Camping & Guesthouse CABINS, CAMPGROUND $
(☎896-9016; www.ninoscamping.com; Rte 119 Km 22.1; campsite/cabins $25/50; ☒) Near Lago Guajataca, this is a nice lakeside option, operated by a friendly family. The little cabins for four to 12 people have everything except sheets and utensils. Discounts are given for longer stays and there's a swimming pool and an activities room on-site. It also rents kayaks and operates fishing ventures for groups.

La Vereda CAMPGROUND $
(campsites per person $7) There are 10 campsites here, on Rte 446, about 5 miles south of Hwy 2. Call the DRNA in San Juan for a permit and to make reservations, or try the Aguadilla office. Like other government-operated campgrounds, getting a permit (or any information at all) can be frustrating.

Getting There & Away

There are no buses to Guajataca. If you're driving, take the narrow Rte 446 south of Hwy 2 and follow it for 5 miles. Bike hire is available at Aquatica Dive & Surf (p216) near the Ramey Base.

Isabela & Around

POP 45,000

Isabela is more famous for its surroundings than its patchwork urban core. Nicknamed the 'Garden of the Northeast' for its local cheeses and elegant Paso Fino horses, the coastline here is wild and rugged, with a handful of classic surfing beaches such as Jobos and Shacks that rival anything in Rincón, especially in the winter. While there's plenty of accommodations and eating joints scattered along Rtes 466 and 4466, the 'scene' here is less cliquey and more isolated. The vistas are spectacular too. After a heavy dose of the ghastly urban sprawl on Hwy 2, the miles of sand dunes, inlets and untrammeled beaches that lie sandwiched between the lashing Atlantic and a 200ft coastal escarpment are a sight for sore eyes. You can scan the water from high cliffs for whales or charter whale-watching tours, which are also available down the coast during the winter.

If you stay off the main roads, Isabela is great cycling country, although there are no nearby rentals. Alternatively, you can explore the web of back roads that skirt the edge of karst country around the Bosque Estatal de Guajataca and nearby Lago Guajataca. The former has a handful of well-signposted

PLAYA JOBOS

What locals refer to as **Playa Jobos** is actually one long coastline made up of different beaches – Jobos is the biggest one, at the intersection of Rtes 466 and 4466. That's also where you will find most of the hotels and restaurants.

hikes (unusual in Puerto Rico), while the latter offers kayaking and fishing.

Activities

Surfing

While Isabela might lack the surfer-chic of Rincón, the waves here are just as legendary. Some say Playa Jobos has the best breaks on the island, while other favorite spots include **Surfer's Beach** (preferred location for local contests, with diverse breaks from multiple directions and strong northwestern swells), **Table Top** (named for a flat, exposed reef that looks like a table with a round barrel coming up against cliffs) and **Gas Chambers** (known as Puerto Rico's best 'right tube,' these waves head right for a sharp and unforgiving cliff). Also check out **Secret Spot**, **Sal Si Puedes**, **Shore Island** and **Las Dunas**. See p34.

To get the scoop on what's breaking and where, stop by **Hang Loose Surf Shop** (☎872-2490; www.hangloosesurfshop.com; Rte 4466 Km 1.2; ⏰11am-5pm Tue-Sat) near Playa Jobos. The shop has a complete selection of gear. Lots of overseas surfers come here to rent boards ($30 a day). You can also rent boards from **Wave Riding Vehicles** (☎890-3351; www.waveridingvehicles.com; Rte 110 Km 7.3; ⏰10am-6pm Mon-Sat). You can get a two-hour lesson at either place for about $65.

Serious surfers will also find a number of custom board builders in the area. Of these, **MHL** (☎609-6198; www.mhlcustom.com; Rte 4466 Km 1.2, beyond Villa Montaña) has an impeccable reputation for hand-crafted boards.

Diving & Snorkeling

La Cueva Submarina Dive Shop DIVING, SNORKELING
(☎872-1390; www.lacuevasubmarina.com; Rte 466 Km 6.3, ⏰8:30am-4pm Thu-Mon) Named after the nearby underwater caves, this outfit is situated on Rte 466 atop a steep hill overlooking Playa Jobos. It offers a complete list of dives and dive courses, including underwater cavern dives for skilled divers ($55), as well as guided snorkeling and scuba safaris for inexperienced divers.

Cycling

Hit the ocean road on or around Rtes 466 and 4466 for some of the best bike rides on the north coast. You'll pass a number of bike-rental places set up at the roadside, where a bike will cost about $20 for half a day. Bike rental and route details are available from Aquatica Dive & Surf on Ramey Base.

Horseback Riding

A horseback ride along a nearly deserted beach is one of the joys of Isabela and an excellent experience. You can take a ride along the fields, dunes and beaches with **Tropical Trail Rides** (☎872-9256; www.tropicaltrailrides.com; Rte 4466 Km 1.8; 2hr rides $45; ⏰twice daily), which works out of stables at Playa Shacks.

Beaches

The wonderfully dramatic crescent of **Playa Jobos** is protected by a large headland of dead coral to the east, and the surf breaks pretty consistently off this point. The site of the 1989 World Surfing Championships, Jobos is a good place to surf or watch professional athletes doing their wave thing. There is also fine swimming off the eastern beach, where the point protects you from the surf. The bar-restaurants on the south side of the cove offer a laid-back après-surf scene, especially on weekends.

Another beach, **Playa Shacks**, lies less than a mile west of Jobos, near Ramey Base on Rte 4466. There are good submarine caves here for snorkeling.

Sleeping

TOP CHOICE **Villa Montaña** RESORT **$$$**
(☎872-9554; www.villamontana.com; Rte 4466 Km 1.2; villas $250-350; P ❄ @ ≋) With its low-profile architecture, secluded setting and plush comforts, this resort is something of an anomaly on Puerto Rico – a high-end stay that works gracefully within its stunning environment. Here, 48 brightly painted plantation-style villas look across the lawn to the tempestuous crash of Playa Shacks. Even better, this place has a fine environmental record and there's an on-site organic garden that is raided daily to season the delicious restaurant food to prove it. Villas are one, two or three bedrooms and are brightly decorated in ebullient Caribbean patterns.

Tucked away amid the tropical foliage, meanwhile, you'll find a tennis court, a gym, a spa and the Moroccan-themed Eclipse restaurant. It also has bikes for guests to borrow. Not surprisingly, accommodations get booked up fast. Though perfect for honeymoons, it also hosts its share of weddings.

Parador Villas del Mar Hau CABINS **$$**
(☎872-2045; www.paradorvillasdelmarhau.com; Rte 466 Km 8.3; cabins $95-165; P❄≋) Places like this barely exist anymore: a gorgeous clutch of brightly painted beach huts scattered like bucolic homesteads along a breathtaking beach where offshore coral islets create bathing lagoons. This rustic retreat has been continuously run by the Hau family for nearly 50 years and aside from the distant glimmer of encroaching condo towers, little has changed. The huts, nestled under wind-gnarled pine trees, have sea-facing decks and basic but comfortable fittings in keeping with the back-to-nature surroundings. Although popular during the summer, off-season this has to be one of the most tranquil places on the island. You can ride a horse, take a cycling tour, kayak, snorkel, hike the beach or sleep undisturbed under a palm tree. The kiteboarding outside the front door is the best on Puerto Rico. The villas are 4 miles west of Isabela.

Hacienda Jibarito ECOLODGE **$$**
(☎280-4040; www.haciendaeljibarito.com; Rte 445 Km 6.4; r $129-279; P❄≋) Opened in 2006, this innovative ecolodge bills itself as an 'agro-tourist complex,' that is, a hotel doubling up as a hacienda (agricultural estate). Although the facilities retain suitably rustic touches such as hammocks, rocking chairs and antique farming implements, it's a bit softer than the back-to-nature experience you get in the hills. Comfortable rooms sport TVs, phones and bathtubs, and a laid-back poolside bar shakes up some refreshing piña coladas. But the hacienda's real forte lies in its beautifully landscaped grounds and positive environmental practices. The adjacent *granja* (farm) – which guests may visit – makes use of its own chickens, cows, shrimp farm and greenhouse to send produce directly to the on-site restaurant. The hacienda is 8 miles south of Isabela heading along Hwy 112.

Hotel Restaurante Ocean Front HOTEL **$$**
(☎872-0444; www.oceanfrontpr.com; Rte 4466 Km 0.1; r $85-150; P❄) Imagine a classic Caribbean-style beach hotel situated on a wild and tempestuous stretch of sand popularly regarded by aficionados as being surfers' heaven. That's the Ocean Front; small, compact, suitably modern but not too flashy. Rooms have balconies and good views of the incoming surf and there's a popular on-site restaurant-bar that hosts occasional live music. Room rates are lowest Monday to Friday. The hotel is situated 5 miles west of Isabela on Playa Jobos.

Hotel El Guajataca HOTEL **$$**
(☎800-964-3065; www.hotelelguajataca.com; Hwy 2 Km 103.8; r $118-162; P❄≋) About 5 miles east of Isabela in Quebradillas, El Guajataca is a run-of-the-mill parador – ie slightly dog-eared rooms, keen-to-please staff and good family facilities – notable for its stupendous north coast setting. Perched on a grassy cliff overlooking the Atlantic, this is Puerto Rico at its wildest and most romantic, although the fairly bland hotel hardly emulates the setting, despite the new 'bed lounge.' There's two nice pools, a tennis court and easy access to a great surfing (but not swimming) beach.

Hotel Lago Vista HOTEL **$$**
(☎896-5487; Hwy 119 Km 22; r $85-135; P❄≋) A few miles inland, on the shore of rural Lago Guajataca, Lago Vista is a rustic country inn with a pool and sun deck. Simple but elegant rooms overlook the placid lake from balconies. It's peaceful and serene, and there's a restaurant serving *comida criolla*.

Parador Vistamar HOTEL **$$**
(☎895-2065; www.paradorvistamar.com; Hwy 2 Km 102; r $75-115; P❄≋) Five miles east of Isabela, this uninspired parador has 55 hilltop rooms, some with balcony views of the Atlantic (across the highway). Fine if you're not fussy, but it's too close to Hwy 2 for comfort.

Eating

Panadería Los Cocos BAKERY, CAFE **$**
(☎895-6932; PR 484 Km 0.2, just north of Hwy 2; sandwiches $3) The rosy-cheeked ladies behind the counter at this bakery will claim that they're baking in Puerto Rico's oldest bakery, a real find on the long drive between the west coast and San Juan. They might be right. The bakery has been cooking continually for 140 years and still uses wood-fired ovens to turn out fresh bread with a thick, dusty crust. Their champion dishes include a slightly sweet bread stuffed with roasted pork, cakes sweetened with fresh fruit and

killer sandwiches. Finding the place can be a little difficult. It is just east of Quebradillas. Look for a sign painted on a surfboard advertising lessons.

Eclipse CARIBBEAN FUSION $$
(☎872-9554; www.villamontana.com; Rte 4466 Km 1.2; dishes $10-36) The alfresco atmosphere – furious waves and gentle breezes, bright tropical flowers and elegantly rustic furniture – is nearly outpaced by the creative flavors of seafood and fresh, locally sourced vegetables at this on-site restaurant of Villa Montaña. Start with a cocktail of house-infused liquor, the fried brie and seaweed salad or the octopus salad with golden plantains before moving on to mains of pan-Latin steak and seafood. The menu changes daily.

Panaderia El Mana CAFETERIA $
(☎872-1475; Rte 466 Km 3; dishes $3-7) After a morning at Jobos, surfers arrive ragged and ravenous to El Mana, a bakery with one of the heartiest home-cooked Puerto Rican lunches on the island. There's nothing much to look at in this dim and scrappy little bakery and it comes (unfortunately) served in Styrofoam take-out, but the rice and beans, pork stew and *comida criolla* standards are excellent and come in enormous portions. To find it, head up the hill from the beach.

Happy Belly's BURGERS, SEAFOOD $
(☎398-9452; Rte 4466; dishes $5-17; ⊙lunch & dinner) When the swell is good you could almost surf right up to the verandah here. Perched above magnificent Playa Jobos, Happy Belly's offers front-row seats to one of Puerto Rico's most visually dazzling surfing 'shows.' The menu is straightforward burgers and fish, but this place is more about setting than scrumptious cuisine. Order a cold Medalla beer and grab a wooden booth among the suntanned surf groupies and boogie boarders. Amazing sunsets are usually only the first spectacle of the evening – this place loves to party.

Hotel Restaurante Ocean Front SEAFOOD $$
(☎872-0444; www.oceanfrontpr.com; Rte 4466 Km 0.1; dishes $6-22; ⊙lunch & dinner) Tiny glowing lights and wavy green plants give this restaurant a relaxed, romantic atmosphere that perfectly complements the seafood dishes. The indoor setting is surprisingly formal, but the deck hosts casual surfers in for a drink. The owner is famous for his secret salmon recipe. Live music nightly. Rooms available.

Cafetín Vista al Lado CAFETERIA $
(☎895-6877; Hwy 453 Km 4.2; dishes $5-10; ⊙lunch & dinner) If you are exploring karst country, stop on the east side of Lago Guajataca for some grilled chicken or pork. You can eat it at a picnic table with a view of the lake and dairy farms. There's also live music.

Information

The nearest information center is at the Aguadilla airport on Ramey Base.

Getting There & Away

The easiest way to access the region, from San Juan or the west coast, is via the four-lane Hwy 22. But to really enjoy this area (and its lack of traffic), you need to get off the main highway and explore the back roads.

No públicos serve these back roads or beach areas such as Playa Jobos.

Aguadilla

POP 15,700

Occupying a small sliver of land wedged between Hwy 2 and the sea, Aguadilla is a small coastal city of patchwork development and surprising contradictions. It's contemporary appeal – including a world-class surf scene and bright marine life – stands in vibrant contrast to Eisenhower-era tract housing and the graying campus of a retired US air-force base. Given its history, it's no surprise that it is a confusing place to navigate, and like many Puerto Rican towns the historic quarter has been largely abandoned in favor of generic out-of-town shopping malls along Hwy 2.

The early colonizers of Aguadilla (founded in 1780) were Spanish loyalists fleeing from the Haitian invasion of Spanish Hispaniola in 1822. By the late 19th century the settlement had become an important port, but in 1918 its fortunes changed for the worse when it was ravaged by the destructive San Fermin earthquake and subsequent tsunami.

Attractions in town are few, though a recent renovation has spruced up the central Plaza Colón. Surfers head north to the unblemished beauty of Crash Boat, Shacks and Jobos beaches, while committed golfers wheel their clubs to the windy Punta Borinquen course built for President Dwight

LOCAL KNOWLEDGE

BIKE-SHOP OWNER, JOSÉ RAFOLS SALLABERRY

There's no full-blown cycling culture, but noncompetitive cycling is becoming ever more popular. Lance Armstrong made an important impression among Americans with his Tour de France wins and this effect has filtered through to Puerto Rico.

Classic Puerto Rico Routes

Cabo Rojo on the southwest of the island offers some of the best on- and off-road routes. Rte 10 between Arecibo and Ponce also has some winding, precipitous terrain. Closer to home, there are some good 50km to 80km rides around the Isabela area in the northwest.

Favorite Ride

Off-roading in the Cabo Rojo area. It mixes technical climbs with smooth stretches and has some pretty views.

Can you tour the island by bicycle?

There's no reason why you shouldn't, as long as you take the normal precautions and stay off the main toll roads. An official 'Vuelta' ride takes place in late November in three stages between San Juan, Mayagüez and Guayama. There's also an organized ride that calls in at each of the island's nine historic lighthouses.

As told to Brendan Sainsbury

Eisenhower. If neither activity is appealing, bypass Aguadilla for Rincón.

Sights & Activities

Ramey Base MILITARY BASE

Vieques, Culebra, Desecheo and Roosevelt Rds; sometimes it's hard to avoid bumping into erstwhile US military anachronisms when you're traveling through Puerto Rico. And, just when you thought you'd had your fill, here comes Ramey, near Aguadilla, a Cold War command base created by the US Air Force in 1939. For 30 years the Americans poured money into Ramey and watched as the surrounding area burgeoned into a populous municipality of 64,000 people. And then in 1973 the base closed, leaving behind a weirdly homogeneous stretch of tract housing, American fast-food restaurants and some beguiling urban development.

Today, the former base hosts the international Aeropuerto Rafael Hernández, a university campus, a couple of hotels, a housing project and the only **ice-skating arena** (☎819-5555; admission $10-13; ⏲9:30am-11pm) in the Caribbean.

If you are traveling to the base from the south, take Hwy 107 north from Hwy 2. This route brings you through what is called Gate 1. The traffic can get a little nutty on this road, so you may want to approach from the east via Hwy 110 (the route to the airport), which brings you through Gate 5. Once you're in, have fun getting lost on the maze of roads that lead you around the airfield, administration buildings and the nearly endless plots of former base housing that have been sold off or rented to Puerto Rican families.

Las Cascadas WATERPARK

(☎819-0950; Hwy 2 Km 126; ⏲10am-5pm Mon-Fri, to 6pm Sat & Sun Mar-Sep; adult/child 4-12yr $19/17.50) Much of the shoreline around Aguadilla can be rough and unswimmable, making this enormous waterpark a godsend for families who need to cool off. The facility is the biggest water park in the Caribbean and a great way to spend an afternoon. While parents get bounced around on the rapids of the Crazy River, kids queue up again and again for the huge slides, navigate the slippery aquatic playground equipment or bob around in the Wave Pools. A pair of speed slides probably provided the most adrenaline-packed rush (though mind the wedgie). The park is part of a bright and clean facility operated by the city of Aguadilla, and there's also a skate park on the premises.

Punta Borinquen Golf GOLF

(☎890-2987; www.puntaborinquengolf.com; green fee $20-35) Although Aguadilla is no Dorado when it comes to golf, it does boast this

ISLA DESECHEO

The island appearing alluringly on the horizon in spectacular Rincón sunsets is Isla Desecheo, a 1-sq-mile knob of prickly cacti and bushy scrub situated 13 miles off Puerto Rico's northwest coast. One of four outlying islands that make up the Puerto Rican archipelago (the others are Culebra, Vieques and Mona), Desecheo was 'discovered' by Columbus in 1493 but remained unnamed until Spanish explorer Nuñez Alvarez de Aragón passed through in 1517. Buccaneers and pirates frequented it during the 16th and 17th centuries to hoard booty and hunt the feral goats introduced by the Spanish, but over the years it's been home to lizards, seabirds and a few monkeys, introduced for an adaptation experiment. From WWII to the early 1950s, Desecheo was – surprise, surprise – used as a bombing range by the US military who left behind a cache of unexploded ordnance, a fact that makes the island remain officially off-limits to visitors (trespassers will be arrested).

But all is not lost. Thanks to its favorable position to the west of the geologically important Puerto Rican Trench, the waters around Desecheo are free from murky river run-off from the main island. As a result the sea here is unusually clear (visibility is generally 30m to 45m), making it one of the best spots for diving in the Caribbean. Desecheo was declared a US Fish and Wildlife Refuge in 1976 and a National Wildlife Refuge in 1983.

6800yd 18-hole course on the former air-force base that was designed for President Dwight D Eisenhower. The course offers a cafeteria, a pro shop, a practice range and lessons. Prices get cheaper later in the day, when the sunset is an added bonus.

Aquatica Dive & Surf CYCLING
(☎890-6071; http://premium.caribe.net/~aquatica; Rte 110 Km 10) Just outside Gate 5 of Ramey Base is one of Puerto Rico's best bike-rental establishments. The staff here can also help you with route planning. There are plenty of decent circuits in the Aguadilla/Isabela area that steer clear of the main roads and incorporate some magnificent rural scenery. There are also a couple of moderately difficult single-track trails in the area, more notable for the incredible scenery than the ride itself.

Beaches

For some swimming, snorkeling and legendary surf breaks, the most popular place to go is **Playa Crash Boat**. It got its name because the air force used to keep rescue boats here to pick up crews from the Strategic Air Command's bombers that didn't make the runway. The beach lies off Hwy 107, halfway between town and the former air base. You will see a sign for Crash Boat that directs you west on the short Hwy 458.

If you are more adventurous and want to avoid the crowds, follow Hwy 107 past the Crash Boat turnoff and onto the base. Eventually, you will see the golf course on your left and a road that heads west through the golf course. Follow this road as it winds down to rough, lonely **Playa Wilderness** and the ruins of what must have been air-force recreation clubs. Surfers like this desolate place, but also congregate up and down the coast.

Sleeping

Courtyard by Marriot Aguadilla HOTEL $$
(☎658-8000; cnr W Parade & W Belt; r $146-194; P❄📶≋👪) Although expectations for a reliable chain are easily met with this newcomer to Aguadilla, two things put it way over the top: a nice casino with a schedule of live performers and events, and a delightful splash park in the courtyard. Parents can blow some of the vacation money in the former, while younger travelers will adore the latter, with its brightly colored slides, fountains and aquatic playground structures. There's also a pool with less toys for adults to enjoy, a fitness room and a snack bar on-site. What the rooms lack in personality is made up for by an exceptional, modern facility.

Cielo Mar Hotel HOTEL $$
(☎882-5959; www.cielomar.com; 84 Av Monemar, Hwy 111; r $90-105; P❄@📶≋👪) In Aguadilla's strung-out hotel strip, the Cielo Mar takes first prize for location. It is situated high atop the area's famous surfing breaks with spectacular views over the town, an old sugar factory, Rincón, Isla Desecheo and those blood-red west coast sunsets. Although the building itself, with its bright orange chocolate-box architecture, is hardly a stunner, the rooms are adequate and the

substantial swimming pool with its huge whale-shaped slide is a hit with the kids.

Parador El Faro HOTEL **$$**
(☎882-8000; Hwy 107 Km 2.1; r $85-155; P❄≋) On a rather nondescript highway between Aguadilla and Ramey Base, El Faro hides some sweet horticultural surprises. The main attraction is the lush tropical grounds – you walk through a vine-covered canopy to get from the swimming pool to your room – plus the ultra-friendly front-desk service and decent on-site restaurant. The 50 rooms are the simple but clean accommodations you have come to expect from an unpretentious parador, but encased in such splendiferous natural surroundings they appear colored with a more luxurious tint.

Parador JB Hidden Village HOTEL **$**
(☎868-8686; Hwy 416, Aguada; r & ste $70-125; P≋) Five miles south of Aguadilla on the way to Rincón you'll see this 33-room parador, which has marble floors, big beds, a restaurant and a pool. Some rooms have kitchenettes.

Parador La Cima HOTEL **$$**
(☎890-2016; www.lacimahotel.com; Hwy 110 Km 9.2; r $85-140; P❄@≋) More motel than hotel, La Cima is on the busy road outside Gate 5 of Ramey Base, with serviceable, if worn, rooms and a number of restaurants within walking distance.

Eating

TOP CHOICE **One Ten Thai** THAI **$**
(☎890-0113; www.onetenthai.com; Hwy 110 Km 7; mains $8-13; ⊙dinner) After all the stick-to-your-ribs Puerto Rican cuisine, it's hard not to instantly fall head over heels for the refreshing flavors of One Ten Thai, a restaurant that began when the owners started doing word-of-mouth Thai meals for friends from their home kitchen. Its ingredients are locally sourced from a community garden and local fishermen. The adjoining microbrew bar has one of the most ambitious beer lists on the entire island (the owner is from America's craft brew mecca, Colorado) and the dishes are simple, elegant and delicious. The small dining area is clearly a DIY affair, but buzzes with great energy.

Platano Loco CARIBBEAN **$**
(☎868-0241; www.platanoloco.aguadaserver.net, in Spanish; off PR 411, Barrio Jagüey; mains $5-13; ⊙lunch & dinner Thu-Sun) First, the good news: the 'Crazy Plantain' serves some of the most inventive lunches in Puerto Rico. *Everything* uses plantains: they are fried in place of bread on a pork sandwich, encase seafood in *mofongo* and come traditionally rolled, mashed and fried. They even pose with other ethnic food – topping spaghetti and filling tacos. On weekends (the only time it's open) families and young couples flock to the 'University of Plantains' for the festive and whimsical menu – words that ably describe the atmosphere. Now, the bad news: this holy grail of awesome requires herculean effort to find (at least it did for us). In a residential area high in the hills above Aquadilla, you might get lost a half-dozen times before reaching it. It has a good map on its website, but without it try this: from Aguadilla, head south (away from the ocean) on PR 411. When you get to the marker for Km 4.0 (about 2km from the intersection with PR 115) start looking for yellow signs. The reward is a wonderful meal and a sweeping hilltop view.

Cocina Creativa CARIBBEAN FUSION **$**
(☎890-1861; Hwy 110 Km 9.2; snacks $5-7, mains $7-14; ⊙9am-5pm; ✎) Tucked rather incongruously behind a gas station on one of the northwest's ubiquitous big box strips, Cocina Creativa boasts a fresh, cozy, homegrown vibe. You can realign your zen here with a kind of organic-meets-European-meets-Jamaican menu and even buy a new pair of flip-flops. Try the yucca and fishcakes, the jerk chicken with mango chutney or the amazing bruschettas.

Wilmer's Caribbean Cuisine CARIBBEAN **$**
(☎629-8442; Hwy 110 Km 7.8; mains $9-14; ⊙lunch & dinner) With purple walls and some flashy art, Wilmer's attempt at ambiance can't go unnoticed: the place looks like the parlor of a vivacious auntie. And so what if the dinner plates come festooned with lots of swiggles of sauce on the plate? The inventive updates of Caribbean standards brim with manic culinary energy. Grilled mahimahi in a fruit salsa and fresh ravioli are both favorites, but the menu is constantly changing things up.

Entertainment

The Cielo Mar Hotel features lightweight rock and salsa bands on weekends for dancing. For a more raucous scene, check out the many American-style bars near Ramey Base.

Information

Departamento de Recursos Naturales y Ambientales (DRNA; Department of Natural Resources & Environment; ☎890-4050-2050)

Puerto Rico Tourism Company (PRTC; ☎890-3315) For more information about this region, check out this helpful office at the Aeropuerto Rafael Hernández, north of town on the old Ramey Base.

Getting There & Away

Scheduled airline services to Aguadilla's Aeropuerto Rafael Hernández change seasonally. Flights come in from New York and Newark (US) and the Dominican Republic about three times a week.

There is a público terminal in town right off the central plaza, if you want to wait around for a ride to your next destination. Expect to pay $20 to San Juan (about three hours).

If you are driving between San Juan and the west coast (and want to avoid rush-hour traffic), consider taking the back road, Hwy 443, which breaks off Hwy 2 just east of town, then rejoins it to the south.

Getting Around

If you have reached Aguadilla by público or plane, you can rent a car to explore the back-country of the surrounding area. Try **Budget** (☎890-1110) at the airport. Cycling is another feasible option.

Central Mountains

POP 350,000

Includes »

Best Places to Eat

- » El Rancho Original (p224)
- » Vaca Brava (p227)
- » Casa Bavaria (p227)
- » Heladería Los Próceres (p227)
- » Hacienda Gripiñas (p231)

Best Places to Stay

- » Las Casas de la Selva & Tropic Ventures (p223)
- » Jájome Terrace (p223)
- » Hacienda Gripiñas (p231)
- » Hacienda Margarita (p227)
- » Parador Villas de Sotomayor (p231)

Why Go?

Those who explore the winding roads of this region find a dramatically different perspective on the island and a chance to commune with Puerto Rico's old soul. Rough around the edges and best approached with a flexible agenda, this is a place of Taíno legends and sugarcane moonshine, muddy hillside towns and misty afternoons.

The whole thing is strung together by the Ruta Panorámica, a vine-covered ribbon of potholed blacktop that rolls like a roller coaster along the island's rugged spine. Following rusty road signs, it passes ragged agricultural towns, humid patches of jungle and cliff-edge vistas where birds of prey glide in lazy circles. Between fog-covered valleys and the sharp scent of fresh-roasted beans, visitors get a whiff of the endangered cultural essence of Puerto Rico – moving decidedly more in time with the less-developed Caribbean neighbors than the paved-over hustle of the States.

When to Go

Unlike the reliably sunny shores, the mountains catch all kinds of weather, and are considerably cooler. Cerro Maravilla in the Toro Negro forest records average temperatures 10°F to 15°F lower than San Juan. In winter, towns in the hills can get downright chilly, sometimes dropping to 45°F. There's no rainy season, per se, but the hills catch clouds and dampness gets in the bones, making layered clothing a must. Mornings are clearer, making simultaneous views of the north and south coast possible. The Ruta Panorámica is often blanketed in mist.

Central Mountains Highlights

1. Load up on fresh, rich coffee and navigate the roller-coaster curves of the **Ruta Panorámica** (p221)

2. Join the spontaneous street party hosted by *lechoneras* (eateries specializing in suckling pig) in **Guavate** (p224)

3. Whiff the aroma of homegrown Puerto Rican coffee in **Hacienda San Pedro** (p230)

4. Bushwhack your way up an overgrown trail in the **Reserva Forestal Toro Negro** (p228)

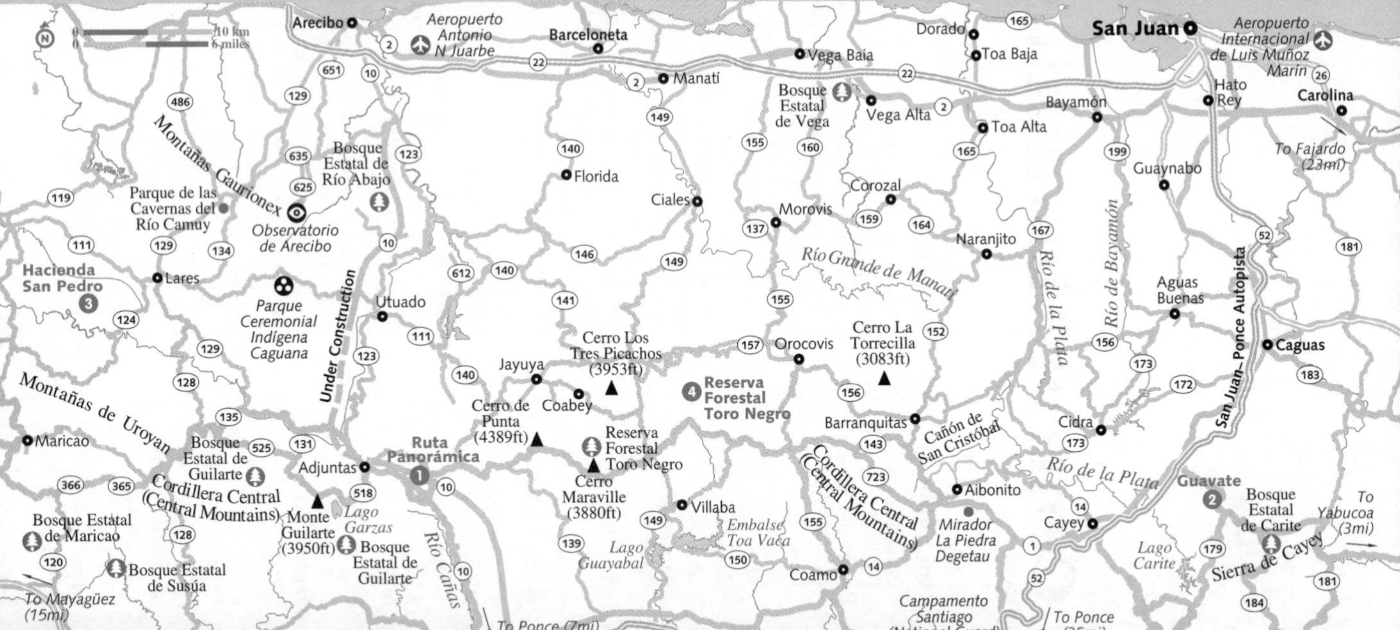

History

Legend has it, native Taíno survived here until the mid-19th century and, even today, Indian traditions run strong in the festivals and artisan workshops scattered along the Ruta Panorámica. In more recent times, notoriety has struck these mountains twice. In 1950 an unsuccessful uprising in Jayuya marked the death knell of the Puerto Rican independence movement as an effective political force. Further scandal erupted in 1978 when two young independence supporters were shot by police posing as revolutionaries on Cerro Maravilla in an incident that uncovered corruption, ballot-box fraud and an alleged FBI cover-up.

HILLS OF INDEPENDENCE

Thanks to their impregnable terrain, the central mountains have long acted as a safe harbor for the rebellious and repressed. Throughout history – from hidden Taínos to domestic terrorists in the late 1970s – these fertile hills and the proletariat farmers who work them have often grown the seeds of revolution. They are still the part of the island where you're likely to encounter the most outspoken advocates for Puerto Rican independence.

Getting There & Around

The Ruta Panorámica, a chain of 40 mountain roads, travels 165 miles across the roof of Puerto Rico, from Yabucoa in the east to Mayagüez in the west. This chapter takes you along this route from east to west. It is generally well marked with distinctive brown road signs and highlighted on almost all commercial maps of the island. If driving, be careful and never drive after dark.

The major towns in the central region such as Aibonito, Barranquitas and Adjuntas are easily accessed by público from either coast. Some of the more remote places, however, are a little more difficult to reach and, if you're without your own car, you may require lifts, taxis or plenty of forward planning. Bikes can be precarious on the Ruta Panorámica, where drivers are famously erratic. Riders should stick to the wider link roads such as Rte 15 between Cayey and Guayama and listen to local advice.

Bosque Estatal de Carite

Less than an hour south of San Juan, the **Bosque Estatal de Carite** (Carite Forest Reserve; ☎747-4545; Rte 184 Km 27.5; ⊙7am-3:30pm Mon-Fri) was created in 1935 to protect the watersheds of various local rivers from erosion and urbanization. Measuring 6000 acres in area, the mountain reserve is easily accessed from the San Juan metro area. It can get crowded on weekends and during the summer when *sanjuaneros* come here to enjoy the 72°F temperatures, green shade, and dozens of *lechonerías* (restaurants specializing in smoky, spit-roasted suckling pig) that line Hwy 184 as it approaches the northern forest entrance. The forest is one of the first points of interest you will hit if you are traversing the Ruta Panorámica east to west.

As with most Puerto Rican forest reserves, facilities are spartan and ranger stations are often unmanned. If you are intending to stay here you'll have to make arrangements in advance, and bring water, insect repellent and food; no supplies are sold inside. The only way to enter the forest is by car. From the north, take Hwy 52 to the Cayey Este exit

RUTA PANORÁMICA

Traveling the Ruta Panorámica can be a fun detour or a maddening frustration. Here, distances suddenly become mysteriously elongated as the island appears to double in size and you crawl along the curving lines of the map at a snail's pace. Drives that would take 20 minutes on the coast turn into two- to three-hour road trips. Only a few brief glimpses of the faraway ocean remind you that you haven't disappeared into the Amazonian jungle. First-timers beware: this is no Sunday-afternoon dawdle. Maneuvering through dense rainforest and sleepy mountain villages, the Ruta's roadsides are populated by posses of stray dogs, escaped chickens, horse-riding *jíbaros* (country people) and – most chillingly – the burnt-out wrecks of hundreds of abandoned cars. The latter should be enough to remind wannabe speed-freaks to steer carefully at all times (at no more than 25mph). Unfortunately, the locals aren't always so fastidious, often taking the precarious hills and tricky chicanes at 35mph or more. Drive defensively and be on your guard, and remember to sound your horn around blind corners.

TAKING A HIKE

Fine, we'll just say it: Puerto Rico can bedevil the ambitious hiker. Despite the lush natural areas and acres of natural reserves there's something about trudging down the trail that just simply doesn't jibe with Puerto Rican culture – one park ranger suggested it was because people don't like getting their shoes dirty! Trails are often unmarked and poorly maintained and there are few reliable maps available locally. If you want to do a lot of hiking it's a good idea to order detailed topographical maps before you leave home, have no expectations for word-of-mouth route suggestions and arrive with an ample supply of patience.

to Hwy 184. From the south, take the Ruta Panorámica from Yabucoa. You can also reach the forest from Patillas on the south coast via Hwy 184.

Sights & Activities

Like many of Puerto Rico's forest reserves, Carite can be a great place for hiking, camping, fishing and cooling off in pools and streams, as long as you're up for a bit of DIY adventure. There are 49 species of bird here – including the endangered native *falcón de sierra* (mountain hawk) – and a variety of trees. If you are passing through the forest on the Ruta Panorámica, you can stop for a picnic at the **Area Recreativa Charco Azul** (9am-6pm), a recreation/camping area near the southeastern entrance on Hwy 184, and take a short walk to the Charco Azul natural pool. You can also stop off at **Area Recreativa Guavate** (9am-4:30pm Mon-Fri, 8am-5pm Sat & Sun) at the northern end for a spot of sunbathing and bird-watching or some local food tasting at the nearby *lechonerías*. The third potential stopping place is the **Area Recreativa Real Patillas** (9am-6pm) on Hwy 184 to the south.

Hiking

Hurricanes have wreaked havoc on Carite's trails in the past and most paths have been destroyed and never cleared. The only trail that's maintained by rangers is Charco Azul, though with a bit of bushwhacking you can probably get through on the El Radar and a couple others that lead upstream from Charco Azul. It's best to phone ahead to check current conditions if you're a serious hiker, though you may well reach a park employee who knows nothing at all about the trails.

At Las Casas de la Selva, managers can provide information and guides for long hikes through Carite, including the six-hour trek through Hero Valley, which descends to a river of slick boulders and is suggested for experienced hikers only.

Charco Azul Trail HIKE

After several storms destroyed many of the trails here, rangers decided to clear and maintain only this one. It's also the most popular and the most easily accessible trail in the reserve. It leads to a hazy blue swimming hole and camping/picnic area of the same name. It is an easy half-mile walk from Hwy 184, near the southeast corner of the forest. The swimming hole is about 15ft deep at the center with a rocky bottom. It can be a madhouse on summer weekends, but relatively lonely in the winter. Beyond the swimming area there is another, far more sketchy trail which leads to the top of Cerro La Santa (2730ft), Carite's highest point. You can also follow the water downstream to a different set of waterfalls and some rocky scrambling.

El Radar Trail HIKE

El Radar trailhead departs to the south, off Hwy 184 near the northwest corner of the forest, and makes a steep, 1-mile climb to the peak of Cerro Balíos. If you look beyond the ugly Doppler radar weather station, you'll be rewarded with vistas of the north and south coasts, and hills that roll off toward El Yunque.

Sleeping & Eating

The options for staying over in the forest are divided between upscale eco lodges and two **camping areas** (campsites per person $4, children under 10 free). At the northwest corner of the reserve is the Guavate Camping Area, with room for six tents and 30 people. Charco Azul, the more attractive choice, is the pondside camping area at the southeast end of the reserve. It can accommodate 10 tents and 50 people. Both areas have toilet and bathing facilities. Reserve 15 days in advance with the **Departamento de Recursos Naturales y Ambientales** (DRNA; p278).

TOP CHOICE **Las Casas de la Selva & Tropic Ventures** CAMPGROUND, CABINS $
(☎839-7318; www.eyeontherainforest.org; Hwy 184 Km 16.1; campsites $15, cabin $50-80) This reserve is on the south slope of the Sierra de Cayey in the Río Grande de Patillas watershed. Once a coffee plantation, it became a sustainable-growth tree farm 20 years ago, and continues to be a leading institution for rainforest study on the island. The 1000-acre reserve is mostly for ecological and environmental research and volunteers, and they often host groups from local schools and the Earthwatch organization. Students of various ages come to work, learn about rainforest ecology and explore (see p288). Ecotourism is not its primary concern, but if there is space, visitors can come for a rustic vacation and sleep in the heart of the forest (tent hire is also available: $25 for two people). Advance arrangements are necessary, preferably through its website, since its phone lines are not reliable. Note: the gate will be locked unless you make a reservation. To find Las Casas de la Selva, follow Hwy 184 southeast toward Patillas through the Bosque Estatal de Carite to Km 16.1, where you will see a sign for the reserve.

Jájome Terrace HOTEL $$
(☎738-4016; www.jajometerrace.com; Rte 15 Km 4.6; r $110-124) Rich in both history and setting, the lush Jájome sits 2800ft up in the mountains of the Cordillera Central with satellite map views over towards Ponce. In business since the 1930s, the place has hosted national icon Luis Muñoz Marín and Miss Universe contestants. Almost wiped out by Hurricane George in 1998, the wooden Jájome was revamped in sturdy brick in 2002 and reopened with its 10 fully renovated rooms and popular open-terrace restaurant fresh with nouveau rustic charm. With no TVs or phones and no cell phone reception, the Jájome can sometimes feel like it's miles from anywhere, particularly from Mondays through Fridays when the restaurant is closed and there may be no other guests. Their loss could be your gain.

ℹ Getting There & Around

While a few públicos pass this way, they can be infrequent. Getting to the insanely popular restaurant strip of Guavate may be your best bet – the forest's northern gate (plus trails and camping access) is less than half a mile from here. The most popular way of seeing the mountains in their entirety is still a rental car.

Aibonito & Around

POP 26,500

Once the de facto capital of Puerto Rico, after the Spanish Governor Romualdo Palacios González established residence here in 1887, Aibonito has long been a retreat for the island's political leaders, its devout people, and the most wealthy. The town has a number of other claims to fame that include being the island's highest town (at about 2000ft), the site of the island's lowest recorded temperature (40°F in 1911) and the home of an impressive flower festival. For all these reasons, and because it's on the Ruta Panorámica, Aibonito is the most visited mountain town in Puerto Rico.

The town has a euphonious name that suggests a Spanish exclamation meaning 'Wow, how beautiful,' but the name is probably derived from a Taíno word that Spanish settlers heard when they arrived here in the 1630s. Today, travelers should associate Aibonito with a very limited definition of beauty. The town itself, which shelters a little less than half of the municipality's 26,500 residents, is something of a mixed bag. It sprawls across a high plateau in a slight rift between surrounding peaks. There are traffic jams every day on the narrow roads at the center of town, as rural families gravitate here for shopping, banking and – naturally – a visit to the drive-thru McDonald's. Thriving flower-growing, poultry-raising and poultry-processing industries have brought prosperity to the region, with little thought to urban planning and only belated attention to the area's natural gifts.

Yet there are two extraordinary natural treasures here. One, Mirador La Piedra Degetau, is a cluster of boulders on a peak bordering the Ruta Panorámica; there are great views from this place. Even more spectacular is the Cañón de San Cristóbal (St Christopher Canyon), which lies north of town in a deep volcanic rift cut into the rolling fields between Aibonito and the neighboring town of Barranquitas.

Aibonito-lovers claim that the weather in their town is perpetually spring-like. They are not exaggerating: the average temperature is 72°F. Gentle showers are common.

Most drivers approach Aibonito via the Ruta Panorámica. A less-traveled and more-dramatic route (if you like hairpin turns) is to take Hwy 173 and Hwy 14 south from Cidra.

WORTH A TRIP

GUAVATE

Puerto Ricans invariably speak of Guavate in reverential tones. During the week, it's just an unkempt strip of scruffy, shack-like restaurants abutting the Carite Forest. But come on weekends for a heady transformation – a free-wheeling atmosphere united around good food, spontaneous dancing and boisterous revelry that earns it the designation of the 'Ruta del Lechón,' Hwy 184.

A cherished place for traditional Puerto Rican cooking, Guavate is the spiritual home of the island's ultimate culinary 'delicacy,' *lechón asado*, or whole roast pig, locally reared and turning on a spit. But first impressions can be deceiving. Although the myriad of *lechoneras* that pepper the roadside might look a little rough around the edges (Styrofoam plates, plastic forks, Formica tables), the crowds tell another story. Everyone from millionaire businessmen to cigar-puffing *jíbaros* (country people) congregate for the best in authentic Puerto Rican cuisine and culture. If it's the island's uninhibited 'soul' you're after, look no further.

The best action takes place on weekend afternoons between 2pm and 9pm, when old-fashioned troubadours entertain the crowds and live salsa, meringue and reggaetón music brings diners to the makeshift dance floors for libidinous grooving. With over a dozen restaurants and stalls all offering similar canteen-style food and service, your best bet is to come hungry and follow the crowds. Standards include *arroz con grandules* (rice and pigeon peas), *pasteles* (mashed plantain and pork) and – brave, this one – *morcillas* (rice and pigs blood).

If you can't choose which *lechonera*, try **El Rancho Original** (Rte 184 Km 27.5; plates $6-7; ⌚10am-8pm Sat & Sun, with variations), where they serve consistently perfect pork that's heavenly, smoky and covered in crispy skin. But, truth be told, the standard on the 'Pork Highway' is very high and most places along the route have avid, dedicated fans who swear their place is the best.

To get to Guavate from San Juan, follow expressway 52 to exit 31, halfway between Caguas and Cayey. Turn east onto Hwy 184.

Sights

TOP CHOICE **Cañón de San Cristóbal** CANYON

The canyon is so unexpected – both in location and appearance – that it may take your breath away. The deep green chasm just drops out of nowhere, its rocky crags hiding the veil of falling water. The canyon is only 5 miles north of Aibonito. Cutting more than 500ft down through the central mountains, you'll probably only see it right as you approach its edge; the rift is so deep and narrow that the fields and hills of the surrounding high-mountain plateau disguise it.

The highest waterfall on the island is here, where the Río Usabón plummets at least 500ft down a sheer cliff into a gorge that is deeper, in many places, than it is wide. For fit outdoor enthusiasts, the descent into the canyon is a first-class thrill, whether you take steep trails or make the technical descent – recommended only for those with mountaineering experience. Not so long ago, San Cristóbal was a garbage dump, but the Conservation Trust of Puerto Rico saved the canyon by buying up most of it for preservation.

You can catch a glimpse of the canyon from a distance by looking east from the intersection of Hwy 725 and Hwy 162. Getting into the canyon is a bit trickier. One way is to take side roads off Hwy 725 or Hwy 7725 and then cross private land to approach the rim of the canyon. It's essential to get permission to cross private property. Cañón de San Cristóbal has sheer cliffs that are prone to erosion and landslides, and the trails into the canyon are a slippery death wish when they get wet (and it rains a lot around here).

The best way to visit the canyon is to plan ahead, make reservations and join an organized trek with **San Cristóbal Hiking Tour** (☎857-2094; www.barranquitaspr.net/tours), run by local historian and geographer Samuel Oliveras Ortiz. Trips run on weekends and holidays and vary from a three- to four-hour basic tour ($90) to a five- to six-hour adrenalin-junkie fest with rock climbing and rappelling ($135 to $160 depending on number of people). You can also visit with **Acampa**

Nature Adventure Tours (☎706-0695; www.acampapr.com), based out of San Juan. Wear secure shoes and layer appropriate clothing that you can take off at the canyon floor, where temperatures can be more than 10°F warmer than up on the brink. Of course, you will need water and snacks for the return trip up the canyon wall.

Mirador La Piedra Degetau NATURAL AREA
This nest of boulders lies on a hilltop alongside the Ruta Panorámica (Hwy 7718 here) at Km 0.7, just south of Aibonito. Once the 'thinking place' of Ponce-born writer Federico Degetau y González, who became the island's first resident commissioner in Washington DC, from 1900 to 1904, this must have been a truly sublime place in its day, with views of the mountains, the Atlantic and the Caribbean. On a clear evening you can actually see cruise ships leaving San Juan more than 20 miles to the north and the lights of Ponce beginning to glow to the south.

Sadly, the natural beauty of the site has been marred by a lookout tower that dwarfs the actual rocks, which huddle like small pebbles to the side. Myriad picnic shelters, a playground and a paved parking lot further hinder the lyrical ruminations of potential poets. It's still an awe-inspiring view but one can't help feeling that Degetau must be turning in his grave.

Festivals & Events

Festival de Flores FLOWER FESTIVAL
The Festival de Flores (Flower Festival) at Aibonito has grown into a major rite of summer during the last 30 years. Today it draws hundreds of commercial growers and amateur horticulturists and tens of thousands of flower-lovers to see the town and surrounding countryside ablaze with roses, carnations, lilies and begonias. Of course, along with the flowers there are food and craft stalls. There's also the requisite beauty pageant. This event takes place at the end of June and often runs into the July 4 holiday (US Independence Day), so you had better plan to get here before the crowds or expect to spend your holiday in a traffic jam. Remember to check the regulations of the Department of Agriculture if you're planning to bring back plants to the United States.

Sleeping & Eating

El Coquí Posada Familiar MOTEL $$
(☎735-3150; Rte 722 Km 7.3; r $80-90) Not the first place in the world you'd expect to find an American-style motel but, there it is, perched over one of those ubiquitous Puerto Rican fast-food joints in the improbable mountain town of Aibonito. The thing is, El Coquí is actually rather good, with amiable service, well-equipped rooms (fridges, microwaves and cable TV), huge beds, and facilities so clean you could safely perform brain surgery in the bathroom. Get takeout from the adjacent mall and nestle down in bed with the Food channel on the tube. It's a good idea to call ahead to let staff know you are coming. El Coquí can be hard to find and the reception is not always staffed.

TOP CHOICE **Tio Pepe's** CARIBBEAN $$
(Hwy 723 Km 0.3; dishes $12-25) This traditional Aibonito favorite is stuck a few miles to the west of the town on a wooded knoll surrounded by trees and flowers. There's a sundeck, function room and regular musical entertainment from passing troubadours and trios. The decor is casually elegant, but nothing too fancy, and the menu is a greatest hits of good old home-style mountain cooking. Pass the *mofongo*.

La Piedra CARIBBEAN $$
(☎735-1034; Hwy 7718 Km 0.7; dishes $10-25; ⊙11am-7pm Wed & Thu, 11am-10pm Fri-Sun) Situated next to the Piedra Degetau Park, this is a long-time mountain institution that also accommodates the recording studios of Radio Cumbre. Yes, that guy at the next table behind the thick pane of reinforced glass isn't a waiter wearing ear muffs; he's broadcasting on the airwaves on 1470AM. The plant-filled restaurant serves up decent food – chicken in a tamarind sauce and chicken broth and *mofongo* are popular. Thanks to its prime Ruta Panorámica location it also acts as a nexus point to chicane weary motorists, Federico Degetau pilgrims, and local walking groups setting off into the

LECHÓN LINGUISTICS

» *Cuerito* – Smoky, crispy pig skin

» *Cuchifrito* – Deep-fried pork delicacies, including ears and tails

» *Morcillas* – Dark pork and rice-stuffed blood sausage

» *Coquito* – Puerto Rican eggnog, made from coconut milk and served around Christmas

Cañon de San Cristóbal. Regardless of what you order for dinner, end with the amazing ginger flan.

Getting There & Away

Públicos will take you to Aibonito from Cayey or Caguas for about $4. These cities have connections to the Río Piedras district of San Juan for another $5.

Barranquitas & Around

One of the most quintessential of Puerto Rico's lofty mountain towns, Barranquitas is a diminutive, picturesque settlement clinging to the muddy slopes of the rain-lashed Cordillera Central. Lying on the north side of the Cañón de San Cristóbal, about a 20-minute drive out of Aibonito on Hwy 162 (or an even shorter detour off of the Ruta Panorámica via Hwy 143), the town is known locally as the Cuna de Próceres (Cradle of Great People) for its historical propensity to produce poets, politicians and governors of national (and international) distinction. Most notable in this list is the legendary Muñoz clan (see boxed text, p228), Puerto Rico's substitute 'royal' family whose evocative mausoleum has made Barranquitas a pilgrimage site for both local patriots and curious visitors.

This is not, however, a fairy-tale village of architectural heirlooms. Hurricanes and fires have ravaged Barranquitas several times (the name translates to 'Place of Little Mud Slides'), and the oldest structures, such as the church, date only from the early 20th century. Barranquitas' charm lies in its narrow streets, tightly packed with shops and houses, which fall away into deep valleys on three sides of the plaza. Indeed, the view as you descend the mountain road into town and the afternoon sun sets the church tower ablaze above the dense architectural jumble of the central neighborhood, is truly memorable.

Sights & Activities

Plaza de Recreo de Barranquitas SQUARE
Barranquita's central plaza is laced with wrought-iron railings, and guarded by the **Parroquia de San Antonio de Padua**, a small church first constructed in 1804. The original church was destroyed by two catastrophic hurricanes (the first of which wiped out the whole town), but was rebuilt in 1933 in a quaint postcolonial style. The church was recently renovated and now gleams amid the surrounding mountain greenery. The centerpiece of the plaza is a decorative wrought-iron gazebo adorned with distinctive art nouveau flourishes and surrounded by four uniquely structured classical fountains. The 19th-century *alcaldía* (town hall) was recently remodeled as well.

Casa Museo Luis Muñoz Rivera MUSEUM
(cnr Calles Muñoz Rivera & Padre Berrios; admission $1; ⏲8:30am-4:20pm Wed-Sun) This tin-roofed house honors the so-called grandfather of Puerto Rico's autonomy movement and the 20th-century architect of the Puerto Rican commonwealth. This is where Luis Muñoz Rivera was born in 1859, and it contains a collection of furniture, letters, photographs and other memorabilia, including his death mask. The coolest thing on display is Muñoz' 1912 Pierce-Arrow, which carried him to his mausoleum.

FREE **Mausoleo Familia Muñoz Rivera** MUSEUM
(7 Calle Padre Berrios; ⏲8:30am-4:20pm Tue-Sun) Just south of the plaza is a family tomb that holds the remains of Muñoz Rivera, his famous son Luis Muñoz Marín and their wives. Photographic displays at the tomb evoke the funeral of Luis Muñoz Marín, but the brightly colored frescos on the walls are an aptly powerful testament to the man himself.

TOP CHOICE **Toro Verde Nature Adventure Park** ADVENTURE PARK
(☎867-7020; www.toroverdepr.com; Carretera 155, Barrio Gato, sector Los Santiago, Orocovis; ⏲8am-6pm Thu-Sun) This new adventure

DON'T MISS

TORO VERDE NATURE ADVENTURE PARK

You're soaring between peaks of central mountains, arms out in front of you like Superman, hundreds of feet over the tree tops. This is no dream; a flight on 'La Bestia,' the 4700-foot long zip line at Toro Verde Nature Adventure Park gives thrill-seekers the rare chance to fly like a bird. It's over in two minutes, but makes a memorable rush, since 'The Beast' is among the longest zip lines in the world. The new adventure park also hosts the only pro-designed single-track mountain biking on the island.

park was completed in 2010, and offers a suite of adventures among a stunning patch of forest near the little town of Orocovis, north of Barranquita. The affordable, adrenaline-soaked zip-line tours and single-track mountain-bike circuit make it the best facility of its kind on the island. There are several zip-line tours to choose from, but even the standard canopy zip-line tour ($75, three hours) is a rush – sending you sailing over a valley connected to eight lines. The longest line on the standard tour is over 2500ft long and 600ft in the air. The other packages on offer are a good option for those who want something a bit different, including the two-minute ride on 'La Bestia' ($50), which harnesses you superman-style into one of the longest zip lines in the world, and a hanging bridges tour ($85, two hours), in which you rush across wildly swinging bridges (while strapped to a safety cable). The 8-mile-long mountain-bike circuit ($25) is far and away the best maintained trail ride on the mountain, designed by pro mountain biker Marla Streb. It's single-track trails are challenging, with lots of tight lines and some good drops. Note that for the zip lines and bridge tour there are weight and age requirements (the youngest available for kids over 12).

WORTH A TRIP

CASA BAVARIA

Although a tour through the Central Mountains makes travelers expect the unexpected, you might not believe your eyes when you stumble on **Casa Bavaria** (☎862-7818; www.casabavaria.com; Carr 155 Km 38.3, Barrio Perchas, Morovis; ⊙lunch-dinner Mon-Sat), a German Creole restaurant. The restaurant is perched 2105ft high in the mountains near Morovis in the center of the island. Something of an off-beat institution, the menu mixes typical cuisine from the Bavarian region of Germany with meaty specialties of Puerto Rico. The outdoor seating and misty views draw bikers and road-trippers galore, and fans include President Bill Clinton, who stopped by in 2008 to order the schnitzel.

Sleeping & Eating

Hacienda Margarita HOTEL $$
(☎854-0414; Rte 152, Km 1.7, Barrio Quebrada Grande, Sector Tres Caminos; r/ste $119/210; ❄☒) Destroyed in a 1998 hurricane, Hacienda Margarita has risen from the ruins with a modern two-story building housing 27 units, a pool, a restaurant and a bar (it hosts live local music most Saturday nights). Rooms feature patios/balconies with views of the surrounding mountains, tiled floors and those ubiquitous flowery bedspreads. Some have rock walls and one has a Jacuzzi. Call the owners for directions, as you have to wind your way through a housing subdivision to find the hotel.

Vaca Brava STEAKS, BBQ $
(☎857-2628; Km PR 9.3 771; mains $10-19; ⊙lunch & dinner Thu-Sun) There's a certain brazen spectacle to the pure carnage at Vaca Brava, an open-air restaurant that serves *enormous* platters of steak, fish and chicken, many constructed in whimsical, carnivorous sculptures. This is a restaurant where gluttony is nearly mandatory. A tame choice would be the *tendedero* (clothesline) – which strings together chicken, sirloin and house-stuffed chorizo and comes sided with golden *tostones* and rice. If you want to test your limits, try the half-stack of beef ribs, some 3ft tall, which seems rather like something out of *The Flintstones*. Masochists should opt for the Vaca Acosta Challenge, an 8-pound platter of sirloin resting on a bed of French fries and soaked in mushroom sauce. Finish it and you'll get it free, but note that previous winners can be counted on one hand (the travel channel's *Man V Food* host Adam Richman was a recent loser). Sure, the unapologetic gluttony is a bit shocking, but it brings a long line of locals, some who wait up to two hours. Just don't end up in the hospital.

Heladería Los Próceres ICE CREAM $
(☎857-4909; 21 Calle Muños Rivera; ⊙9am-9pm) Situated a block from the plaza, this is a classic Puerto Rican ice-cream joint. Milkshakes and 100% natural ice creams are concocted from strawberry, papaya, tamarind and *bizcocho* (sweet pastry). It also serves nachos, *tostados* and coffee.

Getting There & Away

Públicos to and from surrounding towns stop on Calle Padre Berrios, three blocks south of the plaza past the Mausoleo Familia Muñoz Rivera. You'll pay $1 to go to Aibonito, or $8 for the long (plan on four hours) roller-coaster ride to/from San Juan (Río Piedras terminal).

THE MUÑOZ CLAN

While America spawned the legendary Roosevelt dynasty, Puerto Rico produced its very own influential establishment family, the iconic Muñoz clan, two generations of charismatic politicians who changed the course of the island's postcolonial history and set the commonwealth on the road to modernity.

Born in the mountain town of Barranquitas in 1859, Luis Muñoz Rivera was the son of a former town mayor and the grandson of an enterprising Spanish sea captain. With politics planted firmly in his DNA, he formed the Autonomist Party in 1887, an organization that called for Puerto Rican autonomy within the confines of the Spanish colonial system. Three years later he upped the ante further by founding a newspaper, *La Democracia*, to act as a journalistic mouthpiece for his cause.

With the Spanish driven out by a US military government in 1898, Muñoz Rivera switched his focus to the United States. Initially an advocate of outright independence, he dropped his claims in the early 1900s to ensure the replacement of the one-sided Foraker Act by the 1917 Jones Act and a more equitable relationship with the United States. Although Muñoz Rivera died a year before its implementation, he was considered instrumental in drafting the new laws (that granted US citizenship to Puerto Rican nationals) and is still revered as one of Puerto Rico's most important homegrown personalities. His mausoleum in Barranquitas remains an important and oft-visited historical monument.

A chip off his father's block, Rivera's son, Luis Muñoz Marín, was a prodigious poet and journalist who studied law in the United States. Returning to Puerto Rico in 1916, the younger Muñoz joined the socialist party and became a leading advocate for Puerto Rican independence. But, just like his father before him, Luis retracted on his initial promises during a spell as President of the Puerto Rican Senate in the mid-1940s in order to enlist US economic backing for an ambitious industrialization campaign codenamed 'Operation Bootstrap.'

In 1949 Muñoz Marín became Puerto Rico's first democratically elected governor, a position he held for an unprecedented four terms (until 1965). During his time in office he orchestrated Puerto Rico's economic 'miracle,' transforming the island from a poverty-stricken agrarian society into a thriving economic powerhouse based on tourism, manufacturing and pharmaceuticals. Often touted as the 'father of modern Puerto Rico,' Muñoz commanded huge popularity at home for his efforts in tackling poverty while, at the same time, extracting greater freedoms from the United States. Other more nationalistic voices depict him as a turncoat who was coerced out of his independence ideals by a belligerent US military establishment.

Today, the Muñoz legacy is still evident all over Puerto Rico, from the mausoleum and museums of Barranquitas to the island's Aeropuerto Internacional de Luis Muñoz Murín (LMM international airport), named in honor of its most celebrated native son.

Getting Around

Streets are poorly marked and the general populace only uses descriptive addresses, but navigating Barranquitas is pretty easy. Rte 162 becomes Calle Rivera, the main street, and then after passing the plaza it becomes Rte 156 headed east (incidentally, downhill is always east).

Reserva Forestal Toro Negro

Covering 7000 acres and protecting some of Puerto Rico's highest peaks, the Toro Negro Reserve provides a quieter, less-developed alternative to El Yunque. Bisected by some of the steepest and windiest sections of the Ruta Panorámica (Hwy 143 in this section), the area is often shrouded in mist and blanketed by dense jungle foliage. This is where you come to truly escape the tourist throngs of the coast. But don't expect El Yunque's polish. Toro Negro's ragged facilities – which comprise a campground, a few trails and a recreation area – are spartan and poorly staffed and the signs are rough. Rather than just turning up, it's far better to plan ahead and enquire about current conditions at the DRNA in San Juan, as mudslides are common. Properly prepared and with a decent topo map, you should be able to carve out some memorable DIY adventures in the mountains. Those who want an organized trip can go with an organized tour.

Cerro de Punta, at 4389ft, is the tallest point in the reserve and Puerto Rico's highest peak. You can drive most of the way to the top on the Ruta Panorámica or, alternatively, attempt to bushwhack your way up from Jayuya on an infuriatingly unkempt (and vague) trail. Other notable peaks include Monte Jayuya and Cerro Maravilla, where two pro-independence activists were notoriously shot by Puerto Rican police in 1978.

Sights & Activities

Cerro de Punta MOUNTAIN PEAK

Rising to 4389ft, the summit of Cerro de Punta lies in the Toro Negro Forest Reserve just off Hwy 143 (the Ruta Panorámica). Most people drive to the top. Although there's a narrow unmarked, fairly treacherous cement road to the peak itself, it's better to stop in a parking lot on the northern side of Hwy 143 and take the last 1.5 miles by foot, soaking up the sights and sounds of the surrounding jungle. Not surprisingly, the road can be treacherous in bad weather. The summit is crowned by communication towers, though the view north is stupendous – clouds permitting. Cerro de Punta lies in the west of the reserve, almost 10 miles of tortured driving from the Area Recreativa Doña Juana.

The challenge for hikers has nothing to do with the difficulty of the terrain: the absence of marked trails underscores Puerto Rico's disinterest in the activity. Before committing to a hike, understand that you'll waste a lot of time looking for trailheads. Theoretically, a trail leaves from behind the Hacienda Gripiñas, close to the town of Jayuya. If you find it, good luck following it; it is badly signposted and in a poor state of repair. Locals are of little help here – since hiking is so uncommon, most don't know anything about the trail. If you're determined to give it a shot, ask around at the Hacienda Gripiñas and be persistent. The trail is a steep and sweaty two- to three-hour grunt.

Area Recreativa Doña Juana RECREATION AREA

This is the area of about 3 sq miles at the eastern end of the park surrounding the ranger station. You will find picnic sites, toilets, showers, the camping area and a half-dozen short trails branching off Hwy 143. Come here in the winter and the place will probably look empty and abandoned. One trail leads to the swimming pool, open in summer only. Three others lead to the observation tower, less than a half-mile south of the highway.

Hiking

There are approximately 11 miles of trails around Doña Juana, but mostly they are short walks to the swimming pool. Always consult with the ranger station for longer hikes.

Camino El Bolo HIKE

Across from the visitor's center, through the parking lot, you'll spot a narrow trail heading uphill. That's El Bolo, a 2.5-mile jaunt that takes you up to a mountain ridge and great southern views, and then crosses Vereda La Torre to take you even higher. It's best to come down on the same path; the path ends at narrow Hwy 143, which has too many blind corners for a comfortable return.

Vereda La Torre HIKE

A very popular and easy path that starts in the Area Recreativa Doña Juana, La Torre goes up to an observation tower with some great views. The 2-mile trail starts at the picnic tables and slowly gets more hilly and rough as you ascend. You'll see a tiny road feed into Vereda after about 20 minutes of walking – that's Camino El Bolo. Take a slight left to continue on to the observation tower.

Tours

Acampa Nature Adventure Tours HIKING

(☎706-0695; www.acampapr.com; 1221 Av Jesús T Piñero, San Juan) Offers one day hiking/adventure tours to the Toro Negro rainforest. The excursion involves hiking/scrambling along the Quebrada Rosa River, rappelling off a 60ft cliff and zip-lining 200ft across the treetops. Prices start at $149 per person and include transportation from San Juan, equipment and lunch.

Sleeping & Eating

Los Viveros PUBLIC CAMPGROUND $

(Hwy 143 at Km 32.5; campsites per person $4) In the forest, just north of the ranger station in the Area Recreativa Doña Juana, this is a designated camping area with enough space for 14 tents (pretty close together). Note that part of the area is often reserved for groups. You will need a permit from the DRNA in San Juan. Apply 15 days in advance. If you're lingering in this area of the Central Mountains,

SIGNS OF THE TIMES

Don't get ruffled if you can't find signs for the 'official' Ruta Panorámica – signs are often obscured or moved by local business owners hoping to lure traffic.

bring charcoal and lighter fluid so you can cook your food over one of the open-air picnic grills at the Area Recreativa Doña Juana near the east end of Reserva Forestal Toro Negro.

Las Cabañas de Doña Juana BBQ $
(☎897-3981; Hwy 143 Km 30.5) This place is actually a rib joint of sorts on the main Ruta Panorámica. It serves all types of grilled meats for under $10 in little open-air shacks by the roadside. Opening times are sporadic.

Information

The Ruta Panorámica (Hwy 143) is your artery to and from the forest, and it is none too wide. Honk your horn when approaching blind curves and drive with lots of caution.

All of the forest's public facilities lie at the east end of the reserve in the Area Recreativa Doña Juana, clustered in the vicinity of the ranger station at Km 32.4 on Hwy 143.

The **ranger station** (☎867-3040; Hwy 143 Km 32.5; ⌚8am-noon summer, irregular hours winter) has blurry photocopies of park literature, and some of this material is extremely misleading. The trail map lacks useful detail and the compass rose has been rotated so north is not at the top of the page.

You're not likely to get anything better in San Juan from the DRNA, nor is it easy to get USGS maps on the island without ordering through a bookstore. You can get a USGS map from your favorite map supplier in the US or mail-order one on the island.

Barranquitas is an hour away, so you'd better come prepared. Bring plenty of food and water and some insect repellent.

Jayuya

Puerto Rico's unheralded mountain 'capital' lies a few kilometers north of the Ruta Panorámica in an isolated steep-sided valley overlooked by three of the island's highest peaks – Cerro de Punta, Cerro Tres Picachos and Cerro Maravilla. Fiercely traditional and verdantly beautiful, the precipitous geography in this region has protected many of the island's traditions. If you're on a mission to find Puerto Rico's last authentic *jíbaro* (country person), this is a good place to start.

Steeped in Taíno legend, the original settlement of Jayuya had little contact with the rest of the island until 1911, when it was declared a municipality. In 1950 local nationalist leader Blanca Canales led a revolt against US occupation known as the 'Jayuya Uprising.' Rebels sacked the police station, torched the post office and declared a Puerto Rican Republic from the town square. The rebellion lasted just three days before US planes bombed the town, causing widespread destruction. Still, today, Jayuya is one of the island's most un-Americanized towns.

Efforts to keep Taíno culture alive include a festival of music, food, games and a Miss Taíno pageant.

Sights

Jayuya is the heart of coffee country, making a visit to one of the outlying plantations requisite.

TOP CHOICE **Hacienda San Pedro** COFFEE FARM
(☎615-3083; www.cafehsp.com; Rte 144 Km 8.4; ⌚8am-6pm Mon-Sat, 10am-5pm Sun) San Pedro is a small, working coffee farm with an attached museum and tasting room where you can get a fascinating tour of the whole coffee-making process from green bean to dark-roast espresso. The gourmet blends served here are some of the best brews you'll taste anywhere. Rustically packaged beans are sold on-site and there's a small museum. True gourmands can also buy green coffee beans here, to try their hand at roasting.

Casa Museo Canales MUSEUM
(☎828-4094; Rte 144 Km 9.3; adult/child $1/0.50; ⌚noon-4pm Sat & Sun) Nearer to the town center, in a small park in the barrio of Coabey, this reconstructed 19th-century coffee *finca* (rural smallholding) with quintessential *criollo* features once belonged to Jayuya's first major, Rosario Canales. Rosario spawned two famous offspring. His son, Nemesio, is recognized as a great Puerto Rican poet, playwright and political activist who pushed for legal rights for women, while his daughter, Blanca Canales Torresola, became a notorious figure in the Puerto Rican nationalist movement when she led an independence revolt against the American-backed authorities in Jayuya in 1950. The house displays traditional antiques and has a pleasant atmosphere, nestled in the shadow of the surrounding mountains.

Museo del Cemí MUSEUM
(☎828-1241; Rte 144 Km 9.2; adult/child $1/0.50; ⏰9:30-4pm Mon-Fri, to 3pm Sat & Sun) Across the park, this is housed in what is perhaps the oddest building on the island. Designed by Río Piedras architect, Efrén Badia Cabrera, the weird fish-like structure is supposed to represent a gigantic *cemí* or native talisman. The exhibits inside are made up mostly of Taíno artifacts – including a *espátula vomita,* a tool Taíno used to make themselves puke before they took hallucinogenic drugs – and photos of local petroglyphs.

La Piedra Escrita PETROGLYPH
(Rte 144 Km 7.3) Supposedly one of the island's best-preserved native petroglyphs carved on a large rock in the middle of the Río Saliente. Forming a natural bathing pool, it has become a popular stopping-off point for curious (and hot) travelers. There's a small car park and restaurant nearby.

Sleeping & Eating

There are few very basic restaurants in town, though several *panaderías* (bakeries) serve sandwiches.

TOP CHOICE **Hacienda Gripiñas** HOTEL $$
(☎828-1717; www.haciendagripinas.com; Hwy 527 Km 2.5; s/d $111/155; ❄📶🏊) When the winter mist cools things, guests curl up in the common room of Hacienda Gripiñas, a beautifully restored coffee hacienda dating from 1858 that's nestled in the shadow of Cerro de Punta. Guests wander creaking floors between the rooms and sit in wicker rocking chairs on the breezy balconies, pulling their noses out of thick novels to take lunch in the black-and-white tiled dining room. Furnished with antiques and framed historic coffee posters, the hotel has a few modern touches – like wi-fi and a pair of swimming pools – but the historical building is dignified and timeless. But don't expect coastal-style luxury; the rooms are very simple, and some are much nicer than others, so ask to see a few. The three-day packages include meals, but midweek rates are by far the best bargain. Even if you're not staying at Hacienda Gripiñas, its dining room has excellent views and good, if pricy, food.

Posada Jayuya HOTEL $
(☎828-7250; 49 Guillermo Esteves; s/d incl breakfast $69/79; ❄🏊) This place in the town center is a good journeyman sleepover with 27 rooms that include TVs and refrigerators. The air-con might sound like the inside of a 1956 Buick, but at least it'll work, and the passable downstairs restaurant sometimes hosts live music.

Triple G Bar & Grill COMIDA CRIOLLA $
(☎828-9999; Hwy 144 Km 7.3) A small thatched-roof restaurant in the parking lot at La Piedra Escrita, this place serves up the best *comida criolla* in the valley.

Adjuntas

POP 20,000

Although calling Adjuntas the 'Switzerland of Puerto Rico' is a bit of an overstatement, the silhouetted mountains which surround the town earn this attractive agricultural hub a more accurate moniker, the 'town of the sleeping giant.' After the discovery of copper in the area in the 1960s, local community groups fought successfully to prevent their cool subtropical jungle haven from being turned into a huge open-cast mining pit. Instead, today Adjuntas has become something of an environmental steward whose livelihood remains rooted in bananas, coffee and citrus fruits.

Marking the spot where one of the island's major north–south arteries (Hwys 123 and 10) crests the Central Mountains, Adjuntas is a traffic bottleneck in the summer. Be ready for the complicated one-way system and allow plenty of time for delays. The central plaza is a good place to wander while you cool the engine and there are several pizza places on its border for a quick bite.

One of the main attractions in this area is the Bosque Estatal de Guilarte, with a good peak and remote cabins.

Sights

Casa Pueblo (☎829-4842; www.casapueblo.org; 30 Rodolfo Gonzáles; donation $2; ⏰8am-4pm) is Adjuntas' tenacious environmental organization, the primary obstructer of a plan to blight the area with an open-pit mining operation. These days, it also concentrates on sustainability issues and rainforest protection. It has an artisan's shop and grassy butterfly garden. This is an excellent place to inquire about local volunteer opportunities.

Sleeping

Parador Villas de Sotomayor CABINS $$
(☎829-1717; www.paradorvillassotomayor.com; Hwy 123/10 Km 36.3; r $121-$130; 🏊👪) This campus of small cabins along a rock river is

the best spot for families in the area, with an onsite horseback-riding stable, bright swimming pool, basketball and tennis courts and plenty of space to run around. The 26 villas are a bit worn, but undergoing constant upgrade, and they are extremely popular with families throughout the summer. The restaurant and somewhat isolated setting lends it the feel of a previous generation's all-inclusive family summer camp.

Bosque Estatal de Guilarte

This forest, west of Adjuntas, actually consists of a number of parcels of land totaling about 4500 acres. Most of it is rainforest dominated by sierra palms. Coming from the east, you first see Lago Garzas, a popular fishing site. West of the lake, the road rises toward the park's ranger station, near the intersection of Hwys 518 and 131, where there's a picnic area with shelters, cooking grills and toilets. There's also a trail to the top of Monte Guilarte (3950ft) and five cabins.

The **DRNA** (☎829-5767, 724-3647; cabins $20) maintains the basic cabins, toilets and shower facilities. The cabins are slightly dreary but they sleep up to six; cooking facilities are outdoors and there's no electricity. You must bring all of your own gear, including bedding. Make your reservations 15 days in advance with the DRNA in San Juan. You can make an open reservation, which allows flexibility with dates. Camping is not permitted in Guilarte.

Maricao

POP 6200

With a population of fewer than 7000 citizens, Maricao is the smallest municipality on the main island of Puerto Rico, and a gem of a mountain retreat near the western end of the Ruta Panorámica. This is a town of little commerce, with rushing streams, gorges, bridges, terraced houses, switchback roads, and weather so cool and damp that some houses have stone fireplaces to take the nip out of the air. Outside the town there is beautiful mountain terrain and the largest state forest in Puerto Rico, the Bosque Estatal de Maricao.

With its peaks, dark forests and fog, Maricao is just the kind of place in which legends take root. Admirers of Maricao claim that it was the strong coffee grown here that woke up the devil on the island. Another story claims that 2000 Taíno survived here into the 19th century, centuries after the last native Puerto Ricans were thought to have disappeared.

Stopping here for a day or two is probably as close as a traveler can come to experiencing the charms of the legendary *jíbaro*'s existence. Maricao hosts a popular coffee-harvest festival in mid-February, with crafts and traditional coffee-making demonstrations.

Sights & Activities

Bosque Estatal de Maricao FOREST

This forest of more than 10,000 acres lies along the Ruta Panorámica south of Maricao, and the drive is spectacular, with sharp curves snaking over ridges as the mountainsides fall away into steep valleys. Along the drive, there are pull-offs at trailheads leading into the woods or down steep inclines.

Curiously, few of the trails are maintained or mapped and guides are difficult to come by. If you are coming here to hike, bring a topo map from a supplier in the US, or order one from the USGS.

While the landscape is categorized as high-mountain rainforest, scientists note that the 845 species of plant are less 'exuberant' than tropical rainforests such as El Yunque. Birds are the most studied fauna, with 44 identified species. Tanagers, cuckoos and warblers are some of the remarkable types spotted in the forest.

Sleeping

Parque Ecológico Monte de Estado en Maricao CABINS $

(☎873-5632, reservations 622-5200; Hwy 120 Km 13.1; cabins $30-60; 🏊) East of Maricao, this campground has 24 remodeled cabins. Cabin sizes vary from three-person ($15) to six-person ($30) to 12-person ($55) and most have refrigerators, fireplaces and hot water. The area also has a swimming pool, basketball courts, restrooms, showers and an observation tower. Make reservations as far in advance as possible by calling the Compañía de Parques Nacionales (p278) in San Juan.

Getting There & Away

Público vans leave the town's plaza on the Maricao–Mayagüez run and charge $4. As is usually the case, the vans leave when they are full or on the driver's whim. You can approach Maricao from the east or west on the Ruta Panorámica. You can also connect to points north and south via Hwys 119 and 120, which involve a spectacular climb into the mountains on twisting roads.

Understand Puerto Rico

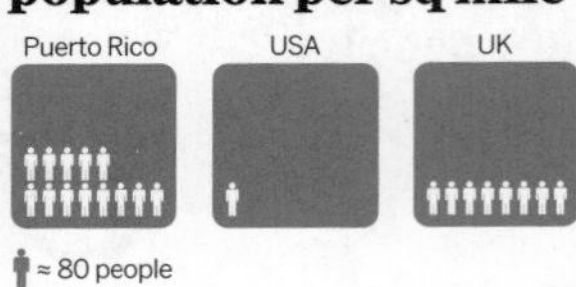

Puerto Rico Today

Fast Facts

» Population: 4.4 million

» Population growth rate: 0.27%

» GDP (per capita): $17,100

» Life expectancy: 78.7 years

» Literacy rate: 94.1%

» Unemployment: 16.4%

» Percentage of adults with cell phones: 73%

» Internet users: 1,222,000

The Economic Downturn

Like so many other places in the world, Puerto Rico's economy was sent in a downwards spiral with the Global Financial Crisis. The effect on the island was immediate and stark: many places included in the previous edition of this guide were found shuttered, with the less touristic south coast particularly hard hit. Unemployment stood above 16% in early 2011, nearly twice the US average. Almost all visible road and infrastructure development projects were next to signs boasting of the Obama administration's 2009 Federal Recovery and Reinvestment Act.

Though Puerto Rico's economy is weak in comparison to most US states, it boasts one of the most dynamic economies in the Caribbean. If you arrive from Jamaica or the Dominican Republic the differences are palpable.

Dreamt up in the 1950s and '60s, Operation Bootstrap succeeded in converting Puerto Rico from an agricultural society into an industrial powerhouse. Tax incentives introduced by prophetic island governor Luis Muñoz Marín led to long-term US investment on the island and growth in both the pharmaceutical and tourism industries. That said, Puerto Rico's per capita GDP is significantly lower than the US's poorest state (Mississippi), and 45% of its population lives below the poverty line.

Environmentalism & Energy

Energy issues have long sparked debate among Puerto Ricans, whose energy costs are twice that of their US neighbors. After a massive explosion disabled the island's only refinery in 2009, the energy crisis has been a constant challenge for environmentalists. A 2010 law promised 12% in renewable energy sources by 2015, but this may not be easy – wind turbines in the southwest were narrowly approved after conservationists protested the impact on the critically endangered Puerto Rican nightjar

Greeting People

» Though the customary greeting for people in Puerto Rico is similar to the US, with a handshake or a quick hug, greetings with acquaintances are a bit more physical and may include a pat on the shoulder or kiss on both cheeks.

Top Books

» **When I Was Puerto Rican** (Esmeralda Santiago) This memoir tackles immigration and cultural assimilation.

» **The Rum Diary** (Hunter S Thompson) A tangled tale of treachery, alcoholism and lust at a San Juan newspaper.

» **La Charca** (The Pond; Manuel Zeno Gandia) This 19th-century novel explores love, murder and the struggle of coffee farmers.

» **Spiks** (Pedro Juan Soto) These short stories concern the struggle of Puerto Rican emigrants to the US in the '50s.

if Puerto Rico were 100 people

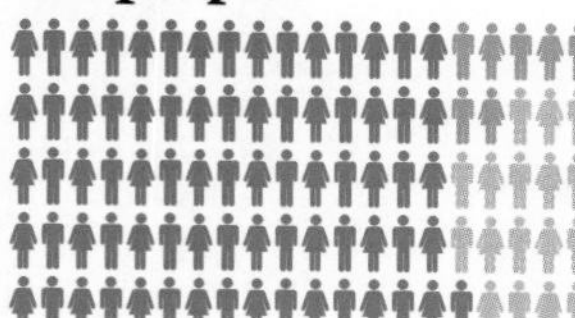

76 would be White*
7 would be Black
4 would be Mixed
13 would be Other

*note that the US census considers Hispanic/Latino ethnicity separately from race; people can choose to identify as Hispanic/Latino in a separate question while identifying with any race.

belief systems

(% of population)

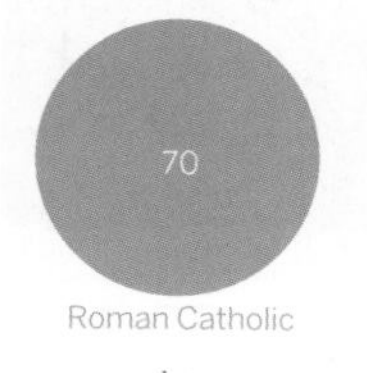

2
Other

10
Athiest/
Irreligious

bird. Most recently, the debate concerns a 92-mile, $450-million natural gas pipeline proposed by Governor Luis Fortuno. Fortuno claims that it would save $1 billion in annual energy costs and reduce 64% of carbon emissions. The problem? The project is plagued with allegations of corruption (the Associated Press reported that the $9.6 million contract was awarded to the governor's childhood friend) and huge protests concerning the route through fragile ecosystems and several archaeological sites.

A Question of Status

A commonwealth of the United States of America, Puerto Rico is a semi-autonomous territory whose constitutional status has long been a political oxymoron. Puerto Ricans enjoy many protections and benefits that US citizens have, but they are not allowed to participate in federal elections and have only a nonvoting 'Resident Commissioner' in the US House of Representatives. Although economic development has become more pressing than any other political issue of late, Puerto Rico's status remains a major point of contention for political leaders.

In recent years, one federally commissioned study after the next has gone through presidential and congressional committees. And while sudden changes to Puerto Rico's status seem unlikely, there is some motion. In April 2010 Congress approved a measure for Puerto Rico's self-determination, which may result in Puerto Rican voters deciding to continue its present form or to move towards statehood or independence.

Even though the debate between statehood, commonwealth or independent nation has animated Puerto Rican dinner tables for years, it can be a real powder keg with visitors. Use lots of tact when inquiring about the position of your Puerto Rican hosts – or, better yet, avoid the topic unless they bring it up.

Top Films

» **Maldeamores** (2007) Luis Guzmán stars in this Benicio del Toro–produced film about love's little ironies.

» **Lo que le pasó a Santiago** (1989) Nominated for an Oscar, this is a mysterious, lyrical tale of unexpected love.

» **Celestino y el vampiro** (2003) A wacky flick about a divorcée and a vampire who bites women on the behind.

» **La guagua aérea** (1993) A rueful comedy about the motives of Puerto Ricans who moved to the US in the '60s.

Political Parties

» **New Progressive Party** Pro-statehood; won 52% in the last gubernatorial election.

» **Popular Democratic Party** Pro-commonwealth; won 41% in the last gubernatorial election.

» **Puerto Rican Independence Party** Pro-independence.

History

Puerto Rico occupies a crucial juncture in the geographical and political history of the Americas. Without a doubt, the most defining event in Puerto Rico's history was the nearly 400 year rule of the Spanish, whose checkered history of colonization, genocide, military triumph and defeat are seen everywhere. Colonized by Spanish explorer Juan Ponce de León in 1508, the island contains the oldest European-founded settlement under US jurisdiction. Long before Sir Walter Raleigh and the Pilgrim Fathers had endeavored to understand the lands across the tempestuous Atlantic, the first granite ramparts of El Morro fort in Old San Juan had already been chiseled into place, guarding one of the safest and easily defended harbors in the Caribbean. Nearly 500 years later, they're still there.

One recent genetic study of 800 Puerto Ricans found 61% had mitochondrial DNA from a female Amerindian ancestor, 27% inherited mitochondrial DNA from a female African ancestor and 12% had mitochondrial DNA from a female European ancestor.

Puerto Rico's history is flavored with contrast and contradiction and it is not easy to quickly grasp. While there are no living indigenous communities, the bloodlines of ancestral Puerto Ricans have been traced to more than half the population. While technically a US commonwealth, some natives still feel the island should be a full-blown American state, others an independent nation, and still more, a compromise solution that is neither of the above. Then there is the singular cultural breakdown: the caustic blending of ancient Taíno with enslaved generations of Africans, melding with European, Caribbean and even Lebanese elements. What you're left with is the beguiling essence of modern Puerto Rico: a proud Caribbean nation with distinctly Latin temperament and abundant cultural exchange with the United States.

Taíno Roots

It's unfortunate that, similar to so many other indigenous peoples of the Americas, the best record of Taíno culture is written by those who would annihilate it. Through the journals of Ramón Pané, a Catalonian friar who was traveling with the second Columbus expedition, we are given a

TIMELINE

2000 BC

Puerto Ferro Man, a native from the Ortoiroid culture that had migrated north from the Orinoco basin in present-day Venezuela, lives on the island of Vieques.

430–250 BC

The Ortoiroids are displaced by the Saladoids, a horticultural people skilled at pottery. Saladoids laid the early building blocks for a singular Caribbean culture.

1000

The Taíno – who also come from the Orinoco basin – emerge as a dominant culture; they name the island Boriken, meaning 'the Great Land of the Valiant and Noble Lord.'

vivid first-hand account of the Taíno lifestyle, customs and religious beliefs. Although told with an unintentionally comic cultural and religious bias, it's precious information and often more accurate than other similar histories in the Americas. In his 1505 *Account of the Antiquities – or Customs – of the Indians,* Pané gives a breathless account of Puerto Rico's native residents, describing cities with wide, straight roads, elaborate religious ritual and small communities of 'artfully made' homes behind walls of woven cane. Their diet was derived from tropical fruit grown in orchards that grew oranges and citron that reminded Pané of the ones in Valencia or Barcelona. The beauty of the Taíno culture only exists as an echo today, but it made an indelible influence on contemporary Puerto Rico.

Juan Ponce de León and the Spanish Discovery of Puerto Rico and Florida, by Robert H Fuson, sheds some light on the man who founded modern Puerto Rico.

Taíno Life on Puerto Rico

We know now that the Taíno were an Arawakan Indian group who had societies that were well established on Puerto Rico and the other Greater Antilles (Cuba, Hispaniola and Jamaica) when Columbus first turned up in the area in 1493. Arawaks first settled the island around AD 700, following a migration north from the Orinoco River delta in present-day Venezuela. By AD 1000 a distinctive Taíno culture had emerged based on agriculture, fishing, hunting and the production of cassava bread.

Pané speaks in depth about the complex religious cosmology of the Taíno, a system that had creation stories that often surprised Pané with their Christian parallels. They believed in a single, eternal god who was omnipresent and invisible, and often also worshiped the mother of this god, who was known by a number of names. Each home held a stone or wood idol, usually about 3ft tall, called a *cemí,* which would receive their prayers. The practice of making these statues translated seamlessly into Christianity. Today *santos* (carved figurines representing saints), of the same height, are available from craftsmen across the island.

The Taínos: The Rise and Decline of the People Who Greeted Columbus, by Irving Rouse, offers a whole book's worth of information on a topic that usually only gets a couple of paragraphs.

The native Taíno belief in the afterlife was quite different from the Christian dogma though, and in it there are some basic elements which would survive in other hybrid religions in the islands. Take for instance the Taíno belief in the walking dead, which bears a certain resemblance to famous tenants of Haitian Vodou. According to Taíno, the dead can return from the afterlife, a place called Coaybay, and walk among the living. In Taíno belief the dead walked through the villages and forests at night so they could eat tropical *guanábana* fruit. They also believed that women from Coaybay could have sexual communions with living men. The only way to tell the living from the dead was to touch someone on the belly, as they believed that the dead had no navel.

The small, round wooden huts of the Taíno people were called *bohios,* where they smoked *cohibas* (cigars) and slept in *hamacas* (hammocks).

1493

On November 19, during his second voyage to the New World, Christopher Columbus lands on Puerto Rico's west coast. He christens the island *San Juan Bautista*.

1508

Juan Ponce de León leads Spanish colonists to Puerto Rico in search of gold. He establishes the island's first colony – Caparra – in the north on swampy land close to San Juan harbor.

» Ponce de León statue

1509

Ponce de León becomes first governor of San Juan Bautista (Puerto Rico) after Spain refuses to grant Columbus' son, Diego, rights to the lands discovered by his (recently deceased) father.

They called their newly adopted island Borinquen (Land of the Noble Lord) and made pottery, wove baskets and carved wood. The native society was relatively democratic and organized around a system of *caciques* (Taíno chiefs) who oversaw a rank of medicine men, subchiefs and, below them, workers.

For leisure, the Taíno built ceremonial ball parks where they played a soccer-like game with a rubber ball between teams of 10 to 30 people. At Tibes near Ponce in the south, and at Caguana near Utuadu in the north, archaeologists discovered impressive courts, marked by rows of massive stone blocks. Drums, maracas and *güiros* provided the game's percussive accompaniment – instruments that resound in Puerto Rican traditional and popular music today.

Colonization of the Taíno

Columbus first saw Puerto Rico on November 19, 1493 – a date simultaneously celebrated and mourned today. Columbus' 17 ships landed somewhere on the island's west coast for water, somewhere in the area near Rincón. But the visit was extremely brief, as Columbus' main base in the region was on Hispaniola (known today as Haiti and the Dominican Republic). There was a period of relative quiet between his 'discovery' of Puerto Rico and the arrival of Ponce de León, who landed on the island in August of 1508. León was here for good; he was sent by the Spanish crown to set up a colonial base for the Caribbean in Puerto Rico and look for gold. At first, León's expedition was amicably received by the chief of all chiefs, a *cacique* called Agüeybana. Agüeybana presided over Borinquen's largest settlement sited on the Guayanilla River near

AGÜEYBANA

Agüeybana (meaning 'Big Sun') was the most powerful *cacique* (Taíno chief) in Puerto Rico when Europeans first discovered the island. A trusting character who was curious about the European travelers, Agüeybana's close relationship with Juan Ponce de León was instrumental in Spanish colonization of the Caribbean. Told in a prophecy about the coming of a 'clothed people,' Agüeybana warmly received the Spanish explorer in 1508; some historical accounts, notably written by the Spanish, claim that he believed the Europeans were deities. He exchanged names with León and hosted a ceremony of friendship and led León and a delegation of his men on a scouting expedition of the island, from which Puerto Rico's first maps were drawn. He eventually even accompanied León on several other expeditions to nearby islands, serving as a cultural liaison with other tribal leaders. But León struggled to convince Agüeybana to assist him with his two main priorities: mining Puerto Rico for gold and converting indigenous people to Christianity.

1511

Subjected to brutal exploitation, the Taíno stage their first unsuccessful revolt against their Spanish overlords. Ponce de León is subsequently replaced as governor in favor of Diego Columbus.

1513

Following the decimation of the local Indian population through disease and outright slaughter, the first West African slaves arrive on the island to work in the new economy.

1521

The city of San Juan is founded on its present site and the island changes its name from San Juan Bautista to Puerto Rico.

1595

With permission from the Queen of England, British privateer Sir Francis Drake attempts to attack and loot San Juan with 26 ships but is repelled by the city's formidable defenses.

present-day Guánica and invited León to a friendship ceremony to welcome the Spanish.

But the good relationship didn't last long. Approximately 100 years before the Spanish arrived, Taíno culture was challenged by the Caribs, a warlike tribe from South America who raided Taíno villages for slaves and fodder for cannibalistic rites. The simmering tensions between the Taíno and Caribs were still evident when Ponce de León took possession of the island and sometimes misinterpreted by the Spanish as Taíno aggression. In reality the Taíno were a friendly, sedentary people who put up little resistance to the new colonizers. Although León's letters to the crown describes this as a period of relative peace, he had difficulty making the Taíno understand that he was now in charge, and indigenous people were understandably resistant to their newfound roles of subservient laborers.

When León was unable to get the Taíno to fall in line with the arduous tasks of mining and farming for the Spanish, Queen Isabella issued an edict in simple terms: 'you will force the said Indians to associate with the Christians of the island.' Though the Spanish crown issued paltry monetary payments for the labor, it was tantamount to slavery.

The first black person to arrive in Puerto Rico was Juan Garrido, a conquistador allied to Juan Ponce de León. He first set foot on the island in 1509.

By 1511 the forced labor and religious conversion of the Taíno had destroyed any shred of initial goodwill which may have existed between tribal leaders and the Spanish. When Agüeybana died, his nephew, called Agüeybana II, took over and tensions came to a head. Though accounts differ about the lead-up to the first Taíno uprising, the most colorful version goes like this: in an effort to test the Spaniards' suggestion of religious protection and life beyond death, Agüeybana II lured a Spanish soldier to a lake where he was promised a number of women would be bathing. Instead, a Taíno warrior drowned him while tribal leaders watched. When tribal leaders were convinced that the Spaniard was dead, they grew confident that they could challenge their new oppressors in battle.

A few small raids on new Spanish settlements in the south went in favor of the Taíno, but as soon as León learned of the incidents, he unleashed his technologically advanced soldiers on the Taíno warriors. The battle that quelled the uprising was shocking in its brutality. An estimated 11,000 Taíno were killed in military campaigns by a Spanish force numbering only 100.

Testimonies vary as to how many Taíno inhabited Borinquen at the time of the Spanish invasion, though most anthropologists place the number between 20,000 and 60,000. In 1515 – after nearly a decade of maltreatment, a failed rebellion, disease and virtual slavery – only 4000 remained. Thirty years later a Spanish bishop put the number at 60. Some historians claim that a small group of Taíno escaped the 16th-century genocide and hid in Puerto Rico's central mountains where they survived until the early 19th century, but there's no proof of this claim.

» Old San Juan city walls

1598

On a revenge mission, George Clifford, earl of Cumberland, lands in Santurce to attack San Juan by land. He occupies the city for several months before an outbreak of dysentery forces retreat.

1598

Spain's Phillip III forbids growing ginger, which is more lucrative for farmers, commonly smuggled and traded for slaves. The king demands they grow sugar to benefit the crown.

While Taíno blood may have all but disappeared in modern Puerto Rico, native traditions live on. Puerto Rican Spanish is dotted with native words like yucca (a root vegetable), iguana, *manatí* (manatee – a sea mammal), maracas and *Ceiba* (Puerto Rico's national tree); and some terms have even found their way into modern English: think *huracan* for hurricane and *hamaca* for hammock.

The Taíno, the island's first people, seem to be simultaneously ubiquitous and wholly absent in contemporary Puerto Rico.

The Invaders

It's easy to imagine Puerto Rico's disparate invaders scheming in the shadowy ports of the Caribbean and the gilded halls of Europe. To evade the guns of El Morro and sack the San Juan harbor would write history – for pirates and princes alike. Not long after the fort was commissioned by Spanish King Charles V in 1539, it came under siege from those seeking strategic power in the Caribbean. Everyone from daring British dandy Francis Drake to storied cutthroats like Blackbeard tried their luck against San Juan's formidable defenses.

One of the colony's earliest invaders, Francis Drake first arrived in Puerto Rico in 1595 pursuing a stricken Spanish galleon – holding two million gold ducats – that took shelter in San Juan harbor. While the plucky Brit may have singed the king of Spain's beard in Cádiz a decade earlier, the Spaniards quickly got revenge in Puerto Rico when they fired a cannonball into Drake's cabin, killing two of his men, and – allegedly – shooting the stool from underneath him. Drake left the island empty-handed and died the following year of dysentery in Panama.

On a stinging revenge mission, San Juan was attacked by the British navy again three years later under the command of the third earl of Cumberland. Learning from Drake's mistakes, Cumberland's 1700-strong army landed in what is now Condado and advanced on the city via land from the east. After a short battle, the city surrendered and the British occupied it for the next 10 weeks, before a dysentery epidemic hit and forced an ignominious withdrawal.

In response to frequent British incursions, San Juan's defensive walls were repeatedly strengthened, a measure that helped repel an ambitious attack by the Netherlands in 1625. Acting under the command of Captain Boudewijn Hendricksz, the Dutch fired over 4000 cannonballs into city walls before landing 2000 men at La Puntilla. Although the invaders managed to occupy the city temporarily and take the Fortaleza palace, the Spanish held El Morro fort and, after less than a month, Hendricksz beat a hasty retreat, razing the city as he went.

San Juan's second great fort, San Cristóbal, was inaugurated in the 1630s and the city saw no more major attacks for almost two centuries.

1625

The Dutch navy besieges San Juan and burns it to the ground, but they are prevented from taking total control by Spanish forces manning the fortifications in El Morro.

RICHARD I'ANSON / LONELY PLANET IMAGES ©

» El Morro

1797

A third and final attempt by the British to take San Juan is led by General Abercromby during the Seven Years' War, but the Spanish once again stand firm.

1825

Spanish authorities hire American schooner *Grampus* to capture 'El Pirata Cofresí', Puerto Rico's nautical Robin Hood, who robbed rich foreign ships to feed Cabo Rojo's poor; he's executed at El Morro.

It wasn't until 1797 that the British, at war again with Spain, tried one last time. Still, even though the armada under the British commander Sir Ralph Abercromby had over 60 ships and 10,000 men they eventually withdrew in bloodied and breathless exasperation. Noble in defeat, Abercromby reported that San Juan could have resisted an attack 10 times greater.

Smuggling, Sugar & Spain

Just look at a map and Puerto Rico's strategic position – between the shores of North, Central and South America – is immediately evident. During Spain's early settlement in the 16th century, the empire knew that Puerto Rican harbors were key to transporting the limitless wealth of the Americas. But the crown's insistence on a centralized government was an

JUAN PONCE DE LEÓN

Soldier, sailor, governor, dreamer and politician, the life story of Juan Ponce de León reads like a *Who's Who* of late-15th- and early-16th-century maritime exploration. Aside from founding the Spanish colony of Puerto Rico in 1508, this daring, yet often short-sighted, Spanish adventurer partook in Columbus' second trans-Atlantic voyage, charted large tracts of the Bahamas, discovered the existence of the Gulf Stream, and was the first recorded European to set foot in what is now known as Florida.

Born in Valladolid, Spain, in 1460, de León served his military apprenticeship fighting against the Moors during the Christian reconquest of Granada in 1492. The following year he arrived in the New World on Columbus' second expedition and settled on the island of Hispaniola, where he was proclaimed deputy governor of the province of Higüey after ruthlessly suppressing a native revolt. Following Columbus' death in 1506, the Spanish crown asked de León to lead the colonization of Borinquen, an island first explored by Columbus in 1493.

Despite initially currying favor with the native Taíno Indians, the Spaniard's relationship with his new neighbors quickly deteriorated. In 1512, after much legal wrangling, the explorer was removed from his governor's post in favor of Columbus' son, Diego, before being given title to explore the lands north of Cuba.

De León, after circumnavigating the Bahamas, elected to divert northwest and, in the process, inadvertently 'discovered' Florida.

After several forays along Florida's coast (which de León thought was an island), the explorer returned to Puerto Rico via Cuba and Guadalupe in 1515 and stayed there for the next six years. In 1521 de León organized another trip to Florida with two ships and 200 people. This time they landed on the west coast of Florida near the Caloosahatchee River but were quickly beaten back by Calusa Indians. Wounded in the thigh by a poisoned arrow, de León was shipped back to Havana where he died in July 1521. His remains were returned to Puerto Rico where they are interred in the Catedral de San Juan.

1850–67

The Puerto Rican liberation movement gathers strength under the inspirational leadership of Ramón Emeterio Betances, a poet, politician, diplomat and eminent surgeon.

1868

Revolutionaries inspired by Betances take the town of Lares and declare a Puerto Rican republic, but the uprising is repelled within hours by Spanish forces sent from nearby San Sebastián.

1873

In the wake of the Grito de Lares, the Spanish authorities institute various political and social reforms in Puerto Rico, including the abolition of slavery.

1898

US forces blockade San Juan and land a 16,000-strong force unopposed at Guánica on the south coast, ending the Spanish-American War; Spain cedes Puerto Rico to the USA.

arrogant political position that would cost Spain dearly, and shape the development of Puerto Rico.

In the mid-1500s Spain insisted that all imports and exports from its growing empire be trafficked through ports in Spain. But Seville was some 2½ months away by sail and the policy was immediately inadequate for controlling the island's many ports. A number of forces – including new Spanish colonies in gold-rich Peru and Mexico – led to the rise of an enormous, well-organized black market in Puerto Rico.

This unchecked flow of goods and money hastened the development of Puerto Rico's *other* ports – Ponce and Arroyo among them – where sugar cane and goods from the Americas were moved out of sight of Spanish authorities.

The power vacuum was quickly filled by merchants operating with their own agenda. Through the 16th and 17th centuries, cities of the south grew rich from trade with Caribbean neighbors – certainly illegal, but completely unknown to the distant king.

Even after Spain gave more power to local authorities in San Juan in the 18th century, the brisk black-market exchange of sugar, ginger and slaves between Puerto Rico and its neighbors (including the young United States) continued in the south, funding many of the majestic homes and fountains tourists visit today.

Mi Puerto Rico, directed by Sharon Simon, contains revelatory stories by poets, abolitionists, revolutionaries and politicians in a fabulous documentary touching on the island's African, Taíno and European ancestry.

DOCUMENTARY

African Roots

As throughout the Caribbean, slavery was the engine of the Puerto Rican economy through the late 18th and early 19th centuries, and has left an indelible mark on Puerto Rican culture. The two types of slaves that were brought to the island – *ladinos,* born and acculturated in Spain, and *bozales* and Yoruba people, brought from Africa – first mined meager gold and silver deposits. Once these deposits were depleted, slaves propped up the sugarcane industry and agriculture on the coastal areas of the island. While the rest of the island's population experienced normal growth, the slave population skyrocketed throughout the late 18th century. A census figure in 1765 shows 5400 slaves in Puerto Rico; by 1830 it had increased to more than 31,000, mainly due to the introduction of new slaves directly from Africa and other parts of the Caribbean. However, despite these increases, by 1795 the majority (more than 60%) of black and mulatto people living in Puerto Rico were free. This trend, unusual for the Caribbean, is often attributed to an asylum policy which granted freedom to fugitive slaves from throughout the region.

By the late 1830s, after years of racial violence in the Caribbean and abolitionist movements, it became clear that slavery was increasingly less justifiable. Sugar barons combined their slave holdings with low-wage workers called *jornaleros* and continued to accrue immense wealth. In

1900

US Congress passes the Foraker Act, granting a US-run government in Puerto Rico; American Charles Allen is installed as governor, aided by an 11-man executive council that includes five Puerto Ricans.

1917

The Jones Act makes Puerto Rico a territory of the US and unilaterally grants islanders US citizenship and a bill of rights; English becomes the official language.

1933

Cockfighting becomes legal in Puerto Rico. Though states in the US and neighboring islands subsequently ban the pastime, its popularity in Puerto Rico booms.

1937

Student *independentistas* (independence advocates) clash with police on Palm Sunday; 20 people die and over 100 are injured in what becomes known as the 'Masacre de Ponce'.

both cases, the exploitation by European whites of African- and island-born blacks and people of mixed race led to the perpetuation of racial myths that laid a foundation for social inequities and racism.

Many slave uprisings occurred and began to intertwine with a political movement for emancipation led by Julio Vizcarrondo, a Puerto Rican abolitionist living in Spain, as well as island-based political leaders such as Segundo Ruiz Belvis, Roman Baldorioty de Castro and Ramón Emeterio Betances. After years of struggle the Spanish National Assembly abolished slavery on March 22, 1873.

Today the cultural echoes from African slaves are still present in Puerto Rican culture, described by the late cultural and social writer Jose Luis González as *el primer piso,* or 'the first floor' of Puerto Rican culture. In its music, art and religious icons, African traditions are powerfully felt. And despite the racial stereotypes and inequalities that continue to exist on the island and within the Puerto Rican diaspora, Puerto Rico has embraced its Afro-Indigenous-Caribbean roots.

Puerto Rico: The Four Storeyed Country and Other Essays, by José Luis González (translated by Gerald Guinness), is a compelling treatise on the importance of African and mestizo peoples in the development of Puerto Rican culture.

From Spanish Colony to American Commonwealth

As two Greater Antilles islands ruled by Spain for nearly four centuries, Cuba and Puerto Rico share a remarkably similar history. Both were colonized in the early 1500s, both retain vestiges of their indigenous Taíno culture, both were heavily influenced by the African slave trade (a cultural stimulant that contributed to their unique hybrid music and distinct Afro-Christian religious beliefs) and both remained Spanish colonies a good 80 years after the rest of Latin America had declared independence. The irony, of course, lies in their different paths after 1898 and the fact that today Puerto Rico is intertwined with the US. Cuba's relationship with the US has only recently warmed since it was considered a former Soviet satellite and 'public enemy number one.' While visitors fly freely between the US and Puerto Rico, Cuba has withstood one of the most draconian (and longest) trade embargos in modern history. So what happened?

Two Wings of the Same Dove

While the bulk of Spain's South American colonies rose up under the leadership of revolutionary emancipator Simón Bolívar in the 1820s, Puerto Rico and Cuba's conservative Creole landowners elected to stay on the sidelines. But, as economic conditions worsened and slavery came to be regarded as an ailing colonial anachronism, the mood started to change.

During the 1860s links were formed between nationalists and revolutionaries on both islands, united by the language and inspired by a common foe. The cultural interchange worked both ways. Great thinkers like

1942

A German submarine fires on Isla de la Mona, a largely uninhabited island off Puerto Rico's west coast. It was one of the few incidents of WWII in the Caribbean.

1948

With US Congressional approval, Puerto Ricans craft their own constitution and elect their first governor, Luis Muñoz Marín, former president of the Senate, who holds the post for 16 years.

1950

A nationalist revolt in the mountain town of Jayuya is suppressed by the US Air Force; in response two nationalists in Washington DC try unsuccessfully to assassinate President Harry Truman.

1952

Constitution of Puerto Rico is approved by referendum, making the island an Estado Libre Associado (a US commonwealth); Puerto Rican flag is flown – legally – for the first time.

The total number of American soldiers killed in Puerto Rico during the Spanish-American War of 1898 was four.

Cuban national hero José Martí drew early inspiration from Puerto Rican surgeon and nationalist Ramón Emeterio Betances, while Mayagüez-born general Juan Rius Rivera later went on to command the Cuban Liberation Army in the 1895–98 war against the Spanish.

It was Puerto Rican nationalists who fired the first shot, proclaiming the abortive Grito de Lares (see p245) in 1868. Following Puerto Rico's lead two weeks later, Cuba's machete-wielding *mambises* (19th-century Cuban independence fighters) unleashed their own independence cry. Both failed, but several key factors led to different outcomes: Puerto Rico's move to independence was launched from an isolated mountain town and spearheaded primarily by intellectuals; Cuba's movement had wider grassroots support and better leadership, sustained with a brutal, though ultimately unsuccessful, 10-year war against the Spanish.

While the rapid defeat in Puerto Rico was a major political setback for the nationalist movement, all was not yet lost. Igniting a second Cuban-Spanish Independence War in 1895, José Martí proclaimed that Cuba and Puerto Rico still stood shoulder to shoulder as 'two wings of the same dove' and, had it not been for the timely intervention of the Americans in 1898 when the Spanish were almost defeated, history could have been very different.

Cuba and Puerto Rico's political divergence began in 1900 when the US Congress passed the Foraker Act (1900), making Puerto Rico the first unincorporated territory of the US. Cuba, meanwhile, thanks to the so-called Teller Amendment (passed through Congress before the Spanish-American War had started), gained nominal independence with some strings attached in 1902.

Former leader of the Puerto Rican Nationalist party, Pedro Albizu Campos was of African, Taíno and Basque descent. He graduated from Harvard University with a law degree in 1921 and was fluent in eight languages.

Resistance to the new arrangement in Puerto Rico was spearheaded by the Partido Unión de Puerto Rico (Union Party), which for years had been calling for a resolution to their lack of fundamental democratic rights. The Union Party was led by Luis Muñoz Rivera, one of the most important political figures in the history of Puerto Rico. But unlike his more radical Cuban contemporaries, such as José Martí and – later on – Fidel Castro, Muñoz Rivera was a diplomat who was willing to compromise with the US on key issues. Under pressure from President Woodrow Wilson he ultimately ceded on his demand for outright independence in favor of greater autonomy via an amendment to the Foraker Act.

In 1917, just months after Muñoz Rivera's death, President Woodrow Wilson signed the Jones Act. It granted US citizenship to all Puerto Ricans and established a bicameral legislature whose decisions could be vetoed by the US president. No Puerto Ricans were involved in the debate over citizenship.

1953

Immigration from Puerto Rico to the US peaks as an estimated 75,000 Puerto Ricans move to New York City. Almost one in 10 New Yorker residents are from Puerto Rico.

1967

Puerto Rico holds first plebiscite on the issue of Puerto Rican statehood, but votes overwhelmingly to remain a commonwealth; the independence parties gain only 1% of the votes

1970

Marisol Maralet becomes the first Puerto Rican to win the title of Miss Universe. Over the next 40 years, four more Puerto Ricans win the title, the most of any country in the contest's history.

1978

Two independence supporters are shot by police posing as revolutionary sympathizers in the Central Mountains; the incident exposes deep political fissures and government corruption.

A Question of Status

Questioned by many before the ink had even dried, the Jones Act failed to provide any long-term solutions. On the contrary, the debate over Puerto Rico's relationship with the US continued to intensify, defining the political careers of two major figures who would emerge on the island in the late 1920s and early '30s: Pedro Albizu Campos, leader of the pro-independence Partido Nacionalista (Nationalist Party); and Luis Muñoz Marín, who established the Partido Popular Democrático (PPD; Popular Democratic Party) in 1938.

As son of the widely respected Muñoz Rivera, Luis Muñoz Marín avoided the radical politics of Albizu, and took a more conciliatory approach to challenging the colonial situation of Puerto Rico. While the US Congress sidestepped the status question, Muñoz Marín's PPD

GRITO DE LARES

As well as boasting the world's largest radio telescope and its youngest-ever boxing champion, Puerto Rico also holds the dubious distinction of having created history's shortest-lived republic. The independent republic of Puerto Rico, proclaimed during the abortive Grito de Lares (Cry of Lares) in 1868, lasted slightly less than 24 hours.

Worn down by slavery, high taxes and the asphyxiating grip of Spain's militaristic rulers, independence advocates in the Caribbean colonies of Puerto Rico and Cuba were in the ascendancy throughout the 1850s and '60s. Ironically, it was the Puerto Ricans who acted first. After several setbacks, an insurrection was planned under the physician of Dr Ramón Emeterio Eteances in the western town of Lares for September 23, 1868.

Meeting at a farm, codenamed Centro Bravo, owned by Venezuelan-born rebel Manuel Rojas on the evening of September 23, over 600 men and women marched defiantly on the small town of Lares near Mayagüez, where they were met with minimal Spanish resistance. Declaring a Puerto Rican republic from the main square, the rebels placed a red, white and blue flag – designed by Betances – on the high altar of the main church and named Francisco Ramírez Medina head of a new provisional government. Fatefully, the glory wasn't to last. Electing next to march on the nearby town of San Sebastián, the poorly armed liberation army walked into a classic Spanish military trap and were quickly seen off by superior firepower. A handful of the militia were killed by Spanish bullets while hundreds more – including Rojas and Medina – were taken prisoner.

While the Grito de Lares was decapitated swiftly and never won widespread grassroots support on the island, the action did lead to some long-term political concessions. In the years that followed, the colonial authorities passed liberal electoral reforms, granted Puerto Rico provincial status and offered Spanish citizenship to all *criollos* (island-born people of European descent). The biggest victory, however, came in 1873 with the abolition of slavery and granting of freedom to over 30,000 previously incarcerated slaves.

1985

A mudslide following Tropical Storm Isabel kills 129 people in the hills near Ponce, making it the island's worst natural disaster in a century.

1990

In an island-wide vote, Puerto Ricans declare Spanish to be the only official language. This is reversed three years later, when the official languages are again English and Spanish.

1999

Major protests break out on the island of Vieques against the US Navy, following the killing of islander David Sane Rodríguez during military target practice.

2000

Puerto Ricans elect ex San Juan mayor Sila Maria Calderón of the Popular Democratic Party as the first woman governor of the commonwealth.

pressed for a plebiscite to allow Puerto Ricans to choose between statehood and independence. In the late 1930s and early 1940s, the majority of the PPD favored independence. However, neither President Franklin D Roosevelt nor the Congress seriously considered it as an option, and laws were enacted to criminalize independence activities such as those waged by the Nationalists.

Rather than take to the mountains to fight – as Fidel Castro later did – Muñoz Marín adopted a strategy that incorporated the status question with other issues affecting the Puerto Rican people, such as the dire economic and social effects of the Great Depression. His deciding moment came in 1946 when he rejected independence and threw his political weight behind an effort to grant the island a new status. In 1948, with Marín's support, Congress granted Puerto Rico the status it has today as a Estado Libre Associado, or ELA, the Free Associated State. This intended to give the island more political autonomy, despite close ties with the US.

A special cask of high-grade rum was set aside by a brewer in 1942 with orders that it be opened only when Puerto Rico becomes an independent nation. When (or if) that happens, free drinks for everyone!

RUM

In 1952 this status description was approved by a referendum held on the island. Voters also approved Puerto Rico's first constitution that was written by islanders. Muñoz Marín became the first governor of Puerto Rico to be elected by Puerto Ricans. The new status and newly granted US citizenship for Puerto Ricans led to what is commonly known as the 'Great Migration.' Attracted to better economic opportunities in the US, Puerto Ricans left the island by the tens of thousands. In 1953 alone an estimated 75,000 Puerto Ricans arrived in New York City. Miami and Chicago also hosted large Puerto Rican populations and the period would forever transform the face of urban communities of the United States.

Nevertheless, despite claims by the new governor and his supporters that the status question was finally resolved with ELA, for all intents and purposes, nothing changed: the US Congress still had plenary powers over Puerto Rico. Although islanders became exempt from paying federal income taxes, they still had no representation in Congress (apart from a nonvoting delegate), could not vote in US national elections, and were still being drafted into the US Armed Forces to fight alongside young Americans in foreign wars.

Blanca Canales, leader of the abortive Jayuya Uprising in 1950, is popularly considered to have been the first woman to have led an armed revolt against the US government.

Over the years a number of referenda and plebiscites have been held, ostensibly to allow the Puerto Rican people to decide the future of the island's status. Two official plebiscites, in 1967 and 1993, resulted in victories for 'commonwealth' status, that is, the ELA. Other votes have been held, with the status options, as well as the approach to self-determination, defined in different ways. All of these popular votes have been shaped by the ruling party at the time of the vote, either the pro-ELA PPD, or the pro-statehood Partido Nuevo Progresista (PNP; New Progres-

2003

After four years of protests and 60 years of occupation, the US Navy pulls out of Vieques; the former military land is promptly designated a US Fish and Wildlife Refuge.

2005

Guerilla pro-independence leader Filiberto Ojeda Rios is killed in a shootout with US federal agents. The incident causes widespread anger and demonstrations on the island.

2006

An acute budgetary crisis forces the shutdown of schools and government offices across the island for two weeks as legislative officials try to address a $740-million deficit in public funds.

2009

Sonia Sotomayor becomes the 111th Justice of the US Supreme Court. Of Puerto Rican descent, Sotomayor is the first Hispanic justice in the history of the court.

sive Party). None of the plebiscites held over the years have been binding for the US Congress.

In 1998, as the island was getting ready to mark the 100th anniversary of US control, another attempt to address the issue came in the form of a bill introduced by Alaskan Republican Don Young. For the first time, Congress acknowledged that the current status was no longer viable. The Young Bill called for a plebiscite on the island where Puerto Ricans would vote on only two status options: either statehood or independence. It did not provide ELA or any other form of 'enhanced commonwealth' as an option, angering members of the PPD. Ultimately, the Young Bill went nowhere. While it was approved in the House by a narrow margin, the Senate never seriously considered it.

In 2010, Congress again took up interest in the constitutionality of Puerto Rico's status, in a complicated set of procedures that would allow Puerto Ricans to again vote to continue or change their political relationship with the US. A congressional task force recommended the vote take place in 2012 and that the congress and president enact legislation based on the results of the vote.

A popular vote in 1990 making Spanish the official language in Puerto Rico was revoked just two years later to reinstate both Spanish and English as joint commonwealth languages.

2010

With numerous raids on drug kingpins and smugglers, the US government steps up its Caribbean drug enforcement. A bust on Puerto Rican police becomes the largest arrest of corrupt police officers in US history.

CHRISTOPHER GROENHOUT / LONELY PLANET IMAGES ©

» Catedral de San Juan

2011

After a long period of economic decline set off by the Global Financial Crisis, Puerto Rico posts its highest rate of unemployment on record, 16.9%.

The Sounds of Puerto Rico

The Puerto Rican Cuatro Project (www.cuatro-pr.org) is a nonprofit organization that has adopted the island's national instrument as a means of keeping its cultural memories alive. Its website is a must for those seeking to learn about Puerto Rican musical traditions, with priceless information on the island's traditional instruments.

The music of Puerto Rico is a sonic reflection of the destination itself, a sound shaped by a proud and dynamic history of revolution, colonialism, and the cultural crosscurrents that blow between the island, New York City, Spain and Africa. Even compared with other destinations in the Caribbean, Puerto Rico is something of an island unto its own.

The sound synonymous with Puerto Rico is certainly the hybrid syncopated patter of salsa, but that which pounds from the open doorways of most of the island's nightspots these days is just as often reggaetón, a blazing blend of hip-hop, Caribbean syncopations and the molar-rattling thud of dancehall.

In fact, the dominance of reggaetón has almost run the hallmark genre of salsa out of island nightclubs entirely, and travelers to the island who imagine themselves sashaying to the beat of a brassy salsa combo every night should be advised: it probably ain't happenin'. Aside from some packed spots in San Juan, scattered destinations around the island and weekly residences at upscale resorts (which don't exactly ooze authenticity), catching traditional music in Puerto Rico is a surprisingly difficult task, especially considering its role in the birth of the art form. The island's sonic movements beyond salsa – heavily rhythmic folk styles such as *bomba y plena, danza,* merengue and cha-cha – are even more obscure, with performances mostly relegated to museum demonstrations and holiday festivals.

Popular Music & its Roots

Menudo was one of the original boy bands conceived by producer Edgardo Diaz in 1977. It went on to record phenomenal worldwide success with a light brand of teen pop music and celebrated former members such as Ricky Martin.

To cram for your history lesson on Puerto Rican music in under four minutes, cue up 'Tradicional A Lo Bravo,' a hugely popular single from Puerto Rican reggaetón hitmaker Tego Calderon. Calderon's rapid-fire lyrical delivery and the pounding syncopated bass line is emblematic of the reggaetón movement, but the song also borrows a little something from the important musical traditions of the island. The brassy horns pay homage to salsa bands from the 1960s. The nylon string guitar nods to colonial traditions and *jíbar*o (rural troubador) music. The loping syncopation of the hand drums reference African-rooted Puerto Rican *bomba*. Somewhere, hidden among Calderon's macho swagger, you'll even hear the grinding scrape of a *güiro,* a percussion instrument made from a notched, hollowed gourd which was a part of the musical battery of indigenous Taíno tribes.

From the lilt of precolonial folk music to the macho assault of reggaetón, Puerto Rican music has always been an evolving part of, not a departure from, past traditions. Puerto Rico is a musical melting pot and remains so today. The island's musical genres can shift as quickly as they are defined, influenced by an ever omnivorous range of influences from the US, Europe and across Latin America. These dynamic hybrids, whether present in reggaetón or contemporary rock, are a fundamental quality of the music. Then and now, these traditions often place as much importance on dancefloor expressions as the sound itself.

Music & Dance in Puerto Rico from the Age of Columbus to Modern Times by Donald and Annie Thompson is a simple timeline of music and dance in Puerto Rico that has great information on the origins of mambo, *son,* salsa and more.

Bomba y Plena

The bewildering conflux of traditions that collide in Puerto Rican music can be seen in the earliest popular music on the island, *bomba y plena,* two distinct yet often associated types of folk music. With origins in European, African and native Caribbean cultures, this is the basis for many of the sounds still associated with Puerto Rico and, like salsa, a musical form inexorably tied with dance.

The most directly African in origin is the *bomba,* a music developed by West and Central African slaves who worked on sugar plantations. A typical *bomba* ensemble included drums made from rum barrels and goatskin, *palitos* or *cuás* (wooden sticks that are hit together or on other wooden surfaces), maracas and sometimes a *güiro.* In the oldest forms (documented as early as the 1680s), dancers led the band, furiously competing with each other and the percussionists in an increasingly frenzied physical and rhythmic display. The tunes ended when either dancer or drummer became too exhausted to continue. Loíza Aldea, on the northeast coast, claims *bomba* as its invention, and the streets rumble with it throughout summer, particularly during the Fiesta de Santiago, its festival for St James the Moor Slayer, which begins during the last week of July and lasts for nine days. Partiers don bright *vejigantes* (Puerto Rican masks) and take to the streets, celebrating all night.

PUERTO RICO PLAYLIST

It's nearly a crime to distil three generations of Puerto Rico's vibrant club music into an iPod playlist, but the following romp includes singles spanning half a century, from classic salsa to contemporary reggaetón. If nothing else, use this as a starter to discover the diverse and unexpected charms of Puerto Rican music.

» Tito Puente: 'Ran Kan Kan,' from *Babarabatiri* (1951)
» Cortijo Y Su Combo: 'El Bombon De Elena,' from *...Invites You to Dance* (1957)
» Celia Cruz: 'Chango Ta Vani,' from *La Incomparable* (1958)
» Willie Colón: 'Te Conozco,' from *Cosa Nuestra* (1969)
» El Gran Combo De Puerto Rico: 'No Hay Cama Pa' Tanta Gente,' from *Nuestra Musica* (1971)
» Ismael Marinda: 'Se Casa La Rumba,' from *Abran Paso!* (1972)
» Eddie Palmieri: 'Nunca Contigo,' from *The Sun of Latin Music* (1973)
» Fania All-Stars: 'Ella Fue (She Was the One),' from *Rhythm Machine* (1977)
» Frankie Ruiz: 'Me Dejo,' from *Mas Grande Que Nunca* (1989)
» Marvin Santiago: 'Fuego A La Jicotea,' from *Fuego A La Jicotea* (1991)
» Vico C: 'Calla,' from *Aquel Que Había Muetro* (1998)
» Yuri Buenaventura: 'Salsa,' from *Yo Soy* (2000)
» Tego Calderon: 'Guasa, Guasa,' from *Abayarde* (2003)
» Daddy Yankee: 'Gasolina,' from *Barrio Fino* (2004)
» Tito el ambino: 'El Tra,' from *It's My Time* (2007)
» Don Chezina: 'Songorocosongo,' from *Tributo Urbano A Hector Lavoe* (2008)
» Calle 13: 'No Hay Nadie Como Tú,' from *Los de Atrás Vienen Conmigo* (2009)
» Kany Garcia: 'Feliz,' from *Boleto De Entrada* (2009)
» Cultura Profética: 'Baja La Tension,' from *La Dulzura* (2010)

Plena, which originated in the more urban region around Ponce, is also drum-based but with lighter textures and a less forceful beat. Introduced by *cocolocos,* slaves who migrated north from islands south of Puerto Rico, *plena* uses an assortment of handheld percussion instruments. Locals once referred to the form as *el periodico cantado* (the sung newspaper), because the songs typically recounted, and often satirized, current events. *Plena* often uses *panderos,* which resemble Irish and Brazilian frame drums, but according to musicologists *panderos* were introduced to the island by Spaniards, who had lifted them from their Moorish neighbors. In its most traditional form, *plena* was performed by a group of singers who accompanied themselves with only the *panderos*. The *plena* beat has strongly syncopated African roots and is a close cousin to calypso, *soca* and dancehall music from Trinidad and Jamaica.

Bomba y plena developed side by side on the coastal lowlands, and inventive musicians eventually realized the call-and-response of *bomba* would work well with *plena*'s satirical lyrical nature, which is why the forms are often played back-to-back by ensembles. If you catch *bomba y plena* today, a historically accurate performance will be rare; in the 1950s a modernization of the sound paved the way for salsa by often adding horns and other European instruments, pan-Caribbean rhythmic elements and the clatter of Cuban percussion.

GENRES

Music of Puerto Rico (www.musicofpuertorico.com) gives an excellent rundown on the complex musical genres of the island including audio clips and printed song lyrics.

Salsa

For most gringos, salsa's definition as a catch-all term for the interconnected jumble of Latin and Afro-Caribbean dances and sounds isn't easy to get a handle on, but for those who live in its areas of origin – Puerto Rico, Cuba and New York City – it's as much a lifestyle as a genre, with cultural complexities that go well beyond the 'spicy' jargon that's often bandied about. If you grew up in any of the above, the instinctual reaction to salsa's buoyancy seems to be in the blood, or at least in the hips. If you grew up elsewhere, try getting acquainted with it by reading between the lines of Yuri Buenaventura's neotraditional anthem, 'Salsa,' where it's called 'the rhythm that gives life.' Or better yet, don't read anything – just get out there and dance.

Salsa tunes might sound vastly different from one another. They can be slow or brisk, flippant or heartrending. Pondering salsa's definition will quickly lead you to the question of where it comes from, and the debate about its Cuban or Puerto Rican origins is as unanswerable as the chicken-and-egg question. Debating this topic is likely to raise the blood pressure of any proud *puertorriqueño* (person from Puerto Rico), but most will concede that salsa was born in the nightclubs of New York City in the 1960s and has deep roots in both Puerto Rico and Cuba.

One of the definitive articles on the origin of the name 'salsa,' the evolution of the music and dance and reviews of iconic recordings can be found at www.salsaroots.com.

The Source of the Sauce

In addition to the mishmash of African traditions that spread through the islands via the slave trade, Cuba's *son* – a traditional style that was widely reintroduced to global audiences in the '90s through *Buena Vista Social Club* – is a crucial ingredient in salsa. Originating in eastern Cuba, *son* first became popular in the 1850s, mixing guitar-based Spanish *cancións* and Afro-Cuban percussion, a fundamental formula that still makes the foundation of many salsa songs. Variations of *son* spread through the islands and became internationally popular throughout the early 20th century, with variations including the rumba, mambo and cha-cha.

Another element of salsa is merengue, which took root in Puerto Rico's neighboring island, the Dominican Republic, where it is the national dance. With its even-paced steps and a signature roll of the hips, it's probably the easiest Latin dance for beginners. Compared with salsa, the rhythmic underpinning has a more rigid structure, and though the music can gallop along at a wild pace, dancers keep their upper body in a graceful, poised stance. It still can get heated, but true merengue is a slightly more controlled dance than typical salsa.

Of all the variations that helped bring salsa into being, none is more important than the mambo – a flamboyant style of music and dance that marries elements of swinging American jazz with *son,* a Cuban musical movement that bridged the gap between underclass work songs and mainstream popular music of the 19th century. Again, the musical dialogue of the Caribbean islands is evident right down to the style's name; mambo is a Haitian word for a voodoo priestess.

Unlike the blurry origins of other traditions, historians credit the creation of mambo to brothers Cachao and Orestes López, who wrote a tune called 'Mambo' in 1938, and Cuban bandleader Pérez Prado, who introduced the complicated dance steps to Havana's La Tropicana nightclub in 1943. What they started in Cuba, Tito Puente (p252), Tito Rodriguez, Machito and Xavier Cugat carried to the US, where it was eagerly embraced by Latino and North American audiences. It even crossed over to Anglo audiences; it was a huge fad in the nightclubs of New York City in the early 1950s. But when diplomatic relations between the US and Cuba became strained after Fidel Castro's revolution in 1959, the spotlight shifted from Cuban to Puerto Rican artists and Cuban expats living in the US.

Among Tito Puente's many honors are five Grammys, a Presidential Commendation medal (for service in WWII) and having a special session of the Puerto Rican Senate dedicated to him.

The Birth & Near-Death of Salsa

So, even if we know that most elements of salsa – which translates literally to 'sauce' – were imported to Puerto Rico, how can it remain one of the country's most prideful exports? Much of that has to do with two artists in New York: Puerto Rican percussionist Tito Puente and Cuban

FIVE FANIA RECORDS MUST-HAVES

The gold standard for salsa recordings often bears the name of Fania Records, a New York label that was started in 1964 by Dominican bandleader Johnny Pacheco and American lawyer Jerry Masucci. Known for funky, soul-dusted LPs of immaculate grooves and a roster that included blockbusting singers and instrumentalists of the genre, Fania made the kings and queens of the era's golden years. These are a few Fania favorites – with a slight bias toward musicians born on Puerto Rican soil.

» Willie Colón and Ruben Blades: *Siembra* (1978) – Nuyorcian trombonist Willie Colón is joined by Panamanian singing icon Blades for this, an essential in any salsa collection. This is the kind of record that parents hand down to their kids.

» Celia Cruz and Johnny Pacheco: *Celia & Johnny* (1974) – Deliriously sassy and brassy as hell, Celia Cruz' breakthrough with arranger Johnny Pacheco (a founder of the brilliant classic salsa label Fania) is stacked with sultry dancefloor burners at every tempo.

» Ismael Miranda: *Asi Se Compone Un Son* (1973) – Aguadilla-born Miranda broke out with this LP's tracks in a romp through salsa standards. Miranda earned wild popularity for his gutsy vocals.

» Fania All-Stars: *Live at the Cheetah Vol. 1* (1971) – Fania's biggest drawing card was its ever-rotating all-stars, a who's-who roster of pan-Caribbean musicians in live, rowdy appearances. In the salsa world this is equivalent to a Dylan–Lennon–Hendrix jam session.

» Ray Barretto: *Acid* (1968) – Nicknamed 'hard hands,' Barretto's furious congas playing took him from the barrios of Spanish Harlem to stages alongside everyone from Charlie Parker to the Rolling Stones. This is his undeniably raw, rock-influenced stomper and the back half of the album has some amazing English-language covers.

vocalist Celia Cruz. By the time these two became household names in the 1960s, the Latin-/Caribbean-influenced style of big-band music, which used congas, bass, cowbells (a Puerto Rican addition), bongos, maracas, a horn section, bass and multiple singers, had come to dominate American social dancing.

In 1964, Johnny Pacheco, a visionary producer, created Fania Records, a record label that began to snap up talented Nuyorican musicians such as trombonist Willie Colón, whose hip-popping music drew rave reviews from critics and brought crowds to the clubs. The only thing the craze lacked was a name. Who came up with salsa? Depending on which story you want to believe, the term itself was either coined in the 1930s by Cuban composer Ignacio Piñerio and revived in the '60s in New York City's club scene, or a 1962 record by Joe Cuba. It wasn't long before Charlie Palmieri, another Nuyorican, released an LP of brightly accented tunes called 'Salsa Na' Mas.' If you're looking for a primer on the classic salsa sound, start here; Palmieri shouts and swings through a set of tunes decorated with lots of sassy flute lines and lilting stings. Scores of Puerto Rican, Cuban and Nuyorican singers became household names in the '60s, and when Carlos Santana's now-ubiquitous rock song 'Oye Como Va' hit the music stores in 1969, it may have marked the crest of the Latin wave.

Though the craze left a mark on American pop and jazz traditions, the crowds dwindled in subsequent decades as musical tastes shifted radically in the late 1970s. While Puerto Rican youth turned to rock-and-roll imports from the US through the '80s, traditionalists celebrated the sappy *salsa romantica* typified by crooners such as José Alberto.

Salsa Today

Though salsa's faithful took plenty of solace in Fania records from the '80s, it wasn't until the 1990s that a modern Nuyorican – salsa crooner Marc Anthony, aka Mr JLo – brought salsa back from the brink of obscurity and into a blinding popular spotlight, braiding its traditional

THE 'BRIDGE' OF TITO PUENTE

Puerto Ricans and Cubans jovially argue over who invented salsa, but the truth is neither island can claim to be the commercial center of salsa success. That honor belongs to the offshore colony known as El Barrio: the Latin Quarter, Spanish Harlem, New York City. In the euphoria following the end of WWII, New York's nightclub scene bloomed as dancers came in droves to the Palladium on 52nd St to bump and grind to the sound of the mambo bands they heard, or dreamed of hearing, in the casinos of Havana, Cuba. At the time, the music carried a basic Latin syncopated beat, punctuated by horn sections that were typical of the great swing bands of Stan Kenton and Count Basie.

Then young Puerto Rican drummer Tito Puente came into the picture. After serving three years in the US Navy and attending New York's Juilliard School of Music, Puente began playing and composing for Cuban bands in New York City. He gained notoriety for spicing up the music with a host of rhythms with roots in Puerto Rican *bomba*. Soon Puente had formed his own band, the Latin Jazz Ensemble, which was playing way beyond the old Cuban templates.

When Fania Records came around, Puente was already a star. Celia Cruz, the late Héctor Lavoe, Eddy Palmieri, Gilberto Santa Rosa, El Gran Combo de Puerto Rico and plenty of other *salseros* have made their mark on the world, but none can quite claim the same place as Tito Puente, who became the face of the salsa boom and bridged cultural divides with his music decades before multiculturalism was even considered a real word. Shortly after the legendary *salsero's* death in 2000, at the age of 77, a stretch of road in Harlem – East 112th St at Lexington Ave – was renamed Tito Puente Way.

elements with those of sleek and shiny modern Latino pop. Long before his wife even conceived of her breakout Latina-influenced 1999 pop album *On the 6,* Anthony's music packed New York's Madison Square Garden several times over with delirious crowds (the DVD of these performances are required viewing in many a Puerto Rican watering hole to this day). Although Lopez and Anthony remain salsa's premier couple, American audiences have also had fleeting infatuations with Ricky Martin (Mr La Vida Loca) and hunky Spaniard Enrique Iglesias. All these artists pay homage to their forbearers with a lot of lip service and fundamental elements – the hand drums and horns, *clavé* rhythms and textured percussion sections. More recent Puerto Rican pop stars, like the smart, jazz-fused group Cultura Profética, pick and choose the elements of the island's traditional sound to weave into contemporary records.

Ricky Martin has released bilingual records since 1999. The most recent of these, *Music+Soul+Sex*, was released in 2011, after sold-out engagements at Madison Square Garden.

But the neo-traditionalist salsa from Bronx-born Puerto Rican singer India and heartthrob crooner Manny Manuel carry the torch from the graying generation who invented it. There are a number of new ensembles who keep turning out the salsa hits in rotation on Puerto Rican radio, though most of them hail from New York City. If you get the opportunity, there's no finer salsa ensemble in the world than El Gran Combo de Puerto Rico, a large group of masters who pack festivals in US and on the island.

Reggaetón

The raucous bastard-child of reggae, salsa and hip-hop is reggaetón, a rough-and-tumble urban sound that took over the unpaved streets of Loíza Aldea, proudly popping its blue collar as the Caribbean's answer to the ethos of American thug life. Recently it's made a wholesale takeover of most dance clubs in the Caribbean and rattles roofs in New York, Chicago and Los Angeles. On a trip to a Puerto Rican nightclub, reggaetón dominates the turntables, and you'll likely wake up the next morning with your ears ringing.

As the name suggests, it draws heavily on reggae, though the simplest reduction of its sound is a Spanish-language hip-hop driven by the crushing bass of Jamaican raga, a bossy, electro-infused spin on reggae. The earliest forms are traced to Panama, thanks to Jamaican laborers who helped build the Panama Canal, but a more aggressive strain of reggaetón developed in urban areas of Puerto Rico in the 1980s, circulated underground on self-released mix tapes. In the 1990s it incorporated thunderous elements of Jamaican raga and came unto its own. Toss in the thud of a drum machine and some X-rated lyrics and you have yourself a bona fide musical revolution.

Unlike most traditionally postured Puerto Rican music/dance combos, reggaetón dancefloors feature a deliriously oversexed free-for-all, with its most popular move known as *perreo,* or dog dance – which leaves little to the imagination. Reggaetón stars such as Tego Calderon, Daddy Yankee, Don Omar and Ivy Queen have played to crowds of thousands in the US and are gradually sneaking on to mainstream urban radio.

Puerto Rican Folk

The earliest folk music on the island started with the percussion and wind instruments of the Taíno, and grew to incorporate elements as disparate as the island's ethnic composition: Spanish guitars, European parlor music and drums, and rhythms from West Africa. All are evident in the DNA of the island's contemporary music, but the long, varied identity of Puerto Rican music incorporates a number of curious indigenous styles and instruments, notably including at least half a dozen guitar-like string instruments that are native to the island, such as the aptly named four-string guitar-like *cuatro.*

In the mountains, sentimental and twangy folk music was played on *cuatros* by rural troubadours, called *jíbaros,* whose costume often includes a ragged straw hat. A number of traditional *jíbaro* songs – mostly rooted in some kind of Western European parlor music – are still popular at island weddings and family gatherings. Of these, the two most worth checking out are the *décima* and *aguinaldo*. The *décima* uses 10-line verses in a tricky rhyme scheme to transform, in the lines of one famous self-referential example, a 'stone into the jewel.' An expert *jíbaro,* such as Florencio Morales Ramos, would be able to improve these on the spot. An *aguinaldo* is sung by groups of wandering carolers at Christmastime, with lyrics that often explain the traditions of the holiday (perhaps unsurprisingly, many of the most famous ones include singing about pork).

Perhaps the most structurally complex of the island's folk music, *danza* is considered Puerto Rico's classical music. *Danza*'s exact lineage is unknown, but it's generally considered to be modeled after *contradanza,* a social music and dance from Europe. *Danza* popularity blossomed in 1840 when it incorporated new music and dance steps called *habaneras* (another export of Cuba), which freed the style of movements. Its expressive nature was wildly popular with youth but quite taboo with parents, and so it was banned for a period. Composer Juan Morel Campos is the national hero of the form; he wrote more than 300 expressive *danzas* before he died at the age of 38.

ANTHEM

Puerto Rico's national anthem, 'La Borinqueña,' is actually a *danza* that was later subtly altered in order to make it sound more grandiose and anthem-like.

Probably the most appealing colonial-era music found on the island is the *décima* – the vehicle through which the *jíbaros* express joy and sorrow.

A *décima* is based on a 10-line poem and requires multiple instruments – the three-, four- and six-stringed guitars known appropriately enough as the *tres, cuatro* and *seis*, and a rhythm section usually comprised of *güiro* and drums. Like other music of the island, a degree of wit and improvisation is expected of the singers. Often a band will have two lead singers who alternate stanzas and try to outdo each other with sizzling rhymes and acrid political statements.

Today, many Puerto Ricans associate *jíbaro* music with Christmas because of *parrandas,* a tradition in which groups of friends stroll from house to house singing joyful *aguinaldos* (Christmas songs set to mountain music) and begging for treats.

Classical

Puerto Rico's offerings for typical classical fare are limited mostly to the San Juan area, where the Orquesta Sinfónica de Puerto Rico (Puerto Rico

PUERTO RICAN MUSIC: ALIVE & KICKING

Through slush and snow, you've been daydreaming all winter about that idyllic Puerto Rican night on the town, when rum flows like water, the band is hot as a tin roof and the likelihood of dislocating something on the dancefloor is high. Catching live traditional music isn't as easy as you might hope, but the following nightspots are the cream of the crop.

» **Nuyorican Café** (p82) San Juan's coziest dancefloor hosts live combos playing traditional favorites

» **Latin Roots** (p83) This is a great place to catch live music and learn to dance salsa. It has free lessons every night.

» **Museo de la Música Puertorriqueña** (p150) Ponce's home of traditional music performances, in a museum setting.

» **Ponce Hilton** (p153) Touristy and a bit tacky, but also the most reliable place for traditional music in the south.

Symphony Orchestra) presents standard orchestral rep and hosts visiting luminaries. The symphony shares a space with a distinguished national opera company at Centro de Bellas Artes (p83), whose guests have included renowned Puerto Rican bassist Justino Diaz.

To see the best classical music the island has to offer you can do no better than a visit during the Festival Casals (p70), held for two weeks every year (dates vary). This festival is certainly the best of its kind in the Caribbean. Recent years have seen performances by the world's most elite string quartets, soloists and chamber ensembles.

The festival is named for cellist Pablo Casals, who despite being born in Barcelona, is considered Puerto Rico's most distinguished son (his mother was from Mayagüez). In the years before WWI, he earned a reputation as the preeminent cellist of his era. Avidly political, he left Spain in 1936 to protest the Franco regime and eventually (in 1956) settled in Puerto Rico, where he lived out the rest of his days. In 1957 he founded the Festival Casals, which is attended by music fans from around the world, and went on to form the Puerto Rico Symphony Orchestra and the Puerto Rico Conservatory of Music.

By the time he died in 1973 at the age of 97, he considered himself – and was considered by his compatriots – to be Puerto Rico's greatest champion of classical music. It could rightly be said that without Casals, Puerto Rico would have been an utter backwater for classical music, like most of its neighboring islands.

Although San Juan's adept classical music culture is the strongest on the island, you'll likely be surprised to hear European classical music traditions in other parts of the island as well. In a country that loves its civic pomp and circumstance, a number of buttoned-up military bands preside over big festivals and ceremonies. Of these, none has a longer tradition than the Banda Municipal de Ponce (Ponce Municipal Band), a volunteer band that has been performing open-air concerts for more than 125 years.

José Feliciano, a six-time Grammy award winner, taught himself to play guitar despite being born blind. He remains one of Puerto Rico's most successful crossover pop stars.

Life in Puerto Rico

Puerto Rican culture is a kaleidoscope with four constantly overlapping elements – Taíno Indian, Spanish, African and American – and as such, the dynamic culture is incredibly hard to classify simply. One side of the street looks like a neighborhood in the Bronx, where oversized SUVs roll through a Burger King drive-thru, the other side is all Latin America, where freshly hacked bunches of bananas are sold out of the back of a truck. And let's face it, that same dichotomy might exist anywhere in the age of globalization.

Welcome to Puerto Rico www.welcome.topuertorico.org is a website set up by a Puerto Rican currently based in Georgia, USA. It provides an excellent in-depth look at the island's culture, history, geography and ecology.

A commonwealth of the United States of America, Puerto Rico is a semi-autonomous territory whose constitutional status has long been a political oxymoron. The island's cultural manifestations are similarly ridden with contradiction. Puerto Ricans love big American cars, but follow loose traffic laws; they serve in numerous foreign wars under the stars and stripes, yet share a closer historical identity to communist Cuba; they export over half of their ebullient population to the east coast of the United States, but still exhibit a fierce loyalty to island they will always call home.

Modern practicalities of the island's political and cultural position have meant that, for three or four generations now, many Puerto Ricans have grown up bouncing between mainland US cities and their beloved

READING UP ON PUERTO RICAN CULTURE

» *Down These Mean Streets*, Piri Thomas – Peppered with the street slang of Spanish Harlem, this classic narrative takes a cold and sober look at the challenges of violence, drugs and racism during the first wave of Puerto Rican immigrants to New York City. It's a gritty classic.

» *Boricuas: Influential Puerto Rican Writings – An Anthology*, edited by Roberto Santiago – This collection of essays and stories presents an incredibly diverse and wide-ranging insight into Puerto Rican authors, many of whom are scarcely translated into English. If you read one book to sample Puerto Rican writing, this is it.

» *The Disenchanted Island – Puerto Rico and the United States in the Twentieth Century*, Ronaldo Fernández – Required reading for Latin American studies students, this chronicle of the island's struggle for independence is passionately told, putting the relationship between Puerto Rico and the United States under a microscope. Fernández showed up on FBI watch lists for his other book, *Macheteros*, which championed the extreme edge of the Puerto Rican separatist movement.

» *Imposing Decency: The Politics of Sexuality and Race in Puerto Rico, 1870–1920*, Eileen J Suárez Findlay – This brassy, bold historical reading of Puerto Rico feminism is rooted in Puerto Rico's working-class sexual revolution during the turbulent years of the American colony.

Borinquen. Even those who stay put assimilate by proxy: young people in a wealthy San Juan suburb may wander the mall past American chain stores and chat about Hollywood blockbusters, while their counterparts living in the uniformly Puerto Rican neighborhoods in New York or Chicago may have a day-to-day existence that more closely resembles Latin America. This makes the full scope of their bilingual and multicultural existence difficult to comprehend for outsiders. Many Puerto Ricans are just as comfortable striding down New York's Fifth Ave during the week for a little shopping, then spending the weekend visiting the *friquitines* (roadside kiosks) with their families at Playa Luquillo.

From Rincón to Vieques, visitors will find Puerto Ricans to be incredibly friendly and open; they like nothing better than to show off their beloved Boriken (the island's Taíno name).

You'll also note that, despite their obsession with American cars and big shopping complexes, Puerto Ricans are much more into genuine experiences than material things. A favorite island pastime is to wade into warm beach waters just before sunset – beer in hand and a few more in the cooler – to shoot the breeze with whoever else is out enjoying the glorious spectacle of changing skies. The next day, there's a good chance the afternoon will be spent standing around the grill (again, usually with a beer in hand) and savoring the scent of a favorite family recipe. Bank executive, schoolteacher, fisherman or even visiting gringo – it doesn't matter who you are, as long as you share an appreciation for how good life can be in Puerto Rico.

And despite the fact that so many people who live on the island have such close economic and familial ties to the United States, there's a very certain sense that life at the pace of the island – slower, more relaxed – is also more meaningful.

Although Puerto Rico shares many characteristics with other Caribbean nations in its food, ethnicity and general laid-back ambience, Spanish colonial and more recent American influences have lent the island certain distinct traits. Despite its close historical and cultural ties to Cuba and the Dominican Republic, Puerto Rico has easily outpaced its former colonial cousins economically, thanks in part to over a century of US aid. As a result, the island has become the most modern in the Caribbean with high-rises, heavy traffic and a high percentage of American tourists.

Annually, five million visitors to Puerto Rico supply the economy with approximately $1.8 billion. More than one third of these tourists are made up of cruise-ship passengers.

Informative website www.boricua.com bills itself as the website for Puerto Ricans by Puerto Ricans, but anyone with more than a passing interest in the island and its worldwide diaspora will find plenty of hidden nuggets here.

Lifestyle

Most Puerto Ricans live a lifestyle that weaves together two primary elements: the commercial and material values of the United States and the social and traditional values of their 'enchanted' island. Because of the strong connection to the mainland United States and inundation by American media, Puerto Ricans have espoused many of the same social values as their cousins in Brooklyn. Even so, the Puerto Rican flags that fly from the fire escapes of Brooklyn leave no doubt that many Puerto Ricans will never fully adopt mainstream American culture.

To look at the figures, about 45% of the island still lives in what the US defines as poverty, but the remaining population is doing quite well – they are the managers of the ever-present pharmaceutical factories, the beneficiaries of the burgeoning tourism business or bankers or business owners in Hato Rey. San Juan is the only city that has much of a middle class – people who do administrative and clerical work in restaurants, hotels, tourism businesses and so on. Many were born in Puerto Rico, raised in the US, then returned to the island after college to find work. Over the years this return migration has been a boon for the island businesses, which need skilled workers, but has made it harder for Puerto Ricans with high-school diplomas to fill those spots. The difficult

According to a recent World Values Survey, Puerto Ricans were among the happiest people on the planet, with a 'happiness rating' of 4.67 out of five. The United States came 15th with a rating of 3.47.

economy of recent years has created formidable hurdles to even Puerto Rico's young and educated set.

A glance beyond the shiny buildings of San Juan will reveal that the effect of the Global Financial Crisis has been felt more acutely in Puerto Rico than other parts of the US. A number of manufacturing jobs left the island over the last five years, taking a number of skilled managers with them and leaving factories to rust in the withering tropical heat. With an unemployment rate of 17% and average salaries around $17,000, many Puerto Ricans can't afford to pay the real-estate taxes the government has been levying of late, and consequently are losing their traditional homes – old farms that have been handed down for generations. Those who left Puerto Rico in their youth and returned to live off an American pension find that their dollars don't stretch quite as far as they used to.

Still, this is the strongest economy in the Caribbean, and you'll see that almost every household owns at least one car. Puerto Rico hasn't quite gotten to the point of having 'two countries' living on the island, but the economic disparities are growing more apparent, especially in the recent years of financial hardship. Tons of fast-food outlets and strip malls cater to the working-class families, while trendy eateries doing fancy *comida criolla* (traditional cooking) pull in not just tourists but also a newly created yuppie class of American-educated 30-somethings enjoying their relative prosperity.

Multiculturalism

Like most Caribbean cultures, Puerto Ricans are an ethnic mix of Native American, European and African genes. About 78% of the island classi-

LIVING WITH UNCLE SAM

Puerto Rico's political status inspires a curious mix of guarded ambivalence and grudging acceptance. For many, the idea of living with Uncle Sam has become more a habit than a passion. Suspended constitutionally between full-blown US state and sovereign independent nation, the island's population remains in a curious state of limbo. It seems as if the people can't decide what they want their country to be. Last put to the vote in 1998, the advocates of statehood were narrowly defeated by supporters of the existing status quo, ie a commonwealth or unincorporated dependent territory of the United States. The various independence parties, meanwhile, continue to come in a distant third. In April of 2010 a presidential commission sought to raise the issue again, though the lousy economy has been the island's main political focus.

Triggered historically by the Grito de Lares in 1868 and reignited briefly in the 1950s, the independence issue has long struggled to gain a critical mass. Compromise is invariably touted as a more desirable modern option. Cemented in the 1952 Constitution Act, the current relationship between Puerto Rico and the US was largely the work of iconic national governor Luís Muñoz Marín. A prophetic democrat, Muñoz believed that to push for political independence from the Americans was a folly akin to economic suicide. Steering a fine line between a free-thinking commonwealth and obedient colonial lapdog during the '50s and '60s, Muñoz successfully lifted the island out of its economic coma. He also professed to have safeguarded Puerto Rico's cultural identity and political 'freedom' for future generations.

It's a sentiment with which many would concur. While few Puerto Ricans play the out-and-out nationalist card these days, most uphold an unspoken cultural resistance toward their neighbors in the north. Ubiquitous shopping malls and Burger Kings aside, the proud *boricuas* have consistently resisted assimilating into mainstream US culture. From the Spanish language to the brassy music to the way they over-enthusiastically drive their cars – patriotic islanders have always been Puerto Rican first and American a distant second. It's a cultural paradigm that looks set to continue for some time yet.

fies itself as white (meaning of Spanish origin, primarily), 8% as black, 10% as mixed or 'other', and 4% as Taíno Indian. Along the coast of Loíza Aldea, where African heritage is most prominent, distinct features from the Yoruba people abound, while in the mountains, a handful of people still claim distant Taíno bloodlines. Many of them are right; advanced ethnographic study of Puerto Ricans in recent years uncovered a strong connection to the island's first settlers.

Puerto Ricans might tell you that ethnic discrimination doesn't exist on their island, but politically correct Spanish speakers may be aghast at some of the names Puerto Ricans use to refer to each other – words like *trigueño* (wheat-colored) and *jabao* (not quite white). It may sound derogatory (and sometimes it is), but it can also simply be a less-than-thoughtful way of identifying someone by a visible physical characteristic, a habit found in much of Latin America. You'll also hear terms like *la blanquita,* for a lighter-skinned woman, or *el gordo* to describe a robust man.

Practice your Spanish by reading *El Nuevo Día,* Puerto Rico's biggest-selling daily newspaper, online at www.elnuevodia.com.

Identifying which terms are racial slurs, rather than descriptive facts, will be a hard distinction for non-islanders to make, and it's wisest to steer clear of all such vernacular. Compared with much of the Caribbean, Puerto Rico is remarkably integrated and even-keeled about ethnicity.

The island's most important challenge is to correct the historical fact that the poorest islanders – those descended from the slaves and laborers who were kept from owning land until the early 20th century – have been short-changed when it comes to higher education. As in the United States, the issue of racial and economic inequality in Puerto Rico – while still visible – has improved immeasurably in the last 40 years. While urban deprivation and a lack of provision of housing are ongoing issues, the relative economic conditions in modern Puerto Rico are significantly better than in most other countries in the Caribbean.

Religion

Like many former Spanish colonies, Roman Catholicism is practiced widely, with an estimated 70% of Puerto Ricans identifying as Catholic. But both Catholics and Protestants – the second-largest religious group – have been widely influenced by centuries of indigenous and African folkloric traditions. Slaves brought from West Africa between the 16th and 19th centuries carried with them a system of animistic beliefs that they passed on through generations of their descendants.

You can hear it in the cadences of the African drums in traditional music like *bomba* and, more recently, in salsa. You also hear African linguistic traditions in dance names like rumba and in variations on Changó (the Yoruba god of fire and war), like *machango, changuero, changuería* and *changuear* (all are island words that relate people, things and behavior to Changó).

El Boricua is an online monthly bilingual cultural magazine for Puerto Ricans worldwide. It can be found at www.elboricua.com.

The *santos* (small carved figurines representing saints) that have been staple products of Puerto Rican artists for centuries descend to some degree from Santería beliefs in the powers of the saints (although many Puerto Ricans may not be aware of the sources of this worship). Many Puerto Ricans keep a collection of their favorite *santos* enshrined in a place of honor in their homes, similar to shrines that West Africa's Yoruba people keep for their *orishas* (spirits), like Yemanjá, the goddess of the sea.

Belief in the magical properties of small carved gods also recalls the island's early inhabitants, the Taíno, who worshipped little stone *cemíes* (figurines) and believed in *jupías,* spirits of the dead who roam the island at night to cause mischief.

Tens of thousands of islanders consult with *curanderos* (healers) when it comes to problems of love, health, employment, finance and revenge.

PUERTO RICO'S BEAUTIES

For all of Puerto Rico's lofty aspirations regarding gender equality, this island absolutely adores the time-honored ritual of good old-fashioned female objectification: the beauty pageant. On most progressive issues of gender equality, Puerto Rico can shame other Latin American countries...at least until it's time to dust off the rhinestone tiara and satin sash and crown a beauty queen. The island's near obsession with beauty pageants has paid off, too. In the big enchilada, the annual Miss Universe pageant, Puerto Ricans are something of a cinch. The island has brought home a stunning five wins in the pageant's history, the most recent in 2006.

Islanders also spend significant amounts of money in *botánicas:* shops that sell herbs, plants, charms, holy water and books on performing spirit rituals.

Women in Puerto Rico

Puerto Rican culture, like much of Latin American, is too often stigmatized as a 'macho' world where women play traditional roles, bearing children, cooking meals and caring for the home. Stereotypes paint Puerto Rican men in a similarly simplistic light – possessive, jealous and prone to wild acts of desperation when in love. Although many women generally perform all those duties (and more) in the most traditional Puerto Rican family structures, recent history has seen the island break significantly with the punitive gender discrimination that can be common in other Latin American countries and throughout the Caribbean. In some sense, both sexes seem to enjoy the drama that comes along with these intertwined roles – pay close attention to couples twirling on the dance floor to a salsa song or, better yet, a steamy bolero, and you'll see clearly what game they are both happily playing. But a more substantive look at Puerto Rican culture reveals a much greater complexity to the role of women in contemporary Puerto Rico.

Puerto Rican women have excelled at business, trade and, most importantly, politics – often with more measurable achievement than their counterparts in the United States. San Juan elected a female mayor decades before a woman won a comparable office in the US, and, in 2000, a woman named Sila Maria Calderón was elected governor of Puerto Rico. She ran on a campaign that promised to end government corruption, and clean house she did.

Other women's issues that tend to be loaded with political and social baggage in the United States have a relatively progressive position in Puerto Rican culture. For instance, abortion is legal in Puerto Rico (although the rest of the Caribbean, outside of Cuba, is uniformly opposed to it). In Puerto Rico, even socially conservative politicians remain acutely aware of the effects of a high birthrate on family living and quality of life. The facts of life are taught early in the home, but it's worth noting that high-school-aged Puerto Rican girls wait longer to have sex. They are also better informed about sex, and use condoms more responsibly when they do have sex, than their American counterparts – and that's according to the US government's own figures. Puerto Rican culture still has plenty of macho myths that pose a challenge to full empowerment of women, but no more so than any other Western culture.

The effect this has on travelers is very noticeable for women traveling alone. Although typical safety precautions should be followed, solo women travelers attract much less attention than in other corners of Latin America.

Puerto Rico's Landscapes

The Land

Cartographers group Puerto Rico with the Caribbean's three largest islands – Cuba, Jamaica and Hispaniola – in the so-called Greater Antilles, the most substantial of a series of islands that dot the waters of the Caribbean and North Atlantic like the trail of a gracefully skipping stone. But at 100 miles long and 35 miles wide, Puerto Rico is quite clearly the Greater Antilles' lesser sidekick, stuck off to the east of Hispaniola at about 18° north latitude, 66° west longitude. With its four principal satellite islands – Mona and Desecheo to the west, Culebra and Vieques to the east – and a host of cays hugging its shores, Puerto Rico claims approximately 3500 sq miles of land, making the commonwealth slightly larger than the Mediterranean island of Corsica and slightly smaller than the US state of Connecticut.

Geology

Like almost all the islands that sprang from the Caribbean Basin, Puerto Rico owes its existence to a series of volcanic events. These eruptions built up layers of lava and igneous rock and created an island with four distinct geographical zones: the central mountains, karst country, the coastal plain and the coastal dry forest. At the heart of the island, running east to west, stands a spine of steep, wooded mountains called the Cordillera Central. The lower slopes of the cordillera give way to foothills, comprising a region on the island's north coast known as 'karst country.' In this part of the island, erosion has worn away the limestone, leaving a karstic terrain of dramatic sinkholes, hillocks and caves.

Forty-five non-navigable rivers and streams rush from the mountains and through the foothills to carve the coastal valleys, particularly on the east and west ends of Puerto Rico, where sugarcane, coconuts and a variety of fruits are cultivated. The island's longest river is the Río Grande de Loíza, which flows north to the coast. Other substantial rivers include the Río Grande de Añasco, the Río Grande de Arecibo and the Río de la Plata.

Little of the island's virgin forest remains, but second- and third-growth forests totaling 140 sq miles now comprise significant woodland reserves, mostly in the center of the island.

The San Fermin earthquake that hit western Puerto Rico in October 1918 measured 7.6 on the Richter scale and triggered a 20ft tsunami. The event caused more than $4 million worth of damage to the cities of Mayagüez and Aguadilla. It killed 116 people.

Territorial Parks & Reserves

Puerto Rico has more than a dozen well-developed and protected wilderness areas, which offer an array of exploration and a few camping opportunities. Most of these protected areas are considered *reservas forestales* (forest reserves) or *bosques estatales* (state forests), although these identifiers are often treated interchangeably in government-issued literature and maps. Commonwealth or US federal agencies administer most of the natural reserves on the island, and admission to these areas is generally free.

Private conservation groups own and operate a few of the nature preserves, including Las Cabezas de San Juan Reserva Natural 'El Faro'; visitors to these places should expect to pay an entrance fee (which is usually under $5). The best time to visit nearly all of the parks is from November to March; however, Bosque Estatal de Guánica is an inviting destination year-round.

The National Astronomy & Ionosphere Center (www.naic.edu) website has information about the Observatorio de Arecibo for the general public as well as academic types.

Major Parks & Reserves

El Yunque National Forest The emerald 28,000-acre highlight of the island's parks is this misty, magnificent rainforest. Dotted with idyllic waterfalls and covered in dense flora, it's home to some of Puerto Rico's most wild and endangered animals. With the island's best trails, its lush forests and sun-splashed peaks are ideal for hiking and mountain biking.

Bosque Estatal de Guánica An immense patch of 10,000 acres on the southwest coast, this huge park is home to a tropical dry-forest ecosystem and a Unesco biosphere forest. Its arid scenery and beautiful birds make it good for hiking, swimming, biking and bird-watching.

Bosque Estatal de Toro Negro This ruggedly beautiful central, mountainous park has landscapes that are only slightly less spectacular than El Yunque's, but none of the infrastructure. If you want to get off the map (literally), this is the place.

Las Cabezas de San Juan Reserva Natural 'El Faro' Another notable coastal preserve is the 316-acre park at the northeast corner of Puerto Rico, where El Faro (Lighthouse) stands guard over the offshore cays. Its paved trails and interpretive centers make this the best park, other than El Yunque, for families. Enjoy coastal views while hiking here, or go kayaking in the mangroves.

Bosque Estatal de Río Abajo Densely forested and dotted with development, this state forest covers 5000 acres in karst country near the Observatorio de Arecibo. It has hiking trails and an aviary, where the Department of Natural Resources is working to reintroduce the Puerto Rican parrot and other endangered species.

Isla Mona The most isolated of Puerto Rico's nature sanctuaries lies about 50 miles east of Mayagüez, across the often-turbulent waters of Pasaje de la Mona. This tabletop island is sometimes called Puerto Rico's Galápagos or Jurassic Park because of its isolation. It's a tag made all the more eerie by the island's 200ft limestone cliffs, honeycomb caves and giant iguanas. Come here for solitude, hiking and caving.

Vieques National Wildlife Refuge Glimmering to the east are the 'Spanish Virgin Islands', Culebra and Vieques, both of which have large tracts of land designated as National Wildlife Refuges under the control of the US Fish & Wildlife Service. At 18,000 acres, the Vieques refuge is the largest protected natural reserve in Puerto Rico and home to wild turtles and sleepy iguanas. Activities here include hiking, cycling, snorkeling, sailing and swimming.

EL YUNQUE

In April 2007, an executive order signed by US President George W Bush rechristened the Caribbean National Forest as El Yunque National Forest to blend in more with Puerto Rico's cultural inheritance.

Other notable parks and reserves include Bosque Estatal de Carite, which offers easy hikes through pristine forest, as well as kayaking and camping, and Reserva Forestal Toro Negro, with its misty mountaintops and wild hiking trails, both in the central mountains; the Bosque Estatal de Guajataca and Parque de las Cavernas del Río Camuy on the north coast, for hiking, caving and petroglyphs; and Culebra National Wildlife Refuge, which US President Theodore Roosevelt signed into law almost 100 years ago.

Organizations

National Park Service (NPS; www.nps.gov) Part of the US Department of the Interior, this federal agency oversees San Juan's El Morro and San Cristóbal forts, which together are classified as the San Juan National Historic Site.

Departamento de Recursos Naturales y Ambientales (DRNA; Department of Natural Resources; www.drna.gobierno.pr, in Spanish) Puerto Rico's fairly disorganized natural resources agency administers all of the island's *bosques estatales* and *reservas forestales,* and issues camping permits. Its main office is in San Juan.

US Forest Service (USFS; ☎campground & reservation info 800-280-2267; www.fs.fed.us) Part of the Department of Agriculture, the USFS manages the use of forests such as El Yunque. National forests are less protected than parks, allowing commercial exploitation in some areas (usually logging or privately owned recreational facilities). Current information about national forests can be obtained from ranger stations (contact information is given in the individual forest sections of this book).

US Fish & Wildlife Service (FWS; www.fws.gov) Puerto Rico maintains regional offices, which can provide information about viewing local wildlife. Their phone numbers appear in the white pages of the local telephone directory under 'US Government, Interior Department,' or you can call the **Federal Information Center** (☎800-688-9889; www.pueblo.gsa.gov).

BIRD-WATCHING

For bird-watchers heading to Puerto Rico or the Caribbean, *A Guide to the Birds of Puerto Rico and the Virgin Islands* by Herbert Raffaele is a must-have. It will help you spy lots of hard-to-find birds in the dense forests of nature reserves.

Environmental Issues

Puerto Rico has long suffered from a number of serious environmental problems, including population growth and rapid urbanization, deforestation, erosion of soil, water pollution and mangrove destruction. While Puerto Ricans still have a long way to go toward undoing generations of damage and preserving their natural resources, the past few decades have seen an increase in the level of awareness, resources and action dedicated to conservation efforts.

Current Environmental Issues

Population growth & urbanization Population growth and rapid urbanization have long posed the greatest threats to the island's environment. And though Puerto Rico's population density was approaching that of Singapore, significant education about family planning and more cautious urban planning has developed in recent years. The current birthrate is quickly approaching zero population growth.

Deforestation & soil erosion Clear-cut logging operations ended in the 20th century, leaving untold acres of rich mountain topsoil plugging the mouths of rivers and streams. In the 1920s and '30s, conservationists and the US colonial government set aside and reforested an extensive network of wilderness reserves, mostly in karst country and the Cordillera Central. Today these reserves are mature forests and cover nearly the entire central part of the island – about one-third of Puerto Rico's landmass. Still, clearing hillside land for housing subdivisions in places such as Guaynabo and Trujillo Alto, both suburbs of San Juan, is a major issue.

Water issues Many streams, rivers and estuaries on the coastal plain have been polluted by agricultural runoff, industry and inadequate sewer systems. Environmental groups lobbying for the cleanup of these cesspools have made little headway. Visitors should not be tempted to swim in rivers, streams or estuaries near the coast (including Bahía de San Juan). If possible, avoid shellfish from these areas.

Mangrove protection Operation Bootstrap rushed to develop business and housing communities and devastated vast mangrove swamps, particularly along the island's north shore. In the 1990s environmentalists saw significant victories in reversing this damage, including the creation of the huge 2883-acre Reserva Nacional de Investigación Estuarina de Bahía de Jobos.

In 2005, the well-known American environmental organization Sierra Club (www.sierraclub.org) welcomed a group of members from Puerto Rico as its 64th chapter.

Heavy-metal pollution The land and sea life around Vieques were literally under siege from the US government during the years of naval bombardment. The US Navy left Vieques in 2003 and the island was deemed a Superfund site shortly after the pullout. Though progress has been made, much of the Vieques National

CONSTRUCTION VERSUS CONSERVATION

Unchecked development has long been Puerto Rico's biggest environmental threat. Big developers and hotel companies regularly eye the country's lush coastline and pristine beaches in search of their next site. As economically beneficial as tourism might be, its continued expansion could lead to a law of diminishing returns. If the Enchanted Island suffers many more reconfigured coastlines or bulldozed palm groves, it will no longer be worthy of its nickname.

Many argue that development – particularly in the tourism sector – has already gone too far. Puerto Rico currently has a higher population density than any of the 50 US states, with an average 1000 people per sq mile. It also supports one of the highest concentrations of roads in the world. Outside of the central mountains, it's rare to drive for more than a mile or two without coming across a housing complex or shopping mall, and the island's peripheral coast road is often more like a parking lot than a highway.

One perennial worry for environmentalists is the flouting of property laws, an occurance that regularly sees buildings going up on protected land. Side-stepping protection laws, large hotel properties often merely act as a cover for future subdivisions and within a couple of years a comparatively new resort will be shuttered up to make way for a housing estate.

Grassroots pressure from conservations has already yielded results, though. In 2007, a proposed condo development was indefinitely blocked by community groups in Loíza Aldea, near San Juan. If realized, this project would have erected an 880-unit gated community, a casino, tennis courts and a beach club at Piñones on one of Puerto Rico's last undeveloped beaches.

Another contentious and resurrected battle is brewing near Luquillo over the pristine land known as the Northeast Ecological Corridor. It is the second most important nesting area in the US for the endangered leatherback turtle, and habitat for threatened species including the West Indian manatee and the Puerto Rican boa. Although it was saved from hotel development a few years ago by a nature reserve designation, this protection was rescinded in 2009, opening up the possibility that this 3000-acre area could be opened up to new development.

Wildlife Refuge is closed to the public until heavy metals, unexploded ordnance and leftover fuels and chemicals can be taken care of.

Conservation Groups

Surfrider Foundation (www.surfrider.org)
Conservation Trust of Puerto Rico (www.fideicomiso.org)
Natural History Society of Puerto Rico (www.naturalhistorypr.org)
Puerto Rican Conservation Foundation (☎787-760-2115)

Wildlife of Puerto Rico

Seeking out the wildlife in Puerto Rico can be rewarding, if you're determined, as the island's tropical environment and high endemism (that's fancy talk for the characteristic of having lots of endemic species) allows visitors to see things that exist nowhere else on earth. The island's jungle mountains and surreal variety of terrain – including some of the wettest and driest forests in the subtropical climate – have a bit of everything. Still, the pleasure for animal lovers will come in modest doses – there are no huge wild beasts, nor skies filled with a riot of brightly colored exotic birds. To get a sense of the quiet charms offered by Puerto Rico's wildlife, consider the island's most famous creature, the humble common coquí. The nocturnal serenade of this small endemic frog is the sound of the island, an ever-present reminder of the island's precious natural environment.

Above and below ground, and under water, *Puerto Rico and Virgin Islands Wildlife Viewing* by David W Nellis gives you all the facts on the flora and fauna of Puerto Rico.

Amphibians & Reptiles

The endless coastline of Puerto Rico is one of its most inviting environments to both human and animal visitors. The most exciting fauna lives along the island's coast. Despite heavy coastal development (see the boxed text, p264), a handful of the island's beaches are still nesting sites for two of the world's most critically endangered turtles, the hawksbill and leatherback sea turtles. An excellent place to view the nesting process is on the isolated northern beaches of the island of Culebra (see p121).

The hawksbill and leatherback sea turtles are among the 25 species of amphibians and 61 reptiles on the island – one of the most diverse collections of such animals in the world. Certainly the most famous amphibian is the tiny but highly vocal coquí frog (its distinctive nighttime croak has been measured at 10 decibels), which has been adopted as a national symbol.

Learn all about the coquí frog and other animals that inhabit Puerto Rico in *Natural Puerto Rico* by Alfonso Silva Lee, an exhaustive but entertaining book on island wildlife.

Iguanas are often kept as semiwild pets and pose unlikely obstacles on numerous Puerto Rican golf courses. The most notable wild species is the Mona ground iguana, which still survives in large numbers on the western island of Mona – often dubbed the Galápagos of the Caribbean because of its unique biological diversity. You'll find other iguana's lazily eyeing your lunch at outdoor cafes on Vieques and Culebra, domesticated to the point where French fries from tourists seem to comprise most of their diet. Refrain from feeding iguanas, however, as food for humans can kill them.

Though not native to the island, spectacled caimans have become somewhat of a pest in the areas around Laguna Tortuguero on the north coast. Introduced as a macho pet in the 1990s, many of these minicrocs were abandoned by their owners and dumped in the vicinity of Puerto

BRIGHT LIGHTS, BLACK WATER

There are seven known regions worldwide that are phosphorescent – meaning they glow in the dark thanks to micro-organisms called dynoflagellates living in the water – but Puerto Rico's are considered among the brightest and the best.

There are three places on the island to see this psychedelic phenomenon: Bahía Mosquito in Vieques, Bahía de Fosforescente at La Parguera and Laguna Grande north of Fajardo. The most abundant of the many organisms in Puerto Rico's 'phosphorous' bays is *Pirodinium bahamense*. The term 'Pirodinium' comes from 'pyro,' meaning fire, and 'dirium,' meaning rotate.

When movement disturbs these creatures, a chemical reaction takes place in their little bodies that makes a flash. Scientists speculate that dynoflagellates have developed this ability to ward off predators.

You can see these micro-organisms flashing like tiny stars in Atlantic waters as far north as New England in summer, but never in the brilliant concentrations appearing in Puerto Rico. Enclosed mangrove bays, where narrow canals limit the exchange of water with the open sea, are the places that let the dynoflagellates breed and concentrate. In a sense, the bay is a big trap and vitamins produced along the shore provide food for the corralled micro-organisms.

Not surprisingly, bioluminescent bays support precarious ecosystems. To avoid damaging them, only book tours with operators who use kayaks or electric motors. Island Adventures (p135) is on Vieques, which has the best bay of the three. Yokahú Kayaks (p106) covers the Fajardo bay, which is the second-best option.

In La Parguera, home to the third bay (p168), most tour operators only use motorized engines and are not recommended. The bioluminescence has been greatly reduced as a consequence. If you're offered a ride, check that it will be in a boat that's safe for the environment.

Rico's only freshwater lake, where they have played havoc with the fragile ecosystem. Local rangers are currently trying to control their numbers.

Puerto Rico boasts 11 varieties of snake, none of which are poisonous. The most impressive is the endemic special boa, which can grow to a length of more than 12ft; it is also endangered, but hikers may spot one in the karst region of northwestern state forests and in El Yunque. Though boas have been long known to feed on bats, scientists only recently discovered that the snakes catch bats in their jaws while hanging at the mouths of caves.

All you need to know about Puerto Rico's insects, reptiles, four-legged mammals and the greenery that they inhabit is in *The Nature of the Islands: Plants and Animals of the Eastern Caribbean* by Virginia Barlow. Very helpful for campers.

Marine Life

Spending time in the water off Puerto Rico's shores at the right time of year can reveal excellent marine life. Pods of humpback whales breed in the island's warm waters in winter. In the late winter of 2010, southern shores off the island also saw more orca (killer whales) than ever before recorded. Local fishermen attribute this to the relatively warm waters of the Caribbean bringing more dolphins for the orca to eat. Most whale-watching tour operators leave from Rincón, usually beginning in early December (see p177) and ending in March.

Though looking for whales may be a hit with tourists, the Antillean manatee (the town of Manatí, on the north coast, is named after the mammal) is perhaps more dear to Puerto Ricans. These so-called sea cows inhabit shallow coastal areas to forage on sea grasses and plants. Manatee numbers have dropped in recent decades due to habitat loss, poaching and entanglement with fishing nets, but they are generally thought to be coming back. To see a manatee, rent a kayak and float along the mangrove-lined shores in the southeast of the island, near Salinas. Despite their lumbering appearance, they can be surprisingly graceful in the water, and have been seen doing somersaults and elegant turns.

Of course, the majority of travelers are captivated by seeing the tropical fish and coral off the island's shores. The continental shelf surrounds Puerto Rico on three sides and blesses the island with warm water and excellent coral reefs, seawalls and underwater features for diving and snorkeling. Especially off the west coast, the water is clear and filled with fish. An abundant supply of sea grass is home to crabs, octopus, starfish and a great variety of fish. Among these, the parrot fish, eels and sea horses are the most exciting. For more about exploring the waters of Puerto Rico, see p33.

Mammals

Very few of the land mammals that make their home in Puerto Rico are native to the island; most mammal species – from cows to rats – have been accidentally or intentionally introduced to the island over the centuries. Of these, rodents are by far the most common animal – scientists estimate that they account for more than 40% of mammals here.

Bats are the only native terrestrial mammal in Puerto Rico. They exist in large numbers in the caves of karst country, but most travelers will only catch glimpses at dusk while visiting Bosque Estatal de Cambalache or the Cavernas del Río Camuy.

But bats and rats aren't the only land mammals, and certainly not the most graceful; Puerto Rico is also home to the distinctive Paso Fino horse, a small-boned, easy-gaited variety. The Paso Finos have been raised in Puerto Rico since the time of the Spanish conquest, when they were introduced to the New World to supply the conquistadores on their expeditions throughout Mexico and the rest of the Americas. They now number 8000 and are unique to Puerto Rico. The horses are most dramatic on the island of Vieques, where they roam in semiwild herds on vast tracts of exmilitary land. Every March, the southern city of Guayama celebrates these animals with parades and rodeo events.

Other mammals of interest to travelers are two small colonies of monkeys, both introduced by scientists. The first lives off Vieques on the 39-acre Cayo Santiago where a group of rhesus monkeys arrived for scientific study in 1938. Today they've burgeoned into a community of more than 900 primates. The second scientific monkey colony that grew out of control is on Isla de Monos off La Parguera, which is a standard part of the tour of the mangrove canals.

Birds & Bugs

With more than 250 species spread over 3500 sq miles, Puerto Rico is an excellent place to dust off your binoculars and engage in a bit of tropical bird-watching. The commonwealth's most famous bird is also one of its rarest: the elusive Puerto Rican parrot. Numbers of the bright-green bird

PARROT

The Puerto Rican parrot is one of the 10 most endangered species in the world, with only an estimated 35 to 40 birds still existing in the wild.

HIKING FOR THE BIRDS

Though land mammals are rare in Puerto Rico, exotic birdlife is abundant, with more than 250 species, 11 of which are endemic and 10 endangered, including the extremely illusive Puerto Rican parrot. The most obvious destination for budding ornithologists is El Yunque National Forest, situated close to the capital. The El Portal Visitors Center (p99) on Hwy 191 has good, basic information on the local birdlife.

The island's richest species diversity can be spied in the Cabo Rojo area, particularly around Las Salinas salt flats, where migratory birds from as far away as Canada populate a unique and highly varied ecosystem. Call in at the Centro Interpretativos Las Salinas de Cabo Rojo (p189) to speak with informed local experts.

For bird-watchers heading to Puerto Rico or the Caribbean, *A Guide to the Birds of Puerto Rico and the Virgin Islands* by Herbert Raffaele is a must-have. It will help you spy lots of hard-to-find birds in the dense forests of nature reserves.

Check out the website www.elyunque.com. As well as excellent information on the island's national forest, this site lists many other activities on the island and is regularly updated with topical environmental news.

were down in the mid teens during the 1970s, but thanks to concerted conservation efforts the population has recovered to a precarious 35 to 40. The parrots still exist in the wild in the El Yunque and Río Abajo forest reserves, although seeing one is akin to winning a lottery ticket. The long-term plan for its recovery aims to have it 'upgraded' to being merely endangered by 2020.

Another endemic bird is the Puerto Rican tody, a small green, yellow and red creature that frequents the moist mountains of the Cordillera Central and the dense thickets of the south coast where it feeds on insects. If you're lucky you'll also encounter various South American families, such as tyrant flycatchers, bananaquits and tanagers.

The coastal dry forest of Guánica might be the biggest draw for serious bird-watchers looking to whittle down their life list. It features more than 130 bird species, comprising largely of songbirds. Some of these are migratory fowl, such as the prairie warbler and the northern parula. Many are nonmigratory species, including the lizard cuckoo and the critically endangered Puerto Rican nightjar. One of the joys of winter beachcombing is watching the aerial acrobatics of brown pelicans as they hunt for fish.

The island also has a supply of unusual flying and crawling insects, including a large tropical relative of the firefly called the *cucubano,* and a centipede measuring more than 6in in length with a sting that can kill. Much to the chagrin of generations of foreign visitors there are zillions of blood-hungry mosquitoes.

Flora

Puerto Rico's tropical climate and unique rain patterns create a veritable greenhouse for a huge variety of plant life, which thrives on tropical heat, tons of rains and lots of moisture in the air. As soon as you leave San Juan's urban zone and head into the mountains, you'll see green everywhere.

Mangrove swamps and coconut groves dominate the north coast, while the El Yunque rainforest, at the east end of the island, supports mahogany trees and more than 50 varieties of wild orchid. Giant ferns thrive in the rainforest as well as in the foothills of karst country, while cacti, mesquite forest and bunchgrass reign on the dry southwest tip of the island, resembling the look of the African savanna. The dry forests near Guánica grow a variety of cacti, thorny scrub brush and plants equipped for harsh, dry conditions.

The hills of the Cordillera Central are densely forested and flowering trees punctuate the landscape. Look for the butterfly tree, with its light-pink flower resembling an orchid, the bright orange exclamation of the African tulip and the deep red of the royal Poinciana, which are cultivated near the Christmas season.

Exotic shade trees have long been valued in this sunny climate, and most of the island's municipal plazas spread beneath canopies of magnificent ceibas or kapoks (silk-cotton tree), the *flamboyán* (poinciana), with its flame-red blossoms, and the African tulip tree.

Islanders often adorn their homes with a profusion of flowers, such as orchids, bougainvillea and poinsettias, and tend lovingly to fruit trees that bear papaya, *uva caleta* (sea grape), *carambola* (star fruit), *panapen* (breadfruit) and *plátano* (plantain). Of course, sugarcane dominates the plantations of the coastal lowlands, while farmers raise coffee on the steep slopes of the Cordillera Central.

Puerto Rico's Cuisine

From first-class dining in Old San Juan to the roadside stalls of Guavate, Puerto Rico's food is far and away the best and most varied in the Caribbean. Foodies can explore five-star 'fusion' cuisine in all the major cities, but the real deal is *comida criolla* (traditional Puerto Rican cuisine). The blend of numerous international influences is as wide-ranging as the Caribbean, African, Spanish and American forces that shape the culture itself.

Staples & Specialties

Meat

First things first: Puerto Ricans adore meat. They smoke it, stew it, fry it and fillet it. They make bold claims about it (apparently modern barbecue descends from the roast pork that the Taíno called *barbicoa*), mash it up with all kinds of starches (*mofongo,* anyone?) and form it into outlandish designs (such as chuletas can-can, fringed like a showgirl's skirt).

But fancy or no-frills, the top of the Puerto Rican food chain is a smoky, savory *lechón asado* (roast suckling pig), which is cooked on a spit over a charcoal fire. When it's done right, the pig is liberally seasoned with a distinctive seasoning called adobo (garlic, oregano, paprika, peppercorns, salt, olive, lime juice and vinegar worked into a paste for seasoning meat). Adobo comes from Spain and is often associated with Filipino food. Then, the meat is basted with achiote (annato seeds) and juice from *naranjas* (the island's sour oranges). Finally, after it's cooked to crispness, the meat is served with *ajili-mójili* (tangy garlic sauce).

For less festive occasions, Puerto Rican dinners include roast *cabro* (kid goat), *ternera* (veal), *pollo* (chicken) or *carne mechada* (roast beef).

The traditional recipes in *A Taste of Puerto Rico* by Yvonne Ortiz are good, but more intriguing are the descriptions of some of the more modern dishes appearing on the island, especially the new emphasis on healthy seafood.

Seafood

Surprisingly, Puerto Ricans don't eat much fish, but a popular way to prepare seafood – from *pulpo* (octopus) to *mero* (sea bass) – is *en escabeche.* This technique yields a fried then chilled seafood, pickled in vinegar, oil, peppercorns, salt, onions, bay leaves and lime juice.

Fried fish is often topped with *mojo isleño* (a piquant sauce of vinegar, tomato sauce, capers and spices). *Jueyes* (land crabs) have long been a staple of islanders who can simply gather them from the beaches. An easy way to enjoy the taste is to eat *empanadillas de jueyes* (crab is picked from the shells, seasoned and baked in a wrap with casabe paste, which is made from yucca). Fish lovers should also try a bowl of *sopón de pescado* (fish soup), with its scent of onions, garlic and a subtle taste of sherry.

A MOVABLE FEAST

Cheap, cheerful and indisputably Puerto Rican, *friquitines*, also known as *quioscos, kioskos* or just plain food stalls, offer some of the island's best cheap snacks. Running the gamut from smoky holes-in-the-wall to mobile trucks that park on the roadside, these kiosks offer fast food that is invariably homemade, locally sourced and tasty.

The island's most famous cluster of permanent *friquitines* (more than 60 or so in all) lines the beachfront at Luquillo (p102). Other more movable feasts operate at weekends in places such as Piñones near San Juan and Boquerón on the west coast, although you can come across them almost anywhere.

Look out for *surullitos* (fried cornmeal and cheese sticks), *empanadillas* (meat or fish turnovers), *alcapurrias* (fritters made with mashed plantains and ground meat) and *bacalaítos* (salt-cod fritters seasoned with oregano, garlic and sweet chili peppers). When it's hot, keep an eye out for *piragüeros*, vendors who s-ell syrupy *piraguas* (cones of shaved ice covered in sweet fruity sauces such as raspberry, guava, tamarind or coconut).

Soups & Stews

Soups and stews fill the working-class cafeterias advertizing *comida criolla* and offer a genuine fusion of Taíno, European and African flavors. Many include island vegetables for texture: *yautia* (tanier; a starchy tuber which is very similar to taro), *batata* (sweet potato), yucca, chayote squash and *grelos* (turnip greens). *Sancocho* (Caribbean soup) blends these vegetables with plantains – peeled and diced – and coarsely chopped tomatoes, green pepper, chilis, cilantro, onion and corn. Cooks then add water, tomato sauce, chopped beef and pork ribs for flavoring.

Another delicious, common dish is *asopao de pollo,* a rich and spicy chicken stew soaked in adobo.

Featuring renowned island chefs, *Puerto Rico: Grand Cuisine of the Caribbean* by José Luis Diaz de Villegas is an excellent exploration of the ways in which *comida criolla* is infused with other culinary cultures.

Fruits

For a tropical island, there's not as much fruit here as you might expect, though Puerto Rico grows and exports bananas, papayas, fresh and processed pineapples, as well as a bewildering variety of exotic tropical fruits. It's also the third-largest producer of citron – behind Italy and Greece – and you'll see a long swath of fields around Adjuntas dedicated to this fruit.

Drinks

Nonalcoholic Drinks

You'll see signs for piña colada (the creamy mix of pineapple juice and coconut cream, sometimes the base of a rum drink) everywhere. This, and other fruit juices, such as *guanábana* juice, are locally made in both carbonated and noncarbonated varieties. *Mavi* is something like root beer, made from the bark of the ironwood tree. As in much of the tropics, beach and street vendors sell *cocos fríos* (chilled green coconuts) to the thirsty.

Coffee, grown in Adjuntas and many of the mountain regions, is a staple at all hours.

Plantains are in such demand on the island they must be imported from the Dominican Republic.

Alcoholic Drinks

Simply put, *ron* (rum) is the national drink. Puerto Rico is the largest producer of rum in the world, and distilleries prop up the island's economy. The headquarters of the Bacardí Rum Factory is in Cataño, but most Puerto Ricans drink locally made Don Q or Castillo.

Because Puerto Rico is a major producer of alcoholic beverages and taxes are low, it is one of the cheapest places to drink in the world. Island-brewed beers generally cost about $2 in bars. The India brand has been around for years; Medalla is a popular light pilsner that many islanders drink like water.

Habits & Customs

There are very few tricks to dining out in Puerto Rico – you can eat with either hand, hold your utensils American or British style, or whatever. Just follow basic manners and you'll get along fine. Breakfast and lunch tend to be quick, and dinner is usually a lingering, social and festive affair. If invited to someone's house, a gift bottle of rum, beer or wine will be well received (more so than flowers). Don't argue when hosts serve you gargantuan portions; as their guest, you get special treatment.

Food is an intrinsic part of Puerto Rican culture, and festivals celebrating regional specialties take place year-round. Some favorites:

Carnaval de Salinas, Salinas April; known for killer seafood.

Festival del Camarón de Río, Moca May; River Shrimp Festival; river shrimp are prepared in every way imaginable.

Festival del Guineo, Lares June; try more than a dozen varieties of bananas.

Puff Pastry Festival, Añasco August; a dessert showdown between island bakeries.

National Plantain Festival, Corozal October; plantains mashed, fried and all ways in between.

Festival del Cetí, Arecibo September; the coastal town feasts on a miniature relative of the sardine.

RECIPES

The website www.ricanrecipes.com specializes in recipes from the Enchanted Island, with a comprehensive list that includes everything from *brazo gitano* to *pollo en fricasé*.

GAMES

Sports

Though the silent, stone-lined Taíno ball courts of Tibes and Caguana pay homage to Puerto Rico's long dedication to sports, they speak nothing of the ferocious energy that fires the competitive spirit of islanders today. For such a geographically small place, Puerto Rico plays a disproportionately large role in modern sport, whether it be through an upset of the fabled American 'Dream Team' at the 2004 Olympics or producing legendary champions on the pitch or in the ring.

During the summer of 2010 Mayagüez was host to the 21st annual Central American and Caribbean Games. It was the third time the island had hosted the regional games and a number of stadiums were built and refurbished for the event, including the 13,000-capacity, $43-million Mayagüez Athletics Stadium.

Baseball

Puerto Rico's official pastime is *béisbol* (baseball), a modern game that bears a vague resemblance to the ceremonial *batú* of Taíno ancestors and draws telling parallels with the island's contemporary economic and cultural relationship with the US. As much as Puerto Rico's beleaguered economy is reliant on support from the US federal government, the Puerto Rican Baseball League is bankrolled by the Major League Baseball (MLB). Players with island roots often make their most significant contributions to the Puerto Rican diaspora while working in New York and Chicago. The pros that rise from the island's embarrassingly empty stadiums are often celebrated as icons when they make it to the big show.

While the official pastime gets plenty of lip service and Puerto Ricans follow the US Major Leagues with some attention, going to a game here can be an eerily quiet event. The 2007–08 season was canceled due to financial difficulties, and when you find yourself as one of a hundred fans among thousands of empty seats, it's easy to see why. Still, every major city has a team in the Puerto Rican league and when the season enters its ascent to the finals, the scene gets a little livelier.

US Major League teams also hold spring training camps in Puerto Rico and regularly use the island's league as a farm team. Early-season exhibition games are held in spring, including the televised San Juan Series, at San Juan's Hiram Bithorn Stadium.

The upside to catching a game here: it can be a terrific cultural experience and it's dirt cheap by American standards. Tickets are usually under $10 and a cold beer will only set you back $3.

Roberto Clemente is probably the most famous Puerto Rican baseball star of all time, with a career batting average of .317. He was posthumously inducted into the Baseball Hall of Fame in 1973 after his death in a plane crash.

Cockfighting

If *béisbol* gets credit as the official sport, *peleas de gallos* (cockfighting) holds strong as the passionate pastime of the people. It's certainly a thorny issue with those who harbor animal rights sympathies, and for good reason. The 'sport' entails placing specially bred and trained *gallos de pelea* (fighting cocks) in a pit to battle each other to the death. It can be terrifying and difficult to watch, but interest goes back thousands of years to ancient Persia, Greece and Rome.

Cockfighting was outlawed when the US occupation of the island began in 1898. After almost four decades underground, cockfighting was once again legalized on the island in the 1930s and remains so to this day.

During the 20-minute, fight the cocks try to peck and slash each other to pieces with sharpened natural spurs, or with steel or plastic spurs taped or tied to their feet, causing feathers to fly and blood to splatter. The fight usually ends with one bird mortally wounded or dead. Then the aficionados collect their winnings or plunk down more money – to get even – on the next fight. Betting usually starts at $100 and goes well into the thousands.

Catcher Yadir Molina is considered among the best defensive catchers in Major League Baseball. In 2010 he became the first player to win the illustrious Fielding Bible Award, for defensive play, with a perfect score of 100 points.

Basketball

Puerto Rico began competing in the Olympic Games in 1948 and has never taken home a gold medal. But at the 2004 summer games, the island made history when the Puerto Rican men's basketball team – in its first showing at the Olympics – upset the USA 'Dream Team' in their opening game, the first defeat of USA men's basketball since the Olympic committee allowed professional NBA players to participate. Facing off against the biggest names in the sport, including LeBron James and Allen Iverson, Puerto Rico was led by a pair of players who sported Utah Jazz jerseys in the regular season, Carlos Arroyo and José Ortiz. The team did not win a medal in the games, but became instant national heroes. Visitors can catch basketball almost year-round, watching teams participating in Puerto Rico's own pro league, the Baloncesto Superior Nacional (www.bsnpr.com) or the international Premiere Basketball League (www.thepbl.com), which has teams from the US and Canada.

SMALL COUNTRY, BIG PUNCH

Puerto Rico has spawned enough fighters to fill its own boxing Hall of Fame, including the youngest world champion in boxing history and one of the sport's greatest-ever knockout specialists.

The standard was set in the 1930s when wily bantamweight Sixto Escobar became the first Puerto Rican to win a world championship belt, knocking out Mexican Baby Casanova in Montreal in 1936. In his homeland, Escobar – from Barceloneta on the north coast – became an overnight hero.

The 1970s introduced the two Wilfredos – Benitez and Gómez. Wilfredo Benitez, nicknamed 'The Radar,' was a Puerto Rican childhood boxing sensation. Raised in New York City, he became the youngest-ever world champion when he defeated Colombian Antonio Cervantes in a World Junior Welterweight championship bout in San Juan in 1976. Benitez, just 17 at the time, defended his title three times before losing to Sugar Ray Leonard in 1979. Gómez, known affectionately as Bazooka, was a punching phenomenon from San Juan who retains one of the highest knockout ratios, with 42 knockouts in 46 fights. Rated number 13 in *Ring* magazine's list of all-time best punchers, Gómez was the subject of the 2003 documentary *Bazooka: The Battles of Wilfredo Gómez*.

As much a showman as a fighter, Hector 'Macho' Camacho was Puerto Rico's most flamboyant star. Born in Bayamón but raised in New York, Camacho aped the style of Muhammad Ali by leaping into the ring dressed as Captain America before a fight. During a 20-year career he fought everyone from Roberto Duran to Julio César Chávez and tested loyalties in his homeland in an all–Puerto Rican world-title fight against Felix Trinidad.

Trinidad, from Cupey Alto, is another modern boxing legend who won world titles at three different weights, including a 1999 victory over Oscar de la Hoya, after which he received a hero's welcome at Luís Muñoz Marín International Airport. He recently passed his mantle over to current superstar Miguel Cotto, part of a famous boxing family dynasty and a product of the famous Bairoa gym in Caguas. Cotto lost his welterweight title in 2008 to Antonio Margarito, only to change divisions and win the light middleweight belt in an exhibition match at Yankee Stadium.

Arts

Literature

Puerto Rico was without a printing press until 1807, and Spain's restrictive rule kept literacy rates low for almost 400 years. But indigenous literature developed nonetheless; the 19th century gave rise to writers who penned the island's identity: Alejandro Tapia y Rivera, Manuel Alonso, Dr Enrique Laguerre and Julia de Burgos.

As more islanders migrated to the US in the 1950s, Puerto Rican 'exiles,' known as Nuyoricans, produced powerful fiction. One of the most successful writers was Pedro Juan Soto, whose 1956 collection *Spiks* (a racial slur aimed at Nuyoricans) depicts life in the New York barrios with biting realism. Luis Piñero, Miguel Algarín and Pedro Pietri started a Latino beatnik movement on Manhattan's Lower East Side at the first Nuyorican Café.

More recently, Esmeralda Santiago's 1986 memoir, *Cuando era puertorriqueña* (When I Was Puerto Rican), became a standard in US schools, and cutting edge literary figures from the Puerto Rican diaspora continue to emerge as vital voices in New York's literary community.

The 1993 movie *Carlito's Way*, starring Al Pacino and Sean Penn, follows the exploits of Carlito Brigante, a Puerto Rican drug dealer in New York who struggles to go straight after his release from prison.

Cinema

Swashbuckling Johnny Depp flicks aren't the only Hollywood productions to exploit Puerto Rico's balmy weather, historic architecture and modern infrastructure. But a homegrown industry only started to flourish in the late 1980s, thanks largely to one director: Jacobo Morales. He wrote, directed and starred in *Dios la cría* (God Created Them). The movie, offering a critical look at Puerto Rican society, was lauded by critics and fans. His next movie, *Lo que le pasó a Santiago* (What Happened to Santiago), won an Academy Award nomination in 1990 for best for-

ICONS OF PUERTO RICAN LITERATURE

» **Alejandro Tapia y Rivera** (1826–82) The 'Father of Puerto Rican literature' wrote poems, stories, essays, novels and plays. Long, allegorical poems include *Sataniada*, 'A Grandiose Epic Dedicated to the Prince of Darkness.'

» **Manuel Alonso** (1822–89) He wrote *El gíbaro* (1849), a collection of vignettes about cockfights, dancing, weddings, politics, race and *espiritismo* (spiritualism) that characterize the island *jíbaro* (an archetypal witty peasant).

» **Julia de Burgos** (1914–53) A major female poet, she responded in outrage when the island became US territory. Her work embodies two fundamental elements of Boricua identity: intense, lyrical connection to nature and fiery politics.

» **Dr Enrique Laguerre** (1906–2005) Puerto Rico's first important international novelist. Published in 1935, *La llamarada* (Blaze of Fire) is set on a sugarcane plantation, where a young intellectual struggles with US corporate exploitation.

TRIO OF PUERTO RICAN FOLK ART

» **Santos** Drawing on the artistic traditions of carved Taíno idols called *cemíes,* these small religious statues represent religious figures and are enshrined in homes to bring spiritual blessings to their keepers.

» **Mundillo** Made only in Spain and Puerto Rico, this fine lace was imported with early nuns, who made and sold it in order to finance schools and orphanages. Renewed interest in island folk arts, generated by the Instituto de Cultura Puertorriqueña, has revived the process.

» **Máscaras** (masks) These frightening and beautiful headpieces are worn at island fiestas, and are popular pieces of folk art. The tradition of masked processions goes back to the Spanish Inquisition, when masqueraders known as *vejigantes* brandished balloon-like objects (called *vejigas;* literally, 'bladders'), terrifying sinners into returning to the church. In Puerto Rico, it merged with masking traditions of African slaves.

eign film. *Linda Sara* (Pretty Sara), his follow-up film in 1994, earned him another.

Director Marcos Zurinaga also made a name for himself in the 1980s, first with *La gran fiesta* (The Big Party) in 1986, which focuses on the last days of San Juan's biggest casino, and the acclaimed *Disappearance of Garcia Lorca* (1997). The most widely distributed and successful Puerto Rican film is probably Luis Molina Casanova's 1993 tragicomedy, *La guagua aérea* (A Flight of Hope), which explores the reasons behind Puerto Ricans' emigration in the 1960s.

Today's celebrity power couple is Jennifer Lopez and Marc Anthony, both Nuyoricans with island ties. Oscar winners Raul Julia – who died in 1994 – and smoldering Benicio del Toro also join the ranks of Puerto Rico's screen celebrities.

The first non-documentary film shot in Puerto Rico was *Un drama en Puerto Rico* by Rafael Colorado D'Assoy, made in 1912. D'Assoy went on to form the Film Industrial Society of Puerto Rico, but his groundbreaking first movie has since been lost.

Visual Arts

San Juan's Museo de San Juan is a symbol of Puerto Rico's dedication to the visual arts, which can be traced back to the early days of Spanish colonization. The first great local artist to emerge was self-taught painter José Campeche (1752–1809). Masterpieces such as *Dama a caballo* (Lady on Horseback) and *Gobernador Ustariz* (Governor Ustariz) demonstrate Campeche's mastery of landscape and portrait painting, often inspired by the story of Jesus.

Another master, Francisco Oller (1833–1917) did not gain recognition until the second half of the 19th century. Oller was very different from Campeche; he studied in France under Gustave Courbet and was influenced by acquaintances including Cézanne. Like his mentor Courbet, Oller dedicated a large body of his work to scenes from humble, everyday island life. Bayamón, Oller's birthplace, maintains a museum to its native son, and many of his works are in San Juan's Museo de Arte de Puerto Rico. Both Oller and Campeche are honored for starting an art movement inspired by Puerto Rican nature and life, and they gave a distinct cultural and artistic identity to the island.

The film *Angel,* written and directed by Jacobo Morales, follows the story of a corrupt police captain and the man he wrongly imprisoned. It narrowly missed out on a 2008 Academy Award nomination.

After a storm of poster art that covered the island in visual and verbal images during the 1950s and '60s, serious painters such as Julio Rosado de Valle, Francisco Rodón and Myrna Báez (b 1931) evolved a new aesthetic in Puerto Rican art, in which images rebel against the tyranny of political and jingoistic slogans.

Today, one of the island's most famous artists is actually a Nuyorican – Rafael Tufiño (1922–2008), who was born in Brooklyn to Puerto Rican parents. Using vivid colors and big canvases, Tufiño was considered the

Rita Moreno, who was born in Humacao in 1931, is the first and only Puerto Rican actress to have won an Academy Award, a Grammy, a Tony and an Emmy.

Better known by the nickname Diplo, Ramón Rivero was the king of Puerto Rican comedy who kept islanders laughing through times of intense economic hardship in the 1940s and '50s. He also starred in one of Puerto Rico's finest films, *Los peloteros* (The Baseball Players).

'Painter of the people' because of his unflinching depiction of poverty on the island. His work has joined the permanent collection of the Museum of Modern Art, the Metropolitan Museum of Art and the Library of Congress.

Myrna Báez is one of a new generation of female artists building on Puerto Rico's traditions to create exciting installation art. Her work is exhibited in many San Juan galleries.

Dance

The rolling gait of salsa is inexorably linked with the Puerto Rican identity, and the island's attitude toward dance often has a refreshing lack of North American reserve.

Over time, many classifiable musical forms – *bomba,* salsa, *plena* and *danza* – have evolved complementary dances based on syncopated rhythms and melodies. An early example was the formal *danza,* an elegant ballroom dance imported from Cuba.

Bomba is another colorful import, with influences brought via African slaves. Boisterously energetic, *bomba* has spawned a plethora of subgenres such as *sica, yuba* and *holandes,* and is both spontaneous and exciting to watch.

Puerto Rico's signature dance is certainly salsa. With its sensuous moves and strong African rhythmic base, it seems like the perfect expression of Puerto Rico's cultural DNA – loose-limbed locals make it look as simple as walking. Salsa is relatively easy to learn, and it is studied around the world.

To see the best Puerto Rican dance, head to San Juan's numerous nightclubs, where steamy Friday dancefloors can only be cooled with icy mojitos.

Survival Guide

Directory A–Z

Accommodations

Although the standard of accommodations is generally better than elsewhere in the Caribbean (although rarely as consistent as the US), prices are generally higher.

For package tourists there are plenty of high-quality resorts, although few are all-inclusive (you must pay extra for food, drink and other activities). Prices for these vary depending on the season and special offers. Elsewhere there's a good system of paradores or midrange accommodations, often in historical buildings or old coffee haciendas. Vacation rentals are a common, economical option for long-term guests or groups. There are no youth hostels in Puerto Rico, and very few dorm-style accommodations. Motels are scarce. Aside from camping, which is difficult and requires organized advanced planning, there's a huge dearth of budget options.

Lodging rates in Puerto Rico vary, sometimes by more than 30%, from season to season and even from day to day, as hotels adjust rates according to perceived demand. In general, rates are highest from December 15 through the end of May. They are also high from mid-June to August, when many island families take their vacations. Rates are lowest from September 1 to December 14. The prices given in this book do not include room taxes, which are 15% at hotels with casinos, and 9% elsewhere.

Camping

Camping is a difficult proposition in Puerto Rico, since reservations have to be made at least 15 days in advance, reservation offices and ranger stations have maddeningly erratic hours and the quality of facility varies greatly.

Beach camping For beach camping and inexpensive cabañas at beachfront facilities of the *centros vacacionales* contact **Compañía de Parques Nacionales** (CPN; National Park Company; ☎787-622-5200, ext 355 or 369; www.parquesnacionalespr.com in Spanish; Apartado Postal No 3207, San Juan, 00904), which allows camping at several public beaches, including Vieques and Culebra.

National Forests & Reservas Forestales (Forest Reserves) Contact the **Departamento de Recursos Naturales y Ambientales** (DRNA; Department of Natural Resources & Environment; ☎787-999-2200; www.drna.gobierno.pr in Spanish; Rte 8838 Km 6.3, Sector El Cinco, Río Piedras) at least 15 days in advance for reservations and a permit. Commonwealth-run forest-reserve campgrounds are likely to have showers and RV hookups available; national forest campgrounds tend to be less developed.

Private camping These are on private property and are usually close to or in a town. Most are designed with RVs in mind; few accept tents.

Rainforest camping At time of research there was an indefinite moratorium on camping within El Yunque National Forest.

Guesthouses

Places calling themselves 'guesthouses' can differ vastly from one to another. While some guesthouses may have as few as two rooms, others may have dozens. One guesthouse may look like a roadside motel, another may be a beach house with a pool, a bar and a restaurant.

The cheapest have rooms for around $75 and may share a bathroom. Pricier places have rooms with private bathrooms, balconies, sun decks and public dining rooms with extensive menus and table

BOOK YOUR STAY ONLINE

For more accommodations reviews by Lonely Planet authors, check out hotels.lonelyplanet.com/puerto-rico. You'll find independent reviews, as well as recommendations on the best places to stay. Best of all, you can book online.

PRACTICALITIES

» **Newspapers & Magazines** *Puerto Rico Breeze* is a biweekly newspaper on gay nightlife in San Juan. *Que Pasa!* is a bimonthly magazine put out by the Puerto Rico Tourism Company (PRTC).

» **TV** American TV is broadcast across the island. Radio is mostly in Spanish; English-language radio station is WOSO San Juan, at 1030AM.

» **Video Systems** Puerto Rico uses VHS videos and DVDs formatted in region code 1, meaning DVDs purchased here will not play in European or Asian DVD players.

» **Weights & Measures** Puerto Rico follows the American imperial system with two exceptions: all distances on road signs are in kilometers and gas is pumped in liters.

service (at extra cost). They may be in a modern structure, quaint country home or urban beach house. Rooms at most guesthouses fall in the $75 to $180 price range, but some cost more than $200.

Hotels

Puerto Rico has many top-end resort hotels and a growing number of boutique options. Major chains represented include Marriott, Hilton and Sheraton. Ecohotels are another growing area, particularly around El Yunque and on Vieques. Ocean Park has some deluxe beachside B&Bs and in recent years Rincón and Boquerón have gone more upmarket.

Few accommodations on the island have rooms under $75, and almost all of these are found in small towns or unsavory neighborhoods of the cities. Rooms are usually small, beds may be saggy and walls may be scuffed, but a minimal level of cleanliness is generally maintained.

Resorts are ubiquitous in Condado and Isla Verde.

Because of changing marketing strategies and seasons, the prices in this guide can be only an approximate guideline at best, though you'll be lucky to find a quality hotel for under $150.

Be prepared to add the 9% room tax, and probably a 10% service charge as well, to quoted rates. Children are often allowed to stay free with their parents, but rules for this vary. If traveling with a family, call and inquire.

Remember advertised hotel prices are not set in stone. If you simply ask about any specials that might apply, you can often save quite a bit of money. Nowadays booking online can also net you a special deal.

In this guide price indicators are used as follows:

Budget	$	Under $80
Midrange	$$	$80 to $200
Top end	$$$	Over $200

Motels

Unfortunately there's no real network of cheap motels in Puerto Rico á la the United States. Such motels that do exist are strictly of the 'rooms-by-the-hour' variety. Not for the average tourist.

Paradores

The Puerto Rico Tourism Company (PRTC) endorses about 20 paradores (inns) scattered across the island and they are a mixed bag. How you view them depends on your expectations. If you're used to upmarket resorts you might find paradores a bit old-fashioned and pokey.

The benefits of staying in paradores are their location in attractive areas (often in historic coffee haciendas), mostly local clientele and relatively low prices.

The disadvantages may include iffy water pressure, basic furnishings and overdue renovations. Prices for rooms in both the endorsed and nominal paradores are comparable to the cost of rooms in guesthouses, ie between $75 and $150.

For reservations, a complete list and pictures of the government-endorsed paradores, contact **Paradores Puertorriqueños** (☎800-866-7827; www.gotopuertorico.com). You can also check with **Puerto Rico Small Inns** (☎787-725-2901; www.puertoricosmallhotels.com).

Vacation Centers

The Commonwealth of Puerto Rico maintains clusters of rental cottages around the island in Arroyo, Boquerón, Añasco, Humacao and Maricao. These *centros vacacionales* are popular with island families on weekends, holidays and summer vacations. Most of the accommodations are two-bedroom condos in attractive new duplex structures. These units are

ALL-INCLUSIVE MEGA RESORTS

» El Conquistador Resort & Golden Door Spa (near Fajardo)

» Río Mar Beach Resort & Spa (near Luquillo)

» Palmas del Mar Resort (near Humacao)

restricted to 'bona fide family groups' only, so groups of friends traveling together may not be accepted.

There is a minimum stay of two nights and a maximum stay of seven. Short-term rates run about $85 a night for a unit that sleeps six, but you may get a special weekly rate from September 1 to May 31 (when island kids are in school).

Bring your own sheets, though some rent them at $15 to $20 per set. Kitchen gear is not included in the price.

Reserve up to 120 days in advance through the Oficina de Reservaciones at the Compañía de Parques Nacionales (p278).

Bargaining

Bargaining is not appreciated or widely practiced in Puerto Rico. There's nothing wrong with asking if there's a discount available at a guesthouse or hotel – especially when there are empty rooms – but full-on haggling over prices in stores is likely to get you nothing but contempt from the shopkeeper.

Business Hours

Reviews in this book won't list business hours unless they differ from these standards. Businesses are usually open 8am to 5pm, but there are certainly no set rules.

Banks	8am-4pm Mon-Fri, 9:45-noon Sat
Bars	2pm-2am Wed-Sat, more days in cities
Government offices	8:30am-4:30pm Mon-Fri
Post offices	8am-4pm Mon-Fri, 8am-1pm Sat
Shops	9am-6pm Mon-Sat, 11am-5pm Sun

Climate

Mayagüez

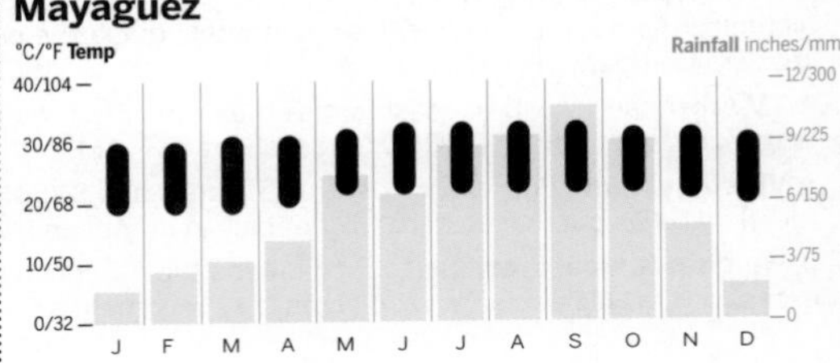

Ponce

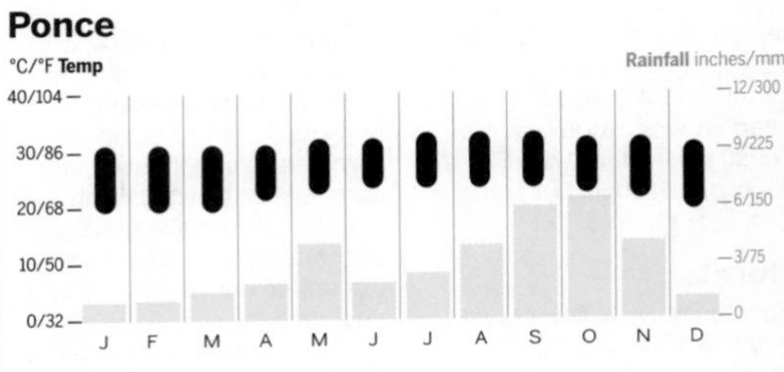

San Juan

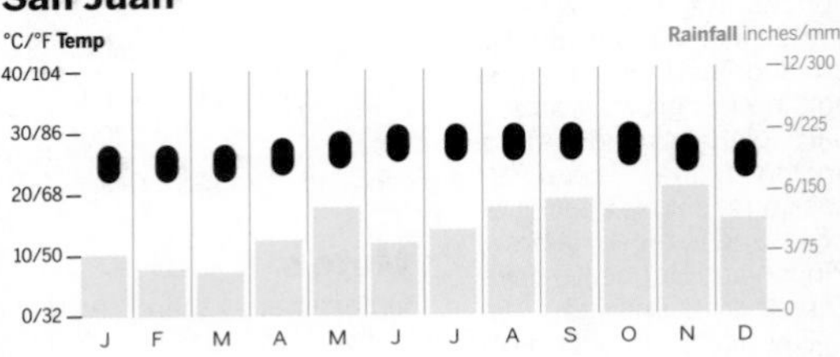

Customs Regulations

Goods brought into the US in greater quantity than the duty free customs allowances are subject to taxes and tariffs and must be declared at customs.

Cigarettes Each person over 18 can bring 200 cigarettes duty free into Puerto Rico or the US.

Currency US law permits you to bring in or take out as much as $10,000 in US or foreign currency, traveler's checks or letters of credit without formality.

Gifts US citizens are allowed to import, duty free, $400 worth of gifts from abroad, while non-US citizens are allowed to bring in $100 worth.

Liquor Each person over the age of 21 can bring 1L of liquor, duty free, into Puerto Rico or the US.

Plants Declare any plants, fruits or vegetables at the airport. The US department of agriculture restricts many island plants.

Electricity

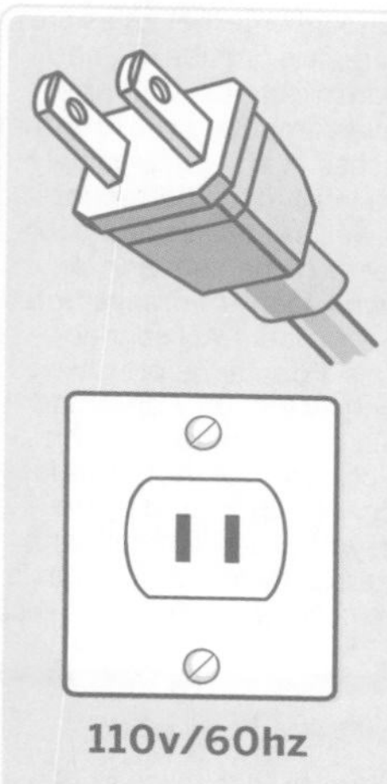

Gambling

Gambling is completely legal in Puerto Rico and takes a variety of forms. Though most of it is confined to the large resort casinos of San Juan, other hotels with smaller casinos exist elsewhere on the island. All casinos will offer a variety of slot machines, and some table games. There is a horse track and cockfighting arena in San Juan. Other places to watch cockfights *(galleras)* elsewhere on the island are largely seedy affairs. You'll likely see vendors selling lottery tickets around the island and a mechanical horse-racing game, with rules similar to roulette, at small town fiestas and along the side of the road.

Gay & Lesbian Travelers

Puerto Rico is probably the most gay-friendly island in the Caribbean. San Juan has a well-developed gay scene, especially in the Condado district, for Puerto Ricans and visitors. Other cities, such as Mayagüez and Ponce, have gay clubs and gay-friendly accommodations as well. Vieques and Culebra have become popular destinations for an international mix of gay and lesbian expatriates and travelers. In the cities and in major resort areas, it is easier for gay men and women to live their lives with a certain amount of openness. As you travel into the middle of the island, it is more difficult to be out, as people are not used to seeing same-sex couples holding hands or displaying affection publicly.

Health

Availability & Cost of Health Care

Many doctors and hospitals expect payment in cash. For emergencies call ☎911. A number of hospitals have emergency rooms, including the following:

Ashford Presbyterian Memorial Community Hospital (☎787-721-2160; 1451 Av Ashford, Condado, San Juan)

General Hospital Dr Ramón Emeterio Betances (☎787-735-8001; Rte 2 Km 157, Mayagüez)

Hospital Manuel Comunitario Dr Pila (☎787-848-5600; Av Las Américas east of Av Hostos, Ponce)

University of Puerto Rico School of Medicine (☎787-758-7910; UPR School of Medicine, A-878 Main Bldg, Medical Sciences Campus, San Juan)

Dengue Fever

Dengue fever is a viral infection found throughout the Caribbean. In Puerto Rico the incidence usually peaks between September and November. Major outbreaks occurred in 1998 and 2010. Dengue is transmitted by Aedes mosquitoes, which often bite during the daytime and are usually found close to human habitations. They breed primarily in artificial water containers such as jars, barrels, plastic containers and discarded tires. Dengue is common in urban environments.

Dengue causes flulike symptoms, including fever, muscle aches, headaches, nausea and vomiting, often followed by a rash. The aches may be quite uncomfortable, but most cases resolve in a few days. Severe cases usually occur in children under age 15 who are experiencing their second dengue infection.

There is no treatment for dengue fever except taking acetaminophen/paracetamol (Tylenol) and drinking fluids. Severe cases may require hospitalization. There is no vaccine. The cornerstone of prevention is protection against insects.

Environmental Hazards

» **Animals** Do not attempt to pet or feed any animal, except domestic animals known to be free of infectious diseases. Spiny sea urchins and coelenterates (coral and jellyfish) are a hazard in some areas.

» **Mosquito Bites** Except for infrequent outbreaks of Dengue fever, mosquito-borne illnesses are usually not a concern in Puerto Rico. A bug spray containing DEET is best to ward off insects, but use sparingly as it kills natural organisms in island bays and inlets.

» **Sun** Stay out of mid-day sun, wear sunglasses and a wide-brimmed hat. Apply sunscreen with SPF 15 or higher, with both UVA and UVB protection, approximately 30 minutes before exposure. Reapply after swimming or vigorous activity.

» **Water** Tap water in Puerto Rico is safe to drink. Those with sensitive stomachs will find purified water abundant, though please consider the environment while buying bottled water.

Pests

» **Cockroaches** These durable pests thrive in the tropical environment, and are not uncommon. Though harmless, they can ruin a meal... especially when they fly.

» **Hookworm** Can be contacted by simply walking barefoot through infected sand or dirt. Public health initiatives have reduced the prevalence of the disease, but the possibility of catching it still exists. Frequent bathing and the use of footwear is the best prevention.

» **Sandflies** Called 'no-see-ums' by islanders. These invisible bugs come out mostly in the early evening. Culebra and Vieques can be particularly thick with them.

Insurance

Regardless of whether you have health or home owners insurance at home, you should buy travel insurance to cover medical expenses, luggage theft or loss and cancellations or delays in your travel arrangements. You should be covered for extreme cases, such as an accident that requires hospital treatment and a flight home. Coverage depends on your insurance and type of ticket, so ask both your insurer and your ticket-issuing agency to explain the finer points. Worldwide travel insurance is available at www.lonelyplanet.com/travel_services. You can buy, extend and claim online anytime – even if you're already on the road.

STA Travel (☎800-777-0112; www.statravel.com) Offers travel insurance options at reasonable prices.

World Nomads (☎www.worldnomads.com) The gold standard of travel-insurance providers, with extremely reasonable rates.

Internet Access

Although internet cafes are quite rare outside of San Juan, most public libraries have computers with internet access. Wi-fi is increasingly available in the better hotels, as well as in cafes and public plazas in medium and large towns. Many midrange hotel rooms offer LAN connections. Popular resort towns such as Rincón, Ponce and Fajardo are extremely connected. In this guide wireless access is indicated by the symbol, while hotels with internet terminals for guests are noted with @.

Legal Matters

» Puerto Rico follows US laws in all criminal and most legislative matters. If you are arrested, you have the same rights as you would on US soil.

» If you are stopped by the police, remember there is no system of paying fines on the spot. Attempting to pay the officer is frowned upon and may result in a charge of bribery.

» Although English is widely spoken, many police do not speak English.

» If you are arrested for more serious offenses, you are allowed to remain silent. All persons who are arrested are legally allowed (and

GAY & LESBIAN RESOURCES

» **Atlantic Beach Hotel** (☎787-721-6900) In Condado, the friendly staff have information on current events in the lesbian and gay community.

» **Gay Yellow Pages** (☎212-674-0120; PO Box 533, Village Station, NY 10014-0533) Has national edition and regional editions.

» **GayCities** (www.puertorico.gaycities.com) Read reviews of hotels, restaurants and clubs written by and for gay travelers.

» **Orgullo Boricua** (www.orgulloboricua.net) Newly launched site with interactive map of gay-friendly attractions and complete listings of pride events and happenings.

» **Puerto Rico Breeze** (☎787-724-3411) Bilingual tabloid of events and listings for accommodations, restaurants, clubs etc, for gay men and lesbians.

INTERNATIONAL VISITORS

Entering the Region

International travelers will most likely fly through New York City or another major city on the east coast of the United States, which has numerous connections to Puerto Rico's airports. If you are arriving by private boat, the same customs and immigrations rules apply, though are much more loosely enforced than at airports. Boats arriving from outside of Puerto Rico's territorial waters should contact customs 24 hours before landing in the territorial waters; see p287.

Embassies & Consulates

Most nations' principal diplomatic representation is in Washington DC. To find out the telephone number of your embassy or consulate in DC, call ☎202-555-1212. Some nations with 'interests' in Puerto Rico maintain consulates and honorary consulates on the island. The foreign consulates in Puerto Rico are in San Juan or the surrounding suburbs.

Austria (☎787-766-0799; Plaza Las Américas, Río Piedras)
Belize (☎787-280-6600; 567 Calle Ramon Gandia, Hato Rey)
Canada (☎787-789-6629; 107 Calle Cereipo Alturas, Guaynabo)
Costa Rica (☎787-723-6227; 1413 Avenida Fernández Juncos, San Juan)
Denmark (☎787-725-2532; 360 Calle San Francisco, San Juan)
Dominican Republic (☎787-725-9550; 1612 Ponce de Leon, 7th fl, Hato Rey)
Finland (☎787-720-0098; D Calle No G 6, Torremolinos, Guaynabo)
France (☎787-725-2527; 206 Calle Del Rosario, Santurce)
Italy (☎787-767-5855; Calle Interamericana 266 Urb, University Gardens)
Netherlands (☎787-759-9400; Mercantil Plaza, Hato Rey)
Spain (☎787-758-6090; Mercantil Plaza, Hato Rey)
Sweden (☎787-778-2377; Menaco Bldg, Hwy 550 No 5, Luchetti Industrial Park Marginal Oeste Park, Bayamon)
Switzerland (☎787-751-3182; 816 Calle Diana, Dos Pinos)
UK (☎787-727-1065; 1509 Calle Lopez Landron, Santurce)
Uruguay (☎787-765-2727; 159 Avenida Chardon, Piso Compañía de Comercio, San Juan)

Money

Major bank offices in San Juan and Ponce will exchange currency from around the world. Foreign travelers are advised to handle all exchange transactions in these cities, as exchange can be difficult elsewhere on the island. There are also exchange desks at the Luis Muñoz Marín International Airport and major resorts.

Post

Sending mail from Puerto Rico is best done through Airmail. Aerogrammes, preprinted sheets that fold into envelopes, are for sale at most post offices. Sending by surface, while inexpensive, can take up to two months to cross the Atlantic and up to three to cross the Pacific.

Telephone

Although the online services from Skype (www.skype.com) are the cheapest and best option for travelers making international calls, prepaid phone cards are also widely available. To call home from Puerto Rico:

» First dial 011, the international dialing prefix.

» Dial the country code of the country you want to call. For Australia, dial 61; the UK, 44; Ireland, 353; New Zealand, 64.

» Dial city or area code and the local number.

given) the right to make one phone call. If you don't have a lawyer or family member to help you, call your embassy. The police will give you the number upon request.

Drinking Laws

Alcohol is deeply ingrained in the island's social scene – more so than parts of the US and Europe. Puerto Rico has few 'blue laws' prohibiting the times and places where alcohol can be consumed.

» The drinking age is 18 on the island – three years younger than in the US!

» Legally you need identification with your photograph on it to prove your age.

» Minors are not permitted in bars and pubs, even to order nonalcoholic beverages.

» Old San Juan has stern laws to stop the drinking in the streets, and violators are subject to heavy fines.

» Driving while under the influence of alcohol will result in stiff fines, jail time and penalties. The legal blood alcohol limit for drivers is 0.08%.

» During fiestas, holidays and special events, roadblocks are sometimes set up to deter drunk drivers.

» Drinking on the beach is legal.

Maps

Travelers who are doing a lot of driving on Puerto Rico's network of central roads, or are interested in cycling or hiking extensively on the island, will require maps that are in greater detail than those provided in this book. While roadmaps are fairly common, including a basic hand-out from many tourist desks, it is essential to order topographical maps before you go to the island, as they are a rarity.

Metro Data (www.metropr.com) Local Puerto Rican map makers that publishes a variety of road and tourist maps. Often the most up-to-date product. Metro Data's *Guía Urbana for San Juan and Ponce* ($15) is by far the most detailed, and is stocked in most San Juan bookstores.

Rand McNally Publishes a foldout road map including detailed city maps of Aguadilla, Arecibo, Caguas, Mayagüez, Ponce and San Juan, as well as the islands of Culebra and Vieques. The map is available at bookstores and newsstands for about $8.

US Geological Survey (USGS; www.usgs.gov) An agency of the US Department of the Interior publishes very detailed topographic maps of Puerto Rico, at various scales up to 1:250,000. Maps at 1:62,500, or approximately 1in = 1 mile, are ideal for backcountry hiking and backpacking. Some bookstores and outdoor-equipment specialists on the island carry a selection of topographic maps.

Media

Puerto Rico's largest newspaper in terms of circulation is *El Nuevo Día,* a Spanish-language periodical founded in Ponce in 1909. It currently circulates in the vicinity of 155,000 copies daily. Its largest competitor is *El Vocero,* a tabloid with more sensationalist news, although its tone has become more serious in recent years. The island's English-language newspaper was the *San Juan Star,* but following the trend of so many other print newspapers, went under in 2008. The loss is great; founded in 1959 the *Star* won a Pulitzer Prize a year after its inception and was famously fictionalized as the *Daily News* in Hunter S Thompson's seminal Puerto Rican novel *The Rum Diary* (p82).

Pets

» Traveling with pets is becoming more common, and some hotels allow small dogs.

» Those who want to travel from the US with their pet will usually have to have the pet flown as cargo.

» As with other customs checkpoints into the US, dogs must be free of evidence of diseases communicable to humans if they are examined at the port of entry.

» Bring a valid rabies vaccination certificate (including a veterinarian's signature).

» Be mindful of your pet, as there are many loose dogs in more rural areas of the island.

» Kenneling the animal is almost impossible, so be sure to make arrangements if you plan to go on long expeditions.

Post

US post office (☎800-275-8777; www.usps.gov) Has branches in almost every Puerto Rican town, providing parcel shipping, postage sales and international express mail.

United Parcel Service (UPS; ☎800-742-5877) and **Federal Express** (FedEx; ☎800-463-3339) operate on the island and are best for parcels and time-sensitive material.

» Use blue mailboxes, available on street corners, for letters and post cards with exact postage.

» Packages that weigh 16oz or over must be sent from a post office.

» Larger towns have branch post offices and post-office centers in some supermarkets and drugstores.

You can have mail sent to you, addressed as 'c/o General Delivery,' at any post office that has its own zip (postal) code. Mail is usually held for 10 days before it's returned to the sender.

» American Express and Thomas Cook also provide mail service for their customers.

Public Holidays

US public holidays are celebrated along with local holidays in Puerto Rico. Banks, schools and government offices (including post offices) are closed, and transportation, museums and other services are on a Sunday schedule. Holidays falling on a weekend are usually observed the following Monday. Nearly all museums in Puerto Rico close on Mondays. Some also remain closed on Tuesdays.

New Year's Day January 1

Three Kings Day (Feast of the Epiphany) January 6

Eugenio María de Hostos' Birthday January 10 – honors the island educator, writer and patriot

Martin Luther King Jr Day Third Monday in January

Presidents' Day Third Monday in February

Emancipation Day March 22 – island slaves were freed on this date in 1873

Palm Sunday Sunday before Easter

Good Friday Friday before Easter

Easter A Sunday in late March/April

José de Diego Day April 18

Memorial Day Last Monday in May

Independence Day/Fourth of July July 4

Luis Muñoz Rivera's Birthday July 18 – honors the island patriot and political leader

Constitution Day July 25

José Celso Barbosa's Birthday July 27

Labor Day First Monday in September

Columbus Day Second Monday in October

Veterans' Day November 11

Thanksgiving Fourth Thursday in November

Christmas Day December 25

Safe Travel

Dangers While Hiking & Camping

» Don't ever head into the forest without leaving someone your planned itinerary.

» Minor cuts and scrapes can get infected easily in this climate; try to hike with disinfectant.

» Getting lost is easy; invest in a good topographical map for serious hikes.

Hazards in the Water

The currents of Puerto Rico's beaches can be deadly, with the biggest hazards being riptides and dangerous ocean currents. Obey all posted signs on beaches. If you get caught in a riptide that carries you away from shore, never panic or swim against it, you'll only get worn out. Instead, swim parallel to the shoreline and when the current lessens make your way back to shore.

Hazards on the Road

Puerto Rican drivers are more aggressive than drivers on the mainland US, and rules of the road are taken as more of a suggestion. Remember to keep your cool and proceed with caution. If you're driving and see a police car with its blue lights on, don't worry, police in Puerto Rico are required to have their lights lit whenever driving. Police will sound a siren during emergencies. Mountain roads can be very narrow, have sudden drop offs, and rough surfaces. Beep before driving into blind curves. If you come to a point in the road too narrow for both cars to pass, the car on the uphill side should reverse and let the other driver pass.

Weather & Natural Disasters

Although somewhat predictable, Puerto Rico can get pounded with tropical storms and hurricanes, which can result in a number of serious disruptions for visitors, including washed-out roads and trails and shuttered attractions. Hurricane season is usually between the beginning of June and the end of November.

CAMPING TIPS

» Bring anything you might need from home; outdoor outfitters are extremely rare on the island.

» Use caution camping alone at a site without a guard. Most CPN sites have guards.

» Camping reservations through state agencies require a valid credit card.

» Summer is high camping season; during other seasons public camping areas are often closed (although sometimes you can just set up camp for free and no one will bother you).

» Getting in touch with the DRNA or CPN isn't always easy; your best bet is to call early and often – someone will eventually pick up the phone.

If you're visiting during this time there's likely nothing to worry about – this also overlaps with peak travel dates for Puerto Rican families on summer vacation – but you'll want to keep an eye on the weather.

Wildlife

Remember all wild animals can be dangerous. Never attempt to feed an animal encountered in the wild. Wild horses roam parts of Vieques, and although they look gentle they can kick, bite and trample. Even small animals are capable of inflicting serious injury or even fatal wounds on unsuspecting tourists. Some also carry rabies. Keep your distance from all wild animals, and that goes double for any mongooses you see in El Yunque. The monkeys and iguanas on some of the cays off the south coast can be downright fierce.

Shopping

Puerto Rico is not a duty-free port. In the last 10 years it has enacted a 5.5% sales tax on all goods.

Coffee Both Adjuntas and Rioja are popular premium coffees with fancy labels and packaging, but islanders say that Puerto Rican coffee is of such high quality that you cannot go wrong buying the local supermarket brands.

Mundillo The intricately woven island-made lace is also a popular souvenir, as are woven hammocks like the ones Columbus admired when he first stopped at Borinquen.

Musical instruments Maracas, fish-shaped *güiros* and four-string guitars named *cuatro* are a few endemic instruments on the island. These can range from cheapie toys to exceptional hand-crafted pieces.

Rum Puerto Rico is the leading producer of rum in the world and a dizzying variety of rum is available in Puerto Rico. It's significantly cheaper here than in the US. Most bottles cost between $6 and $15, depending on size and quality. And there is no limit to how much you can take out of Puerto Rico when you leave, but bear in mind the limits imposed by the country you are next entering.

Santos Probably the most popular purchase, these carved religious figures can cost well over $100.

Surfboards The west coast of Puerto Rico is home to some of the best custom board makers in the world.

Vejigantes Masks typical of those worn in the fiestas at Ponce and Loíza. Island-made macramé and ceramic items are also widely available in the shops catering to tourists.

Telephone

Cell Phones

The good news for American travelers is that all major US cell phone carriers provide service in Puerto Rico, and travelers do not have to suffer high international calling rates. The island is small and the upside of the towers that mar the tops of the central mountains is that coverage is generally very good, especially on the coast. For US travelers, making calls with a cell phone is exactly like being at home. Foreign travelers who are going to be in Puerto Rico for an extended period should look into getting a prepaid cellular phone, widely available from kiosks in shopping malls and ubiquitous cell-phone stores.

From Hotels

Hotels hike up the price of local calls by almost 200%, and long-distance rates are raised between 100% and 200%. Many hotels (especially the more expensive ones) add a service charge of between 50¢ and $1 for each local call made from a room phone, and also add hefty surcharges for long-distance calls. Public pay phones, which can be found in most lobbies, are always cheaper.

Phone Codes

All phone numbers within Puerto Rico consist of a three-digit area code (787) followed by a seven-digit local number. If you are calling locally, just dial the seven-digit number.

» To call the island from the US, dial ☎1 + 787 + the seven-digit number. Call the island from any other overseas destination the same way, after dialing the appropriate code for an international line in your country.

» For directory assistance on the island, dial ☎411.

» For US directory assistance outside Puerto Rico, dial ☎1 + the three-digit area code of the place you want to call + 555-1212. For example, to obtain directory assistance for a toll-free number, dial ☎1-800-555-1212 or 1-888-555-1212.

» If you need Puerto Rican directory assistance while you're outside the country, dial ☎1-787-555-1212.

» The 800, 866 and 888 area codes are designated for toll-free numbers within Puerto Rico, the US and sometimes Canada as well. These calls are free.

Phonecards

Phonecards are available and sold at kiosks, in bodegas and around town.

Time

Puerto Rico is on Atlantic Standard Time. Clocks in this time zone read an hour later than the Eastern Standard Time zone, which encompasses such US cities as New York, Boston, Washington DC and Miami. During Daylight

Saving Time in those cities – from 1am on the first Sunday in April until 2am on the last Sunday of October – the time is the same in Puerto Rico. There is no Daylight Saving Time observed on the island.

When making appointments, most Puerto Ricans generally follow the American style of using a 12-hour clock and adding am or pm to connote morning or afternoon. Occasionally you'll hear the 24-hour clock used, mostly when people are speaking Spanish.

Tourist Information

Puerto Rico Tourism Company (PRTC; www.gotopuertorico.com) is the commonwealth's official tourist bureau and a very good source for thorough brochures on island accommodations, sports, shopping, dining and festivals. The PRTC also sponsors a variety of folk and fine-arts shows around the island. From abroad, you can call any of the PRTC offices worldwide and request a tourist information packet. On the island, call the offices or stop by for up-to-date information and calendars of current events.

Major PRTC offices are located in Aguadilla, Boquerón, Ponce, San Juan and Vieques.

Tours

While nothing can compete with the adventure of planning and executing a wilderness trip on your own, these tour operators can take a lot of the worry out of the adventure and give you a chance to interact with fellow adventure travelers:

Acampa (☎787-706-0695; www.campapr.com; 1211 Av Jesús T Piñero, San Juan) For Isla Mona, Reserva Forestal Toro Negro, El Yunque, Río Camuy or any other adventure spot on the island, Acampa has all the latest gadgets.

Aquatica Dive & Bike Adventures (☎787-890-6071; www.aquatica.cjb.net) Bicycle tours in Aguadilla, Cabo Rojo and Quebradillas, with the option of taking a swim en route.

Aventuras Puerto Rico (☎787-380-8481; www.aventuraspuertorico.com) Kayaking, custom tours, horseback rides and snorkeling around Ponce, Arecibo, Camuy and Isabela.

Aventuras Tierra Adentro (☎787-766-0470; www.aventuraspr.com; 268-A Av Jesús T Piñero, San Juan) Camping, caving, rock climbing and river touring, with a specialty in canyon adventures.

Copladet Nature & Adventure Tours (☎787-765-8595; www.copladet.com) Birding, caving, hiking, horseback riding, kayaking; trips to Isla Caja de Muertos.

Eco Xcursion Aquatica (☎787- 888-2887; ecoxcursion@libertypr.net) Nature-conscious educational tours and outdoor activities including kayaking, cycling, hiking around Fajardo, Luquillo, Ceiba and more.

Encanto Ecotours (☎787-272-0005; www.ecotourspr.com) Mangroves, manatees, turtle nesting; trips to Culebra, Vieques and Isla Mona – this tour group does just about everything on every part of the island.

Travelers with Disabilities

Travel to and around Puerto Rico is becoming easier for people with disabilities. Public buildings (including hotels, restaurants, theaters and museums) are now required by law to be wheelchair-accessible and to have appropriate rest-room facilities. Public transportation services (buses, trains and taxis) must be made accessible to all, including those in wheelchairs, and telephone companies are required to provide relay operators for the hearing impaired.

Many banks now provide ATM instructions in Braille. Curb ramps are common, and some of the busier roadway intersections have audible crossing signals. Playa Luquillo has a beach especially for the mobility-impaired, and ferries to the Spanish Virgin Islands are disabled-accessible.

Larger private and chain hotels have suites for disabled guests. Major car-rental agencies offer hand-controlled models at no extra charge. All major airlines and intercity buses allow guide dogs to accompany passengers.

Information for Travelers With Disabilities

Access-Able Travelers Source (www.access-able.com) Detailed access information.

Mobility International USA (☎541-343-1284; www.miusa.org) Advises disabled travelers on mobility issues. It primarily runs an educational exchange program.

Wheelchair Getaways Rent-A-Car (☎787-726-4023, 800-868-8028) Provides livery service as well as tours of Puerto Rico.

Visas

» You only need a visa to enter Puerto Rico if you need a visa to enter the US, since the commonwealth follows the United States' immigration laws.

» As a commonwealth, Puerto Rico subscribes to all the laws that apply to traveling and border crossing in the United States.

» US citizens can enter the commonwealth with proper proof of citizenship, such as a driver's license with photo ID, a passport or a birth certificate.

» Visitors from other countries must have a valid, scannable passport.

» Countries participating in the Visa Waiver Program – the EU, Australia, New Zealand and much of Latin America – don't need visas to get into Puerto Rico.

» **US State Department** (www.state.gov) has current information about visas, immigration etc.

Volunteering

As a relatively rich country in close geographic and economic proximity to the United States, Puerto Rico offers limited opportunities for volunteering.

Rainforest management The **Earthwatch Institute** (☎1-978-461-0081; www.eyeontherainforest.org) partners with Las Casas de la Selva to run one- to two-week research missions to the Bosque Estatal de Carite, where participants learn forest management skills and aid in the rejuvenation of the tropical rainforest. Volunteers stay in tents in the Casas de la Selva complex inside the park and spend their time planting seedlings, studying trees and monitoring local frog populations. Some of the trips are family friendly.

Turtle watching There are ecological projects on the island of Culebra where the US Fish and Wildlife Refuge runs a volunteer turtle watch on Playa Brava during nesting season. You can access this project through CORALations (☎787-556-6234; www.coralations.com), a nonprofit organization that is involved in coral reef protection in and around the island.

Wildlife protection The **Vieques Conservation and Historical Trust** (www.vcht.com; Calle Flamboyán 138, Esperanza, Vieques) accepts volunteers for a wide variety of projects, including assisting with animals and reefs, maintaining a tank of rescued marine animals, and feeding animals.

Volunteering Resources

Habitat For Humanity (www.volunteermatch.org) Utilizes volunteers for construction and building projects for families and institutions in need.

Idealist.org (www.idealist.org) Lists volunteer positions of a wide variety.

Volunteer Match (www.volunteermatch.org) Helps match prospective volunteers with the organizations that can use them.

Women Travelers

Puerto Rico's status as a US commonwealth means that women have a position in society not dissimilar to the United States. The island has elected many influential women to high political office, including the late San Juan mayor Felisa Rincón de Gautier and ex-Puerto Rico governor Sila María Calderón.

Puerto Rican women crisscross the island all the time by themselves, so you won't be the only solo woman on the ferry or public bus, but as a foreigner you will attract a bit more attention. Most of it will be simple curiosity, but a few may assume you'd much rather be with a man if you could. If you don't want the company, most men will respect a firm but polite 'no thank you.'

Tips for Women Travelers

» Bookstores, found in the Yellow Pages under *Librerías*, are good places to find out about gatherings, readings and meetings.

» The student centers on university campuses often have bulletin boards where you can find or place travel and short-term housing notices.

» One international organization with an affiliate office in Puerto Rico is **Profamilia** (Planned Parenthood; ☎787-765-7373; 117 Padre Las Casas, El Vedado, San Juan). The staff here can refer you to clinics and offer advice on medical issues.

» Information on health and safety issues for women is also available from the government office **Comisión Para Los Asuntos de Mujer** (Commission for Women's Affairs; ☎787-722-2977; 151 Calle San Francisco, Old San Juan).

Transportation

GETTING THERE & AWAY

Getting to Puerto Rico is easy, especially if you're flying in from the US. A spread of carriers make frequent connections between San Juan and New York City and major airline hubs of the US, including Philadelphia, Boston and Miami. Flights, tours and rail tickets can be booked online at www.lonelyplanet.com/bookings.

Entering Puerto Rico

Even if you are continuing immediately to another city, the first airport that you land in is where you must carry out immigration and customs formalities. The customs process can be quick and painless or it can involve a more prolonged exchange between you and officials.

A certain number of passengers are set aside to be searched randomly on just about every flight. You may be tapped, and it may be for no reason other than that your number came up.

Customs officials are mostly focused on excluding those who are likely to work illegally or overstay their welcome in Puerto Rico, so visitors will be asked about their plans and perhaps about whether they have sufficient funds for their stay.

It's a good idea to be able to list an itinerary that will account for the period for which you ask to be admitted, and to be able to show you have $300 to $400 for every week of your intended stay. These days, a couple of major credit cards will go a long way toward establishing 'sufficient funds.'

Remember that the list of items that can't be brought on to airplanes now includes many implements used by divers, campers and hikers. Check the **US State Department** (www.state.gov) for an updated list, and make sure you check those bags.

Passports

Americans visiting Puerto Rico do not need a passport. Non US-citizens traveling to the Commonwealth are required to have a valid passport and an appropriate US visa, if required.

Air

Airports & Airlines

Puerto Rico is the most accessible island in the Caribbean, with three major airports and several small ones. San Juan is served by a number of North American carriers and British Airways has twice-weekly services from London; Iberia flies from Madrid.

Luis Muñoz Marín International Airport (www.san-juan-airport.com) San Juan's recently modernized airport – commonly shortened to LMM – lies just 2 miles beyond the eastern border of the city in the beachfront suburb of Isla Verde.

Aeropuerto Rafael Hernández Aguadilla's airport is at the former Ramey Base on the island's northwest tip. It has some international flights from the US, mainly New York.

Aeropuerto Mercedita Ponce's airport has stepped up its number of flights recently, with direct red-eye service to Chicago and New York.

Aeropuerto Eugenio María de Hostos In Mayagüez, this airport mostly makes regional connections.

San Juan's original airport at Isla Grande, on the Bahía de San Juan in the Miramar district, services private aircraft and the bulk of commuter flights to the Puerto Rican islands of Culebra and Vieques; see p291.

Tickets

Airfares to Caribbean destinations such as Puerto Rico vary tremendously depending on the season you travel, the day of the week you fly, the length of your stay and the flexibility the ticket allows for flight changes and refunds. Still, nothing determines fares more than demand, and when things are slow, regardless of the season, airlines will lower their fares to fill empty seats.

During the holidays, travelers to Puerto Rico will probably find it difficult to get the flights and fares they want unless they plan – and purchase tickets – well in advance. Holiday times include Christmas, New Year's Eve, Easter, Memorial Day, Labor Day and Thanksgiving.

Asia

Most Asian countries offer fairly competitive airfare deals, with Bangkok, Singapore and Hong Kong being the best places to shop around for discount tickets. Hong Kong's travel market can be unpredictable, but some excellent bargains are available if you are lucky.

Australia & New Zealand

Qantas flies to Los Angeles from Sydney, Melbourne (via Sydney or Auckland) and Cairns. United flies to San Francisco from Sydney and Auckland (via Sydney), and also flies to Los Angeles. Connecting flights to San Juan are available. New Zealanders might want to look at www.roundtheworldflights.com, which has lists of carriers from all over the place who fly to Puerto Rico via Wellington.

Caribbean & Latin America

Many flights to San Juan from Central and South America are routed through Miami, Houston or New York. A few countries' international flag carriers fly directly to San Juan from Latin American cities.

Puerto Rico is linked to Antigua, Barbados, Haiti and Jamaica through the following airlines:

Air Sunshine (www.airsunshine.com)

American Airlines (www.aa.com)

Cape Air (www.flycapeair.com)

Caribbean Air Lines (www.caribbean-airlines.com)

UK & Continental Europe

Though London is the travel-discount capital of Europe, there are several other cities where you will find a range of good deals. Generally, there is not much variation in airfare prices from European cities.

USA & Canada

The most popular routes to Puerto Rico from the US are via New York and Miami, but direct flights from about a dozen other cities in the continental US also serve the island. Some carriers now offer continued service through San Juan to Ponce and Aguadilla, or they fly directly into Aguadilla's airport. Almost all major carriers fly to Puerto Rico; jetBlue is currently the most popular and economical option. Canadian discount air-ticket sellers are also known as consolidators, and their airfares tend to be about 10% higher than those sold in the USA.

Sea

Cruise Ship

San Juan is the second-largest port for cruise ships in the western hemisphere (after Miami). More than 24 vessels call San Juan their home port or departure port. More than one million cruise ship passengers pass through San Juan per year. Their ships dock at the piers along Calle La Marina near the Customs House and the Sheraton Old San Juan Hotel & Casino, just a short walk from Old San Juan.

Per diem prices vary according to the standard of the ship, but you will be lucky to pay less than $1700 for a seven-day cruise out of San Juan. However, this price will probably include your airfare and transfers to the ship, as well as all your meals and entertainment.

Cruise Line International Association (CLIA; ☎212-921-0066; www.cruising.org) provides information on cruising and individual lines.

Azamara Club Cruises (☎800-999-9553; www.azamaraclubcruises.com)

Carnival Cruise Lines (☎800-327-9501; www.carnival.com)

Celebrity Cruise Lines (☎800-437-3111; www.celebritycruises.com)

CLIMATE CHANGE & TRAVEL

Every form of transport that relies on carbon-based fuel generates CO², the main cause of human-induced climate change. Modern travel is dependent on aeroplanes, which might use less fuel per kilometer per person than most cars but travel much greater distances. The altitude at which aircraft emit gases (including CO²) and particles also contributes to their climate change impact. Many websites offer 'carbon calculators' that allow people to estimate the carbon emissions generated by their journey and, for those who wish to do so, to offset the impact of the greenhouse gases emitted with contributions to portfolios of climate-friendly initiatives throughout the world. Lonely Planet offsets the carbon footprint of all staff and author travel.

Holland America Line (☎800-628-4855; www.hollandamerica.com)

Norwegian Cruise Line (☎800-327-7030; www2.ncl.com)

Princess Cruises (☎800-421-0522; www.princess.com)

Radisson Seven Seas (☎800-285-1835; www.rssc.com)

Royal Caribbean Cruise Line (☎800-327-6700; www.royalcaribbean.com)

Ferry

TO/FROM THE DOMINICAN REPUBLIC

The oceangoing ferry between Mayagüez, on Puerto Rico's west coast, and Santo Domingo, in the Dominican Republic, had suspended service at the time of research due to a dispute with the Mayagüez Port Authority. The same company, Ferries del Caribe, was running erratic service between Santo Domingo and San Juan, but no regular schedule was available at the time of research.

TO/FROM THE US VIRGIN ISLANDS

Transportation Services Virgin Islands (☎340-776-6282; www.vinow.com) runs an irregular ferry service between Puerto Rico and the US Virgin Islands, with ferries leaving Fajardo twice a month. The Maritime Transportation Authority (ATM) runs regular ferry services from Fajardo to Culebra (p126) and Vieques (p143).

Yacht

Crewing aboard a yacht destined for the West Indies from North America or Europe is a popular way of getting to Puerto Rico.

Marinas are located at most major resorts and at principal ports around the Puerto Rican coast.

Upon reaching the island you *must* clear immigration and customs unless you are coming directly from a US port or the US Virgin Islands.

There are now numerous online clearinghouses for those seeking yacht-crew positions (both experienced and inexperienced mariners). These usually charge a registration fee between $25 and $40.

Yacht Crew Register (www.yachtcrewregister.com)

Crewfinders (www.crewfinders.com)

Tours

Acampa Nature Adventures (www.acampapr.com) Guided hiking, camping and backpacking trips. The most established operator on the island.

AdvenTours (www.adventourspr.com) Hosts a wide variety of tours, including low-impact, supported cycling and cultural tours.

Amazilia Tours (www.amaziliatours.com) Operates birding tours of the island, mostly in the coastal plains and dry forests of the southwest.

EcoQuest (www.ecoquestpr.com) Rappelling trips, zipline trips and adventure tours.

Gold Heron Eco Tours (www.golden-heron.com) Primarily for snorkeling trips, with a good emphasis on sustainability.

Legends of Puerto Rico (www.pureadventurepr.com) Land and water trips.

GETTING AROUND

Air

Because Puerto Rico is such a small island, its domestic air transportation system is basic. Daily flights connect San Juan, Ponce, Aguadilla and Mayagüez. The bulk of Puerto Rico's domestic air traffic links San Juan to the offshore islands of Culebra and Vieques.

Airlines in Puerto Rico

From its Isla Verde location on the eastern edge of San Juan, LMM airport (p289) handles a fair amount of the island's scheduled domestic air traffic.

Isla Grande airport in San Juan's Miramar district, on the Bahía de San Juan, is the center for private aviation as well as Puerto Rico's air-taxi operations. It's also easy and surprisingly affordable to get to Culebra and Vieques from this convenient downtown airport.

Air Flamenco (www.airflamenco.net) Flies routes to destinations in Puerto Rico, including Vieques, Culebra, Ponce and Mayagüez, and other Caribbean islands, such as St Thomas and St Croix.

Vieques Air Link (www.viequesairlink.com) Fares to Vieques are $63 each way; fares to Culebra are about $65.

Bicycle

Bicycles should be considered a recreational, rather than practical, form of transportation for all but the most ambitious travelers. While cycling hasn't traditionally been a popular means of getting around the island, things are changing. Most resorts have at least one bicycle-rental outlet, and independent bicycle supply shops can be found in a few select places. For serious long-distance cycling, bring your own bike. For further cycling tips see p37.

The hazards of cycling in Puerto Rico include nightmare traffic, dangerous drivers and a general lack of awareness about cyclist's needs. Most natives simply aren't used to seeing touring bikes on the road. Never cycle after dark. For further advice contact the Puerto

Rican Cycling Federation (p38).

Boat

Charter Yacht

All of the island's major resorts have marinas where you can charter yachts or powerboats, either with a crew or a 'bareboat.' Crewed boats come with a skipper and crew, and you don't need any prior sailing experience. With bareboat charters, you rent the boat and be your own skipper.

Charter companies include the following:

Caribbean School of Aquatics (www.saildiveparty.com)

Castillo Watersports (www.castillotours.com)

Erin Go Bragh (www.egbc.net)

Sail Caribe (www.sailcaribe.com)

Ferry

Maritime Transportation Authority (ATM; ☎787-863-0705) has large, high-speed ferries that run from Fajardo to Culebra and Vieques. While timetables can be changeable, the boats are generally quick and reliable. See p126 and p143 for details.

Note: reservations go quickly for boats bound for the islands on Friday evening to Saturday morning, and returning to Fajardo on Sunday afternoon to Monday morning, so plan ahead.

Frequency Multiple ferries leave for Vieques and Culebra daily. Ferries between the two islands were suspended at the time of research. In high season island residents get priority over visitors. Schedules change frequently; no reliable information can be found to confirm these on the internet and the phone is often not answered.

Reservation No advance reservations are possible for the ferry to Culebra or Vieques. Ferries do sell out in summer. Arrive one hour early to buy tickets at the ticket office or queue up for the ticket sellers to show up.

Tickets Buy tickets at the dock, one hour before departure. There are no ticket sales on board. In summer, arrive one to two hours prior to departure.

Cars It is not legal to bring a rental car to the island. Rental cars can be parked at a secure lot by the dock.

Food There is no meal service; you can buy drinks and snacks at the ferry terminal. Most locals bring their own food. Drinking alcoholic beverages is officially prohibited, but often occurs.

Bus

See p294 for information on traveling by bus within San Juan. For intertown travel by público (shared taxi), see p295.

Car

Despite the occasional hazards of operating a car in Puerto Rico, driving is currently the most convenient way to get around the countryside, see small towns, cross sprawling suburbs and explore wide, open spaces. This is particularly relevant to roads such as the Ruta Panorámica where public transport is scant and cycling deemed too dangerous. Renting a car is nearly essential for most visitors.

Rental

In orderto rent a car you must meet the following requirements:

» You must be over 21.

» You must have a major credit card.

» You must have a valid driver's license.

» You should have proof of insurance.

All of the major international car-rental companies operate on the island, along with dozens of smaller, local firms. Car-rental agencies are listed in the local Yellow Pages and in the Puerto Rico Tourism Company's (PRTC) publication, *Qué Pasa*. You will find plenty of rental companies at LMM airport, in major cities and in resort towns ringing the island's coast. Agencies in San Juan include the following:

AAA (☎787-791-1465; www.aaacarrentalpr.com)

Alamo (☎787-753-2265, 800-327-9633; www.alamo.com)

Avis (☎800-874-3556; www.avis.com)

Budget (☎787-791-0600, 800-468-5822; www.budget.com)

Charlie Car Rental (☎787-728-2418; www.charliecars.com)

Dollar Rent-A-Car (☎787-591-5500; www.dollar.com)

Hertz (☎787-791-0840, 800-654-3131; www.hertz.com)

National (☎787-791-1805, 800-568-3019; www.nationalcar.com)

Target (☎787-728-1447, 800-934-6457; www.targetrentacar.com)

Thrifty (☎787-253-2525, 800-367-2277; www.thrifty.com)

Wheelchair Getaways Rent-A-Car (☎787-883-0131, 800-868-8028; www.wheelchairgetaways.com)

Rates average as much as $40 per day in high season. Basic insurance will add $20 per day to the base rate. In low season, rates can be as low as $18 per day.

Driver's License

Any valid driver's license can be used to rent and operate a car or scooter in Puerto Rico. If you stay longer than 90 days, residency laws say you have to get a Puerto Rican license.

CAR RENTAL TIPS & TRICKS

» Booking online in advance can save a lot of money. Try www.kayak.com for a comparative overview of rental rates.

» Some major rental car companies are located several miles from the LMM air terminal. Though most have shuttles, be sure they provide transportation to and from the airport.

» Unlike in the US, many airport-based car-rental agencies are not open 24 hours. If you have a late flight home, you'll have to arrange to drop off your car early, or pay an expensive 'airport drop-off fee.'

» Larger companies will accept debit cards, but expect them to put at least a $500 hold on your funds until the car is safely returned.

» If you rent a car from a major airport, it is possible to drop the car off at another location for a small additional fee.

Fuel & Spare Parts

Esso, Shell, Texaco and other major oil companies maintain gas stations across the island. In rural areas, stations usually close on Sunday. Almost everywhere on the island, gas stations generally stay open until about 7pm. At the time of research gas prices were about 10¢ per gallon lower than in the continental US, which is remarkably inexpensive by international standards. You can use credit cards for fuel purchases in all but rural areas. Don't let your tank go dry, though, because the next station could be a long way up the road.

Garages aren't as readily available, so you should always take a spare tire and a jack with you, and carry some water in case the engine overheats.

Itineraries that Won't Require a Car

» **Staying in San Juan** The hassles of traffic, parking and navigating the maze of thoroughfares make using a car in the city a challenge, to say the least.

» **Visiting only Culebra or Vieques** If you are staying only on the islands, the best way to get there is via público or inexpensive interisland flight. Considering the time and hassle, the latter of these is a better option.

Insurance

Liability insurance is required in Puerto Rico, as in most US states. Insurance against damage to the car, called Collision Damage Waiver (CDW) or Loss Damage Waiver (LDW), is usually optional, but will often require you to pay for the first $100 or $500. Some credit-card companies cover car rentals, so extra coverage may not be needed. Always take some insurance – accidents happen far too easily. Most rental agencies prohibit taking a car to Culebra or Vieques.

Road Conditions & Hazards

» Puerto Rico has more cars per square mile than any other place on earth – twice as many as Los Angeles County – so expect traffic jams.

» Puerto Rico has the best roads in the Caribbean.

» Watch out for island animals – dogs, chickens, horses, pigs – that wander across the roads, particularly in the mountains, and on Culebra and Vieques.

» Secondary roads through the mountains are in generally poor condition, with lots of rough surfaces and very narrow passes.

» Carjacking was a problem in the mid-1990s, but incidents have decreased in recent years.

» Police always keep warning lights on. Emergency situations are signaled by a siren.

Puerto Rico's best roads are its Expressway toll roads; these include numbers 22 (San Juan–Arecibo), 66 (San Juan–Canóvanas), 52 (San Juan–Ponce) and 53 (Fajardo–Yabucoa). You must pay a fee on these roads at a booth at one of various entry/exit checkpoints. Prices for two-axle vehicles range from 50¢ to $1.50. It is wise to have the right money available.

The next best roads are the main highways such as Hwys 2 and 3 (which effectively ring the island), Hwy 10 (Arecibo–Ponce) and Hwy 30 (Caguas–Humacao). These roads have two to three lanes in either direction but are infested with traffic lights and are often jam-packed with cars – especially during rush hour. With their ubiquitous shopping malls and unsightly concrete satellite towns, they're hardly the best advert for the island's scenic attractions.

Lesser roads are far more charming, but considerably narrower (often only 1½ lanes wide). Crisscrossing the island's precipitous inland terrain, they are also invariably slow and winding.

ROAD DISTANCES (MILES)

	Aguadilla	Aibonito	Arecibo	Cabo Rojo Point	Fajardo	Mayagüez	Ponce	Rincón
Aibonito	95							
Arecibo	33	61						
Cabo Rojo Point	70	122	70					
Fajardo	115	69	83	145				
Mayagüez	17	80	49	22	142			
Ponce	63	34	45	50	95	46		
Rincón	11	94	43	35	125	14	60	
San Juan	83	46	52	122	38	100	74	93

Bank on an average speed of 25mph in the mountains.

Basic Road Rules

» Driving rules here are basically the same as they are in the US; traffic proceeds along the right side of the road and moves counterclockwise around traffic circles.

» You must be at least 16 years old to drive a car in Puerto Rico.

» It is legal to turn right at a red light, except where signs state otherwise.

» It is legal to ignore red lights (if safe to do so) between midnight and 5am.

» Going more than 10 miles an hour over the speed limit will likely lead to a speeding ticket.

» In rural areas, where speed limits aren't always posted, use common sense.

» Watch for school zones, where the speed limit is 15mph (strictly enforced during school hours).

» Most highway signs employ international symbols, but distances are measured in kilometers, while speed limits are posted in miles per hour.

» Seat belts and motorcycle helmets must be worn; and children younger than four years must travel in child safety seats.

» Carjacking, though rare, is not unheard of in Puerto Rico, so stopping for anyone who waves you down or approaches your vehicle carries significant risk.

» Many island drivers notoriously ignore stoplights and stop signs late at night.

Parking

Finding parking can be a real problem in San Juan. Do not park at curbs painted red or yellow. Parking fees at the hotels average about $20 per day.

Hitchhiking

Hitchhiking is rare in Puerto Rico and not recommended. If you are going to try it, be extremely cautious. Pairs of a man and a woman will likely have the most success getting a ride. For women traveling alone, hitchhiking is too dangerous.

Local Transportation

Bus

Puerto Rico does not have an islandwide bus service. San Juan, however is a different matter and buses are cheap, abundant and well-run there. The system is administered via the **Autoridad Metropolitana de Autobuses** (AMA; Metropolitan Bus Authority; ☎787-767-7979; www.dtop.gov.pr/ama/default.htm, in Spanish) and **Metrobus** (☎787-763-4141). AMA buses and Metobuses charge 75¢ for any destination on their routes; seniors and students are eligible for slightly discounted fares. See p86 for specifics on routes and schedules. Visitors can identify bus stops by an obelisk marker that reads 'Parada' or 'Parada de Guaguas' (Bus Stop). Bus system maps are everywhere.

Metro

» The Tren Urbano (p87) opened in 2005 and shuttles people around San Juan. Tickets are a standard 75¢ one-way.

» It has 16 stations and covers 11 miles from Sa-

GETTING AROUND ON CULEBRA & VIEQUES

Although rental cars from the main island are prohibited on the eastern islands of Culebra and Vieques, you can rent vehicles on both the islands and dozens of 'taxi' vans or públicos will shuttle people around the island for somewhere between $3 and $5 each. Públicos will meet travelers at the docks. Prices for common destinations are usually fixed, and bartering is in bad taste. You can also rent scooters and bicycles on Vieques. Options for transportation are more limited on Culebra.

LOW-IMPACT TRANSPORTATION

» Puerto Rico is a small island and in-country flying is largely superfluous – unless you're the president or in a major hurry. Rather than catching a plane to the outlying islands of Culebra and Vieques, get the scenic 1- to 1½-hour ferry from Fajardo instead.

» San Juan has a great public transportation system that is both far-reaching and cheap, making car hire in the capital largely unnecessary.

» Hire a bike where feasible and discover Puerto Rico's quieter corners on two wheels.

» Resist renting a car on the tiny island of Culebra (there are far too many of them already). Instead, use públicos, a bicycle and your own two feet.

» Aim to take at least one journey on a público and find out what these colorful street-theaters-on-wheels are all about.

» Experience the relative modernity of San Juan's Tren Urbano.

grado Corazon in Santurce to Bayamón.

» Although it still avoids the areas of main tourist interest, there are proposals to extend the route.

» It's the only one of its kind in the Caribbean.

» It currently operates at 13% of its capacity.

Públicos

Públicos are essentially intertown minibuses that run prescribed routes during daylight hours. Traveling via público offers a great local experience, but requires a lot of patience and time. Some públicos make relatively long hauls between places such as San Juan and Ponce or Mayagüez, but most make much shorter trips, providing a link between communities. Públicos usually make their pickups and drop-offs at a van stand on or near a town's central plaza. Travel via públicos takes a long time, as the driver stops frequently to let people on and off. For schedules and fares, inquire at the público stands in town plazas or at San Juan's LMM airport. Públicos are useful for getting around the smaller spread-out municipalities such as Fajardo and Mayagüez.

Frequency Públicos will leave when the van is full. In the early morning and evening, when people are going to and from work, the terminals will be most busy. Some públicos, such as ones that make routes to popular beaches, may only run on the weekend.

Cost Público is by far the most inexpensive way to travel long distances in Puerto Rico. The longest ride on the island will not cost more than $12. Pay extra if you want the driver to take you to a destination that is off the route.

Comfort Van rides are not especially comfortable, as drivers will try to put as many passengers in one van as possible. Vans can be old, stinky and extremely hot and crowded.

Destinations There will be major público terminals near the center of every midsized or large city. The destination will be clearly written in the front window of the van. If you go to an unusual destination, you will likely be stranded for a return trip.

Taxi

Taxis are available in most of the midsized to large cities on the island. In this guidebook, taxi services are listed for major cities. Often, flagging a taxi in a public plaza is faster than calling for one. Drivers almost never use meters, so establish the cost before beginning your journey. San Juan is the exception to this: its government-run 'tourist taxis' have fixed rates for all their trips (see p87).

Language

WANT MORE?

For in-depth language information and handy phrases, check out Lonely Planet's *Latin American Spanish Phrasebook*. You'll find it at **shop.lonelyplanet.com**, or you can buy Lonely Planet's iPhone phrasebooks at the Apple App Store.

Spanish spelling is phonetically consistent, meaning that there's a clear and consistent relationship between what you see in writing and how it's pronounced. Most Latin American Spanish sounds are pronounced the same as their English counterparts – if you read our blue pronunciation guides as if they were English, you'll be understood just fine. Note that the kh in our pronunciation guides is a throaty sound (like the 'ch' in the Scottish *loch*), v and b are similar to the English 'b' (but softer, between a 'v' and a 'b'), and r is strongly rolled. Some Spanish words are written with an acute accent (eg *días*) – this indicates a stressed syllable. In our pronunciation guides, the stressed syllables are in italics. Spanish nouns are marked for gender (masculine or feminine). Endings for adjectives also change to agree with the gender of the noun they modify. Where necessary, both forms are given for the phrases in this chapter, separated by a slash and with the masculine form first, eg *perdido/a* (m/f).

When talking to people familiar to you or younger than you, use the informal form of 'you', *tú*, rather than the polite form *Usted*. In all other cases use the polite form. The polite form is used in the phrases provided in this chapter; where both options are given, they are indicated by the abbreviations 'pol' and 'inf'.

BASICS

Hello.	*Hola.*	o·la
Goodbye.	*Adiós.*	a·*dyos*
How are you?	*¿Qué tal?*	ke tal
Fine, thanks.	*Bien, gracias.*	byen *gra*·syas
Excuse me.	*Perdón.*	per·*don*
Sorry.	*Lo siento.*	lo *syen*·to
Yes./No.	*Sí./No.*	see/no
Please.	*Por favor.*	por fa·*vor*
Thank you.	*Gracias.*	*gra*·syas
You're welcome.	*De nada.*	de *na*·da

My name is ...
Me llamo ... — me *ya*·mo ...

What's your name?
¿Cómo se llama Usted? — *ko*·mo se *ya*·ma *oo*·ste (pol)
¿Cómo te llamas? — *ko*·mo te *ya*·mas (inf)

Do you speak English?
¿Habla inglés? — *a*·bla een·*gles* (pol)
¿Hablas inglés? — *a*·blas een·*gles* (inf)

I (don't) understand.
Yo (no) entiendo. — yo (no) en·*tyen*·do

ACCOMMODATIONS

I'd like to book a room.
Quisiera reservar una habitación. — kee·*sye*·ra re·ser·*var oo*·na a·bee·ta·*syon*

How much is it per night/person?
¿Cuánto cuesta por noche/persona? — *kwan*·to *kwes*·ta por *no*·che/per·*so*·na

Does it include breakfast?
¿Incluye el desayuno? — een·*kloo*·ye el de·sa·*yoo*·no

campsite	*terreno de cámping*	te·*re*·no de *kam*·peeng
hotel	*hotel*	o·*tel*
guesthouse	*pensión*	pen·*syon*
youth hostel	*albergue juvenil*	al·*ber*·ge khoo·ve·*neel*

KEY PATTERNS

To get by in Spanish, mix and match these simple patterns with words of your choice:

When's (the next flight)?
¿Cuándo sale (el próximo vuelo)? — kwan·do sa·le (el prok·see·mo vwe·lo)

Where's (the station)?
¿Dónde está (la estación)? — don·de es·ta (la es·ta·syon)

Where can I (buy a ticket)?
¿Dónde puedo (comprar un billete)? — don·de pwe·do (kom·prar oon bee·ye·te)

Do you have (a map)?
¿Tiene (un mapa)? — tye·ne (oon ma·pa)

Is there (a toilet)?
¿Hay (servicios)? — ai (ser·vee·syos)

I'd like (a coffee).
Quisiera (un café). — kee·sye·ra (oon ka·fe)

I'd like (to hire a car).
Quisiera (alquilar un coche). — kee·sye·ra (al·kee·lar oon ko·che)

Can I (enter)?
¿Se puede (entrar)? — se pwe·de (en·trar)

Could you please (help me)?
¿Puede (ayudarme), por favor? — pwe·de (a·yoo·dar·me) por fa·vor

Do I have to (get a visa)?
¿Necesito (obtener un visado)? — ne·se·see·to (ob·te·ner oon vee·sa·do)

I'd like a ... room.	*Quisiera una habitación ...*	kee·sye·ra oo·na a·bee·ta·syon ...
single	*individual*	een·dee·vee·dwal
double	*doble*	do·ble

air-con	*aire acondicionado*	ai·re a·kon·dee·syo·na·do
bathroom	*baño*	ba·nyo
bed	*cama*	ka·ma
window	*ventana*	ven·ta·na

DIRECTIONS

Where's ...?
¿Dónde está ...? — don·de es·ta ...

What's the address?
¿Cuál es la dirección? — kwal es la dee·rek·syon

Could you please write it down?
¿Puede escribirlo, por favor? — pwe·de es·kree·beer·lo por fa·vor

Can you show me (on the map)?
¿Me lo puede indicar (en el mapa)? — me lo pwe·de een·dee·kar (en el ma·pa)

at the corner	*en la esquina*	en la es·kee·na
at the traffic lights	*en el semáforo*	en el se·ma·fo·ro
behind ...	*detrás de ...*	de·tras de ...
far	*lejos*	le·khos
in front of ...	*enfrente de ...*	en·fren·te de ...
left	*izquierda*	ees·kyer·da
near	*cerca*	ser·ka
next to ...	*al lado de ...*	al la·do de ...
opposite ...	*frente a ...*	fren·te a ...
right	*derecha*	de·re·cha
straight ahead	*todo recto*	to·do rek·to

EATING & DRINKING

What would you recommend?
¿Qué recomienda? — ke re·ko·myen·da

What's in that dish?
¿Que lleva ese plato? — ke ye·va e·se pla·to

I don't eat ...
No como ... — no ko·mo ...

That was delicious!
¡Estaba buenísimo! — es·ta·ba bwe·nee·see·mo

Please bring the bill.
Por favor nos trae la cuenta. — por fa·vor nos tra·e la kwen·ta

Cheers!
¡Salud! — sa·loo

I'd like to book a table for ...	*Quisiera reservar una mesa para ...*	kee·sye·ra re·ser·var oo·na me·sa pa·ra ...
(eight) o'clock	*las (ocho)*	las (o·cho)
(two) people	*(dos) personas*	(dos) per·so·nas

Key Words

appetisers	*aperitivos*	a·pe·ree·tee·vos
bar	*bar*	bar
bottle	*botella*	bo·te·ya
bowl	*bol*	bol
breakfast	*desayuno*	de·sa·yoo·no
cafe	*café*	ka·fe
children's menu	*menú infantil*	me·noo een·fan·teel
cold	*frío*	free·o
dinner	*cena*	se·na
food	*comida*	ko·mee·da
fork	*tenedor*	te·ne·dor
glass	*vaso*	va·so
highchair	*trona*	tro·na

hot (warm)	*caliente*	kal·*yen*·te
knife	*cuchillo*	koo·*chee*·yo
lunch	*comida*	ko·*mee*·da
main course	*segundo plato*	se·*goon*·do *pla*·to
market	*mercado*	mer·*ka*·do
menu (in English)	*menú (en inglés)*	me·*noo* (en een·*gles*)
plate	*plato*	*pla*·to
restaurant	*restaurante*	res·tow·*ran*·te
spoon	*cuchara*	koo·*cha*·ra
supermarket	*supermercado*	soo·per·mer·*ka*·do
vegetarian food	*comida vegetariana*	ko·*mee*·da ve·khe·ta·*rya*·na
with/without	*con/sin*	kon/seen

Meat & Fish

beef	*carne de vaca*	*kar*·ne de *va*·ka
chicken	*pollo*	*po*·yo
duck	*pato*	*pa*·to
fish	*pescado*	pes·*ka*·do
lamb	*cordero*	kor·*de*·ro
pork	*cerdo*	*ser*·do
turkey	*pavo*	*pa*·vo
veal	*ternera*	ter·*ne*·ra

Fruit & Vegetables

apple	*manzana*	man·*sa*·na
apricot	*albaricoque*	al·ba·ree·*ko*·ke
artichoke	*alcachofa*	al·ka·*cho*·fa
asparagus	*espárragos*	es·*pa*·ra·gos
banana	*plátano*	*pla*·ta·no
beans	*judías*	khoo·*dee*·as
beetroot	*remolacha*	re·mo·*la*·cha
cabbage	*col*	kol
carrot	*zanahoria*	sa·na·*o*·rya
celery	*apio*	*a*·pyo
cherry	*cereza*	se·*re*·sa
corn	*maíz*	ma·*ees*
cucumber	*pepino*	pe·*pee*·no
fruit	*fruta*	*froo*·ta
grape	*uvas*	*oo*·vas
lemon	*limón*	lee·*mon*
lentils	*lentejas*	len·*te*·khas
lettuce	*lechuga*	le·*choo*·ga
mushroom	*champiñón*	cham·pee·*nyon*
nuts	*nueces*	*nwe*·ses
onion	*cebolla*	se·*bo*·ya
orange	*naranja*	na·*ran*·kha
peach	*melocotón*	me·lo·ko·*ton*
peas	*guisantes*	gee·*san*·tes
(red/green) pepper	*pimiento (rojo/verde)*	pee·*myen*·to (*ro*·kho/*ver*·de)
pineapple	*piña*	*pee*·nya
plum	*ciruela*	seer·*we*·la
potato	*patata*	pa·*ta*·ta
pumpkin	*calabaza*	ka·la·*ba*·sa
spinach	*espinacas*	es·pee·*na*·kas
strawberry	*fresa*	*fre*·sa
tomato	*tomate*	to·*ma*·te
vegetable	*verdura*	ver·*doo*·ra
watermelon	*sandía*	san·*dee*·a

Signs

Abierto	Open
Cerrado	Closed
Entrada	Entrance
Hombres/Varones	Men
Mujeres/Damas	Women
Prohibido	Prohibited
Salida	Exit
Servicios/Baños	Toilets

Other

bread	*pan*	pan
butter	*mantequilla*	man·te·*kee*·ya
cheese	*queso*	*ke*·so
egg	*huevo*	*we*·vo
honey	*miel*	myel
jam	*mermelada*	mer·me·*la*·da
oil	*aceite*	a·*sey*·te
pasta	*pasta*	*pas*·ta
pepper	*pimienta*	pee·*myen*·ta
rice	*arroz*	a·*ros*
salt	*sal*	sal
sugar	*azúcar*	a·*soo*·kar
vinegar	*vinagre*	vee·*na*·gre

Drinks

beer	*cerveza*	ser·*ve*·sa
coffee	*café*	ka·*fe*
(orange) juice	*zumo (de naranja)*	*soo*·mo (de na·*ran*·kha)
milk	*leche*	*le*·che
tea	*té*	te

(mineral) water	*agua (mineral)*	a·gwa (mee·ne·*ral*)
(red/white) wine	*vino (tinto/ blanco)*	*vee*·no (*teen*·to/ *blan*·ko)

EMERGENCIES

Help!	*¡Socorro!*	so·*ko*·ro
Go away!	*¡Vete!*	*ve*·te

Call ...!	*¡Llame a ...!*	*ya*·me a ...
a doctor	*un médico*	oon *me*·dee·ko
the police	*la policía*	la po·lee·*see*·a

I'm lost.
Estoy perdido/a. es·*toy* per·*dee*·do/a (m/f)

I had an accident.
He tenido un accidente. e te·*nee*·do oon ak·see·*den*·te

I'm ill.
Estoy enfermo/a. es·*toy* en·*fer*·mo/a (m/f)

It hurts here.
Me duele aquí. me *dwe*·le a·*kee*

I'm allergic to (antibiotics).
Soy alérgico/a a (los antibióticos). soy a·*ler*·khee·ko/a a (los an·tee·*byo*·tee·kos) (m/f)

SHOPPING & SERVICES

I'd like to buy ...
Quisiera comprar ... kee·*sye*·ra kom·*prar* ...

I'm just looking.
Sólo estoy mirando. *so*·lo es·*toy* mee·*ran*·do

May I look at it?
¿Puedo verlo? *pwe*·do *ver*·lo

I don't like it.
No me gusta. no me *goos*·ta

How much is it?
¿Cuánto cuesta? *kwan*·to *kwes*·ta

That's too expensive.
Es muy caro. es mooy *ka*·ro

Can you lower the price?
¿Podría bajar un poco el precio? po·*dree*·a ba·*khar* oon *po*·ko el *pre*·syo

There's a mistake in the bill.
Hay un error en la cuenta. ai oon e·*ror* en la *kwen*·ta

Question Words

How?	*¿Cómo?*	*ko*·mo
What?	*¿Qué?*	ke
When?	*¿Cuándo?*	*kwan*·do
Where?	*¿Dónde?*	*don*·de
Who?	*¿Quién?*	kyen
Why?	*¿Por qué?*	por ke

ATM	*cajero automático*	ka·*khe*·ro ow·to·*ma*·tee·ko
credit card	*tarjeta de crédito*	tar·*khe*·ta de *kre*·dee·to
internet cafe	*cibercafé*	see·ber·ka·*fe*
post office	*correos*	ko·*re*·os
tourist office	*oficina de turismo*	o·fee·*see*·na de too·*rees*·mo

TIME & DATES

What time is it?	*¿Qué hora es?*	ke *o*·ra es
It's (10) o'clock.	*Son (las diez).*	son (las dyes)
It's half past (one).	*Es (la una) y media.*	es (la *oo*·na) ee *me*·dya

morning	*mañana*	ma·*nya*·na
afternoon	*tarde*	*tar*·de
evening	*noche*	*no*·che
yesterday	*ayer*	a·*yer*
today	*hoy*	oy
tomorrow	*mañana*	ma·*nya*·na

Monday	*lunes*	*loo*·nes
Tuesday	*martes*	*mar*·tes
Wednesday	*miércoles*	*myer*·ko·les
Thursday	*jueves*	*khwe*·ves
Friday	*viernes*	*vyer*·nes
Saturday	*sábado*	*sa*·ba·do
Sunday	*domingo*	do·*meen*·go

January	*enero*	e·*ne*·ro
February	*febrero*	fe·*bre*·ro
March	*marzo*	*mar*·so
April	*abril*	a·*breel*
May	*mayo*	*ma*·yo
June	*junio*	*khoon*·yo
July	*julio*	*khool*·yo
August	*agosto*	a·*gos*·to
September	*septiembre*	sep·*tyem*·bre
October	*octubre*	ok·*too*·bre
November	*noviembre*	no·*vyem*·bre
December	*diciembre*	dee·*syem*·bre

TRANSPORTATION

Public Transportation

boat	*barco*	*bar*·ko
bus	*autobús*	ow·to·*boos*
plane	*avión*	a·*vyon*
train	*tren*	tren

Numbers

1	*uno*	oo·no
2	*dos*	dos
3	*tres*	tres
4	*cuatro*	*kwa*·tro
5	*cinco*	*seen*·ko
6	*seis*	seys
7	*siete*	*sye*·te
8	*ocho*	*o*·cho
9	*nueve*	*nwe*·ve
10	*diez*	dyes
20	*veinte*	*veyn*·te
30	*treinta*	*treyn*·ta
40	*cuarenta*	kwa·*ren*·ta
50	*cincuenta*	seen·*kwen*·ta
60	*sesenta*	se·*sen*·ta
70	*setenta*	se·*ten*·ta
80	*ochenta*	o·*chen*·ta
90	*noventa*	no·*ven*·ta
100	*cien*	syen
1000	*mil*	meel

first	*primero*	pree·*me*·ro
last	*último*	*ool*·tee·mo
next	*próximo*	*prok*·see·mo

I want to go to ...
Quisiera ir a ... kee·*sye*·ra eer a ...

Does it stop at ...?
¿Para en ...? *pa*·ra en ...

What stop is this?
¿Cuál es esta parada? kwal es *es*·ta pa·*ra*·da

What time does it arrive/leave?
¿A qué hora llega/ sale? a ke *o*·ra *ye*·ga/ *sa*·le

Please tell me when we get to ...
¿Puede avisarme cuando lleguemos a ...? *pwe*·de a·vee·*sar*·me *kwan*·do ye·*ge*·mos a ...

I want to get off here.
Quiero bajarme aquí. *kye*·ro ba·*khar*·me a·*kee*

a ... ticket	*un billete de ...*	oon bee·*ye*·te de ...
1st-class	*primera clase*	pree·*me*·ra *kla*·se
2nd-class	*segunda clase*	se·*goon*·da *kla*·se
one-way	*ida*	*ee*·da
return	*ida y vuelta*	*ee*·da ee *vwel*·ta

airport	*aeropuerto*	a·e·ro·*pwer*·to
aisle seat	*asiento de pasillo*	a·*syen*·to de pa·*see*·yo
bus stop	*parada de autobuses*	pa·*ra*·da de ow·to·*boo*·ses
cancelled	*cancelado*	kan·se·*la*·do
delayed	*retrasado*	re·tra·*sa*·do
platform	*plataforma*	pla·ta·*for*·ma
ticket office	*taquilla*	ta·*kee*·ya
timetable	*horario*	o·*ra*·ryo
train station	*estación de trenes*	es·ta·*syon* de *tre*·nes
window seat	*asiento junto a la ventana*	a·*syen*·to *khoon*·to a la ven·*ta*·na

Driving & Cycling

I'd like to hire a ...	*Quisiera alquilar ...*	kee·*sye*·ra al·kee·*lar* ...
4WD	*un todo-terreno*	oon to·do·te·*re*·no
bicycle	*una bicicleta*	*oo*·na bee·see·*kle*·ta
car	*un coche*	oon *ko*·che
motorcycle	*una moto*	*oo*·na *mo*·to

child seat	*asiento de seguridad para niños*	a·*syen*·to de se·goo·ree·*da* *pa*·ra *nee*·nyos
diesel	*petróleo*	pet·*ro*·le·o
helmet	*casco*	*kas*·ko
hitchhike	*hacer botella*	a·*ser* bo·*te*·ya
mechanic	*mecánico*	me·*ka*·nee·ko
petrol/gas	*gasolina*	ga·so·*lee*·na
service station	*gasolinera*	ga·so·lee·*ne*·ra
truck	*camion*	ka·*myon*

Is this the road to ...?
¿Se va a ... por esta carretera? se va a ... por *es*·ta ka·re·*te*·ra

(How long) Can I park here?
¿(Por cuánto tiempo) Puedo aparcar aquí? (por *kwan*·to *tyem*·po) *pwe*·do a·par·*kar* a·*kee*

The car has broken down (at ...).
El coche se ha averiado (en ...). el *ko*·che se a a·ve·*rya*·do (en ...)

I have a flat tyre.
Tengo un pinchazo. *ten*·go oon peen·*cha*·so

I've run out of petrol.
Me he quedado sin gasolina. me e ke·*da*·do seen ga·so·*lee*·na

GLOSSARY

aldea – village, hamlet
Arcaicos – Archaics; first known inhabitants of Puerto Rico

bahía – bay
balneario – public beach
barrio – neighborhood, city district
bateyes – Taíno ball courts
boca – mouth, entrance
boleros – ballads
bomba – musical form and dance inspired by African rhythms and characterized by call-and-response dialogues between musicians and interpreted by dancers; often considered as a unit with *plena*, as in *bomba y plena*
Boricua – Puerto Rican; a person of Puerto Rican descent
Borinquen – traditional Taíno name for the island of Puerto Rico
bosque estatal – state forest
botánica – shop specializing in herbs, icons and associated charms used in the practice of Santería

cacique – Taíno chief (male or female)
callejón – narrow side street, alleyway
capilla – chapel
Caribs – original colonizers of the Caribbean, for whom the region was named
casa – house
cayos – cays; refers to islets
cemíes – small figurines carved from stone, shell, wood or gold, representing deities worshipped by the Taínos
centros vacacionales – literally 'vacation centers'; form of rental accommodation popular with island families, with facilities ranging from basic wooden cabins on the beach to two-bedroom condos
cerro – hill, mountain
Changó – Yoruba god of fire and war believed to control thunder and lightning; one of several principal deities worshipped in Santería (see also *orishas*)
comida criolla – traditional Puerto Rican cuisine
Compañía de Parques Nacionales – CPN; National Park Company
coquí – a species of tiny tree frog found only in Puerto Rico; the island's mascot
cordillera – a system of mountain ranges
criollo – island-born person of Spanish parentage; in colonial times considered inferior by peninsular Spaniards (see also *mestizo*)
culebrenses – residents of Culebra
curandero – healer

danza – form of piano music and stylized figure-dance with Spanish origins, fused with elements of island folk music
Departamento de Recursos Naturales y Ambientales – DRNA; Department of Natural Resources & Environment

espiritismo – spiritualism
Estado Libre Asociado – associated free state; the term describes Puerto Rico's relationship with the USA

fiesta patronal – the annual celebrations staged in Puerto Rican cities and towns to honor each community's patron saint
fortaleza – fortress
friquitines – roadside kiosks
fuerte – fort

galería – gallery
garitas – turreted sentry towers constructed at intervals along the top of Old San Juan's fortifications
gringo – term used on the island to describe Americans

hacienda – agricultural estate, plantation

iglesia – church
Igneris – Indian group of the Arawakan linguistic group; early settlers of Puerto Rico
independentistas – advocates for Puerto Rican independence

jíbaro – country person, often cast as archetypal Puerto Rican

laguna – lake or lagoon
lechonera – eatery specializing in suckling pig
LMM – abbreviation for San Juan's Luis Muñoz Marín International Airport

malecón – pier, waterfront promenade
máscaras – masks (see also *vejigantes*)
mercado – market
Mesónes Gastronómicos – a Puerto Rico Tourism Company–sponsored program involving a collection of restaurants around the island that feature Puerto Rican cuisine
mestizo – person of mixed ancestry; usually Indian and Spanish (see also *criollo*)
mogotes – hillocks
mundillo – traditional form of intricately woven lace, made only in Puerto Rico and Spain

norte – north
Nuyoricans – Puerto Rican 'exiles' in the US

orishas – Yoruba deities worshipped in Santería, often associated with Catholic saints (see also *Changó*)

palacio – palace
parador – country inn
parque – park
pasaje – passage
pava – typical straw hat of the *jíbaro*
playa – beach
plazuela – small plaza
plena – form of traditional Puerto Rican dance and song that unfolds to distinctly African rhythms beat out with maracas, tambourines and other traditional percussion instruments; often associated with *bomba*
pleneros – *plena* singers
ponceños – residents of Ponce
PRTC – Puerto Rico Tourism Company
públicos – shared taxis, usually minivans equipped with bench seats, which pick up passengers along a prescribed route and provide low-cost local transport islandwide
puerta – gate, door
puerto – port
punta – tip, end

reserva forestal – forest reserve
ron – rum

sanjuaneros – residents of San Juan
Santería – Afro-Caribbean religion representing the syncretism of Catholic and African beliefs, based on the worship of Catholic saints and their associated *Yoruba* deities or *orishas*
santero – an artist who carves *santos*; one of many names for practitioners of the rites of *Santería*
santos – small carved figurines representing saints, enshrined and worshipped by practitioners of *Santería*
sonda – sound
supermercado – supermarket
sur – south

Taínos – indigenous Puerto Ricans
tapones – traffic jams
tienda – store
turismo – tourism
turista – tourist

universidad – university
urgente – urgent

valle – valley
vegetales – vegetables
vejigantes – traditional Puerto Rican masks (see also *máscaras*)
ventana – window
vereda – path, trail
vino – wine

Yoruba – West Africans brought to Puerto Rico as slaves

zoológico – zoo

behind the scenes

SEND US YOUR FEEDBACK

We love to hear from travelers – your comments keep us on our toes and help make our books better. Our well-traveled team reads every word on what you loved or loathed about this book. Although we cannot reply individually to postal submissions, we always guarantee that your feedback goes straight to the appropriate authors, in time for the next edition. Each person who sends us information is thanked in the next edition – and the most useful submissions are rewarded with a free book.

Visit **lonelyplanet.com/contact** to submit your updates and suggestions or to ask for help. Our award-winning website also features inspirational travel stories, news and discussions.

Note: We may edit, reproduce and incorporate your comments in Lonely Planet products such as guidebooks, websites and digital products, so let us know if you don't want your comments reproduced or your name acknowledged. For a copy of our privacy policy visit lonelyplanet.com/privacy.

OUR READERS

Many thanks to the travelers who used the last edition and wrote to us with helpful hints, useful advice and interesting anecdotes:

Karen & Kate & Susanne Andujar Ramirez, Kristina Austlid, Sanne Bogers, Ivan Borisavljevic, Stephanie Calondis, Martha Carnevale, Judy Clark, Chiara Conrado, David Frost, Malakaite Green, Jeanne Holland, Inese Holte, Fei Lauw, Robin Mackay, Marsha Mann, JJ Nino, Annette Parry, Suzette Perez, Stephen Rutenberg, Hannes Schraft, Douglas Smith, Mike Vitiello and Mike White.

AUTHOR THANKS

Nate Cavalieri

Thanks to the 'Dream Team' for the lengthy and heated discussion about desserts of the world and to my excellent colleagues at Lonely Planet. Thanks especially to Florence Chien, my favorite person.

Beth Kohn

So many incredible folks shared their local wisdom this time around, especially Dan and David at Casa de Amistad, Camilla Feibelman of the Sierra Club, Esteban and Emeo at the Andalucía Guest House and Carolyn Krupp of El Yunque National Forest. A standing ovation goes to human dynamo Terrie Hayward at the Palmetto Guesthouse in Culebra. In Lonely Planet–land, huge thanks to Cat Craddock, Alison Lyall, Bruce Evans and Nate Cavalieri. Love to Claude for everything else.

ACKNOWLEDGMENTS

Climate map data adapted from Peel MC, Finlayson BL & McMahon TA (2007) 'Updated World Map of the Köppen-Geiger Climate Classification', *Hydrology and Earth System Sciences*, 11, 163344.

Cover photograph: Playa Crash Boat, near Aguadilla. © Ken Welsh / Photolibrary. Many of the images in this guide are available for licensing from Lonely Planet Images: www.lonelyplanetimages.com.

THIS BOOK

This 5th edition of Lonely Planet's Puerto Rico guidebook was researched and written by Nate Cavalieri and Beth Kohn. The 4th edition was written by Brendan Sainsbury and Nate Cavalieri; Ginger Adams Otis wrote the 3rd edition. This guidebook was commissioned in Lonely Planet's Oakland office, and produced by the following:

Commissioning Editors Catherine Craddock-Carrillo, Kathleen Munnelly

Coordinating Editors Gabrielle Innes, Martine Power

Coordinating Cartographer Valeska Cañas

Coordinating Layout Designer Carol Jackson

Managing Editors Bruce Evans, Annelies Mertens

Managing Cartographers Alison Lyall

Managing Layout Designer Chris Girdler

Assisting Editors Andrea Dobbin, Kim Hutchins, Matty Soccio

Assisting Cartographers Ildiko Bogdanovits, Mark Griffiths

Cover & Internal Image Research Naomi Parker, Aude Vauconsant

Language Content Branislava Vladisavljevic

Thanks to Yvonne Bischofberger, Heather Dickson, Ryan Evans, Joshua Geoghegan, Lisa Knights, Wayne Murphy, Rebecca Skinner, Gina Tsarouhas and Gerard Walker.

index

000 Map pages
000 Photo pages

000 Map pages
000 Photo pages

000 Map pages
000 Photo pages

how to use this book

These symbols will help you find the listings you want:

- Sights
- Beaches
- Activities
- Courses
- Tours
- Festivals & Events
- Sleeping
- Eating
- Drinking
- Entertainment
- Shopping
- Information/ Transport

These symbols give you the vital information for each listing:

- Telephone Numbers
- Opening Hours
- Parking
- Nonsmoking
- Air-Conditioning
- Internet Access
- Wi-Fi Access
- Swimming Pool
- Vegetarian Selection
- English-Language Menu
- Family-Friendly
- Pet-Friendly
- Bus
- Ferry
- Metro
- Subway
- London Tube
- Tram
- Train

Reviews are organised by author preference.

Look out for these icons:

- TOP CHOICE — Our author's recommendation
- FREE — No payment required
- A green or sustainable option

Our authors have nominated these places as demonstrating a strong commitment to sustainability – for example by supporting local communities and producers, operating in an environmentally friendly way, or supporting conservation projects.

Map Legend

Sights
- Beach
- Buddhist
- Castle
- Christian
- Hindu
- Islamic
- Jewish
- Monument
- Museum/Gallery
- Ruin
- Winery/Vineyard
- Zoo
- Other Sight

Activities, Courses & Tours
- Diving/Snorkelling
- Canoeing/Kayaking
- Skiing
- Surfing
- Swimming/Pool
- Walking
- Windsurfing
- Other Activity/ Course/Tour

Sleeping
- Sleeping
- Camping

Eating
- Eating

Drinking
- Drinking
- Cafe

Entertainment
- Entertainment

Shopping
- Shopping

Information
- Post Office
- Tourist Information

Transport
- Airport
- Border Crossing
- Bus
- Cable Car/ Funicular
- Cycling
- Ferry
- Metro
- Monorail
- Parking
- S-Bahn
- Taxi
- Train/Railway
- Tram
- Tube Station
- U-Bahn
- Other Transport

Routes
- Tollway
- Freeway
- Primary
- Secondary
- Tertiary
- Lane
- Unsealed Road
- Plaza/Mall
- Steps
- Tunnel
- Pedestrian Overpass
- Walking Tour
- Walking Tour Detour
- Path

Boundaries
- International
- State/Province
- Disputed
- Regional/Suburb
- Marine Park
- Cliff
- Wall

Population
- Capital (National)
- Capital (State/Province)
- City/Large Town
- Town/Village

Geographic
- Hut/Shelter
- Lighthouse
- Lookout
- Mountain/Volcano
- Oasis
- Park
- Pass
- Picnic Area
- Waterfall

Hydrography
- River/Creek
- Intermittent River
- Swamp/Mangrove
- Reef
- Canal
- Water
- Dry/Salt/ Intermittent Lake
- Glacier

Areas
- Beach/Desert
- Cemetery (Christian)
- Cemetery (Other)
- Park/Forest
- Sportsground
- Sight (Building)
- Top Sight (Building)

OUR STORY

A beat-up old car, a few dollars in the pocket and a sense of adventure. In 1972 that's all Tony and Maureen Wheeler needed for the trip of a lifetime – across Europe and Asia overland to Australia. It took several months, and at the end – broke but inspired – they sat at their kitchen table writing and stapling together their first travel guide, *Across Asia on the Cheap*. Within a week they'd sold 1500 copies. Lonely Planet was born.

Today, Lonely Planet has offices in Melbourne, London and Oakland, with more than 600 staff and writers. We share Tony's belief that 'a great guidebook should do three things: inform, educate and amuse'.

OUR WRITERS

Nate Cavalieri

Coordinating author, Ponce & South Coast, West Coast, North Coast, Central Mountains, Plan Your Trip & Understand Puerto Rico chapters Nate researched the previous edition of Puerto Rico entirely on bicycle, but didn't have the chutzpah to pedal over the Central Mountains this time around. The sting from this defeat was soothed by exploring the beguiling diversity of Puerto Rican pork dishes. His favorite experiences while researching this edition included scanning the waters for manatee from the lighthouse at Cabo Rojo, sharing a Medalla with an on-duty cop at a beach bonfire in Rincón and getting a high five from Sammy, the dancing bull mascot of the San Juan Senadores. Nate's authored a handful of titles for Lonely Planet on California, the western United States, Latin America and international volunteering. After a yearlong trip around the world in 2010, he gets a little taste of Puerto Rico every day while walking through his neighborhood in Brooklyn, New York.

Read more about Nate at:
lonelyplanet.com/members/natecavalieri

Beth Kohn

San Juan, El Yunque & East Coast, Culebra & Vieques Beth has loved Puerto Rico since her first trip here, when she catapulted into a shimmering bioluminescent bay and stayed up for hours listening to the coquí frogs. Her favorite experience this time was tramping up the south road of El Yunque until the jungle swallowed the pavement and her shoes were inundated with water. Next time she'll take some rubber boots and keep going. An author of many Lonely Planet guides, including *Mexico* and *South America on a Shoestring*, you can see more of her written and photographic work at www.bethkohn.com.

Read more about Beth at:
lonelyplanet.com/members/bethkohn

Published by Lonely Planet Publications Pty Ltd
ABN 36 005 607 983
5th edition – Oct 2011
ISBN 978 1 74179 470 0

10 9 8 7 6 5 4 3 2 1
Printed in China